Politics and Faith

Reinhold Niebuhr and Paul Tillich at Union Seminary in New York

MERCER
UNIVERSITY PRESS

Endowed by

TOM WATSON BROWN

and

THE WATSON-BROWN FOUNDATION, INC.

Politics and Faith

Reinhold Niebuhr and Paul Tillich at Union Seminary in New York

Ronald H. Stone

MERCER UNIVERSITY PRESS
MACON, GEORGIA

MUP/ H863

1400 Coleman Avenue
Macon, Georgia 31207

First Edition

Books published by Mercer University Press are printed on acid-free paper that meets the requirements of the American National Standard for Information Sciences—Permanence of Paper for Printed Library Materials.

Mercer University Press is a member of Green Press Initiative (greenpressinitiative.org), a nonprofit organization working to help publishers and printers increase their use of recycled paper and decrease their use of fiber derived from endangered forests. This book is printed on recycled paper.

ISBN 978-0-88146-385-9

Cataloging-in-Publication Data is available from the Library of Congress

Contents

Preface

Religion and politics are intertwined in the foundations of our civilization, from Mesopotamian, Egyptian myths, and divine rulers to Hellenistic philosophy and Hebrew prophecy. In our immediacy religion is decisive in elections and in foreign wars. How shall we relate our ultimate convictions about the meaning of life to our immediate interests in political struggle? Beyond slogans and shouting is there a way through the political morass that can guide our present search? There is no need to pursue simple solutions. These are both ultimate questions and immediate fights. Can we, by turning to the most prominent American theologian and political philosopher of the last century, find guidance for our time and our hopes?

The genius of the political thought and action of Reinhold Niebuhr and Paul Tillich is its relationship to their faith and ethics. They were able to generate political activity and make contributions to political thought while using, but not collapsing their religious faith into their politics. Ultimately politics reflects one's faith, and at its best is correlated with thoughtful ethics. However, there are grievous dangers in merging politics and religion. They resisted this fault while inspiring and directing political responses to the crisis of their times. Faith and ethics have their own reality and are not drawn simply from politics. Politics is its own field, and should not be drawn directly from religion. The relating of politics to faith is more common now than when Niebuhr and Tillich were at the height of their powers. The narrow, fanatical application of religious texts or ideas to politics can produce disastrous results. But technical politics or brutal politics without the guidance of faith or ultimate assumptions and the limits of ethics is either boring or dangerous. Tillich and Niebuhr show the way to best relate the three fields. However, their story is rather complicated and it has its own convulsions. These complexities are in part due to the fact that they lived in wartime and participated in or resisted those wars. The reality of their wartime context to their thought has not been demonstrated adequately before, and this thesis drives the argument of the book.

Reinhold Niebuhr and Paul Tillich are often regarded as the most significant philosophers of America's twentieth century. Niebuhr's claim to such significance is his political philosophy, and Tillich's is his philosophy of religion. Additionally they have competing claims for dominance in theology in the United States. For twenty-two years (1933–1955) they were partners at Union Theological Seminary in New York City. During that period Niebuhr developed his mature political thought and rose to prominence while Tillich was writing his systematic theology. Niebuhr's politics depended upon both his theology and his Christian ethics while Tillich's systematic theology depended upon his philosophy of religion and was also expressed in his Christian ethics and significant political activity and thought.

This volume focuses on their politics, faith, and ethics and is the capstone of my writing. Under the direction of Reinhold Niebuhr, while I was serving as his last graduate assistant, I edited my first book, a book of his essays, *Faith and Politics* (Braziller), my second book was an analysis of his political theory, *Reinhold Niebuhr Prophet to Politicans* (Abingdon and University Press of America). A few years later, I turned toward Tillich and from research in the Tillich archives at Harvard I wrote *Paul Tillich's Radical Political Thought* (John Knox and University Press of America). I followed this by editing a book of his essays, *The Theology of Peace* (Westminster). As I realized how important the context of Union Theological Seminary was to Reinhold Niebuhr, I interpreted his academic teaching and career in *Professor Reinhold Niebuhr* (Westminster). My friend and graduate student, Lon Weaver, and I edited Tillich's wartime radio broadcasts over the Voice of America into Germany and occupied Europe, *Against the Third Reich* (Westminster). This was followed by my collaboration with Mary Ann Stenger on *The Dialogues of Paul Tillich* (Mercer University Press). All of this writing has driven me to discuss their relationship to each other. Now in my retirement, drawing upon those previous studies and new insights and work, I have folded into this volume their politics, faith, and ethics which all have been the subjects of my teaching and other writing. The context of the work is the wars that brought them together and which they interpreted from their base community of Union Theological Seminary in New York City. Though the book necessarily begins earlier than their cooperation at Union Theological seminary and extends past that partnership to the fulfillment of their vocations and end of their lives, it concentrates on their particularly important work at Union from 1933 to 1955.

I acknowledge with thanks the permissions of all those publishers to incorporate revised versions of previously published works into this volume. Reinhold Niebuhr gave permission in 1968 to use any of what he told me and also his papers in my writing. Mutie Tillich Farris receives my thanks for her permission as literary executor for the Tillich estate for permission to use previous work and the papers of Paul Tillich. Also, I thank my dear colleague of all my years at Pittsburgh Theological Seminary and the University of Pittsburgh, Professor Walter Wiest, who was a student of both Tillich and Niebuhr for his improvement of the manuscript. Buried underneath the writing are the resources of the Library of Congress for the Niebuhr papers, the Harvard-Andover Theological Library for the Tillich papers, the Barbour Library of Pittsburgh Theological Seminary, and The Burke Library (Columbia University) at Union Theological Seminary. Finally, I thank the *Journal of Feminist Studies in Religion* 28/1 (Spring, 2012): 89-99. for permission to include material from my essay "Revisiting Valerie Saiving's Challenge to Reinhold Niebuhr."

For my closest friends at Pittsburgh Seminary, Professor Walter E. Wiest and Professor Gonzalo Castillo-Cardenas, colleagues who heard from me about Reinhold Niebuhr and Paul Tillich for four decades

Timeline

1886	Paul Johannes Oskar Tillich, born Starzeddel, Germany, on 20 August
1892	Karl Paul Reinhold Niebuhr, born Wright City, Missouri, on 21 June
1901	Tillich family moves to Berlin and Johannes Tillich accompanies Kaiser Wilhelm II to Jerusalem for dedication of a German church in Gethsemane
1902	Niebuhr family moved to Lincoln, Illinois
1904	Paul Tillich begins university study at Berlin
1906–1907	Tillich, first officer of Wingolf Fellowship
1907–1910	Niebuhr attends *Evangelische Pro-Seminar* in Elmhurst, Illinois
1910–1913	Niebuhr at Eden Seminary; graduates valedictorian
1910	Tillich receives Ph.D. University of Breslau
1911	Tillich pastor in Nauen
1912	Tillich ordained to ministry, receives licentiate in theology at University of Halle
1912–1914	Tillich assistant pastor in Moabit, Berlin
1913–1915	Niebuhr at Yale University: Bachelor of Divinity, 1914; Master of Arts, 1915
1914	World War I begins
1914	Tillich marries Margarethe Wever on 18 September
1914–1918	Tillich serves as army chaplain
1915	Niebuhr begins pastorate in Detroit, Michigan, continues until 1928
1917	Niebuhr appointed executive secretary of Evangelical Synod's War Time Commission, to General War Time Commission, and synod delegate to Federal Council of Churches

1919–1924	Tillich *privatdozent* at University of Berlin, participates in religious socialist discussion circle, and writes on religious socialism, first course on Christianity and society
1921	Tillich divorced from Margarethe Wever
1922	Niebuhr begins writing for the *Christian Century*
1923	Niebuhr's first trip to Europe with Sherwood Eddy's traveling seminar
1924	Tillich marries Hannah Werner Gottschow, becomes associate professor of theology at University of Marburg
1925–1929	Tillich professor of Philosophy at Dresden Institute of Technology
1926	Tillich publishes *The Religious Situation*
1927	Niebuhr publishes *Does Civilization Need Religion?*
1928	Niebuhr joins faculty of Union Theological Seminary and editorial staff of *The World Tomorrow*
1929	Niebuhr publishes *Leaves from the Notebook of a Tamed Cynic*
1929	Tillich and Niebuhr join their respective German and American Socialist Parties
1929–1933	Tillich professor of Philosophy and Sociology at University of Frankfurt
1931	Niebuhr marries Ursula Keppel-Compton at Winchester Cathedral on 22 December
1932	Niebuhr publishes *Moral Man and Immoral Society*
1932	Tillich publishes "Ten Theses on the Church and the Third Reich"
1933	Tillich publishes *The Socialist Decision* and is suspended by German government on 13 April; arrives in NewYork City on 3 November; dismissed from university professorship by Nazi government; on 29 December becomes visiting lecturer at Columbia University and Union Theological Seminary
1935	Niebuhr founds *Radical Religion*
1936	Tillich becomes first chairman of Self-Help for Refugees;

	publishes *On the Boundary*. Delta Cooperative Farm founded; Niebuhr chairman of board of trustees
1937	Niebuhr and Tillich address Conference on Life and Work at Oxford
1937–1940	Tillich associate professor of Philosophical Theology at Union
1939	Niebuhr delivers Gifford Lectures in Scotland
1940	Niebuhr publishes *Christianity and Power Politics*, and resigns from Socialist Party. Tillich becomes American citizen
1940–1955	Tillich professor of Philosophical Theology at Union
1941	Niebuhr founds *Christianity and Crisis* and publishes *Human Nature*, volume 1 of *The Nature and Destiny of Man*
1942	Tillich begins radio broadcasts to Germany
1943	Niebuhr publishes *Human Destiny*, volume 2 of *The Nature and Destiny of Man*; lectures in England; and elected vice-president of Liberal Party
1944	Niebuhr publishes *The Children of Light and the Children of Darkness*
1944	Tillich serves as chair of the Council for a Democratic Germany
1945	Niebuhr serves on Advisory Committee on Occupied Territories for War Department and State Department in Europe
1947	Niebuhr serves as co-chair for founding of Americans for Democratic Action
1948	Niebuhr addresses the founding conference of the World Council of Churches. Tillich has triumphant lecture trip in Europe and publishes *The Protestant Era*
1949	Niebuhr publishes *Faith and History*, gives lecture to UNESCO conference in Paris as a member of the U.S.A. delegation, and participates in a Dean Acheson-called conference at the State Department
1950	Korean War begins in June
1951	Tillich publishes *Systematic Theology*, volume 1. Niebuhr serves

	as official consultant to State Department
1952	Niebuhr suffers crippling stroke in February, publishes *The Irony of American History*. Tillich publishes *The Courage to Be*
1953	Tillich's Gifford Lectures, University of Aberdeen, Niebuhr publishes *Christian Realism* and *Political Problems*
1955	Tillich retires from Union Theological Seminary, becomes University Professor at Harvard until 1962; Niebuhr publishes *The Self and the Dramas of History*
1956	Tillich visits Greece
1957	Tillich publishes *Systematic Theology*, volume 2
1959	Niebuhr publishes *The Structure of Nations and Empires*
1960	Tillich visits Japan and engages in dialogue with Buddhism. Niebuhr retires from Union Theological Seminary and teaches large classes during three succeeding years at Harvard, Princeton, and Barnard
1962	Tillich retires from Harvard and becomes Nuveen Professor of Theology at University of Chicago
1963	Tillich publishes *Systematic Theology*, volume 3; dedicates Paul Tillich Park, New Harmony, Indiana, visits Israel and Egypt
1964	Niebuhr begins seminar in Christian Social Ethics at Union Theological Seminary, and continues it for four years, the last two in his apartment on Riverside Drive.
1965	Tillich's last lecture on history of religion and systematic theology at University of Chicago on 11 October, and dies on 22 October. Niebuhr publishes *Man's Nature and His Communities*
1968	Reinhold and Ursula left apartment on Riverside Drive to reside full-time in Stockbridge, Massachusetts, and published *Faith and Politics*
1969	Niebuhr published with Paul Sigmund *The Democratic Experience*
1971	Niebuhr dies on 1 June.

Paul Tillich and manuscript

(Courtesy of Mutie Tillich Farris)

Paul Tillich on Long Island Beach, inscribed by Hannah Tillich, "Last photo."
(Courtesy of Mutie Tillich Farris)

Reinhold Neibuhr at home on Riverside Drive in New York City in 1960s.

Paul Tillich,Ursula and Reinhold Niebuhr
at Retreat of Fellowship of Socialist Christians, 1930s.
(Courtesy of Mutie Tillich Farris)

Paul Tillich, refugee from Hitler, 1933

(Courtesy of Mutie Tillich Farris)

Reinhold Niebuhr at the airport, 1940.

(Courtesy of Pan American Airline)

Reinhold Niebuhr walks Winnie beside Union Theological Seminary.

(Courtesy of Burke Library of Columbia University at Union Theological Seminary)

Reinhold Niebuhr and Rabbi Dr. Louis Finkelstein
at Jewish Theological Seminary, 1952
(Courtesy of Burke Library)

Reinhold Niebuhr lecturing at Union Theological Seminary, 1952.
(Courtesy of Burke Library)

Hubert Humphrey, Reinhold Niebuhr, and Al Capp
at Americans for Democratic Action, 1949
(Courtesy of Burke Library)

Paul Tillich

(Courtesy of Mutie Tillich Farris)

1

The Great War

An act of terrorism unleashed a chain of developments that would lead to the partnership of Reinhold Niebuhr and Paul Tillich at Union Theological Seminary in New York City. Other events, forces, and acts of human decision, of course, played their part as well. But the assassination of Archduke Franz Ferdinand initiated the great wars of the twentieth century and the terrorism of the Nazi regime in Germany which brought them together. The aftermath of World War II led to the Cold War which divided Germany, and neither Niebuhr nor Tillich would live to see Germany reunited. Nor would they know of the nationalistic passions that murdered the Archduke unleashing another Balkan War as Serbia's ambitions again threatened the peace of Europe. Both of their careers were lived within the shadow of the forces ignited between Slavic and Germanic peoples symbolized in the murder on the bridge in Sarajevo in 1914.

Austria's annexation of Bosnia-Herzegovina was resented by Serbs in Sarajevo and the Serbian government. Behind the assassination was the heritage of the recent Balkan wars of 1912–1913. Growing Serbian nationalism also played its part. Serbia had just retaken Kosovo and Macedonia and forces were pushing to expand greater Serbia. The intelligence service of Serbia and elements of its army conspired to use Serbian nationalists to strike against the Austria dominance in Bosnia. The elaborate assassination plot of June 28, 1914, against the Archduke's tour of Sarajevo was nearly foiled when the first bomb bounced off the folded convertible top of the royal Graf and Stiff sports car disabling the following security car. The Archduke and his wife, Sophie, resumed their inspection tour after the reception in the town hall. Unluckily for them their confused route to visit the hospital took them by the spot on the bridge where Gavrilo Princep had just finished his deli sandwich. He leapt to the running board of the car and fatally shot both the Archduke and Sophie. Police in Serbia and Bosnia soon arrested most of the plotters, and in Sarajevo a trial quickly returned guilty verdicts. But political events dependent upon the interlocking security treaties of the European empires drove events forward. Austrian mobilization against a Serbia unprepared to answer all of the Austrian demands threatened a nervous Russia which was supporting its fellow Slavic and Orthodox neighbor. Russia's defensive mobilization orders against Austria also resulted in its armies facing Germany to mobilize. Germany backed its ally

Austria and felt threatened by the Franco-Russian alliance. The alliances designed for security pulled most of Europe into the downward vortex. The balancing of power collapsed, and the efforts of Great Britain to mediate the disputes and to stop the drift to war failed.

Paul Tillich, a new Doctor of Philosophy, barely had time to celebrate his twenty-eighth birthday and his September marriage before voluntarily joining the army as a chaplain. He like most Germans expected a short victorious war to defend the Fatherland for God and King. He had courted Margarethe Weaver during 1914. He was looking for an academic position after having served for two years as an assistant pastor in the industrial suburbs of Berlin. He had become aware of the alienation of the workers from the church, and he tried to develop methods with his friend Richard Wegener to meet the religious needs of the workers. His own path was leading away from the pastoral role of his successful father. His father, Johannes, had ministered in small towns in rural Prussia where Tillich grew up in peaceful pastoral scenes. His comfortable adolescence was interrupted by the early death of his mother leaving him to be dominated by his rather stern-righteous father. On becoming superintendent of the Brandenburg-Prussia Synod Johannes moved with his family into the exciting environs of Berlin. Paul's loyalties were to God and King with a high respect for the patriarchal ordered world of Germany and his duties to it. His father was both the examiner of the theological students and a sometime chaplain to Emperor Wilhelm II. The leading Berlin Professor, Adolph Harnack, regarded Germany's cause as the just defense of European civilization from the Slavic barbarians. Tillich took unquestioning loyalty to the cause of Germany into the struggle along with the psychological strengths of being almost mature at 28 years of age, formed in his mind, hopeful of a promising vocation, and sure of his Lutheran faith in the king's church.

On the other side of the Atlantic, the assassination had less immediate impact. President Woodrow Wilson, though quite willing to use military force in Latin America, was hesitant to involve the United States in a major European war. He tried to remain legally neutral while supplying Great Britain with munitions, foodstuffs, and machinery. The British blockade made shipments to Germany and its allies impossible. The enforcement of that blockade by England led to severe tensions with the U.S. The sinking of several British ships with American citizens on board deepened the growing hostility to Germany, reinforced by successful British propaganda.

Reinhold Niebuhr had finished his first year at Yale, and was looking forward to pursuing a Master of Arts degree there in preparation for graduate study and a vocation in seminary teaching that his father had unsuccessfully sought. His father's early death that summer deprived him of mentor and beloved parent. His older brother had participated in the war as a correspondent, but on his return to Lincoln, Illinois, the newspaper he edited had financial difficulties and he was released. Reinhold filled his father's pulpit that summer as war clouds darkened and fighting in earnest began in Prussia. The family chose to spend his father's insurance to build a house for Mrs. Lydia Niebuhr, but she was left without other financial support.[1] She became dependent upon Reinhold, the only family member with an income, who soon after his father's demise left for the fall semester at Yale. The dean's return to Germany because of the war helped Niebuhr overcome the deficiency of his lack of a real bachelor of arts degree in his provisional admission to graduate study at Yale. The new dean Wilbur Cross admitted Niebuhr with the stipulation that he achieve an A grade average in his year of studies for the master's degree. Niebuhr's connection to the war awaited the U.S. declaration of war on April 6, 1917. By the end of that summer he had finished his studies at Yale and assumed the pastor's responsibilities at a small mission church of the German Evangelical Synod in Detroit, Michigan. In October he was appointed to the War Welfare Commission of his denomination.[2] As a German-speaking denomination, The German Evangelical Synod of North America was suspect and many of its people and pastors were sympathetic to Germany.

During this period Niebuhr made clear that he was casting his influence in the direction of the Americanization of the denomination. He worked to change the liturgy and publications into English and to aid his denomination in acquiring regular accreditation for its educational institutions. He wrote boldly about the failure of German-Americans to make the best use of their opportunities in America. He particularly singled out the Germans for not supporting the reform movements in America and he contrasted them with the more-progressive roles of Jewish immigrants.

Niebuhr's earlier writings about war had focused on unworthy economic motivations and petty nationalist drives, but he chose to regard the U.S. entry into the war as very unselfish and worthy because of President Wilson's program of changing international relations after victory. While observations of bayonet practice at the army camps he visited troubled him, he participated in his church role in support of the war with enthusiasm.[3] In fact he wore himself out with his travels, speeches, counsels and administration. In January after returning to Detroit he collapsed from exhaustion. Meanwhile Lydia and sister Hulda were holding Bethel Evangelical Church together.

During his early years in the pastorate Reinhold and his mother focused great attention on the education program of Bethel Church, and Reinhold wrote several essays about improving the Sunday schools of the church. While serving on the War Welfare Commission he undertook to enlist the Sunday schools in the war effort. In an essay "The Present Day Task of the Sunday School"[4] he urged the placing of flags in the Sunday school. Furthermore he urged schools to keep in touch with their fighting men by correspondence and presenting the boys who were leaving with New Testaments and literature. Letters from servicemen should be read in Sunday services and every effort made to support charities related to the war effort so "that the services of the whole Evangelical Church will be made available for the men of your church."[5] He urged his church to give up teaching the Sunday school classes in the German language.

Niebuhr's enthusiasm for the war was driven by his acceptance of Woodrow Wilson's claims of the moral nature of the war. He believed that peace-lovers should support the war because Wilson articulated a program to end all war and to found a great international organization that would make war impossible. This idealism of the young Niebuhr is so far from the thought of the mature Niebuhr that most of a paragraph is required to present his thought at the time:

> The test of loyalty at the present time is a very specific one. It is: Do you believe in the justice of the American cause in this great conflict? Answering that question for myself, and, I believe, for most Americans of German descent, I am willing to answer the question without equivocation. I do not believe that any nation ever tried more diligently and honorably to avoid a conflict than our nation did, and, being forced finally to enter, that any nation has ever placed the issue of a conflict upon a higher moral plane than ours. American entrance into the war has given the conflict a new meaning. What began as a crime is ending as a crusade and for the first time in the history of the world we have the inspiring spectacle of a nation making every sacrifice of blood and treasure for aims which do not include territorial ambitions or plans for imperial aggrandizement. Except to the hopelessly prejudiced the word of the president that "we wish nothing for ourselves except what we may share with all free peoples," is convincing.[6]

He was asked by the editors of the student newspaper he had helped found, *The Keryx* , to write an essay on the war. He chose to write on the war and pacifism. He complimented most ministers who had been pacifists on their previous standpoint. He thought in the current campaign to establish an international order for peace through war that even ministers who had been pacifists should support this war. German-Americans, in particular, would be suspect if they objected to this particular war and not to all wars. He respected those who morally refused to sanction any war, but he insisted that would remain a minority position usually available to sectarians or small groups, like the Quakers, who did not have to assume responsibility for the nation's welfare. Churches, he said, were the religious institutions of nations and they had to act responsibly for the nation. They had to speak to the statesman as well as the prophet, and speaking in a statesman-like way required compromise with ethical ideals. But still in this war, "We can be thankful as American Christians that our aims have real moral value inasmuch as they are not selfish or national but are concerned with a new international order and organization."[7] He came close to "just-war" thinking as he insisted that Christian support for a war depended upon the moral aims of the war, and that the ends of the war should contribute to the establishment of peace. He recognized that the outcome of the war depended upon the settlement at the final peace conference. He had a hesitant note that if the conference went back to territorial aggrandizement rather than establishing an international order, the war would have been lost and its goals betrayed. He concluded: "Those who love peace must fashion the forces of war in the interest of their ideal and not content themselves with futile opposition to the war itself."[8]

His diary, edited for publication many years after the war, revealed more ambiguity about the war than any of his publications during the war. In one entry for 1918 he indicated how difficult it was to decide about the war, but two factors inclined him to support it: Wilson's idealistic Fourteen Points and his refusal to let his German origins betray his love for his country. Later in 1918, he tried to resign his position with the War Welfare Commission to take up active duty as a chaplain, but the synod president urged him to stay in the role he was serving, and he complied. In our twenty-first century it is hard to imagine the idealism that followed the U.S. entry into the war under the call to fight to end war and to institute a new international order. Niebuhr's Yale Divinity School faculty lined up behind the idealism. As there were Germans who said "Unless Germany wins the war there is no God," American theologians argued because there was a God the allies with U.S. support would win the war. Some admitted it was for the Germans to choose their own form of government, but that they must confine it to Germany. Others advocated exiling Wilhelm II to some distant isle as Napoleon had been sent to St. Helena. Whereas conservative Christians supported the war because it was part of the Divine order that men fought, and they were accustomed to supporting U.S. wars, the liberals needed more complicated arguments and the Yale Divinity School supplied them. Niebuhr's New Testament professor Benjamin Wisner Bacon proved to his satisfaction that the teaching of nonresistance was a pagan virtue, not a Christian one. The professor of Practical Theology demonstrated why Christian ministers should support the war. Professor Macintosh's arguments in favor of the U.S. entering the war were more subtle than others, but his conclusions about the righteousness of the war were similar. He still feared the cumulative affect of the evil of the war, but he had hopes for a new international order and a more Christian world. He concluded his essay with

> The only safety of the race lies in an essentially Christian international morality, and the only adequate guarantee of this is an essentially Christian personal religion.

Some theologians and ministers drew upon themes of the nobility of sacrifice to support young men in giving their lives for the causes of the war or the nations itself. The Dean of the Divinity school drew upon this motif as well as others to throw his support behind the slaughter in the trenches in France. He recognized that before the war Christianity had not consulted its spiritual and intellectual resources to help people understand the social disorder and factors that led to the war. He noted that Jesus began his ministry quoting Isaiah and addressing the roots of conflict and the social question in his first sermon. He praised the moral response of Christians in America in providing relief and in working through the YMCA and the Red Cross to relieve the suffering. He blamed German materialism for encouraging that country's evil and noted that its science and universities did nothing to prevent the war. He praised Christian statesmen in England for trying to avoid the war and then he praised them for coming into the war.

It was the moral idealism of the war that brought Great Britain and all her distant colonies promptly in line the moment the moral quality of the German government stood revealed in all its hideousness by its outrage upon Belgium.

Similar moral idealism, he claimed, brought the U.S. into the war and supported the young who were to sacrifice their lives to volunteer to take up arms for the right. But the power of the poem he chose to conclude his essay drew both upon idealism and the rush to human sacrifice in a mixture of the ideology that has through history often driven religious people to mix their religion and the sacrifice of their youth."The spirit of our youth has been nobly expressed in those lines on 'The Spires of Oxford' ":

> I saw the spires of Oxford
> As I was passing by,
> The gray spires of Oxford
> Against the pearl-gray sky;
> My heart was with the Oxford men
> Who went abroad to die.
> The years go fast in Oxford,
> The golden years and gay.
> The hoary colleges look down
> On careless boys at play;
> But when the bugles sounded war
> They put their games away.
> They left the peaceful river,
> The cricket field, the quad,

The shaven lawns of Oxford
To seek a bloody sod;
They gave their merry youth away
For country and for God
God rest you happy gentlemen
Who laid your good lives down,
Who took the khaki and the gun
Instead of cap and gown,
God brings you to a fairer place,
Than even Oxford town.
The years go fast in Oxford.

While Niebuhr was moving to support of the war in 1918, in the frontline trenches on the other side of the Atlantic, Paul Tillich having served for three years was disgusted with the war. He had been reading Nietzsche and Marx and coming to understand the class exploitation and less worthy motives of the war. He had buried too many German soldiers in unmarked mass graves and seen too much horror in the battle of Verdun in which 700,000 were killed. His nerves had been weakened and he had been sent for recovery away from the frontline trenches, but he had returned to the slaughter. His doubts about the church increased as it had been part of the establishment that had justified and supported the war. Even his thoughts about God had to change, and God became less the one who determined history but more the symbol of unity and being.

Once following a nervous breakdown he sought to escape the trenches by asking for an appointment by his church in Berlin. It did not work out. He applied for dismissal from the army, it was denied. So he returned to duty. He had a brief period of refreshment, even excitement, as the German forces advanced on the Marne. But that too was short lived as fresh Americans arriving in Europe were integrated into the French forces and thrown into the fray. He was awarded the Iron Cross First Class in June and he took brief prideful pleasure in it. A letter to his father in April of 1918 indicates he was hospitalized again in Berlin. After this hospitalization he did not return to the front. Finally he was assigned as a chaplain to military headquarters in Spandau, Berlin, where he served until the end of the war.[9]

Tillich's first experience with heavy fighting came early in the fall on October 30-31, 1915 when the invading Germans assaulted the heights of Tahure in northeastern France. The goals were not all achieved, and the losses were very heavy. The first days of November were given to visiting the wounded and burying the dead. As Tillich dropped the sticky loam of France onto the coffins of friends in the officer corps, an inner grimness of spirit overcame him. The mass burials of the soldiers deepened his grief. After days of living through such trauma, he knew that a time would come when the numbness that shielded one from the horror of death would break. Occasionally he felt unable to compose a sermon, sometimes claiming that God himself was preaching the message in the slaughter, he pulled himself together to preach after the battle of Tahure. He drew upon Paul from Second Corinthians 4:17-18.

> For this momentary affliction is preparing for us an eternal weight of glory beyond all comparison, because we look not to the things that are seen; for the things that are seen are transient, but the things that are unseen are eternal.

The preacher confessed his inability to speak of things human to his listeners.[10] He preached hoping only the godly word could be heard. If they, the weary veterans and the new replacements concentrated on things visible, they would see suffering and death. His dear war comrades could only despair of the present. Their only recourse rested in meditating on things eternal. The blood-soaked ground of the Champagne held no comfort. But by turning to the invisible, comfort and meaning could be found. They ought to be faithful to themselves for the holy love of the homeland and for the pride of being German and for the bonds of community and for the magnificence of the great German fatherland. All of these things were invisible, but they were true and worth more than comfort. That which is seen is temporary and it passes away; only the unseen endures. He told the soldiers that their heroism had eternity in it.

Then he turned to the question of the fallen comrades and meditated on the despair if death were the end. He comforted the troops with the promise of eternal life, again contrasting the meanness and coarseness of the visible with the beauty and eternity of the invisible. Addressing the new replacements whose shock at the carnage equaled his own, he asked them to look beyond the visible world of war. He feared that the visible reality would cause their hearts to shrink from the task. He called them to realize their brotherhood in arms and to see in every work a service to the great German fatherland, in every suffering the spirit of holy love, and in every death or simple sacrifice, eternal goodness.

In conclusion he called the new troops and the old troops to bind themselves into one spirit of a new flaming enthusiasm, to remain strong and cheerful, and to achieve victory over the external enemy and the enemy within their own hearts. He urged them to concentrate on the invisible, in spite of the visible, because the invisible is eternal.[11]

The sermon does not contain the notes of resignation and defeat that are found in his reports on the months of November and December 1915. The sermon attempts to use belief in an invisible realm of meaning to strengthen men for the visible task before which they quake. Despite claiming divine authority, certain aspects of the sermon, like German-imperial nationalism, do not seem to have been eternal. It is the sermon of an army chaplain and of a chaplain whose world of meaning is crumbling. At the time of the sermon the world had not quite been blown away, but further suffering would overcome it. Many gods have been defeated in battle, and the secure god of bourgeois Germany and of Tillich's young adulthood was about to be defeated.

In May 1916 the Seventh Division with its chaplain went into the trenches of Verdun. Tillich's first weakening of nerves gained him a brief respite from the trenches. His recovery permitted him to take a furlough to deliver a lecture at the University of Halle as he was pursuing a position there. The fighting was interspersed with rest periods and some intellectual work. As a chaplain he demonstrated an empathy with men from all sections of German society and gained a reputation as a creative leader who risked himself in combat to tend to the wounded. In a moment of reflection, he wrote:

> Above all, it [our task] could not concern itself with religious or soul-searching matters. When a well-known officer arrived, unbelievably shaken by a not especially serious wound I held his hand for an hour, remembering now and then previous happy hours until he became quiet. And so, going from man to man, we answered their immediate questions. We let them tell us their fearful experiences—whatever lay first in their hearts.[12]

In October of 1916 he collapsed in battle and was sent to the hospital. His own suffering merged into his consciousness of the dying of hundreds within his sight, millions in the war and an epoch in European civilization. Gradually in the midst of death Tillich began to turn away from his nineteenth-century foundations into a person of the war-torn twentieth century. In November he wrote that he was becoming thoroughly eschatological. Meaning was eschatological. The end came to dominate his mind and he alternated between joy and despair.[13]

He began speculating on a system of the sciences. On leave he turned to art museums and at the front he devoured art books. He read Friedrich Nietzche's *Thus Spake Zarathustra* in the French woods. When the occasion permitted he would decorate houses for parties and join in the excesses of wartime life.

Despite his breakdowns and recurring depression he was more fortunate than the twenty-year old recruits. Erich Maria Remarque's *All Quiet on the Western Front* details how these younger men, without careers, without their families, went to pieces under the pounding bombardment. Tillich had a doctorate; he had a wife, and a promise of a future. He had been grounded in theology and philosophy even though it was changing. Through art and Nietzsche he was discovering a new will to live. Nietzsche's own glimpse of life as an emergence of the will to power had originated in his service in the Franco-

Prussian war of 1870. Tillich's new life took on the character of a Dionysiac style mixed with Christian consciousness. Years later, he would say of Nietzsche: "Although his life was full of misery, in opposition to this he affirmed it infinitely."[14] Tillich began to find his life in his misery. Elements of Nietzsche's understanding of power would remain with Tillich throughout his life and the passionate assertive sense of Nietzsche would contribute to Tillich's own seeking of ecstasy.

The fundamental content of the sermons over five years is orthodox presentation of Lutheran biblical theology with which many of his hearers were familiar. Ninety of these sermons have been published, and one student of the sermons has divided them into five great themes: Christian identity, personal virtue of soldiers, power and weakness, patriotic self-sacrifice, and war and peace.[15] The great themes of God's creative power and his love for each individual are related to the individual's identity in Christian formation. The worth of the soldier's soul was lifted up in many sermons. The destiny of the individual was to find eternity and to realize God intended to be near each person. Christ's coming as a baby and suffering crucifixion were God's way of coming closer to those who were weak and suffering for they could not have survived if God had come in justice and power. The war itself showed that God's Kingdom was not of this world, but was an eschatological reality.

Each soldier was called to be equally responsible before Christ. Still in 1918 he would preach "in the seriousness and holiness of responsibility there is no difference between king and beggar." He preached on the character of the soldier and his responsibility for personal conduct. He urged the soldiers to exhibit courage. As God had blessed Israel with courageous heroes so God had blessed Germany with the royal house of Hohenzollern. He cautioned against hate. For the soldier's duty was to fight the enemy's will that fueled the conflict, not to hate the individual enemy.

The power of the individual soldier came from God, and Christ was the one never-failing source of power. Christ was even spoken of as in much of Christianity as "Lord of holy sword-bearing rage." Power was also needed for the individual life as well as the nation. Consciousness of duty, iron discipline, and order complemented holy enthusiasm, tough will, and joyful humor were themes he preached in 1916.

His sermons were patriotic and recognized the worth of self-sacrifice for the homeland, family, and comrades.

> It is the Fatherland, for which we live and die, which lets our hearts beat more deeply, which is our home soil, which gave first imprint on our souls, which is the mother language in which we think and speak, which is the German essence which goes through us out of which we speak and behave, which is the spirit of the greatness of our people, which is the wonderful,

> hidden and yet living soul of our people which we all take part, which is God among us and with us. We live not by bread alone, and for that reason we are prepared to live and to die for God and Fatherland.[16]

Matthew Lon Weaver's reading of the sermons shows Tillich to be preaching a rather uncritical biblical message of God at war. "Every earthly fighter is a divine fighter, because God's battles are fought out in the roaring wars of nations. Beloved friends that is what turns every battle into a work of, and service to God" The next year he preached: "There is no conflict between Christianity and war. The battle sword and the sword of justice are both of God."[17]

As a chaplain, he believed God was working through the war and that God would seek peace. A prerequisite of peace, he thought was forgiveness, and he feared that human forgiveness had fled the earth. He applauded the German Emperor's plea for peace and his seeking of an armistice. But he feared the peace would be lost. In 1917, he said "Woe to humanity and to future generations, if the hatred and the passion for vengeance and if the lies which make this war so unchivalrous and awful are not overcome by forgiveness!"[18]

The war's continuing slaughter had overcome the early enthusiasm for Tillich's defensive war with Germany fighting the three oppressive surrounding nations of Russia, France, and Britain. The flowers they had received on volunteering and the promises to be home by Christmas 1914 had all withered. The chaplain called to continually reinforce morale had himself first become discouraged, then depressed, and finally broken in spirit. A German scholar of Tillich's works, Erdmann Sturm, found the chaplain to be preaching a war theology that while honorific of the monarchy of the Hohenzollern House, and patriotic, was actually irrational, with an escapist eschatology and view of eternal life, and an escape from temporal life.[18] The American scholar, Ronald MacLennan, is a little less critical than Sturm weighing the context and responsibilities of a chaplain more and noting that Tillich's superiors criticized him for not being more enthusiastic about the war. It is perhaps best to note that Tillich rejected his overly enthusiastic nationalism and developed his thought in directions quite different from his war sermons. Germany changed through revolution in 1918, and Tillich changed even more than the nation.

Niebuhr and Tillich entered the war as idealistic nationalists, though, affirming different ideals and different nationalities. The war was pivotal for them. It is unknown if Tillich's congregations of soldiers killed Americans that carried materials Niebuhr's wartime commission and chaplains had provided, but it seems likely that during the battles of the Marne, Christians influenced by each of them killed each other. Some of the Americans, particularly those from Niebuhr's synod still prayed in German as they died and, of course, Tillich's troops prayed the same prayers. It is hard to believe that, as Tillich counseled, they died without hate for the enemy who bayoneted them. Yet further historical anguish had to occur before the reverends Niebuhr and Tillich became friends and allies.

2

Background of Two German Thinkers

Reinhold Niebuhr thought in the German language of his family until he was finishing his graduate studies at Yale University in 1915 during the war. He then began to resolve to fulfill his vocation in English and to move himself into the American use of English. Some of his professors from Eden Seminary did not make the move and continued to dedicate themselves to promoting German learning and culture in America. Tillich, learning English during his late forties, always continued the Germanic influences in his thinking and accents, but he became incredibly moving in his written and spoken English in his sixties. Even the texts he wrote in German during his later years reflected American-English syntax and became much easier for the Americans to translate than his earlier texts written in Germany. There is no doubt that the classical gymnasiums Tillich attended and his German university education were superior to Reinhold's opportunities in the unaccredited Elmhurst College and Eden Seminary. Niebuhr had attended parochial schools in the German Evangelical Synod until studying for a year in the English-speaking high school in Lincoln, Illinois. Reinhold always admitted he had not had a proper training in English, the social sciences, or physical sciences at Elmhurst. Tillich on the other hand felt competent to begin his book *The System of the Sciences* in his free time during the war. Despite these differences their common heritage in German education must be recognized even if much of Reinhold's was secondhand German learning taught in the Midwest. Both thinkers were influenced by the great Berlin professor Ernst Troeltsch as was Reinhold's younger brother Helmut Richard for whom Reinhold's financial gifts made study in Berlin possible.

One of the strengths Reinhold drew from Elmhurst was a love of learning and a useful familiarity with Shakespeare that worked its way into his sermons. Niebuhr's grades at Elmhurst were not outstanding, but there he began the process that prompted him to earn the distinction of valedictorian at Eden Seminary and to propel him toward further graduate studies at Yale University. Tillich matriculated at the University of Berlin that taught many of the professors for Reinhold both at Eden Theological seminary and at Yale University. The German methods of historical study were becoming dominant in America at the time Reinhold was studying. His German upbringing gave him an advantage that he noted at Yale because he could easily read the important German texts which were closed to his American peers or only available by much hard translating. They had both been congruent with their university professors on their entry into the war. Those in Berlin supported the war wholeheartedly as did the professors of religion at Yale.[1]

Their respective churches both encouraged the war, though Reinhold had several struggles with the German pastors and lay people in the German Evangelical Synod of North America as he pressed the case for the war. These German-speaking Americans were not naturally sympathetic to either American nationalism against Germany or Wilsonian liberalism. To understand either Reinhold or Paul or their relationship it is necessary to understand they were from the same church background. They both grew up on the German biblical texts. Their interpreters have often assumed that in their use of biblical texts they were referring to either the King James or the Revised Standard Version of the Bible familiar to mainline American churches. Often their texts in their sermons or biblical references in writing were their own translations of the German texts with which they grew up. Reinhold particularly made little effort to correspond to the official English translations. Likewise Reinhold was partially formed by the catechism of the Evangelical Synod taught to him in German by his father; it was not significantly different from the catechism that Paul learned from his father. In both cases, not personal religious experience, but the acceptance of the catechism of their respective churches marked their entry into the faith as they grew toward adulthood. *The Konigliches Konsistorium der Provinz Brandenburg* of Tillich was a united church since the reforms of Bismarck united the Calvinistic and Lutheran churches of Prussia in the previous century. Tillich's church was more Lutheran in Prussia than the church Reinhold's father had come out of in West Germany, which lying near Holland, was more Calvinistic. But the Evangelical Synod Reinhold grew up in was a union denomination similar to Tillich's in Prussia, more Lutheran than Calvinistic.

Probably even more formative than their particular denominations which were essentially the same, only one was American-frontier and the other establishment-German, was the fact that they grew to young adulthood sitting in church every Sunday listening to their fathers preach. Both loved their fathers and were formed by them. Niebuhr entered the ministry following his father whom he regarded as the most interesting man in town. Tillich took years to escape the influence of his father, and he might not have made it free except for the trauma of the world war. Both fathers propelled their sons toward higher studies, and those studies distanced them from their fathers and fulfilled paternal dreams. Reinhold's father had sought a vocation teaching in a seminary that he never fulfilled. The influence of Reinhold's father had to take second place to his mother, after Gustav's death in 1914 as Reinhold was preparing to attend Yale. Niebuhr symbolically and literally took the place of this father, being ordained in the same church and filling his pulpit for the rest of the summer. When at his ordination in Lincoln the 'Mantle was laid upon Reinhold" it was the mantle of his father's ministry. Soon he was responsible for supporting his mother and helping the other siblings financially whenever he could. Tillich's father remained his counselor and friend until Tillich was forced to leave Germany in 1933, and he never saw him after that though they corresponded warmly until his father's death. Tillich was shocked by the death of his mother when he was sixteen years of age. He fell into depression, and wondered about his destiny. His acquaintance with Shakespeare left him writing paragraphs reminiscent of the young Hamlet searching himself for the resources to be.

The two of them both had great capacities for friendship. Their union at the same school in 1933 brought all of these heritages together. Also, with his facility in German, Reinhold was one of the few faculty members who could easily converse in colloquial German with Paul.

The theories of their respective dissertations and theses were neither immediately relevant to the war they found themselves in nor to their developed practical work. However no interpretation of the two can ignore their university productions, as in both cases the thought they worked on proved to be very relevant to their mature thought and theory. Some of the irrelevance of their university work to the war and to their participation was due to the fact that neither had yet incorporated the work of their two most important German interlocutors in the social world, Karl Marx and Ernst Troeltsch. Both of them would be deeply moved and influenced by Marx and Troeltsch before they met each other.

Tillich as a student of philosophy learned particularly from Kant, Fichte, and Hegel, but the most important thinker for him was Friedrich Schelling (1775–1854). At the University of Halle he was initiated into German idealism through the teaching and work of Fritz Medicus. While he was serving as a pastor before the war, he worked on his dissertations on Schelling. He conveyed his sense of excitement about Schelling much later in life:

> I recall the unforgettable moment when by chance I came into possession of the very rare first edition of the collected works of Schelling in a bookstore on my way to the University of Berlin. I had no money, but I bought it anyway, and this spending of nonexistent money was probably more important than all the other nonexistent or sometimes existent money that I have spent. For what I learned from Schelling became determinative of my own philosophical and theological development.[2]

The dissertation presented to the University of Breslau for the doctor's degree in philosophy, "The Construction of the History of Religion in Schelling's Positive Religion." was published in 1910. It is breathtaking in scope as in the first part it explains the concept of the potencies, which is the key to Schelling's metaphysic. The implications of the doctrine of the potencies for God, humanity, and world are then expounded in a complete system. In the second part of the dissertation Tillich surveys the history of religion as it has evolved in Schelling's perspective from prehistoric time to the development of the church. In the third part, the implications of all of the foregoing for the philosophies of history and religion are explicated.

His second dissertation for a doctor's degree in theology awarded at the University of Halle in 1912 was entitled: "Mysticism and Guilt Consciousness in Schelling's Philosophical Development." Almost as bold as the first, this tackled two origins of religion; the one in union experiences with God and the other in the arising of guilt consciousness. Whether religion arose from religious experience or guilt was a major problem dividing theological camps, and he thought he had found a solution in a proper understanding of Schelling's metaphysics. By the time Tillich had finished his two doctorates on Schelling and been ordained to the ministry in 1912, many of the foundations for the work of his life had been laid. These foundations sustained him in the trenches even if later he added new contributors to his thought. If he gradually became an existentialist, he found that consistent with the later Schelling, but his existentialism always depended upon essentialism or foundational philosophy and that too he had found in Schelling. Essentialism for Tillich was imbedded in the language as humans expressed themselves in universals.

Hegel was the classic example for Tillich of essentialism. Existentialism expressed the human reality in the world of sin, guilt, and finiteness. Existentialism announced the revolt of the modern human against the illusions of idealism and the self-satisfied view of human nature expressed in the complacency known before World War I by the middle classes. Tillich found this revolt particularly in the contributions of Sigmund Freud, Karl Marx, and Friedrich Nietzsche. He also confessed his debt to the existentialism of the later Friedrich Schelling's critique of Hegel. So Tillich could call himself half essentialist and half existentialist. There are almost a score of points that in summary explicate what Tillich learned from Schelling:

1. The finite is more than finite as it contains in its dimensions echoes of the infinite and its divine origin.
2. Aesthetic intuition can be revelatory of the truth.
3. The infinite has been present in past periods of history and they have their own integrity.
4. The depths of society and humanity reach into the demonic as well as the divine.
5. Theology depends upon philosophy.

6. The power of the unconscious is relevant to both theology and philosophy.
7. Existentialism and Essentialism need each other.
8. Idealist epistemology and the principle of identity are characteristic of Tillich's thinking.
9. The divine requires dynamic categories of movement.
10. Nature-mysticism has its place in theology.
11. Human freedom and a transcendent fall are an issue for Schelling that required continuing work.
12. Elements of the method of correlation are present in the dissertations.
13. The significance of world religions for theology was learned from Schelling very early in Tillich's career and it is not best understood as a late development.
14. Society needs unification beyond bourgeois competition hinted at in Schelling but not apprehended by Tillich until later in the war when he was also influenced by other romanticists.
15, Tillich's developed philosophy of religion is foreshadowed in the dissertations.
16. When the social problem appeared in Tillich's consciousness, its resolution depended on the early work on Schelling's potencies to explicate his solution in the many essays on power and in *Love, Power, and Justice*.
17. The relationship of ontological thought to ethics was necessary for a liberating faith that would sustain one under social crisis. The existential awareness of the social crisis would come only a few years later in the breakdown of Europe in world war.[3]

Tillich's focus on the later Schelling brought him within range of the empirical study of religion which is partially perceivable in his study of world religions in terms of Schelling's observations.[4] Niebuhr turned towards the empirical study of religion at Yale University. But his mentor was found in the work of William James, whose books purchased at the bookstore in New Haven were among his treasured possessions at the end of his life. Niebuhr's Bachelor of Divinity thesis, which with his professor's (Douglass Macintosh) support admitted him to graduate study at Yale, followed the title of James's *The Varieties of Religious Experience* in its title *The Validity of Religious Experience and the Certainity of Religious Knowledge*. Much later in life Niebuhr would provide the foreword to a reprinted edition of James' work. But beyond James' study of religious experience, James' book *Pragmatism* influenced Niebuhr's two Yale theses, his ethical method, and writings for his entire life. Niebuhr brought his German churchmanship and study to the very American William James and used James to reinforce his theology which at Yale was dependent upon philosophical arguments. Niebuhr admitted at Yale that his philosophy was more developed than his theology and so it continued to be, though many interpreters could not see him this way. He did not teach systematic theology at Union Theological Seminary, but ethics and the philosophy of religion that for years he shared with Paul Tillich. His teacher Samuel Press at Eden encouraged his Yale studies, hoping Reinhold would prepare to teach in a seminary. As Reinhold said, he did not fulfill this ambition until thirteen years after leaving Yale.

The first thesis for the Bachelor of Divinity degree recognized that people believed in "supernatural" religion and asked how those beliefs could be authenticated. After all, historical criticism destroyed the authority of scripture on many subjects. Examination of the metaphysics behind much early church Christology weakened the authority of Christ. The necessity of accepting evolutionary theory, upon which biology depended, discredited some views of Christianity's claims to explain creation. He asked in the thesis how faith could be verified philosophically. Assuming the necessity of moral philosophy, he showed how naturalism, in his view, could not provide a basis for the moral life. Idealism failed to provide support for a transcendent God or an adequate moral life philosophy. His final chapter, "The Validity of Religious Ideas," combines several forms of religious apologetics to defend a religion of theism, immortality, freedom, and human ability to reason correctly in matters of religion.

The strongest argument is Kant's, that is, that religious ideas are necessary if the moral order is to make sense. He also comments appreciatively on Ritschl's formulation of the tradition: "It is to this view that we commit ourselves as most satisfactory." This chapter arguing that pragmatism did not need to reject religious beliefs moved on to William James' arguments in *The Will To Believe* explaining that if beliefs were not harmful and, moreover, if they were useful in defending necessary ideas like morality, freedom, and God, they could be trusted in a preliminary way. He had rejected authoritarian religion, naturalism, and idealism, but he thought a realism that looked at actual beliefs of people and found them to function usefully could be defended. Ideas could be regarded as true if they worked to put it in its most pragmatic way. It is hard to tell exactly how convincing this was to either Niebuhr or Macintosh on strictly philosophical grounds. He was arguing from belief to a defense of belief.

Returning home from his first year at Yale, Niebuhr was approached by Carl Vrooman, an assistant secretary of Agriculture, to join Wilson's administration as Vrooman's personal secretary. The salary prospects were much better than Niebuhr could hope to earn in the ministry. Moreover, the failure of his brother, Walter's, newspaper career and the financial needs of his mother pressed upon him. But on learning that he could proceed on toward graduate study with admission as a special student, he planned to return to New Haven.

Niebuhr wrote his Master of Arts thesis and attended classes while serving for a few months a small congregation in Derby, Connecticut. His academic work was mainly in philosophy under the guidance of Douglas Macintosh. Macintosh loaned him books and encouraged him to pursue the doctoral degree. But the needs of the Evangelical Synod for ministers and of his mother for support weighed more heavily and he finished his formal study with the M.A.

The year that Tillich entered the army, Neibuhr won a prize in the church Carnegie Endowment for Peace essay contest on "The Paradox of Patriotism" with a rewritten essay that he had undertaken for Professor Macintosh. Here too he followed William James' argument from his essay "The Moral Equivalent of War." James had argued that though war may be dreadful, it called forth from the individual a willingness to sacrifice in a cause greater than one's own life. As long as humanity did not find a cause greater than a war to give itself to, its fascination and attractiveness to men would remain to sustain the institution. Niebuhr followed James' perspective, but added that if the church could recover its militancy and enthusiasm it would suffice as a cause to give oneself to totally and thereby reduce the attractiveness of war. Certainly the great enthusiasm with which European young men volunteered and went off to the front must have been in his mind. Reinhold's brother Walter had been so attracted to the war as to risk his vocation by going off to serve as a reporter of the war.

Niebuhr's rejection of the war in the essay paralleled other arguments about the war, namely, that it reflected narrow economic interests, irrational patriotism, and petty issues that should have been resolved without further conflict. It was supportive of the American neutralism of the Wilson administration which pretended to be free of the war while shipping supplies to Great Britain. Furthermore the heroic church he described was the church model he was hoping to give his life to totally. Niebuhr's work for the church would throughout his years portray a model of Max Weber's "intraworldly ascetic" who gave himself totally to his chosen vocation to the neglect of health, family, and rest. The church he sought would be one free enough of the world to really challenge the world, but of course it was an ideal not to be realized.

The Master of Arts thesis is a better composition than the copy of his B.D. thesis available in the Library of Congress. The B.D. thesis had spelling and grammatical errors that the Master's is mostly free of, and it would appear that the years of study at Yale had improved his English while he complained that he was losing his German.

"The Christian Contribution to the Doctrine of Immortality" is a study both in New Testament studies and in philosophy of religion. Niebuhr rejects the bodily resurrection of Jesus as a late addition to the New Testament and believes the Christian contribution to the Platonic doctrine of the immortality of the soul is the deepened sense of personality that can be attributed to Jesus' own life and character. The thought of William James from *The Will to Believe* arguments again come into the picture as well as Immanuel Kant's arguments in favor of the immortality of the soul. The thesis marks Niebuhr as the young liberal he was at the time. He regards human optimism highly, lays great stress on individualism, and he does not hesitate to reject traditional Christian doctrine in light of that which is credible to his perception of modern humanity. Furthermore the biblical critics he followed were those acceptable to his own New Testament professors, Bacon and Porter. There is no emphasis on the solidarity of humanity which he would later affirm as supportive of some recognition of the symbol of the resurrection of the body. In his later writing he would argue that Paul's idea of a spiritual resurrection of the body held together the hope that it was a divine, not human, consummation and that the "body" reference implied the consummation not the annulment of the human historical process. Above all he cautioned Christians not to become overly certain about these symbols or their precise explication. The Social Gospel emphasis on social reform did not dominate his interests at Yale, but several themes from this Yale work contributed to the ongoing development of his mind and practice:

1. He was becoming thoroughly Americanized and developing a skill in English.
2. He was a Christian liberal who did not feel bound to tradition if it seemed incredible or oppressive.
3. Theology depended upon philosophy for its intelligibility.
4. Religious experience and not simply revelation was determinative for the vital religious life.
5. The historical criticism of scripture was accepted.
6. The credibility of Christianity as a religion for humanity did not depend on affirmation of the historical accuracy of mythical materials.
7. Peacemaking was a Christian priority, even if the ways were not yet developed satisfactorily.
8. Pragmatism and Christian faith could correlate and assist each other.
9. William James was a thinker Niebuhr would draw upon.
10. The use of "Ideal type" argument learned from both Macintosh and Professor E. Hershey Sneath would remain useful in generalizing huge movements into categories Niebuhr could compare and contrast.
11. The study of Christian ethics in the context of world religions as exemplified by Professor Sneath would remain a method for Niebuhr years later after beginning to teach in a seminary.

3

Between Emperor and Dictator

After the war, both Niebuhr and Tillich returned to church work. Niebuhr went back to his pastorate in Detroit full-time and Tillich took appointment as a city pastor in Berlin. As Tillich had feared, the peace process at Versailles destroyed the Austrian Empire, denied Germany its industrial base, and broke up the Ottoman Empire leaving seeds of discontent in the Balkans where the war had originated. Niebuhr's hopes for a new international order with Wilson's leadership were defeated both by British and French allies and the Republicans in the U.S. Senate. Woodrow Wilson's illness contributed to his inability to persuade the country to join the League of Nations. He wore himself out campaigning for the League of Nations and fell dangerously ill and day-to-day responsibilities for leadership fell on Mrs. Wilson. After Wilson the country was ready for restoration to less ambitious mediocrity and the presidencies of Republicans Warren G. Harding, and Calvin Coolidge followed for the rest of Niebuhr's time in the pastorate. Herbert Hoover defeated Alfred E. Smith the year that Niebuhr finished his pastorate and moved to New York City in 1928.

When serving in his pastor's position, Tillich lectured at the University of Berlin. His first course reflected how the war had thrown him into the social issues of his day. It was entitled "Christianity and the Social Problems of the Present." While Niebuhr was working to drop German from his church's name and to eliminate German from the literature and services of his church, Tillich's church had dropped the name of "King" from its church title substituting the word "Evangelical." But the reforms within the German Church could not go forward very far. The church was threatened by the Socialists' attempt to separate it from the state, and by mounting resistance to the governing party, the church succeeded in keeping its state privileges. Niebuhr's enthusiasm for a Presbyterian plan to unite all of the reformed churches in America into one church also came to nothing. Both of the young pastors were struggling to reform their churches but neither church moved fast enough for them.

In the midst of the revolutionary changes in Germany, Tillich joined a movement for reform of the church that permitted women officers, separated the church from the state, supported the peace movement rather than the state's militant approaches, and favored the new order and developing socialism rather than the old church alliance with capitalism. It called for church rallies to be held throughout the country to form a new parliamentary polity for the church and the replacement of the old bureaucracy. The major part of the church clung to the old verities of the state church in the midst of radical social change in government and society.[1]

The church bureaucracy reacted when a newspaper reported that Tillich had spoken at a rally of the radical Independent Social Democrats. The church superintendent demanded an explanation. Tillich and his friend Richard Wegener responded in a report on "Socialism as a Question of the Church."[2]

The report was divided into sections on Christianity and society, socialism and Christianity, and the church's task regarding socialism. The authors first confessed the independence of the encounter with God and its transcendence of particular social questions, affirming that religion has an inward personal character beyond any particular economic or social form. However, as Christianity carries with it the drive to shape life, they argued, it cannot be regarded as purely personal or inward for it is inevitably involved in society. Historically it has connected itself with the various social orders under which it has lived. Christianity is more inclined toward some orders than others; love has social consequences. The report stated a belief that the egoist competition of capitalism resulting in its militarism is in opposition to Christianity. Furthermore the authors argued that Christianity has greater affinity with socialism than with capitalism. Christianity is challenged to decide whether to move into the emerging social order or to remain in a conservative defense of the old order. The second part of the short paper argued that socialism has no essential fight with religion or Christianity. The atheism of some socialist leaders has been coincidental and unnecessary, they claimed. Socialism needs religion. Socialism may oppose clerical privileges and state-bestowed benefits for the church, but when it understands itself, socialism is not irreligious.

In the third part of the report, Tillich and Wegener argued that the church should adopt a positive attitude toward socialism not to win the workers back to the church, but to change the society. Socialism, they said, is a new ethical ideal emerging from the experience of the working class, and it expresses the proper social ethic of the church.

Superintendent D. Steinhauser did not discuss the report with them. He simply urged Tillich and his friend Richard Wegener not to speak at any more political rallies. He warned them that church people would not like such participation and he did not want to see any amalgamation of politics and religion. Wegener may have been the leader in the episode. He and Tillich remained close friends despite Richard "Dox" Wegener impregnating Tillich's wife twice, once when Tillich was away at the front. Tillich stayed with his wife through the second birth and then proceeded with divorce. Wegener eventually left the ministry and was appointed by Ernst Troeltsch in the Ministry of

Education to a government position. The two remained good friends even in their old age, and "Dox's" correspondence continued after Tillich's migration in 1933. Tillich turned toward a life in the university and only reentered active church life upon his migration to the U.S.

On the relationship of church to socialism, it is interesting to note that after the Second World War he rejoined the Socialist Party of Willy Brandt in Germany, but he kept his church membership in the United Church of Christ which the Niebuhr brothers had helped create out of the previous Evangelical and Reformed synods and the Congregational Church. His efforts to join together the antagonistic church and socialist movement continued even into 1933.

Kairos and Religious Socialism

Tillich's years in Berlin from 1919 to 1924 were the turbulent, chaotic, heady years of the Weimar Republic, and by 1925 some semblance of order was achieved. Tillich resided in Berlin until the spring of 1924, and while sympathetic to the radical Independent Socialists at whose rally he had spoken, his primary political education was in the discussion group of socialist academics that took the name of the Kairos Circle. Tillich's 1922 essay "Kairos" explicates the centrality of this idea in the political philosophy of the group. His essay of 1923, "*Grundlinien des religiosen Sozialismus*" expresses the outlines of his political philosophy at the time. Not all members of the Kairos Circle would accept totally the thought of these essays, but they are representative of Tillich's contributions to the group.

The Kairos Circle was also known as "The Berlin Circle" and it focused on the publication *Blaetter fuer religioesen Sozialismus* (*Leaves for Religious Socialism*) meeting every week or two in a home or a restaurant for discussion. It had evolved out of Social Workers Community under Carl Mennicke, Guenther Dehn, and Tillich's leadership. Guenther Dehn, a member until 1923, wrote that it never grew to more than ten or twelve members. Various commentators list different participants. Most interpreters[3] agree the list of members included Guenther Dehn, Edward Heimann, Adolf Lowe, Hans Hartman, Carl Mennicke, Ludwig Schmidt, Hans Simmons, Arnold Wolfers, and Tillich. The group continued after Tillich left for Marburg, but that move terminated his active leadership in the group. The ideas developed there continued to appear in his thought and Carl Mennicke and Adolf Lowe shared his company and influenced his thought through Frankfurt, and in New York he reunited with Edward Heimann and Adolf Lowe. Mennicke survived the war in concentration camps. Tillich was still sharing wine and conversation with Wolfers at the events around the inauguration of John F. Kennedy in the company of Reinhold Niebuhr. Tillich shared the speaker's platform among the 150 selected guests. Niebuhr, too weak to attend, stayed in the apartment with Wolfers and watched it on television.

The circle was not focused on Tillich's ideas. These were not intellectuals to be dominated and they had quite a few differences. In its membership were found both communists and socialists and both atheists and Christians. Mennicke summarized the groups main topics of conversation as Barth's theology, Marxism, the proletariat, and the shape of the future socialist society. These subjects were discussed in relationship to the turmoil of Berlin's political life.

The 1919 national elections witnessed the overwhelming victory of the Social Democrats. They polled eleven and one-half million votes; their nearest rival was the Catholic Party with almost six million votes. The Liberal Democrats received about five and one-half million. The governing coalition was formed from the three parties and Phillip Scheidemann presided over the coalition cabinet. Friedrich Ebert, the president, promised to rule for all Germans while not forsaking his working-class origins and his socialist principles. The National Constitutional Assembly had met in Weimar partially because of the continuing disorder in Berlin. By August of 1919 it was becoming clear that the Independents and the Communists were not to share in power and that the socialist measures of the new Weimar coalition would be moderate.

The Coalition was assailed by both the extreme right and the extreme left. The crippling pressures came from the victorious allies as they forced the German government to accept the Versailles Treaty. The coalition broke over the acceptance of the new borders, the loss of colonies, the economic reparations, and the insults to the German nation. A new government was formed, but in accepting the Treaty, the Social Democrats were damned from all sides in Germany. The bold new experiment in democracy was being strangled by the victorious democratic nations who seemed unaware that the empire they had opposed in the war had been transformed into a struggling republic. The Treaty of Versailles officially ending the war also lost the peace. The theory spread that a proud Germany had not lost the war on the battlefield but by domestic betrayal. Those who were reluctantly forced to support the Treaty were seen as the traitors.

The constitution was promulgated in August 1919, and in September the government moved to Berlin. The Weimar Constitution was a mixture of socialist and liberal principles reflecting the alliance of Social Democrats and center interests. It was written in the midst of civil disorder, even civil war, and immense powers for the protection of social order were given to the president. The Independent Social Democrats and Nationalists opposed the Constitution from opposite ends of the political spectrum. The hatred between the Independents and the Social Democrats reached a new intensity in January 1920 when rioting before the parliament, resulted in forty-two persons being killed by troops. The Social Democrats' hold on the workers weakened, and hostility to the government from the left deepened.

Political life in Germany stumbled from one crisis to another. Resisting allied demands for the reduction of the army, rightist leaders moved against the government. A brigade occupied Berlin; the government fled and Wolfgang Kapp was installed as head of the revolutionary government. The Social Democrat appeal for a general strike was honored by the unions, and much of German industry stopped. The ineptness of the conspirators, the resistance to the putsch by the proletariat, and the steadfast unity of the constitutional government caused the conspiracy to surrender their positions.

In the Ruhr socialists launched a counterattack that left them in control of several key industrial cities. The French retaliated by occupying Frankfurt on April 6, 1920. The newly formed Mueller government, again a coalition of Center, Democrat, and Social Democrat, was able to secure the withdrawal of France by mid-May. The social disorder was accompanied by the decline in the value of the currency and widespread lawlessness which shook the authority of the government.

The elections of 1920 saw the sharp decline of the voting strength of both the Democrats and the Social Democrats. The center was weakened while both rightist parties and the Independent Social Democrats on the left scored substantial gains. Independents attracted almost five million votes, only slightly behind the Social Democrats of 5.6 million. These elections revealed the trends that were to dominate the Weimar Republic: the eroding of the center and the rise of the extreme parties.

The growth of fighting groups on both sides of the political spectrum increased the instability of the society. Walter Rathenau, the liberal Jewish foreign minister was assassinated by right-wing nationalists on June 24, 1922. "Organization C," the refuge of supporters of the Kapp putsch was responsible. The murderers were caught, but the government, as usual, was unable to enforce stiff penalties against conspirators from the right.

Throughout 1923 strikes and moves for the secession of areas of the Ruhr and Bavaria kept Germany in turmoil. The Hitler-Ludendorf-attempted putsch in 1923 from Munich was suppressed, but the importance of Hitler was underestimated. In the elections of December 1924 the Nazis were so soundly defeated that they appeared to be of little political significance.

In Berlin, the foundations of the world seemed to be shaking. The death throes of the old empire prevented the emergence of a new, solid order. The forces for the new order were divided among middle-class liberal, nationalist, fascist, and radical-left groups. The political issue for the Kairos Circle was: How can we affirm action for decisive change without surrendering to the enthusiasm of the radical activists? Or, how can we mediate between the Marxist determinists and the romantic activists of the left who advocate revolution? Experience taught that action was vital to social change, but the action needed to be in accord with objective social conditions. In religious terms the question around the Kairos Circle was: How does the eternal relate to the temporal? To combine the religious and the political questions from a socialist perspective meant to ask: When are moments of historical action eternally significant?

Tillich's essay "Kairos"[4] attempted to answer these questions. He took the word *Kairos* from the New Testament and interpreted it to mean the "right time." It was more than formal or normal time included in the word *chronos*. He meant the concept to convey the meaning of an absolute demand. At certain moments events forced a decision for action that could become especially fulfilling. Such thinking required a concept that history carried significance and that particular moments allowed for decisive actions. Either Western mechanistic or Eastern mystical thinking were incapable of seizing the significance of particular moments based upon dialectical historical thinking. For Tillich the new socialist order was present in the right time and action for it could secure it in the Weimar Republic and the new could emerge. He didn't mean any state or situation was absolute, all would be relativized, but there were particular moments in which the unconditional broke through and made decisive actions possible. Action had to be carried out in the appropriate historical moment, and yet history did not determine itself. Action was required. The *Kairos* could only seize one and one could give oneself to the call for action when seized by the realization of the *Kairos*. For Tillich the absolute *Kairos* was symbolized by Christ's decisive action of surrendering himself, but there were other *kairoi* in history which could be judged by the *Kairos* of Christ's surrender. In part the essay was a refutation of romantic activists on the left who were constantly called to alter history by action. But it also improved upon the Marxist determinists who would not act, as they placed confidence only in the dialectics of history realizing the revolution. Tillich would develop the concept further, but already here in 1922 was one of his major concepts that would undergird later writings in socialist theory and find its way to his mature theology of *The Systematic Theology*.

In 1924, Tillich's moved to Marburg with his new wife Hannah. His Bohemian lifestyle and socialist politics had alienated him from the established church and the new church had not emerged. Similarly for Germany the election of Paul von Hindenburg to the presidency marked the end of the socialist revolution in 1925. Something like a return to normalcy for Germany was in the air. But the failure of German economics to recover under French pressure and the demands for punishing reparations left instability in the German body politic.

During these years of movement Tillich began writing about "faithful realism." The concept appeared in his *The Religious Situation* of 1926, uniting attention to historical detail (*Realismus*) with a response of faithfulness to the unconditioned. Reinhold Niebuhr had not yet articulated his Christian Realism which was essentially the same movement. Both drew upon Augustine whom Tillich addressed as *Fuhrer* or leader. H. Richard Niebuhr, Tillich's translator of the 1926 volume into English in 1932, suggested that to understand the term one should think first of realism in the history of art or in history generally. Though a focus on particulars was needed, such a focus could not reveal the deeper meanings of faith. Tillich wanted to unite the particulars of historical movement to their deeper religious meaning. The term "realism" also had a history in American theology and at Yale of referring to the reality of God independent of human understanding. Douglas Macintosh, Reinhold's teacher, would use realism in this theological way which was different than Tillich's or Reinhold's later use of it in social or political philosophy. Realism became associated with the Christian ethics of Augustine, taking the needs of the empire seriously but interpreting the history of the Roman Empire in terms of Christian faith in eternal purposes.

In 1927–1928 Tillich wrote two essays on faithful realism. He argued that expressionism and postexpressionism in art exhibited a rebellion against naturalism and idealism. These paintings expressed the depths of reality by breaking natural forms and using color to express "divine and demonic ecstasies." Tillich finds this same attitude of faithful realism in the fight against mystical and technical realism in philosophy of history. The mystical escaped history and the technical reduced it to mechanics and numbers.

In both personal and social relations, faithful realism attempts to unite scientific objectivity with passion for the purpose of transformation. Romanticism tries to escape to a utopia that never was real. *Realpolitik* only manipulates the present without regard to its depths. Faithful realism knows that the unconditional, which is the depth of the human historical situation, cannot be grasped by intellectuality alone.

Tillich uses Schelling to explain his understanding of the unconditioned as the ground and abyss of everything that is. The gap between God and humanity remains. The historical situation can be interpreted so it points in the direction of the unconditional. Tillich compares the interpretation to lightning in a thunderstorm which illuminates all and then leaves it again in darkness. So in faith God grasps humanity, there is a response in ecstasy, and after the illumination the darkness is never the same.

The Demonic

While turning toward Augustine and articulating faithful realism Tillich was also developing his concept of the demonic to illumine history and politics. His 1926 essay, "The Demonic a Contribution to the Interpretation of History,"[5] is his fullest discussion of the idea. The demonic is the form-destroying aspect of reality united dialectically to the form creating reality. It is expressed in primitive art as the force distorting the figures of animals and people in which we recognize the forms, but they are distorted. The potencies of the sexual organs are exaggerated pointing toward orgiastic expression. The orgiastic expression is also found in the rituals before they are tamed and purified. Similarly the history of religion presents phallic cults and holy demons leading even to the laceration-myths or practices and sacral sacrifice of the divinity. In the "Grand Inquisitor" Tillich saw religion making itself absolute, thereby opposing its founder Christ to destroy its foundation. The demonic was destructive, but it lived off the power of the creative or "being." If it were only itself, it participated in the symbol of pure negativity, or Satan, which could have no existence. "Demonry is the form-destroying eruption of the creative base of things."[6]

Art and religion can express the demonic in nature, but they attempt this by having nature rise toward a human form. The demonic comes to fuller expression in human personality and in its possession by forces working through the mind to distort the personality. The criminals portrayed on the nightly T.V. criminal shows come to mind where in most cases the heinous crimes are committed by persons whose personality has become warped. Often the power of the criminal is based upon human strengths which have become distorted and are living off the form of those human powers to break the forms of the mind and of society. After explaining the demonic in primitive and modern art, religion, and personality he turned towards the social demonic which use the power of human creation to destroy those creations. The demonic shows up in economics, church, and state as they misuse their powers to call for destructive sacrifices. Current examples beyond Tillich's time include: (1) Economic overlords calling for the poorest to make sacrifices to restore rational economics (2) Officially celibate priests using their spiritual power to corrupt the young sexually is beyond moral condemnation pointing toward the tendency of the demonic or grotesque to live within disciplined communities of repression to exact a terrible toll on the innocent (3) Young Americans being called to sacrifice their lives in a mistaken war which is partially about ancient religious disputes that they do not understand.

For Tillich at this point, the history of religion is a battle against the demonic expressions found in religion and the peculiar response different religious traditions have to the demonic. Similarly history is the story of the demonic uprising and needing to be put down. Once history is understood as struggle between the powers of creation and those primitive powers destroying or at least attacking the forms of creation, the duty of everyone to resist the demonic is seen as a religious one.

Tillich names two social forms of the demonic. They are the power of autonomous economics expressed in capitalism, and the power of nationalism. Both presuppose form, but they require sacrifices driving towards destruction. The two forces combined to bring about the destruction of the world war. So he saw social demonic power in the union of capitalism and nationalism which had brought about the world war, though temporarily separated, trying to combine again to sustain them and to destroy themselves.

Tillich expressed confidence in the ultimate overcoming of the demonic with the grace of eternity. But in this history the best that could be done was to deny the demonic ultimate victory. All the weapons of resistance against the demonic must be used even without any guarantee of success.

In a few years Tillich would use the demonic to refer to Hitler and Nazism. Many years later the concept would appear almost two dozen times in each of his three works of systematic theology. But in those volumes nationalism and capitalism would not be named as the primary expressions of social demonic. The term has not been used successfully in mainstream American discourse.

Tillich's thought, in this period before Frankfurt, expressed his existentialism, and reflected the influence of Rudolph Bultmann and Martin Heidegger, his Marburg colleagues. But he followed the existential philosophy of Schelling who had coined the term in its individualistic expressions. Tillich was also in dialogue with Marx and he expressed a social existentialism. The human was to a large degree the product of his society. He believed Christianity could only be addressed by a modern person in terms of the concepts of modern society. Christianity, particularly in its Protestant-secular form had contributed so much to society that social questions usually presupposed the heritage of Christianity. The influence of Marx is seen particularly in Tillich's use of the "class struggle."[7] The Socialist Party of Germany (SPD) had evolved into an evolutionary form of democratic socialism that Tillich regarded as naive, and he refrained from joining the SPD until he felt forced to join in 1929 for practical reasons of resistance to various forms of German nationalism. The proletariat was left without security or meaning for their lives.

Tillich never gave up his longing to find meaning for the working class, and he believed it could only be found by a thoroughgoing change of a revolutionary nature that would secure meaning and security for the workers.

Tillich's years in Frankfurt as professor of Philosophy and Sociology were the most prosperous of his academic years in Germany. He no longer had to think about moving and establishing himself in the academic world. But the very context of Frankfurt provided the realities that would lead to his suspension by the Nazi regime in 1933. Frankfurt's reputation as a socialist university was deserved and this was especially true of the Institute for Social Research which Tillich sponsored and collaborated with. Tillich was close to its leading lights who were Marxists trying to integrate Sigmund Freud's thought into their social analysis. Tillich's acquaintance with psychoanalytic theory was deepened here. Though he was close to some Jews in the Kairos Circle in Berlin, here in Frankfurt many more of his friends and allies were Jews. His wife, Hannah, referred to him as "Paulus among the Jews." From these years on he could be regarded as one of the best friends of the Jewish people and he has been memorialized in the Holocaust Museum in Washington, D.C. He was particularly close with Max Horkheimer, Walter Benjamin, and Theodore Adorono. In 1933, he shared in his suspension from Frankfurt with Mannheim, Horkheiemer, and Sinzheimer from the Institute. The young Hans Morgenthau met Tillich at Frankfurt and would much later integrate some of Tillich's philosophic concepts into his political theory as he became one of the best known theorists of world politics during the Cold War.[8]

Frankfurt developed tendencies from Tillich's earlier work and thrust him into opposition to the Nazis as dean of the faculty, as a churchman speaking for Protestantism against the Nazis and tendencies within Protestantism, and as a friend, colleague, and ally of the Jews. He had worked some on Marx and Freud before and had experienced some brief psychoanalysis, but here that work was deepened and ground was laid for his later work in America on mental health issues and their correlation with religion. Though he was more politically active and outspoken than most members of the Institute, he came to appreciate the possibility of critical distance from political involvement which would later find expression when socialism was eclipsed by the Cold War. Finally it was in Frankfurt that he came to realize what Niebuhr called "The Devil's Brew of Hitler." Tillich learned in World War I that he had been taught an inadequate theology, and he spent his years between the revolution overthrowing the emperor and the rise of dictator Hitler developing his new faithful realism on a religious socialist base. Niebuhr was learning his realism in the pastorate in Detroit following the war.

Social Issues at Bethel Evangelical Church

Niebuhr's hopes for a church that would challenge his imagination and take his energies was not fulfilled in his call to the mission congregation of eighteen families at Bethel Evangelical Church in Detroit. He observed from the pulpit in his first Sunday at the church that the congregation was larger than he expected, but its age makeup was interesting. It seemed to be composed mostly of the very elderly and many children. An officer of the church explained after the service that the size of the congregation was due to the special arrangements made for residents of the church retirement home and the orphanage to attend his installation as minister.

His liberal theology and advanced philosophical studies were not of great use to him with the generally conservative German congregation. He had thought that his advanced study should earn him a better call and a larger salary, but he fell back upon the symbolism of the Evangelical synod and the methods of his father and mother to guide the church. The congregation was a mission church and his very meager salary and even the church budget were supplemented by denominational funds at first. The travails and pitfalls of youthful ministry are recorded in the diary he published as he left the parish, *Leaves from the Notebook of a Tamed Cynic*. It still deserves to be read by anyone seeking to enter the ministry. He preached in both German and English until 1919 when the German service was dropped. He had only two years of regular parish ministry from 1915 to 1917 before he was caught up in the necessities of war in the summer of 1918. After the war he soon found himself in demand as a speaker and so he continued the itinerant ministry that had characterized his wartime service. His mother assisted him in maintaining the parish during the week and Hulda and Richard both provided further assistance. In the last years his supporters provided him with three successive young assistant ministers to carry on the local parish work that his developing role made impossible. He tried to be in the parish on the weekends and he succeeded in growing the membership into the 600s, and to preside over the dedication of the new handsome church building. Though this study's concern is his political thought and action, he was a successful compassionate preacher whose voice came to be respected in the rapidly growing auto city of Detroit. Moreover it was his passionate, bold style of speaking which developed from his preaching that led to the demand for his speaking at youth rallies, national YMCA venues, and other public meetings. Social problems encountered in Detroit furnished him with the major themes for his ongoing work in social ethics and politics.

War and Peace

The Great War interrupted his early ministry and projected him onto the national stage for the Evangelical Synod. It encouraged his abandonment of the German background of his denomination and his work to bring his denomination into the mainstream of American culture. Serving on the executive committee of his church's Wartime Commission he crossed the country visiting training camps and explaining his church's support for the American entry in the war. Representing his denomination in New York, he met several of the faculty of Union Theological Seminary also involved in providing support for the ecumenical movement in the war. The liberal ideals with which President Wilson entered the war and tried to implement at Versailles had drawn Niebuhr into the war mentality along with his fellow churchmen and professors of divinity. His engagement with the war policies of his church and his resultant disillusionment on seeing the results of the war while visiting Europe in 1924 on Sherwood Eddy's (1871–1963, a national secretary of the YMCA) traveling seminar led him for the closing years of his pastoral ministry to take a pacifist stance. With his persuasive preaching style of seeming to think through dilemmas while preaching he gained fame as a speaker and his organizational talents gained him a reputation within the pacifist movements, at the same time he was studying and mastering some of the language of international relations. His skill at powerful journalistic writing led him to report on the international travel with Eddy's seminars winning him further influence in the pacifist ranks.

Detroit Race Relations

An attempt by a Black doctor, Dr. Ossian Sweet, to move into a house that he purchased slightly outside of the crowded Negro district led to racist demonstrations outside his home. The police arrested eleven Black Americans after one of the white demonstrators was shot as the mob approached the house. Sweet was accused of murder along with other African-Americans present in the house during the mob riot, and as the case moved toward trial Clarence Darrow and Arthur Garfield Hays rushed to Detroit to join the defense. The incident intersected the campaign for Mayor by John W. Smith and the Klu Klux Klan supported his opponent Charles Bowles. Mayor Smith was also Roman Catholic and antiprohibitionist. Niebuhr and some other liberal ministers spoke out against the racial bigotry that was supporting the Bowles campaign and the major newspapers of Detroit, the *Times* and the *Free Press* both ran Niebuhr's sermon on their front pages. Niebuhr admitted the Protestant origins of the Klu Kiux Klan and asked his listeners to repudiate it.

Mayor Smith remembered the support and the next March appointed Niebuhr to serve as chair of the interracial committee that had not made much progress under its two previous chairs.[9] This appointment was his first major venture into secular affairs since the social reformer, Jane Adams, had asked him to introduce Robert La Follett at the Progressive Party's rally. Among the thousands migrating from the south to automobile jobs in Detroit were veterans of World War I ready to realize some of the freedoms they thought they had fought for in Europe. About 75,000 had migrated to Detroit since the end of the war and the larger migrations were still in the future. Niebuhr accepted the Mayor's appointment to chair the race committee despite the protests of some clergymen that public suspicions of the mayor should disqualify a minister from taking the position. It would not be the last time Niebuhr would work with allies that he could not support wholeheartedly.

Bishop William T. Vernon of the African Methodist Episcopal Church served as vice-chairman of the committee. The committee correlated its work with the Detroit Bureau of Governmental Research's study of the racial situation. Fred Butzel furnished much of the driving force in the committee and he became a lifelong friend of Niebuhr who would often reflect on the integral sense of justice that characterized his Jewish friend. Executives of the Ford Motor Company, lawyers, and physicians also served on the prestigious committee. The committee, using the empirical work of the Bureau of Research, applied its own sense of justice and proposed policies for the city and which they regarded as achievable.

The report urged the creation of a permanent race-relations committee. The permanent committee would work through education to combat racism and be empowered to recommend policies to agencies to overcome discriminatory practices in government, business, education, welfare, real estate, and recreation.

The committee commented on the housing issues. The decline in home prices in integrating neighborhoods was dismissed as a result of fear rather than a necessary condition. While white ownership of black slums was not addressed. Negroes were urged to adopt measures to keep their property in better shape to support housing values. Better integration in the services of real estate agencies was urged, and discrimination in banking practices regarding home mortgages was noted. Lack of more-notable progress in housing related to race was due to the same prejudice that had instigated the mob and the resultant killing and arrests in the Sweet case.

Discrimination in employment was recognized, but voluntary means of correction by labor unions and employers was accepted. Employers were urged to hire more from the minority community, but the presence on the committee of executives from Ford Motor Company and Vulcan Manufacturing Company kept the tone of the report mild. The absence of any executives from the minorities in the education and health work of the city was recorded and temperate recommendations for changes were registered.

The churches were commented on, but without enlisting them in the fight against structural racism. The need for a Black ecumenical church organization was mentioned as was the need for the white churches to aid the African-American churches financially. The report contained no challenge to the segregation of the churches nor could it foresee the leading role the Black churches would later take in overcoming racism.

The report challenged most of the structures of Detroit, but not very much. Still it went further than Detroit was prepared to move. Niebuhr later commented on how these study committees on race issues could not go much beyond the commitments of the power centers of the political body supporting them. Niebuhr's later work would keep him commenting on study commissions on race, but they were to be seen as only one of the levers of reform and not among the more important instruments. More Negroes started attending Bethel Church following the release of the committee's report. June Bingham reported that the Bethel Church board was ready to admit Negroes to membership, but neither the Negroes nor their churches were prepared for the step. Later after Niebuhr's departure, ministers at Bethel would find themselves in deep conflict over the integration of the church as young ministers seemed more concerned to move forward than the leaders of the congregation. Niebuhr himself became outraged at Bethel's refusal to integrate its membership, even though his first response had been to think the young minister had been intemperate and imprudent in the way he handled the issue. Further reflection on this incident is included in the chapter concerning Niebuhr's arrival in New York. According to Christopher Niebuhr, Reinhold's son, John C. Bennett, and Roger Shinn, Niebuhr approached church leaders in Harlem about beginning an ecumenical integrated congregation on the edge of Harlem near Union Theological Seminary when he moved to New York City, and that the leaders of the Black churches discouraged the attempt.

In Detroit Niebuhr kept moving on the race issue by speaking on it in a series of Sunday evening talks on race and by speaking on the subject at Elmhurst College. Before he left he addressed the subject in four of these lectures in 1927 with the titles "Race Relations in Detroit," "What about Negro Crime," "Where shall the Negro live?" and "The Christian conscience and the Race Problem." The talks drew both on the social research of the city's Detroit Bureau of Governmental Research and his deepening theology. In his later life Niebuhr would come to treat racism as an expression of original sin as well as history, and it became one of the main issues of his social concern to the end of his life. Niebuhr's own essay on the report was more expressive than the official report. He detailed the prejudice of the police department against black citizens and recorded the twenty-four shootings of Negroes by the police. He indicated the difficulties of Black citizens finding housing. The unwillingness to employ Black women kept them in miserable poverty. He tried to explode the myth that prejudice was a phenomenon of the South indicting Nordic peoples in general with race prejudice that varied only with historical and social circumstances.

> Race prejudice is one of the greatest challenges to the spirit of real Christianity. The whole validity of the Christian faith is in the balance as men try to solve the race problem. Either there is in Christ neither white nor black or the whole Christian faith becomes absurd.[10]

He went on to indicate that sometimes religion aggravated the race issue. He concluded by calling on young Christians to dedicate themselves to overcoming the race divide within Christianity. The development of his greater sophistication on the subject and his various strategies for working on the race problem of the country will be developed later in this narrative. Already he had learned how to use political power combined with social scientific research and religious imagination to work at liberalizing a community's attitudes on race. As of May 1927, he had seen the mayor respond with the appointment of a permanent committee to improve race relations. Through it all Niebuhr demonstrated his understanding of how deep the problems of racial prejudice were in his people.

The four sermons mentioned above on race were given in his Sunday evening series. He felt he could openly preach or lecture on subjects of controversy in the evening while he kept his Sunday morning sermons more tightly tied to the biblical issues of faith. Often on Sunday evenings he would have guest lecturers on controversial subjects address his congregation and others who would come. It was in the evenings that he would draw out theological themes from literature, and discuss particularly significant books. He continued to discuss literature and religious meanings in his early years at Union Seminary. He first taught with Harry Ward the course in literature and ethics and then he carried it on for a few years as his own course. In 1930–1931 when Bonhoeffer was a visiting fellow, Bonhoeffer was introduced to several Negro authors in Niebuhr's class. Bonhoeffer's published class notes show that he was introduced to Johnson (*Autobiography of an Excoloured Man*); W. E. B. Dubois (*The Souls of Black Folks*); A. Locke (*The New Negro*); C. Cullen (*The Copper Sun*); and B. T. Washington (*Up from Slavery*); and unnamed poetry by Langston Hughes. Other works referred to included antiwar works, Ibsen, Shaw, Lewis, and Dreiser. These lectures on literature, first in Detroit and then at Union, only a few years later, show a side of Niebuhr, the reader of literature and poetry, not often stressed in interpretations of Niebuhr.

The Critique of Henry Ford

Niebuhr's critique of Henry Ford developed late in his Detroit ministry. It followed the events that the editors of the *Christian Century* entitled: "The Battle of Detroit."[11] The American Federation of Labor held its convention in Detroit in October 1926. Niebuhr, as secretary of the committee on industrial relations, and M. C. Pierson, the secretary of the Council of Churches invited clergy members to meet to discuss invitations to church leaders from the A. F. of L. to speak in their churches on Sunday. Eighteen pastors attended the meeting and five invitations to speakers from the labor organization were issued. The Chamber of Commerce protested in its publications and the Building Trade Commission asked that the church decisions be reversed. At a following meeting of the Council of Churches, the secretary of the council explained that the invitations had been the idea of the Federal Council of Churches and that as only five invitations had been given it was a trivial matter that ought not concern the members of the council. Three of the original five invitations were withdrawn and only Niebuhr's Bethel Church and a Unitarian Church went ahead with their programs. Mr. William Green, the president of the A. F. of L. had been invited to speak at an afternoon meeting of the local Y.M.C.A. That meeting was also canceled and Mr. Green was informed that because of a large building project of the Y.M.C.A. to which Mr. Ford and Mr. Kresge were large donors it was deemed wise to withdraw the invitation. The churches and the Y.M.C.A. came in for a flaying at the labor convention.[12] The Federal Council of Churches rallied to uphold the dignity of the churches and sponsored a Sunday afternoon meeting at the First Congregational Church at which Mr. Green spoke. The church had been routed and the freedom of its pulpits challenged even though representatives of the national denominations protested the work of the Chamber of Commerce and the retreat of the Y.M.C.A. Detroit business defended the open shop and made it clear that the real power rested in the wealthy members of the boards of directors that controlled both the Y.M.C.A. and many of the churches. Niebuhr himself had felt the crunch as an organizer of the effort to allow the churches to hear labor speakers. His vision of a courageous church that would take large risks for justice was shown to be in part an illusion. The *Century* editorial summarized: "the churches did show themselves for the most part timid, muddleheaded, and without a word of prophecy."[13]

Niebuhr's first essay on Ford was unsigned as editorials in the *Century* generally were. Under the title "Henry Ford and Industrial Autocracy," Niebuhr attacked the humanitarian reputation of Mr. Ford. He argued that the five-day week was a result of the Ford Company's speedup in which a worker produced in five days what he had originally produced in six days and the worker now received pay for five days. Ford refused to provide unemployment insurance or pensions so the workers' needs fell upon Detroit's philanthropic organizations which Mr. Ford would not support. The drive for efficiency wore the workers out and shortened their working years. He feared that the unions, as unsuccessful as they were, thought only in terms of wages and working hours whereas they needed a message to capture the loyalties of potential members. Both labor and capital needed to try to develop work for the whole person that would promote their dignity and free personality rather than seeing them as cogs in a machine. Niebuhr closed: "Civilization must finally be confronted with the choice between more goods and more good life."[14]

Reacting to the pressure against the churches, Niebuhr signed his second editorial criticizing the moral position of Henry Ford. The essay entitled "How Philanthropic Is Henry Ford?" exposed the meager philanthropic work of the Ford family while noting the large contributions to the Y.M.C.A. and to the hospital which Ford built and maintained. Niebuhr argued that, relative to the cost of living, the average wage for the Ford worker was less than it had been fourteen years earlier. Moreover Ford provided no assistance when it laid off workers or they suffered injuries. He argued that maybe Ford's speedup made engineering and business sense, but that "It shows no consideration for the average man thrown upon the streets because he is unable to keep up."[15]

The purpose of the article was to undercut Ford's carefully cultivated hero status. His reputation as a great humanitarian was undeserved even if he produced a reliable and cheap product and had at one time paid decent wages. The great concentration of wealth built up by Ford was not shared by either stockholders or employees. Niebuhr noted the tendency to ennoble those who were financially successful. A recent poll showed that while Jesus was the most honored person, Napoleon came in second. People wanted to endow important men with moral qualities. He speculated that most Americans wanted to follow both Jesus and Napoleon which he regarded as a dubious mixture. The myth needed to be challenged empirically. Ford's rural-village social views simply applied to a great industrial enterprise obscured the truth. More subtle social philosophies were needed to understand Ford Motor Company.

The short essay caused the Ford Motor Company to react. The secretary of the corporation appealed to a small parts manufacturer who was also the donor of the land Bethel Church stood upon to prevail upon his minister to retract his essay as it was obvious that the *Christian Century* was an anti-Ford journal which had entrapped the young naive minister. Niebuhr was amused by the suggestion that he had been entrapped for he thought that part of the reason for the journal having an anti-Ford bias was due to his previous unsigned editorials in the *Century*. Mr. Hartwig, the manufacturer, assured the Ford executive that after conferring with his minister, Mr. Niebuhr stood ready to retract anything that was proven to be untrue. Feeling the support of his own congregation and the person Ford regarded as most likely to support the auto corporation, Neibuhr published another essay criticizing the pretensions of the company and its owner.

Niebuhr's closing essay reacted to critics who still treated Mr. Ford as a social genius and somewhat of a demigod. Niebuhr gave six accounts of Ford workers who through no fault of their own were forced on to the public welfare rolls of the city. Niebuhr claimed the social agencies of the city were overwhelmed with half of their cases coming from ex-Ford workers. The acclaimed five-day week was being reduced to three- and four-day weeks as the competition from General Motors was taking its toll. The article did not add much to the previous essays, but it raised the threat of unionization while recognizing the need for better union leadership. It appears that Niebuhr needed to continue his criticisms because Ford had tried to silence him with similar tactics as those with which he had muzzled the clergy previously. He concluded:

> In our day of enlightenment it is possible for a man to amass billions and be praised at the same time for the astuteness of his business mind and the generosity of his impulses, even though the groans of his workers may be heard above the din of his machines. Will we ever achieve enough social intelligence to match our mechanical achievements?[16]

Niebuhr's social thought was deepening. He was beginning to think that public industries like Ford Motor Company that demanded the whole society's cooperation should become public in ownership. The influences of his socialist friends and readings were becoming clear. The left-wing of the Social Gospel grew in its attraction to him in the parish. The leadership of the Methodist Bishop McConnell had particular influence upon him in Detroit and his work with the *Christian Century* deepened his connections with the movement, though it is not clear that he had read Walter Rauschenbusch or felt more than his indirect influence. The pacifism he held and his pro-union activities were part of the Social Gospel emphasis, his direct action in race relations came through the contingencies of his urban parish life and his own ethical sensitivity. The book he put together in a summer before leaving the parish reflected his reading of the German masters Weber and Troeltsch which Tillich was also using in the same period. *Does Civilization Need Religion?* reflected their insights and also the philosophy he had studied in graduate school, especially that of Alfred North Whitehead. He struggled against the cynicism of Bertrand Russell and turned toward the Christian Socialism in its British form of R. H. Tawney. The full-blown socialist recognition waited his moving to New York City and its socialist intellectual environment and the depression.

4

The World Tomorrow

During Tillich's tenure at the University of Frankfurt and the deepening crises of the depression and the ascension of Hitler, Niebuhr was arriving at Union, and taking on his work as an editor of the socialist-pacifist journal *The World Tomorrow*. He had been offered a teaching post at Boston University and an editorship at *The Christian Century*, but neither offer drew him away from the Detroit pastorate. The combination of Sherwood Eddy's support at the journal and at the seminary was sufficient for him to leave the Bethel Church. The acceptance of the two roles drew him deeper into socialism and initially deeper into pacifist decision-making circles, but then the realities of the times as he perceived them drew him away from pacifism.

Sherwood Eddy's forms of Christian action were also Reinhold Niebuhr's. Eddy, The Asian secretary for the International Young Men's Christian Association recruited Niebuhr to speak in college chapels, rallies, and at YMCA events around the country. This work demanded Niebuhr spend days away from his Bethel Church pastorate. Some weeks Niebuhr would return to Detroit for the weekends, make pastoral calls, write his sermons, conduct services, and undertake the pastoral work recorded in *Leaves from the Notebook of a Tamed Cynic* until he went on the road again often taking in five to seven speaking engagements before returning by train to Detroit. In addition to recruiting Niebuhr for these talks, Eddy provided several opportunities for the young Niebuhr to obtain international experience in Europe from 1920 on as Niebuhr first joined in then helped lead and translate for Eddy's Christian traveling seminars in which European leaders in church, society, and state met with the seminars. From at least 1927 until he succeeded in the autumn of 1928, Eddy lobbied the president of Union Theological Seminary to find an academic place for the young Niebuhr. President Henry Coffin, also impressed by the young preacher concurred, and after some initial faculty opposition, Niebuhr joined the faculty on a half-time basis in 1928. Eddy raised the funds for Niebuhr's half-time salary at the seminary and the other half was provided as Niebuhr assumed partial editorship of Eddy's journal, *The World Tomorrow*.

Niebuhr's patron was, like himself, a pacifist and a socialist owing much to both Jesus and Marx. Like Niebuhr, he had earlier been a liberal reformer hoping to reform capitalism, but gradually becoming convinced that it needed to be replaced. Eddy wrote in his early biography that a religious social reform movement required three functions: speaking, organizing, and publication. Prior to Eddy's involvement Niebuhr had the first two and had done some writing, but Eddy gradually deepened Niebuhr's role in journalism as he brought him along as editor. Niebuhr served in various editorial capacities with the journal until it ceased publication in 1934. Niebuhr's own position evolved to a less than total pacifism and that created tension with the then-editor (1926–1934) of *The World Tomorrow* Kirby Page (1890–1957; Disciples of Christ minister) who was one the leading pacifists in the country.

Niebuhr was made a contributing editor of *The World Tomorrow* in January 1927. His essay on "Missions and World Peace" appeared in the April issue. He recognized that missionaries were often agents of imperialism pushing American values as much as the gospel. Much of the missionary movement had been sublimated imperialism. In the end he was glad there were missionaries in China as the majority were supporting the Chinese and peacemaking in the current crisis.

Vital Christianity needed to preserve a tension with its society and to uphold its ideals. Niebuhr wrote that Christians would not fulfill their ideals, but it was better to articulate them as purely as possible rather than give up on them because of human failures. Social groups needed to be molded to reflect the ideals of Christianity as much as individuals or the religion would be seen as irrelevant. The essay is quite idealistic, and it lacks the realism about the stubbornness of groups to follow morality that would appear in his major book of 1932.

The January 1928 issue published Harry F. Ward's critical review of Niebuhr's first book *Does Civilization Need Relgion?* Ward, the professor of Christian Ethics at Union Theological Seminary was a fellow contributing editor as were Sherwood Eddy, A. J. Muste, and Norman Thomas. In Ward's opinion, Niebuhr needed more time to reflect, work on his ideas, and learn more from the Communist developments in Russia. Also, Niebuhr failed to show how his recommendations of mysticism or asceticism could translate into practical action which religion so desperately needed. Obviously he had liked Niebuhr's articles on Henry Ford and the one on what the war had done to Niebuhr's mind. Other deficiencies in the volume according to Ward were its failure to use the newer scientific writings of sociology.

Niebuhr of course did not have a high regard for sociology and continued to neglect it as his work turned more toward politics. The classes the two would teach at Union would reflect these ongoing tensions with Niebuhr using less sociology and Ward using more. Their differing evaluations of developments in Russia would bring about the distancing of their work from each other after a period of cooperation.

Ward at first was the dominant professor introducing Niebuhr to teaching. In their first few years together at Union they taught together, but gradually they divided their courses one from another. At the end of his review Ward raised the question whether institutions could provide the talented Niebuhr with space in which to undertake the intellectual work he needed. Such a sentence certainly indicates that Ward knew of the moves Sherwood Eddy was undertaking to bring this pastor from Detroit to a teaching position alongside himself.

Ward left the role of contributing editor after publishing the review. He continued to contribute articles critical of capitalism to the magazine. By 1931 Harry Ward was writing Niebuhr that he had lost interest in the magazine which seemed to him to be of the old world, and he was moving on to the new world.

In April of 1928 Niebuhr was welcomed as one of the three editors of the journal. His commitment as a pastor to social ministry was recognized and he was treated as particularly expert in the areas of race relations, economic matters, and international relations. The same issue announcing his editorship provided a two-page spread advertisement for the book, announced it was the selection of the Religious Book Club, and combined it with a special price subscription to *The World Tomorrow*.

Part of the book, which Ward regarded as too simplistic, was published in the January issue. Niebuhr dealt with the contrast between the spirituality of the East and the applied science of the West. He regarded Buddhism as life-denying and Western religion as having lost its relevance in its inadequate attempts to tame Western greed and practical pursuits of wealth. The more practical aspects of Confucianism were not mentioned. The article was published along with pieces by Sherwood Eddy, Kenneth Latourette, and J. H. Oldham, all of whom were more deeply informed about the state of missions than Niebuhr. In contrast to Latourette, the great historian of missions, Niebuhr was more interested in the ideals of Christianity to humanize life that the missionaries might communicate than he was in notions of salvation through Jesus Christ. He returned to his theme of the need for Western religion to detach itself more thoroughly from Western society if it were to be relevant to the Orient. He noted that unless Western religion gave up its attachment to imperialism, the rise of Japan might drive the West from the Orient.

Niebuhr in 1928 was moving away from his own pacifism as he observed the role of force in industrial relations. His long essay in the May 1928 issue argued that there were many forms of pacifism and that pacifists did not agree among themselves as to its meaning. He stipulated that pacifism meant that the use of force is wrong even though some would regard it as a necessary evil in some situations. While suspicious of the use of force in all situations and hoping for the use of nonviolent forces of social change, he thought that to be a pacifist there must be at least one area in which one renounced the use of violence.

Niebuhr regarded himself as a pacifist at the time, as he rejected armed force among nations as never redemptive. While the use of economic sanctions could not be regarded as a social good, there were some situations in which, though dangerous, they might be justified on moral grounds. Gandhi's boycotts, Chinese boycotts in Hong Kong and the strikes by industrial workers were all regarded by Niebuhr as means of seeking social change preferable on moral grounds to the use of violence. Nonviolent means of social change avoided the confusion of violent means that brought the moral judgment against the rightful struggles to overcome oppression.

Niebuhr's May 1928 essay stressed that cooperation in society and trust had more to do in building societies than violence or force. Cooperation and trusting acts among nations inspired further such acts and strengthened the forces of peace. Distrustful actions engendered similar responses in other nations. Policies of love did not always work, but love tended to increase trust and engender its own victories. He recognized the need for a society to confine its disturbers of the peace. But, even here progressive forces would have to expect martyrs, for societies tended to be self-conservative and would oppress their progressive forces as well as their criminal elements. Here he treated force as redemptive in only a few situations, evil in most, and "dangerous in all situations." The journal continued soliciting articles on pacifism in the following issues, and most of the writers were more pacifist than the role Niebuhr had worked out for himself.

Niebuhr and John Dewey shared back-to-back essays in the October 1928 issue. Dewey's entitled "A Critique of American Civilization" noted the bigotry in race relations, and the corruption of politics, but remained hopeful. He saw that education and potentials for the development of a higher culture were becoming diffused. He thought a new world was being born through mass education and regardless of its quality, its spreading promised new possibilities beyond what Europe could hope to achieve. He thought social criticism was promising results, and he added to the broadening of the benefits of culture his sense that Americans were particularly ready to share the advantages of civilization with each other. He recognized that his optimism was based more on faith than on science, and though he was uneasy about prophecy, he saw promising tendencies beyond the present mendacity and low state of American culture.

Niebuhr's essay, "Why We Need a New Economic Order," was more pessimistic, as he believed the whole public life was corrupted when it was built upon an immoral base. He regarded the large part of the population that suffered grievously from industrial conditions as driven to a cynicism about the moral and spiritual justifications of the present order and its religions. Profits were appropriated individually while the product of industry was a social product. Without change there could be no real health in Western civilization. But the oppressed could not change the system itself. Change depended upon the whole community and upon the elite who could modify or reform the system if they understood its dangers. He was not optimistic about the outcome of revolution in a complex modern society, and he thought the hopes of the radicals for thorough change through revolution "were not borne out by history."

In the essay for December 1928, he asked: "Would Jesus Be a Churchman Today?" He thought that many of the more-sensitive moralists could not compromise enough to associate with the church. He recognized that Jesus remained loyal to his tradition while innovating within his own fellowship. He regarded the racial prejudices and acceptance of the economic order by Catholicism and Protestantism as betrayal of the mind of Jesus. The compromise was necessary, but within Protestantism it almost degenerated into Nordic plutocracy. However, religion as a social force to reform society required some form of organization and the churches should not be abandoned. The task was to make the church an effective agent of social reform. Here the liberalism and low-church theology of Niebuhr were very evident. Despite his years in the pastoral ministry and a lifetime of service in a seminary, it is possible to understand why his critics regarded him as having an inadequate appreciation of the church. However, he was very aware that only recently was the church addressing the barbarous racism of its practice, and it was still unable to qualify the greed of its economic masters.

His contributions to *The World Tomorrow* in 1929 were less extensive than previously. He wrote ten book reviews including volumes by Joseph Stalin and Leon Trotsky. The review of the two competitors for the control of the Russian revolution and the praiseworthy biography *Lenin* by Valeriu Marcu received the most attention and thought by Niebuhr and foreshadowed his lifetime of serious reading of studies of the Soviet Union. His review of John Dewey's collected papers was very short, general, and noncommittal. The review of his own *Leaves from the Notebook of a Tamed Cynic* was by the famous preacher Halford E. Luccock who sensed its relevance to ministry. The book is still read by seminarians in the twenty-first century. In a diary format it presents the trials and tribulations as well as hopes and satisfactions of a young urban minister. As opposed to some critics of Niebuhr's writing, the great storyteller and stylist, Luccock wrote, "Its style sparkles." Appreciating its critical thinking, he compared it favorably to Emerson's journals without the optimism of Emerson

Kirby Page was the usual commentator on international relations in the early years of Niebuhr's association with the journal. Niebuhr's major writing in 1930–1931 was on the economy. He shared with the other editors the conviction that the socialization of the world's economies was one of the major factors that could contribute to peace. He also endorsed the U.S. participation in the League of Nations and the development of other institutions of international order. He was a pacifist encouraging the transformation of the world order for the maintenance of peace.

Niebuhr's first economic essay in *The World Tomorrow* appeared in January 1930, entitled "The Speculative Mania." He attributed the crash of October 29, 1929, to speculation that had pushed the stock marked prices too far beyond the real worth of the manufacturing sector. Increasing unemployment and the denial of the benefits of industrialization to the working class had created an artificial situation. Ownership was unrelated to human ethical concerns and money and stocks both became abstractions quite distant from the human realities which they grew out of in autonomous corporations. The optimism of the business class had created fictitious value which collapsed when exposed. He regarded most of the suggested reforms of the stock market up to that point as of little real use. Greed and the desire of power exploited the abstractness of stock prices and led those holding the stock to resist any increase in the payments to the workers. A total reorganization of the economic life of the nation was called for along with a program to educate the public about the realities of economics.

His next essay on economics in the journal in January of 1931 took on the sanctity of property. It was obvious to him that the corporations were social creations and social in nature and it did not make any sense to him to let the profits from social corporations accrue only to private interests. Again he urged the reorganization of society before the problems inherent in the misdistribution of wealth would lead to the unfortunate results seen in the Russian Revolution. Social goods had to be directed by society, and if they were not, the fates of either Russia or the threatening barbarism in Germany might result. He hoped the forces of the church and education could muster the resolve to lead the society toward a new reality where private property rights were protected only when they served the common good.

He followed the critique of property rights with the essay "Economic Perils to World Peace" (May 1931) with the assertion that "The real root of international conflict lies in the sphere of economics." Tariff barriers, reparations payments by Germany which kept Germany in servitude to the victors, and the depression all threatened the failure of parliamentary government in Germany. With the fascists and the communists both threatening the weak republic, war could be close. He feared most peace activists were not attentive enough to the economics driving the world toward war, and they were far too happy about the Kellogg-Briand Pact. With Russia's industrialization, developing adjustments in trade relations would have to be made here as well or tensions would rise.

He dealt further with Russia in the September 1931 essay "Making Peace with Russia." Russia's deviation from the usual norm of political organization, her growing exports, and her own fears of encirclement and discrimination all increased danger of war with Russia. Fears tended to engender fear as at the outbreak of the World War and care had to be taken to decrease mutual escalating fears. Prudence and goodwill both led to the need to recognize the only government Russia had and to include her in the world of nations. A few pages later, Harry Emerson Fosdick, the preacher at Riverside Church across Claremont Avenue from Union Seminary, described the peace activists as the "Hard-headed Realists" for only they understood the cycle of misery where economics drove toward war and war ruined economics among interdependent nations so that the cycle of poor economy, war, and poor economy continued. So the two thrusts of *The World Tomorrow* for socialism and peace came together in Niebuhr at this point, but would they hold? Even by the end of the year in a book review of *Culture and Education in America* by Harold Rugg, Niebuhr's ambivalence shows. Maybe only economic determinism has the truth as leaders in religion and education seem to have no idea of the resistance social reform will receive from the uneducated and also from among the educated of the privileged elite, he wrote. Obviously he is reflecting on the resistance he has seen to reforms he tried to support, but also some Marxian analysis is threatening his liberal reform instincts.

Niebuhr's *Moral Man and Immoral Society* was advertised in *The World Tomorrow* in 1932 and given away with a new subscription to the journal. In addition to his many book reviews, including a laudatory review of Paul Tillich's *The Religious Situation* translated by his brother, H. Richard Niebuhr, only two essays, both taken from his new book, were published in the journal that year.

Highlander School

Myles Horton's autobiography, *The Long Haul*, presents another dimension of Niebuhr's work. Horton had come to Union from the mountains of Tennessee and he felt very inadequate academically. He was one of four Southerners at the school, all of whom were a little in awe of the well-educated Northerners from fine colleges. He found the friendliness of the young Reinhold Niebuhr to be a big help to him. He explained that most of the students addressed him as Reinie and that Reinie had invited him to join a graduate seminar. After the first day the student thought he understood nothing that the professor was saying. He tried a second day, but during the break he told Professor Niebuhr that he wasn't coming back because he could not understand anything he said. He advised Niebuhr that he would go to the library and use the time reading a book. Niebuhr insisted that Horton understood despite his denials. He then asked the other students who gathered around the conversation whether they understood him. They said they did not understand either. Niebuhr said, then something was wrong, and he insisted Horton stay in the class to help keep it honest.

Horton reported that after that Niebuhr would sometimes ask him in the middle of the class whether he understood.

Horton soaked up New York City with its many worship opportunities and he learned about social action. He spent time going to rallies, strikes, and labor-organizing meetings. He was asked to distribute leaflets for a strike for the International Ladies Garment Workers Union. He was promised union assistance if he were arrested. His hands were cold and he had been warned not to litter or to stand in the street. So he developed a method of shoving the leaflets out from under his sleeve. When a policeman came over and told him he couldn't do that there. He smiled and said,

> Oh yeah, you can hand them out anywhere if you're careful, but you've got to be very careful not to litter, it's against the law to litter. You've got to hold them tight so you don't drop any of them," and all the time I kept giving them out. "See, you hold them this way and push them out."[2]

He played this little song and dance for the second policeman who came over to tell him he couldn't hand out the leaflets, and eventually in amazement they left him alone and he handed out leaflets all day. He joined other demonstrations, learned about unions and became radicalized. He said it was easy to join radical movements with both John Dewey and Reinhold Niebuhr leading the socialist cause. With Niebuhr's encouragement Horton went to Denmark to study labor relations and the cooperative movement. On his return he was more determined than ever to start a school in the Tennessee mountains to inform people about social causes, unionization, and progressive social change. Niebuhr persuaded his patron, Sherwood Eddy, to give Horton the first one hundred dollars for his school. Then using the treasurer of *The World Tomorrow* and the journal's address Niebuhr sent out a fund-raising letter signed by several of his allies from the journal. In part he wrote:

> May 27, 1932
>
> We are writing you in behalf of an educational project which we believe merits the support of all who are interested in more-effective labor leadership and action. Our project is the organization of a Southern Mountains School for the training of labor leaders in the Southern industrial areas. The Southern mountaineers who are being drawn into the coal and textile industries are completely lacking in understanding of the problems of industry and the necessities of labor organization. We believe that neither [the] A. F. of L. nor Communist leadership is adequate to their needs. Our hope is to train *radical* labor leaders who will understand the need of both political and union strategy. Without local leadership a labor movement in the South is impossible. The need for such leadership becomes more urgent when it is realized that the individualistic outlook of the mountain people makes it hard

> for them to understand or accept leadership from without. Naturally, we will make the educational program as broad as possible and try to give the students and the community an understanding of the total problem of modern civilization.
>
> We are proposing to use education as one of the instruments for bringing about a new social order. Assuming that an individual can be integrated by having his interest aroused in a great cause in which he can lose himself, our problems—individual integration, relation of the individual to a new situation, and education for a socialistic society—become one.[3]

Beyond raising funds, Niebuhr served as chair of the advisory board of the school that became the Highlander Center in East Tennessee. In the 1950s the Highlander Center became a focus of the teaching strategy of nonviolent massive civil disobedience for integration of the society. It was here that Rosa Parks, the heroine of the Montgomery bus boycott received training and inspiration. She said:

> I found out for the first time in my adult life that this could be a unified society, that there was such a thing as peoples of differing races and backgrounds meeting together in workshops and living together in peace and harmony.[4]

Later the center was vilified by segregationists who posted pictures of Martin Luther King, Jr. on billboards among some socialists. They identified King as attending a "Communist Training School" at the center's twenty-fifth anniversary party.[5]

Foreboding Year

The World Tomorrow editors found little promise for 1933. Neither the revelry nor the prayers of the New Year's Eve would change the deepening misery of the Depression. The first January issue described the misery, in their opinion, equal to the war years, as due to the deep inequalities in the capitalistic system. The workers received so little they could not buy the products of the manufacturing sector. Once profits plummeted and sales decreased, the lowering values of the industrial base showed how speculative the prices had been. In the panic, everyone lowered prices, creating the slide into depression. The editors had little hope in the election of Roosevelt. The Democratic administration was expected to mitigate the worst suffering, but they were not expected to overcome the Depression. The historical situation was not hopeless, however, and the editors reviewed some of the plans for reconstruction.

The editors could not foresee the capitalistic system correcting itself. Winston Churchill's prophecies of the next war being fought with more horrendous weapons than the last, combined with the demands of the American military for money, threatened both the budget and the peace. They knew the will for peace was present in the world, but concrete steps needed to be taken if war were to be averted. There had to be a large war-resistance movement of people who would not participate in war. The growth of socialism could impede the war forces. Militarism had to be resisted and the budgets for war reduced drastically. The U.S. needed to join the World Court, the League of Nations, and the International Labor Office. The development of international minds had to proceed to strengthen the handling of all of the world's controversial questions so that mutual, not national, interests could predominate.

The militarism of Churchill and those in the U.S. wanting to increase the U.S. Navy were strongly criticized by *The World Tomorrow* editors. Churchill was referred to not only as a hard militarist, but a staunch imperialist. Niebuhr's participation in the editorial process marks his writing at this time as internationalist in the liberal institutional mold with a socialist vision of changing the political economies that drove nations toward war.

Another note penned by Niebuhr under the rubric of "Ex Cathedra" celebrated the success of a Negro boycott against Kroger stores in Toledo that succeeded in winning employment for African-Americans in stores which they patronized. Church participation was a factor in the victory and made clear the real struggle between blacks and whites which had to be recognized as a reality if the churches were to apply Christian ethics to the struggle. The economic coercion used was a necessary tool to win the degree of justice obtained.

In a review of *Civilizing Ourselves: Intellectual Maturity in the Modern World* by Everett Dean Martin, Niebuhr compared religion to poetry:

> There are overbeliefs in all religions which belong to the category of pure illusion. But that does not prove the religious interpretation of the universe to be wholly illusory. Religion is poetry, but poetry is not purely fantasy. It may be that at times. But it may also give insights into reality through which the soul actually comes into significant contact with its world.[7]

Niebuhr's most laudatory review of the year was given to *The History of the Russian Revolution* by Leon Trotsky. Niebuhr regarded it as a brilliant work even if it was dominated by Trotsky's passion to show how his and Lenin's theory fit the historical situation and shaped history. "Quite decidedly this history of Trotsky's is a work that must be read. It is a classic." The review shows Niebuhr's passion for reading about the revolution in the country he had visited three years earlier, but also the ongoing fitting of philosophy of history into an understanding of strategy and tactics.

Fellowship of Reconciliation

Niebuhr chose *The Christian Century* (3 January 1934) to announce his resignation from the Fellowship of Reconciliation. The council of the organization dismissed J. B. Matthews as its executive secretary for his nonagreement with its pacifist principles. An extensive survey was taken of the membership which indicated the voting majority was for its identification as a Christian pacifist organization.

Niebuhr's hold on pacifism had slipped and while he repudiated and promised not to support international war, he could not deny workers the right to resist violence with violence in their struggles. The defense of democracy might also require defense from Nazis or Communists, so he could not regard any principle of nonviolence as absolute. He admitted his pragmatism in social-ethical issues, and he reserved the right to decide on tactics dependent upon the context of the action. He held to his nonpacifism on both Marxian and classical Christian grounds while respecting the Quaker position of the Fellowship as a moral witness. He pointed out the covert violence of the system: "Children do starve and old people do starve to death." Solidarity with the movement for radical social change meant that there was bound to be violence in times of crisis. History contained a certain inevitability of conflict from which one could not hide.

Niebuhr committed himself to the social struggle for justice and hoped that he could grant his opponents a measure of forgiveness, for he knew his own frailty before the demands of God. He thought that the social struggle inevitably involved one in some forms of corruption, and moral consistency would drive one into the monastery, which was not his option.

Tillich's language of the demonic forces at work in the social struggle emerged in Niebuhr's writing and he knew that one had often to choose the lesser evil. This announcement in the *Century* resolved some of the issues so apparent in his writing for *The World Tomorrow* in the last year of its publication and carried forward in a brief way the arguments more developed in the 1932 *Moral Man and Immoral Society*. The divisions within the editorial board were too deep to contain and the journal was in crisis. The advertisements of Niebuhr's *Moral Man and Immoral Society* and Kirby Page's *Individualism and Society* were paralleled on the back cover of the January 4th issue under the title: "The Fellowship Cleavage: Two Interpretations of the Issues Dividing the Fellowship of Reconciliation." Henry van Dusen celebrated the capacity of the journal to keep itself an absolute pacifist journal. H. Richard Niebuhr dissented from the Fellowship board's decision to dismiss the dissenters. To him the pacifism of Jesus meant nonresistance, not only nonviolent resistance, and the journal was very militant in the way it dealt with members of its own fellowship.

In the last issue of *The World Tomorrow* (26 July 1934) Reinhold Niebuhr supported Harold Laski's interpretation of Communism in Russia as a religion.

Of course many Communists who were materialists wanted to deny that Communism was a religion. But to Niebuhr its belief that the dialects of history were determinatively moving in a certain direction with a certain privileged class was not science, but religion. It was a matter of faith to find the meaning in a certain direction of history. The logic of history took on the role of God in classical Western religion. Communism derived part of its power from its faith commitments and it would be weaker without them. Religion was not necessarily good and the fanaticism of Communism was partially based on its privileged knowledge of which class was good and which classes were doomed to failure. He did not think cynicism could save humanity from false passionate idolatries, only the worship of a holy, transcendent God could do that. Communism was not only a bad religion, but also bad politics, and economics. It derived some of its power from its demonic qualities as well as its fanaticism. So the religious faith encouraged fanaticism while also giving it some of its power. Christianity at its best would not completely identify with any political party, but wisdom rested in respecting the relativities of politics while sacrificing some of the passion. Real politics consisted of choosing among relative goods and struggling for them while avoiding demonic fanaticisms.

Earlier in the journal, Niebuhr entitled his response to critics of *Moral Man and Immoral Society* "Optimism and Pessimism." He framed his response around the theme of the need for coercion in society or to change society. He felt his critics missed the recognition that humans coerce each other in their social relations. Moral teachings if not joined to power permitted the oppressors to continue in their roles while tolerating some moral criticism. He feared that the liberal traditions in church and school obscured the realities of coercive force in society. Readers claimed to be shocked by his sense that human struggles would continue in history and that utopia would not arrive through liberal evolution or Marxist revolution. Neither church nor education could change society, even though they could fulfill other functions. Niebuhr entered into a debate with John Haynes Holmes on the interpretation of Gandhi who in Niebuhr's view was an exponent of nonviolent resistance and not an advocate of nonresistance as Holmes believed. Following up on observations he had discussed earlier, he noted how farmers in the Midwest understood that to obtain any fairness they needed to act to stop foreclosures on their farms. Power was subject to inner control of moral ideas as well as counterbalancing power.

Social analysis that did not account for the ongoing power struggles was not very relevant. Niebuhr was advocating a socialist commonwealth, but he knew it would not be a perfect society. He rejected Norman Thomas's suggestion that affluence would eliminate sharp antagonisms in the future. He identified himself as a Marxian who had few illusions about the morality of capitalist culture. He also identified himself as a Christian who went beyond Marxism in knowing that no collective system would eliminate all immorality from the system.

Christian theology interpreted history from the perspective of the absolute and knew that historical forces could not achieve the absolute. It was his particular Christian faith that perceived history as inevitably subject to sin and led him to reject utopias whether liberal or Marxist. He understood that his realism might undercut the social activism of some well-intentioned people. In his book he had hoped that illusions about the creation of a new society might persist until the reforming work was accomplished. But now, only one year later, he regretted that conclusion. Illusions were dangerous and he wished he had concluded his book on that note rather than on suggesting illusions were useful.

In February 1933, Niebuhr could not see how capitalism could be reformed nor did he trust in Marxist utopianism. Paul Tillich had published his *Socialist Decision* which rested its hopes on the concept of expectations for change, a perspective Niebuhr would have found too romantic even though Tillich tried to show the grounds for his expectations to reform both religion and socialism. Before the year was out Niebuhr would join in rescuing Tillich from the consequences of his positions under the National Socialists who were seizing power in Germany. From this point on when Niebuhr said that the greatest mistake of his book was to affirm the temporary utility of illusions, he would remain a constant critic of what he regarded as utopianism. Tillich would continue to use utopian thoughts as an inevitable part of the human condition while Niebuhr had to seek other bases for his social reform agenda.

The very next issue of *The World Tomorrow* (1 March 1933) continued the search under the title "After Capitalism—What?" Niebuhr was convinced that capitalism was dying and that in its failure to share its wealth it deserved to die. Communism and Fascism were competing for the future and he expected most Western nations to fall prey to Fascism even though he was hesitant to predict the future. It was clear to him that Roosevelt could not liberalize the Democratic Party enough to stem the tide, He continued to see hope in the labor movement even though at the present it was hopelessly middle-class in outlook.

Through the long struggles ahead Niebuhr hoped for the emergence of a class-conscious socialistic-inclined labor force to emerge that could in the end defeat Fascism. He did not advocate social revolution and he did not expect parliamentary tactics to be able to change the constitution. Perhaps labor and socialism could in the future achieve a victory through techniques of general strikes or similar actions. Social groups would not cede power without struggle. Within those struggles moral education and idealism had roles to play, but political realism was a better guide to achieving justice because it would not lose sight of the factors of power.

Niebuhr brushed aside the social naiveté of the Mellon-family-supported pastor, Stuart Nye Hutchinson of East Liberty Presbyterian Church in Pittsburgh. Hutchinson had worried about the unemployed being weakened by seeking unemployment relief and he urged them to migrate onto the hundreds of thousands of acres of uncultivated land in the country. Niebuhr regarded the picture of the workers becoming lazy during prosperity as unfair, and he could not see thirteen million workers migrating onto available land. Since the real farmers were already producing more food than they could sell, it seemed unlikely that adding another thirteen million to the farming force would bring any prosperity. While Niebuhr admitted he regarded the picture of the Russian priest forced into begging as indicating a too-rough form of justice, he wanted to recommend some such justice for priests of the church who advocated foolishness for the hungry families of the workers. He wondered if Mr. Hutchinson, shorn of the support of the Mellon millions which had built a new cathedral-like structure for him, would find his own article comforting.

The judgment of Niebuhr on the Reverend Hutchinson may be as critical of a fellow cleric as Niebuhr ever uttered, and he admitted: "My judgment may seem unkind and Pharisaic. But men like Mr. Hutchinson arouse the very devil in me."[8] Niebuhr did note however that some workers were abandoning the struggles of the workplace to move onto farms which had been abandoned to try and support themselves in a self-sufficient economy. This seemed to promise a new peasant class who were trying only to stay alive, if the trend became a movement. The pages of *The World Tomorrow* were dedicated to supporting striking workers in the automobile industry and hoping for better union organization. The president of Harvard's recommendation that wages be lowered to increase buying power was criticized, as were the plans to provide relief for workers by inducting them into the army.

Niebuhr could not see in April of 1933 all that Hitler's ascension would bring, but he entitled his essay: "Hitlerism—A Devil's Brew." He saw Hitler as finding a way of combining the resentment of the Versailles Treaty, anti-Semitism, and an economic reaction that enabled him to win support from the corporate leaders and votes from the poor. His movement was wiping out Communism and liberalism and utilizing anti-Semitism for its goals. While deploring the anti-Semitism, Niebuhr thought the Nazis at the time were more serious about their economic interests and the destruction of social radicals than they were in their anti-Semitic campaigns. Racial prejudice was being used for the seizure of power and for economic gains as it often was in the American South. The same issue of the journal contained data on the lynching of Negroes in the United States from 1890 to 1930.

Niebuhr's book of essays describing the end of capitalism was reviewed in March 1934 by King Gordon who was very threatened by Niebuhr's pessimism about both human nature and society. Gordon did not argue with Niebuhr as much as he described in fearful tones Niebuhr's pessimism about any renewal of Western society. At one point he suggested that Niebuhr sounded more like Spengler than Marx. He concluded with a clever twist: "It should be Reinhold Niebuhr and not his humble critic who says, 'Except the faith of a Christian exceed the faith of a Marxist he shall in no wise enter the Kingdom of Heaven.'" *Reflections on the End of an Era* certainly was Niebuhr's most pessimistic book as he had no hopes that out of the catastrophe would come any quick recovery or resolution. In 1971, shortly before his death, he wrote me saying that the book was too much influenced by the Marxist apocalypse.

His last major essay for *The World Tomorrow* was "The Fellowship of Socialist Christians" in the June 14th issue. He described the purposes of the fellowship, its nondogmatism on certain questions, its nonrequirements of pacifism, its pragmatic character, and its self-taxation purposes for social projects. In retrospect the piece was a signal Niebuhr was moving on in his organizational strategies, he was continuing his writing for *The Christian Century*, and within six months of the closing of *The World Tomorrow* he founded the journal for the Fellowship of *Radical Religion* which looked like the previous journal, but without its absolute pacifist convictions. In the last two issues of *The World Tomorrow* he signed the column "Ex cathedra" which in previous issues had been anonymously signed "Pronuncio." The anonymity had not fooled many readers as his style and judgments were easily recognizable. The last editorial affirmed that a revolutionary socialist party could not be absolute about holding to democratic means, and that violence was a question for pragmatic judgment, not an absolute Christian obligation in the social struggle. Mass movements would sometimes, as in the case of Gandhi, be forced into illegal acts and socialism, as in the recent Detroit conference, could not be fearful of the necessary tactics. Recent events in Germany made clear the need for democratic socialists to fight for their republic once their opponents had abandoned all pretensions of honoring democratic processes. One can almost hear the conversations Niebuhr was having with his new immigrant friend, Paul Tillich, as they discussed in German the fate of democratic Germany now fallen to Hitler. Tillich's "faithful realism" would provide a new conversation partner to Niebuhr which was much closer intellectually, in many ways, than the old editorial board conversations among *The World Tomorrow* crowd.

Sherwood Eddy reflected on his two editors in 1934 as the journal closed. He praised them both. His own pacifism was of the absolute type of rather than the limited, fading pacifism of Niebuhr. He regarded Page as perhaps the most significant pacifist leader of his time in America. He regarded Niebuhr as the prophet of disillusionment of his time. He acknowledged how much he needed the critique of liberalism that Niebuhr provided. He regarded *Moral Man and*

Immoral Society[9] as the most helpful volume he had read in the last decade. In the same pages he also praised Norman Thomas, indicating he was proud to vote for him.

Page led the movement agitating for the outlawing of war. Niebuhr continued into 1936 to speak at Page's peace rallies. They remained friends even after their social analysis drove apart their practical politics. As late as 1936, Eddy involved Niebuhr in the Delta Cooperative Farm, the significant movement for economic cooperative work bridging the racial divide in Mississippi and providing relief to tenant farmers being evicted from the lands they had worked.

Many years later Niebuhr wrote the introduction[10] to Eddy's revised biography, praising him for his extraordinary energy in organizing reform movements and for his uniting of evangelical passion and the quest for social justice. He praised him as a "reincarnation of the spirit of Hebrew prophetism". That was the highest tribute Niebuhr could pay a Christian. Niebuhr also credited Eddy with all his help in providing the assistant ministers for the Bethel congregation, the European tours, and the assistance in bringing him to Union Seminary.

5

Opposition and Migration

The chill in the air and the remaining forlorn leaves on the trees reminded the agents it was fall. They stood beside the road through the forest outside Dresden. Following Gestapo orders based on an informant's claim of the professor's denunciation of the regime, they waited in the cold. But he did not come. He was expected to arrive in a large Packard, chauffeured by the driver of a local industrialist. They did not know him, but they had a small file on him as he had taught in Dresden previously at the technical school, now he was supposedly the suspended dean of the faculty at the "Red University," Frankfurt. But the Gestapo agents knew nothing of Frankfurt or his philosophy, but only that a hair dresser had claimed, her matron had relayed Tillich's comments about the sickness of the regime and the habits of Goering. Ahead of the point of interception, Tillich had been warned they were lying in wait for him. The driver turned the car around and Professor Tillich never fulfilled his luncheon date with his good friends, the Bienerts, whose secretary had delivered the warning.

Paul Tillich had already arranged his family's emigration, and he was only touring the country saying goodbye to old friends and listening to their counsel as to whether he should flee to America or stay. Some urged him to join the underground, trying to form itself, in face of the terror that had emerged since January. Others said his style was too recognizable and that his presence would be a danger to those hiding from the regime as well as to himself. His Jewish and socialist friends on the faculty at Frankfurt were already dismissed or expecting it, and some had fled the country ahead of Tillich. Allies had already been beaten, arrested, sent to camps, or murdered. Other friends had committed suicide after saying goodbye to the Tillichs. He spent most of the day with his friend, and left Dresden in the evening from a suburban station for the train trip to Berlin where it would be easier to hide if that became necessary. In Berlin he was rejoined by his wife Hannah, they arranged for their daughter Erdmutie Christianne to join them, and they prepared themselves for leaving everything else behind. Since being suspended from Frankfurt, he had sought counsel, wandered Germany to say farewell, plotted, considered alternatives to fleeing, and received a visitor from New York.[1]

In the middle of the previous month Horace Friess, at Reinhold Niebuhr's request, had met Tillich briefly at the Heidelberg railroad station. The lanky

Friess, who had attended Tillich's lectures a decade before, shared with the slightly shorter Tillich the plans that had been made at Union Theological Seminary and Columbia University to invite him to come to New York as a lecturer at both institutions. They walked back and forth through the station, two tall, earnest professors deep in conversation, but even more was afoot than philosophical conversation. Faculty members at both institutions were willing to contribute to the cause or to surrender part of their salary so that an adequate stipend and an apartment could be arranged for Tillich who was already studying English. That September day, Tillich did not formally accept the terms of Reinhold Niebuhr's cable of July, but Friess thought his questions indicated he planned to come. Between September and the Gestapo fright in October, tickets had been bought and decisions reached, but the scare on the Dresden Road erased all doubts. Niebuhr had been busy as early as May trying to arrange Tillich's acceptance at Union and Columbia. He and Friess were probably the two at the institutions on Morningside Heights who knew Tillich best. Friess taught German Idealism in the Philosophy department as well as the World Religions course with Herbert Schneider in the same department. Niebuhr had already praised Tillich's first book to be translated into English, *The Religious Situation.*

Tillich would later credit the Niebuhrs for saving his life. Both Niebuhr and Tillich had been warning their readers and listeners of the danger of National Socialism for months, but both were surprised by the political deal that transferred power to Adolph Hitler in January 1933, and the events that allowed him to become chancellor and to seize total power in Germany later that year.

The year earlier, the Nazis had been reduced in political power, and their finances were desperate until bailed out by a coalition of industrialists. The putsch in Prussia had startled them, and their joint venture with the Communists calling a general strike had seemed to discredit them. But the Social Democrats declined even more as they failed to respond with force to either the putsch or the strike, holding on to nonviolent, democratic tactics.

Hitler's move of associating himself with the conservatives to govern paid off when they could not govern. He was able to force himself into the chancellorship surrounded by conservative allies who were not able to prevent his seizing power as events rushed forward at a pace that forced Hindenburg to welcome him to shared power. Hitler was made virtual dictator after the Reichstag fire of February 28. Jewish business was boycotted in April. Trade unions were abolished in May. Political parties were suspended in July, and the Nazi party purged by Hitler. The Vatican Concordat followed, and the German Christians prevailed in July before real church resistance could arise.

Hindenburg's death in August allowed Hitler to merge the offices of chancellor and president, giving him relatively total control. Tillich had done what he could as an academic to stem the tide. He had defended Judaism in his Founders Day Address at the University. He had comforted and physically protected Jewish students, and demanded the expulsion of Nazi thugs from the university. He had put his theological, philosophical, and political criticism of Nazism into print in 1932. In one case, his book on social theory, *The Socialist Decision*, he was subtle, probably few of the Nazis could have understood it. Still it was condemned and placed on the official "Black List." His other writing, "The Church and the Third Reich: Ten Theses" was very direct. The theses were published in a volume edited by Leopold Klotz which also contained moderate and pro-Nazi essays. When the volume, *The Church and the Third Reich: Questions and Demands of German Theologians*[2] was sent to Hitler, a pro-Nazi professor J. Stark condemned it:

> The book in question affords a valuable commentary on the intellectual level of numerous "evangelical" academic theologians. Never have I seen such an accumulation of ignorance, superficiality, presumption and malicious enmity to the German Freedom Movement.3

Tillich's style was to reconcile positions and to include alternatives to his view within his synthetic grasp. However when he saw evil in political movements, he expressed his judgments very clearly in antithesis to them. He had seen the demonic in Hitler's clumsy speech from the platform in Frankfurt, and in the book burning in the central square of his city. The drift of the Nazi rule was terribly wrong, and he saw it leading to the destruction of modern civilization and to war of all against Germany. The starkness of criticism of the Nazis before they concentrated power needs recognition. One of my students from Germany, Andrea Boecherer, translated it for my seminar on Tillich's social thought. Writing as a theologian for Protestantism, in 1932 Tillich contrasted Nazism with Protestantism:

> Protestantism, which opens itself up to National Socialism and rejects Socialism, once more is going to betray its commission to the world.
>
> Seemingly obedient to the phrase that the Kingdom of God is not this world, Protestantism proves itself to be submissive to the victorious forces and their demonic power-as Protestantism often has done in its history.
>
> Insofar as Protestantism justifies nationalism and the ideology of blood and race by a doctrine of the divine order of creation, it abandons its prophetic foundation in favor of a new apparent or veiled paganism. It also betrays its commission to testify to the one God and the one human race.
>
> Insofar as Protestantism gives the consecration of God-given authority to the capitalistic-feudal form of rule—which National Socialism actually protects—it promotes the perpetuation of class conflict, and it betrays its

commission to bear witness against violations and to testify for justice as a measure of every social order.

Protestantism is in the utmost danger of going that way, which will be fatal in the long run. From its beginning, Protestantism has lacked a dominating group independent of secular powers and national separations. It lacks a prophetically founded principle of social criticism. On Lutheran ground, Protestantism lacks the will to shape reality according to the image of the Kingdom of God. In Germany, Protestantism is supported sociologically almost exclusively by the groups that advocate National Socialism, and is therefore ideologically and politically bound to them.

Official declarations of neutrality by ecclesiastical authorities don't alter the actual attitudes of most Protestant groups, theologians, or laypersons, the church takes actions against socialist ministers and congregations, and theologians who resist the pagan National Socialism find no protection in the church.

Protestantism must prove its prophetic-Christian character by setting the Christianity of the cross against the paganism of the swastika. Protestantism must testify that the cross has broken and judged the "holiness" of nation, race, blood, and power.

According to its nature, Protestantism cannot present itself in a certain political movement. It must prove that it is free by allowing Protestants to be members of any political party, even of those that oppose Protestantism as it realizes its religious life. But Protestantism must submit every party—as well as all human and religious activities—to the judgment and hope of the prophetic, early Christian proclamation of the Kingdom of God.

In this way, Protestantism can direct the political wills of those groups that are allied in supporting National Socialism to a goal that is true, just, and appropriate for their social needs. Protestantism can liberate the movement from the demonic powers that today subdue it and that destroy nation and humanity.

After a present increase in church power, an open or clandestine alliance between Protestant churches and the National Socialist Party to suppress Socialism and oppose Catholicism inevitably will lead to future disintegration of German Protestantism.[4]

The thought behind criticism of church opposition to socialism and approval of National Socialism is grounded in Tillich's first paper with his friend Richard Wegener on the Church and Socialism, his first course at the University of Berlin on Christendom and the Social Question, and it is consistent with his final volume of *Systematic Theology* in which the Kingdom of God remains a critical perspective on all totalitarian movements. He saw more clearly than most German church leaders the demonic in National Socialism which was consuming the good, leading the church to betray itself and drifting towards barbarism and chaos. He shows his faithful realism in recognizing the sociological alliance between those supporting National Socialism and the Protestant churches. He was too optimistic in hoping church criticism might free National Socialism of its evil tendencies. He correctly diagnosed the sociological and political dependence of the church and its consequent weakness in facing evil.[5]

The Religious Situation

Adolf Hitler's *Mein Kampf* (1925, 1926) and Paul Tillich's *Die religiose Lage der Gegenwart* (1926; ET: *The Religious Situation*, 1932),[6] attacked the failure of the liberal society from which they came. Tillich's religious socialism was of course, anathema to Hitler, and Hitler's anti-Semitism was antithetical to all Tillich represented. The translation of *The Religious Situation* into English by H. Richard Niebuhr, Reinhold's younger brother, introduced Tillich's thought to the faculties of Columbia University and made possible the invitation to Tillich to come as a lecturer to New York City.

Tillich's book is filled with historically detailed evaluations of many movements in Germany, including science, metaphysics, art, politics, ethics, and religion. The major sources of his argument are the perspectives of his religious socialist circles and the categories of Max Weber and Ernst Troeltsch.

The influence of Weber's classical study, *The Protestant Ethic and the Spirit of Capitalism*, is evident in the central symbol of the book, "The Spirit of Capitalist Society," which was explicitly drawn from Weber. In both authors it is an attempt to capture in an expression the characteristic drive of Western humanity. Tillich calls it "a symbol," but it serves the same function as Weber's "ideal type." Tillich more than Weber, is interested in conquering that attitude of "The Capitalist Spirit"; his socialism is more consistent and thoroughgoing than Weber's reformist liberal, socialism, just as his religious philosophy is deeper and more profound than Weber's agnosticism. Reinhold Niebuhr was using Weber and Troeltsch in his 1927 book *Does Civilization Need Religion?*[7] to criticize liberal society in America.

The spirit of capitalist society, according to Tillich, is the dominance of the world by a particular form of economic activity committed to a view of humanity as competing, finite, consuming, producing units. It is the reduction of human life to mechanical analysis and the utilization of science and technology to promote an economic system committed to the exclusion of the infinite. The capitalistic spirit is the breaking of attitudes of awe toward the material world and the turning of human life toward the endless pursuit of finite things. Tillich opposes the "self-sufficient finitude" that he sees as the motivating force of capitalist society, and he challenges it in terms of response to the unconditional.

The influence of the great theologian and German minister of state in the Department of Education, Ernst Troeltsch, is seen in *The Religious Situation* in the general position that the existing churches have no adequate social response to the twentieth century. Tillich's division of the churches into mysticism, sects, and churches when he analyzes the churches' response to the spirit of capitalism is borrowed from Troeltsch. Tillich also agrees with Troeltsch about the relative ineffectiveness of existing religious socialism, but then he attempts a new synthesis of religion and socialism.

Mysticism both within and outside the churches reminded humanity of eternity, but it lacked the social organization that would make it a social alternative. Through it all Tillich was seeking to reveal a faithful realism that while dealing with the historical particulars could detect in human life the presence of the eternal and guard the transcendence of God from domestication. He appreciated Karl Barth's critique, but felt it had moved too far from its socialist origins and would leave the finite spirit of capitalism untouched in society. He could not tell whether his own and his circle's commitments to realistic, religious socialism would have an effect. His attempt to unite the best of mysticism with the prophetic-ethical expression of Protestantism would remain a theme of his work and still a goal of progressive Protestants in the 21st century.

Does Civilization Need Religion?

Niebuhr wrote his first book in 1926 in the time he could take from his traveling, parish work, and journal publishing. It was, in part, a revision of previously published essays. *Does Civilization Need Religion?* has not been regarded as one of his major works. His Wilsonian liberalism was breaking up that year while Tillich's socialism was fully developed for his work. Niebuhr's first footnote was to Alfred North Whitehead of whom Tillich seemed not to be aware. Tillich was so critical of pragmatism that H. Richard Niebuhr, the translator of *The Religious Situation*, entered a note indicating that Tillich's experience was relevant to the German scene more than it was to the American. Many of the important motifs in Reinhold Niebuhr's book were from his pragmatism inherited from William James. Niebuhr and Tillich shared Ernst Troeltsch's pessimistic analysis of religion. Tillich's book was more analytic and Niebuhr's more prescriptive. Tillich presupposed the eternal and analyzed suggestions of it in several fields of human endeavor. Niebuhr started with Protestantism and sought how it could become more relevant to those fields. Niebuhr hoped to free religion to serve social renewal whereas Tillich saw both society and religion captured by the capitalist spirit that undercuts religion's possibility of renewal. In Tillich's interpretation, until the controlling spirit of the capitalist system is broken, the eternal is ignored and religion is irrelevant.

This early book of Niebuhr's—*Does Civilization Need Religion?*—is not heavily influenced by Augustine or Marx, both of whom would become important later. It encourages idealism as the fruit of religion and sees religious faith as important in grounding the value of the individual against assertions of a nonpersonal universe. Traces of Adolph Harnack and Albrecht Ritschl's liberal

German theology come through as mediated by Niebuhr's father and Eden Seminary. The value theory of Albrecht Ritschl as taught by his Yale Professor Douglas C. Macintosh is present in this book more than in any of his later writings.

The political failure of Wilsonian idealism left Niebuhr treasuring idealism as the fruit of religion while quoting from studies of international politics that were realistic and bleak. He did not expect international institutions to control or qualify substantially the pursuit of great nations' interest. The realism of this early perspective is not grounded in his declining liberal theology and it continues as his theology evolves drastically from 1929 to 1939.

> If religion cannot transform society, it must find its social function in criticizing present realities from some ideal perspective and in presenting the ideal without corruption, so that it may sharpen the conscience and strengthen the faith of each generation.[8]

Niebuhr's chapter on "Transcending and Transforming the World" emphasizes the theme of the book that, to be useful to the world, religion must transcend it and then encourage it critically. No representative of the social gospel is mentioned in the chapter. It is innocent of references to religious socialism or the varied patterns of Social Gospel influence. His declared affection and respect for the social-gospel bishop of Detroit, Bishop McConnell, does not mean he followed him in all of his enthusiasms. In fact the bishop remained critical of Niebuhr's pessimism about society. His Lutheranism and otherworldly dualism at this time kept his thought distinct from the social-gospel movement. This early book affirmed social realism and Christian idealism while regarding Wilsonian political idealism as defunct. In this early volume, the Christian idealism of Niebuhr is that of critic and not that of social-reforming social-gospel thinkers. The phrase "sentimental optimism" appears repeatedly in the book as it is rejected along with "enervating pessimism."

When he contrasts the sentimental quality of religious journals with the anxiety of secular journals he lists as the sources of realism the various crises of his experience in Detroit. He experienced deeply there the brutalities of economic competition, the anarchy of international relations, and the ugliness of racial pride.

The God he follows metaphysically in the book is that of Alfred North Whitehead from *Science and the Modern World* and *Religion in the Making* while he strives to remain open to the pluralism of William James. He appreciates hearing some metaphysical justification for religion while recognizing the God of the Bible, or that the simple believer is not the God of the philosophers. Appreciating metaphysics, his hope is that religion will strengthen moral effort while providing some otherworldly hope.

The long conclusion to the book repeats his arguments and summarizes his hopes that a renewal of religion can contribute toward the moral renewal of society. He preserves his individualism and high expectations of personal ideals when he writes that religion "makes the development of an ethical personality the ultimate goal of human existence."[9]

Niebuhr concludes with affirming hope for an ethical society in which religion and morality reinforce each other. Without ever quoting his favorite prophet Amos, he is affirming Amos's critique of religion that does not support justice. However, the concluding sentences are something of a rhetorical flourish. He is fully aware of the avarice characterizing the "roaring twenties." He has observed that religion of the twenties was not adequately supportive of social reform. He knew economic life was vicious and seldom moral. The racial divisions and injustices of Detroit had not been solved by his report of the Mayor's Racial Commission of 1925. Yet humanity even in its modern failures was, in his judgment, incurably religious in its striving. It deserved and needed a rigorous morality for inspiration and criticism of sorrowful modern society.

As Tillich's 1926 book broke the ground and prepared the way for Reinhold Niebuhr's invitation on behalf of Union Theological Seminary, so Niebuhr's 1927 book enabled Henry Sloane Coffin, Union's President, to call Niebuhr to Union in 1928 with the encouragement of Harry Ward, Union's ethicist, and Sherwood Eddy, Niebuhr's patron. The most decisive difference between the two books was that Tillich had already developed his socialism in terms of "Faithful Realism," but that remained a task that Niebuhr would achieve after arriving at Union. It is ironic to note that neither Niebuhr nor Tillich began their tenure at Union Theological Seminary under normal appointments. Niebuhr's salary was paid for the two first years by his benefactor Sherwood Eddy for whom he worked half-time at editing *The World Tomorrow*. Tillich's first salary was paid by Union faculty members contributing five percent of their salaries to support him, and he spent the first semester studying English.

The books they published showed how they had grown closer together analyzing the collapse of Western economies. Tillich's *The Socialist Decision* was more German than Niebuhr's very American *Moral Man and Immoral Society*, but they were both their primary works in socialist theory. An examination of the two indicates the state of their minds a few months before they met in 1933.

Socialist Theory in 1932

In the midst of the Depression and the growing threat of Nazi supremacy in Germany, Niebuhr and Tillich wrote their major socialist works. They had both warned of the danger of Hitler earlier, but their respective volumes published in

December 1932 and January 1933 preceded Hitler's assumption of the power of the state.

Tillich's book is unaware of developments in America and Niebuhr could not foresee the meaning of Franklin Delano Roosevelt's victory that autumn. The U.S. was trying to isolate itself from the European problems. In both countries, the influence of progressive Christian social movements was at a low ebb. The promises of the previous Social Gospel Movement of the League of Nations and Prohibition were exhausted. Some of the agenda of the Social Gospel in union organization—more fair wages and the termination of child labor—were not yet realized. Both books utilized the newly published manuscripts of the young Karl Marx. Tillich argued, particularly, that the newly published economic and philosophical manuscripts established the humanism of *Das Kapital*, overcame the deterministic interpretations of Marx, and showed both the eschatological and action-oriented aspects of Marxism.

For Tillich, by the end of 1932 Germany's choice would be that of socialism or Nazism. He hoped that democratic socialism, if energized by hopeful action, could call out of Nazism progressive elements to renew Germany. Failing a renewal of socialism to understand its prophetic-eschatological sources of action, the victory of Nazism would bring barbarism and the self-destruction of European civilization through war. Niebuhr's book hoped for socialism also and thought its victory could only reside on the other side of economic collapse and disintegration. He hoped then that a general strike, union action, and a willingness to defend social victories might move the country to socialist reform. Lacking what Tillich called expectation or eschatological-driven action, he thought in his last sentences that perhaps illusion of victory could drive progressives to act for fundamental change.

While Tillich described Hitler as a person of minimal power of being, he recognized the danger of Hitler's charisma. On the other hand, too many of the socialist leaders lacked popular appeal. Many were not psychologically equipped to act decisively. The Prussian putsch in Berlin demonstrated the lack of socialist power.

Tillich's book depended upon two ideal types of political power's sources. The first was the power of origin which resided in the myth of humanity's dependence upon forces of blood, land, soil, nation, etc. The primitive religions of Egypt and Babylon illustrate these sources as the myths supporting the governments, reflect the natural sources of their power as the rising and receding of the Nile River, or the canal irrigation of Babylon that tamed the waters and was reflected in the natural mythology and ritual of the state.

The myths of origin were particularly foundational to the conservative politics of the Junker's ideology, the National Party, the Center Party of the

Roman Catholic Church, and other groups which tended to divinize to some degree the status quo.

The Nazis used the same sources of mythology to attack the present weakness of the socialist-supported Weimar republic. They combined the spirit of revolution with the ancient mythology to attempt to return to the mythical past of a pure Germany. Supposedly this purity of the origins would be restored in a Third German Empire to reflect the apocalyptic third age.

The other source of politics in Tillich's typology was the religious politics of prophetic religion that called on monotheism and justice. Here both Tillich and Niebuhr understood their continuity with prophetic religion in the classical types of Amos and Isaiah. These movements evolved to criticize the powers of origin in terms of justice and the kings who betrayed it or engaged in idolatry. In Greece the power of autonomous reason developed the concept of justice. The Renaissance and the Reformation renewed these critical perspectives though with different accents.

Both socialism and capitalism arose upon the ground of rational-critical politics emphasizing the power of autonomous humanity to develop itself. These modern movements still drew upon the myths of origin, but in a critical way. Modern political thinkers, often skeptical of previous forms of religious politics or the power of myths of origin, underestimated the power of irrational movements dependent upon ecstasy, ritual, and passion. In history these two principles were often mixed in reality. Tillich used the two concepts as principles to try and explain the dynamics of particular parties or movements. Symbols when deeply grounded in important primeval forces often exert more power than rationality in the turmoil of politics and this is especially true when a country is in turmoil. Tillich's politics of symbols is a long way removed from current rational choice models of human behavior. For him Freudian psychological analysis and Marxist understandings of alienation and class warfare had broken through the power of pure rational analysis of human motivations. Nazism relying upon symbols from the imagined depths of German existence was threatening to drive German society back into barbarism while promising a glorious future.

Both Niebuhr and Tillich rejected the concept of liberal society that competition would operate efficiently to encourage humanitarian progress in social development. Whereas their models of society recognized societal harmony, they were more fundamentally models of social conflict rooted in insecurity and greed. Class conflict was real. Losers suffered and sometimes starved. If laissez faire economics failed to produce harmony, but led to imperial competition and depression, social planning was required. Also social-rational organization would need to replace control of the major resources of transportation, mining, means of production, and banking which were now controlled by the oligarchs for profit.

Tillich's argument was that socialism had to decide to act forcefully for its realization. Forces as diverse as the religious and socialist parties, including some of the Nazis, had to choose real socialism. His argument proceeded by ideal type analysis with a particularly high regard for symbolism. Politics for him depended upon an analysis of human nature. Human nature needed to tend to the forces of origin, its rational capacity and its capacity for hopeful action. The focus on origins led to conservative politics or to romantic politics. The focus on the ultimate demand of the consciousness of justice led toward modern politics in its two forms of capitalism and socialism.

Tillich like Niebuhr had joined the socialist party in 1929, and beyond his many abstractions he made it clear in the foreword to *The Socialist Decision* that he intended the Social Democratic Party to carry the future. Reflecting on the humanism of the writing of the young Marx, the book shows how in reality the two types of origins intermixed and produced the variety of parties active in Germany.

Love, power, and justice were all themes of his writing as Tillich explored the recent history of German politics. The solution for Germany would not be the Russian Revolution of 1917, but its own realized form of German socialism. His conclusion was entitled "The Future of Socialism." The conservatism of Germany had no future, capitalism promised only chaos, and Nazism was leading to barbarism. Only a reformed socialism that realized the possibilities of hopeful action or *expectation* promised a human solution. Socialism was for Tillich the principle of the conscious proletariat. The origin-oriented forces must be brought into the alliance. Some conservatives and romantics would have to be persuaded to support the proletariat's action to break into a new future. Socialism had to grasp forces that were adhering to the revolutionary nationalism as the present order broke. In 1932, the Nazis were nearly defeated; only a last-minute financial rescue by nationalist industrialists saved the financially strapped party. Their alliance with the conservatives who thought they could surround Hitler and control him led to his victory through the Reichstag fire and terror. The socialists failed to gain the necessary support and the powers of origin in the conservative-Nazi alliance gave Hitler his opportunity.

Tillich thought he had overcome his earlier utopianism, but *expectation* as a transformative, hopeful action on the part of the Socialist Democratic Party was in 1932 quite utopian. The irrational, conservative-Nazi alliance was more formidable in a depression when strengthened by nationalism. Democratic socialism was an answer, it was Tillich's answer, but for Germany in 1932–1933 it was still utopian. As Tillich finished his socialist-theory book in Germany in 1932, Niebuhr was finishing his in America at the same time.

Niebuhr had started his volume, *Moral Man and Immoral Society* in the summer of 1931, and it came out in December 1932. Its dialectic was between the would-be moral man and the relevant, ambiguous social activism for a new society informed by Christian-Marxist radicalism. The vision of the moral man was that of a disciplined, informed Christian. The social reform called for was that of socialism open to some careful use of violence to achieve its social reforms. The vision of the moral man was individualistic while recognizing community, particularly the church, that of the social reality was of a party in a capitalist world that required social solidarity and planning. The book is often used as a textbook in Christian ethics. In the 1960s it was the only American text included in the theological-ethics University of Oxford exams. However, it is actually a text in socialist theory with a dialectic suggested by the Christian individual. The distance between that individual and socialism was similar, but not identical, to Tillich's perception of the lack of relationship between religion and socialism in Germany. The book showed how the individual could expect moral fulfillment in neither the structures of capitalism nor the socialist organizations trying to overthrow the status quo.

In his introduction, Niebuhr presents his dialectic as that between individuals and the necessities of politics.[10] But, throughout the book it is that of an idealistic individual and the necessities for thorough socialist reform of the nation. His polemic is directed against a list of moralists and educators whom he quotes: John Dewey, John Childs, Kimball Young, Hornell Hart, Floyd Allport, Clarence Case, Arthur Salter, Howard Odum, Justin Nixon, George Stratton, and his senior colleague at Union Seminary, William Adams Brown. He does not think any of them saw the toughness of the struggle to depose the capitalist overlords of their rule and privilege. None of them in his estimate understood the plight of the Negro or the oppression of the worker or the struggle necessary to win their dignity. The targets of his realism, which he feared would be taken for cynicism, were liberals, whether secular or religious, who were overly optimistic in thinking right education or religion would overcome class interest.

Niebuhr's own goal of reformist politics is often expressed as equality. In his more-guarded presentation he puts it: "equal justice is the most rational ultimate objective for society."[11] Those using force for such a goal are on a higher moral level than those using force to sustain traditional human inequality. The moral advantage is with groups like Indians struggling for national independence from Britain or Negroes trying to overcome oppression, and not with their oppressors.

He does not expect victory for justice through purely democratic politics or parliamentary socialism. Farmers cannot be expected to pursue industrial workers' causes consistently. Socialist leaders are too often lured from their socialism by privileges granted by capitalists. Workers may be steered away from socialism by union interests. Joining a coalition government forces compromises upon Socialist parties but they are not powerful enough to govern for long as single parties. Social justice gains can be won through politics; socialist victory cannot.

By 1932, Niebuhr cannot reject totally the use of violence. Politics is about coercion. He writes sensitively and lengthily about the advantages of nonviolent resistance. He is remembered as the foe of pacifism, but he advocates nonviolent resistance in the spirit, if not always in the same terms as Gandhi. His discussion of nonviolent resistance for American Negroes who have no hopes in violent revolution later influenced Martin Luther King, Jr. The Negro must resist with force and he mentions boycotts and selective nonpayment of taxes. He hopes for a Negro-led campaign because white moral sensitivity will never without force concede the Negro his human rights. Religious sensitivity can engender the campaign with humanity and hope which may bring victory.

The cultivation of the human spirit can engender the enthusiasm needed for the social struggle. While hopes for justice may be illusory, the hope encourages the action that can lead to more just compromises. While socialism lost the eschatological expectation that Tillich longed for, the Negroes' revolution nurtured by its religious depths might find it. The degree of his predictive power in 1932 grew out of his own pacifist past, the study of Gandhi, and his recognition of the brutalities of white prejudice and power. Ironically the few paragraphs he wrote about the potential for the Negro struggle proved more accurate than all of his hopes for socialism in America.

Norman Thomas, a former minister, head of the Socialist Party, and the Party's frequent candidate for president of the United States reviewed his friend's book in *The World Tomorrow*.[12] Thomas praised Niebuhr as a leader of the progressives and was cautious in his criticism. Only two years later they would in partnership collaborate in the "Young Turks" capture of the Socialist Party's leadership posts. He pointed to what he regarded as missing aspects of the argument, and he suggested that Niebuhr could have answered the deficiencies. But, he would note the inadequacy in the text's own argument. Niebuhr had written the book the previous year during his engagement and first year of marriage to Ursula to whom the book was dedicated. On 16 July 1931, he had sent Ursula an outline which did not satisfy him, asking her for her suggestions. He noted that it had been so long since he had time for "consistent and constructive thinking" that it was hard to begin his writing.[12]

Thomas opened his argument criticizing Niebuhr for his use of illusion in religion and social philosophy to promote hope for progressive action. Niebuhr, within two years, admitted that his conclusion relying on illusory hopes was too thin. But by then the illusions of the Third Reich had arrived with power. Thomas found more hope in education and the abundance of the product of industrial civilization than did Niebuhr. He also regarded nonviolence as more productive of social reform than Niebuhr had. Differing with Niebuhr on the future of the proletariat, he regarded the middle-class prejudices of the workers as due to social mobility awarded some Americans as well as the pioneer origins of the country. But Thomas's major charge was that the ruthless realism of the Niebuhr's book would encourage defeatism on the part of its readers.

In Niebuhr's lifetime the Socialist Party as a movement toward greater social equality was defeated in the U.S.A. The defeat included his personal loss of two elections as a Socialist candidate. However, the union movement, which became one of Niebuhr's perceived balancing powers to the capitalist-oligarchic spirit, did win some gains for the workers. Also the civil rights movement partially through Martin Luther King, Jr, appropriating some of *Moral Man and Immoral Society* (King's most-quoted book except for Walter Rauschenbusch's *Christianity and the Social Crisis*), moved towards civil rights for African-Americans.

Though the socialist fire of *Moral Man* was drawn from the sources of British Christian Socialism and Karl Marx, the evaluation of the potential of the movement was forced through American pragmatism. Christian socialist that he was, Niebuhr's commitments to pragmatism from William James forced practical judgments and the social forces for practical progress were, in his estimation, inadequate.

In 1931–1932 there were many socialists in the circles of the Niebuhrs. He was defending students engaged in socialist and antiwar demonstrations. He agonized as one of them left the Socialist Party for the Communist Party. In 1930 he had been asked to run as a Socialist for governor of New York, and in 1932 he was anti-Roosevelt and pro-Norman Thomas for the presidency. His Christian pacifism was fading because of his Marxist-inspired views of class conflict. His conviction was expressed that the progress of the proletariat should not be thwarted by limitations of formal democracy or nonviolence. He was still pacifist on the question of international war, but that would disappear under the need for collective security to enforce naval blockade sanctions on oil to thwart Italian imperialism in Africa and Japan in Asia. Two years after the publication of *Moral Man,* he would resign as chairman of the Fellowship of Reconciliation as he would not deny the right of the use of violence to protect striking workers. This should not obscure his Christian preference for nonviolent tactics. He would represent *The World Tomorrow* in 1932 to interview members of Gandhi's circle visiting in London during his wedding visit to England. He wrote to Ursula to allow time for meetings with Gandhi's group indicating that C. E. Andrews "is a good friend of mine."[13] He did not remind her that his own hopes for visiting India were cancelled because of their approaching wedding ceremony in Winchester Cathedral.

Though *Moral Man* was not as Marxist as *The End of an Era* two years later, he wanted to nationalize the major industries of the United States. He felt alone at Union Seminary. He expressed his criticism of the institution in a letter to Ursula and declared he was the only one there "On the left who was right." Harry Ward and he were separating over Ward's enthusiasm about the Soviet Union which both Union professors had visited.

Niebuhr, without Tillich's concept of expectation for the U.S.A., and not seeing the material base for religious socialism, left his text more pessimistic than Tillich's or, as Thomas' review suggests, defeatist. But Thomas was not correct either. In discussion with Niebuhr over an eight-year period, I never saw him give up, there were always possibilities for reform in the future if not now, but there were social actions to be taken now.

His actions in 1932 included: running for Congress, raising funds for the Highlander School, visiting striking coal miners, and participating in founding the Fellowship of Southern Churchmen. (Niebuhr spoke to the 180 persons meeting in May 1934 at Monteagle, Tennessee—the Conference of Younger Churchmen of the South—which then became the Fellowship of Southern Churchmen with Howard Kester as secretary and Thomas Cowan as president.) In 1934, Niebuhr served as chair of the board for the Delta Cooperative Farm. Sam Franklin, moved by *Moral Man and Immoral Society*, returned from the mission field to study with Niebuhr and become director of the farm.

The same struggle over the use of violence that resulted in Niebuhr's resignation as chair of the board for the Fellowship of Reconciliation split the Socialist Party and the editors of *The World Tomorrow* in the next few years. Niebuhr's position drew down upon himself voracious criticism of *Moral Man and Immoral Society* from friends and enemies alike. Richard Fox[14] discusses this criticism thoroughly in his biography, but errs in thinking Niebuhr reduced his activity. As late as 1931, he was elected president of the Fellowship of Reconciliation. He was glad of the opportunity and wrote to his fiancé in England that he thought the Fellowship might be just the kind of organization he needed to maintain contact with the world beyond the church as Harry Ward, his colleague, worked with the American Civil Liberties Union. But in 1932 he shifted his energies out of the Fellowship of Reconciliation in the struggle with pacifism to other para-church organizations which he, himself, led, as he developed Christian Realism.

He had suggested in the preface to *Moral Man and Immoral Society* that the dichotomy suggested in the title was too strong. In the 1960s he acknowledged in a chuckle that John Raines's suggestion that the title of "Immoral Man and a More Immoral Society" was truer to his thought. But then he would have lost Ernst Troeltsch's ring to his words and his own propensity for speaking dialectically while seeking his own unique synthesis.

The title is a little too dialectical and H. Richard Niebuhr reminded him sharply that we sin in both areas of the personal and the social. Reinhold as a Kantian, in part, felt the presence of God in the guilt of the conscience seeking truth. The whole position reflected Niebuhr's realization that as a socialist theoretician he would have to approve of some social tactics that as a Christian he would find personally unacceptable. Heimert Niebuhr wrote:

> I am absolutely thrilled by your book, which I have downed in almost one sitting. But unless the will is freed from our hypocrisy there is no hope for us and that is what you are doing and have done. It is a grand job.

Before he closed his five-page letter he raised four criticisms:

> (1) The sinfulness of the individual person. (2) Reinhold's tendency to regard religion as idealistic, what about Paul, Augustine, Luther, Calvin? (3) "The dualism within the self is intolerable." It's like trying to be "A monk and a bishop at the same time and it cannot be done." (4) "Activism which stresses the immediate results is the cancer of our modern life." "But enough of diversity. I was thrilled by the book. It's really a great piece of work. Well written. Illuminating. Bound to make a big wave. And helpful in many spots as well as in the whole. God bless you for it. Devotedly, Heim
>
> Have you thought of your relationship to Hobbes?[15]

H. Richard's letter was certainly correct in its first two critiques that the book portrayed religion as overly idealistic, forgetting the realism of the center of the theological tradition in Paul, Luther, Calvin, and that the sinfulness of the self was not emphasized properly. His reference to Hobbes is provocative, but the text does not show dependence on Thomas Hobbes. Niebuhr's later source of Christian realism was due much more to Augustine than to Hobbes. In fact he had drawn from his brother's *The Social Sources of Denominationalism* much more than Hobbes, and the major intellectual influences beyond Karl Marx and the British socialists were L. T. Hobhouse, *The Rational Good* and *The Elements of Social Justice* and Ernst Troeltsch's *The Social Teaching of the Christian Churches*, which also underlay H. Richard's first work. Reinhold wrote to John C. Bennett, his colleague, friend, and successor at Union in an undated letter in the early 1930s: "I appreciate you letting me know about Hobhouse. I am sorry to hear of his death. He and Troeltsch have taught me almost all of the little I know."[16] Earlier while working on the book he had corresponded with his fiancé:

> I am rather discouraged because I am making so little progress on my book. I seem to have lost the capacity for conscious thought and the stuff I write is so banal that I throw it in the fire. I have nothing but an outline to show for my labors. Must put the rest of the days I have here on my courses. I

> wonder if that book will ever be finished. Have ploughed through Hobhouse again and marked all the stuff which is grist for my mill and I hope to do the same thing with Troeltsch.[17]

The ideal-real contrast in the book reflected both Troeltsch's sense of how the church sought to express its ideal in the world, but was always forced into compromise. But probably even more important were his own experiences in war, industrial strife, and racial conflict in Detroit. He brought a commitment to social reform as a Christian to the struggles, and in the late twenties and early thirties he expressed this commitment in socialist terms. But he also realized how difficult social reform was to realize. He knew that many liberals dreamed too much of progress and that they minimized the sense of struggle and regular defeat that accompanied a life of social reform. Beyond that his own sense of Christian selfhood engaged him deeply to live the life of moral integrity as best one could. Moral integrity was hard to maintain in the necessities of political struggle, and he refused to minimize that difficulty.

After a stormy trip across the North Atlantic, the Tillichs arrived at their ground floor apartment at Union Theological Seminary on 122 Street near Broadway in New York City. The Tillich family always remembered that Mrs. Urusula Niebuhr was the first to welcome them to their new home. The young, blond English bride had been married less than a year, but she competently settled the refugee family in their ground floor apartment in Knox Hall as if she knew just what to do and had done this regularly. A little more than a year earlier, she had said goodbye to Dietrich Bonhoeffer on his fateful return to his German homeland. He would return one more time to consider teaching in America before his final decision to suffer the fate of his country. That evening a small welcoming party was held for the Tillichs and their daughter, six-year-old Christiane Erdmuthe, by Dr. and Mrs. Horace Friess from Columbia University and the Niebuhrs. The conversation was mostly in German and the new partnership was initiated. Together their power would transcend that of the other outstanding faculty at the Seminary and lift it to its preeminent place in American seminaries' social and theological thought.

Soon Tillich's apartment at Union Theological Seminary became a center for refugees from Germany. Friendships were renewed, politics were discussed, and arrangements to assist other refugees were made. In November 1936, the organization Self-Help for Émigrés from Central Europe was created, and Tillich became its chairman. He labored for the agency for fifteen years as organizer, counselor, and philosopher. The organization was kept open and flexible to respond creatively and immediately to need.[18]

Gradually Tillich came to find meaning in forced emigration and exile. He came to understand emigration as the way that God shattered human securities and so allowed humanity to respond in faith. If God elected people, he separated them from old customs and mores. Abraham became archetypical for the experiences of emigration. God chose Abraham for a special destiny and forced him to emigrate. So, too, Israel had to emigrate to Egypt, and back, to Babylon and back, and into exile in the Western world. Christians were emigrants, separated from both Judaism and paganism.

Tillich interpreted emigration not as a cruel fate, but as a religious category for understanding reality. It witnessed to the exclusiveness of God and to the relativity of all human bonds. By 1936 he could say to a group of refugees.

> Emigration by itself is a protest against the nationalistic disorientation of Christianity and defamation of humanity. The support of émigrés is a support of prophetic protest against the demonic energy of religious nationalism.[19]

Tillich concluded with an appeal to support emigration whether out of Christian love, moral outrage, or for political reasons; but he reminded his audience that there was an ultimate religious truth in the experience of emigration.

6

On the Boundary

Niebuhr's frustration with Tillich's German constructions of the essays collected in the *Interpretation of History* was widely shared. Niebuhr was furious that Richard Savage, the editor for Charles Scribner's Sons had accepted the inadequate translations. However, with Tillich traveling in preparation for the ecumenical council at Oxford, there was only so much Niebuhr with his schedule could accomplish. He wrote to Ursula that he had put in seventy hours of improving the manuscript, and then more time, but the pressures of his editorship, constant speeches, sermons, and committee meetings prevented him from accomplishing more. Of course, there were commentators on Niebuhr who thought his work in the 1930s still revealed that his native language construction was German. Tillich's preface takes a little too lightly Niebuhr's contribution to the project:

> Finally, I want to thank my friend Reinhold Niebuhr without whose help I neither would be in this country nor would I have had the occasion to publish this book. I am indebted to him further for many suggestions which have improved its form and style.[1]

Tillich's autobiographical sketch, "On the Boundary" is the easiest chapter of the volume to read, and it reveals as much as he wished to be revealed to his American audience. It indicates his own penchant for examining things dialectically and leaving the answer to several questions ambiguous as he describes two poles of his life, but protects the center in a cloud of unresolved tension. The choice of title reflects his exiled state at the point that he was abandoning hopes of returning to Germany and beginning to prepare for American citizenship. The outline of twelve characteristics of his life and thought is his, but in this book brief examinations and comparisons with Reinhold Niebuhr will be presented under Tillich's categories.

Two Temperaments

He found his two parents symbolic of his character. His father's Eastern tendency towards melancholy, duty, feudal traditions, and a high sense of sin remained with him and suppressed the more-Western character of his mother's sensuality, love of life, democratic tendencies, and mobility with more emphasis upon rationality. So in part his life was a rebellion against his father which would break through in eruptions sometimes leading to extreme behavior. He did not share with his readers how extreme was his reference to rebellion. He was careful to say the inheritances were not determinative, but rather that they gave him opportunities for his own freedom. His early development, he thought now as he approached fifty years of age, was more under the influence of his father as his mother had died when he was sixteen years old. In Niebuhr whose father died prematurely, the spirit of the father's melancholy, sense of duty, and a severe intuition regarding sin were predominant. He remained very close to his mother, even sharing a home with her until his marriage at forty. Niebuhr's life does not reveal any great sense of conflict except for his workaholic tendencies which often left him exhausted after fulfillment of extraordinary commitments to write, speak, and organize.

Nature and City

Tillich remembered nostalgically his boyhood in small rural towns with fields and animals. This conditioned his receptivity for Schelling's romantic philosophy of nature. Often he wrote by the sea or under the trees and he came to understand the concept of infinity partially through meditation on the ocean, but he found there also the ocean's relentless aggression against the shore. He came to regard an alteration between the city and the country to be necessary for his well-being (he said: "for my existence"). Niebuhr's upbringing also was in the smaller Midwestern town among farmers, and his life like Tillich's was fulfilled in the city with rural escapes to Heath, and Stockbridge, Massachusetts.

Between Classes

Tillich carried, at least since World War I, a high degree of class consciousness. Playing with children in the public schools of the lower classes, he had some associations with the higher classes because of his father's position as pastor. He learned early the antagonisms of the classes in Germany. Migrating through the German *Boheme* class within socialism, he associated with radicals who tended to look down on the lower-middle classes while attempting to identify with the working class. This class consciousness of which he was so aware was less obvious in the United States because of increased social mobility and democratic ideology. His failure to find a proletariat in the U.S. led him to understand finally that his form of socialism was not politically relevant in the U.S. His own sense of duty had been magnified with his father's role of pastor which put him within the Prussian bureaucracy as it had Tillich, first as a chaplain then as a university teacher. As a professor he felt himself to be on the borderline between classes. This was especially true within his own position at the time of a low salary and insecure position at Union in the United States. Most academics never succeed to the social positions of the leading administrators in the universities and certainly not to the positions of the board members of the academic institutions which to a large degree control their fates. Tillich remained conscious of social privilege throughout his life, even when he had obtained a certain degree of privilege himself. His biographers, Wilhelm and Marion Pauck point this out continually from their positions of knowing him personally. It wasn't so much that he was between social classes in his maturity as that he was very conscious of social class and that he moved through different classes and had various relations with members of various classes. Niebuhr's family had known poverty, and several members depended upon his resources from time to time. He was respected for his association with ordinary people. The Jewish newsstand operator across Broadway or the porter in the Hasting Hall dormitory both received his attention. There never was much money in the household, but his intellectual stature gave him contacts with the movers and shakers of American and British society.

Between Reality and Imagination

Writing in America, Tillich was not far from his Bohemian past, and the life of music, art, dress-up parties, and the extremes of that period. His daughter remembers Theodore Adorno coming into their home and playing the songs from "The Three Penny Opera." American readers are best transported into those closing years of the Weimar Republic by "Cabaret," its music and its playfulness with darkness in the background. Tillich admits he had some trouble coming to grips with reality. He wrote about escaping into his imagination from the age of fourteen to seventeen, coping with the death of his beloved mother, and imagining himself in the role of Hamlet. When he protested in *The Socialist Decision*, he admitted he was not only condemning the romanticism of the Nazi movement, but also the romantic-mythical element that he had conquered in himself. During the first World War, he found comfort in art, particularly Botticelli's Madonna, and then in Expressionism. From Expressionism's turning in artistic trends toward Realism, he indicated he picked up his concept of faithful realism so prevalent in his book *The Religious Situation* dedicated to an artist friend. Painting became his appreciated form of art over the usual evangelical pastor's mastery of music which he did not persist in developing. It wasn't that he painted, but that he found comfort in paintings and wrote about it acutely, perhaps prompting the invitation to speak at the dedication of the new wing of the Museum of Modern Art in New York City. Both Niebuhr and Tillich loved and used Shakespeare; Niebuhr frequently quoted from the bard in his writings and sermons, Tillich used him less, but regarded the period of his life in which he identified so with Hamlet as a dangerous experience. Both knew that the world of religion was in part a world of imagination and symbolism,

Niebuhr was more likely to leave it at that level while Tillich tried to explore it more in theory. Niebuhr stuck closer to a disciplined reality though he repeatedly wove his philosophy and presentations of the history of ideas around the polarities of idealism and realism. Niebuhr was the more-active participant in sports in his mature years. Tillich's playfulness is seen in his flirtation with women, and in his seductiveness probably best described with some exaggeration in the book by his wife, *From Time to Time*.[2]

On the Boundary between Theory and Practice

Tillich was known as a person of theory; few thought him a practical man. In his autobiographical presentation he regarded his three years of pastoral work and his four years as army chaplain as years of practical activity. The rest of his career had been dedicated to theory, which he loved. True happiness was in theoretical meditation as Aristotle had recognized. His theoretical bent and his lack of practicality was so extreme that if it had not been for his students recording and organizing, proofreading, and managing the publication, his three volumes of *Systematic Theology* would never have been published. His work on religion and socialism was theoretical as was most of his work for the church. So was his contribution to the Social Democratic Party which he joined in 1929. He proposed reforms for the church, for the university, and for the party, but they would all have to be regarded as theory. Still his theoretical book on politics was perceived as so dangerous that it was immediately placed on the "Black List." He knew that theory and practice were not to be united and though several times he tried to have practical effects, it would seem that what he described as a boundary was on the theoretical side of the divide. Niebuhr, on the other hand, who wrote so many books on the theory of politics, society, and religion, had a practical edge for raising money for the Seminary, causes, publishing, organizing, and practical church work that exceeded Tillich's. Niebuhr also recognized that Tillich knew theology and the history of thought much more thoroughly than he did, and, as previously noted, was a genius at speculation.

Heteronomy and Autonomy

As a Prussian theological student, son of the consistory's examining pastor, Tillich had to fight against heteronymous forces which wanted to bend him to their authority. He won his way through study and challenge before the war broke the pretentious illusions of Germany. Still early in his university career he rejected purely autonomous thought. The term autonomy was important to Tillich. It meant the revolt of humanity in the Renaissance and Reformation to a freedom that was absent from the medieval Roman Catholic system. It was close to Bonhoeffer's phrase of "Humanity come of age." In personal terms it meant the freedom and responsibility of adulthood. It was the opposite of heteronomy or the control of the self or humanity by an outside force. He did not want to fall, as philosophy had historically, into either cynicism or skepticism. His own solution was to work to break through into theonomy as he wrote in *The Religious Situation*. Theonomy was the affirmation of a stance as free humanity realizing the power of the divine. He affirmed a religiously filled criticism which like Protestantism at its best criticized all of its certainties. He admired the possibility that the Catholic church could resist the blandishments of Hitler while most of Protestantism caved in. But he could not surrender to the heteronomy of Catholicism, or even the Confessing church which partially saved Protestant integrity. It exhibited a heteronomy that Tillich could not affirm other than in its resistance to Hitler. He observed in Europe the continuing collapse of democracies and the retreat to totalitarianism and he feared that, as they had not won their own freedom, it was too casually lost. In this essay he wrote the only sentence known to me of his left-leaning earlier political life where he affirms that a "few years before the War, after reaching voting age, I stood on the political left, even though the strongest conservative traditions had to be defied."[3]

He affirmed his own liberal roots in theology on the same page and argued that in spite of all of the deserved critique of liberal economics he could not join in the critique of "liberal thinking" that was all too ordinary:

> I would rather be accused of being "liberalistic" myself, than aid in discounting the great and truly human element in the liberal idea, autonomy, with this disparaging phrase.[4]

Tillich did not know how to integrate needed political authority with the turn to totalitarianism of the masses who could not find meaning in their lives. He thought his essay "Mass and Spirit" had some suggestions as did his piece "The Totalitarian State and the Claim of the Churches," published the previous year in *Social Research*. He was determined to defend the freedom of autonomy, and hoped to contribute along with future generations to the solution of freedom and authority in politics. At this time (1935), he saw the problem in that as the political order needed authority which presupposed group authority the danger of the controlling group dominating the others was ever present.

Democracy was both possible and necessary to prevent abuses of political authority. But in his own experience in the Weimar Republic no group had been able to win power as each group in the democracy thwarted any other. However, totalitarian government had no restrictions to enslaving the groups that were not in power. His suggested solution of esoteric autonomous groups retreating to protect autonomy was not, in his mind, a practical answer at least in a form that he had worked out. So he elected to stay with autonomy. Specifically this had driven him into exile to the alternative polity of the United States, which seemed by balancing powers to have partially resolved the issue.

As noted earlier in *Moral Man and Immoral Society* Niebuhr had not found a satisfactory answer either. He was less plagued by heteronomy than Tillich. Though Niebuhr's father was a German patriarchal figure, he had left Germany for the freedom of the United States. Niebuhr's move to Yale, encouraged by his father who did not live to see his son's matriculation, freed him from much of the provincialism of his Evangelical Synod in the Midwest. Niebuhr, though heavily influenced by several of his professors, as was Tillich, found a lot of freedom in his graduate study and later in the church. His fight for freedom was not as hard as Tillich's nor would it go to the extremes that Tillich chose in his search for radical freedom. Niebuhr knew that America could not achieve much greater justice in terms of equality without the awakening of the working class and their willingness to use some of the methods of revolutionary socialism like industrial sit-downs, and possibly a general strike. Greater justice would require a crisis and then radical action.

In the Depression the crisis was realized, but rather than Niebuhr's radical labor solutions, the nation got pragmatic adjustment through the New Deal which Niebuhr first dismissed and then by 1936 came to accept as he voted for Roosevelt after campaigning for socialism. Both Niebuhr and Tillich achieved a lot of freedom for themselves by accommodation to structures in a relatively free church and a republican representative form of government which they kept trying to influence. By their location in a seminary they found more freedom than that enjoyed by most university professors in establishing their own courses, in freedom of time for self or social causes.. Union Seminary answered only to itself. A president like William Coffin would exert more discipline than his successor Henry Pitney van Dusen, but with both of them there were few disciplines that were not self-imposed. I think for Tillich, who wanted autonomy informed by theonomy, in the 1930s there was probably no better place than where he fortuitously landed.

Theology and Philosophy

Tillich lived on a permeable border between theology and philosophy. He wrote: "As a theologian I tried to remain a philosopher, and conversely so. To have left the border and decided on the one or the other would have been less difficult. But inwardly it was impossible;"[5] He had studied philosophy as a theological student and at Union he was teaching philosophical theology in a Protestant theological seminary. In-between he had been either a theologian or a philosopher, but drawing on methods and substance from both.

At the time of his writing he had not yet arrived at the method of correlation which characterized his first volume of *Systematic Theology*, perhaps his most satisfactory solution to his problem and opportunity for using both. He found after World War I that the existentialism of Heidegger best presented the theological questions in the face of the abyss of Western civilization's loss of meaning. He described his reception of Heidegger as "A sort of Augustinian-colored mysticism" which fascinated him and many other people who were more explicitly believers than was Heidegger. His grasping Heidegger's preservation of both human finitude and human freedom was something that Niebuhr would write about a few years later.

Of course, before he could present existential questions which were seeking the theological answers of Christian faith he had cleared out of his formal thinking much of idealistic philosophy, phenomenology, and Protestant moralistic theology and value theory. Following Rudolf Bultmann, he understood that one could not base faith upon the relative historical answers of New Testament criticism. Troeltsch had brought him deep into the problems of the relativism of all human answers, and he could not accept the ethnocentrism of Troeltsch's answer to the problem. Tillich was led beyond relativism by the encounter with war and revolution to the need for decision in the face of the lack of full knowledge. Nietzche's philosophy of life, the Christian doctrine of justification by faith, and the beginnings of a philosophy of existence from Schelling, all prepared him, he said, to accept and use Heidegger's thought. The theological categories allowed him to move past Heidegger to his own philosophy of religion. The term "border" is a good choice to describe Tillich's relationship of his two fields. Niebuhr walked a similar road, but without the depth of philosophy that Tillich brought. Niebuhr would more often find philosophy not resolving the question of human freedom.He was more critical of the philosophical systems and turned more quickly to the biblical symbols which Tillich would use to support answers from the Christian tradition. Tillich was more inclusive in his use of philosophy; Niebuhr's use of philosophy was more hidden and Niebuhr was more critical of it than Tillich as he constructed his theology.

Church and Society

Tillich confessed how the church from his youth was an indestructible basis for the feelings of sacrament and Christian identity. At the time of his writing he was participating in planning the ecumenical council of 1937, and he could not tell how far this new involvement would lead him. He realized that his German religious socialism was less relevant than before. He mentioned his early pastoral service and his work in writing materials to reach the unchurched German working classes, and how this had not succeeded. He indicated his own alienation from the church because of its repudiation of his religious socialism. He thought in ancient times and in the modern period humanism, which in ancient times was pagan and now was steeped in Christian insight, was and could become a bridge to the intellectuals. For the workers, the bridge would be a religious socialism.

The Barthian theology which was useful to combat the neo-paganism was not itself capable of working through humanism to reach the intellectuals of modernity. Tillich knew that some religious words could not be abandoned even though they would be given new meaning in the present, but some of the concepts of humanism which originally had Christian meaning should not be surrendered to the pagans, but used by the church to convey its message. He conceived of the church both as a manifest or institutional church and also as a latent church of nonchurch Christians and Christian influenced humanists. His category of latent church corresponded to Ernst Troeltsch's third type of Christianity which was neither sect nor church. Many lived inspired by aspects of Christianity while not participating in active church life. The corresponding expression today would be found in those nonchurch people who claim they are Christian in their spirituality, but not religious. Sometimes he found truer expressions of Christianity in the latent church than he did in the institutional church.

Tillich lived in the latent church and tried occasionally to serve the manifest church, but after participation in the Oxford Conference of Church and Society in 1937 his role in the institutional church outside of his preaching, teaching at the Seminary, and worshipping in its chapel services became more limited. Niebuhr, on the other hand, brought his thirteen years of pastoral experience in Detroit to bear in his teaching. The major social issues he addressed were the same ones he had focused on in Detroit ministry: international relations, race relations, and economic justice. He continued to serve on church commissions of all types until retirement, and the early ranks of church social-justice departments were often filled with his students and those influenced by him.

Of course, Niebuhr reached out to intellectuals of the latent church and to workers through political organizations and social action organizations. Niebuhr was more active than Tillich in founding, supporting, and raising money for parachurch organizations like The Highlander School, The Delta Cooperative Farm, Southern Churchmen, etc., but both found service in other organizations which Tillich would have called the latent church. Niebuhr would regularly be found in church on a Sunday morning but Tillich much less so. Niebuhr had written to Ursula on that Easter morning in which he was working on translating Tillich's essays for the *Interpretation of History* that he would be at St. John the Divine Cathedral that afternoon. Tillich's churchmanship became more latent, and though he returned to membership in the German Social Democratic Party, he kept his ministerial authority in the United Church of Christ which he joined in the United States.

Religion and Culture

Tillich was particularly sharp at seeing expressions of the Absolute in artistic creations. He recognized that in appreciating culture it is hard to distinguish the profane and the sacred. In fact he argued that in Protestantism the distinction broke down. The Sistine Chapel paintings, for example, obviously expressed Italian cultural patterns in form while attempting to convey religious meaning in substance. Culture becomes religious whenever it raises critical questions as to meaning, forgiveness, judgment, hinting at the unconditioned beyond the culture. Finding the religious within culture, he was led to a theoretical comprehension of culture in religious terms. Both culture and religion have their own lives but "As the substance of culture is religion, so the form of religion is culture."[6] Therefore in his book *The Religious Situation* (1926, 1932) Tillich examined various forms of culture to find religious meaning in them at the time, and reflected on religion itself only in a section of the book. The increasing secularism of Europe meant that myths of nation and social justice were replacing Christian myths.

He had joined a movement for the renewal of sacraments and liturgy which grew to almost 300 thinkers and clergy. He thought he might find a place there in the Berneuchen Movement (*Berneuchener Bewegung*) to explore the borders between sacrament and culture. Eventually he left Berneuchen as it drifted more into a focus purely on archaic forms of sacrament. In this movement Tillich's deeply religious nature, founded in his family in Eastern Germany's rural parishes, can be glimpsed. But he couldn't retreat into that sacramentalism completely. As he said, he had to remain on the border.

Tillich's primary entry into cultural studies was through paintings that bore religious meaning often in cultural or secular forms. Niebuhr's primary way of entering culture in its higher forms was through literature. He had a penchant for poetry, and in his pastorate he had often presented lectures on novels and other literature. Quotations from John Donne appear in his sermons and letters as do those from Shakespeare. Both of them wrestled with melancholy, and I think Niebuhr found his escape through writing which meant creating his own philosophic literature while, as suggested earlier, Tillich sought meaning in painting at a level not quite realized by philosophy. Literature for Tillich had too much fragmentary philosophy in it while he preferred his own to be organized.

Lutheranism and Socialism

While socialism appeared as a possible outgrowth of Calvinism, it was very foreign to the ethos of Lutheranism. Tillich knew of the earlier Swiss socialism including that of Karl Barth. But he did not regard socialism as a natural bedfellow to Lutheranism. His own piety and thought was definitely Lutheran as it rejected utopianism and emphasized sin, irrationality, and the demonic. His own religious socialism he regarded as foreign to Lutheranism and so its defeat was inevitable. He still thought it right, but just hopeless. The Lutheran theology was expressing its nationalism, as in the thought of his schoolmate friend Emmanuel Hirsch (1886/1888–1972), and its treatment of the Kingdom of God as totally transcendent and otherworldly.

Lutheranism rejected all utopianism and assumed the permanence of human nature. Tillich thought it more realistic to expect the transformation of both human nature and all nature as the biblical prophets had thought. Rather than rejecting the change of society, he thought aspects of improvement could be achieved which were tastes of the Kingdom of God even though the fulfillment of the Kingdom escaped human history. The socialist ideal might be a long way from the fulfillment of the Kingdom of God, but partial fulfillment of socialist goals were not only helpful to humanity but a decision for the Kingdom of God. His previously discussed ideas of the demonic and Kairos both fleshed out his interpretation of history. His theology of history with its assumed drive toward something new made sense of the transformative category of "expectation" which he used as containing the power of change toward human goals. His one official attempt to explain his socialism to his German church was rejected, and except for a few sensitive friends whom he engaged in long-term conversations, most of his socialist colleagues could not go with his religious vision. It was as if he were on a border with guards on both sides shooting at him or at least not recognizing his claims to citizenship.

Niebuhr was building the same bridges with his socialist Christian group which Tillich joined. Niebuhr's church in America was not quite so Lutheran or defeatist. His Evangelical Synod had more Calvinism in it than the old United Church of Prussia. American sectarian Christianity provided more adequate theological grounding for social reform than the more Lutheran Germany. Niebuhr's rejection of optimism baffled his socialist colleagues at first, though it was natural to his theological heritage, and their optimism was more American culture than any formation of theology. American churches were more engaged in the Social Gospel than were the German churches. While the churches in America seemed to be more open to social reform and the German churches prone to capture by nationalism and destructive social philosophies, American society was much less open to socialism than European's were. European socialism was beaten before the war, but rebounded after the war. In America, no party carrying the name socialist could win significant electoral support. They met as socialists with strong religious dimensions. Their religious work outlasted their socialist activity, though both of their societies had been in the convulsions of social change as they encountered one another.

Idealism and Marxism

Tillich would often elect to teach German idealistic philosophy in American universities when given the option of choosing courses. He had been educated in this idealism and it was foundational to his thinking even though many of its assumptions had been exploded by existentialism, including Marxism. Marxism to Tillich was existentialist because it attacked the idealistic presentations of society and exposed the contradictions in capitalist society. It focused on the misery of the human condition under industrialism rather than upon idealistic-rationalistic claims for the economic order.

Tillich wrote that "Above all I am indebted to Kantian criticism." He regarded himself as an idealist in asserting the need for the identification of the subject and the knowledge of the object. His drive to work in a philosophy of freedom was derived from its idealistic roots in recognition of categorical moral demands, and in searching for meaning in society, nature and art. He held there was a correspondence between reality and human spirit expressed in "Meaning." Philosophy as it sought to discover "Meaning" was doing its appropriate work for Tillich. Idealism for Tillich failed when it refused to see its limits and thought it was describing reality as a whole rather than as a partial perception of reality.[7]

Marx, in addition to Kierkegaard, the later Schelling, and Freud showed that humanity was subject to illusions to defend its limited position. Marx's economic materialism revealed the ideological blind spots of the Western world and helped free humanity from its illusions. Economic materialism showed that, to an extent, economics and social situations drove thought. Tillich appreciated Marx for his development of the concept of ideology more than anything else and for the recognition that in crisis truer self-consciousness could emerge. But he remained on the border of Marxism; he appreciated its passion even when he couldn't accept its claims for total explanation and scientific certainty. He reformed Marxism in his own presentation of the concept of socialistic expectation of change in *The Socialist Decision* (1933). He confessed he was not as interested in political parties as in groups that bound themselves together for fellowship. In this the man of theory over practical politics was evident. His explicit denial of party memberships seems a little disingenuous even though it expresses a fundamental attitude of his relationship to socialism. In the same year that he was working on these autobiographical reflections he also penned a more-formal discussion of Marxism for the preparatory work of the upcoming conference on church and society in Oxford.

This 1935 report, "The Christian and the Marxist View of Man" for the Universal Christian Council for Life and Work Research Department,[8] continues the anthropological explorations of *The Socialist Decision* and reveals the analogies between Protestantism and Marxism very clearly. The report is in outline form and many of the references to Tillich's sources are cryptic. He developed a second edition of the paper in 1959 and that version is extant in the Harvard Archive. In that form it appears to be a prospectus of a major study, or a small book. He had continued to publish on Marxism in the United States through the 1930s, 1940s, and 1950s contrary to the assertion by Weisskopf in the American Academy of Arts and Science book *The Thought of Paul Tillich* that "Tillich's socialist writings stem from the time before his emigration to the U.S. and therefore do not cover events after 1933."[9] The report is a reminder that a life-long, primary dialogue partner to Paul Tillich's Protestantism was Marxism. John Stumme has dated the origins of this dialogue to his practical work in "Inner Mission" and church apologetics to the proletariat that led to his debating Karl Liebknecht, who later organized the German Communist Party, on 12 December 1913.[10]

The first section of the paper shows that neither Marxism nor some tendencies in Protestantism have an "articulate anthropology." Their refusal to articulate anthropology in both cases was rooted in their negative evaluation of human existence. However within both, radically critical attitudes developed for healing the ruptures in human existence. Their convergent trends revealed their common prophetic heritage and made comparisons possible.

The second section of the paper outlines the basic ideas of Protestant anthropology showing

> Seven problems of equal importance to Christianity and Marxism: Humanity's original true nature, the transition to a state of contradiction, the character of this contradiction, existence in contradiction, the overcoming of the contradiction, the goals of the perfection of humanity.[11]

The exploration of the seven problems demonstrates that there are structural analogies between prophetic Christianity and Marxism. Tillich does not intend to argue for identity of ideas but to show typologically certain analogies. As the second section had begun, "The galvanizing point of view of Christian-Protestant anthropology is the relation of man to God,"[12] the third section begins, "The controlling viewpoint of all socialist-Marxist anthropology is man's position within society.[13]

The concluding section shows some contradictions between Christianity and Marxism. In each case the fundamental antithesis is one of imminence and transcendence. Christian anthropology is related to God and Marxist anthropology to society. All of the fundamental oppositions can be seen to be an expression of this issue.

Marxism is seen as adopting one element, that of the critical-prophetic motif, while Christianity also preserves the possibilities of mysticism and a certain inward existence distinct from social contradictions. Conditions of the relationship between Marxism and Christianity depend on whether the relationship is exclusive or particular. The first possibility of interpretation leads to a life-and-death struggle. The second interpretation, that of religious socialism, would understand Marxism as the critical-prophetic-imminent tendency of Christianity's own life. Such an interpretation which was Tillich's own would seek to "search for a way of receiving it again into itself." Both Niebuhr and Tillich were working to interpret and receive the benefits of a Marxist critique in Christian social ethics. Niebuhr's attempt at a synthesis would run out before Tillich's and he would undertake the construction of his own anthropology and philosophy of history to replace Marxist anthropology to which Tillich in this paper was drawing analogies. As they worked on the issues, both incorporated Heidegger and Kierkegaard into their systems and preserved the idealism of their younger studies in the philosophies of freedom and studies of the "self" which were not associated so deeply with Marxism. Clearly both Niebuhr and Tillich were shaking off the influence of Marxism, even before they knew it, as they defined the differences between Marxism and Christianity as essentially religious issues of transcendence.

Home and Alien Land

Tillich was not yet an American citizen, and he felt himself deeply German. He was so German that overemphasis on things German betrayed deep insecurities in those emphasizing German nationalism. He insisted he lived on the boundary and that such a position was appropriate for all. He liked to recall Abraham being called by God to leave his land and to trust in the promise of God to go forward in an unknown way. Such was really the way by which those who grasped at transcendence could live. The God of the prophets and Jesus stood against narrow nationalism and called people forth to trust a transcendent promise. Some were literally called to leave home, but others were to stay home and make internal migrations whereby they became critical of the idolatries of nationalism. His writings in the rest of *The Socialist Decision* on power and the demonic detailed his critique of German nationalism and the false nationalisms of Europe which were set on destroying the continent once again. He saw dimly the emerging concept of humanity that transcended nationalism, and in it he saw the idea of the Kingdom of God that was the end of all excessive nationalisms. To some extent the new country in which he could survive was a symbol of the Kingdom as it lived with different nationalities in harmony. He understood the ideal was not realized, but it was a beginning.

> The experience of the four years in the World War was decisive for my attitude. In this experience, the demonic and destructive power of the national

> will to power became manifest particularly for one who went into war enthusiastically and with the firm belief in the justice of the national attitude.[14]

In this biographical reflection, his own exile in Abrahamic terms becomes a criticism of nationalism more than an analysis of his own insecurity in migrating. The concept of humanity was being enforced through the experiences of humanity united and divided through war and economics. Yet its definition was a long way from being realized as the species set itself up in 1935–1936 for another cataclysmic war, and again it would begin in the struggle between Germanic and Slavic peoples. In the same section he would express his gratitude for the hospitality of his new country. His and Niebuhr's work to carry on that hospitality to the refugees from Europe would later grow into the largest of the American nonprofit, nongovernmental refugee agencies. In the closing sentences of his remarkable introduction of himself to his American reading public, he admitted that standing on so many boundaries left him living with many insecurities and an acute awareness of his limits and the limits of human life. He did write briefly in this last section on homelessness, and about how he never could accept pacifism, for power called for the restraint of power by other powers. Yet in that short reflection is a further division between peacemaker and warrior. Both he and Niebuhr had engaged at first in World War I in rather absolute terms, now they were facing a more-violent redoing of that war. He also suffered from posttraumatic disorder from the war as Europe suffered from it. His world would be broken again, and Niebuhr's short period as a pacifist would be dismissed as a mistake. Tillich wrote about the "inability of attaining serenity, security, and perfection." But they were entering a period in which neither the religious forces, nor their socialist forces could restrain the hell that was about to break on them. They were failed by their churches and their political commitments. Still they had to do their work.

Beyond the Boundary

Despite being dismissed by the Nazis for his socialist politics and support of Jews, not all of Tillich's thought was foreign to some Christians who supported Hitler. James Reimer's exhaustive study of the debate between Paul Tillich and the infamous Emmanuel Hirsch showed that elements of Tillich's romanticism, and national identity as a German, and respect for myths of origin were common to both participants in the debate.[15] Hirsch, a long-time friend of Tillich, had read most of his writings and they had mutual respect for each other's differing positions as they evolved their thought. The disruption of their lives by the victory of Nazism in 1933 drove them to emphasize their differences. The split was more political than cultural though their theologies of culture had deep discrepancies also.

Most Protestant clergy welcomed Hitler's victory in 1933, though divisions among the Nazi supporters soon became apparent. There were conservative German Chrisitans, many of whom were united in the *Christlich-Deutsche Bewegung* (CDB). This group was "closer to the Nationalist Party (DNVP)"[16] than to the National Socialists. The CDB attempted to maintain a moderate position of support for Hitler while retaining theological integrity. It folded before the end of 1933, and the more-enthusiastic supporters of Nazism moved into the *Glaubensbewegung Deutsche Christen* (GDC). Emanuel Hirsch was one of the few known theologians who joined the GDC along with Paul Althaus and Friercih Wienke. The GDC was created by the Nazis. It did not have the academic prestige of the CDB, but it was more enthusiastic and committed to the religious-political struggle. Ideology and theology were surrendered in this group to the Nazi attempt to control the church. Hitler supported the GDC in the church elections of July 1933 when the enthusiasm for a unifed church supporting Hitler crested. A third group, the *Kirchenbewegung Deutsche Christen* (KDC) was the most ideologically consistent with Nazism. This group originated in Thuringia in 1927 and represented anti-Semitism and devotion to blood, soil, and *Volk* in their most vehement forms.

The Nazis were unable to completely control the church. Most theologians withdrew from the GDC and gradually repented of their earlier support of Nazi efforts to capture the church. The movement for a German Christianity operated without Hitler's direct support, and church affairs were reduced to chaos. The German Christian movement, however, continued under various names and in different alliances. Hirsch remained committed to the German Christian cause until the end of the war and his attempt to provide a theology for the movement elicited Tillich's attack upon him in 1935.

Hirsch had opposed the Weimar Republic. He had longed for an end to the parliamentary confusion and the mixture of liberalism and Marxism that dominated Germany after the 1918 revolution. He contributed to Christian anti-Semitic tendencies and played down the importance of the Old Testament for Christian theology. With his thought rooted in the nationalist idealism of Fichte, Hirsch developed a political theory that deemphasized the state. His basic concept was of a people or *Volk*, which was created by God. The *Volk* was the bearer of meaning, and when a state did not allow the fulfillment of *Volk*, it could be overthrown. The revolution he justified was, of course, not the founding revolution of the Weimar Republic, but the order that would replace it.

In 1934 Hirsch had his newly published *The Present Cultural Situation in Philosphical and Theological Perspective* sent to Tillich in New York City. Tillich criticized the book in the German journal *Theoogische Blatter* in the form of an open letter that joined personal response to the book with bitter polemic.[17] Hirsch responded in another book, *Christian Freedom and Political Obligation.* Tillich responded again in *Theologische Blatter*, concluding the discussion.[18]

Though at the beginning of this exchange Tillich indicated his personal friendship for Hirsch, he thought it necessary to refute the principal arguments of *The Present Cultural Situation.*[19] Tillich suggested that devotees of the German Christian movement including Hirsch were using categories developed within religious socialism and that they were being distorted. He also deplored Hirsch's refusal to acknowledge the borrowing of the concepts. In particular he suggested Hirsch borrowed the concepts of "Kairos"and "Boundary" as well as general outlines of the intellectual situation. Reimer shows how these concepts may have been common intellectual property to both thinkers; the charge of plagiarism does not seem to be of ultimate importance in this case as much more-important issues were at stake. The essence of Tillich's attack, however, was in uncritically affirming the changes of 1933 Hirsch had surrendered to the demonic-sacramental forces. He accused Hirsch of giving up his vocation as a Protestant theologian in his enthusiasm for a movement and of considering a finite historical movement as an absolute. The Kairos doctrine was thus misused by Hirsch because he ignored the religious reservation about all finite movements. Hirsch forgot the dialectical balance of faithful realism when he was unreservedly critical of the 1918 revolution and unreservedly affirmative of the 1933 revolution. To Tillich the theology of Hirsch seemed to make contemporary events revelatory. Tillich admitted that the previous articulation of the Kairos doctrine had not been adequately guarded from this misuse, but he argued that revelation is first, and it seizes the subject; after that other events are examined in relationship to the original revelation. An event is "in Kairos" only if it corresponds to the original Kairos. A new event does not change the meaning of revelation. Kairos by itself is not revelation; rather it shows a fresh realization of the original. The cross of Christ—and Tillich thanked Hirsch for clarifying this idea for him—is the judge against Hirsch's claim for the "German hour."

Tillich attacked Hirsch for remaining quiet when Jewish businesses were boycotted and for failing to attribute racial legislation, which Hirsch supported, to the simple racial hatred that was infecting Germany. He criticized Hirsch's basic concept of *Volk* as meaningless, it represented no more than the current evil will dominating the German people. He argued that Hirsch had fallen back on primitive sacramental language and had refused to use critical sociological concepts. If there were to be a sacred-blood community as Hirsch argued, asked Tillich, would it not be for a theologian the community of Christians in communion? Hirsch's concept of a "concealed sovereignty" in the *Volk*, Tillich commented, was no more than a way to avoid the antirevolutionary teaching of Lutheran ethics. It was not a responsible concept of a theology of politics, but only an apology for the Protestant rush to support Hitler.

In the closing section of his first letter, Tillich reminded Hirsch that religious socialism taught not only the need for religious social action, but also the need for a religious reservation about social action. He accused Hirsch of ignoring this reservation, falling into an unholy religious enthusiasm for Nazism, and betraying his responsibilities as a theologian.

Tillich's second letter reemphasized this theme saying that Hirsch had even identified the divine with a human realm. On the other hand, Barth had shown the profanity of the political realm, neglecting his earlier religious socialism., Tillich, while agreeing with Barth, sought in the doctrine of Kairos a middle way, which criticized the sacramental, primitive understanding of politics with a prophetic insight, while remaining open to the manifestation of the power of being in historical events. Such manifestations, for Tillich, must be judged by the cross of Christ and the gospel of the coming Kingdom of God. Tillich accused Hirsch of using the two-realm theory of Luther to free the secular realm from prophetic criticism while allowing one to participate with a religious enthusiasm. Tillich's Kairos doctrine was in some ways similar to the two-realm theory of Luther, but it avoided the pitfalls of Hirsch and Barth.

When the Nazi movement tried to capture the religious support in 1933, Hirsch fell into the trap. Barth resolutely opposed such a compromise; but in his opposition, he failed to grasp the deeper significance of some political movements. Tillich tried to maintain a dialectical approach. Practical politics was of a different order from theological politics. A theology of politics, though, had to take seriously the philosophical claims of political ideology which often drifted into religious claims. Tillich had been doing this in his lectures at Frankfurt on the political principles of German political parties. Tillich's debate with Hirsch was both political and theological. Politics, however dominated the practical outcome. Tillich's theology had been driven from Frankfurt by the Nazis. Hirsch would be driven out of the university in 1945 by the victorious allies.[20]

Around the Boundary

Tillich's travel on the continent after lecturing in England took him to Holland, Belgium, Luxembourg, France, Switzerland, and Italy. Twice he could see into Germany, and friends and relatives came out to visit him. While traveling, he wrote a diary for Hannah. She published it five years after his death. *My Travel Diary: 1936* provides the most daily detail of any of his writings. He recorded wines drunk, places visited, meals eaten, strangers and friends encountered, and lectures given.[21] Even with Hitler and Mussolini joining in supporting Franco's revolution in Spain his lectures to arouse Britain had not accomplished much. The British mood of appeasement often opposed him.

On meeting Reinhold in Switzerland, Tillich shared with him the invitation he was considering to join his Berlin friend Adolf Lowe in teaching in Manchester. John Oldham who was encouraging both of them in their preparatory work for the Oxford Conference of Life and Work to be held next year was also encouraging Tillich to stay in Britain. Niebuhr urged him to stay at Union, even though his career was developing slowly there and said: "We will found a school of theology there."[22]

During his European tour, Tillich spoke about the Nazi victory in terms of the disintegration of Western society. He described his own perspective as that of a "tragic dialectic." His pessimism drove him to look for resources of renewal, and he could not find them institutionalized. He called on political and intellectual leaders to covenant together to analyze the situation and to propose avenues of action. He described his idea as a religious order, and it merged elements of retreat from the world with the need to find new proposals for action to meet the situation.[23]

He often discussed the possibility of coup against Hitler and a negotiated settlement with Germany before it was too late. The discussions sometimes considered the possibility of assassinating Hitler. He also encouraged refugees from Germany to start a new life abroad. Germany was behind him now; he was not tempted to return. He was free outside of Germany while on the inside the prison walls were becoming taller and more impregnable.

The diary shows a philosopher who knew that human meaning was constructed by thinking and talk. He gave careful perusal to the good things of life: museums, music, art, churches, dance, food, and wine. He was thinking, talking, absorbing, and trying to understand. He was encouraging both migration and resistance. One can also see the philosopher of nature in the volume as he meditated upon forests, landscapes, mountains, and seas. His league or *Bund* of intellectuals would not come into being, except for a small group that Oldham called together in England.[24]

With differing commitments to speak before the conference, Tillich and Niebuhr traveled separately to the Oxford Conference on Church and Society sponsored by the Life and Work Department, which would become part of the World Conference of Churches. Ursula traveled with Reinhold and they stayed at her college, St. Hughes. Reinhold gave the Bishop Burge Memorial Lecture in London preceding the conference entitled "Does the state or nation belong to God or the Devil." They had traveled earlier than needed and Reinhold had intended to go on to Germany to visit allies and friends. Ursula reported that he was warned by telegram that visiting acquaintances in Germany might be dangerous for them so they left the ship in Plymouth, England.[25]

Niebuhr delivered his presentation to the conference from a few notes conveying a degree of spontaneity to which the delegates were not accustomed.

His wild gestures and the searching of his own mind to the questions he posed for tentative answers impressed the learned group of churchmen. His lecture was almost sermonic in argument as opposed to the carefully outlined, systematic presentation of Tillich. He posed the threat of secularism, as the disavowal of the sacred, to the message of the church. But upon analysis secularism appeared to be the glorification of the human in various guises. On further examination the secularism of the middle class seemed to be the glorification of the bourgeois who ran the world. The secularism of Marxism so useful in social critique, in the end was a mystical glorification of the proletariat. Nazism was the old pagan religion of blood and soil in a new modern, revolutionary guise. He suggested secularism could be understood in the Parable of the Prodigal Son who in his first presentation represents rationalistic humanism in its liberation from the father. As he wasted his substance in riotous living he represented the romantic type of modern humanism, finally when in the famine the son falls into want he represents the modern calamity approaching proud humanity who had rejected the father. If the parable represents modern life, the Christian message is: repent and accept grace instead of pride. The most profound theologies came, he thought, as humanity stumbled into chaos, and perhaps the present degeneration provides such an opportunity. The young pagan nations of Europe faced disruption and the loss of their false religions. In Christian faith there was to be found meaning for history which did not fail, but which provided hope. The preaching of the church needed to admit its own sins and errors. It must avoid the vain glorification of the elder "good" brother in the parable. The church is not the Kingdom of God, and the church becomes profane when it acts self-righteously. The danger was that the offices of the church contained within themselves the temptation to confuse the church with divinity. Paul had resisted this temptation in Acts 14, and the contemporary church had to avoid the mistake also.

The church had profaned itself by pretending that its authority was divine whereas theology is a human discipline as all means of inquiry are human. Theology should not have pretended to confuse its ultimate answers with detailed knowledge of sequences of efficient causation. The church claimed an inappropriate role and secularism had rightly denied it that role. On the other hand, science had tried to deduce ultimate answers from its secular learning. So both science and theology had encroached beyond their competence. Religion had mistakenly claimed literal and historic truth for many of its myths from which it needed to be freed. Also religion had been used to legitimate profane societies and secularism rightly rebelled against such misuse of religious authority. Secularism contained both a useful protest against a false profanity of the church and its own mixtures of contemporary profanity.

He concluded by arguing that the church's judgment of the world had to begin at home. The church must be careful of the temptation of moralism and simple answers. He concluded if the church feels the need for its own repentance; it may be able to address the world with its gospel of a holy, righteous God without making sinful claims for itself. Perhaps it can rebuke the world's sins without becoming satisfied with the sad disillusionment into which the "high hopes of modernity have issued."[26]

Tillich's presentation of "The Kingdom of God and History"[27] was read quietly and deliberately to the Oxford conference. It lacked the gestures and seeming spontaneity of Niebuhr's ruminations around his theme. The theology, though, did not really differ in substance. They were both critics of the futility of their culture's weak response to the forces overtaking it. They both used the Kingdom of God as a symbol to criticize contemporary utopias and to encourage resistance to the evil threatening to overtake them.

Tillich outlined his paper as first the clarification of philosophical concepts; secondly as the theological presentation of the symbol of the Kingdom of God and its relationship to history; and finally as the confrontation with the forces of history today. He believed such reflections grew out of historical action and he identified his own perspective as that of religious socialism. The world was understood as a battleground between the demonic forces and the Kingdom of God that symbolized the final unity and purity of history and, in the present, the forces contending for God against the demonic.

Tillich asserted that the Kingdom of God is the dynamic fulfillment of the ultimate meaning of existence against the contradictions of existence. History, for the Christian, has Christ as its center and salvation has the partial overcoming of the demonic as its history of salvation. It is a history of real battles with victories, but not with the final overcoming of the demonic in history as that is symbolized by the realization of the Kingdom of God. Salvation is fragmentarily realized in history, and the fragments represent the salvation of the Kingdom of God symbol.

Christian action in the world according to Tillich is bipolar. There is the theological meaning of the Kingdom of God and the socially substantive participation in the historical pole which for Tillich is religious socialism. From such a perspective three major forces of the demonic can be named: laissez faire capitalism, nationalism particularly expressed in contemporary European nationalism, and, third, dictatorship expressed most clearly in the Bolshevik dictatorship of Russia. The response of Protestantism to these realities had been so weak that Tillich was willing to suggest that perhaps the Protestant era was ending. Of course, in Tillich's perspective not only Protestantism is threatened but the whole historical existence of contemporary humanity. The Kingdom of God meant not nationalism, but the unity of humanity, not dictatorship but freedom of humanity with human dignity, and it meant not the ruthlessness of capitalism with poverty for most, but the fulfillment of social fairness and regulation of the brutal impulses of decision makers with power. The question of history for the Christian is fulfilled in the symbol of the Kingdom of God, but in the present power must be used to resist the demonic forces that threaten the Kingdom and humanity.

While Tillich was quite clear about his acceptance of evolution as a fundamental quality of nature, he did not see the Kingdom of God being realized by any social evolution. It was in his historical situation primarily a fighting term to win those victories against the demons of capitalism, nationalism, and dictatorship which were possible. The Christian brought a belief in *Karoi* (times of historical decisive actions) to the struggle as well as confidence in the final fulfillment of the symbol of the Kingdom of God.

Tillich's heavy German accent was strange to the listeners as no German theologians had been given visas to attend the ecumenical gathering by the Third Reich. His religious socialism was understood by most, and many affirmed it. The militancy of his speech was foreign to most of his listeners who were dominated by the allies' appeasement. His critiques of capitalism were stronger than many of his audience had heard from ecclesiastical leaders. His rejection of pacifism as irrelevant clearly offended many of his Anglo-Saxon dignitaries at the conference. The gradual drift of Europe into dictatorships had not usually been associated in the churchmen's minds with the rise of the demonic. Thus this address which must be regarded as one of the best of Tillich's theological papers could not be appreciated at the time by of his hearers.

Reinhold Niebuhr remained in essential agreement, and only the previous summer they had deepened their friendship and assured their partnership. The Marxian quality of their socialism and their refusal to settle into the pacifism characteristic of the American Social Gospel was characteristic of Tillich's experience of Lutheranism. Niebuhr had given up on pacifism as he left *The World Tommorow* to found his own journal, *Radical Religion*, about the time of Tillich's migration, and the Nazi seizure of power in Germany. Tillich's early, important reflections on socialism for Americans would be published there as would his first speech on anti-Semitism. The story of that journal is a necessary piece to understanding how their politics and theology developed as they approached their wartime theology. After the Oxford Conference, Tillich would travel to the continent one more time to meet Hannah at Mont Blanc. After that he would not return until a decade later, after the war. Niebuhr would come back in 1939 to deliver his lectures for the Gifford Lectureship in Scotland as war broke out.

7

Radical Religion

Radical Religion's opening page announced it was a publication of Niebuhr's organization, the Fellowship of Socialist Christians, and while some members of that organization were pacifists, the journal was not going to be dogmatic on that issue. The journal expressed the convictions of Niebuhr's most Marxist period, echoing the strong sense of Marxist social analysis of his earlier book *Reflections on the End of an Era*.[1] While Niebuhr still insisted on empiricism and pragmatism, his own vision was shaped by materialistic insights and the expectation of catastrophe. It was during this period of the journal, 1935–1940, that Niebuhr moved beyond Marxism and to a fuller Christian analysis of society under wartime pressures. Niebuhr's assistant editor was Winnifred Wygal; the old editors of *The World* were gone. Bishop Paddock of the Protestant Episcopal Church subsidized the early issues of the journal as it undertook developments for the relief of sharecroppers in the South, support for the Spanish Republic, and other radical social causes with which he identified.

The journal, in its first editorial, indicated its purpose in supporting radical social change giving central attention to the relationship between Marxism and Christianity. It intended to deal with the extent to which a Christian should accept materialism and Marxian economic and social strategies.[2]

Prophetic religion held that no human achievement was ever absolute, as it was corrupted by sin and necessarily finite. Niebuhr used Marxist insights to criticize the pretensions of liberalism, and its sense that the powerful could reform themselves. The utopianism of Marxism needed to be rejected along with the sentimentalism of liberalism. It was necessary to realize that justice required a social struggle. The previous year he had written of the necessity of combining Christianity and politics. In the *Christian Century*[3] he had argued in defense of radical politics, sermons against greed were usually not threatening, but sermons advocating a new order to reduce greed were subject, often, to harsh responses. He explicitly took the side of a former minister in Arkansas who had been dismissed from his church for radical political action. He cautioned radical ministers to be tactful. But more importantly radical Christians needed to demonstrate their faith by their lifestyles and by clear appropriation of their religion of love in their politics. The usual charge of conservatives that radicals should not join their politics to their Christianity reflected the political position of the establishment even when the critics were religiously sincere. Christian socialists could believe that socialism was a requirement of justice in the new technological age while still refusing to dream of a classless society or social perfection. Niebuhr's lead editorial set the tone for the journal.

> We believe that a capitalistic society is destroying itself and, yet that it must be destroyed, lest it reduce in the delirium of its destruction our whole civilization to barbarism. We believe that social ownership of the means of production is the only basis of health and justice for a technical age. We believe that such a society can be established only through a social struggle and that in that struggle we ought to be on the side of the workingman.[4]

The following editorials by Niebuhr made the direction of the journal very clear. In one on the Ethiopian war the League of Nations' sanctions against Italy for invading Ethiopia were in full recognition that Britain's support for the sanctions was partially in defense of its own empire. Even though this application of collective security was ambiguous, still there was a gain in the League's first application or attempted application of collective security. The Italian invasion of Ethiopia was from its colonies on both the north and south sides of the country. After a few months it was stalled by the Ethiopian counteroffensive during the Christmas season. Italy retaliated with poison gas. Soon the native armies were defeated, and Ethiopia and the two Italian colonies were united in a new colony. The occupation was particularly brutal, executing many hostages and war prisoners. The resignation of the Christian pacifist-socialist George Lansbury from leadership of the Labor Party in Britain was unfortunate. It revealed the weakness of pacifist socialism. Lansbury could provide no immediate policy answers because of his ultimate pacifist confession. The world needed relevant policy answers now. Lansbury was celebrated by Niebuhr as a great Christian statesman, but in this case his failure indicated that pacifism was a sure guide only in peaceful times. It provided no guidance for the more-immediate issues of preventing war through economic sanctions. Niebuhr's position revealed that he was no longer even absolutely against international war as he was willing to take the risks of war to avoid or to stop war, in this case to stop imperialistic aggression.

The next editorial was in defense of Angelo Herndon, a Negro, Communist, social activist who had been arrested on false charges, mistried and sentenced to twenty years on the chain gang. Most victims of the gang could only survive ten years of such treatment. Herndon deserved the support of all socially active Christians, even though Niebuhr doubted that many ministers would dare support him. This active assertion of civil rights in the face of Southern racism was a continued feature of Niebuhr's activism and the history of the journal.

The first two essays of the new journal also indicated the alliance between the new refugee professor, Paul Tillich, and Niebuhr. Tillich had been working on religious socialist issues since 1918 and in his essay, "Marx and the Prophetic Tradition" manifested his practical alliance with Niebuhr, whose lead essay was entitled "Is Religion Counter Revolutionary?"

Niebuhr conceded that religion often provided false legitimacy to regimes that did not deserve religious sanction. He admitted that the otherworldliness and dualism of much of Christianity obscured the need for social change. He recognized that aspects of Christian thought discouraged the oppressed from their needful rebellion. Yet he believed that a minority of Christians have found a prophetic religion that criticizes and can transform society. He pointed to revolutionary Calvinism as an example of such a faith. He also recognized that secular movements can become religious in their nature and in defense of their movements. Do not the commissars of Russia act with the authority of priests, bishops, and religious hierarchies? It is consequently the business of radical religion to contend equally against the reactionary tendencies of organized religion and against the misunderstandings of the total human situation in the philosophy, and therefore in the strategies of radicalism.[5]

Tillich's is much more detailed than Niebuhr's, reaching back into the mythology of pre-Christian movements to illustrate how dualism, apocalypticism, and utopianism arose in the human mind and were joined to Christian symbolism. Drawing upon his experience as a religious socialist he shows how traditional Christianity lost its prophetic spirit. The failure of Christianity permitted the rise of a new prophetic spirit in Marxism which unfortunately fell into utopianism. He had tried to resolve this failure in *The Socialist Expectation* but he did not go into his proposed resolution of the dilemma in this republished essay. Even in this early writing the tendency of Tillich to include and transform movements can be contrasted with Niebuhr's tendency to criticize movements and seek alternatives.

Christian Socialism

The journal included letters from the Socialist leader Eugene V. Debbs in jail in Atlanta. A discussion of the last meeting of the the Fellowship of Socialist Christians indicated that most of the lectures at the meeting were included in this first issue of the journal. Also noted was that the previous progressive taxation for dues was being reduced in the society to voluntary contributions. The Methodist church's support of the Social Creed in a clothing industry strike was reported on as well as notice of a minister being dismissed for his social stand for labor. Norman Thomas's address at the founding of a new labor church in Quincy, Massachusetts was also cited. The notes on the Fellowship meeting held at Brookwood Labor College included "That something significant was happening." That spirit characterized the first issue of the new journal.

The second issue reported that though they had not achieved their goal of 1,000 subscriptions, they were more than halfway there, and so they could proceed to publish. Niebuhr's lead editorial discussed the United Front Movement in France to resist Fascism. The question was now the advisability of Christian radicals in the U.S.A. joining common front movements with Communists. After exploring the dangers of cooperation with Communists, Niebuhr thought Christian radicals might join such united fronts if they were certain that they were genuine and all parties could be heard. Other editorials supported the cooperative movements, but indicated the hopes of people like Kagawa of Japan that they could socialize the country through cooperatives were naive. Forces like the Pennsylvania Railroad could only be nationalized by strong central government actions. Kagawa as a liberal hoped to avoid social conflict, but politics concerned power.

Reinhold agreed with Archbishop William Temple that Fascism was a more direct threat to religion than atheistic Communism. Fascism co-opted religion and forced it to serve the idolatry of nationalism. He criticized the social ignorance of the National Manufacturers laissez faire approach to the depression. He affirmed the takeover of the Socialist Party by the young reformers behind Norman Thomas, and hoped it would promote the growth of the party. He decried the exemption of church workers from Social Security and the claim of the universities to escape protecting their workers through Social Security taxes and pensions noting that the faculty and administrators already had their own pension plans. An editorial criticizing the Supreme Court's obstruction of the New Deal found him taking Roosevelt's side, but arguing that the major decisions of the Court were more political than strictly judicial and reflected political interests more than they did a simple reading of the Constitution.

Collective Security

His only major article in the second issue was a dialogue with John Nevin Sayre over the League of Nations sanctions against Italy. Sayre represented a pacifist position that it was unreasonable to try to stop aggression through countervailing force. Niebuhr supported the economic sanctions against Italy by the League while recognizing that French and British imperial interests were served thereby. Both countries had colonies abutting Italian colonies from which the invasion was launched. Niebuhr feared that if collective security could not prevail, the appetites of Italy, Japan, and Germany would be unleashed. If those countries could be contained, perhaps internal pressures within each country might overcome the forces supporting their respective warlords. Niebuhr was not overly sanguine for the use of collective security, but it seemed the best available option. He noted that failure to act because of the immorality of the use of force was impossible as most pacifists accepted the realities of governmental force in protecting their own communities. He also noted that every day he used utensils and ate food which resulted from unjust means of production. The failure of the French to support the British naval attempt in the Mediterranean Sea probably meant the failure of the economic sanctions, but the League needed to develop its potential for police powers. Some of the outlines of his developing realism and pragmatism can be seen in this paragraph from the dialogue:

> The world of sin in which we live is constantly threatened by anarchy because of its sin. One of my tasks is to arrest the anarchy. It is a very grievous error to mistake these tentative balances of power which we construct in order to arrest anarchy, for the Kingdom of God. That is why the Christian pursues his political tasks with humility and in the spirit of contrition. But it is also a serious mistake to imagine that the Kingdom of God is a solution to these political problems.[6]

An Interpretation of Christian Ethics

The editor secured Wilhelm Pauck to review his new book, *An Interpretation of Christian Ethics*. Pauck was very appreciative:

> In conclusion I wish to say that, in my opinion, this book is the richest of Niebuhr's work and one of the most rewarding in recent theological literature. May it have a deep effect upon American Protestant thought.[7]

Pauck understood that Niebuhr was contesting against Christian Orthodoxy and liberalism as well as against Communism and Fascism in his book. He found the book both optimistic and pessimistic. Representing himself as one of the younger generation of theologians he welcomed his dialectic approach which abandoned the older liberalism of religion and culture and sought a new way. Niebuhr's prophetic Christianity improved upon the Barthian movement in Europe which was culturally and politically moribund. The German professor from Chicago was never without his criticism which in Niebuhr's case was that he needed to develop his doctrine of the church more. Pauck noted that the doctrine of the church was an important part of the German church struggle, and he anticipated it would become more important in America also. While noting that Niebuhr realized the need to strengthen his ethic with more theological support, he asked Niebuhr to develop some of his arguments more systematically. He recognized that Niebuhr based his theology mostly upon the doctrine of humanity and philosophy of history.

He noted that Niebuhr acknowledged his indebtedness to Tillich, and reminded his readers that Tillich had some suggestive answers to questions left open by Niebuhr. Ursula Niebuhr, in turn, reviewed the new book by Wilhelm Pauck, Francis Miller, and her brother-in-law H. Richard Niebuhr. All three in slightly different ways sought to declare the church free of the disintegrating culture in which it found itself and to seek out its true task. She thought they did not present solutions to the problem, but that they made the case for a church to find its independent way. She regarded that as a sufficient task for the book *The Church against the World*.[8]

The spring 1936 issue of *Radical Religion* had eight editorials by Niebuhr in which he freely criticizes both sides of the social struggle. It becomes clear through the reading of the editorials how much of Niebuhr's fame and power came from his critique of various social movements and opinions. In the last editorial he praises George Lansbury, The Christian labor leader, whom he had previously attacked. He wanted to make clear that his previous criticism of Lansbury's policies in no way detracted from the great admiration Niebuhr held for Lansbury's combination of Christian faith and social radicalism. Niebuhr was particularly fond of the British labor party and the extent to which Christian faith in England could relate to social radicalism inherent in it from its birth. He had never been anti-English but now, three years after his marriage to the young English student, Ursula Keppel-Compton, his fondness for virtues he could locate in English society and politics became very obvious in his writing.

Other editorials lambasted the president of Yale University, Herbert Hoover, Henry Ford, the United Chamber of Commerce, those who opposed taxes for welfare, the opposition to the estate tax, and Nazi Germany's church leaders for exalting in nationalism. His comments on the international situation revealed increasing realism and his projection of a near inevitability of a major European war inspired by the recent German occupation of the Ruhr. Italy was allowed to digest its African conquests with the vain hope by Britain and France that Italy might help resist Hitler in central Europe. Niebuhr thought that America could hold on to its position of advocating collective security and neutrality even with the tension between the two policies. He was still inveighing against the powerful pacifist movement, but now he was arguing that power to maintain the peace was necessary, and one had to sometimes fight for peace with sinful policies and allies. He wanted to confine the pacifists to the role of a religious symbol, but it was not their business to try to prevent war. International politics lacked most signs of purity. "There seems no longer a possibility of avoiding some kind of hostilities."

The Farm

The most fascinating article in the third issue of *Radical Religion* was Sherwood Eddy's description of his recent trip to the South on behalf of the Tenant Farmers' Union. He found cotton pickers and sharecroppers being exploited and lynched when they protested. He and Sam Franklin were threatened with death and imprisoned. The members of the union were being rapidly evicted from their sharecropping farms. Seeing the immediate need and learning of a farm for sale in Mississippi, Eddy made a down payment on the farm Sam Franklin, a Southerner, settled in to manage the farm which soon had thirty-three families with room for one hundred. Eddy described his talk with Secretary of Agriculture Henry Wallace, and Mrs. Eleanor Roosevelt, both of whom supported the concept of a developing cooperative movement. Eddy's enthusiasm for cooperatives on an integrated basis translated into an appeal for more funds to complete the purchase and to build necessary housing. With this swift response the Delta Cooperative Farm was started, and it would involve Niebuhr deeply over the coming years.

Niebuhr's short essay in the journal was on one of his perennial themes, socialism and progress. Of course, there was growth in society and technical progress, but there was little moral progress. As an adult was more complex than a child so developed forms of society were more complex, but not better than previous forms, or at least they were not morally better. Socialism would mature out of capitalism, but it would still have the problems of politics, greed, and anarchy, though some of the anarchy caused by private ownership of public goods would be eliminated. Where there is centralized power, the problem of justice and injustice will remain, though on a different level. There is no way of to eliminate the problem of power from politics and social morality. The anarchistic pinnacle of communistic dogma is an infantile illusion, which unfortunately many Christians who ought to know better have taken over from Communism.[9]

Sherwood Eddy's essay regarding the plight of the tenant farmers was followed in the next issue of *Radical Religion* by Howard Kerstner's analysis of the fate of blacks subject to the power of the white establishment in the Bible Belt. Sam Franklin added his analysis of the first months of the Delta Cooperative Farm's life in Mississippi. Its first members were mostly refugees from the tenant farmers' attempts at unionization. Franklin described their movement from conditions of vulnerability, similar to slavery, to citizenship at the Farm. He described the philosophy of the Farm in Niebuhr's terms of respecting the limits of human nature, applying an impossible ideal, and achieving limited victories. The Farm identified itself as ministering to the rural proletariat and dealing with the whole health of the most vulnerable. Among the many moving paragraphs of Franklin's essay was the description of worshiping in an integrated setting with the poorest in Mississippi. The announcement that the Fellowship of Socialist Christians' annual contribution to the welfare of labor-church organizations was to be given to the Farm reflected other interest in the plight of the Southern tenant farmers throughout the journal. Sam Franklin moved by study of *Moral*

Man and Immoral Society had interrupted his missionary work in Japan to come to study with Niebuhr and Professor Ward. He followed Niebuhr's advice and studied the cooperative movement in Denmark. On his return to the United States his involvement with Sherwood Eddy with Southern farmers led him to take the management of the Delta Farm which Eddy had purchased as a sanctuary for workers displaced from their farms. It developed into a full-time cooperative with integrated worship, education, and health facilities as well as a cooperative farm. Niebuhr served as chair of the board of directors, and Franklin's later writing credited the farm with following Niebuhr's social philosophy. The farm lasted until it was disbanded during the war with Franklin going into military service. It was continued in the Providence Farm in a nearby county. Providence suffered as had the Delta Farm in being managed by a distant board of directors located in New York and it exhibited many of the problems of cooperative living in a wider society divided by race which the farms were trying to overcome. The Delta Farm suffered from floods, forest fires, and all of the problems associated with the poverty of its members. The failure of outside institutions which owed the farm money for its products also caused internal financial problems. One crisis was resolved by buying the creamery which had gone bankrupt while in debt to the farm. Franklin portrays Niebuhr as deeply involved in the board meeting of 1939 at a time of crisis that was only resolved at the last minute and which Niebuhr called a "photo finish."

Until the Delta Farm was closed during the war it was managed jointly with the Providence Farm in Holmes County, Mississippi which Will D. Campbell discussed in his book *Providence.* Providence continued until the White Citizens Council closed it in 1955 with charges of "Communism" and integration. Niebuhr responded in *Christianity and Crisis* treating the White Citizens Councils as only little better than the Klu Klux Klan. Franklin's analysis of the defeat of the cooperative experiment, which had continued for a score of years, was part of the backlash against the school decision of the Supreme Court in 1954. In the "trial" of the farm by the White Citizens Council the interrogation of four black teenagers arrested for an accusation of speaking obscenely to a white girl was played in a two-hour rendition in which charges of integrated swimming, medical facilities, church, references in discussion to Congress, and the Supreme Court were used to show seditious discussions at the farm. The two basic charges were that the farm was favoring integration and equality in a "Communist" manner.

The 1936 issues of *Radical Religion* accepted Roosevelt's victory, still regarding him as an unknown quantity, but much preferable to the Republican candidate. A long article on socially radical groups in England by Niebuhr noted how much more advanced religious support for socialism was in that country. The gains by the socialist party in the United States would be a long time in the future. The tone of the journal indicates Niebuhr's movement away from the Socialist Party without an announcement of the same or admitting any enthusiasm for his vote for Roosevelt. The journal also noted that progressive Christians in the Northeast of the United States were unable to deliver majorities of their fellow church people for Roosevelt. The supposedly less-enlightened Southern Baptists had produced large majorities for the president.

Creating a Protestant Left

Niebuhr worked to create the United Christian Council for Democracy, and he celebrated its inaugural meeting in Columbus, Ohio that year. Its purpose was to unite the social movements in the Christian Churches beyond what the Federal Council of Churches could accomplish. But only two denominations were organized enough to merge their efforts with the Church League for Industrial Democracy, those being the Methodist Church and the Episcopal Church. The emphasis upon democracy was to encourage the development in the American churches of the need to defend democracy against the emerging tyrannies in Europe, and to promote the recognition that renewal of the social order could happen predominantly in the remaining democracies as the totalitarian emerging governments were turned against socialism. The movement regarded itself as a minority within the official churches who could speak more plainly than the official churches were enabled to speak due to their inclusive nature.

Tillich reported on his findings from his five months in Europe in 1936. He found Europeans believing it was "too late", and that the war was coming. Europe missed its *Kairos* when the democracies created after World War I failed. He reported on talks, interviews, and impressions from the countries of Western Europe bordering on Germany to which he could not return. His diagnosis was one of "fear, uncertainty, and meaninglessness." He couldn't find relevant forces for hope that would combat the deterioration of Europe. "Europe may be desperate about tomorrow, but it can develop hope and strength for the day after tomorrow."[10] Tillich had given his report at the Fellowship of Socialist Christians retreat near Bound Book, New Jersey. A. J. Muste also spoke at the retreat and there was a dialogue between the two Niebuhr brothers on the relationship of religion to politics. The report on the meeting by Norman Sibley indicated that H. Richard Niebuhr saw politics mostly as a restraint on evil. Reinhold indicated possible positive results for humanity through politics. The report emphasized their basic agreements, indicting only this one difference. Probably the difference was not as stark as Mr. Sibley reported, but the words indicate a difference between the two. H. Richard was not as positive about the state as a servant of social justice as Reinhold was, and this in part explains Reinhold's greater emphasis upon politics and H. Richard's greater emphasis upon the church and sociology. The difference could also partially be explained by Reinhold's many more years serving the local church while Richard was reflecting upon it from the university divinity school. In the same issue of *Radical Religion*, Reinhold offered sage advice to the young radical pastor on how he could serve the local church without exhausting its patience over his political participation.

The report on the Fellowship's retreat indicated Sam Franklin had also reviewed progress at the new Delta Cooperative Farm. He indicated that though the state forbids racial equality, the Farm had "stressed and experienced the economic solidarity of whites and blacks."

In the next issue, Niebuhr put his view of the state plainly in an editorial: "The whole sad duty of the political order is to establish justice in a sinful world in which men do not follow the precepts of the Sermon on the Mount."[11] Among those suffering broadsides in Niebuhr's editorials in the Spring 1937 issue were Russia for the "Moscow trials," Norman Vincent Peale for asserting there was a Christian way of solving industrial disputes, the president of Columbia University for objecting to the outlawing of child labor, white neighbors of a woman victim of a young black who wanted him lynched, General Motors for industrial spying, and Henry Ford for blaming bankers for organizing labor, etc.

Niebuhr's essay on Catholicism's alliance with Fascism in Spain remained at a pretty general political-philosophical level. But another essay by a Catholic priest visiting Spain illustrated the denial of religious freedom under the government, and gave examples of Fascist terror against non-Catholic religious institutions in the country. Niebuhr's support for the Republican government against Franco was clear, and he saw it as opening salvos in the coming war as Italian and German forces joined with Franco to overthrow the government.

Niebuhr's editorials were usually critical of trends in church and politics. His writing on the Oxford Conference on Church and State was surprisingly positive. He regarded the reports to be generally solid, though not all agree with the conclusions. After they were amended, the reports recounted the consensus thinking of the delegates rather than individual prophetic leadership. Still, Niebuhr was pleased that in a world in which the church often seemed so reactionary its ecumenical leadership was quite progressive. In commenting on the Conference's threefold possible responses to Christians on war he asked for some more-nuanced statements. The three positions of pacifism, obeying the state, and just-war approaches didn't completely cover the alternatives. It would be more difficult than the report indicated to respect each other's judgments on the war, as war hysteria tended to take over and force judgments of self-righteousness, and Niebuhr hoped the conference could have addressed that reality more strongly. Similarly, he would have appreciated more protection for pacifism during the times of actual war. The journal did not support pacifism as a policy, but Niebuhr argued:

> War is such a terrible catastrophe in modern life that anyone who participates in it ought to do so only with a very uneasy conscience; and his conscience to be kept uneasy by the influence of those who find it impossible to reconcile war with Christ. In that sense pacifists are not fools to be tolerated by the church but witnesses which must be heard.[12]

Another editorial showed less charity for pacifist advice in policy making. A report on a world conference of Quakers at Swarthmore indicated that all international issues could be resolved peacefully. It then proceeded to argue:

> America should agree to concede to Germany, Italy, and Japan the right to develop the natural resources of undeveloped lands for the benefit of the backward people themselves.

Niebuhr regarded the statement as the height of naiveté. However one thought about pacifism, Empires did not develop resources for the benefit of underdeveloped peoples, and there was little evidence that dictators could be satisfied. In a world of anarchy one had to be able to defend oneself. The concessions of Britain in central Europe, though supported by some British realists, promised very little of long-term peace. Other editorials in the journal attacked the Catholic Spanish hierarchy for its age-long lack of pursuit of social justice in Spain and for its support of Franco and his German and Italian allies. The hierarchy's claim of the pursuit of justice did not ring true for Niebuhr who believed the poor of Spain hated the church for its ownership and defense of unjust land practices. The bombing of Guernica disproved in Niebuhr's writing the hierarchy's claim that its allies were pursuing a just war and protecting civilians. The horrors of modern war as illustrated by Japan in China made it even more threatening. Niebuhr's report on his 1937 European travel referred to the difficulties of the British Labour Party in dealing with Spain, and went on from there to comment on the weakness of socialism in Europe with the defeat of the Blum government in France and the inability to intervene or to prevent Nazi and Fascist aggression in Spain. Niebuhr had hopes for policies of collective security, but they had been defeated on three continents with the democratic nations unable to act in the face of more disciplined and authoritarian aggression.

In the winter 1937 issue of *Radical Relgion,* Niebuhr ranged from psychoanalysis and the philosophy of law, to the despair of former utopians giving up on Russia. The issue carried the notes of the Fellowship of Socialist Christians meeting of about forty members and their finalized declaration of principles. While unsure about the collectivization of agriculture and leaving that issue to the future they were quite clear about the need of cooperative development towards social ownership of the major means of production. The objectives were, broadly speaking, to affirm Christian faith and promote socialism among Christians. It is worth noting that with the reorganization of the board of the journal, both the Fellowship's executive committee and the board were balanced between men and women, still most of the writing was undertaken by men. The Fellowship board continued its deep involvement with the Delta Cooperative Farm with financial support and leadership. That involvement and the other allied organizations kept the Fellowship informed and the journal continued to report on lynching.

Lord Robert Cecil in his acceptance speech of the Nobel Peace Prize had argued that international law was for the protection of the weak and that all law had that character. Niebuhr agreed that law occasionally protected the weak from the strong, but he emphasized that law is the rationalization of the balances of power in a society and that it usually favors the ruling oligarchy. Niebuhr thought the argument that law is the basis of peace was usually the position of the satisfied and that it tended to preserve a balance of power either in their favor or with which they could live.

The international situation continued to deteriorate. The Japanese alliance with Germany-Italy predicted the war to come. The League of Nations was impotent before Japanese aggression in China, Italian aggression in Africa, German retaking of the Ruhr, and the German-Italian intervention in Spain to assist Franco's army. The democracies were unwilling to risk action, thereby leaving the advantage to the nondemocratic states. The democracies had economic resources to use, but the resources were dedicated to capitalistic profits and not to peace. Even the democracies were not really democracies, but oligarchies dominated by the rich. Niebuhr expected a German move against Czechoslovakia in the future; eventually England would have to fight, but it was probably not willing to go to war to save Czechoslovakia. He concluded: "Thus the modern tragedy unfolds itself. Like the characters of a Greek drama, each nation helps to bring about ultimate disaster in its very effort to avoid it."[13]

He reported that the newly founded United Christian Council was calling for a boycott of Japanese goods. They were not recommending a governmental boycott yet, but they had hopes that even a personal boycott if followed vigorously could have a hand in encouraging Japan to disgorge its China conquests and end its violent policies. While wanting to avoid self-righteousness and harm to the Japanese people, some action to dissuade Japan was needed.

Niebuhr provided a longer-than-usual editorial on the subject of the renewal of Protestant liturgy and the social conscience. He focused on the pastoral prayer and pled for more structure, more tradition, and more pointed prayers. Later in the journal Howard and Alice Kester, members of the Fellowship from Tennessee, produced a liturgy for concerned social activists. An announcement was also made that the Fellowship of Socialist Christians was preparing a new prayer book for their use. In the next issue of *Radical Religion*, Ursula Niebuhr published a beautiful prayer service, and it was announced she was chairing the committee on producing a prayer and service book for socialist Christians to be published by the Society.

The Roosevelt Administration in 1937 was torn by internal debates as to which direction to go in the Depression, Niebuhr thought far too much ground was being given to the right-wing business interest in the president's council. Given the present difficulties of buying homes and the six million unemployed, Niebuhr called on the Administration to follow the English example and launch a large housing program to meet both needs. He was in favor of a much more-vigorous tax policy to relieve the grief of the unemployed. He saw no gain in more tax cuts for business. He urged Roosevelt to the left, fearing he was tending toward the right.

David Roberts, a faculty member junior to both Tillich and Niebuhr in the Philosophy of Religion department reviewed Niebuhr's new *Beyond Tragedy*. It could not have been an easy task for a philosopher to review a book of fifteen sermonic essays. Roberts claimed that he never understood Niebuhr's method or the use of "true myths" over against rationalism. He admired the power of the book and he summarized the themes he regarded as major. He thought he saw a development in Niebuhr toward deeper theology in each of his books, and he looked forward to the future work Niebuhr was undertaking. He admired Niebuhr's ability to hold hope and realism together, and he thought his version of the faith that could deal with the need for action without absolutism was correct. However, he was bothered by the lack of information about the relevance of the historical Jesus, and he found the mystery of the atonement unclarified. He pled for a little more work on sanctification and the illustration of what historical difference salvation had made. The philosopher was asking for more work by Niebuhr that would show how he avoided the pitfalls of immoral cynicism or over optimism. Niebuhr was laboring on the problem as he thought about the upcoming Gifford Lectures in Scotland. Admittedly his sermons did not fulfill the critiques or questions raised by the young philosopher.

The spring 1938 issue of *Radical Religion* was filled with essays on labor issues, class struggle, the Farm-Labor Alliance in Wisconsin, and cooperative movements. Churches in Japan were chided gently as the German army chaplains had been in the previous issue about their inability to make strong Christian statements under their conditions. The graduate student supervising Tillich's study of English, Carl H. Voss, contributed two book reviews on works of labor organizing.

In an article and an editorial Niebuhr spelled out the meaning of religious socialism as he understood it. It was not an absolute commitment; it was a collection of religious and political decisions made according to the best light then available to them. He recognized that the future might find their contemporary directions mistaken. But they were men not gods and they had to act. The Kingdom of God was the absolute, and it was not reducible to any political program or social goal. The church often tended to identify the status quo with the Kingdom of God, but prophetic religion refused to do so. "Our moral decisions are therefore efforts to realize our Christian imperatives. They must be made even if subsequent history will prove them to be more relative than they now seem."[14]

While noting that religion had both conservative and radical expressions, Niebuhr traced out the radical side of religion favoring Calvinist revolutionaries in his analysis. He thought the Christian socialism of the late-nineteenth and early twentieth century could be seen as a movement for industrial democracy whereas the postwar Christian socialists were more influenced by Marx than their predecessors. He agreed with Marx that capitalism was self-destructive and that overproduction and the struggle for foreign markets would destroy capitalism. He refused to agree with Marxism on several points, but the need for social ownership of the means of production seemed a first step toward a more fair society. At this point he could not regard democracy as an end in itself, and thought it might be damaged in the fight for social justice and common ownership of the means of production. He separated Christian socialists from Marxists in criticizing Marxist utopianism and in refusing to romanticize the Soviet Union. In fact, while probably preferring Russia, he did not regard the difference between Stalin and Hitler as significant enough to justify going to war on one side or the other. He appreciated the Marxist concept of ideology that persuaded people to hide their real interests under idealism and moral platitudes hindering their capacity to judge the economic realities of their time. However, he believed the Christian concept of sin was more thoroughgoing in its critique of human pretensions when it was understood. The Christian socialist could not give loyalty to either Stalin or Trotsky, nor could one expect to ever live in a fulfilled society that did not deserve critique from the perspective of the Kingdom of God.

Niebuhr did not know what to recommend as guidance for the international situation. The world seemed mad. The democracies would not use their economic power, and they were beginning to arm themselves for the conflict that would come because they would not act to prevent it. He still had a little hope for collective sanctions, but Eden's resignation and Britain's willingness to negotiate the fate of Europe with Hitler seemed to close that option. He doubted that the U.S. would be able to isolate itself from a European conflagration due to its economic ties. In a rare sentence for Niebuhr he wrote: "Therefore we find ourselves inclining to abstention not as a matter of absolute pacifist principle but as a matter of immediate policy." Still in the same issue of *Radical Religion* he criticized Roosevelt's one-billion-dollar rearmament program for the Navy as a terrible policy of militarism. He spoke critically of the confusion of the democracies and the Roosevelt administration, but at this point his own policy recommendations were ambiguous, and his analysis was not adequate to provide leadership to his readers in the Fellowship of Socialist Christians. The warlords were moving, bluffing, and annexing, while the democracies were waiting.

Eighty-five attended the spring meeting of the Fellowship of Socialist Christians in 1938. Eduard Heimann, Tillich's economics advisor from Berlin lectured on the difficulty of reconciling agricultural and industrial workers to a coalition for progressive politics. After a discussion of Socialist Party electoral politics, Tillich spoke on the destruction of democracy in Europe and the rise of totalitarian governments. His hope was that the church could preserve values from the humanistic culture while the world went through another dark age. Niebuhr urged the fight for both democratic and socialist values because we could not know how many of our values were going to be defeated in the new pessimistic era coming upon Western civilization. Anglo-American civilization might fare better than Central Europe where democracy was a relatively recent development which was now shutting down. There were various trends in Western civilization and not only that of degeneration. Democracy he regarded as both a luxury and a necessity of justice. Again the more-positive Calvinism of Niebuhr over against the Lutheranism of Tillich appeared in their lectures. Of course, Tillich's realism was grounded in his own losses and in the traumas of battle and politics which he had endured. Niebuhr could see the democratic state as an instrument of justice even though it was a weak one. The minutes reported him as declaring: "We might well accept the creed of later Calvinism that government is necessary because of human sin and that resistance to government is necessary because of the sinfulness of government."[15]

The autumn 1938 issue of *Radical Religion* continued to address the approaching war. Niebuhr assumed the economy of Germany was not adequate to prevail in a war with the allies. He saw Hitler gaining advantages through bluff and the indecision of the allies, but he assumed at some point the allies would resist and war would follow unless Hitler backed down. "Hitler's victory, without a war, therefore confronts us with the possibility of this Nazi madness engulfing the whole continent and finally, by its tribalistic fury, wrecking the last remnants of the traditional European, partly Christian civilization."[16]

He regarded German power, particularly air power as great enough to tempt Hitler to risk a war, even though in the end it would surely destroy him. German hopes for war would surely end in disillusionment, similar to their hopes of 1914.

In other editorials Niebuhr repeated his frequent criticism of the president of Columbia University, Nicholas Butler, who feared increased taxation of the wealthy would ruin democracy. He reported on the misdistribution of national income. The Oxford movement of moral rearmament was criticized for its liberal utopianism and Marxism for its hard utopianism. He wrote again on anti-Semitism to which Mussolini was beginning to initiate a new chapter. Other essays continued the discussion of Christianity and socialism, commented on race relations, and analyzed more fully the changes in the labor movement. By this time he was defending the New Deal from critics mostly on the right, but also against some on the left.

Tillich at Madison Square Garden

Tillich's first major political speech in the U.S.A. at a united front rally in Madison Square Garden on 21 November 1938, was printed in *Radical Religion*. It was accompanied by Eduard Heimann's essay on traditionalism and rationalism making the journal appear almost as if it stemmed from the old Kairos circle of Berlin. Heimann referred to ideas of Tillich published in *The Interpretation of History*, picking up themes of conversation the two had explored in Frankfurt before exile. But the times were much more foreboding, and Tillich's speech addressed the central issue for him in "The Meaning of Anti-Semitism." He spoke both as a German philosopher and as a Christian theologian against Nazism which was intending to destroy both Judaism and Christianity. It was a struggle between the God of Abraham, Jesus, Martin Luther, and the demonic, pretending gods of blood, nation, and soil. He urged his listeners and readers to join in the spirit of the reformer Martin Luther to oppose the contemporary anti-Christ. He called as he did consistently throughout the following war for opposition not to the German people, but opposition to the Nazis who had captured and betrayed Germany. He spoke to the Americans of German descent asking them to remain loyal to the true Germany and not to the usurpers. As chair of a committee he hoped to present the true Germany in an exhibition at the coming World's Fair in New York City. He identified with the persecuted Jews though his own persecution was much less, and near his conclusion he said: "Only those who have voiced an uncompromising no to the persecuting Germany are able to speak an uncompromising yes to the true and persecuted Germany."[17]

His call for unity with persecuted Jews was on the grounds of prophetic religion, humanism, and Christianity and he urged all to fight the evil on the grounds of common dedication to human unity with a dedication to eradicate anti-Semitism. The keynote address at the rally was given by their colleague Harry Ward who was even more disheartened than Niebuhr by the failures of the leadership of Britain and France. He thought the future of democracy would be best preserved by the U.S.A. aligning with Russia and China in the fight against totalitarianism, and he expected socialist gains through the coming war. He, of course, knew of the Russian purges and show trials, but he remained much less critical of the Soviet Union than Niebuhr in *Radical Religion*. In fact, history would develop to where the U.S.A. was aligned with both the Asian powers and with England against the Axis.

Niebuhr's many editorials in the 1938 issues of *Radical Religion* were dedicated to further criticism of the Munich capitulation by the democracies. The *Times* of London came under particular scathing attack in its celebration of British diplomacy that saved the nation from war. The ruling oligarchy of England favored its own economic interests more than it did democracy, and it was blind to the dangers in appeasement as was much of the British intellectual class. The papacy and American Catholic leadership were criticized for their support of Franco in Spain. Niebuhr distanced himself from Karl Barth's assumption that the church would be vanquished in Czechoslovakia while appreciating Barth's perception of the loss to democracy in the surrender of Czechoslovakia. Barth seemed to swing from no political participation to absolute political participation without remaining dialectical. The election results of 1938 defeated progressive governors in the Midwest while choosing the more-progressive governors in California and Oregon. The Socialist defeat in New York where Norman Thomas polled only 31,000 votes seemed to presage the end of socialism as an electoral force in the U.S.A.

The late fall conference of the Fellowship of Socialist Christians drew about one hundred participants at its meeting in Union Seminary. All of the speakers were pessimistic on the theme of the Conference—"The Radical Cause after Munich." The economic difficulties of the Nazi regime were taken as a possible sign of hope. Rationing in Berlin had limited each family to one egg and a quarter-pound of butter per week. Niebuhr found some hope for America in its superior economic base to that of the rest of the world and even in the cultural optimism of America that might help ward off the demagoguery which aided in Europe to overthrow democracy. Appeals were made for Christmas charity for three organizations: German Refugees, aid to Spanish Democracy with Herman Reissig acting as secretary, and the American Bureau for Medical Aid to China. The committee trying to support legislation to ward off American economic support for Japanese militarism was noted.

Niebuhr was in the United Kingdom for the spring and fall terms of 1939 delivering the Gifford Lectures. The pressures on his time for this major work in theology cut into his contributions to the issues of *Radical Religion* for the year. He produced his usual half-dozen editorials for each issue and he mailed in his customary three or four book reviews, but the control of the journal was more in the hands of Winnifred Wygal who failed to gain Niebuhr's confidence as a writer. He was reflecting on changes for the journal. Several issues pled for discussion of the title of the journal, which was held at more than one of their retreats. Niebuhr complained about how hard it was to stay current in the discussion of fast-moving international affairs in a quarterly. Eduard Heimann and other socialist refugees contributed to the journal in his absence. One newcomer was Niebuhr's colleague Professor Harry Ward who spoke at the spring retreat of the Fellowship in Niebuhr's place. The American-educated Englishman regarded England as the great evil in the international mix because of its control of international capital. His differences with Niebuhr were very clear as he argued for an American-Russian alliance in the face of the difficulties of relying upon England. Early in Niebuhr's teaching career they had taught together, but now they each taught their ethics class independently of each other As a Christian-socialist academic from Union there was nothing inappropriate about Ward addressing Niebuhr's group which often sponsored contrary points of view, but their relationship had deteriorated to where Ward spoke there when Niebuhr was out of the country. Ursula and the children had left England early when war broke out, and she reported to the fall retreat of the society on her impressions regarding English social philosophy. She commented on the developments toward war which she had experienced when she was home in 1939. Niebuhr had observed in the summer 1939 issue of *Radical Religion* that Chamberlin was toughening the British position, even resorting to conscription without consulting the Labour Party. He reported on increasing British arousal to the danger of Hitler and the probable unwillingness of Britain to grant Hitler any more gains. The failure of the British-Russian alliance led directly to the German-Russian understanding and the invasion of Poland which brought the allies into war with Germany.

Niebuhr's editorial on the difficulty of working with Communists in United Front organizations noted his own struggles in the Teacher's Union, and His friend Howard Kester's struggle in the Southern Tenant Farmer's Union with the communist-controlled chapter of the Congress of Industrial Organization. While Communists contributed force to the radical cause in each country, their loyalty to Russia always made cooperation difficult. He regarded the tendency of the Communists to see every policy in the light of the interests of Russia as an "unmitigated evil" within the radical movements in each country. Russia was neither a progressive force for socialism nor a protector of democracy. Its recent alliance with Germany was a political choice of defense in light of the democracies' weaknesses. Germany could grant Russia gains in the Baltic and Poland which England had to deny. Comrades had to fall over their old arguments to pretend Russia was innocent whereas Niebuhr thought Christian faith could give a security from which the hypocrisy could be named and mistakes admitted.

Niebuhr had expected war throughout 1939, but he never regarded it as inevitable. As late as the spring issue of the Journal, he had wondered if the increasing British resolve, the implied American support for the allies, and the economic weakness of both Italy and Germany might have given Hitler pause.

He regarded it as accepted that the superior economics of the allies would defeat Hitler in a long war. Hitler's *Blitzkrieg* and air superiority might give him short-term advantages, but the resentment of occupied nations and the economics promised a victory to the European allies in the long run. He wrote about destiny and decision regarding the war and other alternatives that might have developed. But in his mind war had not been inevitable. It required the decisions of oligarchies in control of modern nations. Obviously those controlling the U.S. had not decided upon war, economic support of the allies would probably draw the U.S. into the conflict, but that decision had not been reached. While he reflected on the ambiguities of politics, the weakness of most moral protest against international realities, and the fate of Western civilization in its decline, he reserved his more profound reflections for the lectures he was giving in Scotland.

8

Christian Realism

The political philosophies of liberalism, the social gospel, and Marxism were all criticized by Niebuhr in the1930s. The *Christianity and Power Politics* of 1940 unveiled the realist Niebuhr that had expressed itself in earlier resignation from pacifist causes. Now he was undergirding a realist defense of democracy preparing for war with the nationalism of Germany and Japan with traditional Christian symbolism regarding the nature of history and of human nature. This volume of essays reflected the thought of his first volume of theology to appear the next year, *Human Nature*, and to be followed two years later in the second volume, *Human Destiny*. He had given the lectures in Scotland in 1939 as war enveloped Europe. These two volumes of Niebuhr, given the combined title of *The Nature and Destiny of Man*, are his most systematic theological volumes, and in my opinion the only volumes of his that should be regarded as theology even though much of the method is that of his own distinctive philosophy of religion.

Even more indicative of Niebuhr's change into his mature thought of Christian realism was the publication in February 1941 of his own eight-page journal entitled *Christianity and Crisis: A Christian Journal of Opinion*. In it he broke with the editorial policies of the *Christian Century*, the leading liberal-social gospel journal of Christian thought for which he had so long written. *The Century* persisted in trusting treaties to outlaw war, policies of nonintervention, and of nonpreparation for war. In Niebuhr's mind its pacifism was inadequate to the tragedy of the times and for the need to protect the interests of democracies in a violent world. His rejection of the utopianism of pacifism brought to the fore the streak of realism that had never been absent from his reflections on society since reading Ernst Troeltsch's *The Social Teaching of the Christian Churches* in his parish days. Footnotes in *Does Civilization Need Religion?* (1929) indicate his study of Troeltsch before his volumes on the history of social ethics were translated.

One theme of Troeltsch was the story of the church's changing ethic and its compromises with worldly pressures. The ideals had to bend toward the realities. Niebuhr's commitments to progressive reform continued, but now with an affirmation of Franklin D. Roosevelt's New Deal which he had voted for in 1936 and 1940. The recognition of the ideal compromising with reality came from Troeltsch and the need for approving and working for possible progressive gains came from William James's *Pragamtism*, which he had treasured since using

James so heavily in his two Yale theses in 1914 and 1915. His commitments were now to expanding the reach of social improvement and justice and defending democracy. Even in its ambiguous American form it was a necessary protection for the expansion of human freedom. So to some extent his career from 1940 to his death in 1971 would be spent in defense of democracy in its imperfect historical forms. He became, as his perceptions of history inclined him to become, a wartime theologian as he had been a wartime supervisor of chaplains in World War I. His intellectual origins, travels, and experience inclined him to regard the North Atlantic community as a civilization, and he joined in its defense as a philosopher teaching Christian social ethics. The first issue of *Christianity and Crisis* reveals the meaning of Christian realism.

The journal was dedicated to understanding that war was sin, but that sometimes not to defend civilization against its enemies was the greater evil. The overcoming of evil and disorder in the world was not easy and could not be accomplished by counsels of love. While admitting that Western civilization was imperfect, it was worth defending against the tyranny and slavery of Nazism. While the perfectionist and pacifist interpretations of Christianity were genuinely derived from aspects of the Christian message their interpretations were imperfect. Christian faith in Niebuhr's interpretation demanded the doctrine of the atonement that divine justice went along with forgiveness. The wrath of God's requirement for justice was found in both the Old and New Testaments. The Cross meant that though the divine internal life was not completely understood it involved justice as well as mercy and love. Christians were expected to act humbly as instruments of God's justice in history, and there was no absolute point of innocence from which judgment could be perfect. Christ is the norm for Christian life, but in history it is not perfectly or consistently achieved. Life is to be saved by faith and not works as Paul suggested, argued Niebuhr. For Niebuhr many American Christians were betrayed from reaching adequate political judgments because of a simple moralistic affirmation of pacifism in a violent world. Christians were to live by mercy and seek justice as best they could. Niebuhr was certain that responsibility demanded the protection of Western civilization now even in its imperfections.

> Nazi tyranny intends to annihilate the Jewish race, to subject the nations of Europe to the domination of a "master race": to extirpate the Christian religion, to annul the liberties and legal standards that are the priceless heritage of ages of Christian and humanistic culture, to make truth the prostitute of political power, to seek world domination through its satraps and allies, and generally to destroy the very fabric of our Western civilization.[1]

Niebuhr recognized the need to plan for a future world beyond the immediate war, but the pressing need was to find the will to resist the evil that was pressing upon the world. The task to save the world from tyranny would require resources of faith and repentance, but the failure to act would mean only that other people would have to undertake our responsibility of defense. Practically in 1941, with the nation unable to agree upon going to war, action meant aid to the allies and preparation for the struggle. Niebuhr pushed those practices against those who argued for neutrality and against militarism or the American imperialism that might result from a victorious war. The underlying theology for this short manifesto was present in the understanding of human nature found in *Human Nature* published the same year before the bombing of Pearl Harbor basically overcame the debate.

Human Nature

The invitation to deliver the Gifford Lectures in Scotland in the spring and fall of 1939 drove Niebuhr into his most sustained scholarship and the longest period of research he invested in any book. He started teaching his philosophy of human nature and destiny in 1938, and he continued it until his retirement in 1960. These repeated courses and his course on theological ethics represent his most advanced work in theology of his career. The presuppositions that guided his writing in politics could be found in these courses and books more readily than in his political writing. The lectures are themselves an argument for the verity of the Christian faith as well as the theological limits within which his political thinking would progress. His political perspective was guided by the idea that though humanity could reach spiritual and intellectual heights, it could escape only in theory and mind from the sin involved in human freedom. In politics sin was not irrelevant or overcome; it had to be assumed and protected against. Historical development saw growth in the ambiguous involvement of sin existing parasitically upon the good. Both grew in possibilities and complications. History's meaning was not given within the flux of ever-changing history, but only in human perspectives on history involving a partial transcendence of history by its human subject. Christian faith was one such perspective, and Niebuhr thought it was the most complete as it posited partial fulfillments in each epoch of history and final fulfillment only at the end of history. Such a perspective explained both why people dreamed of a utopia or premature overcoming of evil, and also why such utopias were both projections of the "Best Place," and "No Place." The Christian language for such perspectives was "Original Sin" and the "Kingdom of God."

Niebuhr came to his perspective from his own experience as well as through his mastery of the philosophical and religious language and studies of the Western world. His experience came from the German-Lutheran background of his family. His family of German preachers and farmers had the rather somber perspective associated with German Lutheranism. He worked very hard, and sometimes his overwork drove him to periods of recuperation. In those periods of recovery meditating on self and the world usually at war or in economic depression the leading ideas for his essays and books would emerge. He did not require much sleep, students at the Seminary reported seeing the light for his home study still on at 2:00 and 3:00 a.m., but he required some, and he was usually studying, writing, teaching, or speaking in public. The schedule of public appearances and continual committee meetings while teaching during the week at Union Seminary and then spending most weekends traveling by train to speak several times is too much for any person. In addition to the overwork, Niebuhr's siblings were also plagued by tendencies toward depression, sometimes necessitating therapy. Additionally his European travel in the 1920s and 1930s informed him about the desperation in Europe. The democratic lights illuminated after World War I went out as the twentieth century rushed on to its denouement. United by marriage to an English intellectual, and by academic accomplishment to the British intelligentsia and some British political leaders of the left, his connections to his German farmer family members were depressing as they fell under the sway of political developments in Germany. His friendship and assistance to Paul Tillich in his escape from Hitler's Germany built bridges for him to German intellectuals fleeing Germany. His friendships with American Jews and Jewish refugees from Germany informed him of the horror of European life and, as noted above, of the intention of Nazism to destroy the Jewish people and end Christianity in Europe. Drawn to both Germany and England which were fighting to destroy each other, how could he not be somber?

Beyond the personal experience of his life, he brought to his American listeners and readers, the philosophy of Europe. His sources of Kierkegaard and Heidegger, reflecting the thought of Luther and Augustine confronted his optimistic and sometimes naive American students with existentialism which they were just beginning to hear about. He read and used them from their German sources before they were translated into English. His attacks on liberal theology and culture sounded like Emil Brunner and Karl Barth in Switzerland. Above all he was attacking the liberal myth of progress, especially moral progress. Technological development could be celebrated without needing to think humanity was becoming better or progressing to a realm of plenty and peace. Social changes and technological development cut both ways for good and for evil. He had attacked the capitalist myth of progress for the workers particularly hard during his Marxist-informed socialist period. The workers could not count on progress, what they could hope for was that they could negotiate from a position of power. This realism about industrial civilization, confirmed by his experience in Detroit with Henry Ford, continued throughout his life.

Paul Tillich became known for his method of correlation. He would ask questions about the human condition which had their roots in existential thinking and then attempt to answer those questions from the essential symbolism of Christian faith. Tillich's was a very positive method. He would include in his embrace of faith or ultimate concern everyone from Buddhists to Communists even as they protested against his embrace.

Langdon Gilkey, a student of both Niebuhr and Tillich pointed out that Niebuhr also had a method of correlation. In my judgment, however, his method of correlation was a negative one. He would show that various philosophical alternatives neither protected the consciousness or the dignity of the human self nor provided an adequate social philosophy to protect human freedom. After criticizing the alternatives he would then analyze the central symbols of Christian faith to indicate that they were more adequate in explaining and defending both human responsibility and the transcendence of the human self. Max Stackhouse has spoken powerfully of his deepening of Christian understanding from the study of Niebuhr's analysis of Western thought and the necessity of Christian faith to answer the questions raised by Western thought. For at least two decades seminary students and many undergraduate students grew up sharpening their intellectual tools for understanding Christian faith from reading these two books born in World War II. Niebuhr's point was that without Christian faith the Western world was inadequately equipped to answer its own questions or to preserve itself from its pride and its foolishness.

The many references to the Western world in Niebuhr's formation require only a slight amendment. He did read some of what was available in Eastern thought. The first semester of his history of ethics course was mostly on the ethical reflections of Eastern religion and philosophy, and he studied and wrestled with Gandhi's thought for a considerable period before writing his theology. His own intention to travel and study in India, very similar to Dietrich Bonhoeffer's were interrupted by marriage and family. His colleague Harry Ward traveled widely in the East as did his missionary patron Sherwood Eddy.

Though Niebuhr's correspondence reveals some insecurity in delivering the prestigious lectures, this should not be overemphasized. He found time to prepare them even though the second series had to be completed in the United Kingdom. With a topic as broad as human nature and destiny, he had to bring everything he had learned together. He would draw upon studies at Eden Seminary and Yale to the content of the courses he was teaching at Union.

Niebuhr set himself the task of providing a Christian interpretation of the human situation. He had moved beyond correlating Christian analysis with some form of modern thought. He was no longer working out how Marxist insights can enrich Christian thought. Rather, he was claiming a unique and powerful role for a Christian interpretation on its own terms. Christianity was not to be understood as located somewhere in the foundations of a Western civilization that had advanced beyond it in maturity. Rather, a Christian perspective was more profound than the alternatives—ancient, medieval, or modern. He reflected on biblical insights and traditional theologies, but he interpreted them afresh for his own constructive development of themes. It seems best to regard his work as an exercise in Christian philosophy. He used biblical studies and church history, but he was not writing history or biblical studies. He drew upon many sources, but he was really doing new work. He spoke and then wrote a Christian philosophy for his times concentrating on his favorite issues, human nature and history. In the process, he provided a Christian apologetic, that is, he defended the credibility of Christian thought. If his portraits of humanity and history persuaded his listeners or readers of their truth, then they were already thinking like a Christian. Many readers found his exposition of Christian symbolism persuasive. They found that a Christian ethic for politics had its own foundations and was no longer dependent upon either the assumptions of the liberal culture or its Marxist critics. He entered the public marketplace of ideas with a persuasive and credible Christian message on the themes he developed. Alan Paton, author of *Cry the Beloved Country*, spoke for many when he wrote in his autobiography, "I think him [Niebuhr] to be the wisest man I ever knew, with an understanding of human nature and of human society that no one has equaled in our century."[2]

Readers who saw volume 1, *Human Nature*, emphasizing human sin, were correctly apprehending his intentions. Readers who in the 1960s or 1970s concluded that the picture of sin was overdrawn had forgotten the World War II context. He believed in the relevance of ideas. He believed that illusions about human nature of well-intentioned people, including his own socialist and pacifist friends had aided Hitler's triumphs. He believed the failures of both orthodox and liberal Christianity to present Christian ideas powerfully had allowed the emergence of the cruel parareligious movements of Communism and Nazism. Cynicism combined with romanticism in Nazism was too powerful for Christianity full of liberal illusions or one committed to a past order. The arguments in *Human Nature* are the foundations for the political polemic of *Christianity and Power Politcs*. In his sentence in the conclusion to chapter 1—"The fateful consequence in contemporary political life of Hobbes's cynicism and Nietzsche's nihilism are everywhere apparent"— he is not writing about confusion in undergraduate life. He is addressing the intellectual and moral failure of the Western world unable to organize an adequate response to the horror of Nazism. Finding failures in his survey of Western thought, he returns to a Christian view of human nature that supports progressive, reformist, social policy to defend European civilization against the rising barbarism. The volume still inspires theological students and lay readers alike, but it needs to be seen as dealing with resistance, here of the mind, elsewhere with force to real evil. Therefore the tones about human nature are somber, but they are about Western civilization's inadequate understanding of the evil threatening it.[3]

The lectures began: "Man has always been his most vexing problem. How shall he think of himself?"[4] To his audience of Calvinist Scots at Edinburgh, or to his theological students from the Reformed tradition at Union, this was a familiar beginning. The theology of human nature presented was fundamentally in the Augustinian-Lutheran-Calvinist tradition. There were of course problems with this tradition from past ages, but he taught it as wiser than the modern alternatives. Humanity, he argued in the first chapter and then throughout the book, was best understood in relationship to God. Calvin's *Institutes* had begun by saying, "Nearly all the wisdom we possess, that is to say, true and sound wisdom, consists of two parts: the knowledge of God and of ourselves." In his 1560 French edition Calvin had put it, "In knowing God each of us knows himself."[5] From rooting the understanding of humanity in God emerged the perspective of humanity as finite, created existence with a united body and spirit. The uniqueness of humanity was in relationship to God and in humanity's transcendence of nature, history, and the self. The meanings of personality and individuality were found in God's self-disclosure, culminating in Christ. The sin of humanity was understood as rebellion against God. The sin is found in human freedom, and it spreads from the spiritual to the social dimensions of human life. Because humanity's self-understanding in Christian perspective views humanity's squalor and grandeur in relationship to God, it is able, Niebuhr argued, to look at humanity more adequately than other options.[6]

Critique of Alternatives

Before proceeding with his own perspective on human nature, Niebuhr examines modern alternatives. Neither rationalism nor romanticism could relate vitality and form adequately and they tended to obscure freedom in human nature. Rationalism could not face the reality of evil within humanity. It posited mythological future harmonies which romantic views either of the person in Freud or of society in Marxism destroyed. The developments of Freud, Marx, Engels, and Schopenhauer critiqued twentieth-century civilization, but in Niebuhr they were also critiqued. Modern economics as seen through the thought of either Max Weber's *The Protestant Ethic and the Spirit of Capitalism* or Paul Tillich's *The Religious Situation* enslaved the individual or, in Weber's terms, subjected them to an "Iron Cage." Individuality seemed to be overcome in either capitalism or in nationalism as self-identity was destroyed.

The basic problem Niebuhr found with modern humanity's understanding of itself was in its rejection of the doctrine of original sin. The mythological forms of original sin captured in theology may have seemed absurd to modern technological humanity, but they contained an important truth. Modernity tended to explain away evil rather than realizing it was in itself. Modern thinking tended to place evil in superstition, government, civilization, private property, sexual repression, ignorance, or cultural lag, but it was more basic than any of these expressions. None of the specific locations equipped the historical actors of 1939 to meet the evil overtaking them. His lectures and writing on the innocence-seeking character of modernity relied on wide reading, study, and analysis. Through his survey of modern thought from Hobbes to Whitehead he pushed his thesis: "The easy conscience of modern culture is practically unanimous, but not quite."[7] The rejection of original sin located in human freedom supported optimism, but it was a mistake.

Prophetic Religion

Niebuhr presents a particular perspective on the question of human nature. He focuses on evil in society as did the biblical prophets. It is a Protestant perspective of a critical and world-changing character that he argues for in the middle of the book. It is the philosophical support for a particular form of social ethics. Human nature cannot be adequately comprehended without relating it to God. That relationship is best understood through Christianity, so anthropology drives towards Christology.

He found dim recognitions of God in human consciousness as had Schleiermacher in his recognition of "ultimate dependence" or as his colleague Paul Tillich did in "ultimate concern." The human experience was aware of God in its consciousness of "reverence for majesty" or ultimate sense of dependence, in its moral obligation consciousness, and in the need for forgiveness. The appeal to general religious consciousness is part of the liberal theological tradition. He explicated the three general sources of religion in biblical language of Creator, Judge, and Redeemer. Humanity, of course, rebels against God and suffers historically. The final overcoming of human rebellion is not in the punishment, but in forgiveness. Beyond judgment, mercy and forgiveness are found and here the traditions of atonement and justification are argued for as answers to the human questions about ultimate justice. Forgiveness is the final answer for the social ethics of Christian realism, not the remaking of history. But as Bonhoeffer might say; "Penultimately there is a war to fight." Beyond the biblical symbols, he draws upon Heidegger and Kierkegaard from their German editions as the most profound interpreters, secular and theological respectively. So his listeners in Scotland or in New York City heard an attack on modern convictions, saw the Christian position presented biblically, but also liberally from general human consciousness and then expressed in terms of Christian existentialism drawing upon continental thinkers not yet available in English. The synthesis was his and it presented a Christian basis for action.

The anxiety and melancholy of Kierkegaard's life and his work, *The Cocnept of Anxiety*, met the needs of both Tillich and Niebuhr in the late 1930s. Tillich had read Kierkegaard earlier and Niebuhr consulted him as he prepared for his 1939 Gifford Lectures and the beginning of war. The stress disorders of World War I haunted Tillich as he prepared for war with the Nazi overlords. The melancholy that haunted the Niebuhr family opened Reinhold's mind to suffering self-examination of Kierkegaard's existential psychology. Neither Tillich nor Niebuhr would use anxiety, freedom, finitude, or the demonic exactly as Kierkegaard did; rather they used him in their own way. In the early 1940s Niebuhr was counseling Wystan A. Auden about Tillich's thought, and Auden adapted Tillich's concepts of demonic, *Kairos*, and logos to his poetry. Auden's *Age of Anxiety* utilized the concept of anxiety in his own manner. Ursula Niebuhr has written about a late-night conversation in a coffee shop with Wystan, Reinhold, and herself on Kierkegaard's use of anxiety. The subject became popular in New York intellectual circles with meanings not necessarily found in Kierkegaard. His works were translated into English in the 1930s and 1940s, and they enriched the conversation already begun by Tillich and Niebuhr.

Kierkegaard's writing on the "Concept of Irony" also produced fruit in Niebuhr and Auden's minds as they developed works on irony. Reinhold did not follow Tillich in the use of Kairos as fulfillment of time as fulfillment was a term beyond history for him. Irony fit Niebuhr's theology better and as he moved toward his publication of *The Irony of American History* it came to replace tragedy as a major category. Meanwhile Wystan Auden had written for *Horizon* "On Don Quixote, the Ironic Hero." Later Ursula enlisted him to teach a course on irony at Barnard.

Paragraphs in Wystan Auden's *A Christmas Oratorio*, performed at Union while I was a student there, reflect Niebuhr's influence. Occasionally Auden, himself, would join in the Union Christmas celebrations. Auden had been attracted to pacifism, and Niebuhr showed him a way beyond it. Ursula later chuckled about their postwar assignments in Germany in which Auden received a uniform but Niebuhr did not as his work was more directly tied to the State Department than the War Department. The friendship developed and Auden was often a guest in the Niebuhrs' apartment. He dedicated his volume of poems from 1947 to 1950, *Nomos*, to Reinhold and Ursula Niebuhr.

Human Sin

Niebuhr's course lectures and his writings on sin were those of a Christian theologian, and it should not be surprising if non-Christians were critical of them. A Jewish historian friend of mine told me once how persuaded he was by Niebuhr's analysis of the human situation. Then as we walked by the fountain and statue of Alma Mater in Columbia University's courtyard he said, "I have to make a reverse leap of faith to keep from converting to Christianity." Not enough attention has been paid to the atheist, or Marxist roots of some of the criticism of Niebuhr's perspective.

The perspective on sin in *Human Nature* is systematic and theist. Sin is presented in two expressions: the religious and the moral perspective. The religious meaning of sin is the disbelief in God and the resultant anxiety that causes one to either exalt or deny one's freedom in the search for security. The meaning of sin in the social area is injustice. The grounds for sin are present in human existence and humanity consistently sins by falling prey to the given temptations.

The portrait of sin in *Human Nature* chapters 7 and 8 is among the finest written in Protestant theology, and reawakened the confidence for a generation of Protestant leaders. The pages seemed true in the confrontation with human evil. Sin is basically prideful rebellion against God, as Augustine, Luther, and Calvin all taught. Rebellion expressed as human pride is the "pride of power, or pride of knowledge, or pride of virtue." From these configurations of pride all human institutions are corrupted. Even the needed battle with Nazism expressed human pride.

His writing on sin stays with the thesis of the 1932 book *Moral Man and Immoral Society*—that group egoism is even more corrupting than the egoism or pride of the self. Large political groups tend toward "sinful pride and idolatrous pretension." Germany is used as a particularly heinous example of national idolatry, but Niebuhr treats this idolatry as a consistent tendency in international affairs. The nations pretend to be God and convince many that they are. Fascism and Nazism "have achieved a daemonic form of national self assertion." Such nationalism is incompatible with Christianity. The fact that all people suffer from egoism and pride as do nations does not reduce the need for distinctions. While all have sinned, all sins are not equal. The calculations between a little more justice or injustice must be made, even if the distinctions are made by sinners. Those with power and prestige are usually more guilty. The prophetic protests against the powerful in the Old Testament are continued in the New Testament. All may increase their guilt as they become more powerful. Niebuhr's sentences against the pride of the powerful would please the radical liberation theologian, but the biblical condemnation is not just about social radicalism, it is a message for the perennial human situation. The moral pride of the weak or the social critic can also become dangerous when expressed politically. Still the rich, the rulers, the whites over the blacks and the Germans over the Jews are all particularly guilty.

The victims of oppression suffer from the pride of the oppressor, but if they succeed in becoming the establishment they themselves may become guilty. Kenneth Neal Waltz's book *Man, the State, and War* developed the thesis that most political philosophers who reflect on war place the failure in international politics to achieve peace in one of three places: human nature, the nature of the state, or the international system. Niebuhr's work sees all three to be at fault rendering the struggle for peace particularly difficult and always intersecting with the struggle for power by self-interested parties. It seems overdrawn to argue as John Merscheimer does in *The Tragedy of Great Power Politics* that all significant powers will attempt to increase their influence even at the risk of war. But the struggle for peace is more complicated than Glen Stassen's edited work, *Just Peacemaking,* because the recommended ten just-peacemaking practices will be executed by willful, prideful people or at least by those subject to the national interests of their states. Even if all ten practices were carried forward, some other state in the relatively anarchic international system may begin a war from which there is little chance of avoidance.

Niebuhr's realism about international affairs stems directly from his understanding of sin and its movement through human institutions. But in Niebuhr's thought leaders of nations could also respond slothfully and not recognize the need for defense against encroaching evil. Rather than exerting themselves to maximize institutions people often neglect them, fail to regulate human behavior, and allow institutions to fail or countries to go unprotected. Niebuhr was hoping for a balance between people playing God and refusing to act humanely.

He placed most of the responsibility for the disaster of war upon prideful actors. Likewise, in race relations he emphasized the sin of the oppressor and not that of the oppressed. He did however analyze a subordinate form of sin which picked up practices often labeled sins by the churches. He grouped them in this book under the label of sensuality. These were sexual extremism, gluttony, extravagance, drunkenness, and surrender of the self to physical lusts. These sins he thought were a consequence of undue self-love. The sinful person neglected the love of God and substituted self-abandonment to an addiction. His description of sin as outrageous pride was just right for the situation of the times. However many sins were slighted and in other times, he would receive much criticism for neglecting the sins of the weaker members of society. He only spent a dozen pages on these very personal sins and they may be among the less-satisfying of the book. Neibuhr did not focus on sloth in this book, but he corrected that a few years later with a description of the sins of sloth in *The Irony of American History*. However, his "Serenity Prayer" may be the most used prayer by those suffering from personal addictions. One graduate of Union Theological Seminary wrote me about his church:

> We have twenty-four Alcoholics Anonymous and Narcotics Anonymous groups which use our church building. As the contrapuntal unison recitation

of the "Serenity Prayer" echoes through the halls, I'm sustained by Dr. Niebuhr's insistence the gospel be embodied in practical hope.[8]

The prayer was written the same year, 1943, that the second volume of his study was published. It was a war year. His prayer for wisdom to be able to distinguish between what could be changed and what had to be endured, hopefully with serenity, still remains terribly relevant in both personal and social challenges.

Niebuhr understood *original sin* existentially. He meant by it that the human being not trusting in God became anxious and was tempted by the historical situation to act inappropriately. There is a bias against trusting in God in the human situation faced by ignorance and death. The failure to live trustfully before God is in Augustine and Kierkegaard termed rebellion. The self can find fulfillment only in the living out of human life in accord with true human nature which corresponds to God's will for humanity. Niebuhr chose to express this understanding of the situation paradoxically as sinning inevitably but not necessarily. He wanted to protect both freedom and responsibility for sin. Probably it could have been described without the paradox. The human feelings of guilt and remorse over particular violations of human solidarity or violations of perceived imperatives are sufficient to indicate that all people sin, but in different ways. For Niebuhr the origin of sin is in the refusal to depend in trust on God. His use of pride to name this sin is not a dismissal of all human pride, but the naming of the rebellion against the source of life as pride. This needs to be read dialectically in tension with the opposite denial of God which is to refuse to take responsibility for the life given to one by God. Between "sensuality" in *Nature and Destiny* or "sloth" in *Irony of Ameican History* and their opposite in "pride" in both volumes is contained the misery of humanity which refuses to honor its source in God and seeks alternative means of security.

Niebuhr's name became associated with the term original sin. But he concludes his first volume with a chapter on original justice ("*Justitia Originalis*"). Original justice is the dim human perception of virtues, and that humanity should have done better. It refers to a sense of natural law and even to the classical Christian virtues of faith, hope, and love. Humanity regularly refused to follow its true nature and chose destructive paths. Humanity still had a vague sense of original justice. Niebuhr dismissed both cynicism and utopianism as he laid out his practical methods of striving for justice grounded in Protestant theology. The continuing presence of sin meant that grace was not the power to totally overthrow evil in the world. Grace's power was realized through forgiveness and the resulting power of experiencing that forgiveness. Between the spring lectures of 1939 on human nature and the fall lectures of 1939 on human destiny, the threatened war became a reality.

The publication of his first volume in 1941 was not without criticism. Walter Marshall Horton, for example, after a long accurate summary of volume 1, gently criticized only the pessimism. Georgia Harkness regarded it as Niebuhr's best book but argued that a greater emphasis on Jesus would have provided more direct grounds for confidence in democracy and social action. Her suggestion that Niebuhr's criticism of liberalism was overdrawn and indiscriminate was echoed by James Luther Adams. George F. Thomas asked for a broader understanding of sin, suggesting that greed and sensuality are not best understood as derived from pride. Robert L Calhoun explained that Niebuhr was a powerful preacher-theologian rather than a discriminating scholar. But immediately following Calhoun, that very careful scholar James Luther Adams wrote,

> Not since the days of Benjamin B. Warfield and Charles A. Briggs has America had a theologian who possessed such a grasp of the riches of the Christian theological tradition as does Reinhold Niebuhr.[9]

Adams, a liberal, also hoped Niebuhr's next volume would address his pessimism with more hope and a sense of what the goodness of God can accomplish through humanity.

Paul Tillich, exiled from Germany, did not quarrel with Niebuhr's realism about the current situation. He disagreed with several of Niebuhr's academic judgments about history. He thought Niebuhr perhaps confused religious existential ideas with philosophical-theoretical ideas in his comparisons. This issue still remains in debate among interpreters of Heidegger's existentialism. In general terms, however, he celebrated the book, proclaiming it Niebuhr's best work and suggesting it was the best study of sin in American theology. He concluded, "It is a masterpiece, and it will reintroduce large sections of the present theological generation into the profounder problems of Christian theology."[10]

All major reviewers recognized the significance of the book. The reviewers, of course, revealed their own presuppositions. But, even so, their critiques caught the major difficulties. Niebuhr's historical work was rather polemical. The perspective on sin may have overly focused on pride. The critique of liberalism was overdone, his target was the liberal assumption of social or moral progress. Some thought that resources for the Christian transformation of self and society were neglected. It seems in retrospect that Niebuhr's polemics as a social ethicist are understandable. Calhoun's comment that he wrote in haste is correct, but it was not the haste of the preacher; it was the haste of a prophet seeing the reality of the destructive war and the horror of Nazism.

Larry Rasmussen, the third occupant of the Reinhold Niebuhr chair at Union, indicates his agreement with the reservations concerning Niebuhr's understanding of human nature held by the first two occupants of that chair. Rasmussen sees Roger L. Shinn agreeing with John C. Bennett's comments that Niebuhr dealt less adequately with sloth and indifference than he did with pride. Rasmussen reports: "Shinn goes on to say that while Niebuhr had no peer in analyzing the sins of the powerful, and understanding the dynamic of their inclinations, he says less about people buried in the struggle." He quotes Roger L. Shinn at length from *Man the New Humanism* to establish the point. This issue of criticism has also been made by feminist and third-world theologians. Bennett made the point before the Gifford Lectures. Niebuhr spoke about sloth, and his concern was for the downtrodden, but when he spoke or wrote about sin, it was usually the sin of the powerful and usually the sin characteristic of males. Larry Rasmussen's point made elsewhere by his colleague Beverly Harrison that the limits of Niebuhr's perspective need to be appreciated is both a helpful corrective and a Niebuhrian type of critique.[11]

The context of the lectures with the democracies reacting weakly to the rise of Hitler and the beginnings of this worst war of all time represents one of the limits Harrison suggests. While that perspective is often helpful to reflecting on international relations it may at other times seem overly pessimistic. As Niebuhr revised his work near the end of his retirement teaching, he wanted to soften some of his criticisms of modern culture and let the world see him as the progressive liberal in political thought that matched the theme of his mature work. He admitted that maybe his use of the symbols of sin had offended modern people in a way that he had not intended or no longer intended. On the one hand he regarded it as something of a pedagogical mistake to challenge modern optimism with the symbol of original sin. But on the other he concluded his revision by saying

> I still think the "London Times Supplement," was substantially correct when it wrote some years ago: 'The doctrine of original sin is the only empirically verifiable doctrine of the Christian faith.'[12]

When I challenged him about a professor admitting a pedagogical mistake, He just responded, "Why should a professor be so proud?" At the time he revised his writing he could be a little more gentle about idealism, but it had not emerged again as it did a few years later in the student rebellions of the late 1960s and in the moralism of some liberation theologies.

War and Theology of History

The spring 1939 Gifford Lectures had been preceded by war in Asia and Africa. Niebuhr had urged sanctions, embargoes, and diplomacy to deter Italy and Japan. His organizations responded to these crises and he had written about both. The invasion of Poland in 1939 began the open war in Europe among fascists, communists, and democrats that transmuted into the cold-war struggles over the same land that would continue beyond his death. This context of almost continual war is important for the understanding of Niebuhr. He taught his first course on the theology of history as he was preparing for the Gifford Lectures and writing about the probability of war. The course became a permanent part of his curricular offerings entitled "Human Destiny." The course grew beyond the first notes prepared for the Gifford Lectures and as the war ended and turned into the long Cold War, refinements appeared.

The course growing out of the lectures was not a history course, as was the course on the history of Christian ethics. It was rather a course utilizing intellectual history and constructive philosophy of religion. However, it was a course taught in a Protestant theological seminary by an activist relating to the struggles of war. It was committed both politically and theologically. In fact, its teacher believed there was no general philosophy of history without commitment. History did not explain itself, any perspective on history arose from history and transcended it with a constructive perspective.

There was no reason to be more optimistic about the world situation in the fall of 1939 than there had been in the spring. In fact, in the fall the lectures were given to the accompaniment of the sound of gunfire and falling bombs as a nearby naval base was attacked. Words written only a little later, while Niebuhr was editing the Gifford Lectures, reveal his context. "Western civilization is very, very sick both in terms of its international structure and its domestic policy with each nation."[13] The sickness was partly of the soul. The answers of communism, fascism, liberalism, and Christianity, Catholic or Protestant, were inadequate. He sought fresh intellectual foundations for resistance to evil, new orders of domestic justice and international interdependence.[14]

Meanwhile, his family returned to the United States. June Bingham reminding readers of the delightful dedication of the two volumes to Ursula and the children, shares a story about their son Christopher's return. "The King of England," Christopher said to his grandmother on arrival in the port of New York City, "Told all little American boys they had to go home."[15]

In the lectures on the meaning of history, Niebuhr assumes the philosophical argument of the first volume. The lectures presuppose Christian faith and give Niebuhr's answers to the questions about the meaning of history from a theological perspective.[4]

Niebuhr divides religions into historical and nonhistorical types of religion. Within the historical types, he moves toward those that raise messianic questions to the incompleteness of the meaning of history. Within the historical religions he stays very close to the Hebrew prophets and does not focus on Islam. He finds the beginning in Amos. But he does not locate the answers he needs there. Neither the prophets nor the apocalyptic writers explain adequately how meaning is to be found when the righteous are still unrighteous. Jesus, following Isaiah, seems to Niebuhr to give his own answer of a suffering Messiah. In the symbols of Christ and the Cross, Neibuhr sees the divine suffering accepting the sins of humanity and providing wisdom and power. The suffering love is not triumphant in history, but it reveals the divine will, enabling people to live in history meaningfully. So the answer to the suffering in history is disclosed in Christ.

History is an interim in which there is the possibility to live freely, with new power because of Christ but sin and evil also grow in this human history. Absolute love gives power, but it guarantees no particular victories. In fact, in human history, ethical decisions are made in terms of mutual love and justice, with God's love as an ultimate but not the immediate norm. Within this history, Christians knowing the power in Christ's answer still have to work out their lives prudently and responsibly. One of the ironies of interpretations of Niebuhr is that despite all his care to distinguish between an ultimate of Christ's sacrificial love and that which keeps human life in order, many critics have regarded him as demanding that the weak or poor live sacrificial love. Clearly, for Niebuhr, the poor and weak must organize themselves to achieve whatever degree of justice they can win from those who oppress them.

The law of love is, therefore not a norm of history, in the sense that historical experience justifies it. Historical experience justifies more complex social strategies in which the self, individual and collective, seeks both to preserve its life and to relate it harmoniously to other lives.[16]

The Christian answer to history needs to be inwardly appropriated, because in its acceptance rests its authority. Each aspect of Christian insight reinforces the others. Theologians refer to this as the theological circle. It makes sense when appropriated, and then each aspect reinforces the others. The shattering of human pride provides power to live as humans overcoming some of the affects of sin and receiving forgiveness in one's own incompleteness. Much of Niebuhr's argument is repeating the essence of his theological tradition inherited from the Protestant Reformation. He saw history as meaningful, but pointing beyond itself for fulfillment to God. He hoped that the emphasis on human existential meaning found primarily through justification by faith, would release the person into action and produce a growing sense of solidarity and obligation to the service of humanity.

He pleaded for a synthesis of humanistic hopes for truth and the development of culture though the spirit of the Renaissance, while insisting on the Reformation doctrine that humanity cannot fulfill itself. In these lectures, the atonement that related God's wrath to God's mercy is the answer. History is serious; the good needs to be achieved. Human good is not God's good, but God forgives. Humanity is obligated to help the neighbor, but it cannot perfectly fulfill the obligations, for only God will fulfill humanity.

The major part of *Human Destiny*, the first six chapters, sets forth answers of atonement to the problem of sin in history. The next two apply the answer of seeking fulfillment rigorously, but not believing it to be perfectly achieved. Truth is to be pursued with full rigor. Social reform is an obligation and a continual pursuit not to be fulfilled in history. Both quests are better fulfilled if pretensions of fulfillment are avoided. Truth in religion will never be perfectly achieved so religious tolerance is required.

The longest and strongest chapter in *Human Destiny* is chapter 9, "The Kingdom of God and the Struggle for Justice." It is still relevant seven decades later as a profound introduction to faith and politics. The dialectic moves from God's absolute love and its apprehension by humans to principles of justice perceived in the history of thought to institutions of human order. The formulations of natural law are seen to have been inspired by contingent social processes, whether feudal in the Middle Ages or bourgeois in the 18th century. Still he regards the principles of equality and liberty as developed though the long process of Western history as "transcendent" or "universal principles." They are transcendent and universal, but they vary from time to time reflecting the social realities in which they are conceived. They are never perfectly realized and serve as principles of criticism of the actual social realities. The uses of the terms "universal" and "transcendent" are likely to cause confusion, because they have never been universal in human consciousness and they reflect the social context of the particular thinkers or groups who use them. Occasionally declarations of human rights assert their reality, but more often than not those making the assertions betray by their tolerance of gross inequalities and domination of others that they are only partially serious. What Niebuhr really intended was to make the case for their perception in American democracy the two as regulative principles for a more robust sense of justice in the society. Love motivates the struggle for justice and qualifies it, for in Niebuhr's theology there is no perfect fulfillment of justice. Neither in theory nor practice is justice or its regulative principles free from the influence of self-interest. Still both liberty and equality help to transcend the immediate interests of the powerful in theory. In practice all the ideas are qualified by interest and structured through power. The ethics are a modified Protestant ethic of principles inspired by love and the vision of the Kingdom of God which is not realizable in human history.

Almost half of chapter 9 is material from his history of ethics course on the Christian development of the ideas of the democratic state. He moves from the abstract discussion of justice as it evolved in Western history to the institutions of justice or government in its American form. The Calvinist activism expressed in James Madison's draft of the United States Constitution is credited, along with secular theorists, for fulfilling this development. Given the audience of Scots, Scottish theorists receive a little more (not much) attention in this history than in his usual history.[17] This discussion of the origins and meaning of democracy is one of the themes of Niebuhr which is explored in the next chapter in terms of his lifelong work on the problem.

The preparation and delivery of the lectures in Scotland were exhausting. On returning home, Niebuhr resumed his teaching schedule which had become concentrated due to his absence. He resumed public speaking, founded and edited *Christianity and Crisis*, and published *Christianity and Power Politics*. The overwork led to nervous exhaustion and the need for a two-week furlough. So by 1940 he was able to see the pace of his work catching up with and threatening his health. The work of the lectures would form the basis of his political-social thought for his career, but he would refine that thought further in two books on the themes, *Faith and History* and, after his stroke, *The Self and the Dramas of History*.

The last chapter, "The End of History," discusses the Christian symbols of the end and the fulfillment of history. Here, as at the beginning of the books, he shows how a serious, but not literal reading of the ancient symbols can help dissuade people from trusting in false absolutes or presumptuous claims to control history. The enemy still is the pride of modern humanity, which despite all the evidence believes in salvation through evolutionary moral progress, or thousand-year tyrannies, or revolutionary governments. Events in history relate to God as does the imagined end of history. Since humans imagine the end of history, the proper sorting out of the Christian symbols of the end are important though they should not be taken literally. The Kingdom of God is present in the disclosure of meaning through the Christ event, but it is to be realized not now but at the consummation. He interprets the symbols of the return of Christ, the final judgment, and the resurrection of the body as symbolically capable of expressing the significance of nature, historical action, and the sense of guilt for historical actions. To his mind growth is not moral progress, but history grows towards its end in which continuing evil grows upon the good. The symbol of the final battle between Christ and the evil of the Antichrist means that historical action is significant, and the victory of the good will be realized at the end through struggle. The symbol of Christ as God suffering with humanity in history is significant in demonstrating the meaning of history but that meaning is different than historical fulfillment now. Niebuhr intends his explanation of

Christian symbolism to "prompt men to accept their historical responsibilities gladly." What is really important to him is the confidence found in Paul's writing in Romans 8:38-39:[18]

> For I am persuaded that neither death, nor life, nor angels, nor principalities, nor powers, nor things present, nor things to come, nor height, nor depth, nor any other creature, shall be able to separate us from the love of God, which is in Christ Jesus our Lord.

He finished the editing of the second volume discussing the symbols of Christ's return, the resurrection, and the final judgment, relating each to the incompleteness of history, and the possibility of hope. Interestingly the Kingdom of God, discussed in relationship to political authority as a Christian vision in the preceding lecture is not developed fully, but used to include the three. It is important to recognize that this volume concludes as did his decade earlier work, *Moral Man and Immoral Society*, with hope, but now it is not an illusion, but an outgrowth of Christian life and symbolism.

Thus wisdom about our destiny is dependent upon a humble recognition of the limits of our knowledge and our power. Our most reliable understanding is the fruit of "grace" in which faith completes our ignorance without pretending to possess its certainties as knowledge; and in which contrition mitigates our pride without destroying our hope.[19]

John C. Bennett was very appreciative of the volume. "This volume exceeds my highest expectations. It proves what some of us already believed, that Reinhold Niebuhr is not merely a brilliant diagnostician but that he is also a great constructive theologian."[20] Bennett found the volume to be better balanced than Niebuhr's previous writings. Both the Reformation and Catholicism were critiqued as well as modern Liberalism. The use of reason in theology was defended, while the dangers of pride were acknowledged. The possibilities of human nature were recognized as well as its sin. "The usual talk about Niebuhr's almost-unrelieved pessimism is nonsense."[21]

However, Bennett, soon to be Niebuhr's colleague, had criticisms also. He argued that more emphasis upon the sin of inertia was needed. Others including several feminists would pick this point of critique and develop it the 1980s. How is humanity to be saved from its weakness and inadequacy? Bennett also thought Niebuhr's neglect of the church was unfortunate. Finally the perfectionism of Niebuhr's absolute of sacrificial love seemed, to Bennett, to distance it too much from mutual love. Bennett's reservations about some aspects of Niebuhr's work did not interfere with their friendship and collaboration as Niebuhr worked to bring Bennett to Union. When Bennett could come and was arranging his courses, Niebuhr asked him to emphasize the positive role of the church in developing Bennett's courses. This request of Niebuhr is relevant to defending him against critics who like to score against Niebuhr by saying he did not emphasize this or that doctrine enough. He was a churchman with a low doctrine of the church as appropriate to the United Church of Christ which both he and his brother, H. Richard, helped to create. Reinhold did not write a book about the church, H. Richard wrote three. The church and its various roles were discussed in his classes, often critically, but he asked John Bennett to cover the topic in ways which would compliment his own work. There is quite sufficient material in Reinhold's writing to direct criticism at what he taught or wrote, and there is sufficient criticism of that work in print that it is a little beside the point to criticize what he did not publish. The enduring friendship and partnership contributed to the strength of social ethics at Union and to the health of the school. Bennett once told me that it was a daunting prospect to have to lecture in room 214 between Tillich or Niebuhr or between James Muilenburg and Niebuhr. Bennett was a very careful scholar, and his lectures were delivered modestly. Niebuhr was polemical, brilliant and scintillating. Muilenburg reminded many of his listeners of what an Old Testament prophet should look like in the twentieth century and his lectures had the cadences of the book of Psalms. Tillich read his lectures directly from his typed page and he would entrap his better students who could follow him in an intellectual-fantasy trip into the depths of philosophy.

Though Bennett and Niebuhr (after Niebuhr's retirement, Roger Shinn) had major responsibilities for social ethics, most of the constructive theologians at the seminary wrote books on Christian ethics as well. Tillich contributed two, Paul Lehmann two, John Macquarrie and Daniel Williams each wrote one book on ethics. It was a wonderful ethos for the study of Christian ethics, and while all had some reservations about Niebuhr's approach to the subject, he was their leader and they loved him. Tillich's influence on Niebuhr could be seen in Niebuhr's use of the demonic to refer to Hitler, in his philosophy of history, and in particular insights contributed to him by Tillich. Tillich's existentialism was picked up primarily by John Macquarrie, though as mentioned earlier, Robert McAfee Brown and Daniel Day Williams both used Tillich's *Systematic Theology* in their courses. Brown used his important writings on symbolism as well. Niebuhr's writing on symbolism in religious language was not noted very much, leaving the impression that he was more orthodox than he truly was.[22]

9

World War II

On 1 September 1939, Germany, supported by Russia and Slovakia, invaded Poland from the north, west, and south. Before Warsaw fell in the closing days of September, Russia's invasion followed the German by two weeks, crushing Poland. The Poles fought bravely, but except for a few diesel light tanks their equipment was far inferior and their organization even more so. Poland had tried to defend all of its long borders permitting the Germans to win easy victories by massing their divisions. Poland had not even mobilized by the first of the month and the blitzkreig was too much. The defense beyond the Vistula might have held for longer than four weeks except for the Russian stab in the back. Some of the Polish army escaped to see further fighting against Germany in North Africa, Normandy, and even Norway. The home force would join in the Russian liberation of Poland until it was betrayed by their allies and most of its resisting men sent to Siberia or executed. The entire Polish navy of some sixty ships was saved for the allies as was part of the Polish air force which aided in the defense of Britain. Polish guerrilla forces would resist Germany throughout the war until the disastrous Warsaw uprising. About twenty-two million Poles were subject to German terror, including the execution of intellectuals, officers, and a large part of the population in Hitler's extermination attempts of Poles, Jews, and Gypsies. Thirteen million Poles were subject to Russian occupation. All formal Polish units were defeated by the end of October except for small isolated forces in the east and the south.

The declarations of war by France and the members of the British Commonwealth did not mean much to the Poles who had agreed with their allies to hold out for two weeks until the allies could launch a counterattack in the west. No counterattack came as neither France nor Britain was prepared. Denmark and Norway would fall before effective British countermeasures could be undertaken. France would fall in 1940 and the British narrowly escaped the annihilation of their army at Dunkirk as Belgium and the Netherlands were occupied.

While both Niebuhr and Tillich had expected a European war, Tillich, still a German citizen, waited until his American citizenship in 1940 to speak on American policy. Niebuhr had been warning of the German aggression and speaking against European appeasement, hoping that firm resolution by the allies might prevent the war. In the mid-1930s he had hoped for American neutrality. His policies had encouraged sanctions against aggressors and collective security measures, but by 1939, he doubted his policy recommendations would be pursued by business-oriented democracies. As late as 1938 Niebuhr had thundered against spending by the U.S. for military preparedness. In 1939 he turned toward intervention on behalf of the threatened democracies, but still without advocating U.S. entry into the war. He applauded the U.S. surrendering its neutrality to supply the democracies (by 1941 that was Britain) and supported supplying Britain with fifty destroyers, lend-lease, arming of U.S. merchants, and convoying supply ships to Britain, all initiated by President Roosevelt.

Niebuhr understood such policies along with German submarine warfare would draw the U.S. into the conflict, but dreaded going to war with a divided country. The cost of World War I, strong pacifism, isolationism, and alternative strategic thinking kept Roosevelt from asking for war. The 7 December 1941, foolhardy Japanese raid against Pearl Harbor, and the following German declaration of war sealed the debate. Given the German-Italian-Japanese alliance and Hitler's invasion of Russia nothing could have been more self-defeating than involving the U.S. in the war in alliance with Russia and Britain. The attack on Pearl Harbor changed all of the relevant factors of war against the Axis powers. They probably would have changed eventually, but another year of German warfare against Russia if aided by Japan in the East might have forced Russia out of the war. But after December 7, Russia would undertake most of the fighting and dying for the allied cause, assured that Japan would refrain from attacking. Germany would be forced to fight a two-front war eventually, and Russia was spared the trouble. The U.S. had two wars, but one could be fought defensively and then offensively in a meager way as a secondary front while the main effort was directed to preparing to invade Europe.

Tillich and Niebuhr had their work to undertake; their efforts were multifarious. Niebuhr's *Christianity and Power Politics* of 1940 was directed against pacifism, isolationism, and other policies he regarded as avoiding responsibility. Tillich's chairmanship of the board of *The Protestant* (1941-1943) and the debate over war aims gave voice to the socialist interventionist perspective while Niebuhr resigned from the Socialist Party in 1940 because of its pacifism. Both of them had contacts with the German underground and came under suspicion from the U.S. government. Tillich took his concerns as to how the war should be prosecuted to President Roosevelt. They developed their critique of anti-Semitism and institutionalized it in the Christian Council on Palestine. Niebuhr crossed the Atlantic under either church or government auspices during the war to speak to troops and help organize nongovernmental support for the war. Both Tillich and Niebuhr participated critically in the work of probably the most important committee of the churches on the postwar world chaired by John Foster Dulles, *The Commission on a Just and Durable Peace*, of the Federal Council of Churches. Tillich interpreted the war in more than one hundred broadcasts into German occupied Europe. Niebuhr wrote in 1943 his intellectual defense of democracy, *The Children of Light and the Children of Darkness*, at a time when it was threatened. Tillich chaired the Council for a Democratic Germany of German exiles in an attempt to put forward a plan for a united-democratic Germany. Niebuhr chaired a supporting committee of Americans.

Christianity and Society (1940–1941)

After much polling among its readers the executive committee of *Radical Religion* changed the name of the journal to *Christianity and Society* for the spring issue of 1940. They announced the content would be the same, but were changing the name, hoping the new name would not be as off-putting. The majority of responses had suggested *Prophetic Religion* but Niebuhr thought that was too presumptuous. It was still published by the Fellowship of Socialist Christians and throughout its lifetime it presumed a rather committed readership and a readership of those deeply interested in the Christian contribution to politics and society. Every issue would feature at least one essay specifically on the relationship of the Christian faith to current political discussion. Niebuhr dominated the editorial decisions. Tillich's contributions were not as extensive as Niebuhr's; he had his own journal as early as 1941, and later he had weekly manuscripts to prepare for the Voice of America. However, Tillich's friend,, Eduard Heimann, was a member of the executive committee of the Fellowship and the influence of the German refugees at the New School for Social Research became more prominent, bringing the latest democratic and socialist-German perspectives to the journal. Niebuhr not only paraphrased Heimann at length to criticize Marx in the first issue, but Hans Simons of the New School and a former governor of a German province was the speaker for the spring conference on "The Hazards of a Just Peace in Europe." The first issue was a classic, and it is impossible to think of any Christian journal on contemporary affairs that would be as stimulating as that produced by Niebuhr in 1940. The careful student of Niebuhr who reads through the issues of his four major journals and consults his other published essays elsewhere will understand why he occasionally referred to himself as a journalist.[1]

The first issue published Karl Barth's letter to French Protestants concerning the war. Hitler's aggression had made the war inevitable and he repeated what the French and British prime ministers had both said: "There must be an end to it." He warned against preaching a crusade against Hitler, but Hitler had to be resisted. God had given the sword to political authorities to defend justice, and whatever the other faults of various political bodies the Christian was required to support the political authorities as they defended justice.

> The Churches must with repentance and sobriety pray for a just peace, and with the same repentance and sobriety tell every people that it is necessary and worthwhile to fight and to suffer for this just peace.[2]

He expected Hitler's defeat and wanted the French people to think about what should be done after the particular malignancy of Nazism had been defeated. Measures would have to be taken to insure that Germany's aggression could not be repeated. He hoped the peace would be wiser and more just than the Versailles Treaty even if in some ways it had to be harder. His assessment of the religious roots of the conflict was pointed:

> All nations have their bad dreams. Hitlerism is at present the bad dream of German pagans, whose Christianization in a Lutheran form strengthened certain elements in their paganism.

Barth maintained some sense of God's transcendence from the struggle which he urged all to undertake. God's ways were not humanity's ways. Maybe God would not protect us and we must suffer. If so, it was still necessary to rejoice in God who had his own designs. "We know and must know that God rules as He pleases, and that He makes no mistakes."[3]

Wrestling with Pacifism

Niebuhr was editor and author, sixteen of the forty-four pages of the first issue were his. His main article "Politics and the Christian Ethic" seems to have been written in haste as his editorials often were. It did not really cover the broad subject, but it was basically an argument for realism in political analysis. His first point was that all of life is in conflict and there is no escape from the power struggles of life or from power in politics. Even truth and spirituality when brought into politics join in the power struggle for a perspective to prevail. "All truth is spoken from a perspective."[4] He still thought there was wisdom in the Marxist perspective that truth is used to benefit someone in the struggles of life, but now he said, the idea was more profoundly expressed in the Christian doctrine of sin. Humanity raises the conflicts of life which animals experience to higher levels as issues of honor, glory, and past history enter into the conflicts. Conflicts of life with life are characteristic of family life as well as the broader social life. Some conflicts can be sublimated, and intelligence may help to reduce conflicts. Wise statesmanship can often avoid unnecessary wars, but even in the judiciary there is little impartiality. Judges operate within society, and when societies are openly divided into two parties biased perspectives of the judiciary appear very apparent. One side may yield in conflicts out of persuasion or a desire to not escalate the conflict to a fight. Submission to tyranny is beyond what many are willing to undertake. With Nazism the threat of slavery of peoples was more than many could stand, and they decided resistance was necessary even though the future was uncertain. In Niebuhr's opinion there was no escape from the "war system" because it was part of historic reality. Despite all efforts to mitigate conflict and prevent war, sometimes war cannot be avoided. He wrote all of this while still not advocating U.S. entry into the war.

Niebuhr dealt with nonresistance to evil as a possibility, but would not accept Richard Gregg's argument that Jesus was an advocate of a social program of nonviolence. He thought Gregg's position was that Gandhi was better at nonviolent strategy than Jesus who ended upon the cross. Of course, the argument was eight years before Gandhi's murder by a religious assassin. In developing his argument, elements of a Lutheran "theology of the cross" appeared. The cross is not an alternative to the balance of power and the struggle of life with life, but it reveals the nature of life. Perfect love, Niebuhr argued comes into life as suffering love under the conditions of history. Christ's dying on the cross shows us not what history should be like, but what it is in fact. He deplored arguments that only criticized Europe's mistakes, but could not see the tragedy of Europe. Europe did not need moralistic critique from the safety of the Western shores of the Atlantic. Of course, Niebuhr admitted that human history was not just conflict. Many nations were not aggressive. He noted that nations sometimes yielded advantages to the other alleviating conflict. He didn't believe that history could be changed to bring in the Kingdom of God. History contradicted the Kingdom of God. The Kingdom is the symbol of the love of the cross and the fulfillment of community, but it also reveals the critique of the self-will and self-love of those struggling in history.[5]

The essay is the type of writing that Niebuhr much later would regard as overly realistic. It contained little of the positive Christian contribution to the ethics or understanding of politics other than that the Kingdom of God was not going to be fulfilled in our history and that the ethic of love was deeper than a sentimental social strategy. Principles of justice were not developed. Power was not related to God. The role of forgiveness was not stressed. The transcendence of the struggle Barth had argued for in his letter was neglected. Some of the themes of Niebuhr were in the essay, but it may have been quickly written as a preliminary response to a sharp critique of his nonpacifist ethic. It was a response to Richard Roberts's "Open Letter" published in the same issue.

Roberts' Canada was already at war, and he deplored his church blessing the war. War was by its nature an exercise in mass murder and mendacity, and no Christian ethic should sanction it. He deplored Niebuhr's moral relativism, and while Niebuhr might be able to hold the tension of the ideal and realism together, he doubted that his followers could. For Roberts it was a choice between the revealed righteousness of God and war. He concluded: "But my dear Niebuhr, will you not think it over again?"[6] The editorial note indicated that the editor would try to respond in the next issue.

Niebuhr's eleven pages of editorials in this issue were mostly on the international situation. In terms of a just peace he assumed the desirability of a European federation that could protect France's security while avoiding a conservative government in Germany. He doubted that the united Germans could again be disunited, and he hoped for a collectivist, progressive government for Germany. Both Britain and the U.S. would have to overcome their reluctance to involve themselves in Europe to guarantee a future peace. Future Russian policy was totally unclear. America would have to help economically with the rebuilding of Europe.

In the context of a short protest against the communist-hunting Martin Dies Committee in Congress, he dismissed a rationalist argument by Mr. Stuart Chase that political answers rested in a rationalist approach of everyone learning the art of semantics. His polemic against rationalists in politics still carries weight:

> When will our modern rationalists learn that men are not logical, not because they do not know logic, but because they are capable of standing outside, rather than inside a system of logic, and thus making it the servant of their interests? The basic fault of this rationalism is the identification of personality with reason. Man is more than reason. That is why his actions are usually less than reasonable.[7]

He blamed economic self-interest and pacifism for the refusal of the United States to deny Japan the oil and scrap iron it needed for its Asian offensives. He regarded economic sanctions as the only real alternative to war. He noted that the polls now supported economic sanctions against Japan. Given his previous writing on sanctions against Italy, it must be assumed that he knew these sanctions might not preserve the peace, but rather lead to war.

On domestic issues, he wrote of the sin of the rich who prefer the outdated laissez-faire economics and the slashing of social benefits to the poor. Their devotion to self-interest obscured their judgments of the need of the country and of the ten million unemployed. Self-interest more than ignorance was responsible for the voting patterns of the comfortable in his perspective. He hoped for Roosevelt's reelection, but he also hoped for his independence from the big-city, democrat bosses.

In a major editorial Niebuhr noted orthodox Marxists were reconsidering their Marxism. He then endorsed Eduard Heimann's critique of Marx which went further than Niebuhr, and considerably further than Paul Tillich in distancing himself from Marxism. Niebuhr printed in six points of Heimann's critique:

1. Capitalism led to a separation of ownership and management which Marx had not understood. The Marxist's assumption of the doom of capitalism was not being realized, and the New Deal showed signs of promise for a planned-mixed economy.
2. Modern machinery increased the growth of the middle class not the proletariat.
3. The collectivization of agriculture would be politically suicide in countries where the farmers had some political education.
4. Marx's own writings informed farmers and other middle-class people of the need to avoid alliances that would cut across their interests.
5. The dictatorship of the proletariat was not in the interest of any economic class as the various classes would be better served by pursuing their own interest in alliances and not in subordination to anyone class.
6. Democracy had the right of self-defense, and there was no need to support a dictatorship of any class that sounded more like revenge and power than any move for liberty and justice.

At this point Heimann's economic perspective and analysis was more represented in the journal than Tillich's more Marxist perspective, and Niebuhr's own commitments to Marxist thought were waning, while he was still hoping for a planned economy, nationalization of the means of production, and generous social-welfare policies. By the time he responded to Richard Roberts in the next issue, total war had come.

Norway, Belgium, and Holland were all invaded. Niebuhr's grief at the cost of lives and treasures was expressed in the lead editorial of the summer 1940 issue of *Christianity and Society*. His feelings of impotent rage were pronounced. On one hand he said that only prayer was adequate to the sense of the ultimate tragedy which had come to Europe, but then admitted the quiet of prayer was interrupted by the need to run to the radio to grasp the latest news.

Noting the renomination of his friend Norman Thomas to head the Socialist ticket in the coming fall election, he deplored Socialist official isolationism and indicated he would not be very active in the coming campaign. The failure of the Socialist Party to hold its labor support meant that it would be supported mostly by middle-class radicals of one sort or another. That also meant that socialism in America would have to come through some other avenue than the Socialist Party.[8] It was not clear at the time whether Franklin D. Roosevelt would seek the nomination or not. Niebuhr certainly regarded him as the one best placed to stop the tide of reactionary spirit that was washing over the country. He feared a Republican victory would annul all of the gains labor had won in the previous years and that little would be done to aid the unemployed. He deplored the reactionary policies of the American plutocracy which could be seen in the Chamber of Commerce's campaign to force the states and the cities to supply relief. "Of all the reactionaries in the world, none are quite so blind as our own plutocracy." But despite Niebuhr's fears of Wendell Wilkie's small government emphasis which encouraged big financial centralization, his major writing in the issue was on the failure of Americans to understand the realities of Hitler.

This was particularly illustrated by *The Christian Century* which praised Holland and Belgium for their neutrality in defense of civilization just before they were overrun. Beyond naming parties and journals that failed to understand the times, Niebuhr accused the culture of lacking a sense of the tragic which would have enabled it to see the evil in Hitler threatening the whole culture. But democracies could not combine their consciences with their sense of national interest enough to prepare themselves before being forced into a war. America's situation was different from the little European countries because the threat to America, while real, was still distant. Though the United States was not united enough to risk entering the war, Niebuhr supported Roosevelt's request for another three billion dollars for defense. He wondered if America would wake up soon enough to help save democracy by aiding the allies, noting that at the present the saving of democracy was being decided in Belgium and France. Niebuhr's position of formal neutrality with immense aid to the allies was inherently an unstable position, but it was the road both the administration and Niebuhr advocated.

Niebuhr's response to Richard Roberts' critique was irenic. He admitted he knew pacifists who could debate the issue calmly, but he usually found himself accused of being less than Christian for his nonpacifism. He noted that not all pacifists were full of illusions about the nature of humanity and history, but that most of his opponents were. In focusing on Roberts' argument he said:

> Fully analyzed, the question reveals the theological gulf between pacifism and nonpacifist Christianity. I do not believe that war is merely an 'incident' in history but is a final revelation of the very character of human history.[9]

The redemption of Christ is not the victory over sin, but the forgiveness of sin, and the contradictions of human history were not overcome. The church even in its highest places did not exhibit freedom from sin or sinful history. Niebuhr agreed with Roberts that one had to keep the tension of the relative good and the necessary alive in oneself. But, it was also the business of the "Christian to preserve some relative decency and justice in society against the tyranny and injustice into which society may fall." Niebuhr did not respond directly to Roberts' attempt to hinge his pacifism upon the incarnation, but he argued with him about the meaning of redemption and the Kingdom of God. He acknowledged Roberts' uneasiness with pacifism in Canada that was at war, and he sympathized with the challenge of nonconformity. Niebuhr thought Roberts might be more at ease in the Untied States where many pacifists were intolerant of those Christians who supported more resistance to the Hitler.

Niebuhr's first chapter in *Christianity and Power Politics*[10] was entitled "Why the Christian Church Is Not Pacifist." The thesis of his chapter was that Christianity was much more than "the law of love." He taught that as Christ is the true norm of a Christian's life, it is also true that in a meaningful sense each Christian is a crucifier of Christ. The good news of the Gospel was that there was forgiveness built into the universe and not that we could stop human sin by moral exhortation. Human sin should be regarded as a permanent feature of human life as war was a perennial feature of human history. Christian pacifism was not necessarily heretical. For example the pacifism of the Mennonites who withdrew from political controversy and the manipulation of political power could be seen as an appropriate feature of Christian perfectionism. Much contemporary pacifism assumed that sin could be overcome. Enlightenment thinkers had regarded sin as due to one or another facet of human life rather than understanding it as constitutive of human existence. The belief that humanity was good and that social destructiveness could be overcome by removing one or anther feature of social life, though, was heretical as it rejected the Christian doctrine of sin and the need for grace.

Niebuhr did not enter into technical exegesis of Jesus life or sayings. To him it was clear that Jesus taught an ethic of love universalism and perfectionism. It was much more radical than a political ethic that just stopped at some level of violence and claimed that was the teaching of Jesus. For him the "love your neighbor as yourself" and "be not anxious" were violated every day, and this was particularly true in politics which was about competing interests to a large degree. In interpreting Jesus' ethic in absolute, ideal terms, he preserved a critical principle for all politics. It also freed him to guide political ethics by his interpretation of political philosophy drawn from its history in the Western world.

Government was always involved in coercion and it had to rely ultimately upon force. Its power needed to be checked, and it was also necessary to check ruling classes, and even sometimes to resist tyranny. Tyranny on the international scene too required resistance. Religious absolutism in the form of pacifism encouraged aggression which would eventually lead to war.

Too many Christians had substituted faith in humanity for faith in God's forgiveness. Consequently they were unable to see evil. They hoped preaching and practicing love would overcome evil, but that was not the New Testament teaching. The New Testament interpretation of history is of evil and good intermingling until the end of history where Christ defeats the anti-Christ. Niebuhr was willing to accept the testimony of the Christian pacifist that war was evil, and to respect the witness against it. He only hoped they would not see pacifism as a political agenda with which to confuse the political debate about the best way to resist organized evil as expressed in Hitler's Germany. His essay probably did not persuade many Christians to surrender their pacifism before 7 December 1941, but there is a lot of testimony that his explanation of pacifism and his recognition of the role of Christian realism helped many to join the fight against the Axis thereafter and to understand their vocation as fighters within the terms of Christian faith.

Richard Roberts' critique and plea for Niebuhr to return to pacifism revealed how deeply pacifists who had known Niebuhr as a pacifist resented his Christian realism and acceptance of force in international affairs. Many critiques, some of which I have examined previously were published against him.[11] Perhaps the most severe was that of an activist Mennonite, John Yoder. Yoder's advocacy of an activist pacifism differed from most of his fellow Mennonites who were relatively politically inactive from their farming base. In fact his Mennonite Church censored his personal behavior for which he repented. Yoder's influence is still seen in his former colleague Stanley Hauerwas whom I have critiqued elsewhere.[12] The major difference between Niebuhr and these critics is that he advocates a realistic social ethic and moves the idealism of Jesus' teaching to a transcendent place in his ethics as a critique of realism.

I disagree with all three, I believe Jesus was not thinking very often of a need for a political ethic for his time when the Romans were in control. He criticized those schools of Judaism that had been co-opted by Rome, but not for that co-option. Niebuhr's use of the terms God and the Holy Spirit refer also to the nature of history while Yoder and Hauerwas seem to refer to these symbols for history as independent actors who are deciding history or who could decide history if more followed their versions of Jesus' teaching. Niebuhr's mind holds his version of the idealistic Jesus together with the needs of justice in realistic politics. Yoder and Hauerwas are not very interested in realistic politics as they are imagining a pure community in the Christian church. Such visions of the church are for Niebuhr false estimates of the reality of the church. The most recent scholarship on the issue by Colm McKeogh concludes: "His approach remains persuasive. Niebuhr's ethic of responsibility can be the outcome of an earnest wrestling with the meaning of love in human affairs."[13] McKeogh understands the Catholic Bishops' "The Challenge of Peace God's Promise and our Response" to be attempting to hold pacifism and realism together in tension as Niebuhr succeeded in doing. Perhaps the bishops have a higher regard for political pacifism than did Niebuhr. Though he certainly affirmed the relevance of nonviolent civil protest and disobedience as an admirer of Ghandi and a supporter of King.

By the next issue of *Christianity and Society* (Fall 1940), France had fallen. The threatened invasion of Great Britain was near, but it could not be accomplished given the British air resistance. Niebuhr wrote of British heroism in the savage bombing of London, made possible by their lack of preparation. A Nazi total victory in Europe seemed to have been thwarted, but that was far from a British victory. He wrote of the terrible ambiguity of American hoping for a British victory while remaining neutral. He reserved his greatest scorn for the isolationists and pacifists who resisted more aid to Britain. He wrote repeatedly about the need to respect the pacifist conscience and that in their refusal to be drafted they should be protected. But

> It's this unholy alliance between Christian asceticism and a politics of submission to tyranny which arouses our ire and must prompt our criticism, even though we are unable to express this criticism without sinful presumption.[14]

In the issue he rejected the candidacy of Norman Thomas for its isolationism. When the Socialist Party demanded his support for their foreign policy he resigned his membership and joined the American Labor Party. Wendell Wilkie's conservatism was smoother than that of other Republican candidates, but it was still completely laissez faire and antilabor. Wilkie did not seem to understand the nature and brutality of the Nazi threat. Niebuhr now approved of Roosevelt's foreign policy, except his unwillingness to defy the Catholic hierarchy and act out of his own preferences for the defense of the Spanish Republic. The tilt of Roman Catholicism toward Fascism was criticized, but the left of the church in America which did not share the Vatican's politics was praised. An editorial on the Japanese pact with Italy and Germany was matched later in the journal by a report on the suffering of the Chinese in Shansi written by an anonymous Church of the Brethren refugee worker there. The Germans granting Japan's expansion into the European colonies, Niebuhr thought, was for Japanese help in keeping the U.S.A. out of the war and telegraphed Hitler's thought that the war was now going to be a long one. However, he recognized that the actions by Japan might bring the U.S. into the war sooner rather than later.

He continued his struggle with *The Christian Century*'s isolationism and pacifism. He regarded its defense of Lindbergh's isolationism as giving the advantage morally to Fascism and victory to tyranny. He was thinking of the Fascism of Spain and France being exported with Roman Catholic help to their former colonies and particularly to Latin America. In addition, he saw the difficulty of competing with a Europe organized under Fscism and slave labor. He reported that in Poland workers were being given only food, and he suspected Hitler's drive to reduce the Poles to slaves while exterminating the Jews.

Tillich on Nazism

Young Charles Stinnette, Jr. reported on Tillich's address at the Fellowship of Socialist Christians. Tillich spoke on "The Meaning of the Triumph of Nazism," warning his audience how any analysis makes the speaker reveal his own position on history and current events and may appear propagandistic. Nazism was winning because its opponents were always divided and indecisive. Liberal society was divided and breaking down, giving the opportunity for Nazi victory. The culture had been failing and the Nazis exploited the divisions. The question before America was to what extent the divisions already seen in Europe were determinative for America also. Tillich thought that, at present, whoever won, the future was not bright. Britain might enforce the previous unacceptable national sovereignties if she prevailed and a German victory would produce a new dark age. Stinnette reported that Tillich put his hopes in "the day after tomorrow."

In the winter 1940 issue of *Christianty and Society*, Niebuhr expressed more hope for Britain as she held positions in the Mediterranean, and was enduring the bombing of her cities. He urged the U.S not to loan, but to give Britain billons for defense. He hoped that though nation states could not be eliminated their sovereignty would be abridged after the war. A major article by an assistant professor, Elizabeth P. Lam, on Tillich's concept of ideology continued Niebuhr's effort to promote the standing of his refugee friend. Liston Pope, the assistant professor of ethics at Yale, presented an analysis as pessimistic about overcoming the role of war in human history as anything Reinhold ever wrote. Pope, following Pitrim Sorokin, found that war occurred in about as many years as it was absent. Without placing much confidence in the social science concerning war he wrote: "Whether we like it or not, war in some form is likely to survive at least as long as the basic patterns of Western culture survive."[15]

Joseph Haroutunian then an associate professor of systematic theology at the Presbyterian Theological seminary in Chicago contributed a glowing short review of Niebuhr's new book *Christianity and Power Politics*, agreeing with his argument for full support for resisting tyranny. His one reservation about the book was that it could have expressed a greater appreciation for Divine Providence. Paul Lehmann, then at Eden Seminary, reviewed Haroutunian's book in the same issue, supporting his realistic Protestant theology and argument for the importance of Protestant theology in *Wisdom and Folly in Religion*. Lehmann had been Niebuhr's student and he would eventually, after a brilliant career, find his way back to Union while Niebuhr was in retirement, but still teaching a seminar. There he would write in a rather non-Niebuhrian way his *Transformation of Politics*. Lehmann was characterized by the qualities he praised in Haroutunian of theological rigor and the claims of Protestant theology to express truth.

Niebuhr's lead editorial in the spring 1941 issue of *Christianity and Society*, quoted his favorite prophet, Amos: "Woe unto them that are at ease in Zion." It was an attempt to state the dangers of the present drift into war without seeing the evil that was coming to the country in the form of the victories of Nazism. "Ye have put far away the evil day and caused the set of violence to come near." The west had neglected both justice and adequate preparation to fend off evil and the cost would be great. As he praised the lend-lease bill of aid to the allies in a later editorial, he admitted: "Of course it may lead to war. But failure to take these risks may lead to death." In setting up *Christianity and Crisis* for the general readership it might attract, he left *Christianity and Society* for the more intimate circle of the Fellowship of Socialist Christians. *Christianity and Crisis* was really a war journal while *Chrisitanity and Society* dealt deeply with broader issues. The biweekly publication of the new journal was better at dealing with Niebuhr's immediate concerns than the quarterly.

America was still divided in the summer of 1941. Niebuhr wrote about the British reverses in Libya, the defeats in Yugoslavia and Greece, and what appeared as greater cooperation between Russia and Germany. He deplored the alliances between representatives of the church and reactionary forces of isolationism. He pled for an understanding of life that could avoid both cynicism and sentimentalism. John C. Bennett marked the copy of *Church and Society* I was using to emphasize one of Niebuhr's conclusions: "But we have diluted that faith to such a degree that it has been a source of blindness to us more frequently than a source of light."[17]

More important than Niebuhr's editorials in the summer issue was the announcement of his chairmanship of the Union for Democratic Action. Like *Christianity and Crisis* this was an action to move beyond the Fellowship of Socialist Christians, which he still led, to a broader audience. The new organization was committed to the defense of democratic civilization and also to the winning of greater justice for labor domestically. While the first task was the defeat of Nazism, he argued it must not be done at the price of labor paying an undue burden. Taxation policies and labor policies must be enacted that would guarantee that the forces of capital also sacrifice for the effort. In other editorials he defended the right of labor to use strikes in their power struggles with the owners.

Because some critics of Niebuhr have accused him of neglecting racism during the prewar and war years[18] two things need to be pointed out. Racism during those years was a term often used to refer to anti-Semitism, and Niebuhr was certainly in the front of denouncing and organizing against anti-Semitism. More to the point is the fact that he continued writing against racial discrimination toward the African-American. An example would be the editorial on "The Supreme Court and Jim Crowism" in the summer 1941 issue of *Christianity and Society*. The decision required that Negroes be given equal treatment in interstate transportation. He feared that it would not eliminate "the notoriously unsanitary conditions of the day coaches reserved for Negroes." This partial victory showed to Niebuhr both the limits of the law in achieving justice, and the majesty of the law in establishing political and moral standards This paragraph, though early in the civil-rights struggle, revealed Niebuhr's involvement in the issues, and his sense of how hard the struggle was:

> A complete analysis of the meaning of such a decision must prompt us to both gratitude for constitutional traditions of democracy and to a new determination to realize in life and reality what the law itself cannot achieve.[19]

Niebuhr usually qualified his idealism about all people being equal in the image of God with realism about how difficult it was to persuade the majority to grant rights to the minority. This does not mean that he would not be moved by the greater idealism of a Martin Luther King, Jr.; it meant his theology was different from King's and his expectations for the racist majority to change were less dramatic than the expectations King often expressed in public. King himself became more modest about the gains to be won as he persisted through the struggle toward his own martyrdom in Memphis in 1968.

H. Richard Niebuhr was less an activist, and consequently less an interventionist than his older brother. In the same issue where his brother was pleading for intervention, he wrote: "So regarded the strife between nonresisters and coercionists in the Christian community is not only useless; it is immoral, for in it each group tends to evade its own real moral problems, to escape its duty, and to justify itself."

He certainly indicted his brother in such words, and throughout the essay he argued it is not the act, but the moral and religious context within which one acts that is the issue. It was the church's choice not to take Pilate's place, he argued, but to try to show Pilate how to be just. He tried to take the debate to another level concerning where America was in God's economy, and how to be loyal to the Father of Jesus Christ rather than to publish polemics over intervention or nonintervention in the wars of Europe. The peace of God, not the peace of America, was the concern of the church. The essay was to a certain degree a response in opposition to Reinhold's address at the previous spring conference on the topic "Absolute Religious Commitment and Relative Political

Decisions." Beyond the immediate intervention question were their different approaches to Christian action and in particular international intervention that characterized their dispute in 1932 over boycotting Japan because of its aggression.

In the same issue, Joseph Haroutunian, a frequent contributor, provided a very positive review of H. Richard Niebuhr's new book, *The Meaning of Revelation*. While he praised it as the most worthwhile book on revelation of current Protestantism, he still asked for more tension between reason and faith; perhaps H. Richard reduced the tension too much without giving faith enough weight.

Finally war came on 7 December 1941, with the devastating but futile air attack upon the American fleet at Pearl Harbor and Niebuhr wrote:

> History (God) Has Overtaken Us
> For years we argued whether or not we should go to war. The implicit assumption of all these arguments was that we had the complete power to make the decision. Then history descended upon us and took the decision out of our hands. We might have known that it would be like this. History is not as completely under the control of human decision as either the interventionists or pacifists assumed.[22]

He noted that the Allies and the Axis corresponded to how the world would have lined up before the war if collective security had been able to work, and this costly war could have been spared. Despite the surprise initiating the U.S.A. into the war, he could not but chide *The Christian Century* pacifists who now became militants, and Communists who now supported Britain and the U.S.A. in the war, as well as the Russians for their particular misunderstandings.

Roger Shinn's Choice

Roger Shinn, a Union Seminary student, and Army volunteer wrote from camp on the new morale and direction that characterized those training for the army after the Pearl Harbor bombing. Less than a year before he had published in the *Union Seminary Quarterly Review*, which he had founded, the pacifist testimony of some of his classmates. Eight had refused to register for the draft and they were sentenced to jail for one year and a day. A group of them had gone to work for the American Friends Service Committee in Cooperstown, New York, demonstrating what lives of Christian service could mean while refusing to join the military.

Within the publication was also the diary of his decision by George Houser, one of the leaders of the pacifist group. It showed his decision-making process to accept the prison sentence rather than a ministerial deferment from conscription. The issue of the *Union Review* was quite remarkable for containing the paper of

Albert Einstein on religion and science and Paul Tillich's response in which he chided Einstein for not considering the most critically advanced theologies. Twenty-seven years later Shinn years joined the Union faculty as Niebuhr neared retirement. Niebuhr regarded him as his successor, but John C. Bennett held the Niebuhr Chair and the presidency of the seminary until 1968 with Shinn carrying the heavier load in ethics. Even in this early article, "A Buck Private's Look at the World," Shinn's excellent prose gave promise of his ability which would earn him praise as one of the best writers in the field of Christian ethics. The dispirited quality of the American soldier before the war, Shinn said, was due to the malaise of the American nation and the general weakness of its religion. Shinn feared that the sudden boost in American morale might not last. What was this quick response of the Americans beside the stubborn resolve of the British following Dunkirk, the determination of the Russians in front of Moscow, or the Chinese through ten years of ruthless pressure? He thought the soldiers knew that it would be a hard war, not just a march across the Pacific; he hoped they would find a dogged determination and get over the fanaticism that characterized some of their responses to the news. He hoped the war would bring a contribution toward peace and the abridgement of sovereignty, but that was not driving him. An Allied victory would be better than a Nazi victory and grant Europe a chance for some goodness to emerge, but the future was not known and there was a job at hand.

> History sometimes creates the leaders it demands. It may do so now. The future, we know, will be different from the past. It may be chaos and the uprooting of culture. It may be new life. Our job is to watch and pray, to do what is possible in building plans and ideals. Then the men may arise and the movement emerge which History will seize for the Future. Perhaps it is only a chance. But the God of history, and the God above History, demands it of us, and we can do no other.[23]

That particular paragraph owes more of its thought to Paul Tillich than to Reinhold Niebuhr with whom Shinn would later be more identified. But Shinn was one of a small group of theologians/ethicists who owed much to both Tillich and Niebuhr. Niebuhr's wartime detailed writing would appear more in the new journal *Christianity and Crisis*, and Tillich's role as chairman of the board of *The Protestant* (1941–1943) led him into the question of war aims and how far a noncommunist could move into a united front in a time of war when Russia was an ally.

The Protestant (Digest)

Tillich announced his new American citizenship as of 4 March 1940 in *The Protestant Digest*.[24] It fulfilled his counsel to other migrants to join their new country and participate in its destiny as active citizens. He tried to overcome certain characteristics that seemed provincial in light of his new experiences in America. His greatness consisted, however, in bringing the best of German theology to America and trying to express it in American terms. His most important writings would appear in America in English, but his thought patterns had been established before his migration and before he spoke English.

Kenneth Leslie had attracted Tillich to his journal *The Protestant Digest* (soon to shorten its name to just *The Protestant*) in 1941. An important early essay of Tillich's in the journal was on atheism. Leslie was a rather independent editor, in tension with his editorial board and Paul Tillich its chairman. One of the disputes led Tillich to write a policy statement for the journal in 1942. It is one of Tillich's most succinct statements of the relationship of Christian faith to political action, and it was intended to rein in the editor a little. It appeared under the title "Protestant Principles":

> Protestantism affirms the absolute majesty of God alone and raises prophetic protest against every human claim, ecclesiastical or secular, to absolute truth and authority. Protestantism affirms the Christian message as the ultimate expression of the nature of the Divine and protests all attempts to dissolve this message into a complex of religious experiences, moral demands, and philosophical doctrines.
>
> Protestantism affirms Divine sovereignty over the institutions and doctrines of the Christian churches and protests against attempts to bind the Christian message to the life and law of any historical church. Protestantism affirms the direct reference of the Divine to every element of reality and protests against hierarchical mediations as well as against the separation of a sacred from a secular realm. Protestantism affirms the independent structure of the different spheres of the cultural life and protests against encroachments upon their autonomy by churches and states.
>
> Protestantism affirms the dependence of the spiritual meaning of all cultural activities on their religious foundation and protests against the separation of religious transcendence from cultural immanence. Protestantism while rejecting any definitive or final system of Christian ethics and politics, applies the Christian message to every historical situation as the principle of criticism and demand.[25]

In the next issue of the journal he responded to readers' reactions and provided further interpretation.[25] He wanted to state both the immanence and the transcendence of God. In Protestantism one needed to see that all of life has a religious base, but life was not divine. All religious communities need criticism, but religious symbolism is the best way to express the ultimate. Here he was in agreement with Niebuhr, but Niebuhr adopted largely biblical symbols while Tillich took his terminology more from philosophy, and particularly from his mentor Friedrich Schelling. He wanted to affirm both the world and the church, though both are subjected to criticism. Therefore there can be no absolute answer in politics. This warning was directed to Leslie. Protestantism was not defined by the past, but it was future-oriented even if that future became known as post-Protestant.[26]

Tillich's first statement regarding appropriate war aims appeared in 1941 in *The Protestant Digest.*[27] He blamed the democracies for encouraging Communism by nurturing social injustice and then using Fascism to combat communism. The war was a struggle by Fascism to destroy the humanism of the West, he argued, and the appropriate war aim should be to create a planned economy in a European federation, which while liberal could resist tyranny and give economic security to the masses of people in Europe. Liberal arbitrariness and weakness could be overcome and human freedom preserved, he thought. Nationalism should be reduced by an economic federation. The war aims appeared in serial form in the journal and then published in a pamphlet to further the discussion of goals of the war.[28]

Eventually the sponsors of the journal differed over the editorial position regarding Communism. *The Protestant* folded as a result of the dispute, and Leslie, who was too close to Communism for many on the board, returned to his native Canada. Even though Mrs. Eleanor Roosevelt had endorsed the journal and sent greetings to it on its fourth anniversary dinner at the Waldorf-Astoria Hotel, it had become suspect in the eyes of the more-strident anticommunists.

Before the collapse of the journal, Tillich had taken on the role of an interpreter of the war to occupied Europe for the Office of War Information. Tillich's role in *The Protestant* was a source of suspicion to the Federal Bureau of Investigation. The split among the sponsors of the journal and its board was symptomatic of what happened to another of Tillich's wartime projects, and it foreshadowed the tensions that would divide Germany and the world during the Cold War.[29]

Interpreting the War to England

Christianity and Society announced Niebuhr's absence from the journal because for three months as he was speaking in the United Kingdom, Niebuhr mused that his influence seemed to be greater in England than on the American side of the ocean. His *Nature and Destiny of Man* was being published there and expectations for its sale in the U.K were as high as in the U.S. The society's historical solidarity and the acceptance of socialism in Britain made fertile ground for Niebuhr's messages. Niebuhr set sail on the Queen Mary, and in his first letter to Ursula dated 1 May he told her he was in his tenth day of the voyage. He did not arrive to an unnamed (due to censorship) port until 9 May. Some evasive moves were made by the Queen Mary shifting course in the voyage, but he assured her there had been nothing to fear. He shared a cabin with a flight lieutenant, and on the whole found the trip to be a melancholy one without Ursula's company. A frequent discussion companion was the Welsh playwright, Jack Jones. His days of enforced idleness dragged by, but on arrival in England he had to address the assembly of the Congregational Church and the rest of the trip was a whirlwind of activity. On 22 June 1943, he wrote Ursula: "I have never had such a schedule in my whole life for months on end. [I] have preached eight times, lectured thirty-two times thus far, and written thousands of words and attended twenty small conferences besides."[30] He, of course, visited the sites of London's destruction by German bombers, and on one occasion according to Ursula's report to Charles Brown, he got under a desk with Harold Laski and Edward R. Murrow during an air raid.

The churches of England were the major sponsors of the trip, though the Office of War Information had joined in support and for part of the trip provided a per-diem payment. A *New York Times* reporter hounded him about his support for the New Deal that he had published in *The New Statesman*, arguing that it was inappropriate for him to be speaking for the Office of War Information. Before the trip was over Niebuhr resigned his Office of War Information commission and supported himself from royalty payments which he was receiving from his English publisher. He spoke to both American and British troops and to a variety of Christian socialist meetings. He preached in a variety of cathedrals and churches. In the beginning of July he was honored to receive a Doctor of Divinity Degree from Oxford University. He was delighted to share with Ursula that the speaker referred to him as the husband of one of their graduates from St. Hugh's College. From the many letters he wrote to Ursula, it seems that his most frequent hosts were Sir Stafford Cripps, the labour member of parliament who was in charge of aircraft production in Britain, and Wedgwood Benn, another labour member of parliament. Cripps signed the Russian-British agreement with Molotov in Moscow to pledge their countries to fight together to defeat Germany, refusing to accept any individual peace with Germany until the defeat of Germany was complete. He was also delighted to be the weekend guest of his friend, The archbishop of Canterbury, William Temple, whom he regarded as the best theologian of the Anglican communion. In his writing he praised the archbishop's capacity to synthesize strands of theology to present a reconciling position. He respected the archbishop's lifelong socialist commitments and the fact that he could combine them with leading the Church of England. He delighted in the archbishop's command of social theory and his ability to combine pragmatism with his own version of natural-law theory. Only one year later he would write several "In Memoriam" notices for Dr. Temple, repeating in various forms for *Christianity and Crisis* and *The Nation* what he had written about him while he was living. On 21 June he wrote that his last engagement would be on 10 July and that he was scheduled to return between the 12th and the 18th to take on the summer school at Union from the 19th to the 23rd, preach at Harvard on the 25th and return with Ursula to their summer retreat at Heath, Massachusetts, that Sunday.

He had been interpreting the war in Britain from the perspective of his theology as an American. His speeches at the army camps were in continuity with his role in World War I encouraging chaplains and speaking at camps. Now, though, the war was not to remake the world, but it was a resigned fight to defeat Hitler and squash Germany's attempt to enslave other populations for the Nazi program. On returning home, he would interpret the British role in the war to the Americans, and weave into his international writings insights he had picked up from diplomats, professors, and others while in Britain. For a few months he speculated as to whether Britain would try and play a mediating role between the U.S.S.R. and the U.S.A.

He hoped for a continuation of the collaboration between the Soviet Union and America, but he was not sure it would be possible. It would take an immense amount of wise diplomacy to allow these continental giants with rival political-economic systems to cooperate. As it became clear that the emerging international organization would be an alliance with special privileges for the major powers, he pointed out the need for security for the smaller nations. He hoped that the need for economic integration would lay a foundation for moving toward political integration in Europe. Hopes for a middle way for European economic recovery that would not duplicate either the Russian model or the American model fit into his preferred socialization of the means of production, but not the farms or small businesses.

In 1944, he overestimated Britain's political power, and could not foresee its economic collapse, after the war, leaving a potential vacuum for the U.S.A. to fill. His book of wartime and immediate postwar sermons, *Discerning the Signs of the Times,* was as full of hopes for a new order including the melting of national sovereignty into a world-governing authority as his thought ever reached. However, though he trusted in the goal being someday fulfilled, he could not say whether it was decades or centuries away from realization.

Niebuhr returned to the family cottage in Heath after the summer school. His daughter Elizabeth was recovering from her tonsillectomy which had so distressed Reinhold when he could not get much news about it in England due to wartime communications. His student Dietrich Bonhoeffer had been arrested, but was still alive. Niebuhr had met him on his previous trip to England and offered him teaching posts in America, but Bonhoeffer had gone back to accept his country's destiny, and eventually to try to affect it in a plot against Hitler in which his role was still unknown to the Nazis. Bishop Bell, Bonhoeffer's primary English contact, and who served in the House of Lord's, had informed Niebuhr of the underground's situation. The Germans though defeated at Stalingrad had been counterattacking, and it looked like a long war. In this context Niebuhr penned his wartime prayer for the Sunday service on an envelope:

> **God, give us grace to accept with serenity the things that cannot be changed,**
> **courage to change what should be changed,**
> **and the wisdom to distinguish the one from the other.**

The prayer passed from Reinhold to Dean Howard Robbins who in cooperation with the Federal Council of Churches included it in a book of prayers for the armed services. From there it made its way to Alcoholics Anonymous which changed it for its use. After that it passed into the hands of the postoccupation German Army, and ultimately into kitchen kitsch decorating many households. Various names of alternative authors have been mistakenly assigned to it, but its publication by the Federal Council of Churches for wartime use was its first. His daughter's excellent book, *The Serenity Prayer*, restores to it the original sense of tragedy and decision making in war, and restores the sense of engagement of Niebuhr and his friends with the moral crisis of that time. He was already turning toward his book on the theory of democracy, having abandoned the idea of a book on war and peace while lecturing and meeting in England.

The Commission for a Just and Durable Peace

John Foster Dulles, Secretary of State, 1953–1959, whose temperament and policies seem so far removed from Paul Tillich and Reinhold Niebuhr, had many associations with both of them. Dulles was on the board of directors of Union (1945–1953) during their joint tenure. His father had been a professor at Auburn Seminary in upstate New York which joined Union in New York City. His daughter and son were both graduates of theological seminaries with his son Avery becoming a Roman Catholic cardinal. Henry Pitney van Dusen related to me in 1963 a quip from John Foster Dulles. Dulles had told the president of Union that the problem with the world was that "He [Dulles] should have been president of Union and Henry should have been Secretary of State."

Niebuhr, Tillich and Dulles were all associated in the work of the Oxford Conference on Life and Work of 1937. In 1943, the Federal Council of Churches' Commission on a Just and Durable Peace, to which Reinhold Niebuhr and John C. Bennett contributed, asked Tillich to make a theological presentation to its work. Reinhold must have smiled, knowing the great chasm between the minds of John Foster Dulles and Paul Tillich. Dulles was the chairperson and driving force of the commission's work and it reflected his mind. Tillich chose in three lectures to attack the philosophical basis of the Commission's work in foreign policy. Though the lectures were critical of the Commission's assumptions, the differences in practical conclusions should not be exaggerated. Both Tillich and Niebuhr were supportive of the Commission's work in rallying church support for the United Nations.

Dulles' philosophical mentor, Henri Bergson, had learned some of his philosophy of life from Friedrich Schelling whose thought Tillich had absorbed, and the Commission's work had some of the early Dulles' philosophy of change and world development in it. It lacked Tillich's sense of a world in revolt against the capitalist spirit. Dulles evolved into a hardened proponent of the capitalist spirit against Marxism, in contrast to Tillich's direction. Especially in his campaign for the New York senate, Dulles portrayed a bitter anticommunism. These later differences are present in embryo in Tillich's critique of his host's thought, but the sharp divergences became even more evident after the war. Secretary of State Dulles brought his establishment background (two grandfathers had been preceding secretaries of state), his legal training, his rather legalistic Presbyterianism, and his respect for Woodrow Wilson to bear on U.S. foreign policy. Niebuhr, who had disavowed his former discipleship of Woodrow Wilson, reacted with sharp criticism to the Eisenhower-Dulles foreign policy.

The Commission included leading American Protestant thinkers on foreign policy, among whom were Walter van Kirk and John C. Bennett. In its efforts for the United Nations, the Commission became one of the most effective examples of liberal Protestant thought shaping United States foreign policy. Dulles presented the Commission's findings to the president of the United States, was present at the founding United Nation's conference, and later negotiated the peace treaty with Japan. It has been remarked that it was the only precedent for a chair of a church committee translating it into a secretary-of-state position.

Tillich's first lecture, "Christian Principles and Political Reality," explored the depths of his thinking. It defined and related love, power, and justice to life as the dynamic quality of being. The dynamics of life pushing for change in the foundations of the world situation made the preservation of any status quo impossible. Justice, as the form of the unifying power of being, was in contradiction to the "the durable." The durable might be enforced, but the world was in revolt against the world economic situation, and the durable could not be just for it squashed the required changes.

The second lecture, "The Social Problem of a Just and Durable Peace," focused on a world in revolution. Tillich's analysis described a revolt against the chaos of a world subjected to the Leviathan of monopoly capitalism. Economic insecurity produced meaninglessness and resigned adjustment to heteronomous powers that stifled the human spirit. The way to go was represented by British socialist movements, central European underground movements, democratic socialists in Germany, and New Deal trends in the United States, in alliance with possible liberalizing tendencies in Russia. Liberal planning for state economies was needed. Without gains for the individual to participate meaningfully in the process of production, the war sacrifices would be as much in vain as those of the previous war. The influence of the Frankfurt School, which merged psychological theory with socialist theory, was clearly driving this presentation of Tillich. The meaninglessness presented in so much contemporary art also presaged for him the fate of modern humanity locked into the capitalist spirit. The alliances he hoped for did not develop until many years later and then they were still incomplete. The difficulties of regulating capital, and reforming health care in the United States in the Obama administration showed how the U.S. resisted, much longer than the European countries, trends Tillich was describing. The liberal tendencies he hoped for in the Soviet Union appeared only briefly and they were thwarted early in the twenty-first century.

Tillich's third lecture on "The International Problem of a Just and Durable Peace" moved from social-economic problems to the issue of international relations. Here the development of world history was analyzed. The war itself was creating a world history about which he had started a book in 1933, but never finished nor published. The emerging reality of world history was destructive. By the time of the lecture, he could not hope for world unity, though he believed regional groupings of nations were still possible. Anglo-Saxon domination of the world was a third possibility. Returning to national sovereignty made no sense. The ecumenical movement of the churches was a positive contribution toward the emergence of a world order. But it was a "not yet." It was as it had been: an "underground center of the world historical process." In conclusion he rejected the arrogant concept of a just and durable peace and suggested instead concepts of grace and tragedy. In the early twenty-first century Tillich's prognosis was being realized.

The European economic unity was developing toward political unity, and Anglo-Saxon hegemony was attempted and thwarted by the other empires. Russia, China, India, and the European Union were too diverse and too big to be swallowed. Even the distraction of the United States to war in the heartland of Muslim Asia showed the limits of U.S. power. No peace could be durable, because as Tillich said the dynamics bursting forth in economics, religion, and political movements kept disrupting any imposed peace and the nations were too diverse to agree upon cooperative peace or justice. Tillich's fears of World War II leading to World War III were partially realized as the Cold War developed, and were partially repressed because the reality of hydrogen weapons made any war between the superpowers completely irrational as an act of policy. The serious contributions both Niebuhr and Tillich made toward postwar planning during the war were, of course, eclipsed by the emerging reality of nuclear weapons of which they knew nothing until Japan was bombed. Their colleagues at Columbia and Harvard Universities, and President Roosevelt knew more, but they were not sharing their knowledge as the secret facilities in Chicago, and Los Alamos were being built and staffed.

Tillich gained his one chance to influence President Roosevelt through his friendship with Eleanor Roosevelt. A member of his Council for a Democratic Germany, Trudy Pratt, had introduced him to Mrs. Roosevelt. He had been a guest at Hyde Park, and she arranged a dinner for Tillich and several of the members of the New School at the White House. Versions of Wilhelm Pauck telling the story circulated around Union Theological Seminary. The president joined the group of guests . Wheeling himself to the table he stirred the martinis, a skill of which he was inordinately proud. Pauck's eyes would sparkle and his hands would move in excited delight as he portrayed this event. During the dinner, at a signal from Mrs. Roosevelt who was quite taken with Tillich's ideas for the reconstruction of Germany, Tillich presented a prepared statement about the German underground and the need for a signal from the American government recognizing its legitimacy and hopes for a democratic reconstruction of Germany. German refugees now at the New School followed to supplement Tillich's presentation. But the president excitedly said something to the effect that we have hundreds of thousands of soldiers, thousands of tanks, thousands of bombers and we are about to destroy Germany. German professors should write textbooks for Germany, as we will need textbooks to reeducate Germans after our victory. "I suggest you write these textbooks for them." The Pauck volume suggests Tillich may not have caught all the irony in the president's response.[32]

There was continued after-dinner conversation. Henry Wallace was particularly interested in Tillich's concept of the demonic and he wanted Tillich to explain it. Wallace, of course, was more drawn to socialism than Roosevelt, and he made a better natural after-dinner conversation partner than the president who had to leave the party for work. Members of Tillich's council encouraged by their German contacts with the underground probably overestimated the underground's effectiveness. The highest levels of the U.S. government did not have those contacts and paid less attention to their possibilities.

Council for Democratic Germany

Another forum for Niebuhr and Tillich collaboration was in gathering intellectuals together to advocate for allied policies after the war that would allow a free and democratic Germany to recover. In the late 1930s Reinhold Niebuhr began to raise funds and encourage Karl Hagan (alias Paul Frank), an exiled German socialist leader, in his work of maintaining contact with the

German underground. He had founded Neue Beginnen to succeed the banned Social Democrats. Stafford Cripps had assisted him with British funds, and he was busy assisting refugees, labor leaders, and others opposed to Hitler. Gradually this evolved into an organization with Niebuhr as chair of the American Friends of German Freedom. Eventually Hagan settled in New York and published the organization's newsletter; the group was formed of Niebuhr friends from the Union for Democratic Action, the Fellowship of Socialist Christians. Charles Brown reports that among the other anti-Nazi Germans with whom Niebuhr had contact were George Eliasberg and Barnard Tauer who published *The Silent War* anonymously in 1943 with Niebuhr writing the foreword:

> Their story is valuable for many reasons. It refutes the rising prejudice of those who profess to believe that all Germans are Nazis. It proves with what heroism and resourcefulness many Germans have resisted Hitler's tyranny and still resist it. [It] must certainly convince all but the politically stupid that the reconstruction of German life cannot be achieved without a political program which will allow the forces of residual health in German freedom to achieve the rebirth of Germany from within.[33]

Karl Hagan and Reinhold Niebuhr both supported Tillich in the short-lived Council for a Democratic Germany for which Tillich wrote the opening declaration, "A Program for a Democratic Germany." Unlike Niebuhr's work for the United Democratic Action, the Council included Communists. The Democratic Socialists and the Communists were unable to continue their united front. With developments promising the division of Germany, the group broke apart a little more than a year after it was founded. It was composed mostly of German émigré intellectuals and writers, and it represented Tillich's last attempt to organize a movement for Germany. His participation in the group aroused the FBI's suspicions to a higher level, and led to his being blacklisted by the U.S. Army, preventing his early return to Germany after the war. It may have been among the factors that led to the discontinuance of his radio broadcasts into occupied Europe and Germany. The declaration of the group was published in its own *Bulletin* and in Niebuhr's *Christianity and Crisis*.

The statement hoped for the German people throwing off all of their Nazi rulers. The Nazis were to be completely removed from power and punished. Those who were now in jail who had resisted Hitler needed to be empowered to share the new leadership in Germany. The large landowners, industrialists, and others who supported the Nazis could be removed from power and the German people should not be inhibited from abroad if they undertook such a purging. Policies that would divide the country or enslave the German people would rebound against the peace of Europe which required steps toward economic integration. The economic integration needed to include Germany's industrial capacity for the recovery of Europe and for the payment of such war reparations as were possible. As only the German people could free themselves internally, the reeducation of Germany must be undertaken by democratic people, not attempted by foreigners. All Nazi collaborators and leaders needed to be removed.[34] Tillich was accused of being pro-German, and I think he was while forcefully anti-Nazi. In their organizational work and writing, both Niebuhr and Tillich were developing the fight against Hitler and their own perspectives on the contribution of democracy. In the next two chapters Tillich's perspective against Hitler and Nazism and Niebuhr's perspective on democracy will be presented.

The emphasis upon the organizational work and their journalism for these war years should not obscure their vocation of teaching. They were both busy professors, supervising doctoral students at Columbia and sometimes teaching there as well as their full load of graduate teaching at Union Theological Seminary. The Seminary approved an advanced program in theological education to accelerate the training and education of students for the military chaplaincy, increasing their teaching responsibilities for the war years. Immediately after the war years the enrollment of the seminary jumped to serving returning veterans who were looking for religious meaning to understand the hell they had been through in the war. To take one year as an example, in the academic year 1941–1942 Niebuhr was finishing volume two of *The Nature and Destiny of Man*, and Tillich was beginning his weekly broadcasts into Europe and they were teaching these courses:

Paul Tillich:
History of the Philosophy of Religion:
Term One: Renaissance and Humanism
Term Two: European Enlightenment
Advanced Problems in Systematic Theology
Term One: Existence and Christ
Term Two: Life and the Spirit
Systematic Theology:
The Theology of the Reformers (two semesters)

Reinhold Niebuhr:
Christian Ethics: The Development of Christian Ideals (two semesters)
Christian Ethics:
The Foundation and Application of Christian
Ethical Principles (two semesters)
Christian Ethics Seminar (two semesters)[35]

Niebuhr taught his *Nature and Destiny of Man* as a philosophy of religion course every other year, and Tillich's "Problems in Systematic Theology" course would become volumes one and two of his *Systematic Theology*. Even so their course loads were heavy while they were engaged as public theologians. In these years their vocations could only be summarized as authors, journalists, teachers, and organizers who preached when asked to do so. It might be said Tillich had an additional role as propagandist. That is the subject of the following chapter.

10

A Voice against the Third Reich

Paul Tillich was asked by the Office of War Information to prepare speeches to the German people. From March 1942 through May 1944 he prepared 109 speeches five pages long or about 1,500 words each to be broadcast into Germany. He addressed every speech to "My German Friends." They were broadcast over The Voice of America and the British Broadcasting Corporation.[1]

Tillich's address writing began at an Allied low point in the war, moved through the Axis defeats of 1942, and concluded before D-Day in mid-1944. Throughout this period, Tillich optimistically trusted in the ultimate Allied victory. He was more consistently optimistic about the victory than was Reinhold Niebuhr. He knew that both the United States and the Soviet Union were individually stronger than Germany. With the empire to draw upon, Britain's strength was as great as Japan's, and the less-powerful nations of the world were drawn into functional alliances with the Allies. Tillich regarded the outcome as certain, but to be achieved through much suffering and hard fighting. In terms of population and industrial production, the Allies were too strong for the Axis powers. The military skills of the democrats and the Communists were to be proven as in no way inferior to those of the Nazis, Fascists, and Japanese militarists. Tillich portrayed Adolf Hitler as a gambler who had taken a contest at bad odds. Having lost his gamble, Hitler compulsively tried to repair his losses, but when defeated, his actions turned into an orgy of German self-destruction.

Should we regard Tillich as too optimistic? Many Americans of Tillich's generation also regarded the outcome of the war as a foregone conclusion. Once U.S. production was geared up, more aircraft, tanks, and ships would flow from the North American mills on the invulnerable continent than the Japanese could destroy. In addition to population, materiel, and military intelligence, will was needed to defeat the Axis. Both Japan and Germany, in their terrible excesses, aroused the will to fight in both Communists and democrats.

Tillich's judgments were shrewd, formulated from experience in the trenches of World War I. It is worth remembering that his rank in World War I was higher than either Hitler's or Eisenhower's. By the time of his writing, Hitler's and Japan's mistakes had doomed their regimes. Hitler's Barbarossa invasion of the Soviet Union might have had a chance in 1941 if Japan had struck the Soviets in the East. But Japan's foolish attack on Pearl Harbor and Hitler's declaration of war on the world's strongest industrial power sealed their fate. By March 1942, Tillich could anticipate the Nazi defeat. The turning points for Germany came in North Africa in 1942 and at Stalingrad in early 1943.

Tillich, for his part, was trying to divide the will of his German listeners from the mania of their Nazi rulers. Again and again he struck the theme that Nazism is doomed and that listeners should abandon it. He tried to persuade Germans to stop cooperating with their rulers. The attempt, of course, confronted the obedient character of the good Germans. Just by listening to his broadcasts a German or other European was engaging in resistance. Jakub S. Trojan, a Czech theologian said, "The broadcasts of the Voice of America were very important to us, but we could be executed for listening." The late Professor Eberhard von Waldow of Pittsburgh Theological Seminary related how his father The Reverend Bernd Bastian von Waldow, a pastor in East Pomerania, heard Paul Tillich's wartime broadcasts. Professor von Waldow remembered coming home on leave from his duty as a *Wehrmacht* tank commander, and being told by his father to walk around the house to be sure no one was listening while his father was attending to Paul Tillich's lecture on the BBC. (The Voice of America negotiated with the BBC to have its programs broadcasted over the BBC's medium and longwave transmitters directly to the European continent.) These were much clearer than the shortwave broadcasts transmitted directly to Europe from the United States, according to Holly Cowan Shulman, *The Voice of America Propaganda and Democracy, 1941–1945.*[2]

Resistance to Hitler within Germany was not widespread. Those who engaged in resistance in public were executed or imprisoned. Given the nature of totalitarian rule, resistance had to be in secret to be sustained. Tillich finished writing his addresses before the 20 July 1944 attempt on Hitler's life brought the deadly reprisals against the plotters. Tillich's hopes for Germans taking their fate and liberation into their own hands by overthrowing Nazism were too grand for his suppressed audience. As the war progressed Tillich often called attention to the resistance in Norway, Serbia, France, Poland, and Russia.

To call anti-Nazi activities within Hitler's Germany a resistance movement would be an overstatement. Such a description implies a cohesiveness among those involved that simply did not exist. Most resistance that occurred was undertaken by courageous individuals. Their actions ranged from providing sanctuaries for those fleeing the government, reading illegal literature, or listening to forbidden radio stations. While seemingly minor, all were capital offenses.[3]

Individuals such as Georg Elser and Kurt Gernstein went beyond this. Elser acted alone in his attempt to assassinate Hitler in 1939. Gernstein worked within the system to slow the flow of Zyklon-B to the death camps. Esler was executed.

Gernstein's ambiguous position led to his imprisonment in postwar France where he committed suicide.[4]

The futility of individual resistance was matched by small-scale collective resistance. Discussion groups such as the Wednesday Club, the Solf Circle, and the Kreisau Circle sought to neutralize the oppressive impact of Nazism and to plan for a post-Nazi Germany. Subversive journals such as *Resistance* (published by the Communist Ernst Niekisch) and *Information Journal of the Central Conservative Association* (published by Ewald von Kleist-Schmenzin) were banned in the first years of Nazi rule. Communist resistance began with the invasion of Russia. The Red Orchestra was perhaps the most famous of the Communist groups; fifty-five members were executed when German authorities discovered their shortwave radio signals to the Soviets. Anne Nelson's book indicates that the politics of the group were much broader than Communism included Social Democrats and Jews, and they were intent on proving Nazi atrocities to the outside world.[5] The Edelweiss Pirates and the White Rose were youth resistance groups. The Pirates damaged Nazi property; at the same time, they assisted in rescue and firefighting efforts in bombed German cities. The White Rose, composed of college-age youth, wrote and distributed pamphlets. Its leaders, Hans and Sophie School were caught dispersing their material in Hitler's stronghold of Munich in 1943. They were arrested, tortured, and executed soon thereafter.[6] Adam von Trott, a young German aristocrat, carried a letter of introduction from Sir Stafford Cripps and shared with Niebuhr his plans to attempt a revolution against Hitler. He was later executed.[7]

These scattered collective activities kept hope for change alive among their participants yet they lacked the leverage necessary to affect real change. Such leverage was available only in the German institutions, particularly the civilian government, the Foreign Office, the *Abwehr* (the Nazi intelligence and counterintelligence service), the church, and the army. Each institution had figures who acted heroically against the Nazis. Former Leipzig mayor, Carl Goerdeler, and Social Democrat Party member Julius Leber worked with others to plan for German rule after Hitler. In the Foreign Office, Secretary of State Ernst von Weizaker created a haven for resistance work. At the *Abweh*r Admiral Wilhelm Canaris used his organization to curb Nazi extremism. Under his protection, Hans Oster and Hans von Dohnanyi assembled evidence of Nazi criminality which was destroyed at the time of their arrest. Dietrich Bonhoeffer (Dohnanyi's brother-in-law) became active in the resistance through the Abwehr. Martin Niemoeller from prison was a symbol of church resistance. Church activities prevented the Nazi rule of the church until Hitler lost interest in the struggle. Confessing church members were arrested or sent to their deaths on the Russian front. Their Barthian-inspired confession stiffened church resistance even in those who could not affirm their explicit creed. Bonhoeffer's heroic resistance and execution was one of the boldest actions of church resistance.

The army which might have overthrown Hitler was too used to obeying orders to actively resist. Out of some two thousand generals, only twenty-two of them had any role in resistance to the madness of Hitler. It fell upon the colonels to take significant actions. Very prominent among them was Colonel Claus von Stauffenberg whose assassination attempt on Hitler on 20 July 1944 came very close to success. Tillich's speeches were often calling Germans to resistance, and he addressed people like the above and others he knew of who were resisting Hitler in various ways.

Tillich's first political speech in Madison Square Garden had condemned the anti-Semitism of the Nazis. His intellectual home in Frankfurt had been populated with Jewish intellectuals with whom he shared his dismissal from the university. Anti-Semitism was at the heart of the Nazi movement, so he spoke to it in his first German broadcast. Tillich began his speeches here because the Jewish question was central to his thought.

He spoke particularly to the Protestants of Germany as a German theologian in this first speech. He told them their roots were in Judaism. To attack Judaism was to attack the foundations of Christianity. Their Old Testament, their Jesus, and their Paul were all Jewish. The prophets of the Old Testament were against the idolatry of nationalism which was dominating contemporary Germany. From Judaism came the idea of universal history with meaning. In fighting the Jewish spirit of self- and national-criticism the Nazis are fighting against the best of Judaism. By attacking the prophetic message of meaning in Judaism and humanity they were also attacking the best of Germany. In destroying Judaism they destroy their own humanity. Tillich repeated his friend telling him as the persecution began that "Their blood will come upon us and our children."[8] He would repeat the phrase in other speeches and say that these words have been fulfilled.

Through April and May 1942, he told them of the restored legitimacy of the church in Russia as a partner with the state. The government of Russia was still atheist, but in wartime, Stalin had ended the League for Godlessness and persecution was less direct. Some actions of the Russian state were really more God-like than the pagan leaders of the German state who were acting more irreligiously than the irreligiously led Russian state. He explained how German emphasis upon freedom of the spirit did not join it with freedom of the person. He told them of the heroic resistance of the Norwegian church to Nazi claims, and of the Nazi campaign against human rights. He explained the despair of the German people who could not hope for victory in the war because that meant the continued loss of their own freedom. The despair also arose because of their guilt. Their only way out was through Germany's defeat and their overthrowing the tyranny which too many had welcomed in 1933.

On May 18th he discussed the anniversary of the book burning in 1933. The attempt to burn books had led to the burning of the world. The destruction of books had released a spirit that was hardened by the fires which would eventually defeat those who lit the fires. Much in the books, perhaps, deserved to be burned, but the oppression of the tyranny would return to destroy the tyrant. He described his own witness of the burning in Frankfurt:

> Many of you still have a picture of the events of that day.
>
> I experienced them in a particularly opportune place and want to tell you how they impressed me: meaningfully, awfully, and unforgettably. It was in Frankfort-am-Main. We stood at the window of the "Romer," the old royal residence of the German Kaiser. In the medieval square, the masses thronged, restrained by Brown and Black shirts. A wood pile was stacked. Then we saw columns of torch bearers gushing out of the narrow streets, an endless line, in student and party uniforms. The light of the torches flickered through the darkness and fantastically illuminated the gables of the houses. I was reminded of a painting from the time of the Spanish inquisition. At the end, a cart drawn by two oxen stumbled across the square. It was loaded with the books which were chosen as sacrifices. The pastor of students was striding behind the cart. When it had arrived before the funeral pyre, the pastor climbed into the cart and delivered the speech of condemnation. He threw the first book onto the now ignited piles. Hundreds of other books followed. The flames leaped up high and illuminated the vision that was certainly present. Time had run backward about two hundred years.[9]

Tillich explained how books are dangerous and that the burning of them and of those who wrote them can release the spirit that will overthrow the burner. The spirit released from the book will soon take on body, become a book again and renew its power. Throughout these months he described the Third Reich as having a short life measured not in a thousand years, but certainly in less than two decades.

In his speech of 28 August 1942 Tillich spoke to his German listeners. He denied the arguments of those who would replace German political immaturity with American political leadership. No, to leave Germany politically dependent was dangerous. It had to learn its own political maturity. Its religion, philosophy, and art had to become socially relevant. How had Germany become so politically immature as to surrender to Nazism?

German Evangelical Christianity had disconnected itself from social responsibility in its radical pursuit of otherworldly salvation.

> My friends of the German Evangelical Church! You must take upon yourselves this responsibility, if you want the German nation to come to political maturity! You can no longer speak of the Kingdom of Heaven as otherworldly power that should not have power in this world. For with that you hand this world over to satanic powers such as those that have power today in Germany and that are destroying the church along with the nation.[10]

It is the responsibility of the church to preach and teach the ways of political maturity. The emphasis the church places upon spiritual freedom can obscure the need for political freedom as it has in Germany and this must be overcome for German political development. With this emphasis Tillich hit upon that which was a part of his and Niebuhr's ministry to the church. It was this very political dimension of Niebuhr's teaching that had seemed so strange to the innocent Bonhoeffer when in 1932 he first encountered American theology at Union Theological Seminary with his German Lutheran background.

Germany also tended to separate the political from humanity and government from the nation, but those were false dichotomies. Part of being human is to be political and one's humanity suffers when the political is abandoned to others or to the devil. Political maturity was learned through struggle and so hopefully the German opposition to Hitler would grasp it first; then, maybe in the future, the mature could learn it.

In his next talk, Tillich spoke of how most of the German intellectual class sold itself to the middle-class financial support and the middle class sold the intellectuals to the Nazis.

> We are in the midst of the tragedy of the German intellect; it exalted when it should have condemned; it veiled when it should have unveiled; it kept silent when it should have spoken; it retreated when it should have fought; it betrayed when it should have tolerated. While the bearers of the intellect themselves were unaware of it, they were bought by the ruling powers as civil servants, as successful authors, as famous men, as minions of wealth. Again I must say: this does not apply to all. But perhaps to more than in other civilized nations.[11]

He thought that now German intellectuals understood their own betrayal and that they must become critical and revolutionary or wither. "Now it is summoned to the struggle for liberation and cannot evade it without surrendering itself."

In September, Tillich responded to Goebbels's call for more hatred for the British enemies. The federal propaganda minister thought there were too many Germans listening to the BBC. Tillich urged those who heard his broadcasts not to join the Nazis in their hatred. The Christian message was to call for passionate fighting against the evil of Nazism, but to deny hatred of the enemy. The Nazis understood their differences with Christianity and were planning to destroy the faith. In their fight with the Nazis, Christians must not be seduced into becoming like them in their hatred.

By October 1942, Tillich could interpret Hitler's speech at the opening of the Winter Charity Drive as a major change in Nazi strategy. No longer were the Nazis claiming the world was theirs, but they shifted to the need to defend their conquests. Against that defense internal resistance was rising and the allies were building potential. But for Germans, the Reich of starvation, mass executions, and tyranny was not worth defending. It needed to be opposed. For the previous three years offense was the vision, but now it had changed. The Nazi conquests were immense, but they were both evil and vulnerable. Now the Nazis were only defending their idol of power.

The next week Tillich talked about "power politics" arguing that while the Nazis had promised justice they wanted only power. Power without justice was not sustainable. The Nazis had betrayed justice and everyone knew it. Power could hang on to tools of control for awhile, but without justice the idolatry of power would wane. "Tell the Germans that the idol of power has turned against its worshipers today and will destroy everyone who stands with them"

In November 1942, Tillich lectured in a simple way on the moral order. The immorality of Germany under the Nazis seemed to prevail in the early war. Power, not justice, seemed to be decisive. But the immorality of power without justice ran into resistance from the more moral aspect of the world. The moral order prevailed and the German hopes were dashed against the lines of the moral order.

> You can and should place yourselves on the side of the moral order, against the National Socialist outrage. You should do so inwardly and, as soon as possible, outwardly. You should become instruments of the moral, constructive world and not the immoral, destructive world order.[12]

By the end of 1942, Tillich warned Germany of its approaching defeat. The news of Stalingrad, North Africa, the mobilization of America, and the rising of resistance forces in the occupied countries meant the destruction of German power, cities, and people. But the downfall of Germany would be better for the Germans than their present life in injustice, and he spelled out the crimes of the Nazis:

> I haven't spoken yet of the worst matter: of a crime that Germans are committing daily; of a crime against humankind such as occurs only once in a millennia; of a crime that means bloodguilt for generations for those who are doing it and for those who are tolerating it. The place where it has been taking place for months with evergrowing cruelty is Poland. The victims are

hundreds of thousands of innocent people who have lived among you, whose neighbors and friends you were, with whose children your children played. And other hundreds of thousands are being sacrificed whom you don't know, who have never done you an injustice, who have led a life in poverty and, frequently, in great purity and piety. And today they are being hauled away to mass death by German hangmen, by those who are the trash and the disgrace of the German people, and you are standing by! Can you stand by any longer, German officers, when you still have a sword to use and an honor to lose? Do you know that in France when these unfortunate ones were supposed to be handed over to the German hangman, all the churches became united for the first time in centuries in order to prevent staining the French name with this manhunt? Do you know that the parents whose children were exempt from going along to Poland were handing them over to strangers on the sides of the streets in order to save them from the death that was otherwise certain? Picture, in your souls, those mothers, and calculate the guilt that you are incurring when you are eyewitnesses to it! Do you know that the cattle cars that roll through the German cities with this burden of wretchedness are bolted up for days; that no bread and water is let in, no dying or dead are let out; and that at the end of such a journey, frequently over half of the deportees are lying dead on the ice-cold floor of the car?

And you want to continue to be spectators of that, German clergy, you who are praying for German victory? And do you know that in Poland itself, women and children, old men and the sick are being driven together and being shot down with machine guns? German physicians are found in the camps who inoculate their victims with air bubbles in order to kill them in the most certain and inexpensive way? A shriek went throughout the entire world in these weeks when reports about that came together from all sides! The world is truly growing accustomed to depravity, and yet it listened and cried out when all of this turned from a rumor into an established fact. I can tell you that the hearts of many who sympathized with the truly repressed Germany became numb and hard in those days.[13]

In his Sunday speeches, or sermons, Tillich frequently focused on the holidays of the Christian calendar and addressed his listeners to break with the National Socialist tyranny. In 1942, he contrasted the message of the vulnerable reception of the divine in the human Christ child to the evil of Nazism:

You can't have it both ways. Whoever follows National Socialism must persecute the child in the manger. Whoever obeys the Fuhrer who has become a Fuhrer unto death must turn aside from the star that points to Bethlehem. Whoever respects power above all else must despise the powerlessness of the child in the manger. Whoever preaches hatred must disparage the love that gives of itself, must disparage Christmas. You cannot celebrate Christmas and believe in National Socialism. You cannot serve Christ and the Antichrist. Cut yourselves loose from them and celebrate the fourth-war Christmas as the festival of love that can save you and your children and your nation after the

> sermon of hatred and violence has driven you into the night of this fourth-war winter.[14]

Tillich's radio addresses emphasized the nature of German collective guilt for tolerating or encouraging the Nazis. Other peoples had guilt as well. But Germans had allowed Hitler to capture the country and plunge Europe into war; they had accepted the Nazi racial policies, death trains, and murders of Jews and many others. The ultimate destruction of Germany, Tillich believed, was atonement for the evil into which the Nazis had led the nation. He pled for the Germans to find ways to resist Hitler and to join in their own liberation.

The Nazi regime declared three days of mourning for its defeat at Stalingrad. The government attempted to unify the country with dark arm bands, solemnity, and music. Tillich as a religious leader weighed into the interpretation of the days of mourning. Normally, he said, countries at war do not mourn the loss of a battle. The defeat at Moscow was not mourned. What was going on? Tillich provided his own interpretation.

> With the days of mourning for Stalingrad, the German nation has begun the days of mourning that will not end until the rebirth of Germany. But precisely for this reason, grief is not the end. And precisely for this reason, there is a joy that overcomes grief and a hope that is able to sustain above the restlessness.
>
> This is the way you should feel, my German friends! The days of mourning should be dedicated to mourning the fact that the German nation has fallen into the hands of powers that have led it to shame and misery. The days of mourning should be days of mourning over the triumph of National Socialism in Germany. But at its foundation, there should be a joy and a calmness that comes from the fact that, now, the beginning of the end of these powers has come.[15]

Tillich explained to his listeners in March 1943 how National Socialism attacked the roots of Germany by discrediting its Germanic, Christian, and humanistic sources of life. Nazism attacked the German roots by dismissing the Germanic commitments to chivalry, virtues of justice, and love from the New Testament. Humanism arrived in Germany with Christianity and was particularly developed in the eighteenth and nineteenth centuries.

> There are three things that are relevant to humanism, to the human being as human: reason, human dignity, and humanity. These were the three stars that hung in the sky of the great German Century, and that have now disappeared behind the gray clouds, and the murky fog of National Socialist barbarity.[16]

He interpreted Good Friday and Easter of 1943 for his listeners. As Jews were being hunted and dragged off to their extermination so Jesus was being harassed through Jerusalem. He turned and said: "Do not weep for me but weep for yourselves and for your children." So grief was coming to Germany in its destroyed cities and armies and the suffering would increase as Germany walked through its passion. Easter would come to Germany in its rebirth as it died to the combined evils within National Socialism. Germans would suffer, but they ought not despair for there was hope for the other side of death. The National Socialists in their despair seek death and to unite their death with all those complicit with them. So turn away from them, do not be seduced any further.

He pled with the Germans to see and accept their fate. They had been blinded by their successes, but now these were ending. Only in seeing their fate, accepting it, and willing to live again could they find a future. He described their fate in stark, empirical terms on 19 May 1943.

> When I spoke to you the last time, the German collapse in Africa had already occurred. One hundred thousand German soldiers, nearly a dozen generals, and countless weapons were captured by the Allied nations. The Southern flank of Europe is exposed. Defenseless, the Italian ports wait for crushing attacks from the air. The Italian population is fleeing from the coastal region inland and from the south to the north. Indeed, in the north of Germany, one German city after the other is being turned into an expanse of ruins. And if they are not completely destroyed by the first attack, then follows a second and a third and fourth and so on, until the war industry is made useless and life has become hell for the inhabitants. And there is no letting up, day and night. Will it come to us today? Will I be buried beneath rubble tomorrow? So everyone instinctively asks themselves? And their shaken nerves wait for the warning signal or the interruption of the radio program. Disaster is in the air! Where will it descend?
>
> What does all of this mean? It means that it is not yet the end, but it signifies the beginning of that which is leading, sooner or later, to the end. It means that fate has begun to reveal itself.[17]

His speech of 1 June 1943 is both a sermon and a lecture on world religions. National Socialism is regarded as a national religion with a national god so it must persecute Christianity as a universal religion with one god. Christianity stands for humanity as one and National Socialism understands humanity as tribal with the idolatry of its god to overthrow the other tribal gods. As this dawns among Christians, church resistance to Nazism becomes stronger. In his professorial style, Tillich told his listeners about the collective guilt of all responsible Germans. The destruction of their cities was the price of the justice of atonement. In all human disasters the collective guilt of humanity was exposed.

In the thirty years of war in the twentieth century there was special German guilt; the suffering of the Germans was partial expiation. The Germans knew of the suffering and extermination of the Jews by the Nazis and did not prevent it. The churches spoke not a word in the defense of the Jews. The people permitted the Nazis to rule and with only minor exceptions failed to revolt against Nazis. The war revealed the guilt of all responsible Europeans, but also the particular and collective guilt of the Germans. Even after the war when he returned to speak in liberated Germany his frank speech about the guilt of responsible Germans was not acceptable.

> And today, when the trains with Germans who are fleeing from the cities roll from east to west, this is an atonement for the death trains that, filled with Jewish women and children and old people, drove out of all German cities from west to east to certain death. The German cities slept when the death trains rolled through their train stations with their burden of indescribable misery. Now they are awoken by the fire from heaven; now their inhabitants themselves are filling the trains of misery. We must look all of that in the eye. And I know that you who hear these words have looked at all of this for a long time. I recall that even in the first months of the Hitler dictatorship, Germans with sensitive feelings said, "All of this injustice that is now occurring will come upon us and our children." Now it has come and will come further. The law of guilt and atonement will work itself out further in all who are accessories to the world disaster, in all who are accessories to the German fate.[18]

September 1943 heard Tillich's call for the removal of Hitler. Historically nations paid dearly for the evil of their rulers. Germany had no redeemable future with Hitler at its helm. Earlier he had portrayed Hitler not as a prudent risk-taker but as a gambler who in desperation staked everything on one card. He had gambled and won in Munich, and gambled and lost in invading Poland, but his greatest gamble was the Russian campaign. Hitler even challenged Japan to encourage America into the war. The gamble of taking on the British Empire, the Russian Empire, and American industry was foolish; he did not have extraordinary luck and he lost.

The story of Moses and the plagues inflicted upon Egypt for the idolatry of the arrogant pharaoh told a historical truth. The plagues inflicted upon Germany were more disastrous than those in Egypt, extending beyond the firstborn son to a toll in German families beyond the "firstborn."

> Hitler must now be removed from the German people, not only outwardly but also inwardly. His spirit must be banished from German spirit. The power that he has won over the soul of the youth must be broken. The dreams of German greatness in which he appeared must cease to be dreamed.[19]

Major themes running through many of the addresses were: (1) Germans must rise up, separate themselves from Nazism, and remove the curse of Nazism and (2) while many nations and people are guilty of the unbelievable destruction of the world, the Germans are especially guilty and their continuing punishment will be terrible.

Tillich's phrase of the "fire from heaven" explicitly related by analogy to Sodom and Gomorrah blends the destruction wrought by the Allies to the deserved divine punishment. The vengeful side of God particularly portrayed in the Old Testament and in the New Testament book of Revelation echoes throughout his speeches. Another phrase which places Tillich's language in dialogue with recent themes in theology is his frequent reference to the world war directed against Germany as a war of liberation. Germany requires liberation from its rulers, the Nazis.

He concluded his 1943 speeches with the publication of a German soldier's letter to his sweetheart that detailed how the soldiers were systematically destroying every city and village they retreated from. The soldier said there would be no towns remaining between the Volga and the border. The people, the soldier said, would either freeze to death or starve. The soldier assured his sweetheart that it was better to be bombed in a German city than to have everything destroyed in an evacuated Russian city or town. He called it a war of extermination of the civilians. Tillich called again for the Germans to rise up and separate themselves from the Nazis.

Tillich wrote his radio speeches for the first five months of 1944 as the Allies steadily pushed the Japanese and the German forces back toward their homelands. To his European listeners, he spoke now of the painful passion of Germany and the end of Nazism; themes of liberation dominated his lectures. The ending of his speeches coincided with his founding of the Council for a Democratic Germany (discussed earlier).

German Americans seeking to reach an understanding of policy for a postwar Germany often met in Tillich's apartment at Union Theological Seminary. The concierge at the telephone desk in Hastings Hall on 122nd Street became well acquainted with the names of the German intellectual elite and at least one member of the underground as they came to meet in Tillich's home. The themes of these discussions and later Council policy were echoed in Tillich's speeches: defeat and punish the Nazis, conserve German economic power within a system of European economic integration, allow the democratic forces in Germany to cleanse Germany of Nazis, and insure that the Germans themselves reformed German education.

The Council's basic opposition to extreme measures of punishment for Germany has been criticized, and for a short period Tillich was blacklisted by the

U.S. Army. His speeches were cancelled, and he was excluded from any role in the projects for postwar Germany. Niebuhr who supported Tillich's work in the Council was not treated so roughly. The records of the FBI investigation on Tillich reveal more suspicion of his work on the Council than on any of his other wartime projects. For Tillich his work as president of Self-Help for Émigres from Central Europe provided more satisfaction than the short-lived Council which broke up due to emerging cold-war tensions.

United States' forces continued their difficult but unrelenting movement to liberate the Pacific islands. In the early months of the year, they made gains in New Guinea, New Britain, and the Marshall Islands. In March, they repulsed a Japanese attack on the Solomon Islands. By the spring of 1944, U.S. fleets were dominating the Pacific.

In Europe, the Soviets continued their major advance from the East bearing the brunt of war. By the end of January, the two-year siege of Leningrad was broken. With the Germans in retreat, Soviet forces retook Yalta by mid-April and drove the Germans form the Crimean port of Sevastopol in May.

From the West, British and American bombers continued their efforts against German targets. Late February was the occasion for what became known as the Big Week air raids on cities throughout Germany. While pounding Germany, the Allies also suffered significant losses in the air war. Winston Churchill reported to Parliament that up to that point in the war, the British had lost more than thirty-eight thousand pilots and crewmen and over ten thousand aircraft. The Allies continued their planning and practicing for the June invasion of Europe while trying to deceive the Germans on the place and time.

Anti-Nazi partisan activities increased in German-ruled areas as did the German responses to these actions. Retributive atrocities continued against local communities, especially in the Balkans. One village, Drvar, suffered destruction because it protected Tito until his Allied rescue in May. While beaten down, the Yugoslav partisans were inspired to continue their struggle against the Nazi oppressors.

Tillich wrote his final Voice of America speech the second week of May, less than a month before D-Day. Ten weeks later the plot of Colonel Claus von Stauffenberg to assassinate Hitler failed and the plotters were arrested and soon executed. The speeches of 1944 went beyond merely encouraging the German people to resist and to work for the defeat of their Nazi rulers. Now Tillich's message became an urgent exhortation to them to face their own guilt and to accept honestly the consequences of Nazism's colossal folly.[20]

In January 1944 Tillich decried the Nazi delusion of a coming victory and their claim to have faith in such an impossibility. The way forward after Germany's failure was to admit defeat, admit complicity with the Nazi crimes and then in a smaller and weaker Germany to strive for justice. "Justice exalts a nation" and, in the pursuit of justice, Germany though disarmed and weaker could become great and serve as a model to other nations. As his talks moved into February he described how the Nazis had destroyed the trust upon which community was founded. Even in the family the children were taught to betray and testify against parents. Terror replaced community in Germany. The best community left in Germany was the community of resistance to the Nazis. War that divided nations could also bring them together. The two world wars had destroyed European community. But as the League of Nations came out of World War I, European federation and world community could become agendas for a resurrected Germany after its defeat.

On Palm Sunday 1944 Tillich preached his lecture on the present and coming suffering of the German people, portraying them as the crowd around the crucifixion of Jesus, the innocent sufferer. There were some innocent in Germany who were crucified, but the masses were complicit with the Nazis.

> We all know that the German nation has brought infinite suffering upon other nations, that it allowed itself to be turned into the instrument of one of the most dreadful powers of all time, and that it has in that become the cause of the most frightful war. Even if the extermination of the Jewish people had not taken place, even if the countless atrocities of the Gestapo would not fill the whole world with horror, even then, the extent of innocent suffering which Germany has brought upon other nations would be incredible. Millions have been nailed to the cross of the most profound suffering and the most agonizing death by the henchmen of National Socialism. And the German people stood by and looked on, just as in the old pictures of the crucifixion. "We have been crucified by you," cry out the innocent people from all over the world to the German people. And only very few have the greatness of the innocent one to ask forgiveness for those who are killing them. From the mouths of most of the victims of the Germans come not the word of forgiveness, but the word of curse.[21]

Tillich summed up his contentions in his one hundredth talk on 7 March 1944. His purpose had been to tell them the truth of the German catastrophe, and he felt that now as it approached they had ears to hear that which he had been speaking. The Nazis were defeated and they were preparing to go underground. They still held out a false hope for the defense of Germany. It was impossible. The task for his listeners was still for them to liberate themselves form the Nazi spirit and to prepare for a new Germany free of the Nazis. He intended to hold out the real hope for a Germany resurrected from its defeat and free of Nazism.

On 18 April 1944 he explained: "What had gone wrong in Germany." His proposal was that Germany had never had a significant revolution for freedom. They were a submissive people, and once the Nazis had the government, most Germans submitted. His antidote to the poison: "The German nation's fighting its way to freedom by throwing off Nazi tyranny and by taking its destiny in its own hands." He still hoped for internal German rebellion against the Nazis, but there was not to be very much resistance. Their destiny was really in the hands of the conquering forces, as Tillich knew, even though he hoped for more rebellion against the evil of the rulers of Germany. Hitler had promised not to flee, but he would in 1945 commit suicide after needlessly leading hundreds of thousands more German soldiers to die in the futile defense of a power that was broken. Tillich's hopes for more resistance to Hitler did not come about and the sacrifice of German soldiers and civilians and Allied soldiers continued as more German cities were destroyed. Tillich, taken off the air by the American government as overly pro-German, would continue his fight apart from the government in the Council for a Democratic Germany which would self-destruct as Germany was occupied by two contending forces. Concurrent with Tillich's struggles with the Council to promote a future democracy in Germany, Neibuhr was writing one of his most significant books on the meaning of democracy.

11

A Voice for Democracy

Niebuhr's 1943 thinking about democratic political philosophy for his lectures at Stanford in January 1944, culminated as he signed the foreword for *The Children of Light and the Children of Darkness* in August 1944. In 1943, the outcome of the war though predictable was uncertain. The Allies were not confident enough to create a Western front until June 1944 in the D-Day landings. In the Pacific, American advances following the victory at Midway in June 1942 were limited until late in 1944. The costly victory at Guam in July 1944 gave grounds for confidence. Columbia University's participation in the Manhattan project to initiate the nuclear age was unknown to the theologians though they taught at Columbia. Niebuhr's supporter, Harvard University President James Conant, gave no hint to Niebuhr of the new weapon he was encouraging, though he would complain mightily of Niebuhr's critique of its eventual use. Scientists in the University of Chicago-based work on the atomic bomb signed a petition against its use on civilian targets. But, according to Edward Teller, Robert Oppenheimer would not permit the circulation of the petition at the Los Alamos labs. Oppenheimer reasoned it was the work of the scientists to build it and the vocation of the politicians to decide upon its use. Niebuhr's 1959 foreword to the republication of *The Children of Light* would suggest changes in his thought necessitated by U.S. assumption of postwar world responsibilities and the bomb.

Though *The Children of Light* was regularly used in Christian social ethics classes it was not a book of theological ethics. It was a book of political philosophy like its predecessor, *Moral Man and Immoral Society*. Its major difference from the 1932 argument was in its chapter on property. *Moral Man and Immoral Society* was a work in socialist theory. As late as 1943 Niebuhr had written:

> It is quite obvious that those forms of "private" property which represent primarily social power, and the most potent social power of our day at that, cannot remain in private hands. "The socialization of such property is a *sine qua non* of social justice. On the other hand it is foolish to press the collectivist solution upon all forms of property, agrarian, small trade, etc."[1]

Now, however, in 1944, he surveyed earlier theories by Christian thinkers and noted both positive and negative answers regarding private property. He spent considerable time probing both Marx and Locke on their respective theories of property. Neither, in Niebuhr's judgment, adequately considered the power potentiality of property whether in individual or managerial hands. Abuses occurred in both forms of property. Property's power could be used either defensively or offensively. In modern society, urban apartment houses and large manufacturing firms denied individuals the ownership of either land or the tools of their work. These developments moved toward socialism in Niebuhr's perspective, but no longer unambiguously so.

> There must, in other words, be a continuous debate on the property question in democratic society and a continuous adjustment to new developments. Such a debate is possible, however, only if there is some common denominator between opposing sides.[2]

He did not denounce democratic socialism, nor did he affirm capitalism as his brother H. Richard had recently done. Each question of control of property in a democracy had to be decided on its own merits while maximizing human freedom.

> None of these propositions solves any specific issue of property in a given instance. But together they set the property issue within the framework for democratic procedure. For democracy is a method of finding proximate solutions for insoluble problems.[3]

The lights of democracies, more properly called republics, had been going out in Europe since their establishment following World War I from the dismemberment of the Austrian, Russian, German, and Ottoman Empires. There were not many republican forms of government left in 1943–1944. While Republican forms of government still existed in Latin America many of them were dictatorships in practice. Sweden and Switzerland maintained neutral republics. One could disagree about the proper term for New Zealand, Canada, and Australia in their parliamentary monarchical form existing as part of the British Empire. Niebuhr would think of them along with Britain as democracies. But, of course, in neither Britain nor the United States did other than the privileged oligarchies of money and/or education rule. Niebuhr's friend, R. H. Tawney, the religious socialist from Balliol College and the author of the book *Equality*, had made very clear the limits of British democracy with its privileges of title, inheritance, and education. Niebuhr perceived the growing power of politics to represent the interests of the working class and the impoverished as the New Deal reforms took hold. Still the argument in defense of "Democracy" was really the justification of plutocratic-controlled republics of which the greater number were parliamentary monarchies. Though America had signaled

Philippine independence, it was still a colony established by military repression before the more oppressive Japanese occupation. Niebuhr's own agenda of increasing the power of the people in America was clear, but so was his own realistic appraisal of where power resided. He knew too many millionaires and their power, even in educational institutions' boards of directors, to suggest that he lived in a democracy, meaning rule by the people. Still *The Children of Light* was a wartime book and republics were called democracies in common discourse.

In the foreword, Niebuhr indicated that though he was writing political philosophy without theological expressions, the view of human nature beneath his political views was that of a Christian understanding of human nature. He perhaps should have indicated how modern that conception of human nature was. At the center of his view was the transcendence of human freedom over nature and history. Human beings in his view could accomplish new realities and they were not determined by either nature or God. By understanding that the human self was more than reason, nature, history, or divine determination, one could stand apart from these forces and act. Of course, any of these forces might limit or impinge upon the range of action. Still human action was free. Therefore the essence of developing human community was in the maximization of that human freedom within the order that was necessary to promote freedom. Not surprisingly, in 1943–1944, that gave the edge to republican forms of government.

The synthesis achieved in the revolutionary colonies between enlightenment perspectives on freedom and Calvinist preferences for order to control human sin seemed to Niebuhr to be worthy of defense. Cynicism about human possibilities and morality encouraged tyranny. Sentimentality about overcoming sin or war encouraged vulnerable arrangements that were unstable. The arts of government then were to be enlisted to prudently encourage unity, freedom, and order. Interestingly in this wartime treatise equality as a regulative principle of justice did not receive the same weight as it had in the almost concurrent publication of volume two of *The Nature and Destiny of Man* or in the dozen years earlier *Moral Man and Immoral Society*. Of course, the Nazis were the chief representatives of the children of darkness which also included others who regarded their own self-interested power as the goal of politics. Those ignoring self-interest in the pursuit of the common good were seen as the children of light. Democracy required leadership by those who strive to order life for the common good knowing that in human power it is an impossible task. In politics, "There is no level of human moral or spiritual achievement in which there is not some corruption of inordinate self-love."[4]

Robert M. Brown's designation of Niebuhr as a "pessimistic optimist" fits this book. Democracy he believed had too often been defined and defended by liberal optimists who expected moral progress in human development. Without the modifying provisional pessimism of Christian faith, democracy did not require constant adjustment and realistic defense. But all of recent history showed the need for the reforms of the New Deal and for realistic war policy for its survival. He did not make the argument in the book, but it is also true that without a certain pessimism, humanity cannot understand the need for the Christian promise of salvation through faith. The nature of the human could be fulfilled in democracy and with a right mind it could be defended. He put it in his second most quoted phrase: "Man's capacity for justice makes democracy possible; but man's inclination to injustice makes democracy necessary."[5]

Having overcome his own idealistic liberalism, and in the process of dismissing his Marxism, Niebuhr criticized both as children of light. The liberals, he held, believed that human progress would eclipse the evils of the modern world and the Marxists believed revolution would overcome evil. The evil really was in the self-centered humanity that built this contemporary human life. "The good is, on the other hand, always the harmony of the whole on the various levels."[6] For Niebuhr only divine fulfillment as symbolized in The Kingdom of God would overcome human conflict. The task for the democratic struggle was for responsible people to assume egotism and to manipulate it, deflect it, and organize it for a tolerably harmonious ordered society in which freedom could flourish.

In the succeeding chapters of the book on individual and community, community and private property, and toleration and differing communities, he retells his perspective on the history of Western social theory, and concludes that the ambiguities must be affirmed. No historical perfection is achievable. Democracy is best served by living with tensions and by balancing various interests in compromised solutions.

The frame for his argument of the book came from the great themes of *The Nature and Destiny of Man*. It was human nature to have limited freedom. Sin corrupted that freedom and human institutions. The human task is to build and defend relatively good institutions to encourage freedom. Christian symbolism of fulfillment can encourage the striving for human fulfillment which will not perfectly succeed in history. The argument for a realistic moral theory of government is written in a prose that flows much easier than a similar argument in volume 2 of *The Nature and Destiny of Man*.

Already on the book's second page he had suggested the fall of middle-class civilization. From a middle-class perspective of sixty-five years later such a prediction seems premature. His demand for realism in the defense of democracy seems prophetic. His analysis of the dangers of egotism and pride within the children of light's struggle for reform and freedom has been proven true. The children of light's optimism may have in the long run been more productive of social reform than he could predict in 1944, but, of course, through his efforts some of them were influenced to become more realistic. His plea for toleration of other creeds has produced fruit even in his own changing perspective on Catholicism as it evolved in the century. His recognition of the toughness of the racial prejudice against blacks and Jews has been confirmed while some of it has been overcome by the children of light. His chapter on community and toleration was deservedly rigorous about the difficulty of overcoming racism even in the minds of those struggling to defeat it. The Fellowship of Socialist Christians continued to discuss racism in their retreats, support projects against Southern racism, and include a Negro on their board of directors and in their programs.

A few months after publication of *The Children of Light*, he returned to the subject of racism as the source of the country's "most vicious of all forms of social conflict in the nation." In a major essay he commented on the church's official pronouncements against racism, and he approved of the church using all the psychological and anthropological studies that it needed to prove the stupidity of racism. But more fundamentally the race issue was not the result of stupidity as much as it was of original sin. Racism resulted from the human, in freedom, trying to make oneself and a particular culture God. The idolatry of racism had to be confronted and that was the particular task of the church. The church needed to work on the race issue with deeper resources than the scientific findings that there were "no races" or "no inferior races." The problems lay in the resources of human pride as the basis of "racial bigotry." Enlightenment through science on the race question was useful, but more repentance was needed. The essay showed Niebuhr's usual critique of the church for its sentimentality, and concentration on personal sins rather than the social sin of the nation. Despite scientific findings not reaching the depths of the problem they probably had accomplished more in fact than the church had in dismantling the nation's racism.

World Community

In the concluding chapter of *Children of Light*, Niebuhr recognized that there were significant impulses in major world religions toward universalism and world community. Technology also was pushing people toward a world community as communication distances were reduced.

However, humans found security in their national identities. Beyond the nation-state the world seemed chaotic. Humans were limited creatures influenced by isolating geography, particular languages, traditions of human organization, and in the modern world extreme nationalisms. The achievement of peace in a world community was "the most urgent of all the issues which face our epoch," but it seemed impossible.

Niebuhr feared that humanity would live for a considerable period of time under conditions of international anarchy in which technology, rather than unifying, will make the wars more terrible. The many plans for world government rather ignored that leaders of nations were unable to surrender the sovereignty entrusted to them to defend. The children of light's plans for a uniting world convention ignored the lack of organic community, which was required for government. For Niebuhr, constitutions were dependent upon the organic factors that gave rise to governments and not only upon the need for them. Constitutional solutions in Niebuhr's perspective were the natural fruit of the children of light. Neither could the children of darkness unite the world through armed force as there were three or four powers that would be able to unite to resist any aggressor. Tillich would, a year later, suggest that a liberal-democratic government might try to move towards world supremacy through combining its moral attractiveness with military power and economic power. But Tillich expected resistance to thwart such development. Tillich in various forums and publications pushed for European federation grounded first in economics and then in government. Though both of them supported the United Nations Organization both knew its development depended upon great power cooperation which would be difficult if not impossible to achieve.

The hopes for a world government held by the children of light presupposed a "social contract" theory of government. Neither Tillich nor Niebuhr believed government to have evolved through "social contract." It assumed an illusory voluntarism on the part of national leaders to act at risk to their nations for the common good. Niebuhr's observation of the failed hopes for "collective security" in the 1930s disillusioned him about the capacity of nations to come to the aid of other nations even when the leadership desired to so act. Beneath it all, pride prevented nations from surrendering their particularity to the universal.

Niebuhr thought it probable that the failure of governance in international politics would lead the major powers to fall back upon balance-of-power politics. Such balancing was neither as evil as children of light thought nor as secure as children of darkness wished. Suspicion and fear would undermine such balancing as they had in World War I and lead to the system's breakdown.

Still he found hope in the great powers reorganizing the world after the war. Necessary agreements among the great powers through understandings and treaties would have to contain elements of justice and some minimal checks on the will of each power. The need to include the minor powers would require more agreements combining elements of treaties with justice. From human necessities international agreements pointed the way toward expanding international law and reducing international chaos. As chaos was subdued, order had to emerge, but tyrannical order needed to be avoided.[7] However, in 1944, he saw that agreements might not be reached and that continents could be portioned into two blocs. But a world division seemed to him to be very insecure.

If legal or constitutional checks of significance could not be agreed upon, then the need for moral restraints upon the great powers increased. But the self-righteousness of the great powers made self restraint and self criticism unlikely. He saw the need for responsible involvement of U.S. power in the mix, but he did not refer in the chapter to the end of the British Empire. Nor did he know anything of the terror of the nuclear age which would soon explode upon them. He knew that pure moralism in international politics was not helpful, and at the time feared the self-righteousness of the Russian Communist creed more than he did American pride. He praised British experience in international relations without reference to the seething discontent in many of the British colonies.

World community was necessary, but it was neither realized nor on any near horizon. So humanity would live with the agenda and hopefully work on it without illusions or near-time success. In concluding his chapter he returned to the language of Christian faith. Rather than being pushed by either sentimentality or despair, he urged faith in a mysterious divine power which would work its purposes out. Human striving would be broken, but humans could still trust that there was meaning known to a universal "Divine Power" whose resources are greater than those of men, and whose suffering love can overcome the corruptions of man's achievements, without negating the significance of our striving."[8]

While the affirmation was of an eschatological note, it preserved "the significance of our striving" which would take him back to Germany in 1946 as part of the rebuilding mission of the United States. He followed this up with one meeting with a group called by Secretary of State Dean Acheson and then to meetings with the Advisory Commission on Cultural Policy in Occupied Territories of the State Department. It further involved him in a two-day consultation with the Foreign Policy Planning Staff of George Kennan, earned him mention as a future secretary of state,[9] and saw him journey to Paris as a member of the U.S. delegation to the United Nations Educational, Scientific, Cultural Organization to work on issues of world community. Democracy needed to be worked at by responsible actions in the details of society and government. His examples of action, though little known, may be of equal significance in his perspective on democracy as many of his writings or his teaching of seminary students. Niebuhr never claimed he mastered the art of activist and scholar. Sometimes he reflected that he might have spent too much time in committee meetings to the neglect of his scholarship. Henry Clark's book[10] attempted to weigh the relevance of Niebuhr's life along with his ideas. He found much to admire in his living of his faith and his perspective on politics. While none of us can refrain from thinking that his overwork may have contributed to his debilitating stroke in 1952, his practical commitments regarding democracy need to be taken seriously. Far too many academics do not or cannot involve themselves in sharpening the democracy they write about or live within.

Tillich discovered that the political irrelevance of his colleagues at the University of Frankfurt contributed to their demise and the rise of Nazism. No institution of democracy deserves to be bereft of its academic support and critique. One of the outstanding scholars of Reinhold Niebuhr thinks that his democratic theory needs to be supplemented by responsible actions.[11] In this he is very correct, and the theory needs to be kept in touch with Niebuhr's own actions to understand its commitment to defense, reform, and action in the midst of political ambiguity.

However, this particular book, *The Children of Light and the Children of Darkness*, is a political act itself comparable to Tillich's speeches on the Voice of America. Niebuhr's political theory had a high role for the place of ideas in politics. Wartime was a time of the struggle of ideas and morals as well as high explosives. Politics was too human to be reduced to numbers, statistics, or theoretical models. Politics was human interactions of people who thought about their actions. Of course, they acted for self and group interests and they often acted brutally in terms of power without much regard for conscience. However, they acted out of their worldviews, and Niebuhr was trying to shape worldviews often at a pretty abstract level. Both the children of light and the children of darkness were ideal types or artificial constructions to cover more data than could be actually subsumed under the labels. Still they are useful and we can weigh foreign policy makers as mixtures of both types. We can understand Niebuhr trying to push his ideals forward in realist terms both in his writing and in his speaking to policy makers.

The message he shared with his followers in the circle of the Fellowship of Socialist Christians was more pessimistic than his coverage of world community in *The Children of Light* intended for a different audience.

> But it is now quite apparent that the nations are not going to abridge their sovereignty sufficiently to establish a really stable world order. They may not even achieve a tentative system of mutual security and drift into policies of unilateral security.
>
> At best we may be able to attain a peace which will lay tentative foundations for a tentative peace, upon which a stronger superstructure may or may not be built in future decades. At worst we will fail and make another war in another generation inevitable. In any event the course of history is a more terrible process than the philosophy of this era, including Christian philosophy comprehends.[12]

By the autumn of 1944 Niebuhr could see that neither the worst nor the best would be realized, and he found Roosevelt, who was running for a fourth term, to be decidedly the better candidate in regards to both domestic and foreign policy.

> Thus far both the American and the other international planners in official position have steered a remarkably shrewd course between the dangers of an abstract and impossible international constitutionalism and those of pure power politics.
>
> The Roosevelt administration has in the past sometimes yielded too much to considerations of expediency. But at the moment it is doing remarkably well in steering toward a genuine international accord with due consideration of all the power political realities involved.[13]

Succeeding reflections on the emerging United Nations organization worried about the dominance of the allies of the war over the smaller nations. But perhaps it was as much as one could expect, perhaps the lesser powers would find ways to increase their influence, and it was not at all sure that the major powers alliance would hold. Already tensions between Russia and the West were becoming apparent. He feared Russia's support of radical change in the economies of Europe while the United States holding to traditional capitalism would give Russia the advantage in Europe. After the election, he reflected on college graduates voting two to one for Dewey assigning this rejection of the preferences of their college professors to their economic interest and their locations in the work force. The alliance of labor with big city bosses and Southern democrats proved effective in winning the election, but he did not regard the alliance as one that would hold in the long run. Republicans tended to build their base among the privileged of the Northern cities and the Midwestern farmers. He reflected upon the uneducated in the working class making the wiser decision in rejecting the candidacy of Dewey and used an example which often appeared in his comments in classes at the Seminary:

> The ignorant man may be too ignorant to make a pair of shoes; but not so ignorant that he does not know if a pair of shoes pinches him. Democracy must depend upon the wisdom of pinched toe and the empty belly.[14]

Niebuhr saw the partition of Europe in the releases from the Yalta Conference, and he was wary that such divisions would lead to future conflicts. It did not presage a successful peace, but perhaps it was the only peace that could be obtained given the forces on the ground and the hatreds from the war. The failure to mention any details about Germany seemed to mean that Germany would be reduced in size and partitioned, and probably looted of its industry in the Russian sector. Apparently Germany was to be destroyed. He feared that the injuries of the war and the resultant hate would lead the conquerors to identify all Germans with the Nazis.

He believed in collective guilt and that Germany had already suffered for it. There were many gradations of guilt from collaboration to resistance to a system which one could not escape. There were partial complicity, momentary complicity, inner resistance with some overt opposition, active outward resistance and many other gradations. He guessed there might be three million Nazis, two million anti-Nazis, and the rest were somewhere in between. He did not expect the nations to make many fine distinctions, but rather to pile on in their punishment of Germans. He hoped for better, but he had no high expectations. He hoped the church would witness that "Vengeance is mine, I will repay, sayeth the Lord." Germany had already paid for its sins under the destruction that followed its aggression, and beyond the punishment of the top leaders and war criminals, he was not advocating further punishment.

The World Situation

In 1945, before the initiation of the nuclear age, Tillich published a major chapter on the world situation in a collection of essays. Since 1934 Tillich had met semiannually with a group that called itself the Theological Discussion Group. The gathering included the Niebuhr brothers, Roland Bainton, Robert Calhoun, John Bennett, Henry P. Van Dusen, Douglas Sterre, George F. Thomas, John Mackay, Georgia Harkness, Benjamin Mays, John Knox, Theodore M. Green, Samuel McCrea Cavert, Edwin E. Aubrey, Wilhelm Pauck, and others. Originally a gathering of young theologians, the group gradually came to represent something of an establishment in American theology. Its members considered the group an important channel of cross-fertilization of ideas. The meetings were generally informal and consisted of discussion of scholarly papers.

Henry Van Dusen sensed an emerging consensus among the group, and in 1945 he edited a collection of essays by some of its members entitled *The Christian Answer*.[15] Tillich contributed the lead piece, "The World Situation." The outcome of the war was clear by the time he wrote in 1944, but the atomic bomb and the full split between Russian and the U.S. were not yet known.

Though Van Dusen's introduction to the volume emphasizes the original process by which the essays were written, criticized, and rewritten, the content of Tillich's essay was not really new. Much of his argument is from *The Religious Situation* published in Germany in 1926 and in the U.S. in 1932, and some other conceptual material is from a fragment of an unpublished manuscript. Tillich had begun work on a volume on "Religion and World Politics,"[16] which was to have been published in German by a Dutch publishing house. The outbreak of the war ended the project, though the original fragment is available in Tillich's

German collected works.[16] Tillich's characteristic dialectic disappeared under Van Dusen's editing, and the claims for the ecumenical church seem to owe more to Van Dusen than to Tillich. However, the essay, which has been reprinted[17] several times, remains one of Tillich's most important statements on social philosophy in his American writings.

The work is an attempt to discover the meaning of a revolution that is absorbing the whole world. The determining force of the emerging, interconnected world is the bourgeois triumph over feudalism and its subsequent control over the fate of the world, and more importantly the ensuing revolt against bourgeois life. World War II is presented as the absorption of the world in the struggle of forces arising out of the failure of bourgeois society to provide security and meaning to the people.

Monopoly capitalism armed with technology had created a Leviathan (a biblical term for a monster from the sea used by Thomas Hobbes to represent government) that was nearly irresistible. The chaos of bourgeois economic life and the wars of the twentieth century, says Tillich, refute the myth of laissez-faire harmony, and society is now in revolt against liberal capitalism. In Italy and Germany it is a fascist revolt; in the U.S. and England it takes the form of New Deal planning and mild socialist measures; and in Russia, Communism expresses the revolt. Humanity could not return to capitalism of recurrent depressions, Tillich argues, so planning is inevitable. Tillich, however, hopes for an order that will avoid "totalitarian absolutism" and "liberal individualism." The danger he sees ahead is the modern Leviathan that is totalitarianism through state or corporate bureaucracies.

In "The World Situation," Tillich shows how personality and community evolve together. His analysis ranges over art, family structure, and education, revealing that the political-economic substance of a culture dominates these cultural expressions. Politics and economics are interdependent, he says, and cannot be separated. Much of postwar Christian social ethics would have had more depth if this interdependence of economics and politics had been kept in view.

Throughout the essay, Tillich's concern for structures that would protect the masses from economic insecurity emerges. His own early experience among the workers in Berlin inclines his writing in favor of security for the masses, and he calls for breaking the power of "large vested interests."[18] Christianity, he argued, must be committed in its struggle against dehumanization to an alliance with the masses for economic reorganization of the system.

Tillich was not an absolutist in defense of democracy as a constitutional form of government. He thought that liberal democracy demanded prerequisites that were not present in most of the world. The basic principle of his political ethics was the rendering of justice to the "dignity of every human being."[19] A distinction must be made, he argued, between the constitutional forms of democracy and democracy as the protection of human dignity. Christianity was allied to the latter cause, but not necessarily to any political form. His colleague Reinhold Niebuhr had offered a more thorough defense of democracy. The two were very close in politics, but Niebuhr was the more thoroughgoing democrat in its political forms. Christianity for Tillich should not sanction abstract forms of democracy that hid the "destruction of community and personality."[20]

The old balance of power politics of nineteenth-century Europe was inadequate for the twentieth century. Tillich saw hope resting in a federation of nations not overly dominated by the victorious allies, but the world lacked the unifying spirit to make such a federation a reality. Christianity needed to commit itself to the building of a common spirit within the world. Such a task required an inclusive ecumenical Christianity. Existential and universal truth would need to be unified within an inclusive church if the church were to rise to the occasion demanded by the world situation.

Tillich summarized the situation: A world revolution was underway against a bourgeois order. Christianity had to protect the masses from meaninglessness and insecurity by promoting a new order. Such an agenda required an ecumenical, progressive Christianity, which remained realistic in the midst of tragedy. Tillich's vision during the closing years of the war was essentially the same as during the later years of the Weimar Republic. The victory of an autonomous (revolutionary, self-directed) humanity was affirmed in all its radicalness. Solutions of returning to totalitarian heteronomy (rule by outside forces) were to be avoided even when autonomy was threatening, but humanity had to move on to a theonomous (humanity finding divine resources freely) culture in which a modern solution for people in community could be found.[21]

In his radio speeches Tillich had hoped for the ending of the war before Christmas 1944, but the German defense until Hitler's suicide sacrificed hundreds of thousands more until May of 1945. Neither Tillich nor Niebuhr wanted unbridled capitalism and Communism in a divided Europe to be the conclusion to this horrible tragedy. But by Yalta the jockeying for power positions became apparent and Tillich saw the seeds of the next war taking root in the conclusion of this war. The dismemberment of Germany and the looting of its industry for Russia would further European poverty, insecurity, and German irredentism. Niebuhr wrote of three ways: socialism under totalitarianism as in Russia, capitalism and democracy as in the United States, and his preferred option after the Labour Party's victory—democracy and socialism as in Great Britain.[22] They both wanted democratic socialism for a restored Europe both feared the solution of capitalism and Communism and, of course, neither could see the evolution of Europe to a mixture of democratic socialisms and mixed economies.

By the end of the year, the war would bring Tillich and Niebuhr in their reflections on international politics three pressing moral issues: the bomb, the future of Judaism, and the Cold War.

12

The Bomb

Niebuhr, Tillich, Bennett, and the Bomb

Church leaders and the public knew nothing about the development of the atomic bomb as decisions were made by scientists, military people, and a few civilian officials, particularly President Roosevelt and later Truman. On some other war-related issues, church leaders were ahead of the political leadership. Reinhold Niebuhr, for example, had told of the murder of Jews in camps as early as 1933. Paul Tillich had denounced the anti-Semitism of Nazism before it was understood in the United States. John Foster Dulles, as chairman of the Federal Council of Churches Commission, had met with President Roosevelt advocating an international organization. In 1944–1945 the church was developing American opinion to reverse its shortsighted rejection of the League of Nations, and to support a new and strengthened United Nations. Church leaders had denounced obliteration bombing of cities and questioned demands for unconditional surrender. But on the development of nuclear weapons they were silent in their innocence. On the coming of the new nuclear age they did not see the signs of the times. Paul Tillich's brilliant *The World Situation* published in 1945, for example, has no mention of the new warfare soon to be revealed. Meanwhile the Manhattan project was going ahead across the street from Union Theological Seminary.

In June 1945, the president of Union Seminary and the editorial board of *Christianity and Crisis* had spoken out against the single-minded slogan of unconditional surrender and against obliteration bombing. Henry Pitney van Dusen wrote these two criticisms of the administration in the issue of *Christianity and Crisis* dated 6 August 1945, and quoted Bishop Bell:

> The Rev. George Kennedy Bell, Bishop of Chichester, wrote: There are certain deeds which science should not do. There are certain actions for which scientists should not be made conscripts by any nation. And surely the extermination of any civilian population by any nation is one of these.[1]

By October 1945, Reinhold Niebuhr saw that neither world control of atomic energy nor the outlawing of the bomb was going to be realized. He had some hope for sharing atomic knowledge in a thorough-going settlement of issues with the Soviet Union, but he knew that too was beyond immediate political realization.[2]

The earliest semiofficial church statement on atomic warfare was the release in the spring of 1946 of the report of the Commission on the Relation of the Church to the War in the Light of the Christian Faith. The report is widely referred to by the name of its chairman, Robert L. Calhoun, professor of Historical Theology, Yale University, as the "Calhoun Report." The report involved nearly two dozen leading professors of theology and Christian ethics, mostly from the eastern corridor of schools, including one woman and one African-American. John C. Bennett served as secretary and drafted most of the report. Throughout his long career he would continue to write, teach, and debate on these subjects. Both of the Niebuhr brothers were present.

The theology of the report is theocentric, with God understood as creator, redeemer, and judge. The report, after a theological analytic preface, begins with repentance. "We would begin with an act of contrition. As American Christians we are deeply penitent for the irresponsible use already made of the atomic war."[3]

The "surprise bombings" without warning were specifically regarded as "morally indefensible." Further argument referred to the discussion among scientists of an alternative demonstrative use. Japan's position in 1945 had been hopeless, but the report conceded the bombing may have shortened the war.

The report put the atomic bomb in the context of the preatomic obliteration bombing and rejected the arguments of military necessity alone deciding the issues. They pointed to U.S. Air Force studies which were showing that obliteration bombing had not been, on the whole, a military success. Four theses were put forward: (1) these new methods are intolerable to Christian conscience and Christians need to resist their use; (2) war itself is the problem; (3) the U.S. was urged to stop production of atomic bombs and to promise no first use; and (4) U.N. control of atomic weapons was needed. Through 1945–1946, Niebuhr's editorials in *Christianity and Society* reflected either hope or discouragement as the reports about the difficulties of establishing any international controls on atomic energy became available. By the summer of 1946, he knew that his hopes for a stable peace arrangement over Europe founded on cooperation between East and West had been in vain. There was too much fear and suspicion on both sides, and any suggestion of Western initiatives to accommodate Russian fears were decried as signs of appeasement.

The church's role was in helping the spirit of worldwide community to grow. Penitence for wartime crimes was called for. The temptations to over-punish the vanquished enemies needed to be overcome. Hiroshima and Nagasaki should be rebuilt and the churches could lead the financial drive. The report concluded with the final third being theological analysis of ultimate issues of faith.

Robert C. Batchelder has called attention to the conditioning of the report by World War II with the expectation that war would be total war. Therefore, the war problem itself was attacked. The report focused on the tilting of the advantage to aggressive rather than defensive war and the advantage to the attacker of surprise attack or treachery.

Conant-Niebuhr Exchange

The theologians denouncing the nuclear attacks on Hiroshima and Nagasaki led James Conant, the president of Harvard University, to respond sharply to Reinhold Niebuhr. If Niebuhr had been innocent of knowledge of uranium's potential before the atomic bomb, Conant had led in the development of the bomb from the beginning. Serving as scientific advisor to President Roosevelt and as a member of the "top policy group" on atomic weapons, he at several points had played a central role in advancing the weapons. As an early scientific negotiator with the British he had advised Churchill, as well as Roosevelt, and after the war he would discuss scientific cooperation with Stalin and the use of nuclear energy for peace. Conant was an active interventionist against Nazism before Pearl Harbor and a militant articulator of the policies of unconditional surrender. He approved of the use of the bomb on Hiroshima, as well as the firebombing of Tokyo. His relationship with Niebuhr was one of friendship and admiration. He had courted Niebuhr to come to Harvard as a university professor. Niebuhr's pragmatism and realism were both sympathetic to the president of Harvard's own intellectual commitment. Conant's son, Theodore, described Niebuhr's wartime book, *The Children of Light and the Children of Darkness,* as his father's guiding philosophy. "If he had an equivalent of the Old Testament for an orthodox Jew it was *The Children of Light and the Children of Darkness.*"[4]

Conant would write to Niebuhr three times in March 1946. Conant's letters were personal, but they were also symptomatic of his broader postwar campaigns to justify the bombings. He urged and corrected the McGeorge Bundy ghost-written essay for Stimson justifying the bombing. He tried to stop and participated in altering an MGM film about Hiroshima. He was very active in publicly arguing for correctness of the decision to drop the weapon which he had urged forward and helped to manage. The campaign he and others promoted to win acceptance of the bombing and the weapons was largely victorious. By 1950 most of the church leaders who had condemned the bombing were learning to accept the weapons and deterrence.[5] It awaited further work by ethicists and historians to refute the arguments that the bomb itself stopped the war and led to

Japan's surrender, or that the bomb was necessary to prevent a costly United States' invasion of Japan.

Conant responded to the *New York Times'* account of the Commission of the Federal Council of Churches' report and Niebuhr's participation. Some of Conant's concerns might have been alleviated if he had read the whole report. But, even so, after Niebuhr's responses he had to conclude that the two were still in disagreement.

His first complaint was that the report did not adequately relate the atomic bomb to the accepted practices of strategic or area bombing. If we were to be penitent for the atomic bomb and the incendiary destruction of Tokyo then "the whole method of warfare used against the axis powers" was questioned.

Moreover, he feared that the Protestant leaders would cut themselves off from the majority of American opinion which supported the atomic bomb as "part and parcel of the total operation of that war." Then he asked sarcastically: "Are we to scrap all our armament at once?"[6]

In the last paragraph he states that he is "a great believer in eliminating the atomic bomb as a potential weapon for a surprise through international control."[7] But, of course, that would be very difficult to achieve. A postscript is even more barbed. He mentions recommending Niebuhr's book, *Children of Light and Children of Darkness,* to a clergyman who denounced him for his role in the atomic bomb. But then he adds: "I can't reconcile this book with your signature on the document in question."[8]

Niebuhr's response was irenic. He pointed out that the report made "no absolute distinction" between the levels of destructiveness achieved by different weapons. He referred to the reports mentioning that Air Force studies showed that obliteration bombing was not very effective.

Then he pointed out that the majority of the committee objected to the use of the bomb without warning. They had believed the bomb should have been demonstrated and Japan warned. He then went on to say that the conviction of most of the committee was that the bomb could have eventually been used and justifiably so for the "shortening of the war." The ordinary argument about saving the lives of thousand of American soldiers who would die on the beaches in an invasion was also affirmed. Then he wrote a long paragraph about the guilt that good people incur in defeating tyranny. He signed the report he wrote "to admit the moral ambiguity of all righteous people in history, who are, despite the good they do, involved in antecedent and in marginal guilt."

The tone of Niebuhr's letter is compromising; the tone of the report had been alarming and condemnatory. Sentences of the report were as threatening as Carl Sagan's *The Nuclear Winter*. If Conant had seen the whole church report and not just the newspaper accounts he would have understood that the practice of obliteration bombing was judged immoral and against the laws of God. The line the church leaders wanted to hold after the war between obliteration bombing of cities and attacks on military targets was one that the president of Harvard did not discern or, at least, acknowledge. Neither did President Truman make that distinction in his writing and speeches on the bomb.

Paul Tillich shared the dilemma of the church statements that rejected total war, but did not completely renounce the bomb. The Federal Council report of the Dunn Commission of 1950 saw the need for deterrence and would not give up even the first possible use of the bomb. Batchelder reports that the Catholic moralists who wrote *The Ethics of Atomic War* in 1947 saw the dilemma and affirmed both the immorality of bombing a city and the possible necessity for so doing. Similarly the British Council of Churches' *The Era of Atomic Power* could neither sanction the use of atomic weapons nor demand their abandonment in the present situation. Batchelder believes the Federal Council of Churches' commission of 1950 of which Bennett, Niebuhr, and Tillich were members escaped the dilemma by drawing the line between bombing of cities and other uses of nuclear weapons. The moral distinctions are not between instruments in warfare. Atomic bombs may, under some circumstances, be used, but their indiscriminate use had to be avoided. Niebuhr's introduction to the statement in *Christianity and Crisis* calls attention to four aspects of the report.[9]

> (1) The report is set in context of historical responsibilities to defend Western civilization.
> (2) No absolute distinction among kinds of weapons is made morally. So the report refuses to denounce specifically all possible first uses of atomic weapons.
> (3) The primary task is to avoid war through development of non-Communist worlds, unity of allied nations, and international courage. Preventive war and/or inevitable war understandings are rejected.
> (4) The difference between destruction of military targets and mass destruction of civilian population was central to the report.

Two pacifists on the Dunn Commission who refused to sign the final report published their dissent. The context of the Dunn report was the beginning of the Korean War and though this expressed itself in the sentences affirming the struggle with Communism it failed to note that the present wars were limited and the nuclear weapons, while relevant, were unlikely to be used. Batchelder is very critical of these church studies in their failure to focus on limited wars. The pacifists felt that not enough distinctive Christian guidance was given and that a more thorough theological document was needed. The 1950 document was more aware of the Cold War and the Korean War and less critical of atomic weapons in themselves than the 1946 piece. The church was learning to live with the weapons. The strongest statements of the Dunn Commission were the condemnation of any use of nuclear weapons against massive civilian populations.

Paul Tillich joined Reinhold Niebuhr and John Bennett in signing the report. Niebuhr had endorsed the "no first use of hydrogen weapons" in 1950 while conceding that in the Cold War context the United States could not refrain from developing them after the Soviet Union had detonated the atomic bomb. Seeing the Baruch plan for international control defeated and finding little hope in nuclear disarmament negotiations with the U.S.S.R., he pleaded for restraint in U.S. plans to rely on the bomb.[10] In 1951 while suffering reverses in Korea, Niebuhr pled for avoidance of use of the nuclear weapons. Even though the U.S. position in Asia was very weak, the first responsibility was to avoid nuclear war. Even though agreement with Russia was probably not possible, no fatalism regarding war with Russia should be tolerated by Christians. To assume the inevitably of nuclear war was blasphemous.

In Tillich's own writing he argued that a war fought with nuclear weapons could not be justified. It was not permissible to enter a war which included the intention to use nuclear weapons. Such a war would only bring mutual destruction and no intended goal of the war could be fulfilled. He noted that Western allies could, if they had the will, develop conventional armaments adequate to deter any Communist invasion in Europe. He leaned toward a position of no first use of nuclear weapons as the Commission had declared, but he also allowed the West some ambiguity in announcing such a policy. Until adequate conventional forces were created, "maybe it was safer to keep the Communists uncertain about first use."[11] However, the logic of deterrence meant: "Our intention to answer any nuclear attack with nuclear weapons must be absolutely clear, and it must also be clear that we have the power to do so."[12]

A remarkable short statement by Tillich was published in 1954 in *Pulpit Digest* on the hydrogen bomb. It consisted of only five points. Humanity may destroy itself by the tensions in itself. The meaning of history is not dependent on how humanity is annihilated. Resistance to self-destruction is called forth by all persons who are aware of humanity's suicidal instincts. The resistance must be carried out in all levels of politics, morals, and religions including "a new expression of the ultimate concern which transcends as well as determines historical existence."[13] Finally, the acts of resistance must unite all these different levels of concern and be done with wisdom and courage. The emphasis on resistance to human self-destruction was new and it did not simply follow Niebuhr and Bennett.

The correspondence in the Harvard archive indicates that Tillich was repeatedly requested by the American Friends Service Commission, the National Committee for a Sane Nuclear Policy, and other organizations to endorse their positions against weapons testing and for nuclear disarmament. He refused to give any of the organizations wholehearted support, and he especially resisted their pacifist leanings. He did sign a statement of the Committee for a Sane Nuclear Policy in 1957 calling for arms control and the abolition of nuclear testing. The statement was published in the *New York Times* on 15 November 1957. Other signatures included long-standing pacifists, antiwar activists, religious leaders, Eleanor Roosevelt, and John Bennett whose guidance Tillich often sought on these questions. Reinhold Niebuhr, who was a little more of a cold warrior than John Bennett, refrained from signing, though on most issues Bennett, Niebuhr, and Tillich were agreed. Tillich's Harvard secretary, Grace Leonard, was a member of SANE, and through her influence Tillich agreed to SANE's 1961 use of his statement in the *Pulpit Digest* on resistance to the hydrogen bomb.

After Reinhold Niebuhr's stroke in 1952, John Bennett, the younger colleague of both Niebuhr and Tillich, took the lead in writing the frequent articles and essays on nuclear weapons in *Christianity and Crisis*. Though mindful of the full context of the Cold War, Bennett would focus his direct attention on the problems of the weapons themselves. Niebuhr usually accentuated not the weapons but the conflict that encouraged development of the weapons. Tillich made shorter contributions to the discussion which revealed great passion and deep concern about the problem, but he was not the leader. Bennett's recollection, shortly before his death in 1995, was that Niebuhr's thought provided the leadership on this issue. But it was Bennett who edited the book *Nuclear Weapons and the Conflict of Conscience*. Niebuhr wrote a very laudatory review of it.

Niebuhr's major contribution was the chapter "The Cold War and the Nuclear Dilemma" in his 1959 volume *The Structure of Nations and Empires*. He could find no way out of the dilemma which was the necessity of possessing the weapons and the moral impossibility of using them. All three of the Christian realists recognized the need in a nuclear age for the deterrence, but all of them were horrified at thoughts of first use, preventive war, or preventive strike use of the weapons. Accepting that neither side intended to initiate a major conflict, it could still come upon them. Even so the prospects for either disarmament or arms control seemed minor until the hostilities of the Cold War faded. Capitulation of the allied side seemed unrealistic to Niebuhr, though some in the West advocated it. He did not expect capitulation from the Communist side except in the long range of hundreds of years. Attempts to limit the conflict to tactical weapons in Europe as Kissinger had proposed did not seem realistic to Niebuhr in 1959, though he had hailed Kissinger's book. His one hope was in the waning of the Communist fervor as the original generations of revolutionaries faded from the scene. We were not fated to confront fanatical Communism forever, but Communism was perceived to have advantages in the third world, and he did not see its demise in the foreseeable future. Occasionally, reports of scientific dialogue between scientists from the USA and the USSR, the ABM treaty, or the partial test-ban treaty would raise his hopes that incremental steps might add up to significant progress in relationships with the USSR, but his overall perspective was pessimistic and he expected ongoing conflict mediated by fears of mutual annihilation and processes of diplomacy.

The dangers of the 1961 Berlin crisis led to Paul Tillich's participation in the debates again. It is hard for us to remember the sense of danger that accompanied the Kennedy presidency. I was in Europe during the summer of 1961, and I particularly remember the sense of crisis and the foreboding dark fears of pessimism of Norman Vincent Peale with whom I was visiting in Interlaken. Informed people knew that Berlin was near the crux of the Cold War and that the young president was being tested very threateningly by Khrushchev. Tillich with the realism of his own theology and his central European experience could not regard shifts in the borders of Berlin or its politics as the ultimate issue. His appearance on a panel discussion program of Eleanor Roosevelt's with Henry Kissinger, James Reston, and Max Freedman revealed the deep caution with which Niebuhr, Bennett, and Tillich all regarded the use of nuclear weapons. The panel was dominated by the hard-line cold warriors. A few days later James Reston attacked Tillich (the *New York Times*, 25 October 1961) for Tillich's refusal to approve defending Berlin with nuclear weapons. For Tillich, defense was a moral necessity, but to defend someone in actions which meant their destruction violated the reason for defense. Particularly noteworthy in Tillich's analysis, a theme that appeared elsewhere in his writing, is the insight that even retreat is not the end. Retreat is a normal strategic move. He knew and wrote in *Partisan Review* in 1962 that in the long run the West was militarily superior to the Warsaw Pact nations. The avoidance of retreat was no excuse for relying on nuclear weapons in a suicidal manner.

The Christian realists quickly picked up the debate in November 1961.[14] Bennett led by calling for more significant participation in these nuclear moral issues and cautioning about any violation of the firebreak between conventional and nuclear weapons use. Niebuhr added a short response agreeing that the only use of the weapons for the West was in deterrence or in a second strike to prevent any further attacks by the enemy who had already unleashed nuclear weapons. Kenneth Thompson in the same issue refused to go to the "no first use" position and cautioned Bennett against strident moral protest. Tillich published the statement which had led to the attacks on his recommendation of no defense of his home city of Berlin with nuclear weapons. Tillich's statement was a shortened form of his own formulation of the justified war. Proportionality was built into the requirement that any recourse to war must serve creative justice. Atomic war, he concluded, cannot be justified ethically. Therefore, while defense was required, temporary retreat until the allies could redress the conventional forces was an ordinary tactic and was preferred to any initiation of a nuclear exchange. The criticism directed at the no-first-use policy of these Christian realists was that to telegraph beforehand that you would not defend a vulnerable position with nuclear weapons invited attack. For their part the Christian realists regarded the first use of atomic weapons as wrong and they did not want to be the first to use them ever again.

Summary

The Christian realism of these two thinkers and the additional contributions of Bennett, had several distinctive emphases. The atomic bombing of Hiroshima and Nagasaki was morally wrong. Cities should never be the object of nuclear weapon attack or obliteration bombing in warfare. It was necessary to retain nuclear weapons as long as one's enemy possessed them. It was morally wrong to use nuclear weapons first. The danger of war remained even though neither superpower intended to begin a nuclear exchange. Incremental reduction of the danger of war and the decrease of nuclear terror were possible through creative diplomacy and the probing of the other's position to find out where agreement was possible. They did not foresee any near end to the Cold War, and they did not trust much in disarmament negotiations while the political issues were divisive.

After the assassination of President Kennedy, Tillich's public political role decreased, though he did, as a systematic theologian, issue a denunciation of Goldwater partially because of Goldwater's saber rattling. Niebuhr followed the debates until his death in 1971, growing increasingly concerned about the dominance of the military under Presidents Johnson and Nixon in the context of the Vietnam War. Bennett's debates with Paul Ramsey continued the in-house Christian realist debates. Bennett exalted over the collapse of the USSR and the decrease in the nuclear dangers. In his last Christmas letter he quoted Simeon, "Now let thy servant depart in peace."

In conclusion, there is a lot of wisdom in this Christian realism. During his lifetime some critics who disagreed with Reinhold on the evil of Communism, now think he was more correct than they were. Bennett was not in agreement with criticisms of deterrence as immoral. Its intention to be used under certain circumstances against enemy civilians rendered it morally indefensible for many including the Presbyterian Church, as was argued in my writings, *The Peacemaking Struggle* (1985), *Presbyterians and Peacemaking: Are We Now Called to Resistance* (1985), and *Christian Realism and Peace Making* (1988). Neither Reinhold Niebuhr nor Paul Tillich would have felt free to recommend abandoning deterrence. Niebuhr left it at the dilemma level with the only possible use in a defensive strike. Tillich stayed with the use of war only as an act of creative justice and did not reject deterrence. Some think that the Christian moralist must reject nuclear deterrence morally and then urge creative solutions moving us away from reliance on nuclear weapons. The moral rejection of deterrence does not mean policies of surrender or immediate unilateral disarmament. That is not how policy works. The Christian moralist fulfills the vocation by as clearly as possible saying what is intolerable and working with others to find ways to move out of the morally impossible structures.

Niebuhr warned us as well as anyone about the imponderables, surprises, and ironies of history. Niebuhr did not expect the early end of the Soviet Empire, and he did not live to see it. The collapse was mostly due to the failure of the ideas of Communism and this is quite ironic for a historical materialist system. Maybe he was a little too pessimistic about arms control agreements, but not very much. His optimism was probably more misplaced in his hopes for UNESCO and the Alliance for Progress. At this point it seems useful to note that this Christian Realism was quite different from government policy, though McNamara's strategies on weapons of mass destruction brought the government closer to the realist sense of morality. Though they often found wisdom in Kissinger, Kahn and other mainstream nuclear theorists, their moral reservations and critique were present. Notes of unilateral initiatives recommended by Bennett and Tillich's resistance to nuclear weapons and the necessity of relying on conventional defense took these Christian realists a long way from harder realism or *realpolitik,* and U.S. government policy. Finally, Tillich's refusal to regard even atomic warfare as ultimate kept it in perspective. Ultimately, there was God and not decisions by politicians or generals. The nuclear question intersected the second question left over from the war: the question of Jewish security after the Holocaust.

13

The Jewish Question

The meaning of the term "Zionism" has varied according to the multiple positions of those claiming to be Zionists. The meaning of the term "Christian" also has many meanings. The use of Christian as an adjective modifying Zionism seems peculiar as Zionism is a Jewish movement. It seems better to regard some Christians as pro-Zionist rather than as Zionists. Here in reference to Reinhold Niebuhr and Paul Tillich it means that they come to support the establishment of a "Jewish state" in Israel as Christian theologians. As a Jew can be a Zionist without migrating to Israel or a Christian may be a Marxist-Christian without subscribing to the metaphysics of Karl Marx, so it is possible for a Christian to be pro-Zionist in the sense of supporting Jewish migration to Israel and the consolidation of the Jewish people into a state. Following contemporary usage, Zionism implies more than the "national homeland" of the Balfour declaration and it is not reconcilable with the "unitary, nonsectarian state" of El Fatah.

Zionism may be summarily defined as the Jewish nationalist movement whose endeavors to solve the "Jewish problem" led to the establishment of the "Jewish state" of Israel.[1]

It is not self-evident that American theologians would support Zionism. None of the major church positions could really be regarded as Zionist, though they accept Israel. The tendency of the Christian archaeological community which has worked in Jordan, the American missionary interests, liberation theologians, and official church boards to be pro-Palestinian and slightly hostile to Israeli expansionism is generally recognized.

Friendships with and Respect for Jews

Both Niebuhr and Tillich formed close friendships with Jews who were allied in struggling for social justice. Both of them had grown up in parsonages of German parentage, Niebuhr in Missouri and Illinois and Tillich in Eastern Germany and Berlin. Tillich remembered that though anti-Semitism had been discussed in his home, it had been rejected by his parents. Neither, as youth, of course, was free from the anti-Judaism sentiments their church contexts encouraged. As an adult, Tillich remarked that as a young boy, particularly during Holy Week, he found the anti-Judaism teaching of the church impressed upon him. Reinhold Niebuhr recorded how as a young boy he observed the stereotyping of Jewish businessmen in his Midwestern town. The generous, courteous Jewish merchant was thought of by the Gentiles as atypical; the prosperous, rather pushy Jewish capitalist was regarded as typical. As a young boy who knew few Jews, he had no basis for ignoring or judging such stereotyping.

Their friendships with Jews that are documented are post-World War I. Niebuhr in his last book documented the importance of his friendship in Detroit with Fred Butzel. Niebuhr liked to quote his mentor, the Episcopalian Bishop Charles Williams, a follower of the social gospel who said: "In the weightier matters of social justice there are only two Christians in Detroit, and they are both Jews."[2] Niebuhr reflected on the sources of the social-righteousness he perceived among Jews. He thought that perhaps it should be attributed to the prophetic tradition. He noted that many of the most religious Jews attributed it to the Torah. Butzel, however, who had served with Niebuhr on the Mayor's Race Committee, attributed the passion for social righteousness to their minority status which resulted in suspicion of the establishment and compassion for other minorities. Niebuhr never resolved the issue in his own mind, but noted that Butzel's genius was responsible for the beginning of "my long love affair with the Jewish people."[3]

His respect for the Jews had led him in an early article to contrast their concern for social justice with the relative impotence of German-Americans in supporting any progressive causes. The superiority of Jewish social sensitivity to most Protestant social consciousness was to remain a theme throughout Niebuhr's teaching and writing. The urban pastorate of Detroit was essential to developing Niebuhr's own social realism and part of that mixture was his debt to Jewish friends.

Soon after returning to Berlin in the closing months of World War I Tillich was leading a small discussion group of intellectuals for religious socialism. The group became known as the Kairos Circle, after Tillich's use of the concept. It included Jews, notably Eduard Heimann and Adolf Löwe. They taught the young Christian theologian economics and implanted their influence in his social philosophy. They were to continue as his close friends throughout his life sharing his exile, his wine, and helping to shape his mind. The context of his friendships with Jews is different than Niebuhr's, but also similar in pressing social conflicts, alliances with Jewish leaders, and resulting friendships.

In retrospect the Frankfurt Institute for Social Research dominated by assimilated Jews may be said to have been slow in perceiving the dangers of anti-Semitism prevailing in Germany. After Tillich shared dismissal from the University of Frankfurt with Mannheim, Horkheimmer, and Sinzheimer of the Institute and other Jews, he would help to rally them at his home in exile at Union Seminary in New York City.

Tillich as dean of the philosophy faculty was at the center of the struggle for the University of Frankfurt. When storm troopers attacked Jewish students, he took them to his office for protection and medical aid. He demanded in print the expulsion of students who joined the storm troopers. He was attacked in the *Frankfurter Zeitung* and passages from his *The Socialist Decision* were quoted to prove him an enemy of the new order. Earlier Max Horkheimmer had warned him that certain sentences in *The Socialist Decision* would cost him his life. He was suspended from his post on 13 April 1933. Further consultations with the ministry of education at which Tillich pushed questions concerning governmental attitudes toward Jews and modern culture proved that Tillich's academic career in Germany was over.

These Jewish friends of Niebuhr and Tillich were not necessarily Zionists, but the friendships laid the groundwork for a deep emphatic reaction to the Holocaust and the founding of Israel. Before Herbert Marcuse moved to California, he was often present at Tillich's apartment as were other Jewish friends from the Berlin and Frankfurt days. In later years Abraham Heschel and Reinhold Niebuhr formed a close friendship which had a mutual influence on each other's thought. Gradually traffic between Jewish Theological Seminary and Union Theological Seminary across Broadway increased as mutual trust and respect between their institutions deepened.

The early socialism of the new state drew the respect of both Tillich and Niebuhr. Another strain of these political thinkers inclined them to respect Jewish developments in the land of Israel. Both thinkers relied heavily on the Hebrew prophets in their preaching and teaching. More fundamental, however, was the use of prophetic religion to describe their social theology. They intended that history be taken seriously but not absolutized. They pleaded for active, progressive political involvement that eschewed all fanaticisms and determinisms. Their sympathies for some of Marx's social thought rested on their detection of genuinely prophetic elements within his thought. Their respect for the Hebrew prophets was so great that the term *prophet* is perhaps the best single tribute to Reinhold Niebuhr. He read the contingent in terms of the eternal and fought and pled for justice. The socialist journal that Niebuhr founded, *Radical Religion,* understood itself to be representing the prophetic spirit under the conditions of the twentieth century. Doom was pronounced on the tottering house of capitalism, and justice was demanded in the name of God. Like the prophet Jonah before him Niebuhr was perhaps surprised when Nineveh repented and was spared.

Tillich's Spirit of Judaism

Tillich understood his best work of social philosophy to be derived from the spirit of Judaism. The explicit connections between prophetic religion and social criticism are seen in Tillich's major work on social theory, *The Socialist Decision* (1933). Tillich criticized Nazism's pretensions to be scientific. While admitting its philosophy was powerful poetry tending toward ecstatic and revolutionary apocalypticism, he dismissed it as a serious school of thought. It was a demonic movement in its attempt to make sacred leader, race, party, and space. The only action of integrity for the church was to oppose Nazism. Nazism was understood as an alternative religious attempt to create a system of meaning and solution by a leap back to myths of origin without critical inquiry.

The spirit of Nazism was essentially opposed to the spirit of Judaism which was located in the worship of the God who transcended blood, soil, and communal loyalties, and demanded justice. The pagan myths of origin were broken in the Hebrew Bible and so the Old Testament should be interpreted as opposed by Nazism. The spirit of Judaism was eternally an adversary to the spirit of political romanticism. Myths of origin could still be found in biblical Jewish faith but only in a criticized mode. Christianity and especially the churches of the Reformation had to join with Judaism in the affirmation of the prophetic critique of romanticism. The political romanticism of Nazism was a countermovement against the prophetic in religion and humanism in culture.

Tillich criticized socialism which neglected its prophetic heritage and so lacked the power of expectation. A rediscovery of eschatology would, he thought, show socialism how it could reform its ideology. There were imminent possibilities within the proletariat which had to be emphasized in a call for the transformation of the human situation. In fact, for Tillich the essence of the socialist principle is expectation or political eschatology. The essential point for the argument is that Tillich found in the Hebrew prophets a political eschatology which was necessary for the reform of socialism and to save Germany and the world from the barbarism of the Nazi movement. However, 1933 was too late; socialism was exhausted, capitalism was disgraced and fragmented, conservatism was irrelevant and chaos and war resulted.

In 1933, Niebuhr criticized the churches for their quietism in regard to the "extravagances of Nazi terror." He detailed anti-Semitic atrocities and called for a worldwide Christian protest against the Nazi government. He had only a little respect for the German churches and he thought that sensitivity to the feelings of German Christians ought not to dull the protest. In August 1933, he criticized not only the announced policies of the Nazis but the execution of Jews.

In New York both Tillich and Niebuhr joined with Jewish friends in organizing relief programs for exiles from Germany and in criticizing anti-

Semitism. After becoming an American citizen, Tillich spoke publicly at political rallies beginning in Madison Square Garden as Niebuhr was doing consistently.

Niebuhr's arguments for a Jewish homeland appeared in *The Nation*[4] in 1942. Recognizing Judaism as a nationality as well as a cultural and religious group, he argued for a homeland after the Holocaust. He regarded it as a solution to be contained within British imperial policy and American foreign policy as part of the postwar settlement. Arguments for Jewish rights were set in the context of the need for settlement of Arab claims. He criticized Zionist claims that there would be no "injustices" to Arabs, but he hoped for an overall settlement which would compensate for losses. Later he detailed arguments for joint economic development which would assist Palestinians and assuage the tensions from their losses. These articles and articles by others in his *Christianity and Crisis* set him against the anti-Zionist policies of the *Christian Century* and the immediate past and then current president of Union Theological Seminary.

The increase in Zionist militancy was reflected in the formation of the Christian Council on Palestine in mid-1942. Paul Tillich and Reinhold Niebuhr were joined by three others as the executive committee. Between 1942 and 1946, when it merged into the American Christian Palestine Committee, it recruited 3,000 American clergymen to subscribe to its pro-Zionist principles. In the preface to Waldo Frank's book, *The Jew in Our Day*, Niebuhr argued for political security for the Jews in Palestine "without reference to the final religious problem."[5] Fishman has detailed the political intrigues of these Christian Zionists during the war.[6] Carl Voss, the secretary of the Council, was in the process of writing a book on this story when he died.

When the Anglo-American Committee of Inquiry held hearings in Washington, D.C., Niebuhr testified for the Christian Council in Palestine on 14 January 1946. He argued for a Jewish state and more openness to Jewish immigration in Palestine. The final report of the Committee essentially agreed, as did President Truman, but the British government referred the issue to the United Nations in 1947.

The similarities in the writing of Tillich and Niebuhr on Judaism are striking. They rejected aggressive mission to convert Jews to Christianity. They continued the dialogue with Jewish friends and expressed a willingness to help Jews who were alienated from Judaism to find meaning in Christianity. They both affirmed the need for preserving Judaism against tendencies in Christianity to relapse into paganism.

During the war they both called for the defeat of Germany and urged Western nations to secure the safety of the Jews. Both urged distinctions between the guilt of the regime and the guilt of the German people. Both sought to encourage forces in Germany which could act against Hitler, and both urged restraint in the practice of war and for policies which would encourage resistance within Germany. They came to recognize the need for a homeland for the Jewish people; they were not absolutist about the need for it to be in Israel. As with other Zionists, they debated other options. But the establishment of Israel in 1948 they accepted as fact. Israel was the response to the Holocaust. For them the two are historically tied together. Niebuhr would comment on each of Israel's wars revealing both his love for Israel and his stance against Arab politics. With the aid of secular and religious Jews he founded Americans for Democratic Action which continued political support for Israel among American liberals.

Anti-Semitism and Zionism

Tillich analyzed German guilt for World War II activities against the Jews in 1953 in Berlin. Though he knew Germans did not want to think about their guilt, he regarded it as of the first importance for Germans to come to grips with it. The primary guilt lay upon those directly responsible for the atrocities and, of course, only some Germans were so responsible. A secondary type of guilt derived from failure to act responsibly, and he affirmed that he was guilty of not acting more boldly as the German political situation deteriorated in 1932–1933. Most Germans, he thought, participated in some of the other three types of guilt: the guilt of suppressing knowledge; the forgetting of one's responsibility for the past; and the guilt of regarding the past as over with no consequences for the present. He regarded the guilt that was troubling Germany as operating at psychological depths in much of the population. He urged its recognition and that positive steps be taken to deal with it.

In dealing with Christian anti-Semitism Tillich used an analysis of five types of guilt. In regard to the question of the guilt of Jews for the death of Jesus, he found none of the types of guilt applicable. The accusation that Jews were guilty for the death of Jesus was absurd. His program to free the churches from anti-Semitism involved the review of church publications to purge them of dangerous stereotypes; the emphasis on the Old Testament in the church; the abandonment of the active missionary movement to Jews; the sharing of worship services; the alliance for the struggle for social justice; theological dialogue; and the acceptance of the continuity and authenticity of Jewish faith. The primary witness of the power of Christ to Judaism would be in the demonstration of the quality of life in Christianity that would eradicate the demon of anti-Semitism in the life of the church.

Tillich had known Judaism as the faith of a dispersed people without a land for most of his life. He assisted in the founding of the American Christian Palestine Committee which promoted sympathy for Israel in the U.S. In explaining his pro-Zionist position, he reported how his own position had changed. His earlier teaching that Israel was a people of time without attachment to space was mistaken. Europe was not a secure haven for the Jews; they had to have their own place where they could protect themselves. Assimilation of the Jews in European culture had been a disaster; they had to find their own way. The average Jew was not a prophetic figure who should suffer in dispersion for the world; she was just a person who needed protection.

He accepted Israel as a state, not as fulfillment of a biblical promise. The state of Israel had to be judged as other nations were judged. Israel was a necessary refuge for the survivors of the Holocaust and other expressions of anti-Judaism. His recommendations and hopes for Israel were parallel to his advice to Germans: accept finite borders and develop a sense of national-vocational consciousness within these borders. There is no absolute security; all borders will have some insecurity. Security rests in accepted borders and international understanding across the borders. Solutions will be found through negotiation and compromise that recognize the rights and power of all parties to the dispute.

For Niebuhr, Israel was primarily a refuge for victims of the Holocaust. He regarded it as a responsibility of the United States to protect Israel for reasons of moral responsibility and national interest. He wrote before the Israel-Egypt 1956 War:

> Our nation has a special interest in the preservation of the state of Israel. That interest is not only dictated by national interest in a state devoted to Western democracy and surrounded by Islamic nations in various stages of feudal decay, but is also dictated by humane considerations. For the state of Israel is, whatever its limitations, a heartening adventure in nationhood. It has gathered the Jews of all nations, the remnants of the victims of Hitlerism and other forms of nationalistic persecution, and given them a home of their own. Whatever our political or religious positions may be, it is not possible to withhold admiration, sympathy and respect for such an achievement.[7]

In writing on the strange mixture of secular and religious forces in the modern world Niebuhr regarded the emergence of Israel "as a kind of penance of the world for the awful atrocities committed against the Jews."[8] Furthermore, he noted that injury was done to the Arabs, but still he wrote, "Many Christians are pro-Zionist in the sense that they believe a homeless people require a homeland."[9] Justice still required further work on the rights of the Palestinians.

Niebuhr's writing on Judaism in 1958 in *Pious and Secular America* and his last essay, "Mission and Opportunity: Religion in "Pluralistic Culture," in Louis Finkelstein's volume, *Social Responsibility in an Age of Revolution* (1971), are among the most profound contributions to Christian-Jewish understanding. In the context of the two religious contributions to ethics in the Western world he recognizes that certain issues between the faiths are nonnegotiable and he suggests ways in which both faiths can correct their traditions to promote understanding without proselytizing.

Conclusion

Tillich's death in 1965 and Niebuhr's in 1971 prevent us from knowing how their thought would have evolved vis-à-vis contemporary Israel. A few points are clear, however. Their Zionism did not mean that all Jews should live in Zion. Israel was of the Diaspora as well as Eretz Israel. The creation of Israel was the recreation of a historical nation which was to be evaluated as other nations are evaluated. Israel has a religious history and it is relevant to the present state of Israel, but it is not determinative. For both Tillich and Niebuhr history is radically free and God judges all nations for their unrighteousness. To want to defend the Jewish choice to return to Israel after the Holocaust does not imply absolutism either biblical or secular. It can be done on the basis that Jews were not welcome or secure elsewhere and that the international community of nations recognized the right of Israel to exist.

The genius of Israel does not depend upon the land but on its relationship to a transcendent God who always requires justice. In neither Tillich's nor Niebuhr's thought can borders be regarded as sacrosanct. Borders get changed. They both recognized that our concern for security produces arrogance and blindness, but both recognized the need for security. Defense budgets can tyrannize a people, but people who will not provide for defense in a warring world suffer illusions that Jews cannot afford.

Neither theologian dealt adequately with the plight of Palestinians living within Israel, nor did either address themselves at length to the question of Palestinian refugees. Niebuhr mentioned that Israel's conquest would mean injustice to the Arabs, but he did not develop it in print. Christian ethics, while relating its judgments to historical conditions, must not lose sight of the will of God that all people are to be granted conditions for the flowering of their humanity. Christian reflection favoring the security of Israel must also recognize Palestinian rights and insist that Israel deal more justly with Palestinians inside Israel and on the West Bank.

Neither professor, both of whom died in their seventy-ninth year, lived to see the beginning of stabilization of the Middle East. Both would have welcomed movement towards gradual settlement of Palestinian rights. Both would have accepted the reality that not all political refugees would return and the corresponding recognition for the need for reparations and aid for displaced Palestinians. Niebuhr's regard for justice and Tillich's teaching of the need for finite, secure borders would have led them to oppose Israel's later expansionism. They were harsh critics of anti-Semitism and advocates of compromise toward justice securing peace.

Regarding this important religious political issue of our time, I have been unable to detect how their epistemological, ontological, or aesthetic differences made any difference in their realistic commitment to establishing a Jewish state. Maybe on this issue they did establish a school of thought with consequences, as they had dreamed of doing by the lake in Geneva in 1936.

14

Foundations of Postwar Political Philosophy

Arthur Schlesinger, Jr.'s essay on Niebuhr's political philosophy indicated that a new synthesis had been achieved in Niebuhr's thought in the postwar period.

> The penetrating critic of the Social Gospel and of pragmatism, he ended up, in a sense, the powerful reinterpreter and champion of both. It was the triumph of his remarkable analysis that it took what was valuable in each, rescued each by defining for each the limits of validity, and in the end, gave the essential purpose of both new power and new vitality.[1]

There were aspects of Niebuhr's thought which were not yet clear in 1956 when Schlesinger announced the synthesis. He saw the synthesis, but he could not anticipate how far the new developments in Niebuhr's thought would revise the previous ideas. The failure was not Schlesinger's, but it was an inevitable result of a characteristic of Niebuhr's writing. His brother H. Richard has noted the difficulty of understanding Reinhold Niebuhr due to the obscurity of his presuppositions. "Reinie's thought appears to me to be like a great iceberg of which three-fourths or more is beneath the surface and in which what's expressly said depends on something that is not made explicit"[2]

The publication of *Man's Nature and His Communities* in 1965 brought together the various strands of revision that had been taking place in Niebuhr's political philosophy since the war. The book reveals more clearly than any other work the presuppositions of his political philosophy which were guiding his occasional and theoretical politics. It recants previous polemics against liberalism and reflects the reliance on liberalism and pragmatism which characterized his work. The long essay on political idealism and realism is his solution to the problem he regarded as the most important in political philosophy. It relates the ideals of liberal principles of social morality to the factors in politics that inhibit the realization of those ideals in an attempt to resolve the problem that he had wrestled with since his earliest writing.

The significance of the work for an interpretation of Niebuhr's thought is best expressed in the introduction to the volume.

> This volume of essays on various aspects of man's individual and social existence is intended to serve two purposes, namely, to summarize, and to revise previously held opinions.
>
> The systematic essays are intended to "revise" previously held opinions only in the sense that they seek to give a systematic account to the revisions which have taken place in the author's mind in a whole lifetime of study and of writing books too frequently.[3]

The revisions included nuanced changes in his doctrine of humanity, the understanding of history as ironical, the increased recognition of pragmatism, the renewed appreciation of political liberalism, and a proposed solution to the idealist-realist debate. The analyst should not be misled by the more secular tone of the volume than some of his earlier work for both *Moral Man and Immoral Society* and *The Children of Light and the Children of Darkness* were not explicitly theological either. He knew his wife was planning a book of his sermons and prayers, and his political writings often obscured his theological foundations and limits. The inquirer after the theological foundations needs to investigate his books of sermons, *The Nature and Destiny of Man,* and particularly his class lectures at Union Theological Seminary.

Egoistic Self

The differences between the analysis of human nature in *Man's Nature and His Communities* and *The Nature and Destiny of Man* are due primarily to the disappearance of the theological vocabulary. Human nature is still the subject of the analysis and the focus is still on the political animal, but the style has changed. The later volume translates a theologically inspired view of human nature into nontheological terms. Some theological insights are confirmed through empirical insights, but the reader is not given the impression that the conclusions require theology.

Niebuhr revises his description of the human situation in light of the criticism of his earlier Gifford Lectures. He conceded, perhaps too easily, that the attempt to revive the vocabulary of original sin had been an error. Looking back on his efforts, he said: "But these labors of modern interpretation of traditional religious symbols proved vain."[4]

His growing respect for Erik Erikson's thought is represented by the adoption of some of his language of ego-psychology. The differences between the work of the late 1930s and his last work is partially that of intellectual evolution and primarily a change of style. Throughout his career Niebuhr could write articles in either a secular or a theological mode. The pieces in *Christianity and Society* or *Christianity and Crisis* are characterized by much more frequent usage of theological terms than the articles he wrote concurrently for *The Nation* or *The New Leader*.

As early as 1956, Niebuhr's reply to William J. Wolf's critique of his doctrine of humanity had indicated dissatisfaction with aspects of his own language. He admitted that his formulations "equality of sin and inequality of guilt" and "redeemed in principle but not in fact" were unsatisfactory. Niebuhr's shift in language led to a misunderstanding with Paul Tillich. Tillich reported to a colioquium in honor of Reinhold Niebuhr on 20 October 1961, that Niebuhr had recently admitted he now agreed with Tillich's description of the human situation. Though there still remained differences between them after years of debate, Tillich implied that Niebuhr now agreed with him.

> A week ago we had a wonderful talk in Cambridge for one to two hours, and he said to me quite spontaneously, "I have accepted your point of view in this respect. We cannot use any longer the language of the tradition if we want to communicate anything to the people of our time." As an example he gave me his use of the word *sin,* and especially *original sin,* in his book the words *original sin* shouldn't be used at all. He accepted—if I understand him rightly—something like *universal estrangement* instead of the term *original* or *hereditary sin.*[7]

In reply to Tillich's address, Niebuhr confirmed the former's report about their agreement that traditional theological symbolism was often irrelevant, but disagreed with Tillich's translation of the tradition into his own ontological terms.

> I still think that Paul Tillich's translation of these symbols into the ontological terms essential and existential man is too Plotinian in that it implies, if not asserts, that the whole temporal process is a corruption of the eternal. Thereby one precious biblical concept embodied in the idea of the goodness of creation, may be obscured. I would now rather translate these historic symbols into descriptive rather than ontological terms.[8]

In *Man's Nature and His Communities* Niebuhr's translation of the symbols into descriptive terms (a) retains the emphasis upon freedom of his earlier writing, (b) expresses sin as overly consistent self-seeking, (c) interprets love as self-giving, and (d) discusses grace as the gift of security. True human fulfillment is found when one generously gives oneself to a cause or to another self, but such self-giving presupposes that the self is not desperately seeking its own security. The self is never consistently freed from seeking its own security, but it can presuppose security and relate creatively to others. The impulse toward self-giving is the basis of morality, but morality itself cannot give the self the capacity to relate to others. That capacity comes only as a gift. It is given originally by the healthy family which nurtures and protects the person. But even as the family promotes self-giving by nurturing the relatively secure person, it promotes self-seeking by promoting the family's good at the expense of or at least at the neglect of the good of other families. All personal lives and all achievements of human community reflect this double impulse toward self-giving and self-seeking.

Niebuhr thinks this description of the human condition is consistent with the saying of Jesus: "He who finds his life will lose it, and he who loses his life for my sake will find it."[9] Orthodox doctrine, both Catholic and Protestant, has obscured the insight by distinguishing too sharply between common and saving grace. It has thereby encouraged a view of righteousness within the community which the "long history of religious self-righteousness" refutes.[10] The church has also erred in thinking that self-regard could be suppressed. The perpetual paradox that the human self is both self-giving and self-striving has been hidden. The self fulfills itself by being inclined away from preoccupation with the self by various forms of social pressures and responsibilities.[11]

Niebuhr's analysis continued his battle against claims for the perfection of either the individual or society. It was subject to those charges which had been leveled at him throughout his career, that he did not emphasize strongly enough the sanctification of the individual, the holiness of the church, and the possibilities of human achievement in society. The charges could not imply, however, that Niebuhr had not examined these possibilities. He had examined them in the light of his understanding of humanity and in his own reading of history, and he had found the claims unsupportable.

The analysis of the human situation retained the tough-mindedness of his Marxist and Christian-realist presuppositions. The sober estimate of human possibilities, however, was now set in the context of liberalism. The emphasis upon the continuity between the religious and the secular, or saving grace and common grace, and the openness to psychology indicated the revised direction of his thought. The rigorous apologetic mood of the Gifford Lectures was absent from this book of revisions. Rather than arguing for the greater intellectual adequacy of Christian theology in understanding humanity, he was insisting on complementing theological insights by other methodologies. The tough-mindedness was, to Niebuhr's mind, the fruit of empirical and historical observation as well as the result of either Christian or Marxist presuppositions.

Reflections on History

The word *history* contains a certain ambiguity. It refers both to the events that have occurred and to the records of those events. Niebuhr uses *history* as a series of events in life when he argues that, though history itself is not meaningful, it bears all the meanings which can be found for humans. His writing of history emphasizes the interpretation of events over the recording of the events for their own value.

Niebuhr's focus was on the story and the meaning of the story rather than on the detail of the occurrences. He had many friends who were professional historians, and he was willing to defer to friends like Professors Arthur Schlesinger, Jr. and Wilhelm Pauck on questions of the verification of the events. He did not seek to escape from the discipline of the historians, but neither did he shoulder its burdens. He wrote and waited patiently for specialized historians to correct him if he erred. He tried to stand humbly before the historians while offering to them his understanding of the meaning of the events they tried to verify and relate. In his preface to *The Irony of American History*, he expressed this humility: "I must add that I have no expert competence in the field of American history; and I apologize in advance to the specialists in this field for what are undoubtedly many errors of fact and judgment."[12] Reactions to his writings on the history of America were, of course, mixed. Evidence of the positive response of the historians is noted in Professor Henry F. May's 1968 article on *The Irony of American History*. He began his article: "In 1952 many historians of the United States were deeply impressed by Reinhold Niebuhr's *The Irony of American History*."[13]

Niebuhr's usual practice in arguing for the acceptance of an idea was to trace its history. In discussing *justice* he would trace the idea from its Greek and Hebrew roots, through the early years of Western civilization, to its emergence in medieval Europe, into the complexities and various alternatives of the concept in Reformation, Renaissance, and Enlightenment thought, and for a conclusion he would analyze its contemporary meaning. Or if he were attacking a policy of the government, for example the Vietnam War, he would trace with biting irony the mistakes of the various administrations that had led to the quagmire. So if it is true, that his reflections upon history lacked the precision of careful history, his social criticism and philosophy utilized more historical detail than philosophers usually consider.

The deftness with which he generalized about historical epochs drove both his students and his family to historical research and discussions. The Niebuhrs' family life was often the center of far-ranging debates over the interpretation of history, and what was true history as opposed to sheer interpretation. Mrs. Ursula Niebuhr's Oxford studies in history combined with the discipline of teaching undergraduates of Barnard College often gave her the advantage in debates over historical points. Particularly on British history she often corrected her husband. *The Irony of American History* is dedicated to their son, Christopher, whose approach to historical materials stands in contrast to his father's. Christopher's mind retains massive amounts of the detail and his rapid-fire delivery of the detail overwhelms his listeners. In later years, Christopher often corrected his father to the father's alternating pride and chagrin. After his father's death, Christopher would generously supply corrections to authors who interpreted his father's life and work.

Reinhold decided in 1969 not to offer his seminar at Union Seminary any more. The Niebuhrs sold their apartment on Riverside Drive and retired to their home in Stockbridge, Massachusetts. The white home sat on the side of a hill on the outskirts of the village. Ursula had named their street Yale Hill, and the large front yard provided room for their poodle to run. He continued his writing from the home and, though he dealt with his increasing physical problems, the power of his mind continued into the last days of life. Discussions with visitors in the home would often turn to matters of history. Their son Christopher would join in the talks with a vitality that reminded many of the vitality of the younger Reinhold Niebuhr. Christopher was a master of the details of history and the father wanted to get on to the significant generalizations. Ursula tended to be more modest in her generalizations than Reinhold as she emphasized the counterpoints which force the qualification of the broader generalizations. She laced her conversations with a clever wit which forced one to participate in the encounter every bit as completely as one did when engaged with her husband. The conversations there inevitably involved the problem of the historical, from the history of Stockbridge at which they were all experts through the problems of biblical history in which Ursula had an edge, to the issues of American history in which Christopher mastered the details and Reinhold interpreted. The pace of the dialogue was usually breathtaking, and visitors left the beautiful stone-wood house awed and better informed than upon entry.

The Irony of History

Niebuhr's adoption of irony as a major motif for the interpretation of history is significant. It indicates a trend toward a less dogmatic and more empirical approach to history. He uses fewer Christian symbols to explain history, the liberal ideas of progress are gone and the Marxist catastrophic view of history has been abandoned. History is not regarded as so tragic as it had been previously or in the volume *Beyond Tragedy*.[14] He had not written on irony as a major category for interpreting history until he published *The Irony of American History* in 1952 following his stroke. He had used pathos earlier, and some interpreters confused this use with his interpreting history as ironic.[15] The shift from pathos and tragedy toward irony marked other shifts toward a new openness to human accomplishments in history. "Irony consists of apparently fortuitous incongruities in life, which are discovered upon closer examination, to be not merely fortuitous"[16] He thought that ironical situations could be dissolved as actors became aware of them and the hidden vanities were discovered.

It was the possibility of the United States turning away from the hidden vanities and pretensions of American life that prompted Niebuhr to write on the ironies of American history. He no longer was as bitter in his castigations of America's liberal culture, for he saw that it had realized a higher degree of justice than its critics had thought possible. Yet he still thought the United States was hindered by "pretensions of virtue, wisdom, and power." His book was more the work of a social critic than historian. It was the effort of a social critic who wanted to free his country from illusions which hindered its wise conduct of foreign policy. Niebuhr's use of irony was an attempt to convict the American nation of certain pretensions and thereby to free it for a more creative role in world politics.

Niebuhr's special use of irony is not particularly a theological concept. He relates it to his theology, however, and claims that it is the normative way for Christians to view history.

> Yet the Christian faith tends to make the ironic view of human evil in history the normative one. Its conception of redemption from evil carries it beyond the limits of irony, but its interpretation of the nature of evil in human history is consistently ironic. This consistency is achieved on the basis of the belief that the whole drama of human history is under the scrutiny of a divine judge who laughs at human pretensions without being hostile to human aspirations.
>
> The biblical interpretation of the human situation is ironic, rather than tragic or pathetic, because of its unique formulation of the problem of human freedom.[17]

The Christian view of history is not tragic because it is not necessary that man do evil. He can choose the good, but in his pride he does not. The development of the concept of irony inclined Niebuhr away from the more pessimistic notes of his Marxist writings. Developing the ironical interpretation of history he wrote:

> Nevertheless, a purely tragic view of life is not finally viable. It is, at any rate not the Christian view. According to that view destructiveness is not an inevitable consequence of human creativity. It is not invariably necessary to do evil in order that we may do good.[18]

Niebuhr consistently wrestled with the relationship of the ideal to the real. The writings of Unamuno on the decline of Western civilization had affected him earlier. It was probably Unamuno who had drawn him to the figure of Don Quixote who had refuted the ideals of chivalry by espousing them. Don Quixote was oblivious to the absurdity of his portrayal of the values of the knight errant. But the reader saw the absurdity.[19] As Cervantes had laughed at chivalry through Don Quixote, Niebuhr set out to laugh at the foibles of a bourgeois American culture. The laughter he desired to provoke would be accompanied by understanding of the hidden incongruities of American life. He hoped that an understanding of the ironies of American history would help to dissolve them and to reduce the pride and pretensions of the country. Condemnation of the weakness of the United States accomplished little; the use of irony, he hoped would avoid the hostility of injured pride and result in an "abatement of the pretensions which caused this irony."[20]

Niebuhr piled ironies upon ironies, using the term so frequently that it seemed to lose the rather careful meaning he had given it. The fact that the dreams of agrarian, isolationist innocence of the young America had been reduced to irrelevance by the growth of the United States was regarded as ironical.[21] The American idealists attempt to escape the realities of international politics by articulating schemes for world order was labeled irony. The awareness that the nation had been better able to achieve its security more thoroughly in the days of its youth than in the day of nuclear power was seen as irony.

The height of irony to Niebuhr was that the foe, Marxism, in the hands of the Soviet Union, had transmuted weakness in liberal culture into a dangerous creed that threatened to destroy democracy. The ideas of human control of destiny, equality, human innocence had fueled liberal illusions that combined into a religious-political mythology which threatened humanity. Liberal culture and Communist culture shared illusions and their conquest of the power of nature through science threatened the world. Against the misunderstandings of the Cold War and the discredited mythologies involved in the struggle, Niebuhr responded in the spirit of the scripture: "He that sitteth in the heavens shall laugh" (Psalm 2:4).[22]

An irony of Niebuhr's writing on the ironies of American history was that he gave as little attention as he did to racial strife in his book. In the introduction to his last book he noted the omission: "In the United States we are conscious, as we were not a few years ago, how difficult it is for democratic politics to deal with the problem of race, especially when it is reinforced by economic handicaps."[23] His other writings, editorials, essays focused on the race problem as did the seminar on social ethics he gave in his retirement. But the race problem as such did not penetrate into his writing on the irony of American history in the book. If there is irony in the manifestation of militant blacks charging liberal whites with failure to take their liberal creeds, the Constitution of the United States, and the Declaration of Independence seriously, it is even more ironical to find Neibuhr to whom some militant black theologians looked as an ally, guilty by omission of neglecting blacks in American history.

Niebuhr has not tried to exclude himself from those Americans who are subject to illusions about the American past. James Cone called to my attention that Arthur Schlesinger, Jr. had written Niebuhr before the book's publication of this weakness. Cone also indicated that his source for the warning from Schlesinger was Ursula's publication of his letter to Reinhold. The omission was somewhat corrected by Niebuhr's later chapter in *Pious and Secular America.* Moreover, his major article, "The Negro Minority and Its Fate in a Self-righteous Nation"[24] written during the summer of 1968 in his old age and ill health in the style of his reflection on the ironies of American history, filled the gap left by his books on history.

Somehow he failed to discuss the genocide of the Native American in his book on the irony of American history. He made comments about it in his seminar near the end of his life, but it was not a prevalent reality in his thinking. His hero Abraham Lincoln had participated in the Black Hawk Wars and his home state was named after an Indian tribe, but this original sin of the frontier was basically ignored by the thinking of Niebuhr. He was aware of the racial arrogance of the colonists from Europe in their domination of the world, and in this vein he compared and contrasted the British and Spanish roles in the new world, but his eye was on the conqueror and on the later European immigrants and not on the original inhabitants. Of course, the destruction of the Native American was not really irony; it was tragedy through and through as the Native Americans lost whether they violently resisted or submitted through negotiations. The term irony might have applied to the few Europeans whose good intentions for the Native Americans contributed ironically to their destruction, or to Native Americans who through cooperation with Europeans ironically contributed toward their own destruction.

Pragmatism

In retrospect, Niebuhr's debt to pragmatism can be seen in all periods of his thought. However, he openly stressed the philosophy of pragmatism only after the war. His attacks upon liberalism had obscured the pragmatic quality of his thought, and it had been particularly hidden by Marxist and Christian dogma. The philosophy of William James had been important to Niebuhr as a young student, and Niebuhr's methodological presuppositions continue to reveal the influence of James. In the 1930s Niebuhr cooperated with and argued against John Dewey. In the 1940s he came to appreciate the pragmatic liberalism of President Franklin Roosevelt. In the 1950s he explicitly advocated Christian pragmatism.

Niebuhr's pragmatism is characterized by a rejection of all ideologically consistent political schemes. History is full of novelty, and the stuff of political life cannot be put into neat generalizations. Attempts to state principles of politics on divine, natural, or rational grounds have all been undermined by the relativizing forces of history. Every institution of government should, in Niebuhr's opinion, be regarded pragmatically, that is, the social critic or philosopher should always be aware that an institution that served well in the past may be outdated and require modification. Institutions of government are to be examined, not in the light of Marxist, liberal, or Christian perspectives, but with regard to their usefulness for the common life in a particular situation. This pragmatism forces the teacher of social ethics to refrain from expounding the moral law for political life and inclines the student to study how tentative, regulative, principles of morality function in history. Though occasionally he will protest against the use of any principle in judging politics, his more consistent position is that principled judgments and action on the basis of such judgments are essential. For example, he attacked Barth's "extreme pragmatism which disavows all moral principles" at the time of the Hungarian revolution and Barth's neutrality in 1956.

William James

Unfortunately Niebuhr did not provide a precise record of his debt to William James. His intellectual autobiographies all indicate his move toward pragmatism, but they do not discuss William James. The question of influence is inevitably a difficult question to answer satisfactorily, though one quotation provides a clue to the importance of James: "I stand in the William James tradition. He was both an empiricist and a religious man, and his faith was both the consequence and the presupposition of his pragmatism."[25] Four aspects of Niebuhr's thought reveal sufficient similarities with William James' definition of pragmatism to regard him as a pragmatist even if his exact degree of dependence on James is indeterminable. His thought is strikingly similar to that of James in social ethics, epistemology, and apologetics. His avoidance of optimism and pessimism in the expectations of improvement in the human condition is also foreshadowed in James' meliorism,

In social ethics Niebuhr follows pragmatism. He regards some form of pragmatism or utilitarianism as the best way of making moral judgments about social and political questions.

> When viewing a historic situation all moralists become pragmatists and utilitarians. Some general good, some summum bonum, "the greatest good of the greatest number" or " the most inclusive harmony of all vital capacities" is set up as the criterion of the morality of specific actions and each action is judged with reference to its relation to the ultimate good.
>
> The choice of instruments and immediate objectives which fall between motive and ultimate objectives raises pragmatic issues to such a degree that they may be said to be more political than they are ethical.[26]

Niebuhr's ethic is not simply William James' ethic. It preserves a dualistic note inherited from Augustine and Luther that is not important to James. It is also informed by a vision of Christian perfectionism by which James' ethic was untroubled. The biblical theology Niebuhr found important was insignificant to James. In the practical conclusions reached, it tended to be more consistently "tough-minded" than was the ethic of William James. Niebuhr's writing after 1917 was all in the context of war or the threat of war, James's substitute of a great moral cause for war was inadequate.

Tillich on Epistemology

The authority of Paul Tillich has supported the view that Niebuhr had no epistemology. Tillich began an essay entitled "Reinhold Niebuhr's Doctrine of Knowledge" with the assertion: "The difficulty of writing about Niebuhr's epistemology lies in the fact that there is no such epistemology. Niebuhr does not ask, 'How can I know?' he starts knowing."[27] Tillich then asserts that the omitted factor reappears in disguised form. He argues that Niebuhr's lack of epistemology is the source of his criticism of Tillich's ontology. The remainder of the article criticizes Niebuhr for refusal to accept Tillich's ontology. Niebuhr's thought does appear meager when judged by the canons of Tillich's ontology. Skepticism regarding Tillich's ontology, however, is not the same as the lack of all epistemology. Niebuhr never wrote a formal essay on epistemology, but he considered the issue at length in three books[28] and in several essays on related subjects. Tillich's refusal to acknowledge Niebuhr's consideration of the epistemological question was due partially to his desire to reveal Niebuhr's lack of ontology, but it was also due to the strangeness of Niebuhr's epistemology to Tillich's idealism. Niebuhr stood in the empirical tradition of William James, which was relatively unknown to German idealism.

Niebuhr combines a high degree of skepticism about claims of metaphysical or religious knowledge with a frank acceptance of the achievements of the sciences. Knowledge consists of an awareness of the coherence in life. This coherence is more easily attainable in realms unqualified by human freedom and human self-interest. The skepticism about metaphysical or religious knowledge combines with his understanding of the free but self-interested self to make him a critic of attempts to establish a "scientific morality." On the other hand, he welcomes the refinements in social research which are moving toward greater accuracy in predicting the political behavior of the human subject.[29]

Niebuhr shares the modern world's confidence that the sciences will continue to produce new knowledge. He finds the subject and object dilemma in epistemology rationally unanswerable, but he assumes that there is congruence ultimately.[30] He assumes a large degree of coherence in a basically ordered but unfinished world.[31]

> The whole of reality is characterized by a basic coherence. Things and events are in a vast web of relationships and are known through their relations. Perceptual knowledge is possible only within a framework of conceptual images, which in some sense conform to the structures in which reality is organized. The world is organized or it could not exist; if it is to be known, it must be known through its sequences, coherences, casualties and essences.[32]

If asked, "How do you know?" Niebuhr would answer by describing the process of verifying the idea. The process of verification would involve the coherence of the idea with other ideas, logic, or the observable world.

> It is natural to test the conformity to the particular coherence in which it seems to belong. We are skeptical about ghosts, for instance, because they do not conform to the characteristics of historical reality as we know it.[34]

Niebuhr has confirmed that the following quote from James represents his approach to the question of how we know:[35]

> It matters not to an empiricist from what quarter an hypothesis may come to him; he may have acquired it by fair means or by foul; passion may have whispered or accident suggested it; but if the total drift of thinking continues to affirm it, that is what he means by being true.[36]

Like James, Niebuhr assumes that most of human intellectual achievements represent modifications of previously held ideas. Niebuhr characteristically works through a problem in political thought by assembling the various answers to the problem, checking each possibility, and by accepting the one verified in the sense of cohering to other needed ideas and experience.

One level of Niebuhr's Christian apology is very close to that of James. They both have abandoned traditional natural theology because of dissatisfaction with the arguments for the existence of God and an antagonism toward rational systems which they thought prematurely closed a developing world. Both thinkers recognized an area of life that was beyond the reach of empirical studies. Neither rejected theological statements as meaningless. Both personally possessed lively religious convictions. James' formula sums up one level of their agreement on religious truth:

> If theological ideas prove to have a value for concrete life, they will be true, for pragmatism, in the sense of being good for so much. For how much more they are true, will depend entirely on their relations to the other truths that also have to be acknowledged.[37]

Stanley Hauerwas Misunderstands

Niebuhr used this form of pragmatic apology for theological ideas when he pointed toward the quality of the Christian's life as verification of Christian insight. This form of arguing for Christian faith as seen in the witness of a Christian's life is congruent with pragmatism, and while he may have taken it from William James, it is available elsewhere. Richard Fox and Charles Brown both develop Niebuhr's use of pragmatism. Stanley Hauerwas is the prominent theologian who faults Niebuhr most deeply for relying upon William James. He accepts Fox's misreading that Niebuhr's major work *The Nature and Destiny of Man* is the same argument as his thirty-five-year earlier thesis at Yale. It never occurred to most philosophers or theologians that Niebuhr's method of correlation using his own distinctive biblical theology was the same as William James' argument.

Niebuhr's faith was formed by his life in the church before he ever read William James. He respects the work of Charles Hartshorne and Alfred North Whitehead also, but faith does not depend on philosophy. Stanley Hauerwas falls back on the argument from the quality of life of the witness in his conclusion to *With the Grain of the Universe*.[38] He takes as his examples his colleague John Howard Yoder, the Mennonite theologian, and two Roman Catholics, John Paul II, and Dorothy Day, the radical activist laywoman. Niebuhr's Christian heroes included Martin Luther King, Jr., Baptist preacher and martyr, and Dietrich Bonhoeffer, German Evangelical Church preacher and martyr. Their choices reflect, I think, their differences in ecclesiology. Niebuhr was at home in his German Evangelical Synod which became the United Church of Christ with its liberal, low-church orientations. Hauerwas is not at home in his United Methodist Church, preferring Roman Catholic and Mennonite perspectives.

Hauerwas appreciated Niebuhr's book on his ministry, *Leaves from the Notebook of a Tamed Cynic*, but he particularly criticizes him for his ecclesiology without really going into Niebuhr's work and understanding of the church. The issue as Hauerwas puts it is the difference of a Niebuhr following William James and Ernst Troeltsch addressing mainline Protestant liberalism, and Hauerwas seeking to define the church in terms of a radical pacifism as definitive for the church. Hauerwas perceptively emphasizes the role of William James in shaping Niebuhr's thought. He also taught many readers about the appreciation of Ernst Troeltsch for some of James' insights, and thereby indicates how Niebuhr could and did use both of these early twentieth-century interpreters of religion.

Though Hauerwas mentions Augustine's influence on Niebuhr, he seems to reject Niebuhr's own sense of the importance of Augustine to his thought. He also ignores the influence of Karl Marx on Niebuhr's mind. He notes, but underestimates, the degree to which Niebuhr as a child of the church, son of his pastor father and Sunday-school-superintendent mother, student at two church institutions was formed before he ever got to Yale. There he learned about William James, and had his faith shaped in a particular theological environment that he never rejected. He poured into his church learning the categories of the significant religious interpreters of his day as he learned about them. He learned James from Professor Macintosh at Yale University and Troeltsch when *The Social Teaching of the Christian Churches* was published in German while he was a pastor in Detroit. Hauerwas' Gifford Lectures exposit and criticize William James, first, Reinhold Niebuhr second, then affirm Karl Barth's theology as a prelude to affirming John Howard Yoder's pacifism as constitutive of the Christian Church. The conclusion with Yoder, John Paul II, and Dorothy Day as his witnesses to the faith of the church seems eccentric as two of the three were not really part of the argument of the book, and Yoder had been disciplined by his own church.

The fourth similarity in the thought of James and Niebuhr is the hopeful pragmatism to which the later came in the postwar years. One need not conclude that Niebuhr had once been only a pessimist to recognize a more hopeful note in his analysis of the self and society in his later writings. He did not adopt Spengler and Unamuno's pessimism about Western civilization as his disillusionment with liberalism grew, but he was influenced by them. References to them did not appear in his later writings. The sense of catastrophe followed by utopia in Marx was not tenable. He had argued for the tragic quality of history. His final position was still that of his Christian realism, but in the later writings recognition of pragmatism was clear and it was conjoined to the political liberalism which he had so abused in his earlier writing. His thought about society was now close to the position described by James as meliorism.[39] He could see that some of the conditions of a healthy political order were already present, but so were forces resisting health. The political philosophy of liberalism could be affirmed and the values of liberty, equality, fraternity, and toleration pursued, but the struggle was not over nor was the outcome secure.

The final period of Niebuhr's thought was not a return to his earliest liberal optimism nor was it a continuation of his more pessimistic Christian realism. Of course, conditions for most Americans were much better in the 1950s than in 1938–1939. Labor, for whom Niebuhr spoke, was in a much better place, and before the 1950s expired, some gains had even been made for the African-American population. As in James, pragmatism and liberalism interacted to produce a sober, goal-oriented philosophy which could lay claim to a middle position between optimism and pessimism. Niebuhr's meliorism, however, was closer to James' later category of "tough-minded" political thought. Niebuhr retained a larger degree of eschatological perspective than did James, and he also was more inclined than James to emphasize the inevitable corruption of political community. This higher degree of "tough-mindedness" was one of the chief differences between Niebuhr and John Dewey, the most famous exponent of pragmatism after James.

John Dewey

John Dewey was the aging icon of philosophical and political liberalism when Niebuhr arrived at Union Seminary. Dewey, a shy philosopher in person, expressed himself powerfully in his educational, philosophical, and political writings from his position as professor and later professor emeritus at Columbia. They soon found themselves allied in several liberal causes. Dewey wrote for the journal *The World Tomorrow* which Niebuhr came to New York to edit, and they found themselves serving as officers in the League for Industrial Democracy. They both supported Norman Thomas for president in 1932 while Niebuhr ran for Congress in the district that included both Columbia University and Union Seminary. Niebuhr's first review of John Dewey's work, *Characters and Events* in *World Tomorrow,* was irenic and relatively uncritical. He praised Dewey as a philosopher who left his ivory tower to apply his thought in politics and the other practical affairs of the world.

Niebuhr's lecture in 1930 at the National Educational Association on the Columbia campus was on Dewey's territory and Niebuhr pushed issues of the spiritual dimensions of life beyond that with which Dewey's naturalistic, pragmatic followers were comfortable. While Dewey was aware of his younger ally from the Seminary he did not regard him as a critic of his own form of pragmatism, which while open to a certain religious quality of feeling about his mixture of educational, reforming, democratic pragmatism did not reflect Niebuhr's recognition of a feeling of dependence upon an ultimate or divine power. In 1932, John Dewey attended and spoke at a banquet held in Niebuhr's honor without knowing that Niebuhr had written a polemical broadside against his thought that would be published that year as *Moral Man and Immoral Society.*

Another factor making the following struggle between Neibuhr and Dewey an intramural affair was that the religious educators of Union Seminary were heavily influenced by Dewey. They defended Dewey's thought within the Seminary's own Gothic walls which housed many graduate students from the prosperous overflowing halls of Columbia Teacher's College across Broadway from Niebuhr's office. The arrival of Niebuhr's strong aggressive Christian theology and force of his personality would tip the balance of power within the Seminary towards biblical and theological studies, to the discomfort of the Dewey generation of religious educators at the Seminary.

Dewey's strongest response to Niebuhr was in the pages of *The World Tomorrow*. Niebuhr's essay, "After Capitalism—What?"[41] assumed the death of capitalism, liberalism in politics was exhausted, and Fascism was going to triumph in most Western industrial nations. The efforts of President Roosevelt and liberals to the left of his policies were doomed to failure. In spite of all these predictions Niebuhr saw a future in working with labor towards a parliamentary socialism. He expected that after decades of strengthening socialism the battle would be with Fascism. In his opinion, "neither the parliamentary nor the revolutionary course offers modern society an easy way to the mastery of a technological civilization."[42]

He wrote that orthodox religion was a better guide to the necessary realism for the social struggle than contemporary liberalism. The religious and educational liberals who hoped to eliminate violent struggle from social change were blinded by the illusions of their middle-class complacency. The social struggle was brutal in the present and would become more so. The development of social intelligence had a role in the conflict only if it resisted liberal illusions about sublimating the egoism of groups' defensive politics. Other essays by editors or associate editors in the same pages argued for the honoring of coercive nonviolence in the social struggle or naively thought Hitler's victory probably would not be much worse than the prewar conditions of the Hohenzollern Empire. Niebuhr's realism was not shared by many of the other names on the journal's masthead.

Dewey's counterattack in the next issue of *The World Tomorrow* mentioned Niebuhr by name with an undeserved title in all but two paragraphs. He indicated he was pleading for unity among radicals who wanted fundamental changes in the system. He found Niebuhr's broadsides unhelpful and dangerous to the necessary unity among radicals. He denied any particular designs to defend his own position and asserted that he could not recognize his own position or that of his allies in the naive liberalism that Niebuhr denounced.

His most telling criticisms were leveled at Niebuhr's prophesying the future and arguing from his predictions as to necessary politics. That was not the way to be socially intelligent. He was certainly correct that Niebuhr's predictions were not only esoteric, but often incorrect. Niebuhr, in Dewey's judgment, relied upon general views of history to guide his politics. Such approaches were outdated. Dewey preferred more secular, empirical approaches over the Christian theodicy of history or its antireligious economic deterministic critics. Dewey thought that he probably agreed with the social goals of Niebuhr of a cooperative, fair democratic society. But such goals were more realizable by concentrating on the political needs of the present.

Niebuhr to Dewey seemed "deplorably vague." Dewey said he understood both pacifism and class conflict but that Niebuhr's "position escapes me." He regarded Niebuhr's critique of liberalism as irrelevant to Dewey's own proposals. He concluded by deploring the disunity of the radical and near-radical forces in overcoming the present economic crisis. Niebuhr's polemics to John Dewey's mind did not advance the necessary unity.[43] Though the point was not made by John Dewey, further evidence of such diversity was available in the pages and editorials of the *The World Tomorrow* or in President Roosevelt's cabinet and administration. Dewey would continue to chide Niebuhr for misrepresentation of liberalism's method or at least of Dewey's approach. He also did not believe that Niebuhr's use of "sin" to explain human social failings was helpful. Against Niebuhr's criticisms of politics being expressed as science, Dewey would argue how would one solve the social problem if one did not use the best social science? Methods in the hard sciences had to overcome economic interests as well as in the social sciences and, with effort and the best human intentions. it could be accomplished.

Niebuhr attacked Dewey's thought repeatedly,[44] and the followers of Dewey were not reticent in counterattacking.[45] The interest in the basic disagreements between Niebuhr and Dewey should not obscure their common debt to William James nor the similarities of their thought. They both considered the context in reaching a decision on political policy. They joined in opposing the great systems of philosophical rationalism. Both understood their thought to be in development. Neither gave a completely naturalistic account of the human, for both knew humanity was continuous and discontinuous with nature.[46]

Niebuhr's Marxism fueled his critique in the 1930s and his more developed theological system inspired the critique in the later years. Finally near the end of his vocation, he would admit that his critique of Dewey had been extravagant. By this time he had reconciled his liberalism to his pragmatism. It is not clear that the major interpreters on the Niebuhr-Dewey exchange, Daniel Rice and Stephen Rockefeller,[47] have given full weight to the influence on Niebuhr of Marx in the mid-1930s. In the issue of the journal in 1933 following Dewey's major criticism of Niebuhr, the editors of the journal celebrated the fiftieth anniversary of Karl Marx's death and assumed that he would be the major voice in their preferred politics of socialism. They suggested that he would be the major social scientist, if not thinker, of the twentieth century.

Niebuhr's attack upon Dewey focused on that which creative social intelligence could be expected to accomplish.[48] Niebuhr and Dewey recognized that the social order had always been dominated by force. Dewey hoped that the new social sciences could change the way society was administered. Niebuhr hoped for a radical realignment of the balance of power in society, but he did not expect reason to control force.

> Professor Dewey has a touching faith in the possibility of achieving the same results in the field of social sciences which intelligence achieved in the mastery of nature. The fact that man corrupts his purest visions of disinterested justice in his actual actions seems never to occur to him.[49]

Arthur Schlesinger, Jr. used the following categories to delineate the differences between the two thinkers.

> In the case of Dewey, it should be said that his disdain for the New Deal and his commitment to socialization proceeded naturally enough from his disregard for power in society and from his faith in human rationality and scientific planning; but for Niebuhr, who was realistic about man and who wanted to equilibrate power in society, the commitment to socialization was both the price of indifference to the achievements of piecemeal reform and a symptom of despair. Where Dewey spurned the New Deal because of his optimism about man and his belief in science, Niebuhr seemed to spurn it because of his pessimism about man and his belief in catastrophe.[50]

Schlesinger came close to understanding their common rejection of the New Deal, but the differences are more subtle: the polarities of optimism and pessimism will not stand serious scrutiny any better than Niebuhr's treatment of Dewey as a "child of light." Nor can it be argued convincingly that Dewey disregarded power in society while Niebuhr was indifferent to piecemeal reform. Throughout the decade of the 1930s, Niebuhr wrote editorial after editorial for reform, fought for unpopular causes, and gave himself to left-wing political activity. Certainly he hoped under Marxist influence, for a radical transformation of American society, but this hope did not lead him to oppose reforms for the sake of increasing class polarization. Niebuhr himself did not criticize Dewey for disregarding power but rather for relying too heavily on the possibility of conflicting claims being adjusted through discussion, democracy, and education.[51] Morton White's observation, in the context of criticizing Niebuhr's thought, is closer to the full breadth of the two social philosophers than is Schlesinger: "All we have here is the recognition that men are somewhere between the serpent and the dove, and while Niebuhr puts us closer to the serpent, Dewey puts us closer to the dove."[52]

Dewey and Niebuhr concurred during the depression on the need for a third political party to lead the country into socialism. Richard Fox indicates that Dewey supported Niebuhr's bid for Congress on the Socialist Party ticket. Both expected radical changes in the economy and social structure of the country and thought the changes would come through revolution if not achieved by democratic reforms. Their deep differences were seen in their criticisms of Marxist radicals. Niebuhr criticized them for romantic illusions concerning the possibility of eliminating force from human affairs. Dewey criticized them for lacking a rigorous social science. In their appreciation of democracy the same fundamental difference could be seen. Niebuhr regarded democracy as the best governmental system for the adjustment of power; Dewey praised democracy for enabling the social ideals of men to be tested by experience, making possible the selection of the most rational policy. Dewey attached almost a mystical union of the ideal and the real being realized in democracy. Niebuhr's perspective on democracy was certainly not mystical and the religious for him was not found through politics as it sometimes seemed for Dewey.

For Niebuhr, Dewey's faith in "creative social intelligence" did not take adequate account of how social science was subject to misuse by self-interested parties. Social science was easily converted to ideological uses by those interested in pursuing their own ends. Social Darwinism was widely utilized to defend unregulated, predatory capitalism. Niebuhr was left unimpressed by the analogy of the success of science in nature because he regarded humans as historical beings while Dewey emphasized the continuity of the human and nature. As Dewey put it,

> The intelligent acknowledgment of the continuity of nature, man, and society will alone secure a growth of morals which will be serious without being fanatical, aspiring without sentimentality, adapted to reality without conventionality, sensible without taking the form of calculation of profits, idealistic without being romantic.[53]

Niebuhr emphasized the discontinuity of the human and nature. It was precisely in human freedom over nature that humanity's distinctiveness resided. The study of human history was not subject to the same means of inquiry as those which had proven so fruitful in the study of nature. Niebuhr's charge that the social sciences were not developed to the same extent as the natural sciences was irrefutable. He regarded the theory, that this was due to a "cultural lag" which would be overcome, as the "pathos of liberalism." The social crisis was not due to the lack of research and education, but to the clash of self-interested groups. These groups adopted whatever social science was available for the justification of their own purposes. He admitted the need for reason in planning social action, but he regarded Dewey's ultimate estimate of the hopes for rational arbitration of fundamental social conflicts as overly optimistic.[54]

Niebuhr never wrote extensively on Dewey's approach to international politics. However the gap between their understandings of international affairs was as great as any difference between them. Niebuhr was particularly opposed to schemes for world government or the outlawing of war that obscured what needed to be accomplished now. Dewey revealed a robust confidence in the outlawing of war.[54] He thought the "people" of America had a particularly significant role to play in dismantling the war institution. His analysis focused on the reasonableness and utility of outlawing wars and providing alternative means of settling international disputes. His theory lacked any feel for the Hobbesian state of anarchy which prompted nations to seek desperately their own security. Dewey's political analysis did not adequately analyze the dynamic evils of Hitlerism and Stalinism although both were rather conspicuous.

Niebuhr thought that the failure of educators to realize the seriousness of the mid-1930s social crisis was partially due to the comfort and security of their essentially middle-class position. Similarly, in his opinion, the tendency of the educator to see the solution of the social crisis in the training given to the expert reflected a certain class bias. Liberal hopes that the evolving intelligence of the general community would lead to reform were refuted by the nonexistence of such a community. Society was composed of competing classes, and the perspective of each class was limited by its own economic interests.[55]

Dewey's political model, like Plato's, subordinated class conflict to the needs of education. Class antagonisms could be overcome by rational adjustment, and the rational adjustment of these antagonisms required educational reform. Educational reform and political reform are related and interdependent in both Plato and Dewey. Neibuhr regarded Dewey's tendency to develop "a political theory in the form of a philosophy of education,"[56] and his hopes for resolving political problems through science as attempts to escape from the realm of politics. Niebuhr remained skeptical of all attempts to eliminate political conflicts through some program of increasing social science, but the original source of this skepticism was his Marxist tendency to regard the social sciences as easy prey to ideological perversions. He retained the Marxist sense of ideological justifications reflecting class interests long after he had given up on most Marxist theory. His developed critique of Marxism attacked its pretences to be socially scientific. This polemic against reducing politics to science became one of the defining characteristics of the realist school. Hans Morgenthau's first American book on politics reflected his debt to Niebuhr in criticizing "scientism" in politics.

Christian Pragmatism

In debt to William James and in dialogue with John Dewey, Niebuhr developed a new form of pragmatism by combining it with Christian theology. In an important article he argued that pragmatism was the new direction in the field of Christian political and social ethics.[57] Acceptance of pragmatism meant the dissolution of the traditional dogmas of both the left and the right. Christian pragmatism meant, to Niebuhr, recognition of the complexity of the issues of economics and politics, a commitment to justice, and an acceptance of a sense of responsibility for political life.

The synthesis of pragmatism and theology helped to relativize political programs, by containing them within the hopes of a Christian theology of history. Political policies were no longer to serve absolute ends, but historical projects of importance without illusions. Christian values had been corrupted repeatedly, but properly used they provided intellectual defenses against tyranny, anarchy, and nihilism. Niebuhr particularly relied on references to the authority of God beyond the authority of humans, the moral law revealed as the law of love, the need for love to seek out justice, the dignity of the person, and respect for the institutions that protected and developed human life.

Pragmatists pride themselves upon their openness to helpful contributions from other philosophies. Particularly in the area of political philosophy, pragmatism is open to influence from other schools of thought. For James, Dewey, and Niebuhr, American political liberalism informed their thought. Niebuhr's recognition of pragmatism's dissolution of dogmas of the left and the right is partially intrinsic to pragmatism, partially a renewed confidence in liberalism, and partially a Christian nonchalance about particular social and political dogmas. The Christian influences in Niebuhr's pragmatism were often subtle and stemmed from his theologically grounded doctrines of humanity and history. When he rejected utopianism, he was particularly rejecting the utopian illusions of the Third Reich, Communist classless societies, and laissez-faire economics' promises of prosperity for all. They were rejected on the empirical grounds that their promises were false, and on the theological grounds that the promises were not congruent with Christian perspectives on either human nature or the directions of history.

Liberalism

Niebuhr's tendency to criticize most forcefully options he was tempted by obscured his liberalism and misled some interpreters. His liberalism in politics is rooted deeply in his theology. This connection is seen clearly in the article he wrote on "Freedom" for a theological dictionary.

> The community must give the person a social freedom which corresponds to the essential freedom of human nature, and which enables him to express hopes and ambitions and to engage in interests and vitalities which are not immediately relevant to the collective purposes of the community, but which in the long run enrich the culture and leaven the lump of the community's collective will and purpose.[58]

The connection of liberty-producing political institutions and the freedom of human essential nature is a bold step which many theologians and political philosophers have not taken. The connection between liberalism and the defense of democracy is not found in optimistic interpretations of human possibilities, but in the ambiguous nature of the existential realities of human nature.

Though campaigning some for Norman Thomas in 1936, Niebuhr would finally vote for Roosevelt. Socialism failed more than Roosevelt in foreign policy, and Niebuhr's respect for the pragmatic-liberalism of Roosevelt's New Deal was increasing. Niebuhr wrote that Roosevelt had learned from Wilson's errors and that his commitment of the United States to a continuing role of world responsibility marked a new level of maturity in American foreign policy. He recognized that Roosevelt operated within the framework necessitated by the pride and power of great nations. The concessions were not regarded as simple expediency but a wise recognition of the limits the sovereignty of nations placed upon international politics. Niebuhr's praise for Roosevelt's foreign policy balanced tribute to his political vision and to his command of pragmatic politics. The lend-lease act which drew the United States deeper into the European conflict was particularly praised by Niebuhr as an example of political sagacity.

> Roosevelt was no systematic political thinker; but he saw the main issue clearly and acted upon his convictions with as much consistency as the confused state of American pubic opinion would allow.[59]

Niebuhr judged political ideas by their results. The verification of political theory in terms of its products revealed his deep pragmatism, even though he often introduced such judgments with the words of one of his favorite texts, "By their fruits ye shall know them." Roosevelt became the symbol of pragmatic liberalism for Niebuhr. He would stay with this pragmatic-liberal synthesis utilizing the history of Western political theory, with the parameters he perceived Christian theology permitted, for the rest of his life. It was this combination that won him the respect which, though obscured in the 1970s by the more-radical political doctrines of many of his critics, reemerged in the election of 2008.

Niebuhr told me that he heartily approved of being interpreted as a liberal, and as evidence of his liberal politics pointed to his founding role in the Americans for Democratic Action (ADA).[60] He helped transform the Union for Democratic Action into the broader Americans for Democratic Action and presided with Elmer Davis over the new organization's first conference in Washington, D.C. in 1947. He continued to serve actively as a leader until his illness in 1952 force him to curtail his activities. His initial biographer, June Bingham, was enthralled with the speech she heard him give at a later Chicago convention. Niebuhr was influential in the early hard line that ADA took against communist policy and in insisting that the United States play a responsible role in resisting Communism. In penning the first draft of an ADA statement on foreign policy he wrote:

> The foreign policy of the United States is determined by the responsibilities which we have acquired as the most powerful nation in the free world and by the necessity of exercising our responsibilities in the continual contest with the world-wide tyranny of communism.[61]

Niebuhr viewed ADA as a tool for implementing Roosevelt's pragmatic liberalism on the domestic front and opposing the spread of Marxism and Russian power on the international front. He applauded ADA's struggle to oppose McCarthyism in its inquisition-like hunts of socialists or former members of United Fronts. The combination of realism in foreign policy and the ever broadening development of justice on the home front remained characteristic of Niebuhr's politics.

In retrospect, Niebuhr saw that his critiques of liberalism had been overdone. He had intended to criticize the excesses of liberal optimism and pacifism, and not the liberalism associated with founders of the American republic like James Madison and John Adams. Of course, he was not an economic liberal in the sense of the diverse group represented by Adam Smith, Ayn Rand, or the neoliberal theorists. The economic thought represented in ADA was characteristically Keynesian, emphasizing the government's role in managing the economy and preventing excesses by individuals or corporations. Socialism through a political party would not be achieved in the United States, but much of its program—government aid to education, health, transportation, etc.—would become the program of ADA with candidates like Hubert Humphrey, and Adlai Stevenson. While he was sympathetic to the cooperative movement, his belief in the capacity of politics to dominate economics led him in the direction of maximizing human opportunity through progressive government.[62]

Idealism and Realism

The central problem for Niebuhr in political philosophy was the nature of the relationship between human ideal communities and the real political life. Mistaken answers to the problem, particularly optimistic and moralistic answers, have hindered the formation and execution of United States foreign policy. Niebuhr labored throughout his career, to clarify this relationship. In his earliest days he was an idealist supporting Wilson, but then the international liberalism of Wilson came under criticism first by Marxism, and then by Christian theology. In its most extreme expression, the problem of the ideal and the real was revealed in Niebuhr's Christology; the ideal was powerless to coerce and was crucified by the political powers of the historical situation. In more moderate expressions, the problem was seen in the attempt to persuade wartime leaders to aspire to a more just and well-organized peace than wartime expediency encouraged. Niebuhr's writing at its extremes revealed both the self-giving spirit of Christ and an understanding of the self-seeking strategy of Machiavelli. His major emphasis, however, had been to persuade the American public of the need for a wise and responsible foreign policy.

He had assumed American policy would be self–seeking, and he tried to teach that neither consistent national egoism nor idealistic expressions of national righteousness would best serve American foreign policy. With the assumption of responsibility by the United States in its new superpower role after the war, Niebuhr's major energy turned toward international politics. The longest essay in *Man's Nature and His Communities* returns to this perennial issue in his thought and outlines a balanced approach to the idealist-realist controversy.

The essay on idealism and realism traces the idealistic and realistic motifs from Plato to Hans Morgenthau. The movement in Niebuhr's thought from Christian realism to a greater dependence on a pragmatic-liberal orientation is seen in his increased criticism of Augustine's realism. As late as 1953, though Niebuhr was critical of Augustine, he affirmed his realism. In 1965, Niebuhr was sharply critical of Augustine's realism and identified himself as a "moderate realist" rather than a "realist." The contrast of the tribute to Augustine in 1953 and the criticism of him in 1965 reveals the change in Niebuhr's realism.

> Thus Augustine proves himself a more reliable guide than any known thinker. A generation which finds its communities imperiled and in decay from the smallest and most primordial community, the family, to the largest, and most recent, the potential world community, might well take counsel of Augustine in solving its problems.[63]

The political thought which served as inspiration in 1953 began to appear irrelevant to modern democracies in 1965 as the resources of liberalism penetrated more deeply into Niebuhr's mind.

> An analysis of Augustine's and Luther's dualism and consequent "realism" affecting political communities must yield the negative conclusion that the realism was too consistent to give a true picture of either human nature or the human community, even before the advent of free governments, and *was certainly irrelevant to modern democratic governments.*[64]

The essay improved on his earlier writing on democratic theory by expounding the realism of James Madison. His analysis of power and interest presented the deepest pre-Marxist observations on the influence of class interest and the need to manage rather than eliminate factional interests. Madison represented the common-sense philosophy brought to Princeton by John Witherspoon who not only signed the Declaration of Independence but taught Madison his political theory. Niebuhr's increased respect for Madison reflected his own assurance that political liberalism could be combined with realism and also his view that the institutions of representative government had outlived the optimism that had supported them. The argument of the essay expresses the danger of overly consistent realism or idealism. Humanity is both self-seeking and cooperative. Moral ideals can be achieved only through policies that account for the self-seeking aspirations of various groups. Niebuhr did not expect the full realization of ideals, not even his own liberal democratic ideals of toleration, liberty, and representative government. However one cannot surrender to the lure of cynicism and the wise policy is one that strives to maximize the degree of possible justice. Justice as a principle for Niebuhr consists of both equality and liberty. The goal of a tolerable justice for a society involves the achievement of the maximum possible degree of liberty and equality within a framework of order. The ideals of political liberalism are utilized by Niebuhr, but he tried not to confuse that which is normative with his description of political reality. Political reality is necessarily separated from the ideal, but it is in need of constant improvement and criticism by reference to the ideal.

The pragmatic-liberal synthesis achieved by Niebuhr was a characteristically American way of approaching political reality, and Niebuhr's criticisms of American optimism and moralism are a part of the continuing dialogue in the history of American political thought. His writings on the incongruities of American history have attempted to expose American illusions and in so doing to free the United States to exercise a role of responsible leadership in world politics. His affirmation of the central theologies of Paul, Augustine, Luther, and Calvin and their political consequences kept him a critic of American optimism. His fate as a thinker, assuming responsibility for defending representative governing institutions after World War II, left him defending a country that had become an empire and whose imperialism would expand during the tensions of the Cold War. That is the story of the next chapter.

Paul Tillich, on the other hand, had waged his war against Hitler, and lost his resolve to find a way for a united democratic Germany. The abandonment of the Council for a Democratic Germany, and the refusal of the United States government to permit him a role in the reconstruction of Germany combined with the irrelevance of socialism as a political party to the United States, led him to decrease his actual political work. He continued to speak on socialism when asked. He took bold public stands against McCarthyism and the campaign of Senator Goldwater, but these were rather episodic. While his participation in the nuclear debate was discussed earlier, the full presentation of his theory of justice remains for a later chapter. His major contributions to the theory of politics would be incorporated in his *Systematic Theology*, the production of which dominated the last two decades of his life.

15

Cold War International Relations: The Beginning

The conclusion of World War II in 1945 fundamentally changed international relations. Germany and Japan were in ruins. Their people were hungry and dispirited. In Japan an American General dictated the rules. In Germany a division was enforced. Europe was set back through its loss of industry and the failure of its governmental institutions. China was in turmoil. Asiatic and African peoples who observed their colonial masters defeated began to push more forcefully for freedom from colonization. Russia and the United States stood astride a broken order as the new superpowers.

The destruction and division of Germany discouraged Paul Tillich. His hopes for a democratic-socialist state in Germany seemed defeated. His chairmanship of the émigré Council for a Democratic Germany folded under the beginning Cold War pressures. His political knowledge and instincts were German, and he responded by retreating from his heavy involvement. He never finished his prewar manuscript on world politics and world religions. He continued to make political statements and to lecture on politics when asked, but after World War I he had spoken of a new significant time. After World War II, he spoke of a political vacuum.

His new homeland had ended his political radio speeches into Germany, and it would not use his knowledge for the reconstruction of Germany. He provided support for suffering Germans and continued his work for refugees, but he had to wait until 1948 before he could even return to Germany. Travel to Germany required invitations from German institutions and Army security coverage.

There were sufficient postwar essays on peace to collect into a small book, but his major efforts in international politics were in the past. He heard first about the awful destruction of Germany from visiting Germans and Reinhold Niebuhr who traveled to Germany in 1946 to report on the cultural and educational life under U.S. occupation. By the time of his 1948 journey, his family and friends had left East Germany and the Cold War had taken its postwar shape which would last longer than Paul Tillich's life. Most of the Germans who had lived in the towns of Starzeddel, his birthplace, and Bad Schonfliess, Konigsberg, and Butterielde, the scenes of his childhood, had emigrated to be replaced by Poles. The house in which Tillich was born on 20 August 1886, was turned into a

Roman Catholic rectory, and the thirteenth-century Romanesque church of which Tillich's father was an Evangelical pastor was once again a Roman Catholic Church. Konigsberg had been largely destroyed, and the Friedrich Wilhelm Gymnasium which Tillich attended for two years was in ruins. Bad Schonfliess had escaped the destruction and it remained a minor town surrounded by a medieval wall.

Butterfelde, the scene of Tillich's first romance, engagement, and marriage in 1913, still had sites marking the young Tillich's courtship of Greti Wever. The former Wever estate had been turned into a state-run enterprise. The Russians through the Polish government, had changed the social structure to reflect their values. They interpreted Hitler's movement as mainly an economic expression of collapsing capitalism dependent upon large farmers and industrialists. Socialism of a tyrannical sort without democracy had come to Tillich's homeland which was now part of Poland. The Yalta Conference had hinted at dismemberment of Germany while the Potsdam Conference had urged joint administration of a united Germany. Allied failures and ideologies produced the dismemberment by the time of Tillich's visit to West Germany. The sixty million dead from the war, the massive expulsions of Germans from Poland, Hungary, and Czechoslovakia, the ravages of the Russian armies, and the ineptitude of the occupiers all reinforced Tillich's depression.

Suffering still from the post-traumatic stress disorder from his breakdowns in the horrors of World War I, Tillich returned to his life task of producing a systematic theology. Almost as he had urged his fellow soldiers in the trenches of the Western Front to turn from the slaughter to think on eternal things, so his life moved in that direction to produce a theology true to existential reality as well as the essence of Christian thought. The strongest encouragement came from his American theological students who had been soldiers and chaplains in World War II. They even did much of the early work reducing his lectures into manuscript form for his editing and correcting.

Niebuhr, on the other hand, directed his great energy to postwar international politics. He wrote that he was giving more time to international relations than to theology in his later years. This, of course, was only true of his activities and writing; he was still teaching theological ethics at the Seminary, and writing some on theological themes. Crises including world hunger, nuclear weapons, the Cold War, reconstruction of Germany, relations with Russia, decolonization, the developing United Nations all stimulated his writing. Through serving the government, working in the Americans for Democratic Action, membership on the Council for Foreign Policy, involvement in the World Council of Churches, he developed into a major interpreter of international relations. The major theological basis of his thought on international relations had already been published in *The Nature and Destiny of Man*, and now his writing, speaking and preaching referred often to foreign policy. In summary, the postwar years saw Tillich working more rigorously on publishing his *Systematic Theology*, and Niebuhr engaging international relations. In both cases these decisions were influenced by the Cold War and the division of Germany which neither of them would live to see resolved. Their publications and speeches advanced Union Seminary's public image, and in the 1950s and 1960s it was clearly regarded as the most important seminary in the United States.

In the summer of 1945, Niebuhr's journal, *Christianity and Crisis*, dealt with news about the hunger and shocked condition of the German people. News of concentration camps, church recovery, and economic devastation filled its pages as well as church news from recently freed countries. Editorials and articles detailed hunger and famine among refugees and pled for the lifting of military restrictions that prevented the shipment of food and clothing to Hungary and Germany. Millions of Germans were being forced out of Czechoslovakia and the restored Poland. Thousands were dying alongside the roads from exhaustion and famine. On arriving in the American zone of occupation they were forced into an area which was not self-sufficient in agriculture before the war and in need of food before the arrival of the new refugees. The hope of the occupying power to provide a diet of 1,350 calories per day seemed inadequate and punitive.

The journal argued against further punishment of the country. Often Niebuhr repeated the idea that the Allies had already delivered divine punishment upon German for all of its evil and that though war criminals must be tried, further punishment of Germany was neither helpful nor necessary. In both Eastern and Western Europe, collaborators and the Nazis were hunted down and executed, sometimes by trials and sometimes without. Soon the new governments stopped the process of cleansing as the need for government superseded the thirst for revenge.

By the time of Niebuhr's 1946 inspection tour the tide had turned in the United States from punishment and thorough de-Nazification toward restoration in West Germany. Tillich had written of social revolution, but Communist takeover dominated the social scene in Eastern Europe. At first Stalin's policy had accommodated pluralistic governments since many of the countries had few surviving Communists after Hitler. For a few months the Western allies cooperated with Russia in governing Germany, but soon that ended and the divided country was subject to different social and governing systems.

Reports from the United Nations conference in San Francisco celebrated developments, but noted the tensions between the superpowers. The editors warned against the unconditional surrender policy toward Japan urging readers to write to the president urging the end of unrestricted bombing of Japanese cities. Of course, they had no idea of what awaited Japan in August of 1945. As the war ended Professor Charles Iglehart of the Seminary was requested by General Macarthur to hurry to Japan to advise on the transformation of the Japanese educational system. Three years later a member of the Union Seminary board of directors, John Foster Dulles, would negotiate the peace treaty with Japan that fundamentally disarmed the defeated foe for the long term.

Particularly noteworthy were Niebuhr's editorials on the difficulty of cooperation with Russia in the occupation of Germany. He noted how Russian policies in Eastern Europe would make reconciliation difficult. He warned against war with Russia, not expecting it immediately, but understanding it might come in ten or twenty years. He regarded such a war as a catastrophe. He warned against military domination of policy toward Japan and Germany. Military leaders in both Russia and the United States seemed to be laying plans for an eventual war. Such plans laid in distrust, though maybe necessary, could create the conditions in which nations could slide into an unwanted and unnecessary civil war within European civilization.[1] Niebuhr did not have the term *Cold War* yet, but he warned of its dangers. He opposed the president's request for conscription legislation in November 1945. He understood relations with Russia were deteriorating, but feared legislation that would send threatening signals to Russia. If there were still hope for cooperation it must be maximized. as the central questions were: What about the Russians? What about the bomb? In reality, though, after the defeat of Germany and Japan, both the United States and the U.S.S.R. disarmed the bulk of their armed forces. War was not imminent and trust had to be built to prevent it in the future. According to Niebuhr, the U.S. was strong enough to take risks to strengthen long-term prospects for peace.

Upon learning of the execution of Dietrich Bonhoeffer, who had been a German Fellow at Union, Niebuhr wrote "The Death of a Martyr." He praised Bonhoeffer's theology, his courage, and his political insight. In July 1939 Bonhoeffer had confided to Niebuhr that Hitler would launch his attack upon Poland in September. He had regarded the attack upon Russia as signaling the defeat of Hitler. Niebuhr had secured a teaching post for Bonhoeffer in the Union Seminary summer school so that he could escape Germany as his friends had urged. He reconstructed from memory the letter Dietrich had written him announcing his decision to return to Germany.

> Sitting here in Dr. Coffin's garden I have had time to think and to pray about my situation and that of my nation and to have God's will for me clarified. I have come to the conclusion that I have made a mistake in coming to America. I must live through this difficult period of our national history with the Christian people of Germany. I will have no right to participate in the reconstruction of Christian life in Germany after the war if I do not share the trials of this time with my people. My brothers in the Confessional Synod

> wanted me to go. They may have been right in urging me to do so; but I was wrong in going. Such a decision each man must make for himself. Christians in Germany will face the terrible alternative of either willing the defeat of their nation in order that Christian civilization may survive or willing the victory of their nation and thereby destroying civilization. I know which of these alternatives I must choose; but I cannot make the choice in security.[2]

Niebuhr predicted the rise of the influence of Bonhoeffer's theological thought, and that it would eclipse that of Dr. Niemoeller whose views were being reported so widely since his release from his eight years in a German prison. He also reported on Bonhoeffer's telling Bishop Bell of Chichester in 1942 of the anti-Nazi planned assassination and coup d'etat against Hitler which belatedly occurred in June 1944.

Bishop Bell had been Bonhoeffer's primary contact in his attempt to get the Allies to recognize the reality of German resistance. Bell was, along with Archbishop Temple, one of Niebuhr's chief ecclesiastical contacts in Britain concerning Germany during the war. He joined with Niebuhr in the work of the new Commission on International Relations of the World Council of Churches. Other North Americans on the Committee included John Foster Dulles, and Bishop G. Bromley Oxnam. Niebuhr and Dulles did not agree in their respective methods of relating faith to international politics, but they cooperated in the churches' work in international affairs during the war and until Dulles became the Republican secretary of state under President Eisenhower. Their cooperation at this time is seen in the issue of *Christianity and Crisis* in which Dulles' report on the first meeting of the United Nations shares space with Niebuhr's praise for resolutions of the World Council of Churches' provisional meeting regarding the needs of suffering European populations, helping the transfer of populations, on anti-Semitism, and on Christians of Hebrew ancestry.

The theologians' committee's report on the atomic bomb acknowledged that the plans for the bomb could not be turned over to the United Nations because of distrust of the Russians. That distrust left, according to Niebuhr, only one alternative. That was to enter into a solemn covenant to destroy the American stockpiles and to declare that the United States would never be the first to use the bomb.[3] This rather unilateral disarmament of nuclear weapons was an early position of Niebuhr's and one that he held only until the Russians also possessed the weapon. The commitment to work for a no-first-use policy set him against U.S. military policy, until his death, on an issue that he continued to regard as one of the most important questions facing the U.S. It is worth noting this as a relatively unrecognized early position. This intense involvement in the churches' work for peacemaking is also another facet of Niebuhr's vocation that is under-recognized by many critics.

The same issue that contained Niebuhr's memorandum and a prison poem by Bonhoeffer told of another Union Seminary martyr. Theodore Hume, a 1930 graduate of the seminary was killed in 1943 when his plane was shot down while he was on his way to Sweden to begin to plan postwar reconstruction for the World Council of Churches. The book about him called *Flight to Destiny* was written to inspire youth to join the service of the church for humanitarian aims.

As relations between the United States and the Soviet Union were hardening in 1946–1947, Reinhold was hastening back and forth across the Atlantic helping to build institutions. He worked for the developing World Council of Churches' Commission on International Affairs, spoke to the founding meeting of the British Council of Jews and Christians and traveled with the State and War Departments in Germany as one of fifteen advisors in the U.S. Commission on Cultural Affairs in the Occupied Territories to Germany.

In January 1946, he met with the Anglo-American Commission on Palestine where his testimony was aided by Richard Crossman, the British Member of Parliament who was familiar with Niebuhr's writings. Niebuhr favored the immigration of Jews to Palestine and had as early as 1943 urged the opening of America to Jewish immigration. He argued for recognition of Jewish nationalism even though he conceded it would impose some injustice on the Palestinian Arab population. Though there was an argument that Jewish technology and development could aid Arab development, large Jewish immigration would be seen as an injustice to the Arabs. No perfect solution was possible. "We mustn't say our solution is absolutely a just solution for the other person, but try to make it as perfect as possible."[4]

After finishing the second semester of his ethics course, and the senior thesis seminar at the Seminary, he was off to England to lecture to the founding meeting of the British Council of Christians and Jews. Alan Paton said of his speech on the occasion:

> The big address was given by Reinhold Niebuhr. He was speaking on one of his favorite themes, moral man and immoral society. I had never before heard a speaker who spoke with such apparent ease, who moved his argument forward with every sentence he spoke, who used language that could be understood by any nontheologian, who could be witty and grave in one short sentence, who in fact held his listeners in the hollow of is hand.[5]

His meetings with church leaders and Members of Parliament produced agreements and differences of judgment, particularly as Irgun, the Jewish guerrilla, terrorist militia, headed by the later prime minister Ben-Gurion, blew up the King David Hotel in Jerusalem during the visit.

John Foster Dulles, two bishops, and Niebuhr were the American delegation to the first meeting of the Churches' Commission on International

Affairs in Cambridge, England, in August. Later that fall he defended Dulles from the charges that he had imposed a hard anti-Communist line on this emerging committee for the developing World Council of Churches. In fact, he said the press was uninformed about the meeting and gave the misimpression of a hard line by the American delegation. A continental representative was harder on the Soviets than were the Americans at the meeting

As usual on his visits to England, most of his meetings with politicians were with members of the Labour party who were now in power. Stafford Cripps and Wedgwood Benn the former and present heads of the Air Ministry were particular friends of his. Ecclesiastical issues allied Niebuhr and his wife with the ordination of women which had just been rescinded in the case of a woman minister in Hong Kong. Disputes over the appointment of Anglican Bishops by the Labour government echoed and reconstruction of the Coventry Cathedral were addressed in his letters to his Anglican wife, Ursula. Prime Minster Clement Attlee, who bore the ultimate responsibility for the appointment of these Anglican bishops, told me in an interview at Morningside College in Sioux City, Iowa, in 1955, that he would never have been elected to Parliament if it had not been for the support of socialist Methodists. These easy alliances between socialists and religious people were very close to the model Tillich and Niebuhr advocated for the United States, but the project would not be realized in America. From the English-speaking, consulting, and organizing tour, Niebuhr returned to New York for a week's respite before heading to Washington D.C. for the orientation meetings of the next trip as a member of the United States Commission on Cultural Affairs in Occupied Territories.

His letters to Ursula indicated how often he was tired. 1946 was particularly a year of overwork as he produced more than one hundred occasional pieces (articles of various lengths, editorials, book reviews), and a book of sermonic essays, *Discerning the Signs of the Times,* taught his classes and made two trips to Europe. The trip for the government to Germany brought back memories of his trip after World War I to the French-occupied Ruhr.

The tolerance of the United States for dissent was tested with the appointment of Niebuhr to the Commission on Culture Affairs in the Occupied Territories. An alternative explanation is that forces within the State Department wanted a critic of the U.S. occupation policies on the commission. In the spring he had published a critique of the policies. Both he and Tillich had written before the end of the war on restoring democracy in the reconstruction of Germany. But now in 1946, he called the U.S. approaches stupid, even more stupid than the Russian policies. Many of his articles in this period of his writing called his opponents stupid. It may seem more jarring in the present than it did then. Gary Dorrien refers to this tendency of Niebuhr's without comment in his major history of Christian social ethics, and refrains from using the term himself as he analyzes the various twists and turns of the discipline's development in America.

He criticized blowing up German factory buildings while millions of Germans were homeless, denial of fraternization with the Germans, expecting Germans to live on 1,500 calories a day (up from the earlier figure of 1,350), the policy of displacing five German families from their housing to locate one American officer's family, refusing to restore postal connections with Germany, preventing, for a time, church organizations from sending food to Germany, the scolding nature of U.S. broadcasts into the occupation zones, and the mass dismissal of German workers without adequate investigation of supposed Nazi loyalties. He thought even backward prison wardens had better policies than the U.S. army was pursuing in the defeated country. Statesmanship required wisdom to procure justice and employment in the areas the U.S. controlled so that the people would not be drawn toward Communist propaganda. It was more important to develop wise policies in the areas we controlled than to appease Russia or to threaten Russia, or to negotiate with Russia. But in the present "Russia and America are in a race to determine which is the most stupid in wielding the power which each has won in the past years."[6]

In the orientation for the trip, Reinhold wrote to Ursula that except for her friend Professor White of Michigan and an Iowan the delegation was not very impressive. A sidebar conversation with a State Department representative raised the possibility of Niebuhr's heading up the new UNESCO, the chair of which was reserved for an American, Niebuhr reported to Ursula. From Paris they flew over Berlin, and he wrote home about the city with most of its roofs missing looking like a bees' honeycomb. Conditions of people on the ground were likewise desolate; many seemed to be in shock.

He wrote Ursula on his third evening in Berlin:

> Dearest:
>
> Yesterday after I wrote you we took a tour of the city and saw the destruction at close hand. The inner city of Berlin is a city of the dead. Not a building stands. We stopped at the new imperial chancery which Hitler built and which was destroyed almost completely. The long and high reception rooms of this palace are fantastic in their pretensions. I picked off a piece of mosaic from Hitler's great reception room to take back to the old boy [their son Christopher].

The next day after interviews with the leaders of the occupation, he was off to visit German friends, socialists and churchmen. Especially noteworthy among those he visited were the remnants of the Bonhoeffer family for whom he had gathered rations from the American dispensary. The delegation spent a month visiting many cities and interviewing the leadership both German and American, though it was hard to arrange private meetings for discussions with Germans. German leaders, including Bishop Dibelius, expected war with Russia in the near future. Having faced both death and tyranny for so many years, they were less willing to live under tyranny than to face death.

The trip confirmed Niebuhr's previous judgments of the inadequacy of the American program for Germany, and the difficulties of imposing democracy through force. Many Germans from the resistance were convinced that Russian totalitarianism was worse for them than the Nazis. The mass raping of German women by Russian troops, the looting of property by troops, and the absence of men all left Germans dazed and exhausted. Politics seemed something to be avoided, and the democracy the allies hoped to establish in Germany was received with cynicism by Germans who had lived through the former democracy's surrender to Nazi horror.

In the middle of the trip, Niebuhr received the news from H. Richard that their brother Walter had died. He was grieved that he could not be of help to the family, and he reflected on his elder brothers "sadly confused life." He remembered warmly their genial childhood, and all the pain that Walter's later life had caused the family and especially his wife Beulah. The three theologians of the family, H. Richard, Hulda, and Reinhold all wrote to each other about their brother's death and his successes and many failures. Walter's journalism had been followed by his younger brother, Reinhold. The family had followed with excitement his early successful movie career in silent pictures. His deafness resulting from an insect bite in the expedition against Pancho Villa had doomed his transition to talking pictures, though he attempted it. Reinhold knew of the fragility of family life and personal life, and he was protective of both. His letters to Ursula are warm, full of love, and consistently grateful for their family life. Niebuhr in writings and conversations urged his students to be prudent, faithful, and protective of their family life.

Niebuhr reported his impressions from Germany quickly to his readers. He admitted that the experience was so overwhelming that he was not sure he had organized his thought yet. He reported on three themes. The first was that the army of occupation was offensive in its special privilege, wealth, and general disdain for the people whose homes it was occupying. It was accepted, or tolerated by the Germans who feared the Russians more than they resented American arrogance and condescension.

Secondly, the occupation revealed vindictive passions to be among the worst evils. Care was not taken to recognize that Germans understood how evil the Nazis had been. Wholesale dismissals of the majority of teachers ignored the fact that many of them were only indirectly associated with Nazi guilt. The allies manifested very little sense of guilt though studies revealed that the destruction of cities and civilians added very little to the war effort. All blame was put upon the Germans with the suggestion that the destruction and deaths were a just and righteous punishment.

Thirdly, for his readers of *Christianity and Crisis* he commented on the religious situation in Germany. The German churches had been involved in acts of both valor and betrayal and the results had not yet been sorted out. The Christian roots of Germany were deep, but their spirituality had not been accompanied by a sense of social righteousness that thwarted Nazi paganism. He mentioned moving religious services in Frankfurt and Stuttgart, particularly praising the young Dr. Thiellicke for his thoughtful sermon. Protestant and Catholic cooperation struck a positive note, though he worried that it might be due mostly to their common fear of Communism. There were a few signs of Christian rapprochement with socialism which he welcomed, though he did not expect most Americans to understand it. Karl Barth's warning against the identification of religion with political parties was appreciated. Niebuhr particularly feared conservative movements looking for religious legitimization. He poked fun at Barth's famous Stuttgart address. Barth had claimed: "The Christian faith can be maintained even in a well-regulated band of robbers." Niebuhr mentioned that one of the resisters to Nazism had replied: "Such a judgment is more easily made by one who had little direct experience of the robber band from which we have been liberated."[7]

Niebuhr summarized his general position on Christian faith and international relations in a statement on the subject signed by the editorial board of *Christianity and Crisis*, and others of Niebuhr's supporters. Only John C. Bennett of the editorial board and Niebuhr's close friend, did not sign. The statement emphasized that Christian approaches to international relations were usually more sober than their secular colleagues' approaches because of their consciousness of the stubbornness of nations in pursuing their own interests, and their awareness of the corruption of the human spirit. Repentance rather than despair was called for, and utopian illusions needed to be avoided. The Christian faith urged a sober serenity in which it was known that "neither life nor death nor things present nor things to come can separate us from the love of Christ, which is in Christ Jesus our Lord." Sober serenity was not social peace, but it could contribute to that peace. Hopefully a tolerable peace could be maintained, but efforts to create a world-governing authority were in vain.

Elsewhere, Niebuhr often wrote about the Hobbesian illusions that fear could produce governments where community did not exist. The U.S. had started badly in its use of the atomic bomb. If international control could be established it should be. If not the future of an arms race was ominous indeed. Perhaps for years the world would have to live in atomic insecurity. The comments about colonialism were not far reaching. While the U.S. was urged not to circumvent the principle of trusteeship for economic or strategic gain, there was no urge to condemn all colonialism of the "backward nations." Ten years later a different regard for European colonial powers would cause Bennett and Niebuhr to disagree over the Suez crisis in the pages of the journal.

Niebuhr heard Secretary of State Byrnes's speech in Stuttgart in which he pledged that the United States would stay involved in Europe as long as any other government. The Germans he talked to feared Russia and approved of the speech and the United States' seeming willingness to aid Europe. He indicated that the U.S. and Britain would merge their zones of influence regardless of whatever Russia attempted. It was regarded as a major "Get tough Speech" particularly in light of Churchill's earlier "Iron Curtain" speech in Fulton, Missouri.[8]

Henry A. Wallace who had previously served Roosevelt as Secretary of Agriculture and vice-president was now in the Truman administration as Secretary of Commerce. He spoke on September 12 at a rally in Madison Square Garden arguing for a strengthened United Nations and cooperation with Russia. He feared the line Byrnes had taken would lead to an unnecessary war. In his mind there were two positions, either cooperation and trust of the Soviet Union or distrust and preparing for war. Niebuhr of course favored a third position, which George Kennan had published in *Foreign Affairs* as the famous Mr. X article advocating political containment of the Soviet Union and the avoidance of war through strength. Niebuhr had recently joined the Council on Foreign Relations that had published the article. Henry Wallace was representative of the type of optimistic liberal with whom Niebuhr had been doing battle for a decade and a half.

President Harry Truman at first denied any difference between Byrnes and Wallace. Wallace claimed Truman had read his manuscript and approved of his speech. Byrnes demanded Wallace's resignation and threatened to resign himself if Truman refused to oust Wallace. Niebuhr's Union for Democratic Action secretary, James Loeb, argued for keeping Wallace in the cabinet and proposed a meeting between Wallace and Niebuhr to see if the split in the liberals over foreign policy could be overcome. The meeting was never held.

Niebuhr had strongly backed the recovery of Europe through U.S. economic aid and the necessity of restoring Germany to the world of international legitimacy. Wallace was willing to aid Europe economically, but only through the United Nations and in a manner that included cooperation with Russia. Niebuhr's major article in *Life* set the parameters for the realist-liberal approach to Germany and toward Russia.[9] This essay was excerpted in *Time* and reprinted in *The Reader's Digest* after Secretary Wallace's resignation in September. Niebuhr and Wallace would continue to disagree through 1948 until Wallace's defeat for the presidency as the candidate of the Progressive Party. Years later he would admit he had been mistaken and that his optimism about trustful cooperation with the Soviet Union had been misplaced. But before he came to understand the dangers of the Soviet Union and the massacres of Stalin, he and Niebuhr disagreed also about the correct plan for nuclear control to be offered to the Soviet Union, the Berlin blockade, aid to Greece, the Marshall Plan, and U.S policy toward the Soviet Union 1946–1948.

Niebuhr's parenthetical references to the impossibility of world government that are sprinkled throughout his writings particularly from 1946 to 1948, seem to be directed at the illusions of Henry Wallace who shared the hope for escaping world politics through world government after World War II. Niebuhr's own efforts would be seen in his work as part of the U.S. delegation to United Nations Educational, Scientific and Cultural Organization (UNESCO) later, and in the reference above to the consideration of him for the leadership of UNESCO. This more humble, realistic working toward world community met Niebuhr's own sense of the long-term world development toward community that would have to precede any conceivable world government.

The Union for Democratic Action, which was supportive of Wallace's liberalism for domestic policies, came to oppose him strongly when his run for the presidency threatened to unseat Harry Truman by drawing away Democratic votes in 1948. Niebuhr particularly objected to the united front optimism of Wallace whose Progressive Party was open to collaboration with Communists. Niebuhr had tried to cooperate earlier with Communists within the teacher's union in New York City and his own experience and liberalism persuaded him that such collaboration could not be useful. Wallace's belief that one could guide foreign policy with the "Golden Rule" of Jesus seemed hopelessly naive to Niebuhr.

President Harry Truman also confessed that he resolved the issue of the relationship of morality to foreign policy by claiming that his foreign policy was governed by "The Golden Rule." Truman's statement in light of his World War II policies seem even more disconnected from reality than Wallace's. Truman's realism makes his statement seem like moralistic rhetoric whereas Wallace's seems to come from his deeper, though confused, spiritual roots.

As Niebuhr guided the Union for Democratic Action to broaden its appeal by development into the Americans for Democratic Action, its attitude toward Wallace hardened. Niebuhr and James Loeb both played rough politics to reduce his damage to the Democratic ticket in 1948.[10] Kleinman's discussion of the Wallace-Niebuhr struggle over foreign policy, fails to understand the deep perspectival differences between Niebuhr and Wallace. Kleinman raises but then shies away from Richard Fox's psychological interpretation of Niebuhr's realism about Germany and Russia. But then Kleinman, like his source Richard Fox,, fails to grasp the importance of Niebuhr's developed perspective on international relations and his contribution to the theory of the same for the postwar period in which he lived. Niebuhr's fight with the optimistic liberalism of Wallace and others was deeply rooted in his biblical realism that I have called prophetic realism. This is clearly seen in his book of sermonic essays, *Discerning the Signs of the Times*, published the same year as his critique of Henry Wallace's dissent from the firm policies of the United States in Europe.

Discerning the Signs of the Times

Niebuhr finished the editing of his sermons to universities in December 1945 and it was published in 1946. While the book would serve well as Lenten devotional reading, it contains his political philosophical outlines as well. He describes the chapters of the book as sermonic essays. They actually were sermons preached in college chapels, but they were written in their published form after the sermons and ideas were expanded on and developed in the essays. Niebuhr probably should not be thought of as doing political theology. His theology certainly is not as direct in its political conclusions as either liberation theology or conservative political theology. That is why his theology and outlook on political communities has been appropriated by both progressives and conservatives. His theology sets outlines within which he conducts his political thought which in his case is in a progressive direction. After all, in 1948 he was still hoping that American aid to Europe would be applied in a manner that would socialize the major industrial production of Germany. The programs of both UDA and its successor the early ADA wanted to expand the reforms of the New Deal as much as they could in a socialistic direction. Democratic socialism for Europe was seen as the third way between communism and capitalism represented by the U.S.A. and the U.S.S.R. He tried to balance worldly Christian hope and action with its more eternal dimensions as his version of the Christian faith did not promise worldly success for the completion of Christian hopes, but rather serenity within the worldly tasks.

The title of the book came from Jesus' denunciation of the hypocrites for not being able to discern the meaning of the present, and much of Niebuhr's work in the book kept up the criticism of other perspectives. Both the cynics and the utopians were particular targets. The book represents the mature Niebuhr and to an extent almost the whole of Niebuhr's later thought. Phrases, quotes, and insights from the book were still on his lips in his final seminar in 1968. Whereas Jesus criticized those who could predict the weather, but not discern the meaning of the messianic age, Niebuhr uses the distinction to show how far objective science about nature is from understanding the passions and irrationalities of human nature and human action. The reason used in human affairs is influenced by the total self who is doing the reasoning, and the results reflect the relativity of the perspective of the anxious self. Our judgments about human affairs reflect our own interests. Niebuhr thinks that the virtue of humility from the recognition of God and the recognition of our own sin and inadequacy should guide our judgments and encourage forgiveness. Throughout the book forgiveness of the vanquished foe is seen as a political virtue, and Niebuhr regards it as essential for the healing of Germany. The allies have been the instrument of God's judgment on the Nazi attempt to overthrow the order of the world, but now the repentance of the Germans depends on their being able to see forgiveness in the eyes of the conquerors. God is both the ultimate power which insures that the order of his will can only be challenged so far, but God is also the source of grace and forgiveness which can renew a chastened humanity. Human lives are characterized by hypocrisy; human wisdom for dealing with the traumas is as much a fruit of humility and religious reverence as it is of wisdom gained through knowledge. Both ignorance and pride are the enemies of harmony in human relations.

Niebuhr preached on the text from Ephesians: "Be ye angry, and sin not: Let not the sun go down upon your wrath." He related it seriously if not literally to the war with the Nazis. Anger was appropriate; it was not a Christian idea to deny anger against evil. But it was important not to sin, and it was necessary to get over the anger so that vengeance was not regarded as a virtue. The ruined German cities revealed that Germany had been punished sufficiently. But, whereas criminals still needed to be tried, the people needed to be restored. In Niebuhr's judgment, the Nazi leaders should be tried as society judged its worse criminals. Collective punishment had already been leveled on the society in a terrible way with the cities of Japan and Germany reduced to rubble. Of course, Niebuhr's desire to see Germany redeveloped was prompted by his Germanic heritage, but more profoundly it represented lessons learned from post-World War I. Prolonged vengeance against Germany would only sow seeds for further wars. Here he was expressing his rejection of the plans of Secretary of the Treasury Henry Morgenthau for driving Germany into a peasant-farming economy. Niebuhr's pleas for restoring Germany would also be resented by Henry Wallace in his critique of concern for German rebuilding. Anger as a passion, even a motivation, was not to be ignored, though it was dangerous and could produce evil effects. But anger nurtured and kept alive would produce more evil. Nations tend toward self-righteousness and anger remembered turns into vengeance which stifles repentance and change on the part of the vanquished. The book, finished before he had seen firsthand the destruction of Germany, urged forgiveness and quoted Romans 12:19: "Dearly beloved, avenge not yourselves, but rather give place unto wrath; for it is written, Vengeance is mine; I will repay, saith, the Lord." These words are not only ultimately true but especially relevant at the end of a great conflict in which the vengeance of God upon evil-doers has been more terrible than any which human calculation could have devised.[11]

Niebuhr saw the time as being between a terrible war and fulfillment; he was not as pessimistic as Tillich after the war, but he knew that those who expected a time of fulfillment and order were mistaken. He could echo their hopes for international order, but this would not come about for a long time as the resources for achieving it were not present: "The age of absolute national sovereignty is over, but the age of international order under political instruments, powerful enough to regulate the relations and to compose their competing desires, is not yet born."[12]

None of the great powers in the Security Council of the United Nations was free from insecurity or pride. They would disagree among themselves, and contest the order for their respective views of national interest. A world government of order and justice was needed, but it was not now possible. Periods of historical development required a long time: "Mankind will finally find political instruments and moral resources adequate for a wholesome communal life on a world-wide scale. But generations and centuries may be required to complete the task."[13]

Niebuhr derived primarily from the biblical sources that the danger to nuclear armed nations was pride. Nations reaching beyond their limits and playing like gods to the world would be their nemesis. Statespeople were too ignorant and too prideful to do well in administering the affairs of others. No one was wise enough or good enough to have overwhelming power over others. The realist appreciation of the need for humility was grounded in their estimation of the tendency toward human folly. An aside in his brief paragraph on China was prophetic of the future: "The peace of the world is not served by the dominance of western powers in the affairs of Asia."[14]

In his chapter on the Nemesis of Nations, Niebuhr reflects on the destruction of Egypt and Assyria as prophesied by Ezekiel. In both Greek and Hebrew literature destruction arises from pride. Both Assyria and Egypt exalted themselves and forgot that they were only little powers before the ultimate power. The dictators had fallen as quickly as they had arisen and expressed their pride in ruling others. But the warnings against pride are not only for the losers, but also relevant to the victors. The victors' treatment of the vanquished revealed their pride, and set up their downfall as well. The purpose of prophetic warnings of doom was to encourage nations to change to avoid their downfall. The power of atomic weapons of destruction made prophetic pronouncements against pride more relevant in the modern age. Modern social science could not save modern humanity from in which people forgot their finiteness. Power centered on one nation or in a group of nations focused resentment on those who temporarily were dominant and encouraged their downfall. The very language recorded in Ezekiel is reminiscent of claims made by the victorious nations of World War II. Political shrewdness may enable the strong to avoid the mistakes of thinking they alone control destiny. But the humility needed to realize the danger of political leadership handling the vast new atomic power comes more likely from religious awareness of the sources of humility. Put theologically: "The more men and nations fear the wrath of God, the more they may be brought under the sway of divine mercy."[15]

Niebuhr moved beyond the nemesis of nations to indicate that many peoples hope for peace, the welfare of their own people, and even universal community. The people of Eastern Europe, for example, hoped for freedom beyond the slavery of their recent Nazi-dominated past. Historical hopes however were a mixture of fulfillment and frustration. To fix too seriously on the secular hopes often led to disillusionment and despair. There were degrees of historical fulfillment, but not as much as the enlightenment philosophers dreamed of in the eighteenth century. Christianity too had worldly hopes for peace and community. Its messianic thrusts and the prayer of Jesus that the Kingdom of God would appear pointed toward worldly expectations. Christianity combined its worldly hopes with otherworldly hopes. Accurate expressions of those hopes were both individual and social. Often in church history the two hopes for this world and for another world became separated and the best of the faith was lost. He thought the only adequate expressions of human faith combined both otherworldly and this-worldly expression of hope. The otherworldly hopes could help sustain life when the worldly hopes were frustrated. Niebuhr expected a good deal of frustration as humanity strove for its universal community of peace and adequate justice, and he hoped for a perspective that would encourage the doing of duty even when success seemed far away. Such a position is caught in his life in 1946, working for restoration of ruined Europe, striving for Christian unity through the ecumenical movement, and looking forward to working for the United Nations Educational Scientific Cultural Organization while remaining doubtful about any universal governing authority. For his own generation, he expected frustration and regarded as unjustified even Mortimer Adler's hope for a universal government to bring permanent peace in 500 years. Still the Christian hopes were not to annul worldly striving, but to provide the hope of ultimate fulfillment when the frustrations of human striving for justice were intense. The promise of human fulfillment did not have to be spelled out in much detail; it was sufficient to keep translating the Kingdom of God into the final fulfillment of the human spirit and to engage in the task of moving forward toward more justice and less conflict. We cannot understand completely the meaning of human existence nor fulfill it, but religious hope asserts that meaning.

Meaning is given in faith. Both the present and the future are fulfilled only by faith that one is acting in the presence of the Absolute who utilizes present acts for the process of life. Life flows and part of its meaning is given by the next generations, but the present act has its own value. Another part of its value is in the present in relationship to the total structure of value, relationships, and the valuation of the Absolute. Niebuhr illustrates his point by speaking of the just-war criterion that one can only go to war when success is assured. But there was value in Churchill's resistance to Hitler even if the British had not been successful. It is prudent and therefore moral not to enter into a fight in which resistance is doomed, but often one cannot know the outcome until the struggle is engaged. In the one criterion of the just war he discussed just after the war, he does not agree with the just-war principle. In the popular press and even some ethics textbooks he is regarded as a just-war theorist. Such conclusions should be regarded with distrust. His arguments that some wars can be justifiable are more pragmatic than most of the just-war principles which are generally in the form of rules. But also, beyond pragmatism, there is an obligation to act out of duty in the service of love which in history is understood as justice. One fights evil even when there is little promise of success.

God as the source of life for Christian faith is characterized by power. As the ultimate judge, God is power. God also represents power to limit evil and Niebuhr affirmed that the allies served the God of power in defeating the evil of Nazism. But they participated in the ambiguity of history and their methods were far from perfect. For Niebuhr the paradox of the relationship of love to power is revealed in Christ. Christ interpreted by Niebuhr as the love of God had no power to save himself. God's power demanded justice and God took the consequences of human sin upon himself. Justice requires power, but historically it serves particular interests and therefore government corrupts the power it uses to produce an ordered justice. Perfect love and justice are found only in God where love suffers. In history, love and power are related through justice but also alienated. Characteristically, in this chapter on the relationship of love to power and God to Christ where one would expect the argument to lead to the work of the Holy Spirit, Niebuhr does not go there. The Spirit is omitted for Niebuhr's preferred way of speaking of Christ in the world as suffering love. For Niebuhr power is good, but corrupted inevitably in the world. So his politics will be power politics, but directed to his understanding of the will of God. Therefore there will be a taint of sin the politics Niebuhr recommends and justice is not expected to be fully served.

Much of his effort in the argument is to inform Christians that they can and should use the tool of realistic politics in the pursuit of justice and not become distracted by interpretations that would lure them into fantasies of pure politics. His realism is demonstrated in his oft-repeated interpretation that Jesus was crucified by the best religion and the best law the world had seen. In this picture at the heart of Christian faith could be found the truth about the human situation in relationship to God. He is very aware of the degree to which his narrative is his own interpretation. He expresses it thus: "The truth which is revealed in Christ must be apprehended in faith. Faith as far as it uses our natural endowments, draws on poetic and imaginative capacities rather than rational ones."[16]

The Christian faith, which Niebuhr regards as the correct interpretation of human life, uses symbols to point toward the incompleteness of the human life and to recognize it is only fulfilled in God. In this history there is frustration of the human hopes for fulfillment and harmony. He does not go through the alternative explanations of human life to destroy them as he did in *The Nature and Destiny of Man* only a few years earlier. World War II disabused many of the humanistic optimists of their illusions and he is concerned to give his university chapel congregants—many of them returning veterans—insight into the mystery of the divine which some of the symbols can provide. The power of God to limit evil, the power of forgiveness, meaning beyond the obvious historical chaos, love beyond human vicissitudes made sense when expressed symbolically in biblical terms to his listeners.

His final sermonic essay in the book is also best understood when it is remembered that it was preached to those at the end of World War II. The peace of God is understood as the peace of forgiveness which is accepted. It does not save one from the conflicts, frustrations, and ambiguities of life, but gives one the capacity to live through them with a sense of peace. This was neither a rational nor an escapist peace for Niebuhr. It was beyond rationality, and it was expressed in the picture of the depths of the ocean which still had the tossing waves and mad pursuits of Captain Ahab on the surface. Human serenity to engage in struggle could be found in God's forgiveness. Even as the book was being published, world politics were darkening and beginning the next season of strife.

16

The Cold War Freezes

Forces on the ground basically determined the Cold War boundaries, though there were adjustments. The Allies shut Russia out of final decisions for Italy. The British claimed Greece for the West and resisted a Communist rebellion there. By 1947, The Truman Doctrine supported Britain with financial help and included Turkey in the area to receive U.S. help to thwart Russian designs. Poland, Rumania, and Bulgaria were conceded to Russia without much resistance. Finland and Austria were neutralized as buffers while the Baltic Republics were reabsorbed into the new Russian Empire. Resistance to Russian dominance lasted for a while within the forests of Lithuania. The forces of occupation secured Hungary for Russia, and while the U.S. protested the coup in Czechoslovakia in 1948 there was little the West could do to challenge the outcome. The Marshall Plan of 1948 clarified the American commitment to Western Europe. As Russia tested the atomic bomb in 1949 and Chiang Kai-shek retreated to Taiwan leaving China to a Communist government allied with Russia, the geopolitics of the Cold War and of the lifetimes of Tillich and Niebuhr were set. The nuclear umbrella covering the ideological conflicts of capitalist-democracy and dictatorial-socialism was in place by the end of 1949. Their hopes for democratic socialism would be confined to countries emerging from colonialism and then to its slow development in Europe beginning with the Labour Party's British victory over Churchill after the war. Though there would be two major wars in Asia, and many coups, and revolutions in the Third World, the struggles in Europe would be those of spies, espionage, electoral struggles, and failed rebellions against Moscow. It was a season of near war without open warfare between the major contestants, or of a precarious peace between the superpowers with warfare among and within the client states.

Niebuhr took the spring semester of 1947 to encounter the theological and political thought of Northern European Protestantism and Socialism. He had been expected to give the Olaf Petri Lectures in Sweden in 1939, but the war made that impossible. They were postponed until April 1947. The trip would be his last long separation from Ursula and the family, and his letters are full of messages of love for the family and the pain of being away. His concern for Ursula is shown in his urging her to hire some full-time to help with the home and the youngsters so she could pursue her vocation as college professor. The letters also reflect anxiety for the progress in school of their son, Christopher. Ursula wrote frequently about the independent mindedness of their younger daughter, Elizabeth. He began his trip in Scotland where he received an honorary degree from Edinburgh University. A few days after arriving in Scotland he sent her his revised schedule:

> The schedule now is Feb. 10-12 in Glasgow; Feb. 13-14 St. Andrews; Feb. 15-22 Aberdeen; Feb 23-26 Edinburgh degree, etc. On March 3 I go to Holland till the 11th, March 21 will be in London, then Sweden, Denmark and Sweden. I have a straight passage from Sweden to NYC. April 21.[1]

He gave several lectures at the Universities of Edinburgh, Aberdeen, and St. Andrews in Scotland. He found the academic theology of Scotland to be a rather stuffy Calvinism, but he admired the sharpness of the students and thought they were more in touch with his thought than many of the professors. He met old friends, stayed in their homes occasionally, and dined with many others. Meetings with political leaders were almost as frequent as with ecclesiastical leaders. While he preached in some churches, most events were held in university lecture halls or in university chapels. Requests were often made for British Broadcasting System talks, and he was beleaguered by writers for *Time* who were preparing a cover story on him for the magazine. The interviewers were not particularly apt at understanding American theological issues. The whole procedure was frustrating, and finally his story was bumped for one on George Marshall and his speech at Harvard announcing the economic recovery plan for Europe. When it finally made its appearance in March 1948, the story had been rewritten by Whitaker Chambers. Niebuhr's own intellectual work, aside from the lectures he was giving most days, was in preparation of his paper for the World Council of Churches' study book which had to be submitted by April as his tour ended.

Niebuhr met several professors who filled him in on how a planned economy worked. Also, it became clear to him in England and Scotland that the country was dreadfully impoverished from the war. There did not seem to be a will to hold on to the colonies or bear the financial cost of keeping them within the Empire. Conservative Members of Parliament blamed the financial situation on the unions. His address to Parliament in London had been attended mostly by Conservative M.P.s but most of his personal meetings were with Labour leaders. Stafford Cripps, the godfather of daughter Elizabeth, the Chancellor of the Exchequer, was a favorite conversation partner, and he regarded the Wedgewood Benn family as one of the finest families he ever spent time with. Richard Crossman, the Labour M.P. who had quizzed Niebuhr as a member of the Palestine Committee, entertained him, and their friendship grew. One

Conservative, Richard Butler, the former Conservative Minister of Education, sought Niebuhr out and provided invitations to conversations. On one occasion Butler had asserted he had reformed the educational system of Great Britain on the basis of Niebuhr's *Nature and Destiny of Man*. Ursula, in conversation with me, was doubtful that Reinhold had exerted that much influence through the Conservative Party of her country.

The trip to Holland was particularly fruitful. He was something of a celebrity because three of his books were being published there in Dutch that same month. He found the Protestants to be either Barthian or old-fashioned Calvinists; and many of the younger people took to Niebuhr as a foil against these more orthodox traditions. He couldn't find much creativity in the Protestant political party and he urged them to support the newly formed Labor Party whose leaders he met with on various occasions. He was most enthusiastic about a meeting of the party with the church leadership and workers. The union of the church and the "real proletariat" was something he had been hoping to see accomplished. He felt overused by the Dutch as he was speaking three times a day and attending various formal events as well. Finally he took a day off, and wrote that he had seen there was no need to be killing himself as there were several weeks to go.

He was delighted when there were periods of a few days when he spoke only once per day. He regularly stayed in hotels, and he appreciated it when they were heated. Sometimes he paid for his own hotels, but often the costs were covered. The financial arrangements for the trip were informal, sometimes there was an honorarium and sometimes not. The check of 300 pounds from the BBC for the radio broadcasts relieved him a great deal. He wrote Ursula that he thought the honorarium for the week of lectures in Sweden would cover the cost of Christopher's summer camp, an assist to their always tight budget. He complained gently that the Swiss seemed to assume he was lecturing at the Ecumenical Institut in Bossey near Geneva for his health. He enjoyed the visit there, the view of the Alps, and the international student body. The Institut was new, having been founded after the war for ecumenical studies in the enthusiasm of reuniting the churches. The chateau itself had been donated by the Rockefeller family much in the same way they provided the land for the United Nations in New York City. From Bossey he visited Basel and the father of neoorthodox theology, Karl Barth, before traveling on to Zurich to see Emil Brunner whose son Henry was occupying the guest room in the Niebuhr's apartment in New York City. During this period of absence from home, Niebuhr's letters leave the impression of Ursula languishing under her labors and loneliness. Actually while busy with the children, she was entertaining and meeting the Arnold Toynbees, and seeing Wystan Auden. She and Auden badgered Reinhold in her correspondence to allow the British to publish his

Letters of a Tamed Cynic, while he resisted the overture regarding the book as youthful folly and of unlikely interest to the British reader.

Visits to Barth and Brunner

While traveling, Niebuhr had read Barth's third volume of his *Dogmatics* on creation. Barth met him at the station in Basel and they had four hours of conversation from lunch through afternoon tea. Barth brought Reinhold two letters from Ursula that had been forwarded through him. They focused on their differences which mostly concerned the relationship of faith and reason. Barth, according to Niebuhr, feared he was substituting reason for faith while Niebuhr responded he thought the gospel provided wisdom and grace for the faithful. Barth cautioned Niebuhr about being too critical of others as Barth thought he had been when he wrote his commentary on Romans. Barth believed conversion followed from words of grace rather than condemnation. Barth had no interest in Niebuhr's concerns about the bareness of Reformed worship as he had observed it. Niebuhr felt Barth, like other Swiss, failed to adequately see the power of poetry and imagination in the religious life. Barth was surprised to learn that Niebuhr preached, and he appreciated Niebuhr's report that Urusula regarded his preaching as similar to Schleiermacher's preaching to the cultured despisers of religion. Barth suggested Niebuhr was closer to Brunner than to himself and Niebuhr agreed. Barth thought Niebuhr's writings showed that he had read his works and perhaps learned something from his writings. Ursula many years later gave me Reinhold's faded, paper copy of Barth's 1931 unpublished lectures on ethics, but its route to its place in the Niebuhr library is unknown to me.

From Basel, Niebuhr went on to Zurich for two great days of conversation with Emil Brunner and the hospitality of his warm family. He felt they were among his best days in Europe as he was very much at home there. In later years Emil Brunner's *The Divine Imperative* was a regular part of the ethics curriculum at Union Seminary, and John C. Bennett, Niebuhr's close friend and colleague, regarded it as the most important text in ethics. Brunner's volumes of theology were also part of the first year systematic theology course when Robert Brown, a student of Niebuhr's, taught the course. I thought the dialogue at Union was between Tillich and Brunner as we compared and contrasted their different theologies in that first-year course in 1960 with Robert Brown. Niebuhr was encountered in the first semester of ethics or sometimes in the second semester of theology when the focus was on human nature and Christology. For me the pull for allegiance to a way of thinking was between Niebuhr and Tillich, but Professor Thomas Driver, a generation older at Union Seminary, thought the dialogue or struggle was between Tillich and Barth. Intellectually Niebuhr was closer to Brunner than Tillich, though Tillich and he agreed in political philosophy and action while they both regarded Brunner as a little too conservative and Barth as too transcendent. The intellectual presence of Barth was recognized in faculty members at Union. Professor Smart and maybe some other faculty and some students were regarded as followers of Barth, but other traditions of theology were dominant by my time there in the 1960s. The influence of Karl Barth was dominant at Princeton Theological Seminary and very important at Pittsburgh Theological Seminary where I later taught.

Niebuhr's host in Copenhagen was the head of the Labor Party and also a publisher who was planning on publishing four of his books in Scandinavia. He found himself more comfortable in the worship services in Sweden. The Lutheran Church there was much closer to the original Catholicism than the Reformed Churches where he had worshiped in Scotland, Holland, and Switzerland. In one of his letters to Ursula he described himself as a Lutheran-prophetism mixture. He admitted how much of his preference for higher liturgies were due to his wife's Anglican influence and his own experience in New York City, particularly at the Cathedral of St. John the Divine.

Review of Hans J. Morgenthau

Niebuhr had for years been polemiczing against those who thought social science could solve the social problems or achieve intellectual consequences comparable to those of the natural sciences. His review of Hans J. Morgenthau's *Scientific Man versus Power Politics* permitted him to carry the discussion further. From the time of the review in 1947 their relationship and eventual friendship grew over the distance between Chicago and New York. Morgenthau's colleague at Chicago, Kenneth Thompson, shared Morgenthau's appreciation for Niebuhr and the three of them dominated, along with John Bennett, the academic writing on ethics and international politics from the realistic perspective through the 1950s and 1960s. Niebuhr pursued two arguments from the book. First, that history was very difficult to predict because of the number of variables which did not follow in causation as factors in hard science. Second, the political observer was also a participant, so objectivity was difficult to achieve. He concluded:

> The consequences of the element of contingency on the realm of history and of the relativity in the observers of history make it impossible to reduce the stuff of history to pure rationality. For this reason history will remain a realm of contending social forces, and these forces will embody power and use power. Dr. Morgenthau shows very clearly why it is vain to hope for the gradual elimination of the moral ambiguity of politics through historic development. He contends that every moral action is more ambiguous than the abstract analysis of a moral action and that a political action is doubly ambiguous, for it involves the power impulse of a group. The general thesis is

one which is not unfamiliar to readers of this journal. The book should have a wider acclaim than it will probably get.[2]

Niebuhr's response to the coup in Hungary of the summer of 1947 was quite mild and he censured the hysterical response to the overthrow of the Hungarian government. The Russian occupation of the country had meant that the government would be rendered Communist to serve the security interests of the Soviet Union. He wrote that not much had changed as the Soviets were in control before and after the blow. He wrote that the important issue was to keep France and Germany from going Communist. He criticized the "growing hysteria in America about Russia."[3] Combining realism with faith he argued that the U.S.A.'s strength was adequate, and in any case Christian faith should encourage serenity in the face of political upheaval.

In August 1947, Emil Brunner wrote in Niebuhr's journal of the distress of Germany facing de-industrialization and starvation. In the same issue Niebuhr could praise the promise of the Marshall Plan; finally it seemed Europe would begin to get the help it needed. The Russian refusal to cooperate and its enforcement of Czechoslovakia's withdrawal made it more likely that Congress would fund the plan with the needed billions of dollars. Niebuhr regarded the assistance as the most important decision since the war. He followed the issue in succeeding months urging the adoption of the needed funding of twenty-two billion dollars over a four-year period. The motivation was both in American economic self-interest and humanitarian to aid the needy people. He regarded such a mixture as appropriate. It was the very convergence of self-interest and generosity that gave him hope that the needed funding would be provided.

John Bennett followed Niebuhr's pleas with an essay warning about the danger of members of Congress sabotaging the reduced funding of fourteen billion dollars. Meanwhile *Christianity and Crisis* was supporting church and private aid to the European hungry. The journal kept up a steady drumbeat of support for the Marshall Plan. Finally after the February coup de etat in Czechoslovakia, the plan was passed and funded in April 1948. The Catholic, Socialist alliance in Italy defeated the Communists in the election of 1948, partially because of the promised money from the plan. As Communists refused to cooperate with the plan in Eastern Europe, Western Europe began its economic recovery. Russia took the initiative by blockading Berlin. The corridors between Western Germany and Berlin were closed, and Truman responded boldly with the airlift to support West Berlin. The blockade and responsive airlift lasting into 1949 was one of the more dangerous periods of the Cold War, Russian interception of the American planes could have led to war at a time neither side was yet prepared. Only Stalin knew how close his engineers were to translating the purloined plans for the atomic bomb into a Russian possession, whereas the West took comfort in its atomic monopoly and supposed irresistible power. Niebuhr supported the airlift and the defense of Berlin in his *Life* essay, driving the more pro-Russian liberals further away from the new Americans for Democratic Action (ADA).

Founding the World Council of Churches

The World Council of Churches' opening assembly in August and September of 1948 fell during the Berlin blockade. Niebuhr's colleague on the Commission of Churches in International Affairs, John Foster Dulles, was advising Thomas Dewey in international politics and expected to become secretary of state. Niebuhr criticized Dulles' speech at the assembly as overly legalistic as Tillich had criticized Dulles' work for the Federal Council of Churches. Tillich would have shared the criticisms Niebuhr made in his address against both Dulles and Barth. But Tillich was not there. He had prepared a preconference essay for the conference volume of studies. Tillich had received his U.S. clearance and was lecturing to large crowds in Germany at the time of the Assembly.

Tillich had worked the previous year with the preparatory commission for the Assembly, and he was supported strongly by John Oldham, a British leader in the development of the meeting. Tillich was probably correct in his suspicion that he was excluded from the meeting due to the opposition of his positions by W. A. Visser'T Hooft, General Secretary of the World Council of Churches. He did not participate actively in ecumenical leadership after the Assembly, having worked extensively in it from the 1937 Oxford Council up to Amsterdam. His paper was quite abstract, even for Tillich.

He focused on the failure of Christianity to be the ordering center of the Christian countries of Western civilization. Christianity had been displaced by secularism which he named the principle of immanence, meaning that ultimate reality was not sought, but that meaning was sought only within the competing horizontal forces of modern civilization. The eclipse of Christianity left societies without an ordering principle but only with competing forces that knew no center. Unless Christianity could regain its healing power for the individual and society it would be reduced to only one of the competing forces. This Christianity could not provide wholeness. The tendency to seek solutions in human totalitarian forces was always present when the Christian center was missing. In the competition between Russia and the United States there was no center and the arousing of fundamental issues had no means of resolution.

Tillich believed that the prophets, the New Testament, the Reformation, and neoorthodoxy all separated themselves from allegiance to disintegrating worlds. The problem with Barth's neoorthodoxy was that it escaped to another realm. The task was to show how Christianity was the healing power of this one world. If it could not achieve the grounding of life in the source of ultimate power it would only contribute to the disintegration. Christianity had to conquer the empty individualism within itself without becoming authoritarian. So Western society had to be criticized and the rush toward totalitarian answers opposed. The message of healing was the task of the church as Western society declined: "Christianity is either healing power from the ground of human existence or it is one contributing factor, among others, to the personal and social sickness of our period and will perish with it."[4]

Tillich's argument that the present was a "spiritual vacuum" and that Barthianism was a reaction, but finally an unhelpful one, would not have been acceptable to the general secretary. Tillich's absence left the fight up to Niebuhr who was much more appreciated by Vissar T'Hooft. John C. Bennett, Tillich's colleague in systematic theology, was present and served as secretary for the Commission on God's Design and the Present Disorder of Civilization which also included the Union Seminary connection with Searle Bates, then of Nanking University. Tillich's spiritual presence was confined to a report on his success in Germany by his friend Wilhelm Pauck of Chicago Theological Seminary over beers in an Amsterdam bar with Barth and Niebuhr.

Pauck's paper for the preparatory studies of the conference had stayed at the descriptive level as he analyzed five types of secular alternatives to the gospel message. As placed in the volume, it gave detailed studies of those forces that Tillich described in his paper as the immanence ideologies which denied human transcendence and the need for ultimate references.

Niebuhr was less inclined than Tillich to admire the centeredness of the Middle Ages. He was also less critical than Tillich of secularism for he regarded it as a necessary critique of the pretended absoluteness of the churches. All of the delegates, most of whom felt the horrors of their recent past, were restrained in their hopes for the world. The scars of the war affected Niebuhr deeply as a German speaker, as an observer of the mistakes of Versailles settlement, and the reporter of the horror of the allied occupation of defeated Germany. The morphing of the utopianism of the third and final Reich into leveled cities, hungry children, abused women, and dead or crippled men sobered him almost as much as it did Tillich. But, his task was to call people and the church to work in the dimness before even greater darkness befell European civilization. Already in his 1948 Assembly speech he was asking whether the West would be forced to choose between nuclear apocalypse or submission to tyranny. Differing from Tillich in his activism, he scolded the Barthians for their otherworldly transcendence of the political chaos surrounding them. For his Christian pragmatism the gospel came into history, and for it to be true it had to be historically relevant.

His address to the Assembly, delivered from notes, spoke to the emerging issues of the Assembly as he saw them. First he argued that the secular illusions of liberalism and Marxism had failed. Their failure left their heirs in a civil war which was tearing the world apart. The church had failed and it needed to repent for:

(1) its blessing of all of the sins of the world, even cooperating with Nazism;
(2) part of the church regarded politics as irrelevant and left modern humanity without help to preserve human community;
(3) part of the church has sentimentally advised modern humanity that repentance and love would solve all problems;
(4) part of the church choosing to be relevant fell into moralistic legalism.

The church's repentance should usher in messages of grace, forgiveness, and judgment in terms of love and justice relevant to the social/political struggles of modern humanity. Both community and freedom needed to be encouraged, but one without the other fell into individualism or Communism.

In concluding, he argued that the Gospel gives new life, but does not promise worldly success. Our generation may fail, but even so we must do our duty, and we cannot abandon the world even though it guarantees no success in staving off threatening disaster. He hoped for a saving remnant, but he could not specify its location. There was very little health in contemporary civilization. Having admitted to the civil war on the planet, he feared the consequences. Referring to the search for good people in the cities of Sodom and Gomorrah he saw that their destruction could not be prevented:

> If such a day should come, we will remember that the mystery of God's sovereignty and mercy transcends the fate of empires and civilizations. He will be exalted though they perish. However he does not desire their perdition but rather that they should turn from their evil ways and live, From us he demands that we work while it is day, since the night cometh when no man can work.[5]

Jacques Ellul's speech at the Assembly was as pessimistic as Niebuhr's oration. He too decried the church's many failures. He did not call for repentance, explicitly as Niebuhr had, but he understood the church had lost its power to move contemporary Europe in which the state, totalitarianism and war were increasing their hold on humanity. Niebuhr's speech exists in three versions. The one written for the study volume in 1947 is the less pessimistic, and while the version recorded at the Assembly was more freewheeling and responsive to Barth, it was not as foreboding as the published version of 1953 when the Cold War had settled into harder patterns and Dulles was threatening massive retaliation to Soviet initiatives.

Barth's prepared paper for the conference was shocking as it focused on the congregation as the only true and full expression of the church. He undercut the very idea of a Council of Churches without explicitly making the charge. The New Testament basis for such an approach was made without difficulty as it was only the congregational forms of the church which were alive at the time. Of course, those churches were connected by letters, missionary visits and the Jerusalem council was called to sort out the differences between Paul and his accusers. Niebuhr objected not to that paper, but to Barth's attitude as he perceived it of being beyond politics. In the last sentence of his paper, though, Barth had asserted that the focus on the congregation was the political act that was needed. All of the connections among the Reformed churches Barth served were seen as quite secondary, if not dangerous, in Barth's paper. Perhaps Niebuhr never took seriously enough that Barth was a Swiss and Switzerland played the role of a small neutral country benefitting economically from Europe's wars raging around it as it protected itself in its Alps. Barth's son, Markus Barth, put it to me in a conversation in Pittsburgh where we both served as professors at Pittsburgh Theological Seminary: "Switzerland is a country of cuckoo clocks and fine chocolate." We both knew it was also a country of international banking, legitimate and illegitimate.

There were references in several papers about the division of Europe into two armed camps. The final statement of the conference referred to the possibility of another war; and the realism of the conference reflected the blockade of Berlin which had begun only a few months earlier. Emil Brunner's paper referred to the ongoing sin of humanity and its inability to achieve a world sovereignty to prevent war as "biblical realism." His paper on power was even more brutal in its analysis than Tillich or Niebuhr who were more consistent in affirming the original goodness of power as it derived from and referred to the ultimate power of the creator.

The clearest divisions in the Council reflecting the Cold War were the consecutive papers of John Foster Dulles and Joseph Hromadka. Hromadka was one of the few theologians from the Russian-dominated countries. He would win fame as visiting theologian at Princeton Theological Seminary and as the apologist for the new societies in Eastern Europe. As a leader of the Christian Peace Conference in Prague, he would be seen by many American theologians as too sympathetic to the Soviet Union. On the other hand, his work kept alive bridges between American churches and the churches of the East for dialogue on peace and social justice. In his paper he argued for an appreciation that the Communist power of Russian had borne the weight of the war, liberated Eastern Europe, and overthrown the feudal system which had oppressed them. The history of the East was different than that of the West. Abstract criticism from the West of Eastern European adjustments to Russian power was not helpful.

Western European Christianity had failed Eastern European Christianity many times, and most recently as democracy was allowed to fail in Europe prior to World War II. Abstract commitments to freedom in the West often obscured the reality of oppression exhibited by European countries at home and abroad in their colonial empires. Hromadka pled for speakers like Dulles, without naming him, to appreciate not only Marxist writings but also the reality of Russian history. Russian literature showed a great thirst for liberation from feudalism and Czarist oppression long before the victory of the Bolsheviks. Lenin was a product of this authentic Russian revolutionary tradition. Another speaker, Searle Bates, who would later join Niebuhr and Tillich at Union Theological Seminary as professor of missions, also noted how the poor populations of agricultural workers of Asia could be attracted to the accomplishments of Russia in Asia. The Russian Empire had been, like almost all of Asia, an undeveloped agricultural-workers' nation. Except for selected cities in Europe, it had not matched the expectations of Karl Marx that the revolution would occur in advanced industrial nations.

Dulles' long paper, the longest of the study book for the conference, was in some aspects the finest paper he wrote on the relationship of Christian faith to international politics. His father had been a theologian, and his grandfather and great grandfather had served as secretaries of state. Another grandfather had served in China as a missionary. His son would succeed as a Roman Catholic Cardinal, and his daughter as a Presbyterian director of Christian Education in a Church in New York City. He was an international lawyer by vocation whose diplomatic experience included early service at the Versailles Peace Conference as a secretary to the Chinese delegation.

His church leadership at the time included chairing of the Federal Council of Churches Commission on a Just and Durable Peace, service on the Union Theological seminary board of directors, and membership on the World Council of Churches Commission of the Churches on International Affairs. His opening lines referred to the changing world, and in his early writing on international relations he had emphasized this theme of change. He had studied with the philosopher of change, Henri Bergson, at the University of Paris as a youth, and before his thought hardened into the patterns of the Cold War, he had recommended adjustment to change as a major solvent in international affairs. His thesis was that change needed to be institutionalized. Free societies had accomplished this through government, and the change needed to continue to reform the Western societies and to work for peaceable change in the world. He regarded Britain's decolonization of India as one of major changes accomplished by free societies. There were not enough free societies in the world to guarantee that change could be peaceable. The Soviet program of change was not compatible with that of Christianity. Christianity was committed to peaceable change, and the Soviet Union with its Marxist dogma was determined to achieve a world society through workers' revolution. He regarded the moral law and the United Nations as the major tools of Christianity for advancing the peaceable change that was needed. With those understandings he rolled out a program, not to defend the status quo, but a dynamic program that relying on international law would expand the sphere of free societies. Regional alliances would counteract Soviet exploitation of social ills while reforming the institutions and practices of the West. Hromadka was pleading with the West to accept the changes in the East while Dulles was determined in the name of freedom to prevent those forceful changes from succeeding elsewhere.

He, perhaps, saw more clearly than some of his listeners the price of totalitarianism. The dynamism he urged upon the West in the name of Christianity threatened all of those inclined to defend the status quo. He did not use the words of "rollback" which threatened Eastern Europe as in the days when he was secretary of state, but the program envisaged could be read to suggest that emphasis in embryo. Niebuhr respected his realism and his commitments to change, but Niebuhr's sense of the relativities of moral law was much more thorough than Dulles'. He also had little use for Dulles' legalism. Dulles' paper read more like a legal brief than a church position paper. Dulles' tendency to argue like a lawyer and to expect results reflecting his corporate law experience was more assertive than the normal church policy or position paper. Dulles' American optimism about what American effort could accomplish was also much greater than Niebuhr's realism. He sensed also that Dulles was in a transition from churchman to politician. He complained in his letter to Ursula about Dulles' split between his political (Republican) pessimism and his optimistic Christian program.

> The Sunday formal opening was a sad washout. It was boring and disappointing Bill Pauck and I beguiled the tedium by checking Dulles' German translation of his speech to be delivered today. Dulles has become almost a pacifist in insisting that there must be no war, but there is little relation between his Christian affirmations and his political prognostications for he is very pessimistic. So is everyone else. People over here are talking about war in a month. This is probably foolish but the situation is serious.[6]

John Bennett, serving as secretary, drafted the report for his section on "God's Design and the Present Disorder of Civilization." Bennett's paper had emphasized "The Involvement of the Church" in social service and action. Niebuhr was pulled into the drafting committee of the section on the disorder in international relations, and also onto the final drafting committee for the Council.

Here many of his perennial themes and favorite scriptural quotations appeared, and it certainly reflected his spirit if not his dominance of the drafting committee. An earlier report to Ursula had mentioned that of the four working groups, only those dominated by Barth and Niebuhr seemed to be in order and they were run basically as their seminars. Niebuhr, of course, was glad not to be in the working group on church governance where Barth fought with the Anglo-Catholics and Orthodox on the meaning of the church. Both he and Barth were glad that the Roman Catholics were not present. Barth, for his part according to Niebuhr, referred to Roman Catholicism as a pseudo church which worshiped itself. Niebuhr's letters to Ursula often referred to Barth as well as to the participation of her Anglican mentors and friends. He indicated in one letter that Barth was strangely overly fond of New Testament texts he thought prevented women from becoming priests.

The final statement of the Council in only six paragraphs commended the establishment of the Council, confessed the church's role in the disorder of the world, including the threat of another war, proclaimed Christ as the Word of God needed by the world, noted that the founding of the Council was in vain unless the churches proclaimed God's word for peace and justice, served the suffering, and spoke boldly to those in power about the righteousness found in the Gospel. It noted that people could not save the world which was in God's hands, but that in working the church could set up signs of God's victory. Until the Kingdom of God arrived no powers of hell nor foolishness could separate them from Christ who empowered them in their tasks to "set up the signs" so that humans could realize what God was doing. Some of the specific language, not surprisingly was from Barth, but much of it was from Niebuhr and in between were many words on which both could agree.

Niebuhr complained of tiredness to Ursula. The work of the committees of the Assembly kept him awake at night, but he found energy in the ecumenical meetings. He was sorry Ursula could not share the experience with him. Often he commented on his difficulty with the higher church views of the Anglicans. He mentioned that Archbishop Michael Ramsey had seemed to become much more fixed in his views of the church than he had been before the Oxford Conference of 1937. "Incidentally, what I find simply impossible about his position is precisely the claims he makes for the church when you think of the realities of history."[7] In my later conversations with Michael Ramsey in Oxford in 1966 and Birmingham in a train station tea room in 1982 he remembered both Ursula and Reinhold to me with great warmth. Nevertheless there is no doubt that Niebuhr's favorite archbishop was Temple who furthered the aims of religious socialism in Britain during his tenure in Canterbury.

Tillich's Watchful Waiting

The publication in 1948 of *The Protestant Era* fulfilled Tillich's introduction to the scholarly theological world of the United States. His previous publication, *The Interpretation of History,* had not received much acclaim. His translator, James Luther Adams, had worked on the new translation of two decades of Tillich's essays for years. Its publication was not easy as the essays were heavy and deep and the readership would be limited to the small scholarly world of American Protestantism. The University of Chicago agreed to publish it only after Tillich agreed to publish his forthcoming *Systematic Theology* with that house.[8] The outline of that theology in four parts appeared in the book.[9] The first three parts were existential questions answered by God, Christ, and Spirit. Fourth was the existential question of the meaning of history. The argument of *The Protestant Era* indicates that the problem of history had been Tillich's central concern since World War I through World War II.

Tillich recognized that the rise of Nazism and the war had pushed him more deeply into practical political activity than he had planned. Now, however, following the war he could not find the sense of expectation that followed World War I. The interpretation of history required participation in the struggles of the historical era, and theology reflected the historical situation. If he had sensed that the postwar situation was a moment of crisis and opportunity probably he could not have given himself to the production of the systematic theology which he had alternatively attempted and postponed since World War I. The 1948 volume was interpretation of history but not of the Cold War situation; it represented his previous work. If expectations following World War I were utopian, many of those following World War II were cynical; faithful realism rejected both of them. Now Tillich saw a time of faithful waiting for categories of interpretation to emerge. He lived in a "sacred void" of watchful waiting. His hopes for a spiritual reconstruction of Europe had been dashed by allied policy. His city was occupied by four powers, and at the time of publication Berlin was blockaded and war threatened. Faith and reason needed to coexist in the relevant believer. Reason was confined to the world of existent beings. Faith issued from being grasped through ecstatic intuition by the unconditional. So Tillich's philosophical theology takes reason as far as it ought to go and becomes theology using philosophy through faith.

The arguments for and about religious socialism were relevant politically in Europe where socialist parties, Christian people, and religious political parties had to sort out their relationships. After the war, religion and socialism found ways of cooperating against Communism that they had been unable to achieve earlier. The issues were relevant to thought, but not to practical politics in the U.S.A. Both Tillich's religious socialism and Protestant theology were without party or church but confined to academia. Trends in the United States in the later twentieth century would be toward more socialistic welfare measures and toward more religious life and expression of a form of Protestantism in politics than either Niebuhr or Tillich would have anticipated.

Now he would find increasingly large opportunities and he could write of coming into the "harvest" after his years of planting seeds. Much of that "harvest" was due to the exploitation of the thought of Sigmund Freud, rather than Marx. But he understood the sufferings of the individual to be closely related to the sufferings of society. So even the analysis of the self's movement toward health required the partial healing of the society. Tillich would speak powerfully and helpfully toward the healing of the self. But his self could not be healed. He could live powerfully and radically, more powerfully and radically than most.

He could never escape the very human anxieties of the post-traumatic stress disorder from his sufferings and breakdowns in World War I. The title of one of his most popular postwar books, *The Courage to Be* reveals his own fight within the trenches of Verdun and later in the academic trenches of America to be and to become. Likewise the Bohemian sexual lifestyle accepted by Tillich and his second wife Hannah produced anxiety, guilt, jealousy and conflict through his death, and for Hannah beyond. He lived by the faith he wrote about without resolution in society or self. He knew, not only intellectually but in himself, the demonic as structure and the inescapable power of evil. This understanding of demonic forces in self and society meant that he was existentially equipped to write about the "continuous fight between the divine and demonic powers."[10] In 1948, on the publication of the book and his return to Europe, his writing on history utilized his earlier concepts of theonomy, heteronomy, and autonomy, the demonic and Kairos. But now he was more explicit about Christianity's perspective of "empirical pessimism and eschatological hope."[11]

Niebuhr's writing in 1948 was almost as pessimistic as Tillich's. He entitled an article on Europe "Amid Encircling Gloom." The fall of Czechoslovakia and the "suicide" death of Masaryk shook policy makers in the United States. Niebuhr feared they might overreact militarily. The struggle with Russia was both political and military but the U.S. was overly inclined to react militarily with the President proposing universal military service. Niebuhr endorsed the sentiments of Justice Douglas that the U.S. response needed to encourage social health in Europe through generous policies rather than reliance on military preparations. Niebuhr expected the atomic monopoly was likely to end in the next three to ten years, and argued against those who advocated a preventive war now before the monopoly was lost. Trends in both China and Palestine tightened the circle of gloom in foreign affairs.

While others reported on the World Council of Churches, meetings in *Christianity and Crisis,* Tillich reported on his long trip to Germany.[12] He had gone to lecture in the philosophical faculties of Marburg and Frankfurt, but his trip took him to many other cities and he lectured nearly one hundred times over the summer of 1948. He saw old friends and family, some of whom he could not recognize at first, given his fifteen years absence and the torture engraved in the features of the victims of the war. They had suffered under the Nazi oppression, bombing, the invasion including pillage, street executions, massive practice of rape, and the occupation by unsympathetic victors. Following the starvation of the winter of 1946–1947, illnesses spread. He noted especially the tuberculosis of the children. The Germans were reduced to powerlessness in the realm of politics and the superpowers decided the details of their lives without understanding them. They had suffered a catastrophe of almost unheard of proportions. They felt more victimized than guilty. Tillich found it difficult to lecture or discuss guilt that the Germans were hurrying to ignore. The acceptance of each other in fellowship led to serious conversations, but most refused to accept personal responsibility for the evil of Nazism, even if they had to some degree participated in it to save themselves. Many were finding solace in the absolutism of Catholicism, and Protestant tendencies were running in a more absolute direction than they had previous to Hitler. Tillich wondered if Protestantism could find its way without authoritarian answers.

The Protestant church had not yet found its voice and it had been shattered by Nazism. The fate of his German church encouraged thought that perhaps the Protestant era was at an end. In its Calvinist form it had surrendered to middle-class society and in its Lutheran form in Germany it had surrendered the society to the state. Tillich found himself allied with Germans and Americans who thought Germany had suffered enough and that the better U.S. policy would be to encourage its renewal. He found the messages about love well received, and he lectured often on love, power, and justice. Crowds attended many of his lectures, and his anxieties about whether he as an exile would be accepted gave way to a sense of joy that he was welcomed back. His message from the outside of the carnage could encourage the process of healing among the suffering who met him. In another discussion of his visit he said:

> I saw a sick people, sick as a whole and sick as individuals. Their faces are shaped by burdens too heavy to be carried, by sorrows too deep to be forgotten.But within this nation I found people who were healthy, not because the sickness was not written in their face also. But something else was in them, a healing power making them whole in spite of their sorrow, making them examples for all of us, examples of what could and should happen to us![13]

He proceeded to talk of the sickness of Western society and its need for healing. He found the power of reconciliation to be in the new reality of Jesus Christ whose name was love. Acceptance and reconciliation which helped heal the Germans was needed as well in the victorious United States which bore many signs of social and personal sickness. The acceptance of him by family, scholars, and strangers who came to listen to him, led him to consider returning to Germany. Many teaching offers came to him. But he committed to remain in his new country and to return to German universities to teach often in the summer.

The second book he published in 1948 was quite different from the historical-political essays that Adams had edited. *The Shaking of the Foundations* is a collection of sermons preached on college and university campuses after the war. While issues of the meaning of society and history were still present, the book had a much more personal tone. Freud was more prominent than Marx, and the questions of destiny had more to do with the personal philosophical concerns of his listeners than the social dimension of their lives. The book differed from Niebuhr's book of sermons, not in its apologetic tone for the Christian faith, but in the much greater prominence of the doctrine of the Spirit. The doctrine of the Holy Spirit was almost absent in Niebuhr's preaching and his formal theological writing while in Tillich's sermons it was very prominent in the largest part of *Systematic Theology* published three years later. The sermons resonate with the power of the Eternal Presence and the inescapability of God who is the beginning and end of life. He incorporates even the strident atheist into his embrace inasmuch as the atheist takes the ultimate questions of life earnestly.

The references to the sufferings of the present beyond the personal anxieties often focus on the millions of fleeing refugees in Europe and the starving millions in Asia. The sermons deal with the sufferings of nature often caused by humans, but promise salvation for nature as for humanity in God's purposes. The salvation promised is mostly eschatological, but it is also the power in life in the accepted love of the Eternal in the present. The present is so confused that he cannot tell where the promised renewal will come from. It is a time of waiting, and, he says once, of passionate involvement. But that involvement is not the main emphasis of these sermons. God confronted human sin in Tillich's preaching and condemned it, but Tillich was not providing guidance for action, but for thought. Once he preached:

> Do not ask in this moment what we shall do or how actions shall follow from the New Being from the rest of our souls. Do not ask for you do not ask how the good fruits follow from the goodness of a tree. They follow, action follows being, and new action, better action, stronger action, follows new

being, better being, stronger being. We and our world would be better, truer, and more just, if there were more rest for souls in our world.[14]

The most famous and beloved of his sermons was "You are accepted." He first states that words like *sin* and *grace*, fundamental terms of faith, cannot be superseded, and then he provides his interpretation of them. Sin is the state of separation or estrangement from our true selves, from the ground of our being, and from others. We know we are not true to the deepest side of our nature, there is something missing in our separation. Grace is the reunion of the separated. But it is a fact of life as well as a teaching of the apostle Paul that where sin abounds, the greater reality is grace. The most-sensitive humans know of Nazi atrocities and lynching in the South and still persist. The human is split within itself and feels the power of the instinct of self-destruction. Grace provides a way of acceptance in spite of sin.

As he confessed that he had pursued the thought of acceptance for a long time before preaching upon it, he hinted at autobiographical experiences of compulsions that lasted for decades, of suffering unto despair, of being unable to accept oneself, of harming persons whom one had loved, of being locked in animosity with one whom one could not leave. Then sometimes one realized acceptance, and of being able to live and to accept the other even though harmful to oneself because there was union in the ground of being. Then moments in which one could accept oneself appear. One longs for more such moments, and learns to live the acceptance of self that is given in the ground of being. Sin and grace were powerful words for him, and he understood them as fundamental to life. He pled for more grace for himself and his listeners.[15] He knew his suffering from World War I, the destruction of his world in World War II, and personal estrangement from his wife Hannah. He could accept freedom from traditional Christian morality which could be so repressive. His old loyalties to the rules of his church and his beloved, chaste Wingolf Society still bound him and convicted him in his violation of ordinary marital vows. He transcended the rules of the past, but they still haunted him and drove him to hate himself until he could again find acceptance. But in that tension of his life between estrangement and grace he found power to express his creativity in a most thorough and overwhelmingly radical way. In his next sermon he expressed the struggle as resulting from the modern world choosing freedom to control nature, nationalism, and the secular manner of life. The hidden forces of life rose against these choices in response to the demonic and millions gave themselves to satanic images and sickness unto death. He believed that when a civilization loses its meaning, that lack of a center destroys people who seek a center but cannot find it.

The war ending in the Nuremburg war-crime trials had left Germany empty, and in his talks in Germany he would sometimes share this bleakness. In bombed out Berlin in the middle of 1948 he spoke of the spiritual vacuum. Broken people lacking a convincing faith had turned to nationalism, or to class, or to the leader. All of these had betrayed them. Tillich confessed he had given up on the church and he did not encourage broken Germans to believe they could find a center there. When the political center collapsed, people without their personal centers would be destroyed in the society as they had been during Hitler's reign. People might be healed, but as they tried to enter society again they would be destroyed. In his lecture at the *Technischen Universitat* he refused to give any answer or to suggest a symbol for renewal. He left them waiting with a hope that out of the people, perhaps the young, would come a new symbol to fill the holy emptiness. The vacuum should not be prematurely filled by absolutisms competing for German loyalty, but the emptiness should be endured until the really new appears.[16]

In his American sermon he would say more, asserting that: something new was trying to be born and humanity could after the war only await it. "The saving power is the power of the Eternal within it."[17] Finally he would close the last sermon and the book: "Love never ends."[18] He asked those who were grasped by the power of the divine if they could not perceive the new coming in grace, forgiveness, and love. He had said earlier that neither the Nazis nor Nietzsche—and he could have added the Freud he referenced—could hear the word that would free them from their death instincts. His existentialist preaching contained the word as he focused on death, but not only on death, but on life enlivened by the promise of forgiveness and acceptance.[19]

17

Limits and World Responsibility

Niebuhr's political connections, membership in the Council on Foreign Relations, associations at (UNESCO) and the demand by publishers for his work brought him into prominence in foreign relations at the same time the United States was assuming world responsibility through the struggle with Communism. This movement added to his international church work, advice to policy makers, and personal involvement which continued until his stroke in 1952. His stroke and Adlai Stevenson's defeat in 1952 would limit Niebuhr's contribution to occasional speeches and writing while the work from this period and later combined to increase his influence into the 1960s.

He had advised the U.S. government during the Roosevelt administration on issues of culture and religion, unleashing the security investigations which haunted him for the rest of his life. However, his wartime visit to Britain, his appointment in 1947 to the work in occupied Germany, in 1949 to the U.S. delegation to UNESCO, and the consultations with George Kennan's Policy Planning Staff meetings were his last important government positions. His influence on U.S. policy was indirect through intellectuals reading his work and referring to his perspectives. He never regarded himself as particularly important in the formation of policy, and evaluations of his thought should focus on the cogency of his philosophy of international relations or probably more narrowly on his perspective on United States foreign policy. His colleague in church work in international relations, John Foster Dulles, who was moving into prominence in the policy world at the same time as Niebuhr, needs to be thought of as one whose major influence on action made his ideas interesting. In Niebuhr's case it is the reverse; his ideas are important and sometimes actors merged them with many other factors to influence action. In his report on the UNESCO Conference he confessed that he was an outsider to government who had only been introduced to the processes inside diplomacy. The work of the American delegation was a hybrid combining both civilian voluntary organization input with governmental guidelines. The delegation itself was nominated by the president and approved by the senate.

Niebuhr's perspective on the United Nations and UNESCO had been partially formulated by the failure of the League of Nations, and then by his own work on the commission Dulles chaired for the Federal Council of Churches on a

Just and Durable Peace. His personal reactions to the Paris UNESCO conference of 1949 are found in the letters between Ursula and himself from Paris.

Niebuhr stayed in the Raphael Hotel across from the temporary UNESCO headquarters. He was told he had the room Hitler stayed in while he was in Paris. He was skeptical as the other rooms of the delegation were just as grand. Other American delegates were George Allen, assistant secretary of state; Milton Eisenhower, president of Kansas State University; Luther Evans, librarian of Congress, later secretary general of UNESCO; and Martha Lucas, president of Sweet Briar College. There were also another twenty-four staff members and advisors.[1] The accommodations, many cocktail parties, and the overly sumptuous meals provided contrasts for Reinhold who was used to church conferences.

The days of listening, drafting, consulting and hustling other delegations were very long, and Niebuhr complained to Ursula about the schedule and the number of political speeches. Private conversations around the edge of the formal proceedings provided more insights for his later writings. As Russia did not attend, the debates with Communists were primarily with the representatives from Poland, Czechoslovakia, and Hungary, but informal conversations with delegates from these countries were often very informative. Positions taken by the U.S. government were agreed upon by members of the delegation in advance of speeches,

On returning home Reinhold wrote that the practical work of UNESCO in promoting communication and understanding seemed very fruitful as did the technical help to the developing nations. On the other hand, he thought that ideologically the organization was very weak. Cultural communication was overvalued as a contribution towards peace, and universal-sounding agreements about hopes and rhetoric usually or at least often, only obscured real power struggles among the nations.

He noted that an organization trying to represent the great cultures of the world with one voice would have to be weak because of the cultural-religious pluralism of the world. The attempt of its director to unify world cultures on the basis of scientific humanism was a mistake as the cultures were relative to their own history, and world communication some day would have to address the significant differences between the major religious-cultural systems. He assumed the idealism of the organization would not survive, and he wondered about the fate of the organization as it continued its impossible task of creating a world community in which interests and history divided nations. Still he held out a hope that as the impossible was attempted God might provide a possibility for the development of a world community. The last thought was part of a call for Christians to continue to work with UNESCO while holding out the hope that its work might be deepened and scientific utopianism informed by deeper traditions.[2]

Barth-Niebuhr

Niebuhr's jounal, *Christianity and Crisis,* was regularly full of essays by non-American theologians, and in these years it often carried a section of news on the world-wide Church. One of the more important exchanges continuing the issues from the founding World of Council of Churches Assembly continued in *The Christian Century* in 1948–1949 as Niebuhr and Karl Barth debated the issues in Barth's opening speech over the role of the Bible and social action in the church. Niebuhr worked with biblical themes in his writing for church or religious audiences, encouraging continued social action by Christians informed by social science, social philosophy, history, and economics. Barth worked more closely on inner church themes and wanted theology to be informed much more by careful exegesis. Niebuhr's mixture of biblical themes, loosely interpreted with American pragmatism was not a workable method for Barth who would have liked to have seen his *Church Dogmatics* and its methods more closely consulted.

Barth's address asked the Assembly to reorder its work. The very title of the Assembly, "The World's Disorder and God's Design," revealed the problem. Rather than focusing on the brokenness of the world, the work should be reversed, speaking of God's Kingdom and his righteousness. Barth proposed the work needed to be redone. The Assembly should start over realizing that God's plan or design was already realized. Christians are not some Atlas to hold up the world or to remake it; that has already been done in Christ. Christian confession, not perplexity over social issues, had to be the beginning of their work as an Assembly. He also thought it would have been better to have no services of the Lord's Supper at the Assembly as they could not agree on one celebration.

He also offended others by regarding it as good that the Roman and Moscow branches of the church had not accepted the invitations to send observers. Probably it was a sign that God did not yet want the unity being worked on by the Assembly. Barth thought it was good that the Assembly dealt with evangelism, but he rejected the work of Pauck and Brunner who listed the forces of the secular world in their papers. The church had to be about its confession, not giving credence to the idea that it was a post-Christian world. He recognized that the church in its freedom had a prophetic way to play, but that did not mean laying out economic or political principles for the world to follow; rather it meant asserting its own revolutionary message of the Gospel. He also criticized the preparatory work for not dealing with the problems of capitalism and money and suggested maybe it was this lack that prevented the Moscow church and its political authorities from participating. After all of this he agreed to proceed with the work, hoping it would bear fruit and pleading: "Lord have mercy upon us."[3] There was significant support for Barth's critique, but the work of the Assembly proceeded as designed by its management.

Niebuhr's criticism of Barth's address had appeared in *The Christian Century* before Barth's address was published in the same journal. He had objected to Barth's form of "realized eschatology" that came too close to the position of denying human responsibility for the care of the world and the struggle with evil. He did not want to deny any of Barth's strong affirmations, but rather to argue with the implications of them. It seemed to Niebuhr that St. Paul was concerned to fix the earthly church and that was appropriate work to be undertaken in the circumstances. He reminded Barth of his own injunction that we are men and not God, and that the church needed to interpret the divine judgment that had been imposed on the world in the war. Barth's theology seemed to propose no guidance to Christians who had the daily responsibilities of politics and economics. He found Barth's theology too undialectical: it needed to say more about the world as well as Christ's victory. The Christian, according to Niebuhr, could not flee from responsibility to a biblical position that the struggle was won. Many difficulties confronted the Christian in this history and the church needed to be there providing whatever guidance it could, even risking mistakes.[4] Niebuhr's tone was respectful taking great care to praise Barth's work in resisting the evil of Nazism, but critical of what seemed to be neglect of the practical life in the present.

Barth commented that he did not really recognize his theology in Niebuhr's caricature of it. He had thought Niebuhr understood him in previous conversations, but perhaps he was mistaken. It now seemed that Niebuhr did not grasp his points at all, and he twice referred to Niebuhr as Brutus doing the stabbing. He thought the preparatory work of the conference had lacked a positive vision: it seemed too defensive and he had attempted to correct the deficiency. Barth thought the attitude of representatives of Anglo-Saxon theology, particularly Niebuhr, revealed a too-cavalier attitude toward the Bible which was their central authority. There was too little serious exegetical work in much of the argument, critical of Barth's theology or in the work of the Assembly. Finally, Barth suggested that there was too little appreciation of the mystery which was a dimension of the Bible, and therefore he could not find much of that called Anglo-Saxon theology really very interesting.[5] So the issues between them seemed to be that Barth did not want to speak from a basis of social principles or social analysis and he regarded Niebuhr as not serious enough about his biblical scholarship.

Niebuhr's response labeling Barth's critique "irenic" must have been meant sarcastically. Niebuhr came back with his strongest point that people had to choose between good and less-good decisions, and that Barth's address did not help in that process. Niebuhr recognized more willingness to seek guidance in resources beyond the Bible for ethical guidance and he thought that was necessary. He particularly disagreed with Barth's refusal to move beyond his opposition to ordaining women in the church. He took seriously Paul's injunction that there were in Christ neither men nor women in Christ and overrode Paul's other more time-bound injunctions about women. He thought it was necessary to choose scriptural verses, to exegete the Bible from the whole Bible and to seek the mind of Christ over particular time-bound verses. Choosing passages in light of ethical criteria was dangerous, but not as dangerous as biblical literalism or the affirmation of ancient cultural prejudices, because they were biblical. In his conclusion Niebuhr noted that much wisdom comes from the secular revolt against the church. Even in the dispute concerning women, the secular world had a lot to teach the church about freedom beyond what traditional exegetes had previously been able to find in the scripture. The problem with the Barthian method was that it would overburden the church with irrelevant details from the Bible regarding Christian life which requires a lot of freedom. The other was that the Barthian method would obscure evil too long until it became a monstrous evil requiring heroic witness.[6] With the last sentence, Niebuhr took away some of the praise he had earlier given Barth for resisting Nazism on theological grounds when it infringed upon the freedom of the church. His friend Tillich, of course, had seen the evil earlier and resisted it both politically and theologically. Niebuhr did not need to mention Tillich or his other point that the resistance of the Barthian Confessing church should have been on broader grounds than the freedom of the church in Christ. These differences would continue to divide them and their students throughout their lives.

Streaks of Dawn in the Night

Niebuhr read his critics, and the constant hammering at him for being too pessimistic prompted him to share his hopes for the international situation in a December 1949 essay in *Christianity and Crisis*, but even then it was described as light in the darkness. He found signs of hope:

—The European Recovery Program was succeeding.
—Western Germany was being incorporated into the Western World.
—Though China was bleak, we were freed from supporting the corrupt nationalist China government.
—The Russian Empire in Eastern Europe was insecure. "We can afford to continue a policy of firmness without provocation and hope that ultimately the Russian tide in Europe will recede."[7]

The chances of avoiding a war with Russia were increasing. He believed the best way of avoiding war with Russia was through retaining the ability to negotiate with the Russians while maintaining military superiority. He thought the NATO treaty furthered such superiority and gave the Europeans more confidence that they would not be dragged into a war with Russia or face Russian occupation.

Though much remained to be done, foreign policy was best handled on a case by case approach. Large plans for world government or great constitutional changes in the United Nations were largely irrelevant and distracted attention from what could be accomplished. The themes of the essay are limits and responsibilities.

> From the standpoint of the Christian faith we ought to have some understanding of both the limits of human power in history and of the responsibilities we have within the limits of our power. We are not the "weary and unyielding Atlas" who bears all the world's burdens, but we are by God's grace the most powerful of the world's free nations.[8]

Wars in Asia

The Truman administration acquiesced in the victory of the Red Army in China. Some aid had been provided to the American ally of World War II, the Kuomintang Party of Chiang Kai Shek, but its inability to govern or to attract enough support to keep it in power led the American government to agree to defend it only in its Formosa redoubt. The positions of the Union professors, Niebuhr and Bennett, were in agreement that it was not possible to defend governments in Asia that did not have strong support from the population.

The 25 June 1950 invasion of South Korea by North Korea caught the U.S. by surprise. While Niebuhr opposed widening the war and feared overreaction on the part of the U.S. could lead to a more general war, he supported the conventional war under UN auspices in which the U.S.A. shouldered the major burden. It was another step in containment, though this time containment was primarily a military response. Both Niebuhr and Bennett continued to argue that the main issues in containing Communism in Asia were the moral, political, and economic struggles, but still aggression had to be met when it was within American capacities. Niebuhr published the Americans for Democratic Action program for containment of Communism in Asia in his journal, and followed it up later with the World Council of Churches support for the U.S.A. and UN actions in Korea. Both policies, of course, reflected his own judgments as he had a hand in writing the A.D.A. statement and influence in the W.C.C. position.

The allied victories before the China intervention gave Niebuhr hope that most of the Peninsula could be united with elections conducted under UN auspices to establish a democratic regime. With the intervention of China and the following defeats, he feared for the worse. The outcome of stalemate signified to him what much of the struggle in Asia might look like. He hoped the U.S. would be able to accept frustration in this difficult area of the formerly colonized, and persist in these dim struggles which often could not promise victory. Both Bennett and Niebuhr writing in *Christianity and Crisis* expressed their confidence that Communism would crumble, but before it did the struggle might be very long, and patience was needed. They wanted large aid programs tied to specific reforms in Asian countries that would strengthen their capacity to resist the Communist tide. But they understood the West was at a disadvantage with the populace of Asia, particularly if it could not offer programs towards human dignity and justice for these poor populations.

At the same time that the U.S. was struggling with Korea, Niebuhr was expressing his disdain for French efforts to hold on to its colonies in Indo-China. He did not want the U.S. to back France in what was very likely a futile effort. The French history of colonization doomed it to probable defeat against indigenous forces which happened to be Communist and which probably could count on support from other Communist countries. The geopolitical realities for defense of Western interests on the mainland of Asia were not favorable, in his opinion, though Korea's proximity to Japan balanced somewhat the reality of both China and Russia bordering Korea. Niebuhr could see a U.S. defense line based on Japan, its Southern islands, and the Philippine bases. He regarded comparisons between the defense of Europe and the defense of China or Indo-China to be mistaken analogies. Above all, the reality of atomic weapons and the prospects of hydrogen weapons made any war dangerous and a general war catastrophic. He rejected notions of bringing issues with Russia to a head and found all suggestions of preventive war immoral. An incalculable future was to be much preferred over any war fought with weapons of mass destruction. He commented in passing that many church positions on the new weapons had assumed future wars would feature atomic weapons. The more likely scenario was one of small, frustrating wars with out clear-cut victories.[9]

World Government

The one article Niebuhr published in the Council on Foreign Relations' journal, *Foreign Affairs,* was "The Illusion of World Government." He had reviewed several books on the subject and the issue often came up in classes at the Seminary or in questions following public lectures. The threat of a nuclear war drove people to the inquiry and it was the hope of several peace advocates from Immanuel Kant to the present. That hope was to Niebuhr an illusion because: 1. Governments are not created by people agreeing to do so in a constitutional convention, the social realities of a culture and governing bodies precedes any constitutional arrangements; 2. Governments have only limited ability in forcing a consensus or establishing community. Niebuhr saw governing arrangements arising out of dominant groups and not out of social contracts. He rejected the idea of a social contract because no government had ever been established that way. This incidentally distinguishes him thoroughly from contemporary contract theorists who would like to amend Niebuhr's historical approach to justice with current social-contract moral theories. Though the U.S. Constitution may approach the reality of a social contract, it was formed by colonies that had a common culture and had been engaged in a common war against Britain. The social reality preceded the Constitution as did the Articles of Confederation, but even so it was only finally agreed upon by the terrible experience of the Civil War. Without precedent the idea of world government failed as there were no procedures for denying the states' sovereignty.

Niebuhr observed that governments could not create community through force because the relationship tended to work the other way. Leadership communities formed governments for the good of the community and the leaders. Niebuhr observed how even the power and prestige of modern governments were limited by the mores and customs of the populace. He had seen prohibition defeated by popular protests and illegal acts. The resistance of the population to fair practices among the races was another example of resistance to laws. Governments could lead, but consensus was also important. Government was a construct of prestige and force and the prestige was partially dependent upon moral consensus. Governing succeeded with minimum force when there was social consensus about the meaning of justice. The world lacked such a consensus or the social tissue which could encourage its development. In the present the goal was peace while preserving nontyrannical societies. The development of institutions to weave the world together would be best served without the wasting of energy on dreams of world government. His own efforts were directed toward UNESCO and in the acceptance of the realities of the world reflected in the existing United Nations Organization.[10] Niebuhr told me of a meeting with the planning staff of the State Department in which world-government advocates sat on one side of a table and the planning staff and consultants on the other. After very articulate presentations of why world-government proposals should be seriously considered, George Kennan leaned over to Niebuhr and whispered in his ear: "The difference between the two sides of the table is that we believe in original sin and they don't."

During the early fifties, Niebuhr was realizing that military power had only limited efficacy in the contest with Communism. The French defeat in Vietnam showed that the struggle was caught up in the worldwide revolt against colonialism, and that moral, political, and economic issues were at the heart of the struggle though in some cases military might would be the *ultima ratio*. Niebuhr thought that the U.S. decision to refrain from intervening at the battle of Dienbienphu had been a close call, and that it had primarily been President Eisenhower's good common sense that prevented the intervention. He summarized what he had learned in a speech to the U.S. National Commission for UNESCO in the middle of the decade. The evaluation of U.S resources for the U.S. mission to the world situation required, he argued, an analysis of the dominant world trends. He isolated five factors of the changing world:

> (1) Technology was bringing the nations closer together and making them more dependent. This had both positive and negative trajectories for peace.
> (2) Wars were now more lethal than ever before and this required careful handling to prevent a world catastrophe.
> (3) The demonic religious-political movement of Communism through its utopian illusions and power dynamics threatened continued upheaval in world politics.
> (4) Through the victory in World War II and its economic power the U.S. attained a position of world leadership for which it was badly prepared.
> (5) All of the above were occurring in the midst of a process of great resentment of the former masters' racial and cultural arrogance leaving the Western nations at a disadvantage in the worldwide struggle with Communism.

He thought the factors coming together in a world in revolution presented the U.S. with a unique challenge in its time of leadership. Communism had to be challenged, though carefully because of the danger of nuclear war. He regarded the present as the most severe challenge the nation had ever faced. To the crisis he said: the U.S. brought its religious traditions, its historical traditions, and all of its scientific and cultural knowledge to assist in formulating a response to the crisis. The religious traditions included tolerance, humility, human dignity, and the sense of a divine sovereign. These needed to be informed by the secular disciplines which brought precise judgments of fact to the forming of a perspective so that judgment could be formed by empirical disciplines as well as ultimate perspectives.

His outline for a national perspective included: (1) realism without cynicism; (2) patience and courage; (3) mutuality with allies; (4) a religious discipline which would not dedicate itself to material riches. Living in dire perils, he hoped that all of these resources could be drawn upon for this period of history.[11]

Faith and History

Reflecting on his lectures in Europe in 1947, Niebuhr pulled together materials from 1945 Beecher Lectures at Yale and his lectures in Glasgow, Aberdeen, and Uppsala into a 1949 book, a work of apology for the Christian faith on the meaning of history. As lectures in Scotland in 1939 were shadowed by the approach of World War II, this work on the same subjects had to consider history in light of a possible nuclear apocalypse. The new book, *Faith and History,* also previewed the use of irony which became famous as *The Irony of History*.

Niebuhr's first chapter illustrates through many sources his argument that modern intellectuals place their faith in historical progress. Whether Communist or democrat they believe in the dynamics of history to make human life better if not utopian. Over against this view the conflicts of the twentieth century prove the doctrine to be illusory leaving both sides armed with the potential to obliterate humanity. The refutation of the illusions of the historical overcoming of human conflicts should leave humanity open to hear once again the alternatives of the Christian view of history. The tasks of social control of the financial resources of corporations and the building of institutional regulations to control national sovereignty still remained while he attempted to present a perspective adequate to the evil and dangers of the present.[12]

The second chapter continues the deconstruction of modern narratives of historical progress in terms familiar from his *Human Destiny*. It presents biblical themes symbolically representing a more adequate picture of human behavior and Divine forgiveness.

The third chapter finds a realm of mystery at the beginning and end of scientific analysis which also provides the assumptions of order for the scientific work. Science emerges from primitive attempts to order the universe, and humanity needs science to return to philosophical issues to prevent too easy assumptions of science as adequate explanation for all questions. He's hoping for humility and recognition of the limits of human rationality and powers.

Niebuhr discusses "divine sovereignty" and the purposes of nations together. But the "divine sovereignty" resists the plots of national leaders to seize that sovereignty. Nations rise and fall in a universal history guided by a mysterious sovereign expressed in prophetic faith as a critique of human or national pride. No philosophy including, Arnold Toynbee's, can capture the meaning of history. Universal meaning not found in particular events is provided in faith which protects God from human capture. He admits elements of nationalism are found even in the Hebrew prophets, but insists that at their best in Amos, Jeremiah, and Second Isaiah they refuse nationalistic capture of the divine and pose critiques of the nations, even of Israel.

Despite his earlier distinctions, often people and nations are compared and regarded as similar in their self-centeredness and pride.[13] The struggles, in his view, are primarily with God and only secondarily with each other. There is judgment in the history of personal and national sin, but the judgments are not exact. It is executed through human instruments of power which are ambiguous and imprecise. But Niebuhr recognizes that relatively good nations are also overthrown perhaps through strategic mistakes. For Niebuhr to see history through faith is an option as other philosophies fail. The perspective of Christian faith as it transcends human reason permits humans to interpret history from its perspective. From the revelation, "it is possible to make sense out of life."[14]

Faith and History improves upon the two volumes of *The Nature and Destiny of Man* in its more clear presentation of the same ideas. Niebuhr is operating as a philosopher on the basis of Christian symbols to make a case for Christian faith. The details of the atonement discussion are not necessary to understand that the political person seeking only personal fulfillment corrupts the whole process. The self-seeker is part of the meaning of history as the rebellion against God. In dying to self-seeking through the inward appropriation of the Christ drama, one gains wisdom and power for the life of service to others. For Niebuhr that is the meaning of the new age.

In the book Niebuhr rejects both cultural optimism and pessimism, though he believes the Christian perspective is nearer to the pessimists. But pessimism too has no knowledge of God or a power beyond the human. Repentance can move one from despair to hope and the Gospel has gifts of grace beyond worldly wisdom.[15] The Christian gospel of love and forgiveness is neither ecclesiastical authority nor reason. It is beyond these at the "limits of all systems of meaning."

In his chapter on "False Absolutes" Niebuhr interprets Marxism as a Christian heresy derived from a culture that failed in social justice. In Spain Marxism contended against the false absolutism of Roman Catholicism. The civil war revealed the dangers of absolutisms when allied with other forces in the society. The fury of Western Civilization was often the fury of the pursuit of Christ's goodness by movements that failed to understand that history received God's judgment and could only be fulfilled by mercy and not judgment.[16]

The book repeated much of the history Niebuhr had previously written. The influence of Ernst Troeltsch on his historical perspective is clear from his first book to his last as he retells the story of ideals and realities in Western Civilization. Knowledge, justice, and fulfillment in history are encouraged in their pursuit, but in none of these areas was perfect fulfillment possible. The pursuit of absolute achievement failed and to pretend otherwise was idolatrous. In the failure of historical achievements divine judgment could be glimpsed; still there were mercy and further opportunities to live. No person, organization, nor church could fulfill itself in perfection. For Niebuhr forgiveness and the resultant stance of humility, love, and service were the purpose of life for Christians. Without righteous nations or righteous churches "the saving remnant" unknown clearly to the churches carried the meaning forward as it witnessed against "principalities and powers" of evil in the world. He never would have claimed his own organizations, "Frontier Fellowship." Delta Farm, Union for Democratic Action, Union Theological Seminary, or third party politics were "saving remnants." Their distance from the establishment and their prophetic stances gave evidence of his means of action and meaning. His public advice was often to the elites who determined the directions of American life and policy, but his active organizing remained in these left-of-center groups which represented criticism of both the church and the state.

The Church

The last chapter of the book took up the "The Church and the End of History" more completely than had his previous work. It is the thought of ecumenical Christianity. The church would not be complete without unity, but neither the absolutes of Roman Catholicism nor the disorganized absolutes of the sectarian movements were adequate. The marks of the church were in actions and in the hopeful consciousness of the eschatological nature of the sacraments, particularly baptism and the Lord's Supper. Here Niebuhr was concerned with the need for the church to remain humble to avoid the inevitable dangers of religious pride as in the disputes over the Lord's Supper which had separated the communions at the organizational meeting of the World Council of Churches. While he was confident that "the gates of Hell" could not prevail against the church, its fulfillment was in the unknown interaction of God's eternity and human history. The unknown saints of the saving remnant were the true church, and the historical churches were representative of the ambiguity of religious life. His other writings collected by D. B. Robertson in *Applied Christianity* contain his recommendations for worship, practice, and church organization.

If the church emphasizes its righteousness, it falls into the dangers of becoming the Antichrist of religious pride. A church living in humility by faith, hope, and love finds ways to fulfill its responsibilities for service and courageous witness against evil.[17] The major theme of the chapter is that the historical church is not the fulfillment of the church. It guards against the pretentiousness of the church and the penultimate conclusion of the book is "The secure church is precisely that community of saints, known and unknown, among whom life is constantly transformed because it is always under the divine word."[18]

Despite repeating earlier themes, the book is an excellent restatement of Niebuhr's postwar, Cold War theological understanding. Biographer Charles Brown wrote "*Faith and History*, one of Niebuhr's best-written books, was a clear summation of his theological perspective on history."[19] Brown repeats a conclusion of our conversation that with this work Niebuhr was attempting to do for the Cold War time that which Augustine attempted for the time after the fall of Rome which was to present a theology of history that would sustain thinkers through the times ahead. It becomes, in Brown's exposition, the fulcrum for the important discussion of Augustine's influence on Niebuhr. Paul Merkley who argues strongly that the heart of Niebuhr's political theory is his personal theological perspective regards the book highly.[20] Richard Fox, who seems like

Max Weber to be slightly unmusical in regard to Christian faith, dismisses the book.[21] The difference between the two seems to be in their different perspectives on Niebuhr's faith. Arthur Schlesinger, Niebuhr's personal friend and ally wrote:

> Niebuhr's Faith and History is written with Dr. Niebuhr's usual vigor, erudition, and precision of expression. It is an indispensable contribution to the revolution of our culture with which this age is inevitably concerned and to which Dr. Niebuhr has already played so brilliant and distinguished a role.[22]

The professor's close work with students and the brilliance of the students he attracted is represented in his thanks to the students who helped with the proofreading and indexing of the volume. Roger Shinn, a leading American ethicist would become his successor, John Smith became head of the philosophy department at Yale, and Langdon Gilkey became a dominant American theologian at the University of Chicago.

Ironically, in the very years that Niebuhr was advising on how to resist Communism in the context of a revolutionary world, the government panicking under the losses in Asia and Senator's McCarthy's campaign deepened its investigations of their loyalty. J. Edgar Hoover had won his spurs in the infamous Palmer investigations in the Red Scare following World War I. That grooming plus his own religious views, and something like paranoia, led him throughout the years of his tenure to harass and investigate religious thinkers who dissented from U.S. government policy as he understood it. The most famous of his harassing investigations included Niebuhr, Tillich, Martin Luther King, Jr., and the Berrigan brothers, Daniel and Philip.

18

Under Investigation

The Federal Bureau of Investigation conducted an investigation of Niebuhr in 1951 and 1952. He had sponsored an anti-Joseph McCarthy rally and spoken out against the House UnAmerican Activities Committee, but it was his employment by the Department of State that unleashed the investigation.

The 623 pages released under the Freedom of Information Act identify him as a consultant to the policy planning staff of the Department of State in 1949 and 1950, and list his role as delegate to UNESCO. The investigation was in the context of McCarthy's charges about Communists in the State Department.

The 1951 investigation turned up a previous one in 1942 when he had turned in a voucher for payment of travel when he was advising Archibald MacLeish's office on religion for a pamphlet on one of President Roosevelt's "Four Freedoms." His role as lecturer for the government in England and as a consultant to the Office of War Information was also noted. Once launched, the investigations continued under their own momentum with the information being furnished to other government offices as need was perceived. The investigation did not focus on Niebuhr's advice or service to the government, but on those organizations he had some association with that were under suspicion. Within the reports are various charges of Communist leanings or radical teachings, but little attempt to verify the various charges were evident. The FBI was still collecting material in 1963. The final use of the material seems to have been in 1969 when J. Edgar Hoover sent a summary memo of it to John B. Ehrlichman, counsel to the president, reporting:

> Investigations while largely favorable as to Niebuhr's loyalty, disclosed he had been identified as a member, endorser, or supporter of a large number of organizations cited as Communist fronts which extended over a period of twenty years. Because of his long-standing prominence in Socialist and other left-wing political circles, Dr. Niebuhr has been described as a Christian Revolutionary.[1]

His connections with the American Labor Party, reputed to be under the control of the Communists in Manhattan and the Liberal Party were mentioned. The FBI seemed to have been able to determine when one joined an organization, but unable to learn when or why one left an organization. Hoover's 1963 memo seems ludicrous.

Driving both Hoover and Ehrlichman in October, 1969, however, was probably Niebuhr's August attack on the travesty of the White House Chapel and its ringing pronouncements on White House virtue and American self-righteousness. Niebuhr's article provoked more of a national furor than anything else he wrote the last two years of his life.[2] He had reached down into the depths of his perception of critical Protestant faith and attacked what he regarded as a false piety, covering cruel politics, domestically and in Vietnam. The title "The King's Chapel and the King's Court" was taken from the High Priest Amaziah's silencing of Amos by telling him not to preach justice, for this was the King's chapel and the King's court. Niebuhr's comparison of J. Edgar Hoover to the court priest Amaziah in the article may have been more to the point than he realized at the time of writing.

The investigators interviewed people at Niebuhr's past educational institutions, former neighbors, and acquaintances. They acquired pamphlets from organizations he associated with and collected some of his writings. Many people were interviewed and some of them talked later, much to Niebuhr's embarrassment. An isolationist, for example, tried to discredit Niebuhr with stories that his loyalty was under investigation, while a pastor at a nearby church concluded that Niebuhr was leaving Union for wartime employment in D.C.

The arguments over the investigation involved Archibald MacLeish who had authorized the first investigation. Attorney General Francis Biddle became involved. The matter came to J. Edgar Hoover's attention from Biddle. Niebuhr was allowed to submit his own statement, but he was not permitted to see his own personal file so he refused to submit a statement. The refusal to see his own file came directly from J. Edgar Hoover. The FBI report found seventeen references to Niebuhr in the 1938–1939 House UnAmerican Activities Committee hearings. Later hearings also turned up references to Niebuhr, and he was accused of associating with fourteen groups that had some connections to Communists.

The FBI report finally collected the names of almost two dozen organizations with which Niebuhr had some association which were considered suspicious by some government body. The investigation continued on into the 1960s; sometimes Niebuhr would become aware of it. Stories of FBI agents going through the card catalogue in the library would occasionally surface. Their sources were as varied as reports from someone who heard one of his public lectures, former students, a reference in *The Daily Worker*, or a letter he signed to President Harry Truman protesting the government's loyalty program and the FBI's participation in it.

In December 1951, Hoover was sending telegrams to the New York office demanding they expedite the investigation. Hoover reinforced his request by saying other organs of the government were interested in the investigation of Niebuhr.

Given that Niebuhr was no longer in the employ of the government, Hoover's interest seems irregular, but he had a special place in his investigations for religious figures he regarded with suspicion. The 1952 report from the New York Office was much more responsible than its 1942 predecessor. More testimony was collected from nonfront organizations about Niebuhr's loyalty. His opposition to Communism was much more obvious to the agents than it had been in 1942. The sixty-six page report included references to his resignation from the American Labor Party and from the Socialist Party. One of the agents even excerpted a few pages from the 1932 publication *Moral Man and Immoral Society*.

Some of the nastiest pages in the whole file were contributed by "religious people" who feared Niebuhr's influence in the church. They pleaded for Hoover to investigate this modern "Judas." They asked for information from the investigation so that they could diminish Niebuhr's influence over Sunday school curriculum. Hoover was advised that the Communists would take over America by using Niebuhr to convert the seminaries of the nation to atheism. Hoover for his part could only tell them that FBI files were not available for their use. He, however, occasionally warned his writers as in a note of 7 April 1966, that Niebuhr was well known in "Bureau files for his left-wing activity."

The FBI had information that most of the critics of Niebuhr from the left lacked. The FBI had the records of his party memberships from the Election Bureau that showed his long membership in the Socialist Party, his short tenure as a member of the American Labor party, his three-year membership in the Democratic Party, and then his ongoing membership in the Liberal Party of New York. Though many of those most influenced by him were leaders of the Democratic Party, the actual record of his memberships correlates with the record of his political thought that he was left of the establishment of the Democratic Party.

The files grew over the years in an apparently random fashion. The last entries reported on some of Niebuhr's anti-Vietnam war activities, beginning with the formation of a Minister's Vietnam War committee on 11 July 1963, to protest U.S. policy.

The founding of Clergy and Laity Concerned about Vietnam on 30 January 1967 and Niebuhr's role on the executive committee was reported. He was listed as a sponsor of the Negotiations Now organization's petition, and rally in Philadelphia on 27 July 1967. On 14 October 1969, Niebuhr was associated with a *Sun Times* ad in Chicago by the Business Executives' Move for Vietnam Peace.

Niebuhr's attacks on the internal security apparatus of the Cold War were also noted. One report of the *People's World* of 16 November 1963 listed Niebuhr as asking President Kennedy to lead in repealing the Smith Act of 1940, the McCarran Internal Security Act of 1950, and the Communist Control Act of 1954.

Niebuhr had worked with Communists in some organizations and had struggled to keep Communists from controlling them. When they took control or he regarded some journal as too pro-Soviet he resigned and moved his work elsewhere. He had been a Socialist Party member, a theoretician and a political candidate twice on its ballot. He had written as a self-described Christian Marxist, and at least one Communist publication, *Revolutionary Socialist Review,* had called him "comrade" Niebuhr.

Over all, the FBI investigations were inept. They failed to study his denunciations of Communism or to interview his more important friends in government. All sorts of wild statements were included in the official files. The investigations were partially out of an unnecessary paranoia about "Reds." His loyalty was explicitly and systematically attacked for (1) supporting the democratic forces in Spain against the Fascists; (2) organizing opposition against the Japanese invasion of China; (3) urging diplomatic recognition of Russia; (4) organizing German refugees to work for a democratic and open Germany after the war; (5) opposing U.S. war preparations in the 1930s; (6) opposing the internment of Japanese-Americans in World War II; (7) writing for socialist publications; (8) organizing relief funds for striking workers; (9) working as an officer of the NAACP; (10) supporting the Manhattan Borough president's appointment of a Communist to his staff; and (11) attacking in print the internal loyalty system and the FBI's participation in it. *The Protestant Digest* of which Paul Tillich was the editor-in-chief was regarded as having "faithfully propagated the Communist Party line." Niebuhr resigned from writing for it and Paul Tillich's resignation closed the journal which in their estimation was leaning a little too far to the left, but it was never an agency of Soviet or Communist propaganda. A reading of the journal would have shown the internal struggle which led to the journal's demise.

A study of some of the significant organizations, involvement would have deepened the investigations greatly and made them of more worth. Investigations of the American Labor Party, the New York teacher's union and the League for Industrial Democracy in which they struggled for free and critical social policies would have been helpful. To label those who worked in the ever-shifting world of critical organizations as subversive would have been silly if it had not done so much damage to American politics and the ethos of the country. Many people were slandered, and any review of the charges against Niebuhr reveals many points which eventually became U.S policy or, at least, social wisdom today. Richard Fox has reported that the security investigations of Niebuhr slowed down Ursula's application for American citizenship.

The investigations of Paul Tillich affected his contribution to American thought, and, as they shut down opportunities for him to assist in Germany's postwar recovery. They were reminiscent of pressures he had experienced when Germany turned toward Nazism in 1933 and he fled in exile. Tillich was not investigated for his German socialist work or for his opposition to Hitler. His work in Germany and any substantial references to his German publications or correspondence are absent from his eighty-two-page FBI file. That file opens with papers regarding Walter Winchell's article on Tillich. Winchell, an associate with Joseph McCarthy in fanning the Red scare, was a gossip columnist and a radio news reporter of some reputation with millions of listeners. The writing on him indicates he had dropped out of school in the sixth grade. Winchell had noticed that Paul Tillich was announced as an officer of Christian Action which had among its purposes the fighting of McCarthy and McCarthyism. Christian Action was, of course, the second successor to the Fellowship of Socialist Christians founded by Reinhold Niebuhr and by 1954 it had become less socialistic and more reformist within an assumed capitalist economy while working for mixed economic solutions to welfare and justice issues. There is little distinction between Communism and Socialism in the report. Winchell's piece reads like his rapid-fire radio reports which would be followed by the typing of a telegraph machine to add urgency to his reporting:

> Among the officers of a new outfit, Christian Action, is a "clergyman," Dr. Paul Tillich. This Tillich was once a functionary of the N.Y. branch of the Moscow Free Germany Committee, a Soviet fifth-column outfit formed in 1944. Tillich has numerous Commie Front affiliations listed in the House Un-American Activities records. The new outfit has been formed to combat—that's right—McCarthy and McCarthyism.[3]

The file also contains requests by churches that are fearful of Paul Tillich and requesting information on him or asking that the FBI pay attention to his radical ideas. To its credit, there are no requests for information on him from within his denomination, the United Church of Christ. It is also interesting that the record of his ministry in Berlin or further notices of his ministry have been removed from his file in the Brandenburg Consistory office in Berlin. He never renewed his membership in the clerical ranks of the Evangelical Church of Germany, though he did rejoin the Democratic Socialist Party in Berlin. He was interviewed by the FBI on 17 December 1942.

Tillich's membership in the Guild for German Cultural Freedom in 1937 was noted without any recognition of the Guild's role for anti-Nazi Germans fleeing Hitler. It is as if anything German raised suspicions within the FBI without important distinctions being drawn. Tillich was noted as a founding member of the United Democratic Action, the group led by Niebuhr prior to the formation of the Americans for Democratic Action which merged into ADA. In 1942, his presidency of Self Help for Refugees from Central Europe was noted. It was thought that some of the refugees had suspicious connections, and that their effort to raise money to buy a fighter plane for the United States was to prove their loyalty.

Beyond his official positions, the FBI and Naval Intelligence followed him to some of his vacation spots. He was suspected of frequenting bars in Bar Harbor, Maine, and of showing undo interest in conversations among sailors. His summer trip to Cape Cod was also the object of some surveillance. The Central Intelligence Agency shared some of its reports on Tillich with the FBI as noted in the file.

His associations with Kenneth Leslie were particularly suspect whether it was the editorial work for *The Protestant Digest* or a committee to root out anti-Semitism in American textbooks. Interestingly there is no mention of his White House dinner with the president or his association with Eleanor Roosevelt or her close friends.

The presidency of the Council for a Democratic Germany particularly drew the attention of the FBI as did the advice of Under Secretary of State Adolph Berle to Thomas Mann that he should not associate with the Council. As Tillich's contacts with the German underground became known his mail was intercepted from July 1942 to June 1945.

This practical activity of Paul Tillich in the war period which was not well known in Tillich's theological world kept drawing the attention of those spying on him. He is listed for his work on the Committee to Combat Anti-Semitism, the Immigrant's Victory Council, the American Emergency Conference, Inc. (connected to German underground), International Study for Democratic Reconciliation Advisory Committee, Executive Committee of Christian Council on Palestine, and SANE membership. The FBI also mentions some of his public appearances, but not all and not necessarily the most controversial ones. Shortly before the report concludes, it reports that Tillich was not employable for the reconstruction of Germany after the war.

The report concluded with one obituary, that of the *Daily Worker*, which praised him as a fighter for peace and justice out of his religious socialist insights. It's interesting that the FBI report neglected to include the front-page obituary of the *New York Times*. Some of his protests against harassing by Senator Eastland, the Dies Committee and the House Un-American Activities Committee had also been noted. The file leaves out so much that it would be misleading to any agent reading the file who had no other information on Tillich. In its raw reporting with no interpretation of reports of nonauthoritative sources it remains slanderous. In the future, when the blacked out materials may be examined and other investigations are coordinated with this one, a more adequate picture may emerge. At this point the released material reflects its McCarthy-era origins with very inadequate work. It reveals, however, the political-activist Tillich perhaps better than other sources. The FBI disapproved of his work, but it took it seriously, labeling him in one paragraph as a "Leader of the German underground" in an item from 1944. Theologians and churches in their remembrances of Tillich have hesitated to report on or to analyze this risk-taking, exhausting work of the political Tillich.

19

Tillich's Later Social Ethics

Social Analysis of Tillich's Systematic Theology

Tillich began a systematic theology in 1913, but World War I intervened, and the attempt to build a theology so dependent on his earlier work on Schelling's philosophy was no longer possible after the carnage. The 1913 attempt has been posthumously published in English and German and his lectures on theology at Dresden and Marburg have been published in German, but he did not regard any of these as finished products. He did announce the publication of a theology for 1927, but this announcement of a volume containing both theology and politics was never published. His active social involvement in the events of Germany precluded the further development of his systematic theology. His appointment as a professor of philosophy and sociology in Frankfurt in 1929 finished his plans for a German-language theology. He saved the manuscripts and brought them to America, but when his active political participation dried up after World War II, he began anew. Despite the academic interest in these earlier lecture notes and fragments, the only *Systematic Theology* that Tillich chose to publish is the American three-volume work of the years 1951, 1957, 1963, and its German translation. During the 1950s completing the system was his central passion, and assistants helped him edit his classroom notes to produce it. Parts 2 and 3 were also delivered as the Gifford Lectures in Aberdeen, Scotland in 1953 and 1954. Characteristically, any new or challenging idea would cause him to declare: "I must revise my system." Several professors tell of Tillich walking with them in Boston, New York, or Chicago muttering that he was revising the whole system. Fundamentally, however, the structure of his thought remained unchanged. *Systematic Theology* incorporated other writings and reaffirmed in his theological answers the structure of thought he incorporated from Schelling and classical Christian theology, though the existential questions were from his work in America.

Tillich's intention is seen most clearly in his lectures on the history of Christian thought. He portrayed Hegel and Schleiermacher as having produced great syntheses of modern thought and Christian theology. They demonstrated the truth of the Christian message in terms of modern thought.[1] Their syntheses were rejected by the middle of the nineteenth century, and the influence of the

Ritschlian synthesis, which replaced them, had faded by the end of the nineteenth century. The task was once again to reconcile the modern mind and Christian faith. He had to move beyond the relativism of Ernst Troeltsch and the polemics against synthesis by Karl Barth. He wanted to bring them together in a new way that was honest to the brokenness of the twentieth century. The self-critical humanism of existentialism could pose the questions for volume 1 while the Christian message expressed in terms not that different from the philosophy of Schelling could provide the answers.[2]

Tillich's mind could hold together both the questions and the answers in a system-building way. He noted various possibilities for theological writing from fragments to essays to systems to summae. His own system was less complete than a summae, but it was complete enough to show the consequences of his method and to establish a correlation between his existential analysis of the contemporary situation and his ontological-mystical, theological answers to the questions of the situation.

From Schelling and the mystical-ontological tradition reaching back to Luther, Bohme, Augustine, Origen, John, and Paul, Tillich derived his drive to express the unity of the cosmos despite its diversity. The infinite is expressed in the finite, or being itself supports finite beings. Theology depends upon philosophy, and despite Tillich's efforts to distinguish them in his work, they collapse into each other. Mysticism and ethics are reconciled, and theology must include both. Existentialism depends upon previous insights of essentialism. As Tillich articulates his basic doctrine of God, the reconciliation of the structure of self and world, individualization and participation, dynamics and form, freedom and destiny, being and finitude, all depend upon the ontological tradition in which he stood.

Beneath the structure of his system stands a Christian grasped by the question and reality of God who will not let go of the modern situation. To reconcile his existentialist-essentialist mind with the Christian tradition, the five parts of the system correlate reason and revelation, being and God, existence and Christ, life and Spirit, history and the Kingdom of God. Despite particular problems the beauty and power of the system are evident.

The introduction to *Systematic Theology* claims that the task of systematic theology is to state the truth of the Christian message and to relate that truth to the contemporary situation. It is not the task of the systematic theologian to set forth a political program or a social philosophy. Tillich's volumes of theology do not contain a section on government as John Calvin did in his *Christian Institutes*. *Systematic Theology* is not political theology as found in the theologians of hope of later Germany or in the liberation theologians. However, the second part of his task requires analysis of the contemporary situation, including analysis of humanity's interpretation through sociology, political science, aesthetics, economics, psychology, literature, painting, and so forth. He walks on some narrow lines of distinction as when he writes: "Thus theology is not concerned with the political split between East and West, but it is concerned with the political interpretation of the split."[3] He does not include a section on social ethics. Rather, the system as a whole implies the ethic and reinforces his many other writings on ethics.[4] To show the social thought in *Systematic Theology* it is necessary to examine each part of the work for its political presuppositions and consequences while keeping in view his other political and ethical writings.

The most important consequence of the political interpretation of the contemporary human situation is determinative for the shape of the system. In the opening pages Tillich shows that to surrender theology to the situation is to make the mistake of the German theologians whom he had so bitterly opposed.[5] On the other hand, to pretend that theology is not involved in the situation leads to the dual mistakes of Barth who at first ignored the rise of Nazism and then absolutized opposition to it. The human situation, like an adequate theology, is dialectical. It is an expression of the essence of humanity and the broken existences of humanity. Theology must represent its essential teaching, but in response to the critically interpreted human situation of suffering.

Tillich's theology is written in dialogue with contemporary thinkers. Most of those he had in mind were humanistically educated skeptics. He wrote for the church, but for the church in conversation with contemporary skepticism about religious matters. Most of those for whom he wrote were not socialists or even politically active. Originally, the *Systematic Theology* was taken from the lectures he developed for Union Theological Seminary, and consequently, it was addressed to the skepticism of theological students reflecting the modern situation of World War II and the developing Cold War. Moreover the students most influential in helping with the system were veterans of World War II. While the introduction references Hitler, Nazism, the East-West split, the ambiguities of history, religious nationalism, and political idolatry, it was written to suggest the outlines of the work which attempts to express "the self-manifestation of the divine mystery."[6] The issue is not determining the appropriate means of political thought, but discovering how it is possible to overcome the split between modern consciousness and religious faith. Of course, for Paul Tillich, as for Alexander Solzhenitsyn[7] the restoration of a meaningful faith to the Western world is of utmost political importance. Tillich's religious socialism was seeking the conditions for human fulfillment in reference to the divine or theonomy, so is his *Systematic Theology*.

An example of the correlation of his political philosophy with the structure of *Systematic Theology* is the deriving of the criteria for theology from the Great Commandment: "The Lord, our God, the Lord is one; and you shall love the Lord your God with all your heart, and with all your soul and with all your mind, and with all your strength."[8] From this commandment and from its prior expression in the first of the Ten Commandments, Tillich derived the criterion of ultimate concern for his theology and his need for theology to critique idolatry. His polemics against false absolutes in politics were derived from the same source.

Volume 1, part 1 of the system is his epistemology. In many ways it is the most difficult part of the system for the theological novice, and most readers should start with volume 1, part 2, "Being and God." Part 1, however, does teach that modern "Cognitive dehumanization has produced actual dehumanization."[9] Failures in modern humanity to understand have produced the crisis of modern humanity.

Modern humanity is technologically manipulated. Here he follows his friend and fellow exile from the Institute for Social Research, Max Horkheimer, who had traced the victory of technical reason over ontological reason in *The Eclipse of Reason*.[10] The victory, Tillich points out, encouraged the treatment of people as things rather than as ends. It undercuts any adequate defense of human values and prepared the ground for the erosion of human values in societies dominated by either liberal-capitalist consumerism or Stalinist terror. The movements of romanticism, vitalism, and existentialism all protested controlling technical knowledge in the realm of epistemology and technical manipulation of people in society. As these movements avoided grounding in the self-manifestation of being, however, they were left without criteria of truth and without connections to the values that they wanted to defend. Tillich describes the world of liberal capitalism as the world of empty autonomy, and he labels the world of Marxist domination a world of destructive heteronomy.

> The double fight against an empty autonomy (rebellion) and a destructive heteronomy [legalism] makes the quest for a new theonomy [freedom in the divine] as urgent today as it was at the end of the ancient world. The catastrophe of autonomous reason is complete.[11]

Tillich does not despise technical reason; his point is that it must be guided by the traditions of ontological reason, which runs from Parmenides through Hegel, for the fulfillment of human purposes. Ontological reason explicates the rational character of reality and shows the ends for which technical reason ought to be used. Ontological reason is reason in the service of God for explicating the rational structure of Logos. Under the conditions of human existence, reason is subject to the conflicts of autonomy and heteronomy or rebellion and domination. The resolution of the conflict is found through revelation where the power of being itself is encountered. "Revelation is the manifestation of the depth of reason and the ground of being."[12]

For Tillich there is no conflict between revelation as the disclosure of the depth of being, and reason, as the explication of the structures of being. Reason drives toward the answer of revelation and depends upon revelation for its completeness. Social healing, the restoration of theonomy, or the living in God's saving power, demands that reason and revelation be understood as interrelated. Revelation cannot be against reason; rather it fulfills the reason of the rational thinker in ecstatic, transforming reason.

Even in this formal writing on epistemology Tillich returns to the problem of uniting theory and practice.[13] He concludes that under the conditions of existence the two cannot be perfectly joined, though both the Fourth Gospel and Karl Marx point to the necessity of doing the truth to learn the truth. Humanity practices the way it sees the world, and Tillich's chapter on epistemology is an argument for seeing the world as dependent upon God. Theory and practice seem to be imperfectly joined in history just as salvation and revelation are only imperfectly realized in the lives of those who are possessed by them. Here Niebuhr's and Tillich's sense of the sin or alienation of humanity prevent them from completely joining their religion and their politics. The two are related but not fused. This seems to be the major break between the Social Gospel that preceded them and liberation theology that followed them.

Part 2 of the system is relatively empty of social analysis. The catastrophes of the twentieth century are in the background preventing the credibility of theories of rational providence. The providence of God is an "in spite of." Though the theologian or philosopher cannot escape the relativity of the historical situation, the fact of being, "grasped by the idea of God is not dated."[14] The reflections on ontology in the section on being and on being itself are not heavily influenced by social philosophy. There is a discourse on love, power, and justice reminiscent of the almost contemporary book *Love, Power, and Justice* and of the many lectures he repeated on the subject, but there is nothing new in the section. He goes so far as to say that systematic theology cannot go into the actual problems of social ethics.[15]

The vision of God regarding the whole world prohibits crusades on religious grounds just as that relationship rejects ideas of religious escapism from the world. The dependence of the individual upon the society is clear in the theology of part 2 even though the full implications of that connection will be discussed in part 5. "The destiny of the individual cannot be separated from the destiny of the whole in which it participates."[16] Furthermore he notes as he argued in *The Socialist Decision* in prewar Germany that monotheism emerged in Amos combined with the sense of universal social justice. So, though this part of the system distances itself from reflection on social philosophy, it is clear that his social ethics still, as in his dissertation, depends upon philosophical theology, or in his words, ontology, for their foundations.

Tillich's first Gifford Lectures at Aberdeen in 1953 were published as volume 2 of his system in 1957 containing part 3 of his system, "Existence and Christ." In an introduction he refined his use of being as the fundamental concept for systematic theology and defended his method of apologetic theology. The writing is more polemical than in the first volume. There in the ancient university with its buildings of granite pounded by the North Sea he encountered a less-welcoming but more-theologically informed group of Scots than he usually found in America. The Presbyterian tendency towards biblicism was more pronounced, and the influence of Karl Barth was felt very strongly in that city by the sea. Also the criticism of his first volume had freed him from any illusions that the whole church would accept his theology, so he was freer to express his own theological convictions powerfully. The dialectical relationship he presupposes between the analysis of modern existence and his Christology is expressed in personal terms. His own creative stamp in the writing is more prevalent than before. Except for a few references the volume is apolitical.[17] The issues of Jesus' relationship to political issues are not taken up in depth. In our time much more attention is paid to the political existence of Jesus which was of very little concern to Tillich.

In analyzing the estrangement of human existence, Tillich spends some paragraphs on the problem of collective guilt. Fundamentally he rejects any major meaning of collective guilt, because the group does not decide, individuals within the group make decisions.[18] Guilt applies to the individual actions. There may be a weak sense of individual guilt for holding membership in a group that committed evil acts. He does not want nations accused of collective guilt because of the unjust punishments that may follow. Holding Germany guilty for World War I contributed to the formulation of various national policies that led to World War II. He had constantly argued that those connected with Nazism, particularly its leaders, should be punished, but all Germans should not be punished because of an assertion of "collective guilt."

Parts 4 and 5 of the system appeared as volume 3 in 1963, six years after part 3. The criticism of his Christology in volume 2 resulted in the introduction to volume 3 being the most tentative of any of the introductions. The system was complete, but he noted its fragmentary character and admitted that much of the work was inadequate. In these later years he had become even more anxious about his health and worried whether he would complete the system. Though other work would follow, his vocation was complete with the publication of volume 3 of *Systematic Theology*. In two years he would die. The final volume was dedicated, "For Hannah the Companion of My Life." In their final years their relationship had mellowed somewhat and reconciliation had taken place. The reconciliation participated, however, in the ambiguity of human existence to which he constantly referred. After his death, her anger would boil over in her poetic, fragmentary biography *From Time to Time* detailing their respective affairs and alienated living.

Volume 3, part 4, "Life and the Spirit," presented his existential analysis of life and its answer in the analysis of the reality of Spiritual Presence. It is the longest part of the system and it reveals the mystical roots of Tillich's thought more clearly than other parts of the system. The spiritual presence "is the aspect of God ecstatically presented in the human spirit and implicitly in everything which constitutes the dimension of the spirit."[16] The length and power of the writing, along with his lengthy critique of Christocentric theologies, certainly permits the observation that the third person of the trinity dominates the second in the system. The dominance of the spirit, the control of ontology, and the exposure of the mysticism led Niebuhr to say according to popular seminary gossip, "He's even more heretical than I thought he was." On the other hand, Niebuhr was relentlessly criticized for lacking a doctrine of the Holy Spirit.

Tillich explores psychoanalysis, existentialism, the church, culture, morality, and religion under the rubrics of the ambiguity of life and the Spiritual Presence. Often the discussion in the volume repeats his smaller, less-technical works. Aside from the discussion of social ethics and the repetition of the themes of love and justice there are only a dozen or so references to issues of social philosophy. The terms demonic and theonomy reveal their origins in the religious socialist movement, but there is no argument for any particular socialist realization. The discussion of theory and praxis obscures its importance in the circles of Marxist-inspired social criticism. The issues of social philosophy, Tillich decided, belonged to the categories of historical existence so they were put into part 5. Tillich's criticism of Protestantism's overemphasis of male symbolism and his own hints of the correction of this distortion, though brief, have provided some of the most helpful insights from the volume and been the basis for much feminist work until the present time.[20]

Tillich's system comes to its end and its fulfillment in the discussion of the ambiguity of history and the Kingdom of God in part 5. Tillich regards the Kingdom of God as "a most important symbol"; he does not call it the most important symbol. It is an especially important symbol for ecclesiastical and political life. The pressures of ecclesiastical life toward absolutism have eclipsed the symbol, which is a guard against that very absolutism. Despite the difficulties, Tillich affirms its revival in the social gospel movement in America and identifies its importance in his own articulation of religious socialism in Germany.[21] Also, the Kingdom of God is a difficult symbol because it has both historical and transhistorical aspects. He looks for its reinstatement as a powerful symbol in the dialogue with Eastern religions.[22] He believes that the memory that Jesus' message was the preaching of the Kingdom of God and that every repetition of the "Lord's Prayer" petitions for its coming should encourage its revival despite its difficulties. The emergence of political and liberation theologies since Tillich's writing confirms his hopes for the revival of this symbol even if these theologies have not always guarded the concept from utopianism.

Tillich's writing on history passionately rejects philosophies of history characterized as progress, utopian transcendental, and nonhistorical. In his view humanity is in history, and no one escapes its influence. The political element is central to history, and the fight for freedom is carried out most significantly in the political realm. Marxist interpretations of history are not obvious, and even the importance of economics is downplayed here. History is life in existence and reflects all of the ambiguities of life. There are structures, but human freedom and chance can undo or overthrow structures. There is a drive in history toward centralization, newness, fulfillment, and universality, says Tillich, but these characteristics of the Kingdom of God are only partially realized in history. The Kingdom of God is the answer to the agonies of history.

Humanity's political organization reveals the drive toward centralization and universality in the building of empires. The empires express a particular vocational consciousness such as Great Britain's attempt to represent a Christian humanism, as well as the will to power. But the vocational consciousness of imperial groups is resisted by various consciousnesses of the oppressed. Even in the ruling group, the necessities of ruling come into conflict with the vocational consciousness of the empire. These ambiguities prevent any imperial power from surviving forever. They have their day and pass.

Historical self-creativity is expressed as new forces and new ideas emerge to oppose the old. If a system is not structured to allow the new to emerge, pressures and contradictions build to the point of revolution. "There are situations in which only a revolution (not always a bloody one) can achieve the breakthrough to a new creation."[23] Tillich notes the dangers of revolutionary purpose being betrayed by the dynamics of the revolutionary process. He is no romanticizer of revolution, but he explicitly rejects the ecclesiastical tendency to oppose revolution. Paul's caution about opposing government in Romans 13, he argues, was directed against apocalyptic enthusiasts, not against revolutionary forces about to install a new order to replace a decaying one. Revolution, like empire, participates in historical ambiguity.

Tillich, like Niebuhr, aims for overcoming both cynicism and utopianism in his writing on politics in the *Systematic Theology*.[24] He advocates the politics of responsibility in Max Weber's sense of responsible politics. History produces drives to transcend its ambiguities and these drives are expressed in mythologies of the "Third Stage," or "Third Reich," or "Age of Reason," or "Classless Society." In history, however, these myths fail. Even limited attempts at absolutism must fail as, for example a political party in Russia, or the church in

Rome. Though the failures can produce cynicism, Tillich urges action against the various forms of the demonic.

Democracy, for him, is also an ambiguous political expression, but it is the best way of protecting human freedom within an organized group.[25] In modern society, Tillich argues, freedom must be preserved in the political sphere or it will be lost in other realms as well. Techniques of representation, control of communications, and party bureaucracies reduce the freedom of the individual to participate creatively in society. Majority rule can be misused to deprive minorities of expression. Democracy in practice is fully ambiguous, Tillich acknowledges, but when confronted with various forms of totalitarianism, democracy is clearly more successful than dictatorships in nurturing individual creativity. Democracy's tendency toward mass conformity nonetheless presents a very real danger to creativity, in some cases even more danger than an absolutism that elicits opposition.

The risk of this emphasis on the ambiguity of history, and fragmentary fulfillment in history is that it will lead to a politics of complacency as Niebuhr had argued in *Moral Man and Immoral Society*. The tension between the presence of the Kingdom of God in the achievement of authentic democracy and the not-yet-fulfilled Kingdom of God in the failures of democracy is difficult to maintain even when the theoretical need for such tension is perceived. Satisfied forces in the church and in the government will pervert the tension into satisfaction with the status quo. Tillich emphasizes this danger in the *Systematic Theology*, making one of his infrequent references to the Marxist philosopher Ernst Bloch and his "restatement of the 'principle of hope.' " The emergence of hope in opposition to smug complacency Tillich regards as a victory for the "fighting Kingdom of God." In discussing Bloch, he refers to "movements of expectation," which was his own central term for socialism in *The Socialist Decision*.[27] He cannot leave the discussion, however, without again pointing to the tendency in such movements to forget the presence—even if fragmentary—of the reality of the Kingdom of God. Elsewhere during the same period he was writing the *Systematic Theology*, Tillich called for the victory of the "spirit of utopianism" over utopianism.[28] Here in part 5 of the system we have essentially the same point: The Kingdom of God as the Spiritual Presence of God is real in human history; it drives humanity to fulfill creativity, universality, and community, but the fulfillment does not come completely in history. The ambiguities of history, including the fragmentary realization of the Kingdom, drive humanity toward answers that are found in the Kingdom as the end of history or as eternal life.

The *Systematic Theology* achieves its aim to present a synthesis of existentialism and essentialism in terms of Schelling's philosophy of religion in loyalty to Christian theology. The apologetic power of the system is impressive, especially to those inclined toward the religious-mystical side of Protestant theology, but who desire a realistic ethic. There are, of course, other Protestant traditions and theologies of higher Christology or more-biblical terminology. Tillich, however, has produced a powerful system of God as "Being Itself," Christ as New Being, and the Spirit as Spiritual Presence while he contributed to the revival of the symbol of the Kingdom of God as a central symbol for social theology.

The *Systematic Theology* was written in conversation with Tillich's sources reaching back to his early work in Germany, but it was written mainly for American students of theology in the 1950s and 1960s. These were the students who lived during the Truman and Eisenhower administrations, but at Union Seminary most of these students were politically following Adlai Stevenson, Hubert Humphrey, and in 1960, John F. Kennedy. Their political ideals reflected those of the Americans for Democratic Action; they read *Christianity and Crisis* and participated in the Cold War as liberal democrats. The students were neither socialists nor revolutionaries.

Tillich, being more disengaged, did not support the Cold War perspective of his friend Reinhold Niebuhr. But he and Niebuhr both engaged in criticism of the House of Representatives Un-American Activities Committee. Tillich supported non-ideological organizations working to improve race relations and in the protection of civil rights. His thought does not reflect any acceptance of laissez-faire capitalism, but leans toward supporting mixed economic models. He held to a personal view of religious socialism as the contemporary meaning of theonomous society, but his listeners and readers were not interested and he muted the references to it in the *Systematic Theology*. During the Eisenhower era the advocacy of religious socialism would have been utopian and in his maturity he was determined not to be utopian. If the seminaries and divinity schools had contained more Third World students who were conscious revolutionaries, more blacks, or more radical feminists, his theology would have been written with them more in mind, but his closest students were the returning World War II veterans. As he wrote in the U.S.A. he did not have a proletariat in view. Without a proletariat, social theology becomes—as his did—a theology to fight against dehumanizing forces in the society rather than for the total restructuring of the country.

Dehumanization in Society

While welcoming technical developments, Tillich feared the dehumanizing effects of modern technological society. In an essay celebrating the founding of Christian Action in a volume serving as a tribute to Reinhold Niebuhr, Tillich tried to show a way to resist the process of dehumanization.[29] He saw the existentialism movement in Kierkegaard, Marx, and Nietzsche as a protest against the reduction of a person to a thing. The protest was profound, but it failed.

Tillich hoped for the development of groups that could resist the mass conformity in modern society that compelled people to surrender their personal creativity. In the essay he recommended to groups like Christian Action, to which he belonged, a retreat from and an attack on modern society. The "partial nonparticipation" in the structure of modern society, he argued, was best grounded in the "new Reality" represented in the Christian message and elsewhere. The retreat was an affirmation of the religious reservation about the world; the attack could be expressed in a "rebellion of life" against forces that degraded the person. The attack also had to continue the fight for social justice. As Nietzsche represented the rebellion of life and Marx the struggle for social justice against capitalist society, so Kierkegaard represented the seeking of the ultimate roots of personal identity. Withdrawal from the clutches of technical-capitalist society was necessary if one were to hope to act against that society. And while the withdrawal was to religious resources, the attack was one in which allies were sought within the technical society to fight its dehumanizing aspects. The person could finally be defended only by a "personal encounter with the ground of everything personal."[30]

Tillich was, of course, part of technical society and his transcendence was only partial. His refusal to accept the conditions of contemporary social or religious life is clearly seen in his essay. In fact, this statement shows perhaps more clearly than the *Systematic Theology* the part of the modern mind with which he was correlated. His correlations were with the modern mind in rebellion against the dominating trends.

His acceptance of much of the technical-scientific development is seen in his celebration of the new perspectives coming to humanity through space exploration. The space program, harnessed to military competition, strengthened antidemocratic tendencies within the United States. Yet, he affirmed the program because it expressed the creativity of humanity. It contained immense dangers, but the threat of danger was not a reason to stop development. Eventually, "space exploration will be judged in the light of the meaning of life in all its dimensions."[31] The political process would sort out the priorities of the nation as reflected by the operative forces in the system. He hoped that the humanistic elements in society would insist on values other than those simply residing in the drive to push as far as possible. The nonhumanistic forces in society were prevalent, but because they were not self-sufficient, rebellion against them could be expected. Tillich did not live long enough to see the beginnings of mass revolt by American youth against the technological system or to see their defeat and return to quietism. His judgment that the political system itself would arrange the priorities of the nation regarding space exploration was correct. Like all other exceptionally creative human endeavors, space exploration caused his spirit to soar, but the program itself remained ambiguous.

Christian Ethics

Tillich experienced a moralism in America that was quite different than the uninhibited academic life of revolutionary Germany within his social circles. He commented on this in a 1955 lecture shortly before his retirement from Union and his move to Harvard.[32] The morals of his personal life were as far removed from those of Union at the time as his politics were from J. Edgar Hoover's fear of his radicalness. Christopher Niebuhr, Reinhold's son, has told me that his father was glad that his behavior became widely known only after he had moved to Harvard, so that it did not become an issue for Union Seminary. In the lecture Tillich distinguished between moralism, morality, and ethics. *Moralism* was the oppression on the human self of a foreign ethical code backed up by authority either internal or external. *Morality* was the human being acting according to his essential human self toward fulfillment. *Ethics* was the science of morality. The lecture, from beginning to end, attacked moralism as a human oppression represented in many different systems. Moral systems were relative to the historical situation and the groups that controlled the moral discourse. Yet as Kant had taught, the moral imperative or categorical imperative which truly represented the essential nature of the human being was an unconditional imperative to be followed. The category was a universal characteristic of the human whereas the particular stipulations of the moral imperative would vary from situation to situation or from society to society. There were elements of Kant in the ethical theories of both Niebuhr and Tillich, but Tillich pushed toward human fulfillment whereas Niebuhr emphasized duty more. Tillich would allow more negative impulses into the self in its decision making to avoid repression. Niebuhr feared the idolatry-making capacities of the self a little more and would stress more than Tillich the duties of restricting the self for the good of the other. Niebuhr as an ethicist was inclined to teach a traditional Protestant sexual morality for the sake of the family whereas Tillich feared repression and encouraged risk taking. Niebuhr's family was generally happy; Ursula would confess to students that they were very happy in marriage. Tillich's married life was terrible, full of jealousy and rage at infidelity and the denial of it. Both of the Tillichs knew that their family morality was a failure and he found much of the genius of his Lutheran piety in forgiveness. His oft-repeated refrain that the grace of God was experienced in the acceptance of the unacceptable referred more to his own personal experience than most of the thousands who listened to his later lectures ever knew. Luther had established the family as the norm for Protestant clergy with a force equal, almost, to the Roman Catholic insistence on celibacy for professional religious leadership. Tillich could maintain the form, but it covered his failures as the formal priesthood covered the shambles of formal chastity within Roman Catholicism. Tillich was certainly correct that moral systems are relative, but the theologian or ethicist must be able to find, affirm, and live out, even with some transgressions to be overcome, a moral life within the relativities of the pluralism of moral systems and common immorality.

The breakdown of the great Hegelian synthesis in the hands of Schelling, Nietzsche, Feuerbach, Freud, and Marx convinced Tillich that human thought is never complete. He found this lack of completeness particularly to be the case in Christian ethics. He learned a great deal from Ernst Troeltsch about the historical relativity of Christian ethical judgments. Tillich began a 1962 lecture in Dallas with the assertion that there was not any one accepted system of Christian ethics. The whole direction of his thought inclined him to the conclusion that there would never be a final, authoritative system of Christian ethics. In World War I. he experienced the ideological misapplication of his beloved Lutheran tradition as most of the Lutheran forces supported the war and lined up on the side of social reaction after the war. Though Religious Socialism became for him a working social ethic, he always kept it in a tentative position by his loyalty to the essence of the Reformation. That essence which he described as the "Protestant Principle" was the stubborn insistence that no moral practice or ethical system could take the place of the absolute. The dual love commandment of Jesus expressed the Protestant principle and, though itself absolute, was not law in any ordinary sense. Rather, it was a summary of Christian ethics, the meaning of which was not immediately obvious for most ethical situations. The Christian ethic was always in the process of being worked out, and Tillich plunged into the fray of ethical debate with his usual vigor.

Recent essays on Tillich's ethics have labeled his method as an "ontological self-realization ethic,"[33] as a metaphysical ethic,"[34] and as an ethic of theology of culture.[35] It is true that nearly everything Tillich wrote can be related to his constructive ontology developed from Schelling, but it is not true that his ethic is deduced from his ontology. His ethic is more complicated in form than the labeling of it as a metaphysical ethic permits. In *Das System der Wissenschaft* (*The System of the Sciences*, 1923) he distinguished ethics from metaphysics, the social sciences, and theology.

Ethics as a discipline cannot be known in itself, he said. It only becomes an object of knowledge when it is placed in a frame of reference. The necessary frame of reference for Tillich was a system, and the role of ethics in his mind when he wrote it in his later years was consistent with *The System of the Sciences*. In this ambitious undertaking, he attempted to perceive the unity of all of the sciences. Ethics was conceived of as belonging to the mental sciences, distinguished from the sciences of being, and the sciences of thought, and it should not be reduced to logic or empirical studies. His tripartite division of the sciences was also expressed as sciences of form, or ideal science, the sciences of objects, or real science, and the sciences of norms or normative science.

Tillich considered the subsuming of ethics in theories of sociology to have weakened the understanding of ethics as the active direction toward the unconditional. Destruction of the ethos reduced ethics to morality, that is, the theory of compulsory behavior in the context of the conditional. The dignity of ethics could be perceived by understanding it as the science of the ethos, that is, the understanding of practical activity moving toward the realization of the unconditional. Therefore the place of ethics in the practical realm was analogous to that of metaphysics in the theoretical realm. Ethics as the science of the ethos expresses itself in transcendent symbols and knows that its unconditional view is not to be realized concretely. Ethics can analyze the content of community apart from any particular realization of it.

Tillich was concerned to protect the relative autonomy of the social sciences. Since Tillich's early writing the sciences have exploded in their proliferation and development. He would willingly use all of them in research appropriate to their methods. Their goals, however, should come from ethics. Ethics then would be referred to in ontology or philosophy, or intellectual history, but it had its own role in shaping the goals of the community. Tillich was concerned to protect the relative autonomy of ethics while placing it in a larger scheme of meaning, but it was definitely neither theology nor metaphysics. In a seminary context Christian ethics at Union Seminary had a role in both philosophy of religion, and in systematic theology at a formal level, but its major work would be in the area of Christian ethics which had evolved from Niebuhr's earlier appointment in Applied Theology. Most of the theologians at Union would write treatises on Christian ethics while leaving the practical application of it up to the Christian ethicists who often held positions in either philosophy of religion or systematic theology as well.

Tillich shared in the movement of vitalism, expressed differently in Schelling, Nietzsche, and Bergson. Ethics was not to be reduced to a morality that confined, but was to reveal the way to fulfillment of the self in the community. Within the ambiguities of life and the struggle of various beings to fulfill life, that which was moral was the act in which the potential to be a person was realized.[36] Recognition of the drive for fulfillment of the self in community gave his thought a radical direction in terms of both personal morality and social morality. This recurring motif in his writing on ethics could lead to the conclusion that his life was a teleological or goal-oriented ethic, but there are deontological or rule-elements also. This model of beings struggling for the fulfillment of their power to be gave his ethics realism, but he also saw that it was in the struggle that the need for justice was found. The encounter of person with person demanded justice, that is, an arrangement that would allow both to flourish. Similarly, among classes and nations, the need for justice arose so that all could find fulfillment in relationship with one another.

As a follower of Troeltsch, Tillich knew that Christian ethical judgments had changed through the centuries on almost every major ethical theme. As he sought for an absolute amidst relativity, he could only find one: the commandment to love the neighbor as the self. This commandment grounded in the first commandment, of course, contained within itself the requirements of justice and the need for wisdom. Love, justice, and wisdom, then, were the norms that worked together in a properly ethical decision.

Tillich's ethic reflects his life, and an adequate treatment of his ethic must mention the experiences that broke his life leaving him to personify vulnerability. The experience of World War I shattered his political complacency and his Lutheran conservatism, leaving him suffering from post-traumatic stress disorder. The seduction of his first wife by his close friend while he was at the Western front shattered his conventional sexual morality. His experiences among the workers and the revolution in Germany broke his aristocratic tendencies. The disaster of Nazism destroyed his German academic community, and the occupation of his homeland by the Russians after World War II made his exile permanent. The presence of anti-Semitism in Wingolf drove him to resign from his beloved fraternity and the ongoing struggles alienated him from many of his friends. Tempermentally, he was inclined to a philosophical idealism, but the destruction of so many of the foundations of his life tore him from his roots. Only his faith kept him a faithful realist rather than a cynic.

Elements of his Lutheran heritage remained even after all the shocks. His ethic retained a provisional dualism, distinguishing along with his friend Niebuhr between the moral expectations appropriate to groups and to individuals. He was never attracted to the Christian pacifism of many American social activists, and his social realism owes much to his Lutheran roots. On the other hand, his socialism and concern for social justice on theological grounds set him apart from the conservative Brandenburg Lutheranism in which he grew up.

Paul Tillich, like many people of courage, was also subject to fears. Late in his life at the height of his personal success, he did not emphasize the full radicalness of his earlier Christian Marxism. On occasion, he would suppress the republication of a socialist piece that he felt was irrelevant to the present and potentially dangerous to his career. However, he never denied his earlier socialism and often explicitly defended it before conservative audiences.

In the realm of personal morality he hinted in his lectures that he was exploring new paths of personal fulfillment. He explicitly attacked conventional morality. He regarded divorce as a possible demand of agape. He dealt with the idea of sexual relations with partners other than the marriage partner, and he discussed the possessive sexual jealousy that undercuts relationships.[37] Here he only hinted at the radicalness of his life and it took the publication of his wife's memoirs to reveal the meaning of clues found in his lectures. It should be stated also that he often commented on how difficult it was to discuss sexual problems nonlegalistically. He acknowledged the incompleteness and failure of both his theory and practice in the realms of politics and sexuality. It seems best to regard him as a man who defied convention and who paid the price of that risk in loneliness and suffering. The price was one that he mentioned as the cost of the search for unconventional patterns of life.

His boldest move in theoretical ethics was an essay entitled "The Transmoral Conscience."[38] He analyzed the meaning of conscience in scripture and philosophy, and he found the transcendence of the conscience in Nietzsche and Heidegger dangerous. His own tentative formulation of the transmoral conscience was grounded in Luther's idea of justification by faith and not by the correspondence of an act to conscience. He concluded that any sensitive conscience will be an uneasy conscience. Transmoral could mean either the claim of morality beyond moral law or the destruction of morality. Tillich's conclusions affirmed transmoral conscience in the former sense, that is, the conscience that acted creatively for justice even while setting aside accepted canons of justice.

Despite the complexity of the biographical formulation of Tillich's ethic and the wide range of sources from which it is drawn, the form of his ethical reflection for moral action is clear and consistent. The structure is threefold: first the ultimate principle of Christian ethics is agape, which is known as the law of human nature; the second part of the structure is human wisdom represented in laws, moral principles, and guidelines; third is the concrete situation in which the actor takes upon oneself the risk of moral decision. This pattern of love, law, and situation is present in most of Tillich's later ethical writing.

Agape is the one universal element of the human moral situation in Tillich's view. Occasionally, he describes the universal element as "the human self." The seeming ambivalence in his ethics, of course, derives from his claim that a properly conducted analysis of human nature reveals love as the essence of life. In much of his writing, however, it seems that the experience of love is the starting point of the analysis: "In man's (human) experience of love the nature of life becomes manifest."[39]

The second level of the theory accepts the relativity of all moral principles unless they are alternative formulations of agape, which in itself includes justice and the honoring of a person as a person. Moral principles, or middle axioms, are not despised, but they are considered relative. They are useful as guidelines, and if they embody agape and meet the situation, they may be the ground upon which the moral decision maker acts.

The third ingredient—the situation—requires a loving receptiveness of the part of the decision maker. It is at this point that the tools of the social and psychological sciences have their greatest, importance for Tillich. His anti-moralism demands that as many of the particulars of the situation as possible be considered. In the situation rested the contradiction of Tillich's marriage and promiscuity. He believed his vocational situation prohibited divorce, as did Hannah's dependence upon him. However, his history of promiscuity provided some fulfillment, comfort, and escape from the demons of his human insecurity. Human relations of depth with the other sex often led him into violating the marriage with Hannah, as did her promiscuity. It was an unsatisfactory situation, but he lived with it in ways that betrayed his own ethic of agape which included his relations with his wife, and his whole system allowed him to live with the brokenness of life and failures while remaining incredibly productive and creative. In a different historical situation divorce could have freed him to still support the dependent Hannah, at least financially, while freeing him to live with integrity as a single unmarried person. But in their situation of codependence, his vulnerability, and his vocation, such an option was probably beyond him. The consequences of such a break were revealed with Hannah's publication, after his death, of the angry volume *From Time to Time* from which his reputation has not recovered.

In Tillich's published ethic, there is no security; there is only the risk of moral decision and the comfort that trust in the power of forgiveness brings. The development of the ethic in terms of love, power, and justice is undertaken in the next chapter along with an analysis of the same conceptions in Reinhold Niebuhr's thought.

20

On Justice

Niebuhr's first book on the renewal of society echoed themes of brotherhood, social values, and equality more than it focused on justice. The term *justice* in *Does Civilization Need Religion?*[1] referred to the criminal justice system and the hope that the tendency to inflict vengeance could be restrained. Less than four years later his volume of socialist theory, *Moral Man and Immoral Society* informed by the work of R. H. Tawney, *Equality*, and according to his own record even more by L. T. Hobhouse's *The Elements of Social Justice*, affirms justice as: "From each according to his ability and to each according to his needs." He calls the formula that of equal justice an ideal. He recognizes it has never been achieved, and that it is impossible to realize. The choice of trying to realize it through democratic evolution or revolution tends to depend upon one's world view, and not on an absolute moral difference. Whether the formula is accredited to the New Testament or Marxism or both it still remains an ideal. Justice as an ideal has different formulations in various social arrangements. In the case of this demand for equality from the proletarian, it is inspired partially by the new class consciousness, and by their recognition that they are the sufferers of industrial society's inequality.

There is little in Niebuhr's thought that would deny a Harvard professor's concept of the social contract of disinterested parties creating a balanced vision of fairness and calling it justice. But of course it is only one dated view from the perspective of late-twentieth-century academia. Likewise, he would not forcefully attack a Yale Professor's view that the demand for human rights, based on the one reference in Genesis to the image of God in humanity, is the basis of human rights which through history evolved into a concept of justice built out of human rights theory. Similarly, he would not have the same reading of history nor regard the ideal as having particular relevance to the social struggles which have produced in Western histories the various social arrangements for which humans have settled. His own view is more akin to that of John Wesley who looking at the social contract theories of the France of his century regarded them as absurd, because clearly the discourse about law and justice reflected the arrangements forced upon people by the stronger winners of the social struggle who set the rules for others.

The rational theory of social contract of John Rawls' disinterested people fails, because disinterested people have never established a social contract nor been disinterested either. The divine-command theory of human rights of Nicholas Wolterstorff fails because the biblical commandments and the biblical myths of the relationship of the divine to the human place all of their injunctions in particularly Hebrew accents reflecting more the meaning of their time than the clear injunctions of the divine. The relativizing of the Sabbath commandment of the Ten Commandments by Jesus, or Paul claiming that Christians did not need to honor special days, and the shift from the Sabbath to worship on Sunday by the early church show how an absolute divine commandment of morality falls apart even within the scripture. Of course, Niebuhr did not reply to these posthumous theoreticians of justice, Rawls or Wolterstorff,[2] but his writings on the historical relativity of particular systems of morality make the deduction of his critique of these systems relatively straightforward and obvious.

The human has an idea of perfection or original justice which is mythically present in the Garden of Eden story. The image of God for Niebuhr means the essence of humanity which is not found in a pure form in history but only in a sinful condition. The requirements of original justice are too high for historical humanity and so, "There is no justice, even in a sinful world which can be regarded as finally normative."[3]

The mature ethic of Niebuhr adds freedom as a requirement of human nature to the principle of equality while recognizing that under historical conditions no theory or historical settlement is final. The essential human nature keeps pushing for a system of acceptance and love which humanity cannot manage. The ideal, which in his earliest writings he hoped might be realized, and which in his socialist writings required a revolution achieved violently or perhaps nonviolently is now expressed in the essential nature of humanity in tension with its human existence as a permanent problem. The competitive forces in a society could be cajoled into accepting a tolerable system of justice which while far from perfect could, in a democratic organization, achieve degrees of freedom beyond what a tyrannical system could achieve. "There is therefore, no historic structure of justice which can either fulfill the law of love or rest content in its inability to do so."[4]

Further refinements in the dialogic approach to justice as expressing the tension between love and justice in society would emerge, but the basic pattern was set by his 1941 *Human Nature*. The understanding of his approach requires a consideration of his actual struggles for justice in race relations, social policy, and economics. Also, as he works through the history of ideas in many of his volumes he uses the basic paradigm of Troeltsch of ideal and compromise. Niebuhr's interpretation of various thinkers reveals his concepts of justice and social reality. Many collections of Niebuhr's writing on social policies have been edited, and all of them differ from Tillich's primary writing on the theme as he stays closer to that which Niebuhr described as the essential nature of humanity.

The most significant study of Niebuhr's use of the term *justice* is Harlan Beckley's examination of the concepts of justice in Walter Rauschenbusch, John Ryan and Niebuhr, in *Passion for Justice.*[5] Beckley wisely uses Niebuhr's tendency to use the categories of ideal and real to frame his discussion. He recognizes that Niebuhr never developed a theory of justice, but he believes he has a concept of justice which he utilizes for his commitment to social reform. He explicates this concept of "justice as a strategy for approximating the social ideal entailed by Christian love under the actual conditions in which the ideal transcends all historical possibilities."[6] He furthermore contends that this basic concept of justice continued throughout his realist writings even though he gave it more substantial theological grounding in his Gifford Lectures of 1939. I think he is correct that Niebuhr uses the concept of justice as a strategy for progressive social reform, but I think his actual texts show more meanings of justice than Beckley's book considers. Also it was unfortunate that Beckley concluded his study of Niebuhr in the mid-1950s as Niebuhr had still more to contribute to the discussion of justice.

The comparisons to Rauschenbusch and Ryan make use of Rauschenbusch's pre-World War I writings compared to Niebuhr's in the mid-1950s when the situation of American labor had fundamentally changed and the years of Harry Truman's administration showed a prosperity by the American middle class that they had never before perceived. The same mistake is made in comparing Ryan's critique of the New Deal in the 1930s to Niebuhr's acceptance of it as a social improvement in the mid-1950s. Niebuhr was as critical as Ryan of the New Deal in 1935, even though for different reasons inspired by Niebuhr's socialist critique. Likewise, throughout Beckley's argument not enough account is taken of time; many of Niebuhr's changes in recommendations were due to the historical changes in America more than they were to theological changes or adjustments in his thought. I think his discussion of Niebuhr shows that Beckley was probably following sources not-well-enough informed when he repeats the critique that Niebuhr: "seemingly lacked grounds for advocating specific policy reforms."[7] On the preceding page he had explained, "There are numerous plausible explanations for Niebuhr's lack of attention to domestic reforms."[8] It is very hard to know what such sentences intend as in all probability, there is no record of advocacy for domestic reform than that of Niebuhr.

An example would be James Cone's assertion after teaching the thought of Reinhold Niebuhr for several years that there is no better white theologian on advocacy for racial justice than Reinhold Niebuhr.[9] D. B. Robertson's edited book *Love and Justice*[10] provides chapters of rather detailed social reforms by Niebuhr on health reform, economic issues, labor law, race relations, tax policies, peace terms, trials of war criminals, weapons, the United Nations, peace aims, neutrality legislation, resettlement of Jews, inflation, and education. His social reforms as spelled out further in journals and letters through the 1960s have not yet been fulfilled. It may be that some of these proposals, especially the post-World War II ones, are not as radical as Beckley thinks he should have made in light of Rauschenbusch and Ryan's earlier proposals. But that would be a different argument than the assertion that he did not make detailed proposals for reform. Beckley seems fond of Ryan's proposals for economic democracy, but for Niebuhr that was a stretch beyond American reach. Post-World War II Niebuhr affirmed mixed economies while affirming policies that his opponents labeled socialist even if he was refraining from so labeling them. Also Beckley affirms Rauschenbusch's enthusiasm for the cooperative movements, but while criticizing Niebuhr for not sharing this commitment, he neglects that Niebuhr actually helped found a cooperative movement for interracial justice in the tough country of the Mississippi Delta, helped manage it as chair of the board and to fund it through the Fellowship of Socialist Christians. Finally it was shut down by the furor of the White Citizen's Councils in Mississippi. The executive director of the Cooperative recorded that it was Niebuhr's thoughts about justice, Christian social ethics, and economy that inspired the cooperative venture. Niebuhr knew however that it was a model and not any solution to the American economic problems. There is evidence of testimony that significant figures in Roosevelt's New Deal agricultural policies regarded it as a model for some of their attempts to change U.S. agricultural policy.[11]

While I appreciate Beckley's analysis, and I think he is correct that justice for Niebuhr was one more strategy rather than a precise theory, I think Niebuhr's specific proposals for reform were more thorough than Beckley credits. The concept has both a fuller statement and his use of justice has more variety than Beckley surveys. First to its various uses, Ursula Niebuhr edited a book of his prayers and sermons posthumously; published under the title of *Justice and Mercy*.[12] The book contains many different uses of the term justice. There is a use of the term *justice* to mean that exploited workers may learn to labor for a more fair world in which no one will suffer from poverty. There is a prayer that all who work in the world of market may do justice and refrain from fraud. The meaning seems to be that they would honor their vocation and act within the rules of their vocations. There are prayers that the authorities will act with a spirit of justice meaning they will work for the common good. There is a prayer that all rulers will recognize a sense of judgment that stands beyond the rules of the judges of the earth. There is a prayer for a day of justice so that the community of nations can be built up. There are several references to divine judgment or the justice of God. A prayer for achieving justice has reference to ending tyrannies, overthrowing the great of the earth, delivering the desolate, granting respect to the lowly, peace, and a plea for working with God's providence to achieve justice. A reference to a petition for a "just peace" includes that leaders will find wisdom to fashion the structures of peace. The references to justice call for community, human effort, and humility. A prayer for justice and mercy is so the people will not be without hope. He prays for a new day in which the sovereignty of God will be recognized and the people find justice and peace. The two terms peace and justice are often linked in his prayers. In one prayer is the sentence "Your judgments are more severe and your mercy is greater than the justice and goodness of the world." So in these prayers *justice* is a concept with different meanings including at least human systems, concepts of justice, concepts beyond human justice, and divine justice. It is both an ideal and human reality in some instances. It even seems to partake of the absolute with God and the relative in human societies. In class near the end of his career he would regard justice as near the absolute of love, but note its relativity in human affairs and be most concerned that any structures regarded as just contain elements of a tolerable order and the pressure of the regulative principles of equality and liberty. The prayers contained many references to community which was also a major theme of his Christian social ethics and a reference and theme in his last book *Man's Nature and His Communities*.

One of the more fulsome statements of justice by Niebuhr surrounded by theological reflection on agape is:

> The real problem of a social ethic is how to make justice with its calculations of rights, the instrument of love, that is of the primal love commandment which enjoins us to be responsible for our neighbor. The problem of a Christian social ethic is how to profit from both the heights of its idealism and the depth of its realism in constructing systems of order and justice which provide for a tolerable harmony in communities of selfish men, who may or may not be touched by the divine law "written into their hearts."[13]

Subsequent to those defining paragraphs, Niebuhr indicated his enthusiasm for the social policy of the Amsterdam Conference in which he had been active. In his mind it moved toward pragmatism in Christian social ethics. In particular it avoided dogmatism in economic policy favoring solutions of a mixed economic type which avoided the rigorous ideological positions of capitalism or Communism. Though he had favored socialist practices for the recovery of Europe after World War II, he came to see the future of the industrial West in mixed economies. He was enthusiastic about the socialism in Britain, but he understood America's history prevented it from moving so quickly. He supported socialized medicine in both its British and Truman plans while recognizing that some payment for medical treatment by the patients would assist in avoiding overuse of the health facilities. He lived to see the postwar prosperity of the American middle class and the movement toward justice for unionized workers in basic industries. During the Richard Nixon administration, he saw significant movement toward social-welfare policies which he appreciated, and he affirmed the Nixon plans for a negative income tax to assist the poor. He did not live to see the doldrums of the Carter presidency in the midst of an oil crisis, or the privatization and anti-union policies of the presidency of Reagan. He probably could not have imagined the racist policies and the reduction of the influence of the middle-class that characterized the closing years of the century.

The decline of the percentage of the GDP going toward the middle class and working class accompanied the decline of the union movement which for Niebuhr had been a large part of his social strategy. To him the welfare tendencies of the Johnson administration were seen as real gains thwarted somewhat by the Vietnam War. His sense of confidence of movement toward economic justice in the U.S.A. was drawn from the success of the Truman Administration in solidifying gains of the New Deal and social progress. He would not have been shocked by the resurgence of Republican conservatism and fear of socialism in the 1990s and early twentieth century; all gains were subject to reversal. The acceptance of the Johnson Administration of many liberal policies which only decades before had seemed impossible inclined him to think many of the toughest victories had been won in mainstream American economic policy. He expected economic gains for blacks to be a much longer struggle for justice; once he suggested it might take 100 years. Perhaps a semi-concluding comment on Niebuhr's post-World War II perspective on economic justice is that it should not be seen as too distinctive. Most of the Americans for Democratic Action, union leaders, and liberal intellectuals held the same sense that a lot had been achieved and the rest could come through democratic processes reforming the nation.

Another Christian policy wonk with a less-developed formal Christian ethic put it in his 1948 inaugural speech: "All men have a right to equal justice under the law and equal opportunity to share in the common good." That sentence of Harry Truman falls within the orbit of Niebuhr's thought. Truman regarded himself as left of center, continuing and expanding the liberal policies of Franklin Roosevelt. Niebuhr hoped his friend Adlai Stevenson would continue left of center political leadership within the presidency. Progressive politics advanced the development of justice for Niebuhr.

> A second problem for me, arising from my Edinburgh lectures, had to do with my strong conviction that a realist conception of human nature should be made the servant of an ethic of progressive justice and should not be made

> into a bastion of conservatism, particularly a conservatism that defends unjust privileges.
>
> I might define this conviction as the guiding principle throughout my mature life of the relation of religious responsibility to political affairs.[14]

Two pages later in the midst of his final revisions of his thought, he credits John Milton for adding the principle of freedom or liberty to the classical regulative principle of equality regarding his concept of justice.

In her discussion of Niebuhr's thoughts on justice Karen Lebacqz expresses her sympathy for my suggestion that now Niebuhr's thought could be deepened regarding the Third World by the passions of liberation theology.[15] Lebacqz then explores liberation theology, particularly that of Gustavo Gutierrez and Jose Miranda. After visiting several liberation theology projects in Latin America with my colleague and friend Gonzalo Castillo-Cardenas, I became convinced that liberation theology of was really fit for Latin America and particularly where it promised a turn to socialism. Such had been the Peruvian context for Gustavo Gutierrez in the 1960s. I still believe American political theologians need to listen to the voices of the poor mediated by liberation theologians from the Third World and to the voices of liberation theology in the United States from feminist, Hispanic, and black voices even though we work to carry out our reform strategies in terms of American political wisdom interpreted through realist eyes informed by Reinhold Niebuhr.

Robin Lovin repeatedly stresses the complexity of Christian Realist theory in his two academic books on the subject distinguishing between Reinhold Niebuhr and broader Christian Realism.[16] In the first volume he interprets Niebuhr's theory of justice very handily, and the first page of his second book and the conclusion to that volume on "Politics, Faith, and a Meaningful Moral Life" are among the best summaries of Christian Realism written. He understands Niebuhr as seeing justice expressing Christian love in human reality under the conditions of finitude and sin.

> Precisely because complete justice is identical with a human good in which everyone would participate, however, it is impossible to achieve; and it is when we try to create human good on the scale of nations and empires that we become most acutely aware of our limitation.[17]

Justice is part of the strategy of achieving human good, and he explains it in terms of Niebuhr's two regulative principles of justice—equality and freedom. He notes that in some places other regulative principles are mentioned by Niebuhr—community, order, and peace. The earlier Niebuhr in the 1930s, usually referred to the solitary principle of equal justice, adding freedom as he became more profoundly convinced of the virtues of democratic government after the New Deal and World War II. He notes Niebuhr's use of absolute and relative justice. He recognizes the historical scope of principles of justice and quotes Niebuhr on "They [Principles of justice] are the product of social wisdom and unwisdom."[18]

In the same paragraph Niebuhr had denied that principle of justice in society was derived from some first principle of justice or developed like science or mathematics as they are subject to passions and interests. Yet it is not all relative. There are realities underlying human discourse about God, politics, and theology. My own interpretation of Niebuhr may be a bit more relativistic than Lovin's who does not emphasize how dependent Niebuhr's moral and political judgment is from his reading of the very contingent, interpreted history of ideas. My tutor at Oxford in the history of political ideas was a liberal theorist, John Plamenatz, who advised me to choose between theology or politics and not to try to do both. This was just the choice Niebuhr refused. Lovin's second book is an attempt to reconcile Christian Realist theory and liberal political theory like that of John Rawls and others. He does it well as they both have a place in the political market-place of ideas. In actual political practice they can cooperate or oppose each other depending upon the issue.

Among liberal political theorists, Plamenatz's colleague Isaiah Berlin, is more easily reconcilable with Christian Realism than John Plamenatz. Plamenatz's magnum *opus, Man and Society*, in two volumes, argues that political theorists' ideas are distinguishable from and can be separated from their world vision. Berlin, a close friend of Niebuhr, was much more open to the relevance of the thinker's world vision or ontology having a place in theory. Lovin correlates his examination of both his discussion of justice and the comparison of Christian Realism to political liberal theory particularly to the thought of John Rawls. There is a similarity in that both qualify their principles of equality with recognition of society's need to reward service differently based on different social functions. However, it seems to me that Rawl's theory depends ultimately upon his myth of non-self-interested, rational people entering into an imaginary social contract. To a religious studies perspective informed by Niebuhr this is akin to affirming principles of justice for the Garden of Eden. In actuality principles of justice are formed this side of the Angel separating us from the garden of innocence. Niebuhr's theory is far less tidy, and more historical and open to change as the new contingencies of history impact our thinking.

Lovin's careful work on Niebuhr is marred by his omitting in his two references[19] to Niebuhr's conclusion in *Moral Man and Immoral Society* that there is a need for madness in the mind for social change, that Niebuhr repented of this closing sentence the very next year. This may be a substantive issue. The utopian hopes that Lovin seems to be open to were rejected by Niebuhr because he associated hard utopian hopes with Fascism and Communism and soft utopian hopes with irrelevant schemes for pacifist world order. In consideration of the new realities of our post-Communist collapse, the utopian hopes of militant Islamists imposing rigid Islamic law on the world or of America imposing its order on the world are doomed to failure. In their clash hundreds of thousands can die and practical human work toward creating a better, more fair world can be set back. Niebuhr knew of the inevitable human spirit to fulfill dreams in his political realism, but he also knew of its dangers. His colleague Paul Tillich who shared his realism may have handled the problem of utopia more profoundly.

D. B. Robertson, Niebuhr's bibliographer, stresses the necessary incompleteness and variety of Niebuhr's concepts of justice. Justice like knowledge in the humanities reflects the perceptions and interests of those defining it. Justice is produced in society by political processes and politics represents more the clash of interests than a meeting of the minds. He frames his introduction in terms of Niebuhr's most important problem, giving him the title for his edited book *Love and Justice*.[21]

The love of one's neighbor promotes the seeking of justice for the neighbor. The blacks and the workers, two neighbors that Niebuhr particularly sought justice for, he met in his ministry in Detroit. In New York City he added a focus on the Jews to these concerns for neighbors. Throughout his career he sought more freedom and equality for those three groups. The essays chosen by D. B. Robertson show his strategies and the concrete political and legal remedies he sought for these three groups. He recommended some rather detailed strategies for the churches. But except for the black churches which had some resemblance by analogy to his beloved sectarian reformers of the Cromwellian revolution he did not expect much direct leadership from the churches. Robertson quotes Niebuhr as saying a son of the black church, Martin Luther King, Jr., is "the most creative Protestant white or black." He pled for relevant ministry and preaching and directed his pleas for racial justice particularly to Billy Graham. He argued for union power to redress the injustices imposed on workers and traveled with church investigating teams into situations of labor-management conflict. He analyzed in print detailed legislation and court decisions for both blacks and laborers hoping for legal gains that would promote justice while prudentially seeking to avoid backlash. He urged justice for Jews and Japanese decrying government policy on immigration and incarceration.

His published essays named those who violated justice and praised those who strove effectively to advance justice in all three campaigns for Negroes, laborers, and Jews. Particularly in the labor struggles he used both analysis of statistics, wages and suffering and published personal stories of injustice. As the Truman administration pushed first for the Fair Employment Act, his own judgment was that the antilynching and poll tax-removal legislation should have been laws to push forward first. Southern support could have been garnered for those pieces of legislation. Maybe Fair Employment legislation would have to await more state action before it could become national policy. Often in dealing with legislative matters his arguments extend to an analysis of the enemies as well as the moral arguments favoring legislative acts.

Similarly, in going into detail knowing that immigration policy for the Jews to the U.S.A. would not be generous in the post-World War II America, he pled for immigration of Jews to Palestine under the British mandate with a policy development of compensation to the Arab population. For him anti-Semitism had to be fought on two fronts, both within the U.S.A. and in recognizing the Jews as a nation needing their own homeland.

In addition to these three justice issues, Robertson's excellent edited work also contained essays on national politics and international politics. The collection might also permit critics to rethink their critique of Niebuhr's lack of a precise dogma of the church while appreciating his continual application of the criteria of love and justice to the real churches he counseled. While the various denominations, sects, and historical issues would prevent him from thinking any one doctrine of the church could be universal, judgments could be made about church subservience to capitalist overlords, its racism and its anti-Semitism.

Merle Longwood[21] concluded his careful paper on Niebuhr's reflections on distributive justice with a need for Paul Ramsey's term of "love transforming justice," which means approximately Niebuhr's use of "higher justice" or "imaginative justice." The goal of loving the neighbor as the self in social relations is probably beyond human capacity consistently, but it recognizes the goal of one person counting as equal with another person in the things they need for their full contribution to society. This recognition is close to Niebuhr's use of justice in many instances.

Paul Tillich on Justice

Justice was not a central term in Paul Tillich's polemic against capitalism. He did not often judge capitalism by the criteria of justice; rather, he assumed the contradictions within capitalism were going to destroy it. He regarded the spirit of capitalism as the proclamation of a self-sufficent finitude, and his basic argument with it was that it was not open to the experience of the unconditioned. Capitalism encouraged alienation, competition, meaninglessness, and it was self-destructive. Justice became a central concept for Tillich as the Marxist analysis faded in the American context.

There are exceptions to the above generalizations. Three of Tillich's earlier writings include justice: "Grundlinen des Religiosen Socialismus" (1923); "Man and Society in Religious Socialism" (1943); and *Die Sociallstiche Entscheidung* (1932). These writings do not push the discussion of justice to the ontological depths of his later work. The 1943 essay is more reflective of the American political discussions while the earliest essay is still very Hegelian. Justice is not used as a concept to attack capitalism in the way Reinhold Niebuhr was using it at the same time.

According to the 1943 essay, human nature bears the claim that every human being be recognized as a person.[23] There is a natural equality that is the equality of claim to express one's creativity—later he would say "power of being." "This is the ultimate criterion of justice."[24] Justice concedes to finitude that the contingent characteristics of human existence prevent absolute equality. But justice requires that all accidental differences—by which Tillich meant gender, race, intelligence, strength, birth—ought not infringe upon the essential equality. Therefore, all the structures that reinforce essential inequality would be opposed. Fascism, monopolistic capitalism, and class-determined education all result in dehumanization, or the violation of the opportunities to express one's power of being, and were opposed to justice.

Justice plays an important role In Tillich's most profound socialist writing. *Die Socialtische Entscheidung* (*The Socialist Decision*) was written in 1932 under the impact of the revolutionary seizure of power in Berlin by Chancellor Franz von Papen and the romantic-revolutionary gains by the Nazis. In Tillich's analysis, neither party represented the claims of justice. They both appealed to myths of origin of life and not to a future shaped by the principles of justice. Tillich argued for an understanding of socialism that would be religious in its respect for the origins of being and prophetic in its insistence on justice. Still, justice, though not elaborated, is essential. The call of the future is that of justice. Justice is the demand arising in human consciousness that calls for the future to be different. Justice requires expectation. As Tillich puts it, "The ought is the fulfillment of the is, Justice is the true power of being."[25]

Justice means "the dignity of being free of being the bearer of fulfillment implied in the origin. This recognition of the equal dignity of the 'Thou' and the 'I' is justice."[26] Here, though not stated, is the definition of justice as the second commandment of Jesus: "Love your neighbor as yourself." Similarly to the religious reader the trusting in expectation echoes the daily prayer of "Thy Kingdom come." Tillich's argument in the book depends upon the proletariat's realizing possibilities of transforming the historical situation. The book is committed to the possibilities of the proletariat. Of course, very few of the proletariat could have understood the book if they had been exposed to it. Nazi suppression of the book through "Blacklisting" it made any attempt at reading it impossible or nearly so.

Additionally in the same volume Tillich develops a perspective of justice sounding a bit like Jean-Jacques Rousseau as he expands beyond the "Thou-I" encounter. Justice is found in consent to the social contract. Consent to power in the long run depends upon the recognition of a tolerable justice in the contract.

> Consent is given because those who ascent to the exercise of power consider the way in which the unified will is executed to be just. The exercise of power appears to be just when all members of a society can acknowledge that their own will is contained in the will of the whole.[27]

Consent to governing power could be coerced without a sense of justice if the rulers were willing to utilize terror as were both the Nazis and the Junker class. In fact the Nazi's coercion without justice led to the suppression of the book that argued justice was necessary.

Tillich produced his most systematic work on justice in the American context with the publication of *Love, Power, and Justice* in 1954. Here he unites reflection on three concepts on which he had worked for years. He wanted to find a way between cynics who would reduce justice to the meaning given by the powerful and idealists who would assert the demands of justice without reference to power. He sought to overcome the dichotomies in Protestant ethics between justice and love without collapsing them into each other.

The method of the volume may be confusing.[28] The method seems to me to be that of conceptual analysis of basic categories of ethics and politics. Tillich asserts that such elaboration is ontology. Consequently he calls what I would regard as conceptual analysis of terms that also have ontological implications as ontology. Niebuhr, on the other hand, looks for the meaning of justice in different historical epochs and traces its evolution to his own formulations.

"Justice is the form in which the power of being actualizes itself."[29] In Tillich's ontology all beings drive toward actualizing themselves under the conditions of finitude. This drive toward fulfillment produces competition, and justice is the form that allows this competition for life without destroying the whole.

The principle of justice is love that contains: (a) adequacy, (b) equality, (c) personality, and (d) liberty. Tillich raises the issues of community, but decides not to list it within his formal definition of justice. All through the discussion, he reflects ontologically upon the concepts while drawing some of his meanings from history, and stipulating his own preferred meanings.

The principles of justice are applied at various levels of justice. He lists: (a) the intrinsic, (b) the tributive including distributive, attributive, and retributive, and (c) the transforming. The transforming level of justice reveals the biblical roots of Tillich's discussion of justice. Creative or transforming justice is the form of reuniting love that does that which is necessary for the reunion of beings.

Love does not do more than justice demands, but love is the ultimate principle of justice. Love reunites; justice preserves what is to be united. It is the form in which and through which love performs its work. Justice in its ultimate meaning is creative justice, and creative justice is the form of reuniting love.[30]

Tillich's theory of justice presupposes his entire systematic reflection in terms of ontology. Hegel and especially his fragment on love lies in the background, along with the I-Thou of Buber, and the social contract of Rousseau. The need for consent to government in terms of a sense of justice reveals his socialist commitments for a strong affirmation of the positive functions of government. His meaning of justice preserves the sense of the need for radical expectation and a drive for reform. The socialist presuppositions are not argued particularly in the book, but it can be read in those terms.

Tillich always wished that Niebuhr would make his ontology more explicit and he criticized him for not so doing. The American theological world could see the biblical and American sources of Niebuhr's concept of justice more clearly than they could adopt Tillich's language. Wilhelm Pauck argued explicitly that Niebuhr did not need to adopt Tillich's language. Niebuhr feared that human freedom would be obscured if the discussion was confined to the ontology of Tillich. Tillich for his part tried to reassure the American thinkers that his ontology was dynamic and that his theory of justice contained liberty for the human spirit. Niebuhr's historical rendering of justice and Tillich's philosophical concept came close in their meanings. Tillich's reflections in this volume deserve the name of a theory of justice, and it seems less dependent upon myth than that of Rawls, and while it is more directly dependent upon Christian theology than Wolterstorff, it is less dependent upon the myth of creation and God's image than the latter. Previous examinations of liberation theologies have shown that Tillich has a more complete theory of justice in his American writings than the liberation theologians. On the other hand, his earlier writing as a revolutionary socialist is closer to the radical demands for social change of the liberation theologians than his later more complete theory. Both Niebuhr's and Tillich's writings on needed reform in the U.S.A. were beyond that which the society was ready to grant as they argued for the end of all privilege and for only functional differences in rewards for certain types of production and work. Tillich's argument for the end of privileged education may have gone further than Niebuhr, but he did not develop it. R. H. Tawney, Niebuhr's ally, had explicitly argued to end private education. On the other hand, I don't know that Tillich ever explicitly argued for or campaigned for universal health care as Niebuhr did. Both were explicit about the need for racial and gender equality as part of their meaning of justice, and though Tillich's writings about the need for the social security of the masses were mostly in his earlier socialist writing, his membership in the German Democratic Socialist Party after the war continued the tradition even if it could not be completely realized. Niebuhr's writing for the empowerment of blacks called for a negative income tax to correct some of the inequality in America. The year before he died, he wrote to the Bicentennial Commission of the U.S. saying that the inequality of the black population was one of the three great issues for the nation to face during its bicentennial celebration.[31]

In terms of racial justice it is fair to say that though Tillich lent his name to the cause of racial justice for blacks, and explicitly demanded it in the name of justice in his theoretical writings, Blacks like Martin Luther King, Jr. and George Kelsey carried his conceptual development further in their practice than he did. His primary work in racial justice was against the anti-Semitism of his day and his work with Jewish intellectual allies from Berlin to Chicago. There is some use of Tillich by James Cone, but he explicitly drew much more for his later teaching from the work of Reinhold Niebuhr than Tillich.

There is learning to be gained from Niebuhr's work in race relations for students of social justice. The major learning is that the malignancy from racism must be fought continually with a variety of tools and social strategies. His included moral teaching, integrated education, economic boycott, governmental study commissions, civil rights legislation, cooperative, interracial economic institutions, boycotts, divestment strategies, antipoverty legislation, universal health care, personal relations, church action, writing, rallies, and demonstrations. His realism and tendency to account for the enemies' actions would have prevented him, in his time, from dreaming of an American black president.

John C. Bennett told me that when Niebuhr came to Union in 1928, he hoped to found an interracial church on the edge of Harlem, but that friendly black clergy dissuaded him. It was shortly after that that he became enraged at his Bethel Church in Detroit for explicitly denying membership to blacks who asked to join the church. As a pastor in the church, he had encouraged Negro attendance, but the challenge of membership never came up during his tenure. The letter he wrote to the elders of his church for failing to meet the challenge deserves to be recorded even though it does not use the word justice.

To The Church Council January 22, 1930
Bethel Evangelical Church
Detroit Michigan

Gentlemen and Brethren:

My first reaction on hearing the disappointing news from your annual meeting was one of such complete despair that I decided to resign my membership in Bethel Church immediately. I felt that your action was a repudiation of my ministry and that I might as well repudiate the church.

After my head cleared and cooled a little I decided that I would not resign, first because I would not like to have those who shared my conviction in this issue to do so and I have no right to do what I would not like to have them do; and secondly I felt that after all I can not very well repudiate a church which grew up largely under my ministry and which, if it reveals such weaknesses in its life, may well ascribe them to defects in my ministry as much as to any limitations of its own. I have always believed that race prejudice is one of the most serious evils in our day with which the Christian gospel must deal. I have often stated that explicitly. In fact I did it in season and out of season. Why no serious objection should ever have been raised to this emphasis when the congregation felt in its heart as it proved in its vote is a mystery to me. But I do not see how any church can put up bars against members of another racial group who apply for inclusion in its fellowship. The number who would apply would probably never be large. We would never have been forced to meet the ultimate test which I am willing to admit no congregation at the present time would be able to face. But to refuse to take the next step seems to me to be clearly an act of apostasy. It weakens the faith of all sensitive people in the moral power and the goodwill of the church.

I recognize the fact, of course, that this action might never have been taken if passions had not been needlessly aroused. But I am unwilling to follow my first inclinations of throwing the full responsibility for these high passions upon what I believed to have been unpedagogical methods in the presentation of the issue. These methods may be criticized but it remains a fact nevertheless that prominent members of the church did everything in their power to fan latent race prejudices into a hot flame. If there should is anything more unchristian than that kind of procedure I do not know what it is.

I did not intend when I started this letter to reopen any acrimonious controversy. I shall therefore not follow my argument any further. I conclude merely by saying that I am hurt and pained to my innermost being by your action. Whether I shall ever preach in your pulpit again is a real question in my mind. Meanwhile I will hope and pray that the Lord will soften your hearts and help you to see how much harm has been done by your action to the cause of Christ everywhere. You may be sure that among other things every antichristian journal in the Eastern world will make full use of this bit of history in which we are all involved to prove that Christians have never really accepted the Lord of love whom they profess to serve.

Yours sincerely,
Reinhold Niebuhr[32]

Three years earlier, Niebuhr had tried to lead the congregation forward on the race issue, preaching a series of evening sermons drawing upon his work as chair of the Mayor's Commission on Race Relations. The furor in Bethel which led to the dismissal of Niebuhr's young replacement, Adelbert Helm, could not be quieted and even Niebuhr's influence was not enough to reinstate the Reverend Mr. Helm. Niebuhr agonized over whether his leadership on race relations had been forthright at the church. Richard Fox noted how often in *Leaves from the Notebook of a Tamed Cynic* Niebuhr had worried about his own lack of a prophetic enough ministry.[33] In this letter he mentions his earlier blaming of Pastor Helm for lack of tact on the issue. Apparently Mr. Helm did make the issue a defining issue for the congregation which refused his leadership. In other writings Niebuhr often noted how many ministers in the South lost their pulpits for forthright stands on race relations. Ministers of my acquaintance also lost their churches over race relations in the 1960s in the North.

In the twenty-first century the church still remains mostly segregated in America. Here and there churches have successfully integrated, but particularly in the American church, racism as a child of slavery still remains the original sin to be combated. My efforts combined with other Union students to break down the structures of division based on race in the Methodist Church of the 1960s were approved of by Niebuhr's colleague and friend John C. Bennett, but he did not expect immediate success. Niebuhr, himself, was supportive of students and colleagues who took actions to break down racial barriers in the South and the North. Preaching on race or demonstrating for church integration were still highly controversial in the 1960s and disapproval by church authorities for leadership in integration was still the rule. After sitting with Dorothee Sölle in an all-white congregation in Pittsburgh, I defended Niebuhr's defeated efforts to prevail at Bethel in accepting Negroes as members. The German liberation theologian could not excuse his failure, but she was teaching in the 1980s in one of the significantly integrated seminaries in the U.S.A., Union Theological Seminary in New York City. After three decades of struggling for racial justice I understood better than the visitor the necessity of continued "slow boring of hard boards" in racial justice in the U.S.A., but I appreciated her more pure critique.[34]

21

Political Philosophy in the Cold War

The year 1952 opened with Niebuhr suffering a stroke that left him semiparalyzed on his left side and suffering from depression. He would never regain the full use of his left arm, and he would combat the depression for the rest of his life with it receding and returning. Though his speech was affected and sometimes slurred, he retained enough use of his voice to finish out his teaching responsibilities until the mandatory retirement age of 68 and then to continue teaching to large crowds at Harvard, Yale, Princeton, and Barnard. Finally he returned to Union to conduct a seminar in the English Gothic quadrangle next to the bookstore and then in his home on Riverside Drive through 1968. However his days of frenetic circuit-riding preaching and lecturing in the chapels and colleges of the nation were over. He did not have the energy to sustain his projects of the Frontier Fellowship and *Christianity and Society* for long. He recovered to continue his writing, but now his manuscripts typed with one hand on the new typewriter provided by his supporters needed more proofing than previously by his editors. He reduced his role in the Americans for Democratic Action, and John C. Bennett took a larger role in *Christiainity and Crisis.* His days of advising the State Department came to an end. His friend and foe, John Foster Dulles, would win the secretary of state position. Dr. van Dusen confided to me that Dulles wondered why Niebuhr was so critical of him whereas Dulles had never criticized Niebuhr in public. Dr. van Dusen edited a volume of Dulles's speeches, *The Spiritual Legacy of John Foster Dulles* which was a tribute to this son of the manse who had fathered both a Roman Catholic cardinal and a Presbyterian religious educator.

Tillich could not find hope for politics during the Eisenhower residency. His homeland was divided and his own points of origin were under Russian control. He would make contributions to political thought during the eight years of Republican domination, and his hopes would be renewed by President Kennedy and then crushed at Dallas. Tillich's socialism had no future in America that he could ascertain. Columbia intellectuals would joke that the loss of President Eisenhower from the University was also their country's loss. For Tillich there seemed to be no political future for his socialism with the Republicans in control of the administration, and his primary work would not be in politics, but the finishing of his systematic theology and contributions to

American theology of culture. Tillich's influence in the field of religion would eventually come to outshine Niebuhr in this decade before Tillich's death.

Niebuhr's major role after his stroke would be as a writer, but even here his best work was behind him. His four greatest books—*Moral Man and Immoral Society*; *The Children of Light and the Children of Darkness*; *The Nature and Destiny of Man*; and *The Irony of American History*—were all written before his stroke and declining health. However, he continued to build upon his reputation as a political thinker, and though his next half-dozen books would not achieve the eminence of his previous work, they made a contribution and fleshed out his legacy of democratic political theory and his reflections on the human self. His essays were widely sought and he wrote on a variety of topics.

This chapter focuses upon Niebuhr's political theory and particularly upon the theory of international relations. He worked as a commentator and thinker from a theological perspective on international relations in the context of the Cold War from the Korean War through the Suez crisis, the Cuban crisis, to the Vietnam War. It was, as Thomas Hobbes would call it, a season of war. That did not mean it was always war, but as a season can be known as a rainy season even if there are some drier periods during the season this was a season of war. His faith made him a Christian, and the character of the times encouraged him to draw out the realist perspective of Christianity. The Cold War eclipsed the previous Marxist coloring of his thought, and though he had served as a representative to UNESCO, the internationalist trends in his thought were also reduced by the Cold War. Over the whole period the nuclear competition with the Soviet Union and the Middle Eastern issues discussed in previous chapters flavored his thinking, and he was not permitted to see the solution of the first nor all of the dangers of the second. In his later writing with Paul Sigmund he would face the issues of the Russian competition for the future of the Third World which was still an undecided contest at the time of his death in 1971. Throughout this period he would help lead liberal thinking of the anti-Communist type while some conservatives would also claim his influence. The new-left emerging in the 1960s was relatively hostile to his liberal thought and to his realism.

His teaching was impaired, and the whirlwind travels were concluded; now he could contribute through his writing, and he kept that up at nearly the same pace as before his strokes. He would never fully recover. He was left semiparalyzed on the left side, and he was subject to recurring depressions of varying severity. His doctors tried to limit the hours he would work, and they succeeded in reducing them.

Father of Political Realism

Niebuhr's role as one of the leaders of American political realism has been widely recognized.[1] Of course, realism is far older than Niebuhr; it can be traced to the Old Testament prophets, Aristotle, Augustine, Machiavelli, and scores of other political thinkers. George F. Kennan entitled Niebuhr "the father of us all" meaning the British and American political realists of the twentieth century[2] while speaking to Kenneth W. Thompson about a memorial article for Niebuhr. Niebuhr's *Moral Man and Immoral Society* preceded by half a decade the turn toward realism of *The Nation* and *The New Leader*. Though other leaders appeared in E. H. Carr, Nicholas J. Spikman, and Hans Morgenthau, Niebuhr's was the first significant volume of the new school. Writing in 1941, John C. Bennett recognized Niebuhr as the initiator of a new movement in political and theological thought.

> In this country Niebuhr has been the spearhead of a new tendency toward what is often called "realism" among American religious thinkers. More effectively than any one else in America he mediates to us insights that are common assumptions in European theology and he does so with much moderation.[3]

There is a second sense in which Niebuhr can be regarded as the father of political realism. His thought laid the foundations of political realist philosophy in the concept of humanity. The dependence of Hans J. Morgenthau on Niebuhr has been confessed, and the content and notes of *Scientific Man vs. Power Politics* document that dependence. Though the realists display many differences, they agree that the meaning of humanity is important for political theory. All of them reflect some debt to Niebuhr at this point.

Kenneth W. Thompson regards the early years of the Policy Planning Staff of the State Department, founded in 1947 by General Marshall, as the period in which the realists most clearly influenced policy. The Policy Planning Staff brought together George F. Kennan, Paul H. Nitze, Louis J. Halle, C. B. Marshall, Dorothy Fosdick, and as occasional advisors Hans J. Morgenthau and Reinhold Niebuhr. Thompson believes common elements can be deduced from the writings of these thinkers, all of which appear prominently in Niebuhr's thought, and he is willing to use them as standards for the definition of realism. They are (1) the tendency to avoid moral absolutes in international politics; (2) a rejection of the escape from power politics attempted by writers on international relations in the 1920s and 1930s; (3) a distrust of concepts of human perfection and moral progress in human affairs; (4) a passion for the study and interpretation of history; and (5) the conviction that a rather explicit conception of the human being is helpful to political thought.[4]

The divisions within the realist school are hard to categorize except in particular debates over a specific policy. Theodore R. Weber has tried to describe a two-party split within the realist school.[5] He thought they divided on the question of the application of moral norms to political life. One group he labeled prudential realists and the other casuistic realists. Perhaps the one group emphasized the consequences of the action and the other focused more on the use of moral norms.[6] Niebuhr's polemics may have obscured the dialectical balance he sought and various tendencies have shown up in one thinker or another, but characteristic of the moral realists Weber describes is their tendency to use both principles and pragmatism.

Raymond Aron has criticized the realists for "mixing theory and praxeology."[7] He believed that this mixing contributed to their failure to make rigorous distinctions between historical particulars and the permanent characteristics of international politics. The realists have tried to distinguish the contingent from the perennial in international politics. Such an attempt is the chief purpose of Niebuhr's major work on the theoretical side, *The Structure of Nations and Empires*. Aron is correct, however, in his assertion that they mix theoretical insights and practical considerations. In fact, they judge theoretical insights by practical results and tend to explain practice in terms of broad theoretical considerations. The school has demonstrated an affinity for moving in and out of political power and the academic community. Its major journalist, Walter Lippmann, published works on social philosophy, and its major theologian wrote hundreds of journalistic pieces. The school and Reinhold Niebuhr in particular, have favored the form of the political essay that combines theoretical reflections and policy recommendations. This merging of theory and practice is a distinguishable feature of the Policy Planning Staff as was its commitment to the development of "an applicable body of theory."[8]

The United States' National Interest

The United States and its allies dominated the world at the end of World War II; no nation could directly challenge the will of the Allies. The common interest of the Allies, however, had consisted primarily in the defeat of the Axis. From the alliance came the protagonists of the next chapter of the struggle between sovereign nations. Niebuhr had hope for continued postwar cooperation and the building of new structures of order,[9] but tensions among the Allies during the war convinced him that the major powers would try after the war to advance their own interests and that the most desirable state achievable would be a relatively stable balancing of power.[10]

The collapse of the wartime alliance led to the Cold War, one of the three chief characteristics of international politics in mid-twentieth century. The rivalry between the two major nations was aggravated by the revolutionary ideology of Communism. The utilization of Communist perspectives by the Soviet Union made it a more complex and dangerous opponent than Nazi Germany. The Cold War, in Niebuhr's analysis was a struggle to preserve the values and institutions of Western civilization from the revolutionary fervor of a dangerous creed. There is no evidence that Neibuhr ever advocated the rollback of Communism where it existed, but he did hope for the withering of Communist appetite for active revolution. He was a consistent cold warrior (that is, he advocated serious competition in all spheres to meet the Communist challenge), but he did not permit the Cold War to become a preoccupation that blinded him to other foreign-policy considerations. Later he spoke of the dangers of over-aggressive anti-Communism.

The second major characteristic of international politics in the postwar period was the revolution in military technology. The nuclear weapon and intercontinental ballistic missile altered significantly the way international problems were met.[11] The problem of security was particularly heightened for the United States, and the two major protagonists ironically became the guarantors of each other's survival. J. Robert Oppenheimer's simile captures the way Niebuhr regarded the irony of nuclear deterrence.

> We may anticipate a series of affairs in which the two Great Powers will each be in a position to put an end to the civilization and life of the other, though not without risking its own. We may be likened to two scorpions in a bottle, each capable of killing the other, but only at the risk of his own life.[12]

The issue confronting Niebuhr was not only how the United States should act regarding a series of issues around nuclear weapons, but whether the whole character of international politics had changed.

The third characteristic of the political situation after the war was the merging of the movements for nationalism and modernization in the non-European world. European nationalism was transplanted to the colonial world and combined with the revolution of rising expectations to unleash revolutionary political forces. In Niebuhr's mind, United States national interest required encouraging this process without sacrificing international order and the loyalties of European allies.

The challenge of the three revolutions combined with the traditional features of international politics to confront a new military world power with awesome responsibilities. United States foreign policy was primarily a response to these revolutionary developments, though it was responsible for the development of nuclear weapons and it had abetted the nationalist movements. Niebuhr expected United States foreign policy to pursue the interests of the American people. He understood those interests would be defined by the political-economic oligarchy of the country. As a moderate realist or a pragmatic liberal, he defined those interests very broadly.

The primary goal of United States foreign policy was the preservation of order, not the secure order of domestic politics but rather a more or less stable balance of power that would prevent the breakdown of the system. The United States ought not, in the pursuit of order, to assume the responsibility of policing the world to quell all revolutions or all threats of war.[13] He advocated the development of effective international institutions for the resolution of disputes between nations, but the absence of world community thwarted such development. If all nations had a stake in preserving order, the United States--as the most powerful and wealthy nation—had additional reasons for preventing the breakdown of the present system. Niebuhr understood the interests of the United States in preserving the present system, but he also saw the instability and injustice of the system. His writing on international politics pressed for reforms in trade policies and international organizations, and for the reduction of international competition while at the same time preserving the system. His writing did not pretend to an impartial objectivity but represented the demands of a liberal American who was keenly aware of America's interest in the system. He assumed that United States imperialism, in the sense of exercising responsibilities commensurate with power, would give American foreign policy the character of defending the outlines of the status quo[14] against forces that threatened the system with disorder.

The national interest is a term Niebuhr used to express the goals of foreign policy. Each political actor has his individual view regarding the national interest. Argument about the national interest is always in order, and through the administration a country acts to fulfill the national interest, yet anyone's concept of the national interest may be mistaken.

The three revolutions influenced Niebuhr's understanding of the United States' national interest. Before anything else the national interest required the avoidance of nuclear annihilation. This interest was in harmony with the interests of the Soviet Union. The nuclear stalemate realized the identity of the human and the imperial interests in the avoidance of nuclear war.[15] The uniting of national interests through nuclear deterrence has been regarded by Niebuhr as the "final revelation of the incongruity of human existence."[16] However, neither the incongruity nor the dread of nuclear war led Niebuhr to expect significant progress in the dismantling of the deterrent.

> Each lacks the capacity or inclination to sacrifice its own interests for the good of mankind since such a sacrifice would mean capitulation to the adversary. Both lack sufficient mutual trust to engage in a large-scale partnership of peace. But the ideological chasm between has been bridged by their common sense of responsibility for avoiding nuclear catastrophe. The negotiated limited test-ban agreement may be the first step in politically acknowledging this common responsibility.[17]

The second major United States interest is the preservation of open societies that have not succumbed to Communist control. In his last book Niebuhr admitted the difficulty of maintaining open societies. He did not regard either the liberal ideology of the West or the Marxist ideology suitable for the needs of the developing nations. He stressed that each country had its individual needs and urged that dogmatism about development be avoided. Still as the only country strong enough to deter Communism it fell upon the United States to aid in the defense of open societies. His critique of United States Vietnam policy,[18] for example, was not directed against United States aid to countries resisting Communism, but against the particulars of the policy.

The Democratic Experience

In his retirement, Niebuhr taught a course with Paul Sigmund at Harvard on the origins and future of democracy. Later he brought the course at Barnard19 College in 1963. His conclusions about the future of democratic government in the developing nations were not optimistic. However, his plainly expressed preferences were for open societies that presupposed some forms of elections, representative institutions, checks on governmental power, and nationalism as opposed to the pseudo universalism of the Cold War rivals. He also expressed hopes for some forms of socialism to insure that a large part of the national product would be reinvested in machine tools and the infrastructure necessary for industrialization.20 He regarded nationalism as the chief bulwark against Communism and the need for social capital accumulation as a counter to the excesses of liberalism. His survey of the developing nations convinced him that the nations were emerging in a post-liberal and post-Marxist age. The major contest would not be between capitalism and Communism, but between various open societies and dogmatisms that did not fit the patterns discovered in history.[21]

Niebuhr did not consider it his task to articulate the needs of the developing nations. He hoped for open societies, but he saw that the future of democracy was precarious. He assumed that most of the emerging nations would try socialism, but he knew that socialism combined with military leadership would tend toward tyranny. He did not regard it as the responsibility of the United States to promote a particular social order around the world. The United States interest would best be served by countering overt Communist imperialism but allowing the developing nations to evolve their own answers to their needs.[22]

Power

There are three basic attitudes toward power in Niebuhr's political thought. Power is in one sense morally neutral. It is simply the vitality of life and is almost synonymous with energy. In this meaning Niebuhr uses the balance of power to mean the state of equilibrium that permits the vitalities of social forces to be expressed without annulling any one of them.[23] A second use of power regards it as the outgrowth of human pride and false attempts to gain security through the domination of others.[24] This use of power has led Niebuhr frequently to speak of power as equivalent to force.[25] The third use of power is to treat it as a necessary expression of social organization and cohesion.[26] Given his understanding of human nature, he believed an organizing power is needed to prevent social chaos. In this sense, power has a more positive moral connotation than in the first two uses. Depending upon the particular context, power may be regarded by Niebuhr as morally neutral, negative, or positive.

Not only the moral connotations of power but its meaning varies with the context in Niebuhr's writing. The importance of the term *power* to his political thought, however, requires that the central meaning of the term be understood. Niebuhr characteristically notes that "the contest of power is the heart of political life."[27] Here in this sense, which is fundamental to Niebuhr's thought, power means the capacity to realize one's purposes either through authority or force. The struggle that characterizes politics is for the control of the institutions and forces that permit one to realize goals. It is not always clear in Niebuhr's writing that power includes the goal factor; often it appears that he is thinking only of the control of institutions or forces. But the goal factor is presupposed in Niebuhr's thought by his concept of human nature which insists that every political self has certain interests which one is trying to maximize.

Commentators on Niebuhr's political philosophy have underestimated the subtlety of his understanding of power. Harry R. Davis's dissertation[28] and his later edited work on Niebuhr are examples of a tendency to oversimplify Niebuhr's thought by (1) neglecting the chronological developments of his thought and (2) oversystematizing his thought. Davis argued that Niebuhr's political philosophy allowed for three types of social power: military, priestly, and economic.29 Davis recognized that occasionally Niebuhr hinted there was a fourth type of ideological power, but he pointed to the recurrent listing of three types of social power as evidence of their basic position in Niebuhr's thought.30 According to Davis, Niebuhr regarded economic power as the dominant form of power: "it is a major point with Niebuhr the political radical that in the modern period economic power dominates society (an obvious modification from Marx)."[31]

Niebuhr's own writing indicates that though he may have listed at various times, three, four, or five types of expressions of power as of special importance, his thought emphasizes the limitless combinations of factors which produce political power: "The spiritual and physical factors of man are able in their unity and interrelation to create an endless variety of types and combinations of power, from that of pure reason to that of physical force."[32]

Niebuhr's testimony that economic power is not, in the Marxian or any other important sense, the dominant form of power reflects his abandonment of Marxist categories of political philosophy.

> The modern belief that economic power is the most basic form and that all other forms are derived from it is erroneous.
>
> The struggle in congress over the tax bill is a harbinger of another new development in modern society. It indicates the gradual ascendancy of politics over economics. The war has greatly enhanced the supremacy of political over economic society.[33]

Though Davis eliminated some of the subtlety and complexity in his presentation of Niebuhr's understanding of power and mistakenly regarded a passing stage in Niebuhr's development as normative for his thought, he saw the centrality of the struggle for power to Niebuhr's political philosophy. He also emphasized the connections between Niebuhr's philosophy of human nature and his theory of politics.34

In general Niebuhr views activity in the political arena as a collectivized, complicated and grandiose version of the individual's attempt to overcome his insecurity by dominion over his fellows.[35] All communities are, in Niebuhr's thought, representative of a balance of power. That is, humanity covertly lives in a state of anarchy with each individual pursuing self-interest and trying to achieve a false security.[36] Social peace or order is a temporary achievement that is never final. The peace achieved is not the peace of God, but a mere armistice.[37] The armistice is based upon the balance of power, that is, some adjustments and accommodations of interest have been agreed upon by the major contending forces. All such conditions are regarded as tentative and the "principle of the balance of power is always pregnant with the possibility of anarchy."[38]

Though the balance of power does not play as significant a role in Niebuhr's thought as it does in other realists, it still has an important role.[39] A balance of power in the domestic sphere represents order enforced by the authority of the dominant group. In the international sphere the balance of power represents an accommodation of interests of nations relative to their power that is sufficient to prevent major wars as long as it holds. The international arena lacks the organization that can coerce submission and require that the system be protected. The maintenance of a tolerable degree of order in international relations therefore devolves upon the major countries. They must exercise their responsibilities for the order of the world while attempting to refrain from excessively exploiting their advantaged positions. During World War II, Niebuhr's writing on the reconstruction of the postwar world emphasized the relationship between America's responsible assumption of a position of power and the need to overcome anarchy.

> The world must find a way of avoiding complete anarchy in its international life; and America must find a way of using its great power responsibly. These two needs are organically related; for the world problem cannot be solved if America does not accept its full share of responsibility in solving it.[40]

The old balance of power had been destroyed by the two world wars; the choice now is between a new balance or continued anarchy. Throughout the war Niebuhr pleaded with his reading public to accept the responsibilities that the United States' new role gave her.[41] He recognized that to assume the task of shaping a new world order would expose the country to the charge of imperialism. He counseled against both isolationism and imperialism[42] in the postwar period, but he insisted that a new balance of power required active United States involvement. Even while counseling the United States to accept its role as a world power, he warned of the dangers of pride.[43]

In the postwar world, he saw a bipolar balance of power develop that was secured by the presence of nuclear terror. The balance differed from previous European balances in that it was worldwide, bipolar, and enforced by nuclear weapons. It had a similarity to previous European balances for the United States in that it remained important to the United States that no one power dominate Europe. The responsibilities of the United States left it no option other than to try to maintain this new order. There was no assurance this new order was stable or secure. Niebuhr's comments on international issues from the period of the Korean armistice until his death in 1971 were under the influence of this stand off between the Soviet Union and the United States.

Imperialism

Niebuhr understood the United States as an empire. After all it had displaced the Indian nations, conquered and annexed part of the Mexican Empire, absorbing some of its people, and taken territories from the British, Spanish, French, and Russian empires. After the Spanish-American war of his childhood it had expanded across the oceans. As he grew to maturity its economic outreach expanded its power, and the two world wars had married its economic power to its military power. His Augustinian theology led him to understand that Christianity had come to maturity in an empire. Appreciation of Charles Cochrane's book *Christianity and Classical Culture* in his discussion circles encouraged him to think of empire as the context for much of his own thought. He also regarded the Soviet Union as an empire and it never occurred to him to think of the United States as the sole empire. Empires had preceded nation states and he thought of them as an intermediary form in the present between nation states and the unrealized world community.

The concept of empire came to bear heavy weight in the political philosophy of the last stage of his career. *The Structure of Nations and Empires,* his most formal work in the theory of international relations, does not provide an all-embracing system or a complete model for thinking about international relations, but it analyzes the phenomenon of empire in many of its expressions. It argued that there are discernable patterns by which strong nations relate to weaker nations and it made an effort to isolate discernable patterns of imperialism.[44] The practical efforts of Niebuhr came through as he related the struggle between the U.S.S.R. and the U.S.A. to perennial and contingent aspects of imperial competition.[45] He noted that the terms were difficult to use in contemporary political discourse.[46] He used the terms to refer to patterns of hegemony exercised by one nation over another. For *Structures of Nations* it was a recurring pattern within the international system, and one of the most important characteristics of the Cold War.[47] Despite the liberal and/or Marxist criticism of imperialism the respective empires exercised hegemonic control by military force, economics, and diplomacy over other members of their alliances.

Niebuhr's understanding of imperialism is closely related to his concept of power, and it contains a note of imperialism's inevitability. Strong nations tend to impose their will upon weaker nations. The conflict among motives often gives the stronger nations a sense of universality to their claims that the weaker nations regard as hypocrisy, but actually the claims reflect the mixture of motives that characterize imperialism.[48] The motivations of missionary, economic, and political are usually present and mixed in imperial ventures. The missionary implies the export of an ideology that the imperial empire may regard as universal. The economic motivation does not necessarily mean that the empire profits, but it indicates only that important interests in the empire can profit from the imperial actions.[49]

Political motivations can be as broad as self-defense or the seeking of prestige or the maximization of power.50 National strength for Niebuhr almost inevitably tends towards imperialism and its rationalization.[51] The moral ambiguity of imperialism reflects the domination inherent in the political process even though it accentuates it because of the cross-cultural domination.[52]

He meant to say that his survey of the forms of imperialism showed that their claims for universality were overstated and the legacy of European imperialism had beneficial aspects as well as harmful accents. He thought that though empires were never as beneficial as their ideological supporters claimed they were only seldom as evil as their nationalist critics supposed. Both of the major rivals in the Cold War had historic critical postures toward imperialism, and consequently always reflected contradictions from that ideology in actual actions of imperial dimensions.[53] Rivalry between the two empires was unavoidable, but Niebuhr hoped to provide a perspective on the Cold War that would free the American public from fanatically regarding the Soviet Union as a unique, unalloyed evil. The new empire did have unprecedented features, but he believed an emphasis on the "perennial and constant factors" of the rivalry between the two empires would encourage the wisdom needed for a long period of competitive coexistence.

Niebuhr's own attitude toward American imperialism had shifted. Prior to World War II, he had seen the developments toward American imperialism and had warned against it. He had particularly feared that a combination of American military might with its economic power would be dangerous to world peace. Noting the British labour party's opposition to imperialism he had hoped for such a position developing in the United States.[54]

During World War II he had adjusted to the realities of the U.S.'s new power and, rejecting isolationism, hoped for responsible use of the power. Eventually imperialism came to mean the "the exercise of the responsibilities of power."[55] The imperative was to contain Communism while avoiding nuclear war. Questions of imperialism were involved in the cases of Suez and Vietnam.

Suez

Tensions developed between the United States and Egypt in 1955–1956. Nasser's regime was distrusted by the Republican Administration, and John Foster Dulles' refusal to go ahead with loan guarantees for the Aswan dam led Egypt to seek help from the Soviet Union for the ambitious project. The shift in the alliance led Nasser to nationalize the Suez Canal. Dulles led the West in a series of negotiating positions, none of which persuaded Nasser to return the canal to its British-French overlords. Niebuhr was writing in *Christianity and Crisis* and *The New Leader* on the need for bold leadership for economic development in the region to avoid war.[56] Like a prophet Niebuhr called for justice in the area to avoid the threat of war, but he thought a catastrophe was likely; the writing also affirmed Niebuhr's strong pro-Israel position.[57]

Great Britain, France, and Israel surprised the United States by invading Egypt. Allen Dulles, director of the CIA, said he did not know of the invasion before the combined fleets sailed from Cyprus, and John Foster Dulles reacted with outrage. He demanded in the name of the United Nations that the invading cease, and both the Soviet Union and the Untied states applied pressure on the Europeans and the Israelis to withdraw. The realists revealed their internal divisions by splitting over the crisis. Hans Morgenthau and Niebuhr criticized the U.S. attack upon their allies, while John Bennett, Searle Bates, and others in the *Christianity and Crisis* community supported the secretary of state. Niebuhr and Morgenthau weighed the Western alliance as more important than the anticolonialism of the others. Niebuhr and Morgenthau criticized Dulles severely for his moralism and legalism, and refused to take the critiques of the Western powers from the Third World very seriously. The issue was made more complex by the Soviet Union's invasion of Hungary to which the West in disarray was unable to respond, aside from moral denunciations. Niebuhr thought Dulles mistakenly regarded the United Nations as an agency of action rather than as a forum for negotiations. He criticized the secretary's moralism and political-economic pressure that collapsed the governments of France and Britain.

Before the year was out Niebuhr attacked the Administration for not understanding the responsibility of the West to utilize its power to protect its interests abroad. He listed seven great errors of U.S. foreign policy: (1) the United States failed to recognize that the European economy required the Middle East's oil; (2) the United States failed to grant the overriding importance of its Atlantic alliance and played to the sympathies of the uncommitted; (3) the United States failed to recognize that the dynamism of the Egyptian dictatorship could only be constrained by power; (4) the United States crippled its diplomacy by adopting a policy of "absolute pacifism"; (5) the Administration entertained illusions about the Soviet Union shattered only by the invasion of Hungary; (6) the United States had acted upon a "misconception of United Nations as a supergovernment"; and (7) the United States policy toward China was a failure based upon official fictions.[58]

All of the points except the fifth and seventh are related to Niebuhr's convictions regarding the importance of the North Atlantic alliance and his conviction that imperial nations ought to recognize their power and attendant responsibilities and utilize force where necessary to secure their interests. John C. Bennett, Niebuhr's colleague and friend, who usually followed Niebuhr disagreed sharply on Suez. He regarded it as outrageous that Britain and France would use force to secure their colonial economic advantages. He was more sensitive to the criticism of the Third World, and generally more responsive to the claims of other nations against the United States than Niebuhr. The disagreement among the board members of Niebuhr's journal was also unusual. The rift between Dulles and Niebuhr would continue, and it reflected the deep differences between their forms of Christian realism as Dulles really was more moralistic and more committed to the United Nations than Niebuhr. Sometimes Dulles' brash legal manner was more assertive of legal claims and moralistic arguments than Niebuhr would feel comfortable making. Niebuhr may have seen more deeply than Dulles the tangle of motivations that allied the U.S. with the U.S.S.R. in forcing the Europeans and Israelis out of Suez. But Niebuhr may not have seen deeply into his own Anglophile and pro-Zionist positions that colored his response to the Egyptian assertiveness.[59] Despite his French beret which he wore jauntingly upon his head when he walked his two French poodles, probably no one accused Niebuhr of being particularly biased in favor of French politics. Niebuhr had already argued that the U.S should not support the French in Indochina as their colonial cause there was doomed to defeat. At one point Niebuhr suggested it would have been better to follow the Canadian position of objecting to the use of invasion forces, and then have let the British and French have their presumed victory at the canal.

Vietnam War

Niebuhr's willingness to have the U.S. accept the responsibilities of power in the postwar world was balanced by his argument that the United States should not attempt to arbitrate the fate of the Third World. Containment did not mean total responsibility for fighting all Communist expansion in his view. His response to the war in Vietnam is consistent with his political philosophy, but his changing responses indicate his need to see flexible policies which can change to meet new situations or evidence.

In the midst of the civil war in China he indicated that though the United States should help to rebuild the war-ravaged countries, there were limits beyond which the United States ought not to go. The Nationalist government appeared to Niebuhr to be weak and corrupt. The problems of China could not be solved by the United States and he advocated that the United States accept its inability to accomplish its goals: "It is not possible for even the most generous external aid to create health in a nation. If there is residual health there it is possible to increase it. In China the residual health seems totally lacking."[60]

The criticism of the United States attempt to prop up China revealed some of the themes he would apply later in the case of Vietnam. He pressed his readers to rediscover the limits of American reach. He pointed to a sense of humility as one of the most important contributions of the religious conscience to the dialogue concerning American foreign policy.[61]

> If there is anything that we can contribute from the standpoint of Christian faith to a nation as powerful as ours it would be a sense of its impotence and lack of majesty before the Supreme Majesty which governs the nations. It is intolerable to imagine an America so powerful that we are held responsible for historical events in every part of the globe beyond our knowledge or contriving. Nothing is more dangerous to a powerful nation than the temptation to obscure the limits of its power. It will be our undoing if we imagine ourselves the masters of contemporary history.[62]

Though he did not share the passion of many American liberals for decolonization, Niebuhr regarded the French effort to regain Indochina against the rising forces of nationalism as ill-conceived. After losing moral prestige in Asia the French could not hold their colonies with armed force.[63] American meddling in Vietnam in 1955 led Niebuhr to write an essay condemning the tendency of the United States to rely too heavily upon military force in Asia. The poverty of the American cause in Vietnam was exposed by the resentment of the West, the disunity within the country, the inefficiency of the government, and the widespread opposition to Bao Dai. An article on"The Limits of Military Power" contained one major note of equivocation: Niebuhr criticized the United States for being overly preoccupied with its "defense perimeter" in Asia to the extent of ignoring the political complexities of the continent.[64] Later in the same article he emphasized the disinterested quality of the American involvement in Vietnam.[65] At least we were more disinterested than the French, he wrote. Maybe he was writing too quickly; it is difficult to affirm both of those propositions. Niebuhr's view of the United States. involvement in Vietnam was one of vague uneasiness. While conscious of the dangers of prideful use of power, he did not regard Vietnam as a primary threat to American interests.

In 1963, while the U.S. involvement in Vietnam publicly was limited to advice and support of the government and army of South Vietnam, Niebuhr questioned the wisdom of committing American prestige to the defense of President Ngo Din Diem. He did not that year urge an abandonment of United States policy in Vietnam, but he regarded the policy as very precarious. He admitted that sometimes for strategic reasons the U.S.A. had to support dubious leaders. He quoted President Franklin D. Roosevelt who had said of a Central American dictator ally they "may be bastards, but at least they are our bastards."[66] However, Diem's regime was so unjust and unpopular that the United States was suffering a loss of prestige by supporting it.

In 1963 Union Theological students registered their protests against the policies of Vietnam's ruling family by demonstrations at Idlewild Airport in New York City against Mrs. Nhu's tour of the U.S.A. Events began to move quickly as Diem was assassinated with CIA support, and then President Kennedy was assassinated. That same year the F.B.I recorded Niebuhr's leadership in the Minister's Vietnam Committee as of 11 July 1963, which was committed to opposing the Administration's policy.

His criticism of United States policy became more forceful, but he wondered if the United States could have escaped involvement. His hopes for a settlement of the conflict altered as various suggestions were made public.[67] He came to distrust Administration announcements as to the facts about the war, and he attacked the Administration's pretensions of virtues in the conflict.[68]

As late as January 1965, he entertained questions whether the administration was serving interests of the United States which it could not make public.[69] His public strictures against the Administration were moderated by his awareness of not having all the information the policy makers possessed. He attacked the Administration for its lack of candor and for its failure to make a case for the policy in Vietnam. He became convinced in 1966 that it was highly unlikely that the Johnson administration could extricate itself from its policy of escalation. He did not believe that a military victory at an acceptable cost was possible. A 1967 lecture arranged by President Bennett and myself for Niebuhr drew his most scathing refutation of the Administration's arguments for its policy of war in Vietnam, and produced escalating protests by the students against the war with several of them taking great risks in opposition and going to prison for refusing to register for the draft after turning down their ministerial education exemptions. Others among the involved faculty and students participated with extraordinary effort in the electoral politics of 1967–1968. Some of those who entered electoral politics in 1968 found themselves participating in civil disobedience at a later point as the war continued into the Nixon years. President John C. Bennett broke the presidential traditions at Union by being arrested himself in a protest against the draft for the war. Nonviolent civil disobedience by younger faculty and Niebuhr admirers like The Reverend William Sloane Coffin of Yale University became part of opposition to the war. Probably as important as the civil disobedience was the organizing of Clergy and Laity Concerned about Vietnam, one of the leading antiwar organizations and lobbies. It was originally organized in the apartment of the seminary president. Niebuhr served on the executive committee as he could in his declining health. Niebuhr's criticism was largely directed at the administration's defense of its policies. Lacking the information that the policymakers had, he did not try to map out an alternative policy, but in his opinion he had sufficient information to expose the shallowness of the administration's arguments.

He hoped for an alternative to the Administration for the 1968 election, and he supported Senator McCarthy's opposition to the president. His analysis of both major parties provided little comfort for finding a way out of the "quagmire"[70] of Vietnam. In his dark mood he speculated in a letter to Will Scarlet that maybe for the first time he would not vote. In another letter he admitted he would consider voting for Governor Rockefeller if General Gavin could provide him with a realistic plan for withdrawing from the war.[71] He sympathized with my working for Governor Rockefeller's campaign to stop Richard Nixon's candidacy after I wrote materials for him following the assassination of Senator Robert Kennedy. Niebuhr had withheld endorsing Kennedy because of a prior pledge to Senator McCarthy to desist from doing so until after the primaries. Despite public and private criticism of Senator Humphrey for clinging so closely to President Johnson, he cheered his late breakaway from the Johnson policies in Vietnam and endorsed his candidacy.

Niebuhr attacked the ideas that self-determination and democracy were being defended in Vietnam. He rejected the concept that the security of the United States rested upon fighting a war in Vietnam.[72] Niebuhr acknowledged there were certain imperial interests that might have been forwarded by a successful defense of South Vietnam. However, these possible imperial interests of safe harbors, forward bases in anticipation of war with China, and a military presence on the mainland to increase security for other non-Communist nations were not admitted by the Administration as being reasons for American involvement.[73] In a published interview, Niebuhr implied that in his estimation such interests were not worth the struggle being waged and that the war failed to meet the just-war criterion of proportionality.[74]

Niebuhr did not and could not advocate without contradicting major motifs in his thought an admission of defeat at the hands of the Viet Cong or an abrupt withdrawal. His essays emphasized the need for a downgrading of the importance of the ideological interest in the war. He hoped for a compromise settlement which would have protected the imperial interests of Russia, China, and the U.S.A., and minimized the loss to the United States of its prestige which seemed to be the chief American interest. After a moderate period of giving the newly elected Nixon Administration a chance to de-escalate the war, his sharpest criticism was directed against the policies of Richard Nixon and Henry Kissinger.

Morality and Foreign Policy

Niebuhr wrote about morality and international politics from the perspective of an American defending Western culture from Nazism first and then Communism. His perspective was not an attempt to encompass all international politics, but to reflect upon United States policy. His writing included observations of other nations, but his focus was on the United States. His most far-reaching study of the conduct of nations, *The Structure of Nations and Empires* was undertaken to illuminate concrete problems facing the United States in the Cold War.[75] This tendency to confine his discussions about the morality of international relations to the United States reflects his appreciation of the hazards of making moral judgments about other nations. His judgments about the morality of American foreign policy often were indebted to citizens of other countries with whom he had contact. Reference to wise foreign opinion served in his thought as a corrective against the narrow pursuit of national interest. The transcendent perspective from which Niebuhr judged American conduct was his interpretation of Christian faith, and not that of the community of nations or international public opinion.

Niebuhr's early writing on the morality of international relations had been largely on the hypocritical use of morality as ideology to obscure the pursuit of national interest.[76] The final period of his thought saw an important change. The difference is partially due to a shift of thought, but it is also dependent upon the shifting character of his opponents. In *Moral Man and Immoral Society* he had attacked liberal illusions about the degree to which politics could be conducted morally. In *Man's Nature and His Communities* he leveled criticism at realists, including his own followers who too easily dismissed the influence of morality. In both volumes, however, he was trying to unite the perspectives of the moralists and the realists.

The basic limiting factor on morality in international politics is the anarchic situation. Each nation lacking security pursues its own increase in power however it can. In this condition morality is often used as ideological cover for the pursuit of power. The nation-states' natural and necessary pursuit of self-interest in the midst of an almost anarchic situation is increased by the interests of its citizens. The nation-state receives the loyalties of its citizens and combines their various hopes for glory, power, and prestige in a political process which acts on the international scene to further those hopes. The function of fulfilling the role of an alter ego for millions of citizens also reduces the role of morality in international politics.

A third limiting force moving moral judgments toward ideology is the various drives of particular individuals and groups. Though imperialism may not have paid for either the British Empire or the American empire it made certain powerful men wealthy. Though particular policies might be regarded as contrary to morality or the national interest, they could be serving particular interests within the government or the careers of particular people.

A fourth factor in making morality less relevant to international politics than to personal life is the absence of other sanctions that function in personal relations. The forces of law, custom, and religion do not exert the same degree of control over international policies as they exert in interpersonal relations. Niebuhr's writing about the morality of the United States foreign policy was characterized by an acute sense for hypocrisy.

Since nations constitute an extreme case of the sinful pride of groups, perhaps the best that can be expected of them is that they should justify their hypocrisies by a slight measure of real international achievement, and learn how to do justice to wider interests than their wont, while they pursue their own.[77]

Basic to his philosophy was the conviction that people could be expected to hide their self-interested motivations behind a veil of moral-sounding justifications. He probed behind the moral protestations of statesmen for the real interest they were pursuing—whether power, prestige, security, or economic gain. This expectation of hypocrisy led him to expose it and to insist that the proper role of morality could be understood only when its limitations were recognized.

Another reason for Niebuhr's modesty in claiming a role for morality in foreign policy was his fear of ideological crusades. In the postwar period he advocated that the United States accept worldwide responsibilities, but he urged that such responsibilities be accepted humbly and in full acknowledgment of the self-interested character of the role. His critique of President Johnson's treatment of the war in Vietnam included the charge that American foreign policy was suffering from undue reverence for the principle of self-determination of nations. The policy in Vietnam reflected the hypocritical use of moral language to obscure hegemonic interests. The ideological commitment led to a crusade beyond the rationally calculable national interest. Idealism or too simple an affirmation of morality in international politics led to confusion and hypocrisy.

> Our engagement in Vietnam has consequently forced the Administration to create a series of obvious fictions or myths calculated to obscure the hiatus between our idealism and our hegemonic responsibilities. Unfortunately these myths and pretensions of our foreign policy are not sufficiently credible to obscure our real hegemonic purposes.[78]

Politics remained for Niebuhr the realm in which the interests of power-seeking men and groups interact with the arena of conscience. He developed discriminate standards of justice and he criticized Augustine for refusing to do so. Niebuhr regarded such standards for political life as ambiguous and contingent because of his respect for the absolute ethic of Jesus and the degree to which history proved all principles of social morality relative to their culture.

The historical relativity of the principles and the particular problems involved in relating morality and international politics, and the hypocritical use of morality by statesmen did not drive him to cynicism. His thought bordered on cynicism and made use of it, but his aim was to discover a way to make moral claims relevant to international politics. The moral pretensions of certain British statesmen and imperial spokesmen were intolerable, but the moral cynicism that characterized the German attempt to build an empire was far more dangerous.[79]

The bulk of Niebuhr's formal writing on the morality of sovereign states is a record of the hypocritical pretensions of the state and the limitations of morality in international relations. However, he has not hesitated in his occasional writings to judge nations, particularly the United States, for violating moral standards. The positive statements that he made about the relationship of morality to international politics reveal the foundations of his moral philosophy. The pursuit of one's interest must be harmonized with the interests of others to be moral. Recognition of the equal claims of others is the beginning of moral reflection. Niebuhr did not demand the impossible that a nation sacrifice its own interests. The beginning of moral and wise foreign policy, however, is the recognition of and consideration for the interests of other nations.

> The force of "alter-egoism" is, however, so strong on the national level that it is almost universally recognized that a nation cannot simply espouse a more universal value at the expense of its interests. The highest morality

possible for a nation seems to be not a sacrifice of its interests, but a prudent self-interest, which knows how to find the point of concurrence between its interests and the most universal interests.[80]

Niebuhr's concern is to avoid the errors of either overly consistent realism or idealism. He does not want to obscure the latent capacity for moral action on the part of either self-regarding men or nations. Neither did he want to exaggerate the factors that prompt people and nations to act for the good of the whole community. A sense of justice does qualify the pursuit of national self-interest, and it often works to broaden the definition of national interest. Such a sense of justice is derived from religious and moral sources as well as from a brave respect for the opinion of other nations based, for example, on United Nations resolutions or public-opinion polls. The wise and moral statesperson will seek ways to accommodate conflicting interest and to define national interest humbly as to allow for accommodations. Competition is inevitable in an unstructured world beset by rival ideologies, none of which is adequate for organizing the whole, but it need not be violent and it can be limited if it is violent. Finally the relevance of morality to the struggle for power and peace depends upon the prudence of the actors. The moral act in foreign policy is the wise act which considers the interests of those affected by the act. The "good" in international politics is, in Santayana's phrase, "the harmony of the whole which does not destroy the vitality of the parts."[81]

Hans J. Morgenthau

Niebuhr regarded Hans Morgenthau's work on international relations as very similar to his own. The two realists often found themselves allied in political controversy and academic debate. Niebuhr helped to introduce him to scholars who had avoided him because of a suspicion of Machiavellian tendencies in his thought.

Their relationship had been one of mutual dependence and friendship. Their letters to each other were very complimentary, and they reviewed each other's works. Morgenthau made a trip to visit Niebuhr during the last months of his life along with his colleague Kenneth Thompson. On the question of the relationship of morality to politics, however, there were differences. In his desire to discriminate between the requirements of ethics and political action, Morgenthau stated the Christian ethic in extreme terms. At the Reinhold Niebuhr Colloquium at the Cathedral of St. John the Divine, Morgenthau argued, "It is impossible, if I may put in somewhat extreme and striking terms, to be a successful politician and a good Christian."[82] Niebuhr's earlier writing contains statements almost as extreme, but by emphasizing the Christian social teaching on justice and responsibility for order, his thought reduced the impossibility to a tension-filled possibility. The church's norms of social justice and responsibility are more relevant to political problems than the perfectionism Niebuhr saw in Jesus' teaching. Niebuhr thought that Morgenthau's statement of the dichotomy conceded too much to the Christian perfectionists.[83] Morgenthau's emphasis on the gap between "the moral ideal and the facts of political life" moderated the temptation to pretense and hypocrisy. Morgenthau confessed a reluctance to evaluate politics morally. He requested: "cosmic humility with regard to the moral evaluation of the actions of states. To know that states are subject to the moral law is one thing; to pretend to know what is morally required of states in a particular situation is quite another."[84]

In political life, morality functions as a judgment but only infrequently as a goal for Morgenthau. Formally stated, Morgenthau's morality is deontological and not teleological. The teleological elements of his prescriptions for foreign policy are stated in terms of the national interest. In his concern to distinguish political realism from legalistic-moralistic approaches to international politics, he insisted upon the autonomy of the political sphere.[85] Students of Morgenthau's thought find a degree of ambivalence in his relationship of interest and principle.[86] The overall impact of Morgenthau's writing is to maintain a separation of the political sphere and the moral sphere, though judgments are made about the immorality of politics. Especially in regard to his strident support for Israel and for immigration of Jews from Russia, moral and even ethnic factors came to have influence in his strongly advocated politics. In his later life his strong commitments to Judaism became pronounced even though Judaism in his daily life and commitments to Jewish education had been obvious earlier. He had endured abuse as a Jew in Europe and his migration to America was due to the anti-Semitism of Europe. Moral judgments are sometimes relevant to policy, but Morgenthau provided few criteria for deciding whether morals were relevant or not. Niebuhr insisted that moral considerations are relevant to every stage of the policy-making process, and his theory was less consistently realistic than Morgenthau's. He could not grant to any realm the relative autonomy that Morgenthau granted to politics. To the extent that there was a gap between a realistic political analysis and moral concerns, Niebuhr wanted to bridge it: "In a sense the bridging of this chasm by putting political realism into the service of justice, however defined, remains one of the paramount problems of an adequate political ethic."[87]

Niebuhr agreed with Morgenthau that the pursuit of national interest is the dominant motive of foreign policy, but he thought that in his concern to isolate the dominant motive Morgenthau obscured the degree to which statespeople act out of higher loyalties. He thought Morgenthau's description of the human situation also obscured the relationship of power to love. Power and love are not opposite responses of the human self. The pursuit of power is a corruption of the love impulse. The will to power is not a substitute for love according to Niebuhr, but a corruption of a desire to serve the community.[88] Morgenthau's use of Tillich for his ontological reflections confused the issue more, for in Tillich power and love were more dependent upon each other than they were in Niebuhr. Niebuhr emphasized human creative and destructive tendencies, whereas Morgenthau's view of human nature was more tragic. For example he wrote

> There can be no actual denial of lust for power without denying the very conditions of human existence in this world. There is no escape from the evil of power, regardless of what one does. Whenever we act with reference to our fellow men we must sin.[89]

This is a tragic description of human power. Divorced from any transcendent ethic by his sinfulness, human political action is doomed to produce evil. Niebuhr insists upon the mixture of good and evil and finds politics like human morality ambiguous rather than evil.

A final point of difference between the two realists is their degree of commitment to the pursuit of national interest. Niebuhr accepts as adequately descriptive the statement that nations pursue their national interests defined in terms of power. Morgenthau accepts the statement both descriptively and prescriptively. He insists not only that they do but that they should pursue their national interest on both moral and political grounds. Addressing the Truman Administration he wrote "And above all remember always that it is not only a political necessity but also a moral duty for a nation to follow in its dealings with other nations but one guiding star, one standard, one rule for action: the National Interest.[90]

Niebuhr urged that the understanding of the national interest be continually broadened. The egoism of the state can be expected, but it cannot be accepted as normative; it is the recognition of norms beyond the national interest that helps to qualify the nation's egoism and to assist it in achieving what may be regarded as enlightened self-interest. Against certain extreme statements by Morgenthau, Niebuhr argues that norms are not derived from political practice but from moral and ultimately religious sources. A narrowly conceived pursuit of the national interest is poor politics in Niebuhr's analysis, as well as immoral. A nation which is overly concerned about its own interests will tend to define those interests narrowly. It will fail to realize the degree to which its well-being is connected to the well-being of other nations. Against Morgenthau he argued, "Nations as well as individuals stand under the law 'Whoever seeketh to gain his life will lose it' "[91]

Niebuhr's criticism of Morgenthau[92] indicated a move within the realist school to look again at the possibilities as well as the limitations of morality for international politics. Morgenthau's attacks upon the Johnson Administration's Vietnam policies revealed more clearly than his formal writing on the subject his own willingness to allow moral arguments to bear a significant influence in international politics. Realism had moderated its stance and it is no longer as inclined as it once was to place itself in a polar position to idealism. Niebuhr inclined to regard both realism and idealism as inadequate in his last book and to claim the middle ground of "moderate realism."

Democratic Prospects

Niebuhr continued in his retirement to reflect upon the problems that had exercised him in his teaching career, and in 1969 he published another book on politics.[93] At Harvard in 1962, he taught a course jointly with Paul E. Sigmund, analyzing democracy as a theory and system of government, and discussing its future in the developing nations of the world. These class notes yielded the book *The Democratic Experience: Past and Prospects.*[94]

The genesis of the book was in the early 1960s during the bloom of the promises of the Kennedy era. It was conceived and planned before the intractability of the race problem was generally perceived as clearly as it was in the late 1960s. The malaise of the Vietnam War had not yet spread to rust away the confidence of the citizens of the United States in her purposes. Paul Sigmund working with Niebuhr's outline and general concepts completed the book when Niebuhr's health prohibited him from finishing it. Sigmund's influence and style are more noticeable in part 2, on the developing nations than in part 1, democracy in the West. Sigmund's contributions made it possible to reflect on the specifics of the recent developments in the developing nations of Latin America and Africa. The discussion of the particulars of the origin of the book explains some of the weaknesses when it is examined in the context of the year of its publication. The consideration of the date of the lectures also makes it necessary to consider *Man's Nature and His Communities* (1965) as reflecting the later thoughts rather than that of *The Democratic Experience* (1969).

The book brings together many themes of Niebuhr's earlier thought on democratic politics. Its purpose is both to support the concept of democracy for those countries that possessed its prerequisites and to argue that democracy could not be superimposed upon societies which lack the conditions of democracy. The authors described their position as a "pessimistic faith in the democratic idea."[95] They admitted the dangers and problems of democratic government to be sizable but they found alternative forms of government less attractive. Communist utopians and democratic utopians both were judged to be productive of illusions that threatened human ability to regulate common life.

Niebuhr treated the utopian claims of Marxists and democrats similarly when they spoke of freedom from fear or absolute egalitarianism. He trusted that democrats would be wiser and safer for avoiding political slogans while seeing the dangers of Marxist utopianism. The title of his first chapter, "Democracy and Communism: Two Utopian Ideologies," overstated his case. There are large elements of sober political thought in both systems. Marx had some utopian notions, and Niebuhr had some eschatological ones, but neither Marx nor Niebuhr can be dismissed as utopian or otherworldly. Humans seem to live by visions as well as by systems of production, and both Niebuhr and Marx knew it when they were not politicizing against the illusions of others. Niebuhr recognized the fact of vision as a perennial feature of American life, and he could have reflected longer on why this was so. Is it true that most societies have some utopian expressions that give to a lesser or greater degree some legitimacy to the reality which exists? Is the role of a utopian vision as a mythological support for social change or revolution always a negative element? Tillich, though less utopian than Marx, saw utopian aspects of thought as a perennial aspect of modern humanity and one that needed to be used critically. Niebuhr noted: "Some deep current in the American tradition must undoubtedly account for the persistence of this note in our national life."[96] The issue may not be the need to destroy utopian illusions but to analyze them for their usefulness in promoting desired values.

Democracy has many possible meanings and the authors do not pin it down to any particular definition. They used it to cover various forms of the republican form of organization of government, constitutional monarchies, and to encompass the governments of France, the United Kingdom, Japan, India, the United States, Mexico, et al. It is often used synonymously with their term "free government" which they define at least functionally. A " 'free government' was one outside the Communist orbit which presupposes national unity, protects individual rights, has independent institutions, competitive elections, and enough political equilibrium to begin to meet issues of social justice."[97] The book was written against the Cold War background that contrasted democracy and Communism as polar concepts, the one incarnated in the U.S.A. and the other in the Soviet Union.[98] The book lacked the subtlety that had characterized Niebuhr's earlier writing. Some of the book had been developed for an earlier project and while the concepts worked, I thought as I listened to the lectures at Barnard in 1963 for a large undergraduate course, they were not as developed as seminars I took with Niebuhr at a later date. The publisher Frederick A. Praeger had a history of publishing Russian authors and a lot of books on Communism, and later fell under suspicion for secretly publishing books for the C.I.A. It was quite a different location for a book by Niebuhr who had previously published mostly at Scribner's. The utilization of the same terms for so many different governments gave the terms equivocal character. Maybe the equivocation and generalization were necessary for polemical purposes of the Cold War, but they were confusing if applied to the early development of representative government in Europe and to modern republics or to both the governments of Lenin's Soviet Union and North Vietnam.

The authors discussed the contributions of pre-democratic Europe to the conditions necessary for the emergence of democracy. Three factors were regarded as necessary: (1) unity of the nation which could hold conflicting subnational groups together; (2) humanism expressed in terms of individual rights and values; and (3) a balance of power that permitted the development of a tolerable level of social justice.[99]

Their analysis of the situations in the world led them to a mixed prognosis for the future of democracy. It was expected to remain more of an ideal than a reality. Authoritarianism seemed destined to hold sway in Communist states. Though they expected democratic leaders and particular historical contingencies to allow for democratic growth in some of the developing nations, a more common phenomenon would be the predicted cycles of alternating democracies and dictatorships.[100] They were not pessimistic about democracy in Western Europe and North America, but its future in the rest of the world was an embattled one.

The book had three major weaknesses: the failure to address the problems that racism, imperialism, and militarism created for the United States. The criticism here is reserved to the interrelated issues of imperialism and militarism. Niebuhr's frank acceptance of the role of imperialism for the United States is a fresh dose of candor in the discussion of foreign policy, but it has all sorts of baggage in the Third World.

The authors spoke of a coming crisis in Latin America, but their hopes that it could be avoided were very clear.[101] Their hopes were based upon political parties like Chile's Christian Democrats, progress in Venezuela and Colombia, and the cooperative support of the United States for democracy in Latin America. The author's support for the Alliance for Progress and their rejection of Castro-type solutions distinguished them from the left which regarded the United States as "the principle obstacle to the establishment of meaningful democracy in Latin America.[102]

It is possible to agree with the authors that a judgment on the influence of the United States on Latin American democracy is a mixed one[103] and still deplore the pattern of U.S. exploitation in Latin America. The regard of revolutions as dangerous to U.S. interests may have hidden the dangers of imperialism from these scholars. Their two ideal types of Communism and democracy disguised the problems confronting Latin America. Democracy has been in many countries, as the authors recognized, a front for a decaying feudal system blended with laissez-faire economic structures. Social change may have to come through revolutionary measures that will sometimes be mixed with

Marxist overtones and elements. The possibilities of evolving something resembling social justice out of such societies may have been more relevant than speculating how American capitalism can produce a democratic system in Latin America. The World Council of Churches wisely used the term "responsible society" instead of democracy as a goal for social development in the Third World. The term with its connotations of state direction, pluralism, and civil liberties, and resistance to foreign exploitation may have been a better goal for Latin America in the 1960s than democracy. Post-Niebuhrian neoliberalism, the collapse of the Soviet Union, and globalization were all developments beyond the scope of this Cold War book. Some of Niebuhr's comments indicate he foresaw technology driving the economic forces to closer integration, but he did not anticipate any collapse of the Soviet Union to be near, and he could not have imagined neoliberal, sometimes called neoconservative thinkers claiming any authority from his writings for their retrogressive, imperialistic policies. The hopes of both Tillich and himself for democratic, mixed-economic societies were postponed, but in the twenty-first century they still seem relevant.

The second criticism of the volume, that it failed to wrestle with the danger to American society of the increasing militarism, is based upon both the general omission of the problem and upon Niebuhr's specific disavowal of the problem. "The result of this subordination of military power to civil authority was to eliminate the military oligarchy as an important part of the power structure in free societies."[104] The neglect of the growing military influence on American institutions was due partially to the fact that in 1961, when the course was first given, or even in 1963 when the course was last given, the problem was not as apparent as it was in 1969, when the book was finally published. This interpretation is partially supported by statements that Niebuhr made elsewhere. For example, in an interview published in 1969 he responded to a question regarding the realistic possibility of stopping the military and industry from building the anti-ballistic missile system then under debate in the Senate:

> Well, I don't know. I'm not enough of an expert on all the details. I think that the dominance of the military, whether in the ABM system or in Vietnam War, is nearly overwhelming. I think that Ike was quite right at the end of his term when he warned against what he called the military-industrial complex. After all we've got a budget of which fifty percent goes to the military, and military expenses account for many of the high production rates that reduce unemployment and so forth.
>
> So these are fantastic problems that American technological society faces. The question is, "What will the President do in relationship with the Joint Chiefs of Staff.[105]

Further evidence that Niebuhr too was becoming increasingly alarmed over the expansion of the military is his response to my criticism of his book on this problem. He wrote: "You are right; in light of Viet Nam my confidence in the subjection of military to political authority is too simple."[106]

Niebuhr's overall political philosophy is not endangered by the evidence that the offices of the Pentagon had come to dominate "the largest network of submanagement and industrial resources in the world."[107] There is a threat in the continuation of the escalation of military influence. The end of the Cold War did not present the peace dividend to the country The intersection of failed diplomacy with Iraq, two wars, and rising Islamic militancy left the country unsure of itself and its institutions one decade into the new century. The combined problems of racism, imperialism, and militarism force a less-sanguine picture of the prospects of democracy than the volume provided. Niebuhr's preference of democracy is not invalidated; his faith in it was after all a pessimistic faith which found it less objectionable than other forms of government. The measures necessary to keep democracy in the United States are more radical than Niebuhr could see in his lifetime. Neither Niebuhr nor Sigmund recognized the rise of Islamic militancy in the Arab world in the few pages they granted to discuss the Middle East in the book. There is no indication in the book that U.S. support of Israel's policies would raise problems threatening to the well-being and democracy of the United States. The pressures of globalization, the sacrifice of human rights for the war against terrorism, the deregulation of business under neoconservative guidance, all have deepened the problem of democracy since Niebuhr's time.

Peacemaking and Realism[118]

The Cold War shaped Niebuhr's thought about international politics which was his major preoccupation during the 1960s. He was thinking as a Christian pragmatist with a progressive social vision. As a pragmatist he focused pretty consistently on history and in his case on the history of ideas concerning nations, empires, power, and peace. The hope for peace in a warring world was biblically derived from the prophets who also focused on international crises. It was enriched by his New Testament theology regarding Jesus Christ and his perspective on Jesus' teaching.

He regarded principles of international morality as important, but unable to control the relativities of particular situations. The primary Christian contributions came through its perspective on the human, the limits of history, the necessity for forgiveness, and the limitations of the perspective of self-interested persons and nations. Politics resembled art more than science, and the imponderables of historical events resisted perfect or all-conclusive answers. He was not antisocial-science; it was rather that he did not expect it to resolve human complexities or the surprises of freedom. Some of his more important essays concerned the mythology of the competing empires and the myths that dominated U.S. foreign policy. Religious faith found meaning beyond tragedy, but many of the acts of human history were tragic. Given various biblical visions of peace, and the passions of the contemporary churches for peace, the issue of this section is how does Reinhold Niebuhr's Christian realism contribute to peacemaking?

Reinhold Niebuhr's debates with Christian pacifists and his polemics against idealists in politics have obscured his commitment to the search for peace. His fate is not too different from that of Hans J. Morgenthau whose passion for peace is seen in the title of his famous text, *Politics among Nations: The Struggle for Power and Peace*. Power was central to international politics for both Niebuhr and Morgenthau, but their goal was peace. Both opposed vigorously the United States' war in Vietnam. The other direct use of U.S. military force abroad during Niebuhr's later years was President Johnson's intervention in the Dominican Republic. Niebuhr opposed that incursion in print also.[109]

Still the major critique of Niebuhr's public policy positions during his lifetime resided in his thought regarding the Cold War. Probably only consistent pacifists would deny his support of the U.S. participation in World Wars I and II. American opinion divided around the U.S. position in the Korean War. Walter LaFeber regarded Niebuhr as one of the main systematic thinkers who contributed to the philosophy of the American cold warriors. His *America, Russia, and the Cold War* attributes immense influence to Niebuhr in shaping the American thinking about the Cold War.

A fellow theologian, John M. Swomley, accuses Niebuhr of providing "the religious rationale for the military policy that created the contemporary American empire and the policy of global intervention culminating in the war in Vietnam."[110] Building on the insight of Charles West he suggested that Christian Realism served an ideological role in justifying American empire. The record shows that Niebuhr consciously provided rationale for competition with the Soviet Union while he explicitly attacked the Vietnam policy. One of his more-famous essays, "The King's Chapel and the King's Court," explicitly attacked the attempt by the Nixon administration to religiously legitimize its policies.[111]

As argued earlier, Niebuhr had hoped during World War II for postwar cooperation among the allies, but tensions between the U.S.S.R. and the Western allies convinced him during the war that both sides would try to advance their own interests. The collapse of the wartime alliance led him to regard the Soviet Union as a dangerous opponent. Its creed and policies encouraged him to believe that it was important to rally the United States to assume responsibility after the war and to oppose the presumed ambitions of the Soviet Union. The role of Niebuhr in leading American liberals to oppose Communism is well known. As he had provided arguments for the opposition to Nazism before and during World War, he supported opposing Communism while avoiding war.

He perceived the process of maintaining competitive existence between the U.S. and the U.S.S.R. as necessary to maintaining peace. "There cannot be war between us without mutual annihilation. There must not be war."[112] He envisaged the tension existing for decades or longer. There could be no resolution through war, but neither party to the competition could be expected to surrender its respective myths or ideologies. Wise diplomacy was the most important element in maintaining the uneasy partnership in preventing nuclear war. He had no great confidence in education, cultural exchanges, religious impulses, or disarmament plans to eliminate the competition of the two continental empires competing for influence and interests in the world. This view of the world as two empires locked in a struggle was not the world he would have wished for, but it was the world he perceived. It was also a world subjected to the winds of revolutionary demands flowing through the undeveloped world, and a world made more dangerous and unified by technology.

He warned of the danger of overreliance on military power. The tendency to build defense pacts in Asia revealed little understanding of the political complexities there. Military force could be effective in crises, but without political forces of cohesion military force could accomplish little. Overreliance on military force was a temptation to a nation as wealthy as the U.S., but it could contribute to political embarrassment. Military force for Niebuhr was a means of last resort or for deterrence, but the American temptation was to use it as meat-ax where subtlety was required. The understanding of the needs of a population required wise statecraft not primarily military power.[113]

The real task of preserving the nuclear stalemate rested in the political sphere. He noted that technical miscalculation might bring about the nuclear catastrophe, but his primary concern was in political miscalculation. A defeat in some vital area might tempt one side or the other in hysteria to resort to nuclear weapons. This I think was the central reason for his continual reference to the "balance of power" in the post-World War II situation. He often described it as a "nuclear umbrella"; competition could go on, but it must be limited so as not to threaten the vital interests of the other party. Of course, it was not balance of power in any pre-nuclear meaning of the term, but an arrangement ironically stumbled into, which did not secure peace in any deep sense, but at least avoided the nuclear holocaust: "World peace requires that the dynamic of this strange political movement be contained, its ambition to control the world be frustrated, and its revolutionary ardors be tamed by firm and patient resistance."[114]

Niebuhr regarded the complex and threatening postwar world as requiring "shrewder calculations of both ideological power factors than we are accustomed to give them."[115] How shrewd was Reinhold Niebuhr? Was he just a journalist commenting on the world in countless editorials, articles, and numerous books on empire, power, and American history. Or was he trying to have a political affect? I think he was being very political in his writing. He wrote in a major essay on the theory of international politics: "If power is identical with authority, it follows that the climate of a culture of its "ideology," which sanctions a particular type of authority, is really the ultimate source of power."[116]

Niebuhr knew that the facts did not interpret themselves. The complexities of the international world had to be reduced to be graspable and put into perspective to become politically relevant. Niebuhr did not write much about method in either theology or international politics. But what he wrote about myth, symbol, and ideology reveals that he knew that in their articulation resided power. The expression itself was a creative act even as it remained loyal to the best of one's ability, to the materials being discussed. Millions of events were occurring in the world but he would write, "Thus modern history is fated to be governed by the contrasting myths of the two superpowers."[117]

He knew that these myths were not easily changed and that he was powerless to affect the mythology or perspective of the Soviet Union. He did set out to affect the mythology of the United States and to affect the perspective of the United States in its understanding of the Soviet Union. So his critics who accused him of presenting his version of an ideology for United States' participation in the Cold War are correct. The perspective he presented, however, was one of a precarious partnership between the two countries in preserving a nuclear peace while engaged in other struggles. The contest Niebuhr envisaged was primarily ideological. Finally, authority rested on a governing group's ability not only to ensure order but to deliver or promise a tolerably just society.

In the ideological struggle he felt that the United States, with its ties with the colonial powers and its own problems of race and social justice, was at a temporary disadvantage in the developing world. However, the creed and actual accomplishments of Marxism were so badly flawed that he believed that patient resistance would eventually encourage other governments to find their own solutions without succumbing to alliances with Communist powers.

Technological aid and economic aid were among the major contributions the United States could make to the health of the poorer nations. In 1962 he would regard the ability of a democratic process to provide funds for aid as "the litmus test of the capacity of a democracy to survive in the contest"[118]

Elsewhere I have criticized Niebuhr's overly optimistic expectations for the Alliance for Progress.[119] It was unfortunate that his critic, John M. Swomley, Jr.[120] took part of the paragraph in which Niebuhr was arguing for a strong interventionist policy in Latin America in the terms of the Alliance for Progress as evidence of the advocacy of imperial self-interest, and neglected to mention that his use of the economic power was for the attempted land reform and education. For the sake of changes in the oligarchic practices of Latin America he urged intervention, overriding liberal reservations about anti-imperialism. To Niebuhr, the United States was an empire in struggle. He hoped for Latin American reforms in the spirit of John F. Kennedy, but neither Niebuhr's support for liberal reforms nor the later liberation theologies' hope for socialist revolution could overthrow the oligarchic, semifeudal societies of Latin America. Critics have often found fault with Niebuhr as if he were responsible for the empire or for the struggle. Certainly his views shaped some perspectives on the empire and the struggle, but they were rooted in reality as well as perspective. A sympathetic reading of Niebuhr's writing finds him urging a cautious policy of statecraft, the upbuilding of the developing world, a nuclear partnership, a decrease in American reliance on military power, outright rejection of U.S. policy in Vietnam as early as 1963 and sober earlier warnings and disassociation from the French effort there. His politics criticized those responsible for the war and tried to change the political leadership of the country vis-á-vis the war.

Competitive coexistence in Niebuhr's perspective called for ideological debate. Hence, while he tried to clarify and reform American ideology by interpreting its religious and secular elements, he criticized the pretensions and illusions of Marxism severely. This criticism of Marxism can be seen as fueling the Cold War. However, in Niebuhr's perspective it was exactly the ideological debate that needed to be carried on in order to follow Senator Fulbright's idea of not trying to "to redress ideological deficiencies with military power."[121] He feared the dominance of the military-industrial complex and criticized its dominance of the United States economy and resisted journalistically some of its demands for new systems.[122]

Doves in the peace movements will probably never be at ease with Niebuhr. He believed with Augustine that sometimes force had to be used to win the peace. He wrote for *Life* magazine in 1948 an essay "For Peace We Must Risk War." He believed deterrence often preserved the peace though it was not a sure method. His resignation from the presidency of the Fellowship of Reconciliation and his essays criticizing pacifism earned him the enmity of the pacifists. He respected the nonpolitical witness of religious pacifists, but he raised doubts about their participation in debating international political issues.

On questions of disarmament he was not a dreamer. His own history had witnessed the difficulty of disarmament plans in the early twentieth century. He regarded the ban on nuclear testing as a great achievement, as he thought the attempt to stop the development of the anti-ballistic missile race was a gain. The nonproliferation treaty seemed to him to be of dubious worth because it represented the satisfaction of the "haves" and the repression of the "have nots."[123] Community needed to precede disarmament or, at least, accompany it in its formation. The formation of international community was significantly begun in the work of UNESCO in which he had served as a delegate, but finally it would require the moderation of the revolutionary ardor of Communism, the development of the Third World, and wise diplomacy on the part of the Atlantic Alliance. So there were no guarantees of peace.

The building of community as seen in the work of UNESCO was flawed. The flaws revealed the spiritual nature of contemporary humanity. Modern humanity had to find ways of continuing to build community across international borders and to avoid discouragement when it failed to completer the tasks. His comment on UNESCO stands as his attitude toward building world community.

> Here is an organization which seeks to realize the impossible: a world community. It must not regard this end as simple possibility; but neither can it dismiss the task as impossibility. It stands, therefore, constantly at the final limits of the human situation where the possible and the impossible are curiously intermingled and where it is difficult to distinguish between God's and our possibilities.[124]

The significance of the tribute to UNESCO is its recognition of the two traditions of idealism and realism in Niebuhr. Usually he expressed the realism to safeguard against the dangers he perceived in the moralism of American foreign policy. His foremost concern during the Cold War, however, was the securing of peace. He believed that the pursuit of peace required realism and the recognition of the role of military power in preserving the ambiguous peace of 1945–1971. Secondary concerns included human economic development in the poor world countries, human rights, and the development of world community. It was this combination, I believe, that led a politician with a good deal of idealism like Adlai Stevenson to regard Niebuhr as a possible secretary of state and to say: "If I had been elected president, Reinhold Niebuhr would have been become my secretary of state."[125] The expression was made without regard to Niebuhr's health which would have made this quite impossible in 1952, but it expressed the respect with which his thought and work was held by the anti-Communist liberals during the 1950s.

Shortly before the 1960 election year he wrote of "The Democratic Elite and the American Foreign Policy."[126] He praised Walter Lippmann's perspective in the volume dedicated to honor him, but he had his reservations. He rejected both Lippmann's hope for a stronger presidency in foreign policy and his recommendation of natural law as the basis for reforming American morality. While Lippmann regretted the influence of the Congress in foreign policy, Niebuhr regarded the slowing down of decision making as an advantage and the Parliament's ability to limit the risk taking of the Administration as an advantage for democracies. His particular recommendations for spreading the learning of history and languages were unexceptional, though they reflect his approach to diplomacy. Democracy needed to develop elite groups answerable to the democratic process to guide foreign policy and other policies. Those elites were needed in several fields. Educators had much to contribute towards developing the elite who could guide the country and they were found both as academics and as journalists who informed the country. The elite also consisted of the general public to the extent they could be brought to learn to rethink the general presuppositions that were needed to guide U.S. foreign policy. More interesting were his suggestions that comparing Communism to Nazism was unhelpful, and the recognition that the Soviet Union was changing. He recognized that the Soviet Union did not want war and that Communism developed differently in various cultures and evolved with time. He noted the growth of Russian technological power particularly in the field of missiles and rockets. Also, rather than calling on the workers of the world to unite in revolution, it was furnishing training to the third world in technical competence. Despite the successes of the Soviet Union that disinclined it from pursuing war, the dangers of miscalculations still threatened the world. Competition and coexistence, as hard as they were to manage, gave the best hope for living through the tensions. In conclusion he praised the wise journalists who interpreted the world situation to their readers, with particular praise for Walter Lippmann.

22

Myth and Meaning

Niebuhr's primary essay on myth, "Faith as the Sense of Meaning in Human Existence"[1] was written the year after Paul Tillich's death (1965). His appropriation of his particular concept of myth probably had its origins in his helping translate Paul Tillich's *Interpretation of History* (1936) which contained a short section "Myth and History." The interpretation of historical dynamics, according to Tillich, required a myth of the entry of the divine into historical events. These ancient practices could be seen to continue in modern movements that based themselves in interpretations of history. In the same year he was revising a bad translation of Tillich's book used this concept of myth as a principle for interpreting liberalism and Marxism in his publication *Reflections on the End of an Era* (1934). Niebuhr expressed his gratitude to his new colleague in the preface to his *Interpretation of Christian Ethics* (1935). The significant intellectual debt to Tillich is evident in Niebuhr's use of "prophetic religion" as Tillich used it in *Die Sozialtische Entscheidung* (1933) The critical perspective of the prophets criticizing Jewish nationalism through ethics and monotheism became a major thread throughout the book. Also, the blistering attack upon Emmanuel Hirsch, Tillich's friend and opponent of the 1930s, echoed Tillich's critique and fight with the German theologians supporting Hitler.

Another debt is Niebuhr's borrowing of the term "demonic" from Tillich. The idea that the ethical imperative reveals the goodness of life probably came from Tillich. The idea that in life our ethic connects us with the essence of "life as harmony with life" is very close to Tillich's conception of love revealing the truth about life. The language of essence contrasting with existence is familiar to readers of Tillich, also. Shortly thereafter he published in a Festschrift for his professor, Douglass C. Macintosh, his essay "The Truth in Myths" (1937).[2] This use of myth, shaped his presentation of biblical religion throughout his major theological works of *Nature and Destiny of Man*.

His essay of 1966 critiqued the Death of God Theologians for not proposing alternative systems of meaning for those they wanted to destroy. He noted that previous atheists like Freud, Nietzsche, and Marx had provided alternative mythical systems for the one they debunked. To Niebuhr religious symbols or myths expressed trust in the meaningfulness of life while protecting a penumbra of mystery surrounding life. Together these insights into mystery and meaning protected life from despair or overconfidence in human power. He approved of Bultmann's demythologizing if not of his individualism, and he sought to articulate through biblical myths a realm of meaning for life. If the religious would not attach themselves to pre-Enlightenment literalism, cooperation with secularists who were not overconfident in their secularism could provide partnership to preserve an open society.

The dedication of books on the Death of God to Tillich said more about Tillich being dead than it did about God to Niebuhr. In Tillich's thought, debates about the existence or nonexistence of God were irrelevant. He wondered whether their presuppositions were of a Tillichian mysticism or the atheism of French pre-revolutionary philosophers.

To Niebuhr all language about God was symbolic, and it pointed toward the mysterious origins and ends of existence. The symbols combined into the more developed myths upon which his theology reflected—first human nature, and then human social life. He called his developed concepts of sin, eschatology, atonement, and redemption, biblical religion in that the biblical images were related to the whole realm of social sciences, literature, and humanistic knowledge and less so to the purer sciences. Langdon Gilkey has presented the most systematic analysis of Niebuhr's theology in his *On Niebuhr a Theological Study*.[3] Niebuhr believed humanity had many intuitions about the meaning of life regarding morality and judgment, human dependence upon a source of life, life beyond death, and the overall meaning of human history. The questions raised by these intuitions could be answered by vital religious traditions in language that related human life to eternal life. Such a relationship was rationally best described in paradoxical language as mythical language was used to answer existential questions. Both Tillich and Niebuhr provided religious answers to these human questions, but Niebuhr's answers were provided more often in biblical mythological terms while Tillich's answers were framed in his formal writing in ontological language. His sermons use the ordinary biblical language of Protestantism as well as new concepts related more closely to his ontology.

In his last years at Union, Tillich wrote a book attacking Niebuhr's use of biblical myth, and argued that his form of philosophy, ontology, was necessary to present the biblical truths. This was a repetition of the argument Tillich often made against his friend. In his essay on the Death of God theologies, Niebuhr expressed his fears of Tillich's position. He thought Tillich equated finitude with sin in regarding the creation as equivalent to the fall. Niebuhr wanted more of a distinction between the goodness of the human and sinful humanity than Tillich's transition from the essential human to the existential human provided. He feared his Neoplatonic mysticism would neglect history and not be of much use to the Western insistence that history be regarded seriously.

He was not certain that Tillich's claim for one non-metaphorical definition of God was successful. In this piece, one year after Tillich's death, most of the issues between the two remained. He complimented Tillich on his translation of traditional theological terms into vocabulary for modern humanity. They were trying to provide modern humanity with a sense of meaning and trust equivalent to the church language of faith. Niebuhr was suspicious of humanity's capacity to experience pure being and was more inclined to stay with the traditional language from biblical images even when it required paradoxical expression of mythical language.

In his last book, Niebuhr in the face of criticism even seemed willing to abandon "original sin" and to move toward more empirical terms for the human situation. This suggestion seemed casual as he had won the argument for at least "sin" as descriptive of humanity. Maybe "original" needed to be jettisoned. Probably other forms of sin which he sometimes used: sensuality, sloth, lust, concupiscence, idolatry needed to be discussed more and "pride" less. Pride in its various expressions covered many of the forms of sin displayed by the powerful in academia, church, and politics, but it was less applicable to the dehumanization of those without power. But these elaborations could be undertaken in amending and not discarding his language. The insights from which he criticized both Paul Tillich and the Death of God theologians were present in his first essay on myth published thirty years earlier.

In the earlier essay, he argued science had destroyed the literal reliability of the myths that abounded in religion. Modern humanity understood itself in scientific terms and gave up on myths as accurate history or science. Those who had engaged in demythologizing were on the right track in freeing religion from the unbelievable. However, in failing to distinguish primitive myth which needed to be forsaken from authentic myth, apologists for religion surrendered too much. Myths or stories of God making man from clay and breathing life into the clay to create a human being were obviously biologically improbable. But the creation myth revealed humanity's sense of dependence, and it preserved the sense of God as involved in the world but not identical with it. When combined with myths on consummation of the world, the world had a mythical quality of a beginning and an ending with a sense of meaning beyond the world which could be related to historical senses of meaning. Ethics had a reference point and life could be conceived organically rather than mechanically.

For Niebuhr, religion preserved values and gave a mythical grounding for them as values were affirmed in the myths. For example, "the image of God" in humanity could become the grounding for human rights struggles as well as for the freedom of religion. Human rights could be seen as having value beyond social contracts of government concession of the rights. Of course mythology could be harmful as well as useful and it was the philosopher or theologian's role to keep the ultimate mythical sources of human life promoting human dignity. He regarded the modern idea of "progress" as a myth that obscured the social struggle and blinded people to the possibility of historical catastrophes.

It is sometimes hard when reading Niebuhr or Tillich to discern the reality of God underlying the myth in their more technical discussions. John Bennett would say: "Never doubt the reality of God behind Niebuhr's discussions of our language forcing us to use symbolic and mythical language." Even in that first essay on myth he would write: "God is in other words, both the ultimate ground of reality and its ultimate goal." Most scholars who doubted the reality of which they spoke never heard Tillich preach or Niebuhr pray.

Niebuhr's essay criticizing Tillich's presentation of sin in ontological language was published in 1952.[4] Niebuhr preferred the more biblical language distinguishing between creation and the human fall into sin. He feared Tillich's rendition of the myth into ontological language made the fall inevitable while Niebuhr thought both the Bible and human experience made more of a distinction between our humanness and our sinfulness. He found Tillich's interpretation of the myth understanding sin as separation, occurring with the move from potentiality into existence, made sin too fateful. Admittedly there was an element of fate in sin, but human responsibility for sin needed more protection than Tillich allowed. Tillich's response pointed to various biblical stories including the myth of the Garden of Eden that presupposed sin or temptation to sin. Humanity was more transcendent of nature for Niebuhr than for Tillich who had more of a place for nature in his theology than Niebuhr. Tillich insisted that he maintained human responsibility for sin, but that sin was basically estrangement or separation from being itself, or God. Sin for Niebuhr was the false exaltation of the self, and original sin was foundational to all of biblical thought and the best guide to human experience. He appreciated but did not accept Tillich's drama of human existence as the move from unity before creation to unity after the end of history. Niebuhr was writing with Tillich's first volume of his systematic theology in hand. He was also using Tillich's "Propositions" (a privately circulated document), and awaiting Tillich's second volume where he generously accepted that some of his questions might be answered. Tillich's response to Niebuhr was brief and he did not meet all of Niebuhr's points, but soon he was working on another book to resolve in philosophy's favor issues raised by Niebuhr and others.

Tillich wrote in the preface in 1955:

> The philosophical language I am using in my theological work has often been critically contrasted with the concrete imagery of the biblical language. The larger part of this book describes the contrast in its most radical form. But I do not draw the consequence expressed by some of my critics that theology has to restrain itself from using philosophical terms. It is my conviction that

this is neither possible nor desirable and that the attempt to do it leads to self-deception or primitivism.[5]

He was referring here more to fundamentalists and some of Barth's followers than he was to Niebuhr, but in his rejection of the term "metaphysical speculation" by his critics a few pages later he had in mind Niebuhr's essay contrasting biblical faith and ontological speculation. Niebuhr would agree with Tillich's assertion that we cannot avoid philosophy. His argument was over the mode of presentation of Christian faith and his assertion that historical, poetic, and dramatic presentations were more appropriate means than Tillich's particular ontology. He feared ontology in Tillich's presentation obscured the radical freedom for human nature he wanted to assert. He was afraid Tillich lost some aspects of human responsibility for sin if sin were understood primarily as separation from being itself. Niebuhr wanted two stories, one of creation and one of the fall, Tillich seemed to collapse them into one story in Niebuhr's perspective. Niebuhr had tried to meet Tillich on his own ground in arguing that his use of essence and existence were confusing and that Tillich had made logical mistakes. He also challenged his idea that the one nonsymbolic statement was that God was being itself. Niebuhr was more at home in philosophy, broadly considered to include moral philosophy and political philosophy than he was in systematic theology. They agreed that Christian faith was expressed in myths and that theological references were symbolic language. Through all their discussions, the basic issue was over sin, freedom, responsibility, and mode of expression. In his posthumously published critique of Niebuhr he added the disagreement over epistemology.

The issue here was different epistemologies, one American pragmatic and one German idealist, not really the lack of epistemology. In his response Niebuhr thought they were into the old argument about faith and reason. He thought Tillich misunderstood his defense of Hebrew historical modes of thought. Niebuhr appreciated reason in both its classical and technical senses, but he thought both the human self and the divine self were better presented in terms that preserved the freedom of both beyond ontological categories. Ontology was inadequate, Niebuhr thought, to comprehend the irregularities of history and the dramas of the self in sin and forgiveness.[7] In a reply to Gustave Weigel in the same volume, he wrote: "I do not know how it is possible to believe anything pertaining to God and eternity literally."[8] Then he explained he did not mean God was a term with only subjective meaning, and he distinguished himself from Bultmann who failed to distinguish between primitive myth and permanent myth. Tillich's early German writing on myth and symbolism had utilized the concepts to explain the driving ideological forces of political movements and Niebuhr used the terms in the same way. They both explained how empires and controlling oligarchies in those empires relied on mythological speech to motivate themselves as well as to motivate their followers. Tillich had earlier projected in Germany a volume that would explain both theological and political symbolism, but the volume was never published. The analysis of German political movements in *Die Sozialtische Entschiedung* (1933) carried through the symbolic explanation of the ideas of the contending parties. Niebuhr's writing on myth of 1937 and his later writing on the myths of the Cold War reflected this earlier work of Tillich.

Tillich's writing on symbolism and myth in America dropped his earlier use of the Unconditional from his *Religionsphilosophe* (1925), and the theory was developed in the face of criticism of American philosophers. Specialists in Tillich's use of symbols find differences between the volumes 1 and 2 of *Systematic Theology*.[9] Despite its evolution and presentation in many different works, the presentation in *Dynamics of Faith* (1957) captures the central meanings in a readable form for the American reader. Symbols are the language of religions for Tillich, and they are brought together in myths that relate one symbol to another. Theology uses concepts to reflect upon the religious symbols that mediate between the experience of the Holy and the human expressions of being grasped by the Holy. To speak of the infinite beyond space and time still requires language that moves from the world of the finite to its depths in the ground of its being. Religious objects or words are like the flag or the pledge of allegiance to the flag which take ordinary words and give them ultimate or nearly ultimate meaning.

Tillich listed six characteristics of symbols: (1) They point beyond themselves. (2) Symbols participate in the power of that which they symbolize. An example would be the Moslem reaction to Danish cartoons of the Prophet. (3) Symbols open human beings up to levels of experience that would otherwise not be available to them. (4) Symbols reveal aspects of human life otherwise not approachable by them. Here he is more Jungian then Freudian as he believes there are levels of the human unconsciousness approachable through symbolism. (5) Acceptance of symbols depends on the individual or group unconscious recognition of them. They are not easily created or destroyed. (6) Symbols have their own life and their acceptance comes and goes as they answer or fail to answer human needs and longing.[10]

Religious symbols point to human ultimate concerns. The ultimate concerns may be of gods, or politics, or success, or lust, or other values. They are truly ultimate or not idolatrous if they are of that which is a matter of being or nonbeing. While one can live without an ultimate concern or even participate with many religious concerns symbolized by many gods, such lives are for Tillich disorganized. The word "God" means ultimate concern; "God" is the symbol for God. The Christian myths organize the symbols of Christianity around that which is ultimate. But even the Christian symbols must be demythologized to recognize the place of the ultimate concern. Bibles, sacraments, special holy sites are mythological and must be demythologized to recognize the truly ultimate or God. So Tillich's theology is radically monotheistic, but even beyond the word for God is the reality or the God beyond God. There are different ways of denying the mythological character of the symbols of faith. The naive acceptance of myth is part of human experience, and Tillich does not criticize it. Repression of the symbolic language by those who have sensed its symbolic truth is for Tillich dangerous as it represents the split in the human personality that accepts literalness on authority rather than affirming myths as myth or broken myth. Myth is a natural part of the human mind like science or art, and it needs to be understood in its own right rather than affirmed as existing on some literal level. To reduce God to the literal level of existing things in space and time is to deny the reality of God.

Langdon Gilkey, who accepted the Tillich-Niebuhr understanding of religious language as symbolic language, feared that the two levels of literalism were prevailing among more and more Americans. Many lived in a world that Tillich doubted it was possible for modern humanity to live in, that is the world of pre-Enlightenment criticism that accepted myths as the world they lived within. The other literalism was those who suspected the religious language of Christianity was mythological like other religious language but denied it to protect themselves. Long after American Christians surrendered the idea that government and its stories were literally given by God they wanted to hold to the myth that religion or at least their form of American religion was given by God. For both Niebuhr and Tillich both government and religion were part of the human response to living in God's world.

Niebuhr's intuitive sense of the human dependence upon a creation that he believed God provided, his sense of the need for judgment in history even if by sources beyond history, and his sense of the reforming power of democracy leading toward a rough justice seemed to be stronger than Tillich's. He was a little more at home in this world. But his symbolism was less rich than Tillich's religious world. Niebuhr never felt the need to develop a system to symbolize the spirit while Tillich's largest part of his system is on the Spiritual Presence. The doctrine of the Kingdom of God is much fuller in Tillich's *Systematic Theology* than in Niebuhr's *Nature and Destiny of Man*. Though Niebuhr taught the ethics of world religions, he would never enter as deeply into the mythology of world religions as Tillich. However, Tillich in reducing his political writing and action after leaving Union in 1955 did not keep up the symbolic and mythological analysis of society that characterized Niebuhr's late-life writing. While Tillich was expectantly waiting, Niebuhr was acting and very aware of the important changes being won in improving the lot of the black minority and the working class in the U.S.A. With his original homeland split between Russia and the U.S.A. power struggles, Tillich offered less guidance for the history-shaping Cold War than did Niebuhr who majored in the subject. Tillich's major contribution in symbols and politics in this period was an unconscious one.

In 1965 (the year of his death) The United States Supreme Court quoted Tillich's *Systematic Theology* in ruling on a case of conscientious objection to the Vietnam War. The court ruled in favor of Daniel Seeger who claimed that he was entitled to a conscientious objector status even though he did not base it upon conventional belief in a divine being. Previous to this case, belief in a Supreme Being was necessary for a conscientious-objector status to war. The Supreme Court depended on volume 2 of the *Systematic Theology* where Tillich had argued that the affirmation of meaning is an affirmation of the "God above God" or the power of being. This idea in Tillich's theology thus became the basis for extending the rights of many American pacifists who before the decision had been unable to claim the privileges of conscientious objection on religious grounds. Tillich had agreed to testify for the Americans for Civil Liberties on this issue of broader religious rights for nontheists. There is irony in the thought of this nonpacifist Christian's thought being used to win rights for American pacifists, but for both Niebuhr and Tillich who respected conscientious objection to war, irony is central to history.

The Christian myth as he interpreted it gave Niebuhr an adequate sense of meaning for history that modern humanity needed. Though he referred often to the secularity of his age, he refused to provide a secular theology. Similarly he would not collapse the myths of religion into the mythology of politics though he examined myths in both fields. As Tillich noted, failure in the political field leads to failure in the other areas of civilization.

Gary Dorrien's thorough discussion of the role of myth in contemporary theology in *The Word as True Myth*[11] moves quickly through Niebuhr and Tillich to their use by Langdon Gilkey in a lengthy discussion. He rightly sees Gilkey as returning to the basic discussions of his two teachers throughout his wide dialogic exploration of other philosophies of religion. Gilkey published more on the exploration of other schools than did his one-time colleague Roger Shinn. Shinn stayed closer to Niebuhr and used Tillich, but by being in their environment of Union Theological Seminary he ventured less far out than Gilkey roamed. Other than Gilkey, Shinn would be the major theological ethicist to use both of their approaches. Though I often shared platforms with Langdon Gilkey in college and professional-society celebrations of the centenary of Tillich's birth, and on one occasion used his eyeglasses, we evaluated the political relevance of the Tillich/Niebuhr tradition differently. He did not seem to know much about the Tillich political tradition, and he was tempted to move in the liberation direction rather than the Niebuhr direction for later politics.[12] On reviewing his book *On Niebuhr* for the University of Chicago Press, I urged that the volume that began with the politics of *Moral Man and Immoral Society* conclude with a discussion of Niebuhr's mature politics. Such a final conclusion was not included.

Dorrien's suggestion in *The Word as True Myth* that he would move in the direction of Barth and C. S. Lewis as interpreters of myth even if Barth would call it saga seems to me to be a dead end. There is way too much in Barth that supports a less-than-critical reception of Scripture even if this is not his intention. The use of either Lewis or Barth for guidance of the American empire seems unlikely. There is nothing in Tillich and Niebuhr that prohibits their being used together other than their choice of different philosophic preferences that in Christian theology is not the decisive choice. Tillich's German idealism would always remain strange to Niebuhr, and Niebuhr's pragmatism was inadequate to Tillich, but they shared existentialism, and more importantly the proto-Lutheran emphasis upon forgiveness through faith in Christ. The role of Jesus as the bearer of the myth of Christ was decisive for both of them. Dorrien's conclusion praising Barth for recognizing that the mystery of God could not be known and recognizing that in Christ the hidden God is known through faith could as well be said of Niebuhr/Tillich. Neither of them would disagree with Dorrien's earlier comment on Barth and of himself: "If Christianity is true, it is true as true myth."[13]

A thesis of this study is that both Niebuhr and Tillich must be understood as theologians during times of war. Dorrien suggested that their theology written during war and depression was not so relevant in times of peace and prosperity. Actually, they never were so fortunate to see such a time. The Cold War with its threat of nuclear apocalypse continued and they responded to it. Niebuhr's late writing like the later speeches of Martin Luther king, Jr. called attention to the desperate poverty of the minority black population. Ironically two of my major criticisms of them would be that Tillich de-emphasized the political realm, which he recognized as centrally important, during the years he was writing his theology of the Holy Spirit, and Niebuhr never developed a theology of the Holy Spirit, leaving his theology more dualistic than Trinitarian.

The next two chapters deal with criticisms of the two thinkers before concluding with a chapter on the meaning of their legacy.

23

Criticism of Niebuhr on Faith and Politics

Niebuhr's thought at the end of his life was shaped by the Cold War situation as well as Christian faith and his immense learning. In 1971, he could not see the Cold War's climax or the relatively peaceful transition of the Soviet Union into disparate nations. South African apartheid was not yet collapsing, the Irish troubles were still in the news, the war in Vietnam dragged on and on, and the reconciliation of the races in America still seemed a hundred years away. Though the mainline denominations had installed social action agencies and many of their positions were filled by his students or disciples, their witness was still shaky and often timid. The ecumenical movement held more promise at the end of the 1960s than it would in the future, and his influence was still a leading factor in the social theologies of the World Council of Churches where his student Paul Abrecht directed the social studies of the organization. His journal, *Christianity and Crisis* was flourishing though already trends to alter it were underway. Two significant black scholars had joined the large faculty at Union Theological Seminary, young women were winning positions and the Seminary was often regarded as the best school in the United States for a liberal theological education. With President Bennett and Dean Shinn, the school was guided by Niebuhrian thought, though it was cracking around the edges under pressures from students of the new-left agitated by the Vietnam War and by the Students for Democratic Society revolt at Columbia University across Broadway Avenue. The 1968 election turmoil coupled with the assassinations of Kennedy and King unleashed responses of anger and utopianism that were not congenial to Niebuhr's incremental reform politics.

Shortly before he died, he had written an essay "Indicting Two Generations." It was very critical of those around Presidents Johnson and Kennedy who had left us in the quagmire of Vietnam. It also attacked the student revolution on the campuses coming down particularly hard on their Maoist and Marxist illusions. I thought I had successfully repressed the piece in conversation with Niebuhr, but it came out in *The New Leader*. Thankfully the students who might have felt indicted did not read *The New Leader*.

At the time Niebuhr had been talking not to the young college students, but to the faculty of Union and Columbia on Morningside Heights who were discomforted by the occupation of their offices and the disruption of the campuses. Niebuhr's influence among anti-Communist liberal academics and churchmen had grown so large that his critique of the war was outweighed by the chorus who blamed him or his thought for influencing many of the advisors who defended the war. Some liberal-progressive faculty even at Union in their frustration started making utopian projections and faulting Niebuhrian realism for being too close to the establishment. This internal critique began during his later retirement years and intensified soon after his death. The Vietnam War and its resultant political confusion led many young, idealistic students to seek comfort in various schemes of utopian politics. A few would change and staff the think tanks of the new right. Others continued to express relatively nonpolitical life choices. Some continued in utopian directions, and some returned to try and resurrect the vital center. Eyal J.Naveh analyzed the rise of this utopianism against Niebuhr as well as anyone in his 2002 book, *Reinhold Niebuhr and Non-Utopian Liberalism* and in "Beyond Illusion and Despair: Niebuhr's Liberal Legacy in a Divided American Culture."[1]

The students in the 1970s to some degree lost faith in their professor mentors, and they became open to more far-reaching programs of social justice. Experience in the civil rights movement and its frustrations led white and black activists to turn toward black power and the liberation theology of James Cone. The brutality of American opposition to radical social change in Latin America made it possible for liberal Americans to be attracted to liberation theology. Experience in the student revolts and the Civil Rights movement fueled the feminist critique of male theologies and assumptions. All of these movements were developed by first-rate scholarship that challenged the older reigning Niebuhr paradigms. Each expressed impatience for social change for the sake of justice, and undertook to overthrow the older, more incremental understandings of reform movements.

It did not really matter in the fury that Niebuhr had done as much to analyze race relations and to struggle for justice for the minorities as any white churchman. His critics forgot that he early had argued for and struggled for women's ordination, or that he had opposed the president's intervention in the Dominican Republic. It seemed irrelevant that he supported democratic reform movements in Latin America by Christian Democrats, influenced President Kennedy in ambassadorial appointments, and gave intellectual support to the Alliance for Progress. Other paradigms that could express more anger and more far-reaching gains for justice were needed, or so it seemed.

Those who followed Niebuhr in teaching social ethics at Union as holders of the Niebuhr chair all criticized Niebuhr for not emphasizing hope for social change more than he did. Bennett and others had been urging him to incorporate more hopeful analysis since before the Gifford Lectures of 1939. Shinn and Rasmussen had noted that he did not focus his analysis of sin on those who lives were caught in the oppression. Later it became the mainstream of feminist criticism that he failed to represent the experience of women under male patriarchy. His dialectic between pride and sloth from *The Irony of American History* meets some of these critiques. There are endless combinations of human sin between the poles of pride and sloth, but maybe these two poles of revolt against the source of life, God, provide a way of comprehending human failure in a Christian perspective.

Later, he admitted, the New Deal and follow-up liberal reforms accomplished more than he expected in the struggle for justice. However, with his political eye on developments in Europe, how much more room for hope was there than he announced in 1939? The claims of Wilsonian liberalism had proven hollow; the hopes of Russian Marxism were fraudulent; the hopes of the European Social Democrats were broken; and the hopes of the Nazis were demonic illusion. Billy Graham and Norman Vincent Peale ran with the American current of optimism and certain blindness to American social sin. Niebuhr could not go there; the most he could see by the 1950s was that organized labor with governmental support had won some battles toward more economic justice. But the seriousness of the Cold War armed with nuclear weapons combined with the misuse of American military power in Vietnam, Cuba, Lebanon, and the Dominican Republic could not provide grounds for optimism. The trajectory of optimism in America may have been stronger than he knew, but he could only criticize it and present that which he regarded as a more Christian worldly pessimism or, as Douglas Hall and Larry Rasmussen have argued, a theology of the cross. His social strategies, however, were to undertake a progressive liberal agenda from American traditions working within the American social world and political system. His realism grounded in Christian theology conditioned and limited his hopes for victories in the social struggle, but love in the pursuit of justice drove him and those influenced by him to continue the struggle and to participate in some historical victories.

A symposium held at Union in 1943 had echoed the critique that Niebuhr's realism needed more forceful presentations of social hope. The 1968 panel on Christian Realism at Union expressed some of the same critique. The discussion was published as "Christian Realism: Retrospect and Prospect" in *Christianity and Crisis.*[2] The panel consisted of John C. Bennett, Richard Shaull, Alan Geyer, Tom F. Driver, Roger L. Shinn, Harvey G. Cox, and Robert W. Lynn. I had been asked to participate, but I was out of the city on that date. Underlying the discussion was the assumption that a social philosophy relevant to the 1940s and 1950s would need to be revised for the late 1960s and 1970s. All the panel members knew that Christian realism was flexible and open to revision. They undertook to discuss how it could best evolve. Bennett, the member closest to Niebuhr by long association, said that changes in the Communist world, the need for revolutionary change in much of the world, the U.S. tendency to become a counterrevolutionary power, and the dangers of nuclear war demanded that Christian realism change its position from its earlier Cold War stance. All panelists agreed on the desperate straits of the American Republic in the late 1960s. Many of them found Christian realism unable to adjust to the changing technological situation, revolution, and the imaginative lifestyles of the Cultural Revolution. Occasionally they suggested Christian realism had a conservative tendency, but they knew that charge was irrelevant to Niebuhr. They were more agreed that the realist style was one of prudent action while for some of them the times called for revolutionary action. While realism asked the professors to play the role of responsible statesmen, a couple of them were more inclined to imagine themselves as revolutionaries.

Several of the theologians, particularly Driver, Cox, and Shaull, exhibited uneasiness over the lack of imagination in Christian realism. They called for the return of utopianism and apocalyptic motifs. Others were suspicious of apocalypticism in politics. Though the panel could not agree, there was a tendency to express a need for greater hope than realism provided. Hope not buoyed by illusion is a needed resource for desperate people who need motivation to continue the struggle against forbidding odds. Though uneasiness about Christian realism had provoked the occasion, the discussion indicated it had not yet been replaced as a social ethic. With a few minor exceptions the uneasiness could not be translated into workable alternatives or paradigms of understanding. Moreover while there had usually been women on the board of *Christianity and Crisis* under Niebuhr's active leadership, none were on the panel. It was male uneasiness driving the discussion; a revolt by women would soon produce an alternative view.

Feminist Criticism

Valerie Saving Goldstein published her important essay, "The Human Situation: a Feminist View," in 1960, more than a decade after she had submitted a version of it as a term paper at Union Theological Seminary. Though students at the Seminary in the 1960s were unaware of the paper, it became a defining icon in the feminist movement after Judith Plaskow commented on it in her 1980 study. *Sex, Sin, and Grace: Women's Experience and the Theologies of Reinhold Niebuhr and Paul Tillich.* Goldstein, then teaching at Hobart and William Smith College, did not enter deeply into the tradition out of which Niebuhr was writing or into the type of detailed logical argument that characterized the later work by Plaskow. Rather she noted the differing roles of gender identity discovered by Margaret Mead and Ruth Benedict in different cultures. She regarded these differences as human developments from biological differences. Women's roles as developing children, sexual beings, and mothers distinguished their experiences from the more active assertive roles of male biological development.

Recent history had also developed culture in a way that inclined the male to even more competitiveness and anxiety. Goldstein also suggested the role of woman in Western civilization had left her closer to nature while pushing the male into a role more transcendent of nature. The male drive for completeness left him more prey to the sin of pride than was the woman whose underdevelopment might better rest in her acceptance of her identity with nature and lack of struggle for fulfillment. Together these factors left the dilemma of the woman to be the opposite of the male's, and this difference had been missed by current theologians, particularly Niebuhr and Anders Nygren.

Studies by David Riesman, Lionell Trilling, and Hannah Arendt indicated to her that we might be entering a new era that could be regarded as the feminism of culture and if so, male models of theology that missed the experience of women would become irrelevant. She was certainly correct that Niebuhr had not emphasized the extent to which women's experience might require a less universal view of sin. Her criticisms were put gently, but they suggested the need for a new model to explain women's reality beyond that which Niebuhr was using. Ironically, her suggestion as to what theologians should be doing practically fit Niebuhr's relationship with his working wife perfectly.

One might expect of theologians that they at least not add to these pressures. One might even expect them to support and encourage the woman who desires to be both a woman and an individual in her own right, a separate person some part of whose mind and feelings are inviolable, some part of whose time belongs strictly to herself in whose house there is, to use Virginia Woolf's marvelous image, "a room of one's own." Yet theology, to the extent that it has defined the human condition on the basis of masculine experience, continues to speak of such desires as sin or temptation to sin. If such a woman believes the theologians, she will try to strangle those impulses in herself.

Goldstein was basically saying if we are getting it together and challenging the status quo do not make it any more difficult for us with male-defined universals that basically only reflect male sin. She noted that much male and female experience was the same, and she omitted any reflection on the war context of the thought. Niebuhr's warnings about pride apply to both men and women in politics, to Margaret Thatcher and Sarah Palin as well as to Winston Churchill and Eleanor Roosevelt, but the political person is not the whole of humanity either. But even more centrally he was utilizing a major myth and its interpretation to explain why political actors were so dangerous and cruel.

Judith Plaskow builds on the insight of Valerie Saving Goldstein, but advances the argument considerably. Plaskow is one of the few authors who discusses both Tillich and Niebuhr, and she explores the intricacies of their respective theologies. The presentation of both of their theologies and an analysis of women's experience in one dissertation is an unusually bold effort.

The breadth of her dissertation meant that she could not present the experience of the men she was studying. Nor could she explore the experience of their most intimate relationships with women. Neither Tillich nor Niebuhr regarded "experience" as a primary source of theology. Plaskow treats "experience" as a primary determinate of the adequacy of theology. So their methods are different and Plaskow's method becomes determinative for her criticism of Niebuhr and Tillich. Women's "experience" controls the argument, and the experiences Niebuhr and Tillich have of women are not very relevant. The argument of this book is that they both were significantly influenced by their experiences of war from 1914 to their deaths. Plaskow does not touch on the wartime context. Our methods and sources are different also.

Plaskow's model of women's experience is drawn from many sources, particularly from feminist sources which neither Tillich nor Niebuhr consulted. She takes care to argue that "Martha" of Doris Lessing's early novels of *Children of Violence* is not universal woman, but a particular woman. Still she uses her as an "image of a twentieth-century woman-person."[6] "Martha" is a thinly disguised reference to the historical life of Doris Lessing, who grew out of her childhood, adolescence, and early adulthood to become one of the great writers of the twentieth century. Of course, in the context of Christian theology, Martha is also the woman of the New Testament who busied herself overly much with the details of domestic life and protested her sister's dalliance with Jesus' conversation. Jesus seemed distressed over Martha's obsession with domestic details. Lessing like Plaskow herself became an intellectual influencing many. Lessing , the school dropout, colonial white woman raised in Africa, did not remain stunted by the oppression; she overcame, so to speak. Lessing with her Nobel Prize in literature did not remain as "Martha" of Plaskow's 1980 book; she flourished. She became the Communist wife of an Eastern European ambassador to Uganda. She could even refuse Queen Elizabeth's honor of making her a dame of the British Empire because there was no longer a British Empire. All of this is to say it is hard to build a lasting dissertation argument on personal experience before the trajectory of the personal experience is complete or nearly complete.

Niebuhr's published work describes the limitations put upon Ursula's academic career by the reality of domestic life and children in a manner for which Plaskow would have sympathy. Still, as a published author, chair of Barnard College's Religion Department, and feisty presence on Morningside Heights of New York City, she was far from Plaskow's "Martha" and more like Lessing or Plaskow herself. Neither of the other two major women in Niebuhr's life—his mother, Lydia, nor sister Hulda, as leaders of Christian churches developing resources from Scripture seem that similar to "Martha" either. Rather they used the New Testament story of Mary and Martha as grounds for their development of their spiritual side and roles as educators and administrators in the church.

Tillich's wife, Hannah—artist, writer, mother, refugee, and strong feminine presence—does not fit Plaskow's mold of "women's experience" very well either. Tillich's women friends that I have known also resemble much more the successful writer Doris Lessing than the repressed "Martha" of Plaskow's book. So if experience drawn from personal sources is a slippery source, we can ask: does Plaskow's method allow her to appreciate the experience of Tillich's interrogation of biblical myths from the ground of German idealism and existentialism or Niebuhr's preaching of Christian faith from the foundations of American pragmatism? How do we write a dissertation on women's experience critiquing male theologians without examining, explicitly, our own experience or that of our original sources, or the fuller story of women writers whose characters we use?

Another part of the problem is that both Niebuhr and Tillich used the Bible from a perspective of Christian faith. Most of the Bible was written by men in a patriarchcal society and its suggestions for women's liberation are few, though more than mid-twentieth-century theologians knew. Feminists have taught the discipline the need for a hermeneutical suspicion to uncover the male bias of the authors of the biblical stories. Neither Tillich nor Niebuhr interrogated the Scriptures or their own writings for male presuppositions. Plaskow's appreciation for the work of Mary Daly opens up the broader subject of the patriarchal, often-cruel role organized religion has played in supporting human society's repression of women.

As a father of an artist daughter, member of the Peace Corps in Africa, who works on the borders of technology, society, and art, I am very grateful to feminist scholarship and activism for breaking some of the barriers to women. She is more than she would have been but for the feminist revolt. As a young professor, I was asked to chair the committee to advance opportunities for women in the Seminary—and we succeeded. Of course, in a Niebuhrian perspective we compromised with the ideals, but barriers to women were obliterated and the student body became more than half female in most of our seminaries. As my adult life was always in the context of the ministry of women pastors, I have been blessed to see how the patriarchal structure of sin in religion can be overcome, but in the Near East in Jewish, some Christian, and Moslem services of worship I still see the religious separation and discrimination and I know a little about how far humanity needs to move to overthrow religious oppression of women. In fact only a few religious bodies permit women to hold positions as ministers, priests, or leaders. The gains of women in religion are to be celebrated, but they bring us into a different historical epoch and some of the feminist critiques of the earlier years seem overdone and some of the promises of a new world seem utopian.

But as Plaskow particularly focused on discussions of Episcopal church ordination of women, she needed to know that Niebuhr was engaged in the struggle long before the issue she raises surfaced, and he criticized his friend Archbishop Temple for failing to permit the ordination of women. Ursula, also managed to preach in a Church of England cathedral before ordination was possible. My reading of the theologies of Tillich and Niebuhr is that they did not distinguish between the sins of men and women, though their denunciations of the sins of men were far stronger as men participated more in the oppression. I do not think it is helpful to apply Niebuhr's categories of sloth or sensuality to women and pride to men. In our human experience, in moments of decision, in our limited human freedom, we may act either to renounce that freedom and to become less than a free human being or exaggerate it and act like little gods. Both responses and the millions of combined responses that make up the human spectrum are applicable to both men and women.

Many of these failures can be seen from a theological perspective to result from inadequate faith in God. The less power men have the more their failures tend to resemble sloth or sensuality. The more power women have the more their failures tend to resemble Niebuhr's four levels of prideful acts. Plaskow's point that their theologies neither understood nor empowered women to overthrow their oppressors is accepted, and Plaskow's argument that they too easily universalized male experience is important. Her critique ranged far beyond Goldstein's important points and other points of criticism deserve attention.

In concluding her presentation of women's experience, she asked: "Have these theologians appropriated and do they perpetuate the mythology of the society in which they write, or do they speak from a broader perspective?"[7] Certainly the answer is they perpetuate aspects of the cultural myths they were taught and they also attempt to reform those myths and the structures that inform them. For example, after World War I, Tillich participated in a move to reform the church. He was a pastor, so supported the mythology surrounding the church, but he participated in a movement and signed a statement in 1919 that called for the election of woman officers. I would add that the election of women elders in my own congregation has done more to equalize the gender roles in the congregation than any shift in vocabulary or theological adjustments that have resulted from the power shifts.

The Niebuhrs' adjustment of the domestic responsibilities of their home so that Ursula could be free to teach a generation of women undergraduates an empowering religious understanding of self and society, probably was more important than any pronouncements Niebuhr made on women's ordination.

A pivotal argument for Plaskow is that Niebuhr's focus on pride as the premier expression of sin from his Augustinian-Reformation tradition is a mistake. It suggested to her "that self-aggression and the struggle for self-definition are sins."[8] But this is not a conclusion drawn from Niebuhr's writings or his life. Nor does he assert that "sensuality" or the surrender of freedom is particularly women's sin. That is Plaskow's definition, perhaps drawn from Saving and de Beauvoir, neither of whom share Niebuhr's perspective. Niebuhr tended to see the sin of the oppressor rather than the victim. Plaskow's argument cannot help but blame the victim even if only by implication. By 1980, as a published author and college professor, even though she may suffer some discrimination as a woman, she is among the elite.

Plaskow helpfully noted that Niebuhr's writings argued that equality required improvement in the status of women and she listed some of these in footnotes. She commented on his criticism of Karl Barth for opposing the ordination of women. She also noted Niebuhr's repeated references to the arrogance of men encroaching on any proposal for full equality for women. She then added: "Surely this lesson must be applied to his theology as well."[8]

She found his understanding of grace weak when applied to women who assented to their secondary place in society. She thought his doctrine of the church was inadequate. Rachel Headley King's argument that his theology omitted the Holy Spirit was regarded as important. She thought his last book, *Man's Nature and His Communities*, found resources of community as a method of grace more than in his earlier work. Still his theology did not provide an adequate vision of a better society. There seemed to be more resources in both nature and community than his thought accounted for in its discussions of sin and grace. There probably are more resources in both community and nature than Niebuhr perceived for the healing of human life. However, he wanted to avoid both naturalism and romanticism about community. Women's voices still remind us of the atrocities against women in male-dominated communities. Nature's havoc still destroys people and their aspirations. The corporate (communal) exploitation of nature may still destroy the living space for humanity. Finally there is no reason to ignore the corruption of community life, and even Doris Lessing's holding on to Communism until 1954 indicates how blind humans can be to the corruption in their primary communities.

She finds Tillich's theology more affirmative of women's needs than Niebuhr's. Neglecting to go into Tillich's experiences with women or women's experiences with Tillich, she still finds his thought inadequate when measured by her model of women's experience. Their methods are radically different as she uses her model of women's experience to criticize his theology derived from existential questions to the Christian tradition from the Bible through German philosophical developments. There is no way the two methods can complement each other. The Bible is foreign to her model as it includes the tale of both Mary and Martha and not just "Martha." Its portrayals of women vary from Jezebel, the queen, who has her opponent executed so the royals can seize his vineyard, to the Virgin Mary.

Obviously the Western white woman of Plaskow's reference should not be judged by ancient biblical standards as some religious fanatics would try to do, and as some religious communities have selectively enforced some biblical practices from the time of the writing of Scripture. Intellectually the judgment against one model of theology from presuppositions from another model also has its difficulties.

Plaskow finds many confusions and inconsistencies within Tillich's developed arguments, but her main criticism is that he swallows up women's experience within his theological monism. She is looking for the self-actualizing woman while Tillich's hoped-for development in women would be that they would not be autonomous as Plaskow wishes but theonomous or at home in the realized religious person. She wrote: "his failure convincingly to establish the preservation of finite individuality in the experience of grace leaves ungrounded the human experience of unestranged, individuation, growth, and change."[9]

The problem, as Plaskow noted in a quotation from Ray Hart, is that Tillich's theology is radically God-centered and that whatever he says about estrangement comes back to inclusion through faith in the union with God. The theology is too monistic or the doctrine of God dominates human experience too much. Here is the fundamental division between Tillich and this critic, his thought is too God-centered and that leaves the picture of humanity as not fulfilled in solitary, autonomy from God. Nor is the individual person unestranged as Plaskow hopes. For Tillich's part this God-centeredness and the reasoning about it is what he thought theology was all about. The goal for all human beings in his thought was not enlightenment rebellion, but the return to God-centeredness or theonomy.

If Plaskow's critique of Niebuhr and Tillich is as I suspect alien from the Christian tradition, Susan Nelson presents her critique in *Beyond Servanthood* as within Christianity. Her use of Lessing's character of "Martha" from her early work seems in line with Plaskow's use of the same character to describe women's experience. She wants to reform the Christian tradition to reveal its liberating possibilities for women. She believes the issue for women is not the over exaltation of the self and pride but the failure under pressure to adequately develop the strengths of the self. She builds on the work of psychology and theologies of Rosemary Radford Ruether and Elisabeth Schussler-Fiorenza to find the resources within Christianity to call for the free self of women who can speak in their own voices. Her own voice is clearly within the liberation theology of white Western women. In her own experience of theological education she found help in reclaiming her authentic liberating voice and she sees it in the vocation of women seminarians who now outnumber males in many North American seminaries. Obviously her later experiences, if not all of her women mentors, were within the smaller part of Christianity that ordains women to ministry. Whether the totally male-dominated Roman Catholicism or Eastern Orthodoxy can support liberating calls to full Christian vocation and leadership remains doubtful. The sickness of religious misogyny as represented in the pope's appeal for forgiveness over child abuse by male priests, whose mothers could not aspire to religious leadership in the Roman Catholic Church, raises anew the possibility of liberating words from that hierarchically structured body. Is not the enforced male celibacy designed to strengthen the hierarchy? Women's liberation that will provide the criteria for judging theologies is the coming into fullness of women that will allow them to speak with their own authority in the overthrow of patriarchy. From within my own antiauthoritarian realism, I suspect the overthrow of the very ill patriarchy of the bulk of Christianity is far from realizable in this century.

I do not agree with my late friend and teacher Henry Clark that "the feminist critique of Niebuhr's concept of sin as sensuality is somewhat trivial."[9] I think however Clark is correct that with all of Reinhold Niebuhr's emphasis on creativity, freedom, and the correction of power to destroy hierarchies he would have abhorred the idea that his theology was in any way hindering the freedom of women. Niebuhr held that the human self was free by nature and that the human needed to be freed in society to develop its life. Nelson finds women not to be free by nature because the prevalence of patriarchy reduces the human self towards negativity. Niebuhr seems to believe that the self can be free even in prison and that it is the oppressive structures that need to be torn down. Woman, I believe in Nelson's anthropology needs to be called into freedom and that she wants to find language in the church to empower that freedom. She believes that the symbols of service and altruism are not basically freeing for women, because women have been oppressed by being expected to serve others and by being criticized for acts of assertiveness rather than altruism. One sees that the expectation of women to serve does reinforce the character type that Lessing found in "Martha." But beyond exploitation, the service of Jesus in healing, teaching, and organizing out of love seem like characteristics of the Christian life for those who would, as Nelson wants, become friends in community with Jesus. The defense of self-centeredness in Nelson's argument seems harder to sustain than many of her other wise points. Could not that oft-repeated point of Niebuhr, that the overpursuit of self-interest leads to self-destruction, be wisdom? He made the point both for personal relations and for international affairs.

Nelson's chapter 4 is interesting as in her dissertation for Claremont Graduate School she criticizes three prominent theologians from Union Theological Seminary on their understanding of love. Her criticism of Niebuhr here is mild. She understands that the self he says has to be broken and cast aside is the old sinful self either of self-abnegation or of prideful disregard for others. It is not clear that she grasps that both of these expressions of sinful development are due to "unbelief." For Niebuhr sin is the failure to live as a human, and I do not think she would disagree with that conclusion. Her worry is that Niebuhr reinforces altruism and service as marks of the Christian life, but a full reading of Niebuhr would convince any reader that Niebuhr too wants the responsible self to act freely in community.

She interprets Niebuhr's understanding of life in Christ to be that of self-sacrifice. I think that is a misunderstanding. Niebuhr knew that selves must look out for themselves and insist on justice for themselves and use power to win justice for their communities. The self-sacrifice of Christ in the atoning act of the cross was the highest expression of divine love and therefore ultimately normative. But human life was life among many penultimate decisions where human persons had to be protected, and actions were not to be self-sacrificing but acts toward justice. His oft-repeated goal of acting to balance powers for the sake of justice was not self-sacrificial. Some of her sentences acknowledge that Niebuhr is not interested in the negating of the self, but she strangely persists in thinking he recommends a life of self-sacrifice. Some early Christian martyrs chose self-sacrifice and needed to be cautioned against it, but this is not Niebuhr's problem. She may exaggerate Niebuhr's use of self-sacrifice as a characteristic of the Christian life; it is an ultimate religious norm expressed in the cross and consequently a principle of judgment on human life, but it is not seen as a daily ethic, or pragmatic wisdom, or as a guide for people or groups needing liberation. She is correct when she says Niebuhr assumes the self. More focus on what he described as sloth or sensuality would put one in touch with his sense of the need to remove all barriers to human development including self-imposed ones. However an ethic of self-care or hedonism was something that he thought needed resistance, because that is the way to the war of all against all. The love commandment was the basis for the deontological elements in his ethics. Nelson's conclusion seems to want to include both the freedom of the developed self and the love ethic. I suspect that is what Niebuhr was trying to say, and what Jesus said pretty clearly.

She found Tillich in *Love, Justice, and Power* to represent adequately the idea that love needed to be related to justice and that the self needed to be preserved within just structures. Her discussion of Tillich is very brief and its purpose in the chapter is difficult to discern, but it seems to be a fuller statement than Niebuhr's work to the affect that love presupposes independent selves. Love requires justice that presupposes free selves. If the realization of love requires developed selfhood, Nelson argues then the characteristics of complete Christian life contain selfhood as well as love, service, and altruism. As long as the requirements of selfhood are not too stringent this is probably correct. But the self required for Christian life cannot be presupposed to be equivalent to the requirements of a woman holding a Ph.D. in Religious Studies. There are very incomplete selves in church services accepting forgiveness for themselves who may exhibit love and altruism without full autonomy. On one occasion, I drove and chaperoned a van load of mentally challenged adults to Washington D.C. for a long weekend vacation. They were Christians. As we sat in the balcony of the U.S. Senate, I realized how much better off the country would be for a while if these disinterested, loving citizens could control the reins of government for a few days even if they were not up to the high standards of self-interested, centeredness of Nelson. Their disinterestedness dismissed the self-interestedness of politicians and the resultant meanness. They could have governed for all. During the trip they cautioned each other about misbehavior that might endanger the beauty of the trip or a return trip for all. Of course, they were only relatively innocent. Something more than innocence is needed to govern and the virtues of wisdom and prudence would have been needed to supplement their relative innocence. In a real scenario they would have been exploited, but it is a fond act of imagination to dream of being governed by folks with very little inclination to grasp power and benefits for themselves.

As noted earlier, Tillich's ethic is more one of fulfillment than is Niebuhr's. Niebuhr's full discourse included more elements of rules, limits, and laws than Tillich's. Tillich could and can be more easily used by the theology of women's liberation than Niebuhr. Tillich's hope that ethics would be God-centered presupposing the relativizing of all other rules and living for personal fulfillment runs high risk of chaos.

Nelson's earlier writing on Niebuhr was more hostile. She confessed how guilty she had been made to feel as a woman and decided that the classical Christian condition was responsible for her guilt. She assumed Niebuhr was representative of the tradition and that his doctrine of sin contributed to the pain women felt. She recognized that for him sin originated in lack of trust in God and that he expressed sin in bipolar concepts of pride and sensuality. As pride as rebellion against God was seen by him as the primary sin which underlay even the secondary form of sin, sensuality, she argued he lost his original insight regarding the escapist character of sensuality. She thought the model of sin could be better explained if the second form of sin was named the "sin of hiding." She continued to develop this concept throughout her career as a theologian. Also, she regarded this second form of sin or hiding as the characteristic sin of women. If they could see that they sinned by failing to develop themselves toward freedom, then they could confess properly and within Christianity begin to develop their own power. She thought his theory tended to forget what she called the sin of hiding and developed only the sin of pride, thereby confusing women for whom pride was not the primary issue. His thought neither judged her sin of hiding nor called one out to escape from it. In her conclusion she calls for finding in "herself a faith in a deity who judges her passivity and escapism and who beckons her onward."[10] She ended calling for a transformed world, that oppression be fought and that a vision beyond violence and guilt be realized. Her expectations were rather un-Niebuhrian.

Probably Tillich was correct that for most of us guilt will be overcome through our acceptance in faith that the unacceptable are forgiven and accepted by the source of life. None of this is to deny that women's theology and the liberation movement are transforming Protestant seminaries and impacting churches in the United States and that the gains throughout the country for justice toward women have been tremendous. This is partially because of a change in consciousness and partially through the incremental changes that are possible in politics in reforming the structures.

These feminist writers are on to the deficiency noted by so many writers that Niebuhr's anthropology may not encourage the weak as well as it criticizes the powerful. However, the feminists run the danger of oversimplification in their dichotomous presentation of male and female experience in the Western, white world. Marjorie Suchocki underscores this weakness when she gently adds to their models of women's experience the addition of oppressed men or the marginalized escaping the burden of free selfhood.[11] She makes the addition without criticism, implying it to be their positions, but it is not exactly what they said; they spoke of women's experience in light of anthropology, psychology, and "Martha," Lessing's character's, experience. Lessing herself became aware of feminists use of her character to oversimplify the human story and she protested against being identified as a feminist writer and said:

> What the feminists want from me is something they haven't examined because it comes from religion. They want me to bear witness. What they would really like me to say is, "Ha Sisters, I stand by you side by side in your struggle toward the golden dawn where all those beastly men are no more." Do they really want people to make oversimplified statements about men and women? In fact they do. I've come with great regret to this conclusion.[12]

It was unfortunate that feminists mentioned above based so much on Lesssing's character of "Martha." Plaskow also referenced her character Kate Brown, but Martha remained the primary figure and example of women's experience. Women's experience in other Lessing characters, as for example

"Sarah" in *Love, Again,* experienced life quite differently than the portrayal of "Martha" in the earlier novels.

Marjorie Suchocki appreciated the critique of the three feminists in exposing deficiencies in Niebuhr and Tillich's understandings of sin. Taking Niebuhr as representative of twentieth-century interpretations of sin, she deepened the criticism. Following a method of natural-theology argument, which was already permeated with Christian symbolism, she reasoned differently than Niebuhr and Tillich who assume the Christian symbols and then reason.

So the nature-spirit Protestant theology of Albrecht Ritschl taught to Niebuhr by Douglass Macintosh and reflected in the *Nature and Destiny of Man* is abandoned for a more naturalistic philosophy, and sin becomes more of a rebellion against nature than against God. The unnecessary violence of humanity is the basis of sin from which anxiety arises. She is as serious about sin as is Niebuhr, but it is rooted more in nature and less in the distinctive human realm of spirit or mind. At this point he would worry about the naturalistic explanation losing the human responsibility for sin.

Suchocki's presentation is strong in its utilization of science to explain the natural origins of the human mammal's use of violence, and particularly insightful in showing how the scars of violence linger in victims and perpetrators. Her relational theology is adept at explaining the connections within society of acts of violence as acts against creation's well-being. Her newspaper accounts of violence prefacing each chapter root her reflections in the reality of violence. Though her evolutionary account is already dated by more recent science, her instinct to tell the story of human evolution of violence from natural origins is an improvement over Niebuhr. Her distance from political philosophy, on the other hand, means she does not deal with violence in recorded history and its politics as well as Niebuhr.

Her focus on violence as the primal sin rather than rebellion against God means, I think, that she does not deal as well as Niebuhr with greed, envy, pride in its various forms, alcoholism, structural economic abuse, perversions of religion, and so forth, as expressions of sin. Taking his understanding of sin as the refusal to be free humanity trusting God may still provide a "spiritual' emphasis on sin that energizes the political struggle for justice and human resolve in community to overcome the personal sins.

In our history Niebuhr's emphasis upon diplomacy, structures, and balance of powers, and progressive movements may still do more to alleviate some unnecessary violence than Suchocki's hope for forgiveness. History is still understood by the followers of Niebuhr as the symbol of crucifixion reflecting cruelty of violence in religion and imperial order as well as forgiveness.

Her taking Niebuhr and Tillich together in their existential theology concerning sin is wise. As Ursula Niebuhr has emphasized, existentialism was part of their community's discourse. Both their time and conversation partners kept them focused on anxiety. They correlated that anxiety with the fear of death more than with violence. They observed less violence domestically than that which Suchocki observes and more internationally, some of which they believed they had to support. Both Hitler's forces and Stalin's forces had to be countered and the relevance of forgiveness was not obvious. With Augustine they thought violence sometimes is overcome with more violence, though Suhocki is correct that peace achieved violently lays the ground for further violence. However, national weakness also encourages aggression. Even in American cities order depends in part upon the violence police use as agents of the state that claims for itself a lawful monopoly on the means of violence. The guilt surrounding violence may imply, as she suggests, a necessary vision of a good nonviolent society, but their philosophies of history and humanity do not permit them to envisage such a society until humanity and history are transformed. Their theologies are both more practical and less visionary than those of Nelson and Suchocki.

Canadians put on a particularly good celebration of the centenary of Niebuhr's birth in 1992 at McGill University. Aurelia Takcas Fule's paper summarized the work of several feminists on Niebuhr. She particularly focused on Plaskow's work, but also referred to work by Beverly Wildung Harrison, Judith Vaughan, Susan Nelson Dunfee, Daphine Hampson, and Valerie Saving. She noted that the rise of inclusive language in recent decades in publishing and liturgy was a symbol of the feminist gains since Niebuhr's time. After beginning her essay with a description of the human situation as seen through Niebuhr's theology, she explored feminism to examine the adequacy of his picture of the human. Was it really drawn from the male experience and inadequate to describe the female experience? Here she found mixed results of "less than careful reading" of Niebuhr and also helpful insights and corrections. Quoting Saving on sin, she said the specific feminine forms of sin are better suggested by such items as triviality, distractibility, and diffuseness; lack of organizing center or focus; dependence on others for one's own self-definition; sentimentality, gossipy, sociality; and mistrust of reason; in short underdevelopment or negation of the self. To some of us, this does not seem like a list for the confessional. Our response is more like what a pity, what a waste."[13]

She doubted that "self" was being used in the same way by Niebuhr and his critics. His use seemed to come from the theological tradition and that of his critics from psychology or therapeutic concerns. Different views of the human also implied different conceptions of God and more was at stake in the debates than male and female differences or similarities. She thought the argument was not with Reinhold Niebuhr as much as it was with the main Christian tradition. The evidence of women's experience she feared was taken not from women, but from a very limited sample of Western, white, middle-class experience. She also thought categories of race and class were not sufficiently used in claiming ground in human experience by the critics.

Fule's work in the World Council of Churches perspective seemed to give her a broader perspective than that of the feminist critics for evaluating the human. Still she recognized that the search for differences in male and female experience was a post-Niebuhr phenomenon and it needed to be approached with vigor. Feminism had made real gains for women. Though many feminists had left the church, feminism needed to be understood and utilized by the church. She claimed that much of the best feminist scholarship had been accomplished by the women working on Scripture, and then in an ironic twist, she quoted Phyllis Trible's interpretation of the fall in Genesis which shows the woman being the active one, and the man going along with her, rather than with God, in a sort of dumb, silent, brutish manner. The male of the story illustrates weakness, and she quoted Trible's comment that there are many varieties of response that contribute to transgression.

Pre-feminist Criticism of Niebuhr

Niebuhr was able to reply to his critics in the 1961 volume edited by Charles Kegley and Robert W. Bretall, though there were no women's voices in that volume or in some of the other succeeding collections of essays on his thought.[14]

He responded generously to his friend, Emil Brunner, chiding him on the need for footnotes crediting Brunner's influence on his ideas. He apologized even though there were footnotes to Brunner in the criticized volumes. Their friendship was close, Brunner's son had stayed in the Niebuhr's apartment while studying at Union, and Niebuhr had enjoyed his pre-war visit to Brunner immensely. Niebuhr noted that though his ethics differed he felt closer to Brunner than to some other European neo-orthodox thinkers and he admitted that Brunner's work, particularly *Man in Revolt*, had influenced him.

Niebuhr recognized in response to Paul Tillich that Tillich for two decades influenced his thought and taught him a great deal. However, he did not accept Tillich's critique that he needed a different epistemology and ontology. Niebuhr did not believe epistemology could get you to the Christian faith in the divine mystery of Christ. He feared that ontology (philosophy of being) would obscure human freedom and the dynamics of the human self. He preferred the dynamic of the biblical presentation to ontology. Tillich was correct that Niebuhr was preoccupied with the "self," but the story of freedom of the divine self and the human self seemed to Niebuhr to be what Christianity was concerned to understand. He would not concede to Tillich that he overemphasized the Hebrew contribution to Christian faith. He intended to recognize both the Greek and the Hebrew contributions to Christian faith while preserving the freedom of both God and "self" more dramatically than he believed possible under the science of ontology. Both theologians discussed human nature and the fall, but Tillich's emphasis upon the ground of being or being itself related Tillich more closely to the doctrines of creation. Tillich's thought came closer to the philosophy of nature than Niebuhr's. Earlier I have argued that if Niebuhr had placed "original righteousness" before his discussion of "original sin" he might have escaped some of the continuing criticism that his philosophy of the human was too pessimistic. However, Niebuhr perceived the need to correct American social science, sentimentality and over-optimism about human rationality so that adequate strategies for social justice could be developed in light of the actual human misery of the twentieth century.

He appreciated John C. Bennett's history of his social ethics and pointed out that any conservative tendencies in his thought were due to an increasing appreciation of the historical factors that limit human ability to create a new world. Some of the Enlightenment voluntarism and especially its modern form in Communism rode too roughshod over the historical limitations given to existing communities. Earlier in correspondence with Bennett he had indicated his lack of interest in Bennett's suggestion that he write a systematic Christian social ethics for two reasons: he was more interested in the immediate social issues than he was in system building; and he understood his brother, H. Richard Niebuhr, had an ambition to write a systematic Christian ethic.

Through his greater exposure to the poor nations in the world through ecumenical meetings and his own travel, Bennett was becoming more deeply aware than Niebuhr of the revolutionary needs and passions of the world's poor. Bennett was less passionate in his condemnation of Communism, emphasizing the changing nature of Communism and its varied expressions in different nations. Niebuhr was probably more deeply Eurocentric than Bennett, but that shading of a difference should not be overemphasized as both were exposed to Third World visitors at Union Theological Seminary. Bennett had studied at Oxford, but Niebuhr's command of German gave him access denied to Bennett and even before Niebuhr paved the way to Union faculty membership for Bennett, he had urged him to take more seriously German scholarship, particularly regarding mythology. Furthermore all criticisms of Niebuhr's Eurocentrism need qualification with the reminder that Niebuhr taught the course on the ethical thinking of different world religions, that his reading in the literature of the Third World was immense, and students from the Third World and leaders of the churches would visit him when they came to New York City. Near the end of Niebuhr's life, Bennett was president of Union Theological

Seminary, and the three of us often discussed political issues in person or over the phone. Bennett had become more radical than Niebuhr. His last book in retirement was entitled *The Radical Imperative* and it showed openness to socially radical theologies that Niebuhr was not sharing. Bennett, with whom I taught Niebuhr's course on "Moral Issues in International Relations," was always a little more of the progressive liberal than Niebuhr. I joined Bennett in thinking that Niebuhr's critique of Communism was overdone, but after 1989, when Russians could criticize their own history publicly, many of their critiques went beyond Niebuhr.

Niebuhr responded generously to Paul Ramsey's criticism of *An Interpretation of Christian Ethics* by indicating that he had moved far beyond his early work. He had no interest in defending it. This abandonment of this earlier Marxist-colored work should be a warning to all of those who try to understand his thinking through heavy use of the volume. He had indicated in the later reissuing of the book that he thought it was badly flawed. His phrase of "love beyond law" was faulty as Ramsey argued. He thought there was an essential human nature, but that natural laws were too bound to the times and thought of the elites that formulated them to be regarded as universal. Part of the essential nature of humanity was freedom, and that very freedom meant that natural laws were always relative. Niebuhr in ethics was closer to situationalism or contextualism than Ramsey, though that was not his position. Also, his substantial ethical conclusions were more progressive than those of Ramsey. Whether that was more due to Ramsey's reliance on natural law or his Southern Methodist origins or the Princeton University academic context, I do not know. During the Vietnam War Ramsey became very hostile to Niebuhr's criticism of U.S. policy. Later he saw the futility of the war and apologized.

Niebuhr regarded Arthur Schlesinger, Jr. and Kenneth Thompson as friendly critics and he accepted Schlesinger's interpretation of his intellectual evolution. He agreed also that he had been too slow to accept the pragmatic gains of the New Deal as he was subject to socialist illusions with which he had criticized his earlier liberalism. So beyond using first liberalism, then a Marxist social democratic position to criticize the optimism of liberalism, he had moved on to support a more pragmatic, progressive social policy with his deepened Christian theology. His Christian realism chastened the optimism of the social gospel in an attempt to improve its social consequences of progressive reform.

Kenneth Thompson, while affirming his deep appreciation of Niebuhr's political thought, challenged Niebuhr's lack of definitions about central terms. Niebuhr was more inclined to paint a narrative picture than he was to use rigorous definitions. Niebuhr also kept his understandings of American values more closely related to national interest than did Thompson. Thompson, a realist after Hans Morgenthau, wanted to define politics clearly as the pursuit of interest in terms of power. Niebuhr's uses of realism were in Thompson's perspective too vague and sometimes contradictory. Niebuhr could not accept deriving political ethics from political practice, but required that the normative ethical tradition has its own history and its own sources. Thompson continued throughout his career studying Niebuhr's writing and worrying about the best relationship of ethics to international politics. Niebuhr was consistently stronger on the ethical reflection than Thompson, though they often agreed on practical issues. On the Suez crisis, for example, Niebuhr, Thompson, and Morgenthau had lined up against Bennett and Bates of the editorial board of *Christianity and Crisis*. Niebuhr did not reply to Thompson about the need for more careful definitions, though it was an appropriate criticism. Thompson's later writings on nuclear issues and Vietnam would distance his positions from both of his mentors, Niebuhr and Morgenthau.

Under criticism, Niebuhr admitted that two of his formulations, "equality of sin and inequality of guilt" and "redeemed in principle and not in fact" were inadequate to express his theology. Professors William Wolf and Richard Kroner were given credit for pointing out the difficulties in those formulations. But Niebuhr wanted to resist Professor Wolf's criticism of the inadequacy of Niebuhr's understanding of the church. He argued that he had gradually come to appreciate it more as a community of grace and the bearer of the preaching of the word. However as this is one of the two major criticisms of the lack of development in Niebuhr's thought, it needs to be remembered that Wolf was speaking from his context in an Episcopalian seminary. Roman Catholic, Episcopalian, and Methodist critics of Niebuhr's understanding of the church need to be careful that they are not just repeating differences of the conflicts in English history over polity.

Niebuhr's church in which he served as a minister within a local parish for thirteen years had a congregational doctrine of the church. He should not be held to standards of churches with bishops. His seminary was ecumenical, having fled the orthodoxy of early twentieth-century Presbyterianism, and he worked doggedly for the ecumenical church movement. It is awkward for Methodist laymen who have little experience serving a church as a minister to criticize a minister of the United Church of Christ for sounding like a low churchman, which he is by definition. Similarly Episcopal priests must know that by definition their views on the church, no matter how disparate, probably do not correspond to the low-church polity of churches merged from Evangelical and Reformed synods and the Congregational Church as was the United Church of Christ. My own experience of serving in Roman Catholic, United Church of Christ, Lutheran, Presbyterian, and ecumenical institutions is that you put on different hats in different histories and practice the toleration of a John Milton, which Niebuhr often referred to in his writing and speaking.

Niebuhr's declining of positions offered at Harvard and Yale Universities was in part due to his vocation in the church which he thought could be better served at the Seminary. The critics that often repeat the criticism that Niebuhr's understanding of the church is inadequate must be reminded of the reality of their own social location rather than assuming they, in their particular denomination or sect, have the truth about the church. He faced the issue again in responding to Father Weigel's criticism that Protestantism faced the dangers of subjective, individual interpretation. Niebuhr regarded theology as under the discipline of the church, but that allowed great freedom. The authority of the Catholic Church could be envied, but that authority created problems of pretension and the stifling of criticism which should begin first within the household of God. He did not believe the differences between Catholicism and Protestantism could be resolved.

Alan Richardson's insistence that the miracles, the fall from grace, the virgin birth and the physical resurrection must be true historically could not really be accepted by Niebuhr. These issues for Niebuhr are the poetry of religion. His attempt to distinguish between myth as ancient saga and perennial myths that reveal the actual human situation before God, he feared would not be sufficient for Richardson. Niebuhr does not believe that the great themes of religion can be expressed except symbolically or ritually or as social symbolism of the Christian community. Richardson and all literalists must understand themselves as in disagreement with Niebuhr no matter how much they appreciate his contributions to Christian theology and apologetics.

Niebuhr conceded that Professor Daniel D. Williams was correct in that his polemics against liberalism had gone too far. He had meant to criticize theological liberalism's overly optimistic picture of the human situation and not all of the gains of liberalism from which he himself benefited. He disagreed with Williams' critique that he found meaning outside of history only in eschatology. In Niebuhr's perspective meaning was found in history and the historical differences were decisively important. But there were promised realms of fulfillment which were better understood eschatologically for they could not be realized in history. Also he thought Williams misunderstood his attempt to distinguish mutual love from agape love.

In response to Paul Scherer's suggestions that more of the positive message of the gospel was needed, Niebuhr conceded that he had presented too pessimistic a picture of the human situation, but that the unrelieved optimism of American culture had so penetrated American Christianity as to falsify it. He was not sure how he could have preached a more positive message to have found contact with the culture without betraying the gospel. He admitted that in preaching so much on the human predicament and divine judgment that the divine mercy may not have been developed enough in his sermons.

Niebuhr believed that the greatest differences between thinkers in the volume of criticism were between himself and Professor Henry Nelson Wieman's religious naturalism. Niebuhr thought classical Christian faith preserved more dynamic places, both for the human person and for the divine person, than Wiemans' location of the divine within the process permitted. He thought Wieman drew more upon Dewey's naturalism than upon Whitehead whom he argued respected the mystery of the divine beyond the process. Elsewhere in the volume, Niebuhr indicated his respect for the metaphysics of W. E. Hocking. Several places within his writings Niebuhr affirmed the metaphysical contributions of process philosophy, but the reduction of the human drama to naturalism was an exaggeration he always resisted. I am sure Niebuhr would have chuckled at a comment I heard at an American Academy of Religion meeting in Chicago where in response to John Cobb's presentation of his political theology, it was suggested that in politics all of us process philosophers are "Children of Light."

Niebuhr's response to E. A. Burtt's questions were in part responses to Buddhism in which Burtt specialized. Niebuhr thought there was one major biblical interpretation of sin in which men surrender the image of God and worship the forms of the creatures as Paul stated in Romans 1. He conceded that he might not adequately express resources found in other religions, but he thought truth lay within the Christian presentation of the freedom of the human situation and the drama of fall and redemption of the self, rather than in the denial of the self as found in Buddhism, He had to testify to the truth he found in Christianity. To accept a religion was an existential commitment and while one hoped to be able to appreciate other traditions, one had to express the truth as one found it and committed to it. Niebuhr had referred to Burtt's questions as friendly, but Burtt really pounded him on his narrow Protestant perspective, given the wealth of the Eastern religions and philosophies. Niebuhr has in personal letters referred to his insecurity about his own teaching of the ethical traditions of non-Western religions, but I wonder why he never at least mentioned that he tried to understand and teach beyond his own Protestant faith. Niebuhr's commitments also involved him in the leadership of the doctoral study of religions at Columbia University which required the study of non-Christian religions. Burtt's challenge of activist pacifism to Niebuhr's realism, forced him to reiterate the relevance of love to political problems and the need for all sorts of discriminate responses to political issues, But Burtt's appeal to the example of Gandhi provoked Niebuhr to the starkest critique of Gandhi he made in print.

> I do not think that Gandhi, to whom Burtt refers, has taught us anything new on this perplexing problem [relating love to justice]. He made the

> pretensions of sainthood into an instrument of political power that may have seemed plausible in the environment of India, but it must be ultimately intolerable anywhere.[15]

The comment preceded King's use of active nonviolent strategies in a way reminiscent of Niebuhr's 1932 recommendation of activist nonviolence to Negroes in the manner of Gandhi. I think it was the escape from the responsibilities of making careful choices about the use of violence to protect humanity under conditions of violence that provoked Niebuhr. Generally his comments about Gandhi, after Niebuhr had abandoned pacifism, were more discriminate. In any case the religious violence which led to Gandhi's assassination and to the murderous aftermath of British withdrawal from India point not only to evil, but to the ambiguous results of nonviolent power strategies.

The final critiques that Niebuhr responded to were Jewish. Alexander J. Burnstein thought Niebuhr badly overplayed the role of sin, and presented far too dark a picture of humanity for Judaism. Niebuhr was spared the necessity of arguing with the rabbi when his friend Abraham I. Heschel presented a Jewish vision of the human as pessimistic as Niebuhr's view in a "Hebrew Evaluation of Reinhold Niebuhr." Niebuhr concluded the volume by thanking his critics and witnessing that he had learned from their labors and that he hoped to incorporate their suggestions into his work if he had a few more creative years to work. His response was, as the editors noted, after a period of grave illness in which they had not known whether they would have his contributions or not.

The bishop of New York City, H. W. B. Donegan, introduced the colloquium on Reinhold Niebuhr's thought in the Cathedral of St. John the Divine on 20 October 1961, stating that it was their purpose to honor Reinhold Niebuhr. However the three professors who spoke, Paul Tillich, John C. Bennett, and Hans J. Morgenthau, also brought criticism. Niebuhr's absence was partially due to his ill health as Roger Shinn explained, but he had also agreed to preach at Harvard that Sunday and so he stayed in Cambridge. The introduction by Harold R. Landon to the volume of essays was more honorific than the lecturers, who as Niebuhr's longtime friends, brought their critiques as well as their tributes. He thought it was the combination of Niebuhr and Tillich in the 1930s that balanced European theologies appeal with the American. The theological atmosphere of the days of their partnership was very heady and the times called out for their theological responses. Niebuhr exposed human sin more clearly than anyone else in the season of anxiety in economic depression, Nazism, and war. In Landon's presentation sin was balanced by grace. Though Niebuhr would not move into Landon's full Episcopalian affirmation of the church, he thought no one had served the church better. Of course the reality of sin prevented Niebuhr from affirming a full vision of a good society or the highest sentiments about the church. Still he knew the church was where the preached word could witness to Christ and equip Christians for their worldly vocations.

Commenting on the partnership between Tillich and Niebuhr, he regarded them as closer than most supposed at the very heart of their theologies. Both knew they had faith, but they acknowledged they had it only imperfectly. They recognized one lived by grace and not possession of the divine or the full truth. Their task was to point toward Jesus as the Christ and not to claim that they had the final truth. Landon did not want to resolve their differences over ontological language, and he asserted perhaps they both were right. The use of ontology might create a more consistent position, but it might also obscure moral responsibility. His closing words were an introduction to the person:

> Reinhold Niebuhr was for more than thirty years a teacher, and part of the rich legacy he left behind is a whole generation of students who remember him most of all as a human being so free of pretence, so honest in soul. So humble in mind, so reverent in spirit. His sister, Hulda, has a book of stories for children with the title *Greatness Passing By*. The participants in the Reinhold Niebuhr Colloquium, as well as countless men and women who knew and loved Reinhold Niebuhr apply to him the words of John Drinkwater's poem. "Those who worship greatness passing by are themselves great." Those of us who knew and loved Reinhold Niebuhr knew a great human being who changed theology and spoke with the power of a prophet in our time.'[16]

Tillich spoke intimately and forcefully of Niebuhr beginning with Niebuhr's invitation to him to come to New York, and of Ursula meeting them at the apartment which Union professors had furnished with some of their own furniture. He recounted how for two years while Reinhold was writing *The Nature and Destiny of Man* they walked and discussed the issues of the volumes. According to Tillich they lived nearly together, walked together, and talked together. Gradually their differences became more apparent as Niebuhr's social-ethical passions distinguished him from Tillich whose classical philosophical interests were developing in relation to psychological health. Tillich decided to talk mostly about their understanding of human nature on which they basically agreed. Tillich had tried to develop a middle way between the utopianism of Social Democracy and Lutheran transcendentalism, but Hitler had ended that stage. Later on in Europe it was partially realized. Meanwhile Niebuhr was revolutionizing American theology with his attacks on the optimism of the Social Gospel and liberalism. As they started to systematize their thought the differences became clear. He wanted Niebuhr to rely more on rational thought rather than to lean so heavily upon biblical symbols. He thought to make the symbols intelligible required ontology or a philosophy of being. He thought Niebuhr presupposed some ontology like Tillich drew from Heidegger, but Niebuhr would never admit it. He thought from their most recent conversation in July that Niebuhr was also moving away from the term "original sin" toward universal estrangement. Tillich welcomed this. He also said he appreciated Niebuhr's coming to see that words of grace were needed by modern humans more than descriptions of sin and the human predicament. He praised Niebuhr for being willing to change while still keeping to his basic position with which Tillich agreed. He also criticized Niebuhr for not appreciating more the connections between the human and nature. He thought Niebuhr often did not respect the context of various philosophers' thought. Niebuhr needed to see them more in their own time and to appreciate their contexts to become more appreciative. "But it was a great experience and decisive for my own development to have this ever ongoing talk with him as a friend."[17]

Professors John Hutchison, Willhelm Pauck, and Richard Kroner all defended Niebuhr from the need to use Tillich's systematic ontology. Daniel D. Williams also questioned him on his ontology, and thought Niebuhr was not devaluing reason, but starting with revelation. Tillich took the opportunity to contrast his way with Karl Barth's method which started from revelation while Tillich tried to start from below in the human experience as, Barth's daughter had pointed out recently.

On further reflection. Tillich said Niebuhr made his impact in criticism of the culture with his doctrine of sin. It was timely. One needed to be consistent, but what was consistently worked out did not make the impact. One speaks to the situation and Niebuhr hit the situation directly. The force with which one is received depends not only on what is said, but also where the listeners reside. To John MacKay he admitted he and Niebuhr were in the same boat in that they confessed justification through faith while still remaining sinners. There is a new being in Christ, but even if the divine spirit is working in us we cannot claim to possess it. If MacKay meant to be critical in his question of Niebuhr, it applied to his own thought as well, Tillich said.

John C. Bennett's lecture "Reinhold Niebuhr's Contribution to Christian Ethics" carefully discussed Niebuhr's doctrine of the human and his contribution to the formation of norms. Bennett when questioned indicated sometimes he could not distinguish his thought from Niebuhr's judgments. One commentator has indicated the works of Bennett's later evolved intellectual life appeared as if Reinhold had lived another twenty-four years. He emphasized especially Niebuhr's social activism, as he worked constantly to found and nuture institutions; he was not simply an academic. Additionally his life as a professional teacher, fifteen years as a minister, and one who continued to preach while teaching needed emphasis. However, his journalism has not been adequately appreciated as he labored robustly to turn out several editorials, reviews, essays, and comments each week. After praising his colleague and explaining him, he raised three questions for Niebuhr's further work noting how Niebuhr's thought kept changing. (1) Could Niebuhr develop more resources to provide hope and morale for people in the struggle for social justice? (2) Could Niebuhr or people who share his general outlook return to the questions of economic justice that had characterized Niebuhr's work as a socialist? His recent attention to political issues overshadowed the need for thought on economic issues. (3) Is there is a need for more development of social ethics to provide norms rather than drifting into an adjunct of the defense of the American republic? Bennett explicated this in reference to the dangers of nuclear war. Bennett noted that Niebuhr had agreed with Tillich's recent refusal to justify a nuclear defense of Berlin.[18]

Wilhelm Pauck pushed the usual criticism that Niebuhr's doctrine of the church seemed undeveloped. Pauck noted that Tillich and Niebuhr belonged to the same church, the United Church of Christ, without mentioning that he belonged there also. Bennett responded in terms of Niebuhr's activity in the church and that Niebuhr believed the church was where the word of grace was preached and that the church bore the revelation. Pauck thought his doctrine of the church was "strangely spiritual" and that it conflicted with his real activity. Jacob Taubes reflecting his own skepticism did not find enough Christian structure in his thought. Others asked for more of a social vision and Bennett's suggestion that a final solution vision was not possible for Niebuhr's thought did not satisfy the critics. Paul Tillich thanked John Bennett for correcting the one-sided polemic against Communism that Niebuhr provided in the pages of *Christianity and Crisis*. It was noted that Niebuhr's thought because of its Cold War edge was not of help to people behind the Iron Curtain. Bennett agreed that Niebuhr's thought was closely associated with advising and in thinking about politics for the American scene in a time of Cold War crisis. Hans J. Morgenthau would later say that it was of the nature of politics that great political philosophy was related to particular contingent political problems, and that to state that Niebuhr was closely related to the Cold War was no political criticism at all.

Morgenthau's own paper was entitled "The influence of Reinhold Niebuhr in American Political Life and Thought." He gave Niebuhr the credit for establishing the relevance of the political humans' inevitable struggle for power which he thought had been neglected in American political thought. Niebuhr's awareness of the limits of the political mind and his suspicions of politics as a science were important contributions to human thought. The contingencies of history and the freedom of the human actor made reliable prediction impossible. For example, our knowledge of what Khrushchev would initiate over the Berlin problem was largely a matter of historically informed hunches. We neither understood the actions of our opponents nor the outcomes of our own actions. Consequently the refusal of Niebuhr to provide a vision or a social blueprint was a virtue; it was better to work pragmatically from case to case. Historically visions usually were not fulfilled and they could often provoke tragedies as in the recent cases of Nazism and Communism. Morgenthau thought Niebuhr's book *The Structure of Nations and Empires* was particularly helpful on the role of ideology in international politics. He concluded by saying, "Let me say in conclusion that I have always considered Reinhold Niebuhr the greatest living political philosopher of America, perhaps the only creative political philosopher since Calhoun."[19]

Later Niebuhr responded to his friend's criticism humbly:

> One suspects that friendship has dulled their critical faculties, or that they have concluded that a colloquium about the thought of an aged colleague is so much like a funeral that the axiom applies: "About the dead speak nothing but good."[20]

He thought Bennett presented his thought more systematically than he could, and he wondered if the organizational life he had undertaken had kept him from the harder scholastic life. He admitted to feelings of inferiority among real scholars. He did not want to move into Tillich's Platonic or Neoplatonic description of human sin as the movement from essence to existence. He preferred a description such as describing "the paradox of the human freedom and its corruption by the mastery of the anxious self over the rational capacities." Modern humanity like Enlightenment philosophers too easily regarded the rational faculties as masters rather than as servants of the self. He and Morgenthau basically agreed, but Morgenthau's contrast between Christian life and political life was a little too extreme. The Christian politician had to live by relative standards of justice and not only by the absolutes of the Sermon on the Mount. The community, after all, had a right to protection. He was concerned to describe the moral ambiguities of politics in a manner that does not eliminate the moral realities. He refused to provide the general principles Eduard Heimann asked for or the visions other critics requested. He described himself as a pragmatist who tried to be guided by principles as they evolved in Western political philosophy: "A Christian engaged in political philosophy can do no more than to seek to prevent premature solutions of insoluble problems, hoping that time will make some solutions possible tomorrow which are not possible today."[21]

The paragraph, though, given in general terms was his response to the Cold War in 1961. Let's act so as to live through it so that in the future solutions to the problem may present themselves. In 1961, neither premature retreat from involvement nor war, as some advocated, were responsible.

Democratic Socialist Criticism

The democratic-socialist criticism of Niebuhr was generally more sympathetic to Karl Marx's thought than Niebuhr. They had more far-reaching changes for the social direction of the United States than Niebuhr advocated in his later days. Many of them disagreed with Niebuhr's interpretation and criticism of Marx. They tended to be more enthusiastic than Niebuhr about socialist revolution in the Third World, and they thought his support for the United States in the Cold War was over done. Cornell West, who advocated a democratic-socialist, revolutionary stance, is in some ways representative of the democratic-socialist criticism. The issues are somewhat subtle when Niebuhr is carefully read and the neoconservative appropriation of some of his themes is dismissed as a misunderstanding of his politics. His great admirers in England were members of the Labour government, not the Tory party. He was not an establishment Democrat, but a member of the Liberal Party of New York State. His followers in the Democratic Party were on the left wing: Hubert Humphrey, Birch Bayh, Adlai Stevenson, and Arthur Schlesinger, Jr. The two presidents who claimed him as their philosophic mentor, Jimmy Carter and Barack Obama, were progressive though they recognized the need to govern from the center-left.

Those closest to Niebuhr would have been sympathetic to the left-wing coalition that Cornell West dreamed about. While West may not advocate nationalization of the major means of production, specific recommendations as issues for the left now were unemployment, national health care, maldistribution of wealth and taxation issues, and finally the elevation of the issues of homelessness and poverty to the status of moral issues exposing the control of the business class. Niebuhr's writings address all of these concerns without the heightened consciousness of class or race which give punch to West's rhetoric.[22] Their differences might have led them to vote differently in primaries, but probably not in national elections.

For my own part, I doubt that I would have voted differently from West in the primaries either. When I was writing a book criticizing the United States' policies of counterrevolution in the early 1970s it never occurred to me that academics would regard Niebuhr as anti-revolution per se.[23] He had opposed the most recent intervention by the U.S.A. in the Dominican Republic, and did not seem to be justifying the U.S. domination of Latin America, as West asserts. His writing was critical of the feudal economic structures of Latin America and during the Kennedy administration he was advocating thorough change in Latin America if not supporting socialist revolution ideologically. He was certainly too optimistic about what the Alliance for Progress could ever achieve, but accusing Niebuhr of being too optimistic is not a staple of the socialist-democratic critique.

On rhetoric: West is certainly moralistic and passionate in his outrage whereas Niebuhr's writing often has a coolness and a distance that is quite different from West. In part it is the difference in preaching in white mainline pulpits and black church pulpits that one would suspect from two Christian preachers. A respect for the Stoic contribution to Christian social ethics is even reflected in his powerful "Serenity prayer," "God give us grace to accept with serenity things we cannot change." Beyond the differences in rhetoric, West's suggestion that Niebuhr's British marriage influenced his Eurocentrism would have to be qualified by West's admitting that he writes such sentences from his African marriage perspective biasing his critique from an Afrocentric position.

There simply is no doubt that Niebuhr's home and love is in Western civilization and that is the source of his ideas. I think West is in error to portray Niebuhr's dialectic as between ideology and realism, certainly it was between idealism and realism and both are to a degree ideological. A revolutionary-democratic socialist position is ideological as is Niebuhr's Christian-pragmatic realism. West doubts that the concepts of balance of power and national interest are free of ideology, and I think they are used ideologically and the values employed by those who use them are crucial. But certainly Niebuhr, Kennan, and Morgenthau are correct that it is a U.S. national interest to prohibit any hostile power from dominating Europe.

Niebuhr and West agree that America began to replace England as a world power following World War I and that this American hegemony was partially realized after World War II, though never completed. West resists this hegemony. Niebuhr thinks it devolved on the U.S.A. due to weakness in most of the previously dominant powers after World War II and the need to resist Russian expansion. Niebuhr assumes American dominance in his lifetime and West advocates its overthrow. West correctly understands Niebuhr as Eurocentric including America in his perspective, and I think West's perspective is more inclusive of the Third World democratic-socialist perspective.

Time has perhaps passed by West's 1987 critique. The Cold War ended with the collapse of Marxism. I witnessed this in Prague in 1983, when a member of the Russian Academy of Sciences in a dialogue with me on the radio could no longer defend scientific Marxism. His colleagues from Eastern Europe around the lunch table in a Communist-run labor retreat center made fun of Marxist economics. Two years earlier in India my advocacy of a mixed economy for India's human economic development was ridiculed by Marxist colleagues at our college as only a view of a "mixed-up economy." Shortly before the fall of the wall, an East German economist took me around Berlin to show me the empty shelves of grocery stores and said our economy isn't working. While Niebuhr had criticized Marxism as bad religion and bad politics, in the end its economics did not work either.

The Cold War concluded earlier than Morgenthau and Niebuhr believed it would, approximately on George Kennan's "Mr. X" essay's schedule. It concluded with their predictions of Marxist collapse. There were terrible casualties in the Cold War, but though there was evil perpetrated on the Western side of the divide, millions were killed within Communist societies and millions of others were treated inhumanely. The realists resisted both those who argued for "Red or Dead" arguing for and contributing to an ideological struggle and for limited, necessary military responses. The conclusion of the Cold War has to be accepted as an American success even though the reasons for its concluding were due to Russian failures. The technology of warfare and the ideological differences between the two competing empires were developed to the point of making a war likely as it was in Berlin in 1961, and Cuba in 1962. It is not academically honest to criticize Christian realists for wars they actually opposed, like Vietnam, even if others used some of their ideas in new frameworks to support those struggles. As West suggests it is the foreign policy differences that divide some of the liberals on left from those more influenced by Marxism, and even cause the liberals within the democratic left to divide.

West chooses as his case for Niebuhr's "ignorance" and "blindness" his support of Israel. Here, as argued earlier, Niebuhr noted that the Palestinians would suffer, and he suggested some plans to alleviate that suffering and contribute to Arab development. The plans were not ever developed by governments. Niebuhr may have been too hopeful about Israeli prudence, and not known about intentions of the founders to take all of Palestine at the expense of the Arabs. Neither Tillich nor Niebuhr foresaw the stubborn Arab resistance to their displacement. Within the Americas, it has taken unto the present day for Europeans to subdue the Native Americans. Tillich did not write about American history, but it is sad that Niebuhr's writing is lacking in any reflection on this American tragedy. The tale of the Palestinians under Israel's half-century occupation resembles in many ways the tragedy of the American Indian who lost the land whether one submitted nonviolently, fought organized wars, attempted legal recourse, or engaged in terrorist resistance. The difference is the Arabs within Israel, in Gaza, and in the West Bank equal in population the Israelis so they cannot be so simply displaced. Their numbers, including the Diaspora, outnumber the Jews in Palestine, though I believe including the numbers in the Jewish Diaspora would outnumber the Arabs from Palestine and their descendants. Niebuhr's very early support of a Jewish homeland eventually became U.S. policy, but there is nothing inherent in Niebuhr's political philosophy that does not permit sympathy for justice for the Arabs evolving to sharp critique of Israel and pressures against the Israeli occupation.

Oscar Cole Arnal, a Canadian socialist professor, regretted Niebuhr's later politics of realist compromise.[24] He preferred the earlier socialist Niebuhr and he feared Niebuhr had lost the transforming edge of the gospel. Niebuhr, for Arnal, had been too locked into his politics of the sinful actor and not aware enough of the power of peace, reconciliation, and transformation of the gospel. Arnel preferred the more radical politics of elements of the Francophone Catholics of Quebec. He thought of Niebuhr as a great social-activist prophet. However, his doctrine of sin, used to criticize both the oppressor and the revolutionary, too easily reinforced the status quo. Arnal, given his Canadian experience as a socialist, deplored Niebuhr's defense of middle-class democracy and especially his role as an interpreter of America's need to contend against Russia in the Cold War. He also thought that Niebuhr too easily surrendered to America's support for non-democracies against the Soviet Union. He wrote that Niebuhr was overly critical of the social gains in Russia and Eastern Europe under Communism. Though he identified his critique as a socialist one in the essay, he failed to criticize Niebuhr's support for a pragmatic mixed economic model that post-New Deal and Canadian reforms developed on the continent. Arnal praised the more radical communitarian efforts of liberation theology and movements led by socialist priests in Canada. Niebuhr's preference for pragmatic compromise owed a great deal to Ernst Troeltsch who taught compromise was of the essence of Christianity's dealing with politics.

Paul Merkley, another Canadian socialist scholar provided the most complete account of Niebuhr's political activity to the date of its publication in 1975. He regarded Niebuhr as the important political thinker of the 1940–1950s, and as the outstanding American theologian who improved substantially upon the Europeans. He stressed his various roles in advising government, basing some of his conclusions upon an interview with Niebuhr in 1962. However, as a socialist, he thought Niebuhr became too complacent during the Cold War about the achievement of social justice in the United States. When Niebuhr referred to a tolerable social justice being achieved he was referring to the power of the union movement and the living standards achieved by the manufacturing and unionized class of workers. Merkeley knew Niebuhr never gave up his mixed economic preferences from *The Children of Light and the Children of Darkness*, but during the Korean War period his Cold-War positions hardened and he became complacent about the brokered understandings between the strong union movements and the owner class. He regarded Niebuhr's role in turning his small Union for Democratic Action into the larger and more powerful Americans for Democratic Action as brilliant, and he credited Niebuhr with a large role in helping ex-socialists move into the Liberal Party of New York State which provided a place for some unions and also for ex-socialist intellectuals. Even in the earlier *Children of Light* he had moved into piecemeal socialist reforms rather than dreaming of a socialist election victory. In Niebuhr's estimate the forces of bourgeois ownership and individualism were much stronger in the United States than in Europe. Merkley criticized Niebuhr for abusing the term *socialist*, but he also wrote that Niebuhr did not surrender his goals of piecemeal socialist reform. He noted that Niebuhr's de-emphasis upon socialism was in part due to his greater focus on nuclear competition and the Cold War. He recognized that Niebuhr after his strokes was confined to many less hours of work, and that his fame grew about the same time he had less energy to push through to new conclusions. On the subject of the movement away from socialism, Merkley concluded:

> For Niebuhr it would be too late in the day for reinstatement on the left—though that is where his heart was in the end. The frailty of his health in the sixties excluded any opportunity for more than a few gestures of revision of his long-published opinions.[25]

Niebuhr's criticism of socialism is like his criticism of liberalism, it is a movement in which he retains great stock. But neither was adequate for guiding foreign policy and both had suffered from illusions. The frequent refrain of liberals or socialists that Niebuhr needed to develop a vision of public virtue (Richard Fox) or the common good, or a social vision (Rosemary Reuther) were all mistaken. Society, like the individual, remained fallen; the modest transformations for the good that could be won were still subject to human corruption. Democracy could receive Christian support as a solid option for human and Christian lives. It was worth defending and giving one's life for, but it remained subject to many abuses and in its American form it needlessly encouraged human underdevelopment. Niebuhr was not so interested in projections of either human perfection or social fulfillment, but in working out human duties as they were understood from the position of the love-justice dialectic in a world in disarray. Merkley understood that Niebuhr's theology expressed in his politics provided a way for a human life engaged in the lifelong struggle for justice without needing to succumb to illusions.

Beverly Harrison developed one of the most serious critiques of Niebuhr from her neo-Marxist, socialist theoretical base. Her work is original and influential in her doctoral students and their ongoing roles in American academia. She was a student in Niebuhr's classes a few years earlier than I, and she knew a younger, stronger Niebuhr than the man I knew personally. Her evaluation of Niebuhr's teaching was much more critical than most of the students who responded to my earlier survey of his Union Theological Seminary students. Many years after taking his course on "Christianity and Communism" she was particularly critical of the course, but said having the previous Russian Prime Minister A. F. Kerenski in the class made it worth the price of admission..

Harrison, like Niebuhr, states her criticisms strongly, and the reader must be careful not to overreact to her biting use of language which is partially fueled by her anger over the oppression of her gender. An example might be "Niebuhr was then also prototypical liberal male chauvinist" or "Like many a male ethicist, Niebuhr, romanticized the family."[26] The historical situation does affect these judgments as Niebuhr in his lifetime saw women win the vote, and improve their roles in the economy. She has read about his hoping for more gender equality in the church, but she does not quote him on these subjects; also she needed to analyze his criticism of his friend Archbishop Temple's rejection of women's ordination in the Anglican Communion, and explain more fully the disagreement with Barth over women's ordination. He did comment on unjust power relations within the family, even if he thought the woman's capacity to bear and nurse children affected their roles significantly. The fact that his own family relations were so good did incline both him and his wife to comment very favorably on family life, but he also new of the chaos of family through the suffering of relatives, and the many persons he counseled. He resisted overly rationalistic feminist criticism as he resisted overly rationalistic social theory in general.

Harrison is correct that Niebuhr favored political theory over sociology for understanding the human situation. I think her development of the relevance of recent sociological theory for Christian social ethics and his reliance on political theory is fundamental to their differences and also to some extent to the differences between Reinhold Niebuhr and his much more sociologically influenced brother, Helmut Richard. Harrison and Reinhold Niebuhr do not usually quote the same sources.

Harrison tends to announce her conclusions on Niebuhr and Marx rather than to show the work behind the conclusions, though her footnotes refer to the work of her doctoral students on the subject. My early essays on Marx were influenced by study of Marx at Oxford under John Plamenatz and Isaiah Berlin while reading the works of Marx as well as Bennett and Niebuhr at Union.[27] My impressions of Marxism come from dialogue with self-described Marxist philosophers and activists in Eastern Europe (Christian Peace Conference), Asia (Syrian government officials and Chinese), Latin America (Liberation theologians and activists in Peru, Chile, Argentina, Mexico, and Brazil) and these sources are different than Harrison's. Our perspectives are necessarily different. Maybe her sources are better, but I think she is overly critical of Niebuhr.

Her claim that Niebuhr's use of political power is ahistorical is not supported by the sources in the footnote referring to books edited by Landon, a comment by Bennett, one of my books, and Hoffmann's critique. There are various criticisms of realism in those books, but not that he is ahistorical. Her doctoral students have repeated the criticism that Niebuhr is ahistorical, and I have never been able to figure out what they have meant as I know of no ethicist who has written so much, so critically about history. There is no intention here to defend everything Niebuhr has said about history or to deny he often speaks abstractly without providing full contextual references, but there is a lot of history in his writings, and he probably has had more following in American historigraphical discussions than any other philosopher of religion.

She is mistaken in her repetition that Niebuhr's mature positions were at "the middle of the political spectrum" or at the "service of the middle-of-the-road reform"[28] unless she is considering Stalin's agricultural purges, and Mao's "cultural revolution" to represent one end of the spectrum. Niebuhr's later recommendations of socialized health care, negative income tax, heavy taxes on the wealthy, regulation of corporations by political policies, divestment from corporations profiting from South Africa, use of boycotts for integration, support for civil disobedience vis-à-vis U.S. policy do not appear to be middle of the road in American politics. Americans for Democratic Action and the Liberal Party are not usually considered as middle of the political spectrum. J. Edgar Hoover's representation of Niebuhr as a "Christian Revolutionary" was overdone, but middle-of the-road is not fair.

Harrison's criticism that Niebuhr did not enter deeply into Marx's criticism of religion is a good point. Though, even here, some qualification is needed as he provided the longest lasting introduction to the writings of Marx on religion for a generation of students. I included that essay of his on Marx to show that Marx was one of his sources in the last edited volume of his writings which he approved.[29]

Care in this discussion is needed because a journal in South Africa has published essays credited to Niebuhr on Adam Smith and Karl Marx and of the two of them on religion which he did not write. The essays were found in the Niebuhr papers in the Library of Congress and the editor assumed they were by Niebuhr. Though the style of writing and sources used are very un-Niebuhrian they published them under his name which is not on the manuscripts.[30]

Harrison is entering into a methodological debate with Niebuhr, while he was entering into an ideological debate during the Cold War hoping to discredit the intellectual underpinnings of a dangerous nuclear-armed opponent. She can call attention to the economic achievement of Russia and China under their forms of economy that Niebuhr neglected. In hindsight Niebuhr's neglect of any economic gains under collectivism in those two countries was probably wise, as one economy collapsed and the other had to radically change. The cruelty of the agricultural policies of Stalin and the Great Leap Forward of Mao must not be ignored when discussing economic gains. Their issues are different. She is correct, I think, that Niebuhr saw Marx as representing a form of "scientific positivism," though I do not remember that he ever used that term for Marx. But even if she is correct, many of the Marxists that I had dialogue with have represented Marxism as the final form of economic science. We do not agree on whether Marx had a philosophy of history. I think both Niebuhr and Marx regarded history philosophically and that both were also empiricists. Karl Marx's *Grundrisse*[31] is widely interpreted as a philosophy of history and for that matter Niebuhr read the early *Economic-Philosophic Manuscripts* of 1844 as philosophy of history.

She is certainly correct that Niebuhr was a critic of sociology, but not as acute a critic as she is of Max Weber whom Niebuhr trusted somewhat. Niebuhr adapted Marx's notion of ideological distortion of social theory to his later view of human sin coloring every theory for the self-interest it protected, and so continued to use some of Marx's mind in his own reflections without, in the later years, giving Marx credit. I do not know whether Harrison would agree here or whether she would find it interesting. In our last brief exchange on Marxism, I found liberation theologians I met in South America to be heavily influenced by Marxism, and she disagreed. It is certainly true of our mutual friend Gustavo Gutierrez whose *Liberation and Change*[32] reflects the thought of Karl Marx he learned in Louvain University and also in its indigenous form in Peru. Professor Larry Rasmussen, Harrison's colleague, summarized her criticisms of Niebuhr on Marx in his introduction to *Reinhold Niebuhr: Theologian of Public Life*[33] while admitting there was much to be debated in this matter. While Niebuhr in the 1930s would describe himself as both a Marxist and a Christian, his scholarship on Christianity was far the deeper of the two subjects. In a letter to me in 1971 he referred to *The End of an Era* as his most Marxist book and disassociated himself from its arguments. The predominance of the Christian thought in his mind, along with the remnants of liberalism untouched by his Marxism would soon dissolve his Marxist apocalyptic thoughts, and he became a severe critic of Marxism.

Critics of Niebuhr on the Cold War

The murderous reign of Stalin, the reforms of Roosevelt, and the Stalin-Hitler pact of 1939 freed Niebuhr to deepen his criticism of the Soviet Union. His senior colleague Harry Ward persisted in his appreciation of the Soviet Union while Niebuhr as early as late 1946 was becoming very critical. During the Cold War he was both anti-Marxist and anti-Communist. His anti-Communist polemics fit the religious agenda of the American administrations to enlist religion in the fight against Communism. Despite the disarray of the religious opinion about issues of the Cold War, all administrations tried to enlist religious forces against atheistic Communism, and most helped. William Imboden's recent book *Religion and American Foreign Policy, 1945–1960: The Soul of Containment*[34] explicates the many intersections of power and religion that characterized the Cold War. Niebuhr's problem with Marxism was at its heart a theological issue. The Cold War was to a great degree a religious struggle for many of the most prominent American cold warriors. The book contains many aspects of the religious struggle that we would not have learned in Niebuhr's "Christianity and Communism" course including Stalin's instructions to Andre Gromyko as Russian ambassador to attend American worship services each Sunday to find out what was going on in the country. In Niebuhr's case the use of his thought by cold warriors served the mutual interests of the U.S. government and Niebuhr's own agenda of contending with Communism. Of course, it did not interfere with Niebuhr's polemicizing about the need to recognize China or to oppose the Vietnam War.

A political scientist from New Zealand weighs Niebuhr's influence very heavily in rallying American support for Cold-War policies. Even more than Hans Morgenthau, he regards Niebuhr as the leading spokesman persuading policymakers as opposed to political scientists to follow political realism in dealing with the Soviet Union. Campbell Craig thought Niebuhr's realism collapsed under the pressure of the probability of thermonuclear warfare. Craig believed that realism required the willingness to go to total war for the sake of national defense. Niebuhr's argument for the development of the hydrogen bomb to counter the probability of Russian similar development and his unwillingness to renounce nuclear deterrence implied to Craig total-war realism. Obviously Niebuhr rejected nuclear war as immoral in his developed position so he must have scrapped his realism.[35] As the dilemma came upon the older, suffering Niebuhr, he could not think his way through the quandary with his realism according to Craig. Actually Christian realism for Niebuhr did not justify total war, and Niebuhr was much less of a just war theoretician than Craig imagined. Niebuhr and Bennett criticized bombardment of cities in the total war of 1939–1945. They rejected "unconditional surrender" demands and criticized the bombing of Hiroshima and Nagasaki as discussed in chapter 13. Regarding later developments they argued for no first use of nuclear weapons in opposition to U.S. government policy and they became critical of planning for limited nuclear war.

Niebuhr hoped that deterrence and diplomacy would enable the U.S. to blunder through the Cold War until Communism waned and Russia changed. Despite the dangers of nuclear war in Berlin (1961) and Cuba (1962) wise heads prevailed and nuclear stalemate revealed its strengths to contain a risk-taking Nikita Khrushchev. Gorbachev and Reagan hoped for total nuclear disarmament, but that was illusory. Gradually the major stockpiles were somewhat reduced under the umbrella of nuclear cooperation. Niebuhr never surrendered to

Campbell's world-government vision of Thomas Hobbes's new Leviathan emerging out of fear of nuclear war

Niebuhr's friend Hans Morgenthau made dreamy statements of such an outcome. Paul Tillich refusing the utopianism of Campbell and others had foreseen formations of nations federating or the possibility of a liberal-democracy domination of the world. The federation eventually appeared in Europe, but the Soviet Union's imperial federation broke up. Both corporate power and international terrorist alliances would challenge the nation-state models, but in our time the world structure features three significant empires, and nation-states organized in loose regional organizations, and weaker international organizations. Niebuhr's book title of *The Structure of Nations and Empires* captures our current political reality when the modifying influence of corporations and organizations is recognized. The economic realities are tending to shift toward international corporation dominance, but in the empires of China and Russia the state still dominates, and in the recent American economic crisis, the role of the government was decisive in rescue. The fourth center of power, the European Union, still exhibits pluralistic decision making, with the French and German governments featured as dominant actors.

Kenneth Thompson usually sided with Morgenthau in the *Christianity and Crisis* debates. He urged John C. Bennett to be a little more cautious in his moral judgments. He saw Niebuhr becoming a less strident cold warrior after the Korean War even though he had less enthusiasm than Morgenthau and Lippmann about rapprochement with the Soviet Union over Germany early in the Cold War. Niebuhr, according to Thompson used national interest as the realists did, but he had a broader view including the country's goals and moral values than Morgenthau. Gradually, he came to appreciate the possibility of change in the Soviet Union, though he did not live to see the thoroughgoing change. He recognized Niebuhr's influence on the realist theoreticians E. H. Carr and Hans Morgenthau and that it was less on George Kennan and Hubert Butterfield. Thompson's view that Niebuhr is still widely used in international relations studies differs from my perspective and information that realism as a whole and Niebuhr in particular are used much less in international relations studies than previously. Thompson draws his evidence from his own students and it is natural that they would be more inclined than most students toward Niebuhr, because Thompson is now more of a devotee than a critic. His point that more dissertations are written on Niebuhr than other figures is, I suspect, accurate, but I cannot corroborate his evidence on this point. Thompson recalls Niebuhr's presence among practioners and scholars of international relations, and also how he used material from many meetings to advance and modify his views. He quoted Walter Lippmann as saying after a Washington conference on theories of international relations in which the elderly Niebuhr had participated: "How many generations will it be before we see his equal again."[36]

Previous books have concerned critiques of realism by Stanley Hoffmann, Raymond Aron, Kenneth Waltz, and others.[37] Recognition is needed that realism in its various forms has not dominated international relations studies since the end of the Cold War. Realism was thought of in American history during times of conflict with threatening forms of totalitarianism and to that degree was most relevant to those times of conflict. Its relevance to the conflicts of the present will be explored in the discussion of its legacy. One major effort to refine the thought of those realists identified with Niebuhr, Carr, Morgenthau, and, interestingly, Isaiah Berlin has been seen in the work of the Australian political scientist Roger D. Spegele. He was neither impressed with the work of the positivist social scientists who regarded themselves as realists nor the revolutionary or emancipatory realists. He articulated what he thought was an improvement over the common sense realists mentioned above.

Spegele developed four theses: (1) The state and state-system are the fundamental realities to be investigated by international relations; (2) biological evolution of the human animal needs to be given a more prominent place in international relations; (3) a modest conception of historical research is needed for international relations studies; and (4) the moral and non-moral variables need to be considered in international relations.[38] He accepts the common sense realist view of state interaction and is asking for a realistic moral perspective to inform it. He accepts pluralism, but wants to avoid the nihilism of absolute relativism. Niebuhr or Tillich would only reject his heavy weight on the biological sciences; they assumed them, but the interesting factors for them as for Spegele were in the human realm. There is no major fight, he just had not made much use of Niebuhr's writings on human nature and history. His view remained traditional value-oriented realism as was the Christian realism of Niebuhr. Evaluative realism seems to me to be equivalent to what elsewhere has been described as moral realism or that which I have developed using the Jewish Morgenthau and the Christian Niebuhr as prophetic realism.[39]

The development of international relations since Niebuhr inclines me to think he could have been more open to positive changes than he revealed. The Irish-British questions of Northern Ireland seem to have been relaxed, the Soviet Union collapsed sooner than he would have thought, and apartheid came to a peaceful end in South Africa. He has admitted that some of his prognostication was too pessimistic. As discussed earlier, this was partially due to the times, partially to a family tendency toward depression, the depression of his health for nineteen years, and partially because of the need to awaken America from its illusions of progress, superiority, and prosperity. Still as a moral philosopher he was committed to the reform of human conduct. The judgment of his dear friend, interpreter, and student Robert MacAfee Brown that he was really a pessimist-optimist deserves respect. His views of politics were dependent ultimately on his theological convictions and these contain at least one major lacuna. He neglected to develop the doctrine of the Holy Spirit which is what the spiritual reality of the universe can unleash when it is realized in its human agents. In the three positive surprises mentioned—Ireland, Russia, and South Africa—religious forces and human agents inspired by Christ were active as well as material economic factors and material power considerations. His colleague Paul Tillich developed the doctrine of the Holy Spirit in its relationship to the human phenomenon very completely in his theology, and our argument now turns toward the criticism of Tillich's politics and its theological support.

24

Criticism of Tillich on Faith and Politics

In hindsight the criticism of Tillich's "Ten Theses on the Church and the Third Reich" by Hitler's philosophic henchmen in 1933 makes Tillich appear heroic. He was among the earliest of the Christian theologians to defy Hitler on the grounds of Christian theology. His record as a religious-socialist theoretician and journalist resulted in his very early removal in 1933 from his position as dean of the faculty and professor of Philosophy and Sociology at Frankfurt. The brief interlude in which he sought to find an alternative position in Germany for resistance was dangerous, and his colleague Max Horkheimer had told him that his book, *The Socialist Decision*, would cost him his life. The burning of the book by his opponents represents a consequence that social critics and theologians in the United States have not had to face. His philosophy of religious socialism was defeated in Germany and while he found a home for it for a few years in Reinhold Niebuhr's Fellowship of Socialist Christians, the evolution of that group towards reformist politics following World War II left Tillich without a social base for this thought. As he failed to find a revolutionary proletariat in the United States, religious socialism remained a vision for him, but not a political program. The idea of religious socialism was related to several other central concepts of his thought: the demonic, the Kairos, and eschatology. These would be present in his *Systematic Theology* without connections to religious socialism. The lack of religious socialism in his later written works and his tendency to develop the relations of psychology to theology was regarded as something of a failure by John Stumme, John Marsden, Eduard Heimann, Jose Miguez Bonino, and many others who had appreciated the contribution of his religious-socialist writings.

Liberation theology, particularly in its Latin American varieties continued to express socialism related to religion, but they tended to ignore the possible connections between their work and the earlier work of Tillich. The use of his doctrine of the Kairos as a unique time where something of the eternal of decisive social importance breaks into finite human history has been used by religious groups opposing oppression. The Presbyterian Church (U.S.A.) utilized it in 1980 to oppose militarism and nuclearism; it was echoed in South Africa by Christians against apartheid, and then in Central America by Christians opposed to North American dominance, and in 2009 by Christians in Palestine in opposition to Israel's occupation oppression. Several formally Christian-focused countries in Europe have moved into largely socialist practices which have received Christian support and opposition. Israel began as a socialist state with religious support as well as secular Zionist support. India's socialism has been supported by Gandhian and explicitly Hindu forces. Even in the most capitalist country of the United States, policies once regarded as socialist receive the support of churches as well as opposition from Christians. Those supportive of explicitly socialist policies may wish that Tillich could have continued his philosophy of religious socialism in more developed writings. But one socialist friend, Adolf Lowe, saw it differently. He said "God wanted Tillich to write his theology." That was the way Tillich also saw it and he produced for his host country his *Systematic Theology* in his later years.

It can be said that Niebuhr's major contributions after his stroke in 1952 were in the fields of democratic politics, U.S. foreign policy, and in elaborating a platform of reformist politics through U.D.A., A.D.A., the Liberal Party, *Christianity and Crisis*, and so forth. Whereas, Tillich was contributing especially in his writing and speaking to the strengthening of religious faith in his last years at Union Seminary and after his retirement in 1955. He continued after leaving Union to speak out on civil liberties, against nuclear weapons, and against the conditions of modernity that reduced humanity to objects subject to economic, social pressures, and against right-wing politicians, for example, Senator Barry Goldwater. However, more attention to democratic political reforms would have been in continuity with his earlier attention to the central area of politics. But American politics was not his natural political environment and his vocational choice was to write his theology in his last years.

José Miguez Bonino criticized Tillich for his limitations as a Northern European theologian. He seemed provincial to Miguez who noted he picked up the Christian Realism associated with Niebuhr in North America, but he regarded him as largely continuing his limited German heritage.

> I say this not only because he did not travel south of the Tropic of Cancer and did not refer at all as far as I know, to contemporary Southern countries and peoples. More important he was fully anchored as a theologian of the North Atlantic world as the center of "world history."[1]

Anne Bennett had made a similar point about Tillich announcing a "sacred void" in a time of European stagnation while the rest of the world was winning its independence from European colonialism. Anne criticized Tillich for thinking nothing of the divine was being accomplished at the moment when blacks were beginning to win civil rights in the U.S.A., and colored peoples the world over were wining freedom.

While I'm inclined to sustain Bennett and Miquez's critique, John Thatamanil takes some of the sting out of it, by reminding critiques of Tillich's openness to Japanese religion, and his important dialogues with Zen Buddhist masters in the U.S.A. and in Japan. His hopes to overcome his provincialism by interrogating his theology with Eastern perspectives were a bold move: "A full forty years after Tillich's passing, few Christian theologians, postmodern or otherwise have engaged another religious tradition with the seriousness with which Tillich engaged Buddhism."[2]

Marc Boss claims Mircea Eliade as the authority that Tillich was very serious in his hope to correct his theology, and he reminds his readers that Tillich knew Buddhist experts from 1951 through his ten-week trip to Japan in 1959, and that he continued to work on the issue through his Bampton Lectures of 1961 at Columbia which I heard. His famous last lecture in Chicago continued the conversation about the significance of non-Christian religions for Christian theology.[3] The depth of the recorded dialogues show that Tillich, even if Eurocentric, knew there was a meaningful world beyond his and in his last years he pursued it in depth, echoing his primitive, earlier work on Schelling's reflections on world religions in his youthful dissertation. Niebuhr too falls prey to the same criticism with the qualifications made earlier in this volume concerning his reading, writing, acquaintances, and teaching. Niebuhr critiqued some of the failures of European colonialism. But neither thinker acknowledged the full debt Europe owed to China or Islam or to the wealth African slaves produced for Western civilization. Slight technical advantages of the West freed them to commit terrible outrages against the rest of the world. Western domination and violence against the world was obscured for both thinkers in their basic Eurocentrism.

Feminist Critique

Tillich, only a little less than Niebuhr, has spawned a small industry of feminist critique of his work. Rachel Sophia Broad's essay[4] is only the most recent of these works.

At first glance, one would assume, Tillich's record obviated the need for the critique. He advocated church offices for women in the revolutionary church he advocated in 1918. In *The Socialist Decision* he advocated a religious socialism freed from patriarchalism, and argued that socialism could not fall back into the retrogressive patterns of German patriarchy, his ministry was in a woman-ordaining church, and in significant passages in his *Systematic Theology* volume 3[5] he argues for nongender stereotypical language for God. He suggests the doctrine of the trinity must remain open to new symbolic development that can better incorporate elements of the symbols of the female. He reflects on the near divinization of Mary in Roman Catholicism and reveals concerns about the exclusive maleness of God in Judaism and Protestantism. He explicitly addressed the presence of both female and male symbolism in the self-sacrifice motif and in the Holy Spirit. Ann Belford Ulanov, who knew Tillich well, commented on these developments:

> Tillich's frequent use of the image of embracing or holding "ground" of being points to the reality of this love, which he sees as imbued with the 'feminine element of being." He was one of the first theologians to insist on inclusion of such a feminine element of being in our traditional masculine concepts of God."[6]

There is no reason to think his suggestions in 1963 would remain the currency of the twenty-first century, but they require notation and further development.

However, much turns on the decision about experience as a source or medium of theology. For Tillich experience is a medium and this obviously means his birth into a patriarchal society and his maleness colored his theology, as the birth of a woman into a more-equal society and her female experience will color her theology as she reaches for inclusiveness. But some feminist theology elevates experience into a source of theology. Then the interpretation of experience becomes crucial and theology tends toward identity theology which has dangers of idolatry within it. Rachel Baard's essay only suggests the tensions within feminist theology between "equality" feminism and "difference feminism"[7] To my mind this translates into the differences between the justice-feminism of Harrison and the nature-feminism of Plaskow. At the time of this writing, I am more sympathetic to the justice-feminism because the different nature-feminism of Plaskow and Nelson seems to be built too exclusively on one model of women's experience whereas there are a multitude of feminine models of experience just as there are many different male models. Lessing's criticism of the religious-simple models, to my mind, overturns the simple model of her character "Martha" as the model for women. Baard's conclusion, that women and men including Tillich's theology have much to learn from each other, seems appropriate.[8]

Hannah's Book

One feminist responding to the careful essay of Owen Thomas on the questions of morality relating to Heidegger and Tillich introduced the concept of "A Hermeneutic of Revulsion."[9] This running away from Tillich's thought by women has been a widespread revolt of women students upon reading Hannah Tillich's disclosures of her suffering and the unconventional marriage they sustained. Julie A. Lamm wrote: "I am revolted by the sadistic element present in his relationships with some women and present also in his pornographic taste."[9] She said she wasn't revolted by his failure to live up to an ideal monogamous marriage as Hannah apparently didn't desire or expect that. Mainstream Christians were shocked to learn of the report of his promiscuity, and if they did not read the book, *From Time to Time* they did not learn of Hannah's own affairs, heterosexual and homosexual, or of their Bohemian values drawn from the Frankfurt lifestyle of the Weimar Republic. The generation of scholars older than I was shocked by the reports of Tillich's affairs, whereas my generation was not so shocked by the affairs as the number of them described by Hannah and her suffering. The use of pornography was still troubling to my colleagues. A sensitive report shared with me by a young artist of another generation, learning of a later Harvard Divinity School dean's dismissal for pornography on his Divinity School computer, was "Doesn't everyone have pornography on their computer?" Responses to the disclosures by Hannah were received differently by different generations and by each gender. Feminist reaction was strongly critical of Tillich, and I think it was out of sympathy for the deep hurt to his wife which cries out from the pages of her powerful book. Feminist scholars, like their male colleagues, know of inappropriate sexuality within academia and are generally not offended by it. But the rampant promiscuity of Tillich, who was held in such high esteem, offended many within the academy.

The sexual norms of the three American communities of Tillich have changed in our lifetimes. Harvard Divinity School, Union Theological Seminary, and the University of Chicago Divinity School are open to homosexual behavior now whereas they were not in Tillich's time. None of these theological centers would now worry about nonmarital sexual practices which were not destructive. Extramarital sexual expression openly practiced would probably not be tolerated in leaders of the institutions, but is generally ignored among the general population of faculty, students, or staff of the institutions unless it became a public issue or involves harassment. But in the 1930s–1950s at Union, knowledge of Tillich's behavior would have cost him his position. The knowledge of it caused an uproar at Harvard Divinity School in the 1960s and similar behavior cost his closest assistant his position, as disclosed by that assistant publicly to the North American Paul Tillich Society. Apparently knowledge of Tillich's behavior prevented an invitation being extended to Tillich in the 1940s from the Divinity School of the University of Chicago. The secrets Tillich failed to preserve point toward the contradiction between his dependence upon certain communal responsibilities and his lifestyle. He accepted the community's "bread and salt" but did not follow its expectations. Particularly at Union with its "church" atmosphere and close faculty-student living, such a violation of personal expression against communal expectations or the ethos of Union in that time is a moral violation.

Hannah's book revealed her continuing anger at Paul after his death. Despite reported reconciliation as they aged, her anger boiled over. Other written documents in the Tillich archives at Harvard confirm her ongoing rage. Their son Rene Tillich spoke on the subject of his parents conflicts at Harvard in 1998. His testimony tends to confirm Rollo May's account that many of the relationships that Hannah denounced as adulterous were not explicitly sexual. Rene describes her obsession with sexuality founded in a mind influenced by Freudianism and her own sexual abuse as a child. Her book flows between fantasy and narrative and the lines are often blurred. Critics who attack Tillich on his sexuality need at least to read beyond the wife's rage and the psychoanalytically informed son's report.[10] Rene, in part, was defining himself and his family by his counter report. He never denied that Tillich had affairs, many of them, but he had another perspective derived from his years as a psychotherapist. He had warm, loving memories of his childhood. Though his father was often absent, he has treasured memories of his time with his father and special holiday trips with him. He testifies that Paul loved Hannah and that Hannah loved him in the beginning, but he is not sure that she did by the end of her life. According to Rene, Hannah attacked Paul repeatedly in the home. Paul's response was quiet endurance. They discussed divorce but did not carry through on it. Rene said that Paul stayed in the marriage because he loved Hannah and he practiced the art of survival or *realpolitik* in the family. He sent the children away to good schools, Rene thinks, to shield them from Hannah. In Rene's opinion Paul made the best decision for all members of the family by resisting divorce. He didn't approve of men who dismissed their wives for younger women.

"My knowledge of Paul's sexuality was far more forced on me by Hannah than in any way experienced with Paul. But Hannah saw almost everything through the lens of sex."[10] From about the time he was five years old, Rene's mother talked to him obsessively about sex. As an adult molested as a child, Rene thinks she had "a tendency to sexualize her experience and distort reality, particularly in the sexual realm."[11] He believes "they agreed sexual involvement with others was permitted," but that she came not to like it and in her obsession she wrote sexual novels, sent him pornographic materials, and talked approvingly of prostitutes. Rene wrote approvingly of Rollo May's interpretation that Tillich found vitality in relationships with women whether sexual or not and that this energy drove his intellectual work. Tillich according to the son was not outspoken at home and the rest of the family drowned him out. Only at Christmas he asserted himself by controlling the decoration of the Christmas tree and reading the Christmas story before the opening of presents. There wasn't a lot of joy in the Tillich family and Rene mentions teasing his father about being a workaholic. He thinks his work held him together.

Rene believes Tillich overcame estrangement and lived a life of love, and he testifies to it from his own knowledge. Tillich's struggle with estrangement was a lifelong task and it was complicated by his overly stern father, early death of mother, trauma of war, betrayal and early divorce, and the forced emigration. The resultant nightmares, anxiety, and a possible love addiction did not cripple him and he overcame with his work and honesty about himself to himself. Rene would argue that as Freud analyzed himself in working out his theories, Paul developed his own theories "giving himself a talking cure.[12] Rene diagnosed his own father according to the *Diagnostic and Statistical Manual IV* as "having anxiety and depression, post-traumatic stress syndrome from the war, and paraphilia, and I would diagnose him on Axis II as a narcissistic character with dissociative features."[13]

The younger Tillich continued his case study and related the elder's fascination with love triangles as a way of avoiding over-commitment, but still allowing him to experience love and to gain the strength to work. The work in turn covered his neuroses as he himself has described in his sermons. Technical literature on male sexuality is brought into the discussion in a way that undercut Tillich's own theological exploration of libido and love. He had mentioned a dissociative tendency in Paul by which he could write theology even if an emotional storm were going on around him. He could experience love without falling too deeply into love in a way that would destroy him. He thinks that in his older years some of these tendencies weakened along with the narcissistic drives and that he could relax more with Hannah and things became more pleasant with them. Perhaps he was simply less driven by libido. He concluded by saying that he could not understand the ongoing bitterness by Hannah and that he thanked his father for his own sanity resulting from the steadiness and love that Paul had given him.[14] I am not competent to judge the psychoanalytic judgments of either Rollo May or Rene Tillich. I think I appreciate Hannah's anger over and her sense of rejection by Paul, but I would not read her own story of bitterness and fantasy as an accurate description of Paul. Rather I understand him as a person radically wounded by the years of war, preparation of war, Nazism, and continuing Cold War suffering post-traumatic stress syndrome who lived from the Bohemian sexually distorted years into a straighter America increasing his sense of guilt. The academic life gave him time and adoring feminine presence to act out whatever inadequacies in his upbringing and marriage urged him toward. His question about whether his love life was a failure or a new way is best answered by accepting the term "failure." Sociologically he was as driven by the "Protestant work ethic" as he was by the urging of the libido to overcome the emptiness which he feared. Beneath even the work ethic was the radical drive to overcome the German world which failed him in World War I and to find a new way towards a theonomous society. So on the other side of accepting his failures, the ongoing task is to develop any helpful trajectories his methods and visions entail.

Mary Ann Stenger's writing on feminism and theology indicates, while Tillich's personal life may cause the reader to use caution in applying Tillich's theology, the theory should be examined for its own validity.[15] She notes its use by many feminists and also the criticism of its abstractness and patriarchal inheritances from the Christian tradition, but she is hopeful feminist development will remove the objectionable while using his theory of correlation and symbols for the development of future theology. Beyond the use of his understanding of symbolism and the method of correlation for asking new questions and finding new answers she reflects on his use of justice and power. Changing symbolism alone does not necessarily advance justice. Theology must include empowering insights that keep the eyes on the power relations between genders to develop towards a more inclusive justice.

Tillich's use of the Protestant Principle to criticize idolatrous religious practices is one of her tools for criticizing the idolatry of favoring males for priesthood. Here the finite maleness becomes an absolute barrier to the full religious development of the priesthood. Confronting the idolatry and the absoluteness of the church on this issue, placing maleness above race, moral character, or ability or even religious sensibility, Tillich's terms are useful. The critique of idolatry can also be useful to feminists who in their movement might be tempted to make absolute their own perspectives. So accepting human ambiguity and the relativeness of human theological insight, she notes how feminists have used Tillich to begin their liberation and advocates that where his insights are helpful they be used. Stenger never made the point, but her elaboration of the usefulness of Tillich's major categories for feminist development indicates the advantage of Tillich's thought over Niebuhr's in this aspect of future promise. There is a flexibility in ontology that the more biblical themes lack, though Niebuhr's own development of symbolism has room for movement beyond the biblical patriarchy. Stenger's emphasis upon justice and power as primary categories for Tillich indicates the need for the closing section of criticism on Tillich which is his political philosophy.

Political Philosophy

It is more appropriate to refer to Tillich's contribution to political philosophy than to politics as his influence has been as a thinker and as a developer of political philosophy. Americans tend to think of him as a philosophical theologian and many are surprised to learn that in Frankfurt he was a professor of Philosophy and Sociology and his last invitation to teach was at the New School as a professor of Social Research. Roger Shinn, dean at Union at the time, also reports he intended to stay in an apartment at the Seminary and teach one course there while serving the New School in New York City. Most of the American writing on Tillich's political philosophy has been on his *The*

Socialist Decision, and his untranslated German social-theoretical writings are largely unknown in the U.S.A. The essays by Roger Shinn, Walter Weisskopf, and Dennis McCann in *The Thought of Paul Tillich* focus on *The Socialist Decision.* John Stumme's study of *Socialism in Theological Perspective: A study of Paul Tillich 1918–1933* is the major study of the earlier socialist Tillich. Work by Eduard Heimann and the Paucks have also contributed to an interest in Tillich's political philosophy. James Luther Adams has written several pieces on Tillich's socialism, and his edited *Political Expectations* has provided translations of many of the relevant early German essays.

The annual volume of the Papers of the North American Paul Tillich Society regularly feature essays on various aspects of Tillich's political thought. My edited collections of essays *Theology of Peace* and, with Matthew Lon Weaver, *Against the Third Reich,* have made some of the work of Tillich on these subjects more generally available. My own attempt at a comprehensive presentation of Tillich's social thought preceded these volumes in *Paul Tillich's Radical Social Thought.* The Shinn, Weisskopf, and McCann essays contribute now to overcoming my lack of dissent from Tillich's social thought in my earlier book. Tillich's immanent eschatology of *The Socialist Decision* captured in his resolution of contradictions in socialism by "expectation" was too optimistic, or in Tillich's terms, utopian. His romanticism and German expressionism fueled his hopes for socialism to the point where he spoke of the *Kairos* in world-transforming terms relative to the events of the Weimar Republic years. He knew it was an existential decision, but certainly he was wrong. Weimar could not work because of outside political pressures, the punishment of the Versailles Treaty, and the economic depression. The punitive forces of conservatism and revolutionaries were too strong, and the concept of "expectation" or the romantic idea that socialism and religion would reconcile in Germany was fantasy in the 1920s.

Similarly in the United States after the war the prosperity and gains in civil rights, and the recovery of Europe encouraged by the Marshall Plan, and the consolidation of the gains of the New Deal were not a void. There was neither chaos nor void, but limited gains in protecting the poor, limited gains in civil rights which would inspire the revolts of the 1960s, and the ambiguities of American social life until his death in 1965. The critics assess this problem differently. Roger Shinn gently suggests more empirical work needed to inform his political thought. Dennis McCann stresses that Tillich's socialist vision was a personal vision and dependent upon Tillich's own complex personal experience and religious vision and that without entering into those dimensions it may not be a secure guide for modern times. Weisskopf, though finding Tillich's thought suggestive for analyzing the "crisis of the West," believed that its peculiar structure was dependent upon Tillich's German experience and therefore limited. *Kairos* obviously relates to social expectations and is future directed.

Hindsight tells us that it is always a risk to use the term announcing a social fulfillment in time.

Francis Ching-Wah Yip[16] has contributed two valuable notes of critique to Tillich's social thought. In addition to his Eurocentrism, Tillich's economic thought is thought to be overly focused on the cultural aspects. Tillich needed more focus on the very real material, and production aspects of economy. This is to say he needed more of Karl Marx, not less. He tended to focus on the spirit of capitalism rather than on the system of production. Therefore his critique of capitalistic modernity was not as realistic as it needed to be. He failed to spell out the underside of capitalism which caused much suffering in Europe and more in the rest of the world. Francis Ching-Wah Yip turned to Jurgen Moltmann to supplement Tillich's critique of capitalism and to expose the suffering and meaningless of the other subjected to the domination of capitalistic modernity.

The criticism of Tillich's personal vision of utopia and religious socialism may obscure his very creative reflections on utopia and his practical political activity, so it is useful to consider the concept of utopia in Tillich before concluding the book on the note of their legacies.

On the Boundary of Utopia and Politics

Paul Tillich was more comfortable with his activity in German politics than with his American political role. In 1951, he returned to Germany to present four lectures at The *Deutsche Hochschule fur Politik*[17] in Berlin on the topic of utopia. The theme of those lectures of utopia provides a perspective for an interpretation of Tillich's politics. His politics like his thought in general was characterized by boldness and risk taking. This boldness was partially due to the fact that he was more a person of theory than one of action, though his activity in politics was considerably more than most of his contemporary philosophers or theologians in both countries. He was not active in local politics in any way that I know of, but he addressed politics at its refined and highest levels in both of his countries. It may be important to note also that he was a refugee from Germany as it gained its infamous role as the most important country in Europe and in America as it gained its role as the most important country in the world. It is not surprising that as a German philosopher in both Germany and America that he would keep rewriting his frequent lectures and papers on *power*. But politics for him was never just *Realpolitik,* it always referred to the depth of humanity or to the human essence. This human essence was the first meaning of utopia to Tillich. Humanity was in part utopian because it was of human nature to be so. This is one of his great differences from his mentor in American politics, Reinhold Niebuhr. They never spoke about it in their infrequent public dialogues, but it remained one of their disagreements. Niebuhr polemicized against the utopias of Germany's Third Reich, and against the Russian-Marxist utopia of the Soviet Union and against utopia in general. Tillich would express the weaknesses of utopia, but also its strengths. Tillich's sometime attempts to unite politics and utopia failed, as they must fail, but from the struggle came political courage and fascinating political theory.

Perhaps his most important assertion about utopia is that it is characteristic of humanity's being. It is neither a fantastic delusion nor a temporary phenomenon. It expresses the situation of humanity as finite freedom. The freedom means the possibility to act as a whole-centered person; the finitude means that in all actions the threat of nonbeing is discovered. Political existence is necessarily a threatened existence and the systems that deny this threat, as both churches and political movements are tempted to with promises of eternity or nonfallibility, are shown by history to be subject to nonbeing. Political existence like human existence is a combination of anxiety and courage. Utopia expresses the ideal possibilities of human existence, but it is an ideal. Usually it has both a backward look to an imagined utopia which really reflects the essence of humanity, and a forward look to the expression of a paradise or a new reality in the future. Most utopias show this triadic movement. There is the corrupt present, the essentially good past, and a promise of a new, better future. In Tillich's mind both classical Christianity and much of existentialism and pragmatism denied the real possibility of utopia now in this history. But classical Christian thought had the notion of a millennium or thousand years, and this was used to attack other classical ideas. From this arose much of the revolutionary ideology of restoration of human life to what it was originally and was meant to be. There is also the secularized bourgeois idea of utopia as progress within history.

Tillich's second lecture, "Historical and Unhistorical Thinking," is mostly about unhistorical thinking which cannot have a notion of a historical utopia. The historical types of thinking can find utopia in an idealized past, in a revolutionary future, or in a notion of progress. The unhistorical types he discusses include classical mysticism, naturalism, and existentialism. But these movements have elements of historical thinking, and various forms of utopianism begin to emerge. Historical thinking emerged triumphant in the West, but even here the religions and ideology of space remained an influence. Tillich came to see that Israel requires a space, he knows that Rome was a space as well as a philosophy of history, and even in Marxism, Moscow became the centered place. He raises the question, are both pragmatism and process philosophy which do not really contain a utopia, perhaps more realistic than philosophies of history which preserve the utopian element?

His third presentation took up "Religious and Secular Utopias" in which he made it clear that the original meaning of utopia was "no place" and that the word was a symbol without location in either time or space. The first principle of utopia was that it was the *negation of the negative.* The elimination of the negative allowed the symbol to express the ideal and to expose the negatives of the society in which it was articulated. The negativities were derived both from finitude and estrangement, but the presentation of the myth of life in paradise served as social criticism. While Tillich talked about the utopia of the conquest of death in its various expressions, he understood that the school was particularly interested in his discussing social utopias. But even after mentioning social utopia, he remained pretty much at an abstract level indicating that the biblical social utopias involved not only the removal of social evils but the reconciliation of the human with nature, of men with women, of nature with nature. The social sphere could not be isolated from interpersonal relations or nature as they all were interdependent. The social utopia to be useful could not deny power as all social relations have power issues, but they could deny the exploitation of the hierarchy and challenge the authorities.

The most useful forms of utopia for Western society had expressed either an egalitarian-political agenda or an organic-political agenda. The first is in danger of anarchism and the second of reaction and conservatism. He opted for forms of utopia that held together individual renewal as well as social renewal and which contained elements of both historical and transhistorical thinking. The kingdom of God was the traditional Christian utopia which held together these different aspects of utopia.

His final lecture dealt with "Critique and Justification of Utopia." On the positive side, utopia expressed the truth of the human situation. It is fruitful in that the anticipation and encouragement of human fulfillment has power to change reality. The power comes from being true to the essence of humanity and encouraging its fulfillment. But on the negative side of utopia, usually the symbol does not show how estranged humanity overcomes estranged humanity. Niebuhr in criticizing the failed utopia of Marx said that it was as if Marx pulled the new society out of estrangement like a magician would pull a rabbit out of a hat. Therefore, to an extent, utopia was unfruitful. Utopia holds up possibilities, but it sometimes confuses possibilities with impossibilities. Also utopia may be impotent and lead to disillusionment. Tillich noted in 1951 how the affirmation of utopian goals without the power to change society could lead to terrorism as an expression of the disillusioned. Also in the disillusion space of emptiness, demonic forces may rush in to prey upon the society. Beyond the negativity of utopia, Tillich in his mature years looked for a way to transcend the negativity of utopia. For Tillich, revolutionary socialism was the movement of utopia after World War I, but it was opposed by the transcendental utopianism of Lutheranism. His discussion group worked with the church-socialism conflict and also with the problem of timing and utopian actions. Eventually they found the concept of *Kairos* to be a way to express fulfillment at particular times while still recognizing the problems of finitude and estrangement. Utopia was affirmed but they hoped without its illusions. They found that their continued insistence about the reality of ambiguity in history subjected them to the ongoing critique of the absolute utopians, but in retrospect, he believed they had been correct. At the moment he was speaking, he thought the right moment for action for the realization of something of the Kingdom of God was far in the future. It was important, he thought, to express utopia in its truth, but to guard against its untruth. He concluded by saying: "Or, as I could perhaps say in summation of all four lectures on utopia: *It is the spirit of utopia that conquers utopia.*"[18]

25

Legacies

On the grand staircase in the University of Berlin are the words: "The philosophers have interpreted the world in various ways, the point, however, is to change it." The thesis in German, of course, is the eleventh thesis of Karl Marx on the thought of Ludwig Feuerbach. It was placed there during the Communist regime and it was still there in 2002 after the reuniting of Berlin. Roger Shinn, Niebuhr's successor, asserted that Tillich never forgot the thesis.[1] Niebuhr and Tillich were inspired by their Christian faith and world events to live out the thesis as they could and in some significant ways they succeeded.

Before he retired from Union, Paul Tillich joined in a significant essay in honoring Niebuhr in a 1953 volume, *Christian Faith and Social Action*. Editor John Hutchinson described their collaboration in the organization Christian Action, the successor to Frontier Fellowship and the Fellowship of Socialist Christians. Though Niebuhr led, it provided a fellowship for Paul Tillich to replace his socialist groups of Germany. Their purpose was to critique the failure of social concern and action by Christian Churches, the illusions of the social gospel, Marxism, and secular humanism. To replace these, they developed understandings of biblical faith for Christian social action.

Tillich emphasized his conviction that Christian faith inspired social action for justice while providing a sanctuary from the turmoil so that the world would not conquer faith. For both Niebuhr and Tillich the Christian had resources of forgiveness and trust that were strange in politics. One engaged in active pursuit of justice for the neighbor out of love. But in faith there were absolute resources whereas in politics there were possible relative gains. Politics and faith were not the same, though faith knowing love and hope had resources for political action.

However, it must be said that their Christian realism differed from the liberation theologies that would follow them and critique them at this point. Human liberation was an important goal for the struggles of Niebuhr and Tillich, for example, the liberation of Europe, but it was not the faith. Faith endured with or without liberation and provided resources for the achievement of liberation. But human gains of liberation remained ambiguous as in the American, French, and Russian revolutions. Some interpretations of Christian faith are relatively apolitical, others almost totally political. These two lived and taught a vigorous commitment to politics for the common good or justice, but with a Christian reservation about politics, and Christian resources for life beyond politics. Such a stance is appropriate for the United States in which the possibilities for achieving greater justice through democratic politics are both threatened and promising.

By 1953, they both recognized they lived in a mixed economy and that both pure socialism and pure capitalism were irrelevant. The technological modern age was threatening to human freedom in their "free" society, and in their enemy, the "totalitarian society." Tillich's article, in the 1953 volume, particularly attacked the threat of technological modernity subduing the human spirit. Their political actions were now pragmatic and less ideological than in their earlier writings. Niebuhr, in the years remaining after his strokes, would exhibit less social vision and more pragmatism than Tillich. It can also be said vis-à-vis Marx's thesis against Feuerbach that Tillich's understanding of the world was focusing his energy on changing American theology while Niebuhr was using American philosophy in the service of faith to change America's perception of the world.

Vernon Holloway's essay in the same book, "Utopianism and Realism in Foreign Policy" reflected his debt to both thinkers. His contribution as a former staff member of the Congregational Church's Council for Christian Social Action points to the legacy they left in the Council. For many years all of its staff leaders were clearly influenced by Niebuhr and several had studied with him. This Niebuhrian-Tillichian influence was important in the Federal Council of Churches, the National Council of Churches, and the World Council of Churches social action work in the 1970s. In the Council for Christian Social Action it was dominant. In the Presbyterian Church social action it has been dominant unto the present.

Other writers in the volume including Shinn and Bennett carried Niebuhr and Tillich's work forward at Union Theological Seminary. It was heavily critiqued in the 1970s–1980s by liberation theologians and emerging identity theologies. It began reasserting itself in the 1990s and the beginning of the twenty-first century. Their legacy never disappeared from Union, but it was forced to coexist with the more radical forms of theology and suffered severe criticisms in *Christianity and Crisis* after the magazine turned toward more cultural analysis and became more radical after Niebuhr's resignation from the editorial board. Many theologians carried a mixture of liberation and realist motifs in their minds. John C. Bennett became more open to liberation theology, and Robert MacAfee Brown moved toward the liberation group while retaining respect and affection for Niebuhr and his approach. Gustavo Gutierrez, the father of Latin American liberation theology also knew the reality of human suffering and the disappointments of political repression.

Union Seminary reduced its faculty under the burdens of maintaining facilities on Broadway on Morningside Heights, and though a street would be named Reinhold Niebuhr Place his influence declined in the shrinking faculty and student body. After his strokes his organization, Christian Action, closed with some of its influence moving into the forenamed church social-action agencies. White Citizen Councils drove the Providence Farm to abandon its cooperative-interracial life in the 1950s and Niebuhr could not continue his Southern work after 1952. The Americans for Democratic Action (ADA) had absorbed his Union for Democratic Action and through its director James Loeb becoming director of ADA Niebuhr's influence continued. Democratic presidential candidates most reflecting Niebuhr's thought, Adlai Stevenson and Hubert H. Humphrey, could not win the presidency. Jimmy Carter and Barack Obama on the other hand claimed Niebuhr's influence, but its final significance in the thought of these two presidents is unclear. Niebuhr was widely blamed for the mistakes of a whole group of realists surrounding the presidencies of Kennedy and Johnson. The more radical promises of liberation theology to change society were attractive to many realists and their students who understood themselves as change agents. But liberation theology, except for the feminist expressions, was not stable enough to persuade middle-class Americans to support it.

Promises were not fulfilled for blacks or Latin Americans. If they refused to give up their politics they returned towards the ambiguous pursuit of social change mixing hope and recognition of resistance to justice in progressive social action. As Niebuhr and Tillich had seen more clearly than many of the enthusiasts for the social gospel the presence of radical evil in the world, liberation theology proclaimed more forcefully the particular oppressive injustices toward women, blacks, and Third World peoples. Liberation theologians saw the evil in the ambiguities of democratic practice which Niebuhr and Tillich had spent their lives defending against Nazism and Communism. Its hopes were more far-reaching than Niebuhr's and it carried forward the utopianism which Tillich had overcome.

Some of the liberation analysis informed by neo-Marxism discomforted Niebuhr when he saw the first signs of it in student radicals on the Columbia campus in 1968. However, Gustavo Gutierrez turned toward an analysis of Job limiting his theology of liberation work under pressure from the church hierarchy. Also, James Cone's love of teaching courses on Reinhold Niebuhr's thought may be signs among many others of the need to separate and relate Christian faith to politics. Neither Cone nor Gutierrez as fundamental leaders of liberation theology neglected the analysis of power or the ambiguities of church and political life.

Tillich sometimes applied his theology directly to extreme politics. His wartime speeches to German-speaking Europe often move directly to religious judgments against the Nazis. In his editorials he denounced the Goldwater candidacy specifically as a theologian because of the extreme bellicosity of his rhetoric and those associated with the right-wing campaign. Ordinarily though, both Niebuhr and Tillich speak to issues of politics in terms of liberty, equality, justice, order, and power. Theology shapes their perspectives on history and the nature of humanity, but they hesitate to throw religious enthusiasm or special revelation into the political fray. They find resources of forgiveness, humility, compassion, and serenity in religious faith, but their application of these Christian virtues is not directly to politics. President Kennedy tried to directly disassociate his Roman Catholicism from his politics and Senator Santorum tries to directly connect his Roman Catholic faith to his politics. For both Niebuhr and Tillich it is a more complicated process moving through social ethical judgments, political philosophy and then policy and party strategies. However, the question remains as to the direction of this generation of theologically informed leaders: Will they turn their faith toward socially responsible action or will they be seduced by the less-educated Christianity that subsumes the social evil of America underneath its presentation of a socially uncritical gospel?

Faith

Niebuhr and Tillich were both in the Lutheran tradition of salvation by grace through faith alone. For Niebuhr it meant believing in the center of one's self that the creator, judge, and redeemer of humanity is trustworthy. A text that appears in many of his sermons was shared with me as we discussed the end of his life. The essential goodness of God shines through Jesus Christ and one can therefore be "persuaded that neither life nor death—are able to separate us from the love of God, which is in Jesus Christ our Lord."[1] Faith in the greatness of God is required before one can teach humility. The Christian interpretation emphasized forgiveness, because the squalor of human life kept us from acting well. There is a peace that the actor could have which was a peace beyond one's own achievements or the quality of the times. It was a peace that could bestow serenity in the midst of great conflicts and injustices that one could not overcome. The text I heard most often from Niebuhr when he was arguing that faith provided a serenity beyond any secular fulfillment or triumph was from Paul: "For whether we live, we live unto the Lord; or whether we die we die unto the Lord; whether we live therefore or die we are the Lord's" (Romans 14:8). Their interpretation of God was through both Jesus as the Christ and God as understood by the Hebrew prophets. Their monotheistic faiths as the ultimate presuppositions for both social ethics and politics were among their greatest legacies.

Faith gave more of a sense of trust in God's overcoming one's incompleteness than an explanation of how exactly this was accomplished. Early in his ministry, Niebuhr came to believe that Christian faith needed two resources to be persuasive to modern humanity: to show its relevance to the problems of human existence and an adequate metaphysic. Later his pragmatism allowed him to value less the metaphysic. Whenever he turned to metaphysical arguments, he preferred the process style of argumentation of Whitehead and Hartshorne over Tillich's ontology. The openness of process philosophy and its unfinished character of human history seemed to preserve the radicalness of human freedom better than Tillich's philosophy of being to him. Niebuhr's own vocation demonstrated the relevance of Christian faith to the problems of the American empire in the twenty-first century. Niebuhr would turn down invitations to leave Union Seminary and accept offered positions at Harvard and Yale because of the service to the church that could be rendered through the seminary. But while their greatest contributions to students were through their seminary teaching, both gave of their time to guide dissertations at Columbia University in international relations, religion, and philosophy. For them teaching at the university was a complement to their seminary teaching. After retirement from the seminary both taught in the universities, and produced books while finishing their careers. Niebuhr's closing years of teaching were back at the seminary, and Tillich intended to return to teach a class at Union in accepting the position at the New School, but death thwarted his planned return.

Tillich also showed the relevance of Christian faith to the imperial struggles of the twentieth and twenty-first centuries. His understanding of faith was that in the realization of being grasped by an ultimate concern, one could through Christian symbolism believe one's broken self was accepted. Neither theologian denied the realization of faith through other religions or traditions, but for them it was through Christian faith that these realities were known. They understood the moves to faith by Luther and Kierkegaard, but for both of them their Christian faith came through family life, Christian education, and confirmation. Through all their wanderings, they were sons of the German Christian families into which they were born.

Tillich explained the Christian symbolism well and rationally in his *Systematic Theology*, yet the move from existential anguished questions to the Christian theological circle required faith. Tillich provided a version of a believing metaphysic that Niebuhr thought Christianity needed, but it was apprehended by the believer and not the one who remained with the existential anguish alone.

The character of their faith is best grasped through their sermons and their prayers. Through the diligence of Ursula, Niebuhr's *Justice and Mercy* provides many of his prayers. We have fewer prayers from Tillich, but the one Tillich offered in the conclusion to the *Eternal Now* is a profound prayer of thanksgiving. He offers to God, the eternal source of our being, thanks for life and the blessings of life, accepting before the infinite the finiteness and dependence of humanity.[3]

Because of their polemics against liberalism and their use of traditional symbolism Tillich and Niebuhr were often thought of as neoorthodox. This was unfortunate as they were, each in their own way, using liberal methods in biblical criticism, historical criticism, and contemporary reflections on symbol and myth to attempt something new. Though Tillich would often use new symbols to contain old meanings, he would in his sermons often revert to the traditional language of Protestantism. Both followed existentialism in asserting a freedom for humanity that previous theological generations had not presupposed. Both were at home using modern science.

Gary Dorrien describes their work as using myth to describe truth about the human situation before God.[4] This is helpful. They both followed Rudolf Bultmann, but after demythologizing biblical symbols so they could be used by modern believers, they remythologized their insights. Niebuhr's sermons stayed closer to the biblical terminology which he interpreted in a powerful way. Tillich utilized German idealism to undergird his fresh vision of the Christian life. Both were using biblical myth to explain the religious human drama, but behind their myths were intellectual models drawn in their own way from their liberal theological education, the modern world, their own heritage, and other philosophies to explain and make bearable the traumas of the twentieth century. They were to the best of their ability, which they realized was limited, making the Christian narrative relevant and persuasive. Niebuhr worked more by criticizing other theories while Tillich worked by absorbing other philosophies and showing how Christian symbolism could explain reality better. More thoroughly than most thinkers they showed how alternative perspectives unconsciously borrowed from Christianity or reflected their own assumptions. Freud would explain too much through sex and dreams based upon his own traumas in these areas. Marx would explain too much though focusing on economics and translating it into materialism. Sociologists like Emil Durkheim would replace God with society. Contemporary scientists build models from their own limited presuppositions which may or may not included divine references, though they may be filled with other unseen realities like parallel universes. Much of the work of Tillich and Niebuhr can be understood as using aspects of these and other modern thinkers while providing Christian alternatives to their misjudgments regarding the faith. Humans as thinkers tend to build intellectual models from their own specialties while Niebuhr and Tillich argue the whole human drama is better explained by interpretation from Scripture and the history of thought.

Their social realism is dependent upon the Augustinian stream of theology which formed them from their inheritances of Luther and Calvin. They confessed their dependence upon this stream of theology and were less impressed with the rationalism coming into Christianity from Aristotle and finding expression in

Thomas Aquinas and his heirs. Though they taught about or lectured on non-Christian religious materials, their thought remained within Western paradigms.

Interestingly among those focusing on the major differences between them few noted the absence of any sense in Niebuhr of the importance of the doctrine of the Spirit whereas Tillich integrates his system with the doctrine of the Spirit. In the upsurge of interest in the Spirit and various spirtualities, this guarantees Tillich a more lasting influence in the religious field. While he was formulating his doctrine of the Spirit, Niebuhr was further developing his political thought and so Niebuhr's influence will continue to be the greater in the realms of international political theory and in social philosophy. They both used the symbol of the Kingdom of God, but it had a more positive influence in Tillich whereas Niebuhr used it in the sense of finality or *telos*, and as a principle of critique of other religious or secular utopias. In Tillich it reinforced the sense of historical hope and took on life as a fighting symbol against negative social movements which called forth resistance. Many social activists have felt the Kingdom of God realized with others in resisting evil trajectories in society of racism, militarism, and dominance. It seems wise to supplement Niebuhr at this point with Tillich's insights about the Kingdom of God, and to recognize it also means the rule of God or participation in the Kingdom of all of those who take Christian life and its requirements upon themselves. For both of them the myths were taken very seriously, but not literally. For example: The story of Adam and Eve, while teaching us little about history, conveys the truth of the human estrangement from God by humanity's free act. The truth underlying the myths is best represented in Niebuhr's *The Nature and Destiny of Man* and Tillich's *Systematic Theology*. The power of the myths is best captured in their sermons. Their sermons, persuasive when preached years ago, are still powerful guides to contemporary devotional life.

Peacemaking and Realism

It was their fate to live in times of war. They both lived in empires. They both provided religious support for the first struggle between their respective empires, Germany and the United States, and for the second struggle of World War II. Neither one was tempted to deny the responsibilities of the empires, but both sought to understand and encourage realistic peacemaking. After his short-lived time as a pacifist, Niebuhr resigned from the Fellowship of Reconciliation and sought international security through the advocacy of robust collective security. He could never put full trust in either the League of Nations or the United Nations, but he pled for the League of Nations' action, and participated in building the climate in the United States for the United Nations and then served in UNESCO. Similarly Tillich supported the development of a world organization and the federation of Europe as the Second World War drew towards its climax. They joined in criticizing allied demands for unconditional surrender and the bombing of cities during World War II, and argued for international control of nuclear weapons. Failing control they supported diplomatic efforts and rejected first use of the bomb by the United States. Niebuhr urged patient, nonfanatical opposition to Communism and ideological debate with Marxist thought. They criticized overly militaristic responses by the United States and Niebuhr opposed the war in Vietnam much earlier than most. His support and service for Clergy and Laity Concerned about Vietnam is representative of the fact that both knew active Christian ministry required support for parachurch organizations which could take action more easily than the established churches. Characteristically they not only spoke and wrote, but organized. While Tillich's active organization had ended with the Council for Democratic Germany, he did not refrain from endorsing the work of antiwar organizations as well as organizations working to improve the movement for racial justice.

Serious peacemaking requires recognition of the problems of empires and the need to reduce their threat as possible. It requires criticism and action against nuclear and other weapons of mass destruction. Diplomacy, without neglecting balancing of power, is the preferred method of realism toward peacemaking. Niebuhr would often say that humility regarding our knowledge of others and their needs and aspirations was a vital requirement for diplomacy. Tillich would point to the dynamics of history, its flux and vitality which required flexibility on the part of national leaders rather than dogmatism or attempts to control the world.

One of Tillich's last comments on international politics dealt with the inadequate perspective of Pope John XXIII's utopian hopes for peace on earth.[5] The conditions within humanity could not promise any such eternal peace on earth. There were grounds for hope including the threat of nuclear weapons to humanity. Such fear may restrain violence. Human community was slowly developing across nations and religions. The technical union of humanity also had some seeds of promise within it though there were dangers in technology itself. Some developing legal institutions increased the chances for peace. But beyond legal structures human love or *eros* needed to develop to increase human compassion.

Both made remarkable statements about nuclear weapons at various times which were discussed in the previous chapter on the bomb. Niebuhr's proposal to the U.S. Bicentennial Commission, before his death, listed three issues that the Commission should focus on in their planning for the celebration: the control of nuclear weapons, improvement in race relations, and attention to the threats to the environment.[6] During Niebuhr's lifetime there was no escape from competitive coexistence. War was the danger that had to be prevented. In the period of the struggle he argued against American overreliance on military solutions, and recognized the need for building international legal structures to reduce the danger. But the economic interests rooted in the ideological conflict between America and Russia made the transfer of ultimate power to any international body impossible. His eye, as noted previously, was on the conflict between the superpowers. It had to be managed. His last book about democracy preceded the current emphasis upon peace among the democracies, but the Third World which he surveyed was not his primary emphasis. He urged technological and economic aid for the developing world, but he felt the Soviet Union had an edge in the competition for the poor world's allegiance. His articles on America's relationship with Asia saw the advantages the Chinese possessed, and he was dubious about trying to export American political power to that vast area. He recognized that the world was tiring of the Cold War, ideological conflict, and economic rivalries. His frequent notice that the world was moving toward mixed economic solutions based more on pragmatism, in retrospect, seems prophetic. Socialism and capitalism have had their fights and there may be more, but knowledgeable people understand that the issues of the Cold War are past.

Tillich and Niebuhr participated in those struggles even longer than they fought Nazism, and in general they counseled well, and their policies avoided the war, and peace of a sort could arrive when the Soviet Union fell years after their deaths. Niebuhr's thoroughly developed philosophy of the Cold War and Tillich's intermittent comments provided the right balance. The Soviet Union needed to be deterred from risking war while the U.S.A. had to avoid overreacting militarily to communist gains. Their teaching was a forceful policy for a rough, tolerable stalemate until conditions would change to make war improbable. Given the new technology of war and the strong ideological and national self-interests pushing the ideologies, their sense of deterrence and prudence seems to me to have been the best strategic policy. Mistakes were made, and the U.S.A. participated in blunders and cruelties at the tactical level. At the strategic level both the Russians and the Americans survived and opportunities were given for humanity to find better ways forward after the Cold War.

Economic Ethics

Few Christian ethicists wrote as much about economic issues as Niebuhr and Tillich. Tillich's contribution to this subject concluded with his turning toward his *Systematic Theology* and Niebuhr reduced his writing on economics following his stroke in 1952.

Most of the earlier writing had been undertaken as religiously inspired socialists. Neither one was well trained in economics or understood much about fiscal policy which is so important in modern-day economic policy making. Niebuhr's resignation from the Socialist Party in 1940 over foreign policy differences foreshadowed his later lifetime passions for international issues and philosophy of foreign policy. Tillich rejoined the Socialist Democratic Party in Germany after the war, but ended his published contributions to socialist theory. Niebuhr's contributions to the policy platform of the Americans for Democratic Action and three essays a decade apart in 1953 and 1963 represent his major contributions to economic thought for that period. Though there are a few incidental reflections after 1963, he added nothing new to the work of earlier decades.

The three essays: "Christian Faith and Social Action," "The Christian Faith and the Economic Life of Liberal Society" of 1953, and "The Development of a Social Ethic in the Ecumenical Movement" of 1963 present different aspects of the same argument. History has led humanity past the old arguments of laissez-faire capitalism and revolutionary socialism. Christian thinkers in the United States through the evolution of the Fellowship of Socialist Christians to Christian Action have come to understand that beyond those old debates pragmatic decisions about government regulation of capitalism is the preferred method.

Theologically pragmatic decisions beyond Christian theology need to be made, but in the light of the Christian understanding of the sin of humanity as well as great cooperative possibilities of humanity. The love ethic is the law of human nature, but self-love is dominant in history and so decisions need to be made for justice which recognizes both of these elements. The ecumenical movement's refusal to opt for either socialism or capitalism was seen as wise, and Christians needed to see the dangers in both. Unchecked power in economic centralization in the corporations or private ownership is dangerous as is economic centralization in governmental agencies. Pragmatism in Niebuhr's terms here becomes ad hoc advice depending upon the situation in light of his basic perspective upon humanity.

In the same period he wrote a long piece on the need for democratic measures within unions while celebrating the results of the power of the unions in winning economic gains for the workers and lifting the standard of living of the whole nation. He suggested there were reasons for nationalizing the coal industry in Britain which might not apply in the steel industry. His own thought had been influential in the ecumenical conferences he discussed from Oxford, through Amsterdam to Evanston. Also of course the conclusions he reported vis-à-vis Christian Action were of his own making. But the general historical trend he reported was a matter of his observation. Many would disagree with the directions he perceived from his own place in the Liberal Party. He still refused to join the Democratic Party of the presidents whose directions he regarded as positive: Truman (more or less), Kennedy enthusiastically, and the domestic policies of Johnson. His socialist convictions had, under pressure from historical developments, turned to support for the welfare, mixed-economy state. He tended to think "independent" governmental institutions like the Tennessee Valley Authority were better than centralized governmental control because they were less likely to be subject to political manipulation or control.

While both Tillich and Niebuhr favored, supported, and led nongovernmental agencies for human welfare including cooperatives, refugee resettlement programs, and unions, their critics are correct that they favored state action to correct the injustices of the poor. They were reformers in their maturity, not revolutionaries, though they were supportive of revolution in particular cases and Tillich argued the case for revolution even in his *Systematic Theology*. Niebuhr approved of the Bank Campaign to change U.S.A. policy toward South Africa through economic pressure and his journal *Christianity and Crisis* transferred its small account, as mentioned earlier, to a community owned bank in Harlem. This action of Niebuhr's journal was the first institutional response to the student-led initiative of the Bank Campaign begun by Union and Yale theological students. This was consistent with his recommendations since 1932 to use economic pressures for racial and social justice causes and his support for economic sanctions and boycotts to achieve some of the aims of peace. They were feared by conservatives and the FBI as dangerous leftists, but that is really a misunderstanding. Europe would achieve basically their advocated mixed economies with fuller welfare policies than the United States could achieve. Their homeland of the United States had too many forces resisting their preferred solutions and they understood that reality. Tillich died in the years of the Johnson Administration and Niebuhr in the Nixon years, and so neither had to deal with the more right-wing policies of President Reagan or the Bush Administrations.

Since his time many students of Niebuhr and of John C. Bennett and Roger L. Shinn, his successors, have worked on the economic aspects of the justice struggle. Bob Stivers, a leader in ecological ethics has suggested there are resources for balancing corporate power including nonviolent political demonstrations, political organization, international political organization, labor organization, deconstruction academic work by intellectuals, and nongovernmental organizations, investigative journalism, church corporate responsibility work, and the sensitizing of corporate managers.[8] Gary Dorrien, an admiring critic and successor in the Niebuhr Chair at Union, develops arguments for the earlier social gospel agenda of economic democracy.[9] Shinn, one of the first of the professors to develop ecological ethics was succeeded in the Niebuhr Chair by Larry Rasmussen who developed further the field of ecological ethics and has been a critic of corporate power, along with Stivers, as both argued for developing policies of a humane, sustainable society. Professor Max Stackhouse at Princeton, who owed his realism and much of his thought to Niebuhr and Tillich emphasized the contributions to human welfare that corporations were making and also argued for their assuming ethical responsibility for their actions. An admirer, Ambassador Michael Novak at the American Enterprise Institute, developed the pro-corporate, market side of Niebuhr's arguments without the same enthusiasm for Niebuhr's government side of the mixed economy. Mark Lewis Taylor creatively uses the socialist perspectives of Paul Tillich to promote the social justice side of the argument critical of the American economy.[10]

Neither Tillich nor Niebuhr actually answers questions of economic justice for the present. They both knew that faith could not project answers to those questions. Their perspectives are still relevant in the intellectual debates at the general attitudinal level rather than the technical economic level at which neither were expert.

Henry Clark, one of the better economically informed Christian ethicists concludes that Niebuhr's solution in the 1950s to accept a welfare state fueled by mixed economies became the dominant position among Christian ethicists in the 1960s and 1970s. Most of them included Niebuhr's convictions that the fight against poverty had to be renewed and funded. Some were inclined to push further for democratic socialist conclusions and few of the Christian ethicists in the Society of Christian Ethics (the main professional society of the field) would have supported the country's drift to the right in the 1970s. Major thinkers like Michael Novak, Max Stackhouse, and Richard Neuhaus who supported the rightward trend, received little support from their academic colleagues. The more left-wing critics of various liberation positions received more support from the academics, but by the turn of the century the progressiveness of Niebuhr seemed to have carried the day. Henry Clark was careful to point out that various voices need to be heard. Among the progressives, more radical voices can project what moderate scholarship can refine and aspects of which they can support for further development. In particular he welcomed the non-Niebuhrian Third World critiques of capitalism like those represented in the World Council of Churches attacking corporate-capitalist power. Corporate power and its ethos revealed in the scandals of the first decade of the twenty-first century need critique and to be balanced by the powers Stivers suggested above. However, critical perspectives like the Presbyterian Church official policy of "Just Globalization" are wiser and more responsive to Niebuhr's warnings than World Council of Churches' recent publications on economics which are more informed by neo-Marxist categories. Clark is more optimistic about the left-wing ecumenical tendencies and, though acknowledging Michael Harrington's conclusion that democratic socialism will not prevail in our lifetime, also echoes Rosemary Ruether that there is every reason to keep trying.[11] He believes that democratic socialists are quite close to Niebuhr's overall agenda and urges that we drop the labels. Our economic fate is to live in a mixed economy as does most of the world with various shades of mixture. The task is to structure the economy so that all can share in the sustainable necessities of a good, human life while limiting greed and balancing power. Tendencies are running in other directions in the U.S.A., and the populace is so uninformed in political economy and ethics that support for the broad array of needed policies is weak.

Race Ethics

Paul Tillich's major intervention in race relations was in his defense of Jews. Here his activities were heroic and grounded in friendship. Particularly from his years in the academic circles of Berlin he associated with Jewish intellectuals in his socialist discussion groups. These contacts continued and expanded in Frankfurt in the Institute for Social Research. His writing identified the prophetic spirit which was decisive for modernity in its Hebrew origins, and he insisted Christianity was dependent upon its Hebrew roots for its integrity. His major university address was on the subject of the Jewish contribution to German culture, and he defended Jewish students at the university physically and in print.

For him the horrors of Nazism were rooted in its anti-Semitism and in its repudiation of modern humanism and learning. His distance from other early Christian opposition to Nazism was in his commitments to defend Judaism and in his political activities with socialist Jews. His labors in émigré organizations were dedicated to all opponents of Nazism including Jews. His first political speech in New York City and his first political broadcast on the Voice of America were both against the sin of anti-Semitism. At Columbia University he was involved with Jewish scholars, and the FBI particularly investigated his service, along with Niebuhr, on committees to eliminate anti-Semitism from school and church textbooks. Friendship with and use of the thought of Martin Buber led him, near the end of his life, to Israel to dialogue once again with the scholar.

There are records of his financial support for NAACP causes. His prowling of night clubs in Harlem contributed both to his infamy and appreciation depending upon one's perspective. His influence is obvious in the early Black theology of George Kelsey and in the later Black power theology of James Cone. Martin Luther King, Jr., following Kelsey and his faculty from Boston University, utilized his thought on power, love, and justice in the civil rights struggle and his ontological method in his doctoral dissertation. Love is at the heart of his theology and love requires power be used for the justice of the neighbor. Tillich blessed the civil rights struggle and his thought was adopted by many Christians in explaining why the struggle was an appropriate Christian cause and the means of the struggle needed to be realistic.

Niebuhr's involvement with American blacks began about the same period as Tillich's alliances with Jews, in the 1920s. Niebuhr's chairing the Race Relations Commission for Detroit led to his lifelong friendship with Fred Butzel, a Jewish lawyer on the commission. From this friendship grew Niebuhr's great respect for Jewish social righteousness. To his funeral in Stockbridge I shared a car trip with Abraham Heschel and his daughter Susanne from New York City. Ursula would write movingly that Abraham was Reinhold's closest friend in his last years. She was particularly pleased with her husband's final essay for the president of Jewish Theological Seminary's book, "Mission and Opportunity: Religion in a Pluralistic Culture." Dr. Finkelstein graciously invited me to the seder at the Jewish Theological Seminary in appreciation of his own friendship with Niebuhr. Niebuhr's friendships and partnerships with Jews carried on throughout his career and they returned the respect and honor he showed to them. Similarly students from Jewish and Union theological seminaries cooperated and supported each other in the civil rights struggles and demonstrations. Niebuhr's own relationships with his German relatives were disrupted by their anti-Semitism. The Niebuhr household was never hesitant to rally to the support of Israel from before its existence to its last wars during his lifetime. The continuing support of Ursula for Israel was unflagging.

Throughout this study, aspects of Niebuhr's support for the empowerment of American blacks have been noted. Most significant were his leadership of the Detroit Commission on Race Relations, the Delta Farm in Mississippi, passages in *Moral Man and Immoral Society* on strategies for winning justice for blacks, the influence on Martin Luther King. Jr., and his continual writing and speaking on the need for full justice for blacks.[13]

In previous writing I have emphasized how his work in race relations shows his full theories of progressive social action. He brought the need for racial justice into his teaching and preaching. He utilized social research to inform his approach to social change. His recommendations, while remaining realistic, stretched beyond present practice. He built political and social coalitions for social change and nurtured the organizations personally and financially. He urged government pressures for justice. He urged the churches to act, but understood parachurch organizations would have to carry the agendas further than the regular churches could. He used mixtures of Christian ethics and American values in his pressure for justice. He supported nonviolent civil disobedience for justice. The struggle for justice had to be carried on within many different arenas at the same time.

My chief regret regarding his contribution to racial justice is that he neglected to carry it forward in his major books beyond *Moral Man and Immoral Society*, and the short chapter in *Pious and Secular America*. It is noticeably underdeveloped in *The Irony of American History*. Before publication his friend

Arthur Schlesinger, Jr. criticized the omission as James Cone pointed out to me. Schlessinger failed to criticize Niebuhr's omission when he reviewed the book in Niebuhr's journal. The book is also lamentably absent any reference to the destruction of the Native-American population of the continent. The chapter on "tribalism" in the last volume, *Man's Nature and His Communities*, is not forceful enough in denouncing the evil done to the black community. By 1960, when I arrived at Union Theological Seminary, support for the civil rights movement was in the ethos. Two of the younger faculty had just returned from action in integrating airport facilities in the South, and a supportive picketing of the Woolworth Store on 125th Street in Harlem was underway. A tutor on Christian ethics was soon harassed and threatened as a "Freedom Rider" in the integration of the bus lines in the South. Niebuhr was part of the movement, though he regretted that his only actions could be through writing and encouraging due to his crippled state.

An essay he wrote in the summer of 1963 reflected support for the movement, but his own recognition that blacks had to carry the struggle forward. It was published a few weeks before the Martin Luther King, Jr. inspired March on Washington.

> The simplest explanation for the increasingly urgent demonstrations of the blacks against disfranchisement, segregation in school and church, lunch counters and public conveyance, and against every public custom that affronts the dignity of the human being, is that the Negro feels—as we all ought to feel—that a century is a long time to wait for the elimination of the "American dilemma." If we recognize that the present situation is more unbearable to the victims of injustice than it is offensive to the conscience of men, we are confronted by the hardness of the human heart, even among those whose hearts have been softened by human sympathy and the stirrings of conscience. Try as we will we cannot feel the pain of others as vividly as they do.[14]

The essay proceeded to support the legislation on civil rights proposed, but not adopted until 1964. He praised the Negro church for its support of the civil rights movement and criticized the white church for its tardy responses to the issues. He hoped for the passing of the legislation, expecting a great struggle over it as the white supremacists became more desperate in opposition. Yet he doubted that the recalcitrant would be moved by the law as they had resisted the court decisions to integrate the schools for a decade. Custom had great resources for resisting both the law of the land and the law of conscience. He still hoped the church might help in moving those resisting justice.

James Baldwin

The Sixteenth Street Baptist Church in Birmingham was bombed on 15 September 1963. The following week the Protestant Council of New York City presented a dialogue between James Baldwin and Reinhold Niebuhr moderated by Thomas Kilgore minister of the Friendship Baptist Church and the director of the Southern Christian Leadership Conference in New York City.[15] They were both asked to comment on a faceless representation of Christ from the ruin of the church. To Baldwin it suggested the need for a new representation of Christ because the picture of the alabaster Christ had failed. Niebuhr said he agreed with Baldwin on the moral failure and continued:

> This moral crisis that we live in, as far as the church is concerned, represents a failure of the church, particularly the Protestant church. Catholicism, that's another problem, and it hasn't been as failing in the racial situation as Protestantism has. As far as the church is concerned, I think we have to admit first of all that we have miserably failed to give the Christian message a real content, a real face, the face of Christ. I think I feel a little hesitant to say love, because I think one of the failings of the Protestant church is always to say love when we are dealing with group relations, when we ought to speak of justice. The Negro doesn't love the white man collectively or the white man the Negro collectively. The thing is the pope, Pope John, was more right than we Protestants when in his encyclical he said, "Let love be the motive, but justice is the instrument." We have got to realize in Protestant Christianity that there is such a thing as the motive of love with justice as the instrument of this love. And justice means respect for the other person across racial boundaries. We haven't comprehended the real mystery of group prejudice.

In response to a follow-up question, he said:

> Well, this is a revolution, of course. And the significant thing is that the Negro church has been significant. The Negro church has been the leadership of this movement, or one of the many leaders because, also there are secular movements as well as the Christian movement. It is the *white* church that has failed. The Negro church has revitalized itself in this crisis. I should say that from my standpoint Martin Luther King is one of great Americans of our day; and for this reason: that he has related nonviolence to resistance.

Baldwin responded when requested:

> What I think is that there is a very great paradox occurring in this country now. What you say about the Negro church for example, is, I think, entirely true. Martin has used the Negro church really as a kind of tool, not only to

> liberate Negroes but to liberate the entire country They are the only people in the country at the moment who believe either in Christianity or in the country, and are the most despised minority in it. It is ironical, I am trying to say, that the people who were slaves here, the most beaten and despised people here, and for so long, should be at this moment, and I mean this, absolutely the only hope this country has. It doesn't have any other.

Niebuhr's response elaborated on his thesis that it was a revolutionary situation and that though the Negroes had to bear the burden of the revolutionary situation, they could count on some from other groups assisting them. Continuing he said:

> Now, I think that is the significant thing in our present revolutionary situation. You could say that the Negro is the only genuine proletarian, speaking socially, in America. He is the revolutionist; he has got to be the revolutionist. He has got to recapture many of our revolutionary traditions and Christian traditions and moral traditions. And nevertheless we can't quite, I think you are not—if I have read you correctly, and I have read, I think, almost everything you have written—you are not throwing out the white man as white man.

Baldwin responded:

> No, no, no. I don't mean to say that. But I do mean to say this—that the bulk of the white Protestant majority in this country, the white Christian majority in this country, has exhibited a really staggering level of irresponsibility, an immoral washing of the hands. And really because segregation means among other things, they do not know what goes on in my kitchen, you know? I don't mean to say the white populace are villains or devils or anything like that. They are irresponsible.

Niebuhr, not quite hearing asked: "They are irresponsible, you say?" Baldwin:

> Yes. They are morally irresponsible, criminally irresponsible. But this is their country too. What I want to say is that I don't suppose that everyone in Birmingham, who lives in Birmingham, are monstrous people. But there may be silent people, you know, and that is a crime in itself. That's what I mean.

Interestingly, it was Baldwin who moved the conversation to economics and politics insisting that it was the people's responsibility to move the issues to Washington, D.C. to stop urban "removal." The neighborhoods needed to be integrated and the schools would follow. Full employment was needed; it was twice as bad among Negroes. He was not concerned about being liked by political opponents, but the structure of the country needed to be changed. His criticism of the American people was that they allowed a political vacuum to appear which the racists seized. Niebuhr when asked about theology, agreed with Baldwin that the church had failed, and that the Protestant church suffered from its individualism and its failure to struggle for justice.

Baldwin had called for a boycott of Christmas to commemorate the Birmingham martyrs and Niebuhr was sympathetic to the concept. Niebuhr praised James Reston's power analysis of Birmingham and his call for the powerful national companies to act and to create the communication needed between the white and black communities. The moderator had seen a sign in a picket line at the United Nations reading "Arm the Negroes." He asked the two respondents about it. Baldwin noted the irony of the country loving violence in its structures, in its entertainment, but being repulsed by the sight of a Negro with a gun. Niebuhr affirmed we were in a revolution which means violence, but that this revolution was occurring in a legal system. They sparred a little about the legal system and its tendency to be violent to the Negro. Niebuhr concluded the discussion with this remark:

> Now this is a paradoxical situation but I wouldn't say that the answer is violence for the Negro. I would honor the principle of nonviolence not from purely moral reasons, as Mr. Baldwin quite rightly says, we honor the Revolutionary war and the Civil War, etc.,—but because it is pragmatically the only way that a minority group can deal with a majority group.

Baldwin was the stronger of the two on the subject. Niebuhr was informed, but less political than Baldwin who resided mostly in Paris in self-imposed exile. Niebuhr's discussion of the nonviolent revolution was deep, but Baldwin's politics at one level seemed more relevant. The dialogue with Baldwin is the only written record of sustained dialogue with a leading, radical Black intellectual. Martin Halliwell reconstructed a dialogue with Martin Luther King, Jr. but it was only of King's learning from Niebuhr's works throughout his education and Niebuhr learning from King how much could be accomplished through Christian use of massive non-violent, civil protest in America. Niebuhr had much to learn from King about the power of hope and the relationship of eschatology to social change. Unfortunately the two never had a face-to-face conversation. However, further events in 1963 would move the situation to where the pressure of disturbances in the street could lead to later civil-rights legislation, but without the economic gains for Negroes that Baldwin hoped to see. Niebuhr's essay on race in 1968 would address economic and political issues that Baldwin put forward in 1963.

Seminar

Niebuhr's lecture on race in December 1964 at Union Theological Seminary correspondened with the writing he was doing on the book that appeared in 1965. In *Man's Nature and His Communities* he dealt with racism under the heading "Man's Tribalism as One Source of His Inhumanity." The post-retirement seminar was held in room 1014 across the hall from the bookstore. His student assistant was John Raines who translated his experience as a freedom rider in integrating the bus lines in the South to organizing Union students for social action for integration. The chapter on tribalism dealt with many conflicts beyond the race issue in the U.S.A. whereas the lecture dealt only with the local situation. He argued Christianity is the inheritor of human universalism from the Stoics and also from Hebrew universalism as seen in Amos. Paul preached universalism from the Stoics to the Athenians, God "made from one every nation of men to live on all the face of the earth." Also from his letter to the Galatians: "There is neither Jew nor Greek; there is neither slave nor free; there is neither male nor female; for you all are one in Christ Jesus." Unfortunately the Christian universalism set them against the Jews and led to the history of Christian anti-Judaism. Contemporary anthropological universalism as in Ruth Benedict shows that race is a historical and not a biological construct. The historical differences distinguishing one group from another are greater than any of the biological markers used to distinguish one race from another.

Racism is as close to original sin as any expression of sin. The pride taken in the "we" group excludes the other. As the "other" moves towards the "we" group and adopts its tribalism character it receives more toleration. Majorities tend to have a high degree of prejudice, but minorities display it also. Niebuhr finally resigned from the Conference of Jews and Christians because he felt the overflagellation of Christians in the organization obscured the universalistic tendencies toward prejudice.

Anti-Semitism, he argued, was rooted in racial, religious, and economic motivations. The forcing of the Jews into money lending in Europe fostered the resentments of those who borrowed money. Money lenders are usually regarded as dishonest by those who need to borrow money. The populist movements translated the resentment of the money lenders to this country. Jews were often regarded as dishonest even though their record for civil justice often puts Christians to shame.

Cardinal Bea asked Rabbi Heschel about racial prejudice against Jews while he was working on the memo to the Vatican Council for its consideration about Jews and the killing of Christ. The Jewish community presented a memo to the Roman Catholic Council, and then reacted negatively when the schema on the subject was postponed. Heschel commented on the conservatism of the Spanish bishops who were willing to say that: "Not many Jews killed Jesus." W. D. Davies had influenced Niebuhr to see how the Gospel of Matthew contrasted the law of Jesus as superior to the law of Moses, and the other gospels contained the seeds of early church-Jewish conflict.

The human situation of being divided into tribes, groups, and nations tainted all of our judgments. We evaluate others by our own standards. Black theologians today would probably accuse Niebuhr of such taint while recalling his frequent references to backwardness of the race caused by years of slavery and repression. Pictures of Niebuhr, before his stroke, on the Delta Cooperative Farm which ministered to and organized poor tenant farmers, many of whom could not read, signals some of the explanation, if not justification for some of Niebuhr's observations.

As he turned in the lecture toward the discrimination against the Negro, he emhasized the difficulty of the American problem given the suffering under the previous condition of servitude and the resultant cultural backwardness marked by the identifiable color differences. The dilemma was rooted in the history illustrated by Thomas Jefferson's declaration of equality while fathering mulattoes from his own slave women. Slavery was deeply embedded in states where Jeffersonian democracy and Christian evangelism were very strong and prominent. The Methodist and Baptist churches with their perfectionist and sectarian ideals could not resist slavery. Evangelicalism sank into legalism as it tried to prove it was really good as a church. It was forced to confront its failure to face the social evil in its midst, but basically it failed to approach fulfillment of the love commandment.

Robert Penn Warren's *Heritage of Civil War* admitted we were forced to be one nation, but could not restore the Negro nor solve the racial issue. The free society according to Jefferson was based upon an educated electorate. But the Negro received neither education nor the vote after reconstruction, spoiling the whole system. Niebuhr then worked through the Hayes-Tilden election and the deal in 1871 that abandoned reconstruction for Southern votes. Until 1954, the Supreme Court bowed to election returns and failed to enforce the ideas of equality which it pronounced. Niebuhr cautioned against over-optimism about court decisions as he believed that when overwhelming support of custom meets law, custom would prevail. Later many of his cautionary statements about gains through court decisions would receive sharp criticism. Such caution was natural to one who thought in organic terms of functionalism as well as normative concerns of ethics. He experienced personally the backlash he feared in the overthrow of the Delta Farm's succeeding farm, Providence.

He cautioned Southern preachers as to keeping their pulpits, but he saw some of them allied with him lose their church positions. As a student deeply involved in the civil rights struggles I believe I was more optimistic than Niebuhr about the court cases, but in retrospect observing the segregated public schools in the South and the North, Niebuhr's pessimism was realistic. Still he was saying in the seminar in 1963: "Why should we have the Negro revolt in 1963?" He said the Supreme Court decisions gave the Negroes hope and revolutions often depend upon the twin factors of hope and desperation. Also, the rise of the articulate element in the Negro population furthers the struggle, and the sit-ins are very important. The final use of Federal power by the Kennedys also encourages hope.

Racial injustice was perceived as a violation of natural law, and Roman Catholicism has a feeling for the social substance of society through long experience. He reiterated the Catholic superiority to the Protestant response to the civil rights struggle, saying the strong connections within the system reveal the witness of the total church against the local church. Such rigor debunks the congregational principles of the seventeenth century still seen in Protestantism. The local prejudices of the laity can control the independent local church. The weak response of the Protestant church to the racial issues also reveals weaknesses of Protestant social conscience. Here we have had a real simple issue in conflict with the love ethic, and we bungled it badly. Evangelical emphasis upon conversion has hindered the movement. It called people back to the moral standards of the deficient church community. The sins of culture were not understood or dealt with through evangelism. He thought the Negro church had been subject to all forms of corruption represented and criticized differently by James Baldwin and Adam Clayton Powell. Its passion for social justice, however, has redeemed the Negro church. Martin Luther King, Jr. who has led the movement is a moral hero revealing how grand a human can be, but he also spreads illusions. The need to struggle for civil rights also shows how terrible humanity can become. It is a hard question to determine whether illusion is necessary for social change and progress.[16]

In 1965, Niebuhr was asked to contribute a foreword to *Mississippi Black Paper* by the Council of Federated Organizations, an organization dedicated to registering Mississippi Negroes to vote. The book was a collection of affidavits and statements which revealed the horrible conditions of official justice in the state of Mississippi. The documents exposed the brutality of the police and the injustice of the courts. "On the evidence of these affidavits, it seems that that there are no limits to inhumanity, cruelty and sheer caprice in a closed society, once social and communal restraints are no longer in force."[17] According to Niebuhr the documents proved the absolute need for the Civil Rights Bill for the country's well-being. Law had to be enforced on Mississippi which he compared to Nazi Germany and South Africa in inhumanity and brutality. He concluded:

> There are no quick or simple ways to eliminate the monstrous injustices revealed in these pages, but perhaps these affidavits will suggest to their readers that justice in Mississippi is corrupted to such a degree that without aid from the outside it is doomed.[18]

Among the half-dozen other pieces on race relations finishing out the last half-decade of his life, the most important on civil rights for African-Americans was "The Negro Minority and Its Fate in a Self-Righteous Nation."[19] Here in a small denominational publication of his own church he analyzed the violence of the ghettoes that erupted in 1967–1968. He based much of his analysis upon the report of the National Advisory Commission's recommendations to the country after the riots. The failure of the education system in the cities was emphasized along with the unemployment of young Negroes. Promised reforms had not come or they had come too late for the poor, underfed, unemployed, uneducated Negro population. He then detailed American illusions which contributed to the complacency and resistance of the white community to injustice. The Negro from the first slave days to the present had been kept at the bottom of the ladder by the white society. Denied the free land awarded many by the Homestead Act, they were kept in poverty, denied the vote, and discriminated against at every level.

Both the courts and Martin Luther King, Jr.'s boycotts were given credit for initiating revolutionary hope among the downtrodden Negro minority. He denied that the riots of 1966–1967 were part of the revolution, but rather indicated that the changing attitude of the nation had come too late to alleviate festering frustration. The gap between the ideology of freedom of the nation and its reality was too great. He noted it was the business of the church to remind the nation of its moral responsibilities. The Protestant churches had failed while the Catholics did a little better. Neither Jeffersonian democracy nor evangelical Christianity was equal to the task of moral guidance within their societies. Both idealisms became sources of complacency within the nation on racial injustice. It was fortunate that some interracial congregations had grown, and he believed the groundwork for the movement had some of its origins in integrated denominational and interdenominational conferences. The churches had a responsibility to contribute to the reform of the welfare system, and the idea of a "negative income tax" was needed to assure all families of at least a minimal income for living. More scholarships to assure quality education for Negroes were a national priority. Other priorities of the National Commission needed to set the agenda for the returning congress to address. Without congressional response, more rioting should be expected. Echoing the address of Martin Luther King, Jr., he explained that addressing the needs of the Negro was certainly a greater priority than the futile war in Vietnam which cost billions. "After almost two centuries of broken promises and pledges our debt to our Negro minority is immense and obvious, and its burden lies heavy upon our consciences."[20]

The agenda, more than forty years later remains much the same as Niebuhr argued in 1968. William Julius Wilson in *More than Just Race* returns to the need for affirming dignity or human appreciation to the Black and the provision of income, preferably through dignified work, to the black population. Barack Obama's agenda focuses on improving education, and his administration is trying to find a way to return to employment after the financial scandals which drove the country into recession. However the failures of education, employment, drug addiction, and gun policy have made the ghettoes intolerable. Now the guns and drugs destroy the youth individually rather than uniting some few of them in rioting. Niebuhr's analysis recognized white supremacy and the resultant anger and saw the riots as political action even if disconnected from the civil rights movement. While we probably recognize the economic needs that Niebuhr saw, the assassination of King denied the probability of the further success of the most successful tactic in Black advancement, the massive, nonviolent civil protest and disobedience in the name of religious insight from the black church and Gandhi's religious nonviolence. Niebuhr's organic sense of society and sin led him to suspect the gains in race relations would be less than the more militant blacks hoped for and he was criticized for words of caution and prudence. However in the 1960s, he called both for economic support for the impoverished black family, and for the government to use discipline in recalcitrant states to force social justice upon those racist elements in the society. Andrew Young saw Niebuhr and Tillich as the underlying intellectual force of the civil right's movement for Martin:

> I want to begin by saying that there was always a misunderstanding of what Martin Luther King was about. I remember one night when someone came at him with some of the strict presuppositions of Ghandian nonviolence, and he responded about three o'clock in the morning with the most brilliant lecture I have ever heard on *The Nature and Destiny of Man*, Reinhold Niebuhr, the thinking of John Bennett, and *Christianity and Crisis*. He reminded us that he had done his Ph.D. thesis on Paul Tillich, and you realized how everything he did was formulated more out of a sense of Christian realism and out of the historic black reality of the Christian church, in the Southern part of the United States, than I think the press had ever really understood.
>
> We always tried to make nonviolence something that was very idealistic and ethereal for the saints to live by, and never really understood as Dr. Niebuhr said as far back as *Moral Man and Immoral Society*, that nonviolent power and economic withdrawal would be the means that the black community might eventually use to gain justice.[21]

The last document listing Niebuhr's priorities was a memo sent with Mrs. Niebuhr's assistance to the American Revolution Bicentennial Commission in 1970. He urged the Commission to consider the ambiguities of American history with special reference to the slave problem and the contradiction with the nation's ideals. Secondly, he wanted a discussion of the growth and strength of the system in its 200-year history, and finally a discussion of problems and possibilities. In part 3 he listed as problems and challenges of the future:

> The elimination of the last remnants of injustice, which slavery had introduced into our democratic society and which since the Supreme Court Decision of 1954, became more and more urgent.
>
> Our responsibility for saving the environment and eliminating the pollution of air and waters created by modern industry.
>
> Our most important opportunity and responsibility is to come to terms with the problem created by the contrast between the degrees of our imperial power as one of the two superpowers in an atomic age and our responsibility for avoiding a nuclear catastrophe by our uneasy partnership with the Russian superpower.
>
> We are thus spiritually and morally committed to concern ourselves with problems which are created by the inevitable contradiction between our pride of power and our pride of virtue.[22]

The recognition of justice for the impoverished minority is no surprise in Niebuhr's list of priorities. Everyone who knew him would recognize that the last years of his life were given to problems of international relations and the Cold War in a search for both peace and resistance to Soviet imperialism. The highlighting of ecological concerns is surprising on a list of three priorities, though it was deserved. The development of moral consciousness around the issue would depend upon his students though, particularly Roger L. Shinn, Larry Rasmussen, and Robert L. Stivers. Tillich was also, at his end, writing about peace in his participation in the colloquium on "Pacem en Terris," in his writing on nuclear weapons and technology, and in his final essay on hope. A reading and comparison of their latter sermons shows Tillich dealing more with the encounter with the divine and Niebuhr dealing more with the international political issues.

In their respective last year of work Tillich was talking about the importance of world religions to understanding Christianity and Niebuhr wrote about Jewish-Christian relations in a major essay. They both worked on the Jewish-Christian relations issues while Tillich went further in his dialogues with Buddhism and Niebuhr, mostly, stayed at the introductory level of world religions in his teaching of the ethics of other world religions. Tillich's *Christianity and the Encounter of the World Religions* shows that his dialogue was still nurtured by the Lutheran traditions of his boyhood faith. Christopher

Niebuhr, Reinhold's son, sent the last manuscript found in Niebuhr's typewriter after his death to the Library of Congress. It was on Martin Luther and in particular on Luther's critique of the Roman Catholic Church in the Reformation.

Niebuhr's wide-ranging participation in justice in race relations indicated his strategy and persistence in social action was deeper, and longer lasting than Tillich's. Tillich's intellectual engagement with Marxism was the more profound of the two and must rank as one of the most thorough engagements with Karl Marx by a Christian philosopher, Niebuhr's navigation of the dangers of the Cold War was more thorough than Tillich's relative disengagement from it. Though both emphasized the contributions of religion to personal development, Tillich contributed more to psychology of religion than Niebuhr who contributed more to social philosophy. Not everyone would see it this way. Nathan Scott, Jr. credits Niebuhr's reflections on the self to be his greatest contribution:

> Yet that side of the Gifford Lectures which is likely to make the greatest final claim on future arbiters of intellectual ferment in the first half of this century is that which entails the great feat of imagination represented by Niebuhr's analysis of selfhood. For it is in this dimension of his thought as one of the greatest of Christian "psychologists" of the modern period, that he most nearly proves his parity with Pascal and Kierkegaard.[23]

Tillich, as Niebuhr said, was considered the greatest of the philosophers of religion in his time. They remained friends, and if Tillich could have taken up residence at Union in 1965 as he planned, it would have been fascinating to see how these two closely allied in Tillich's time at Union from 1933 to 1955 would have evolved.

Their greatness also resides in another dimension. They turned their traumas into creativity. Tillich's nervous breakdowns in battle in World War I and the resultant post-traumatic stress disorder still forty years later could drive him to awake screaming, an experience many veterans know. Niebuhr's repeated collapses from overwork preceded the strokes which separated him from death by almost a score of years. He was crippled, but with only one hand to type and a stumbling gait he could defy the Federal Bureau of Investigation and frighten the White House with his critiques of its folly in a misplaced war. Both men turned their suffering into immense creativity.

They also rose above other weaknesses. Tillich's world, meaning, and order were broken by the war, and still he arose from it to create a new synthesis in philosophy of religion which gave structure to his Christian systematic theology. Niebuhr drove through his inadequate, Midwestern preparation in the German language to achieve intellectual genius, and then turned that into a Christian social philosophy which stood the test of time as he evolved and the nation changed. The vulnerabilities of the man were first published, I think, by Richard

Fox who had early access to his personal letters. Fox detailed his early insecurities very well, but perhaps failed to understand Niebuhr's contributions as well as several of us who knew of his genius, before we learned of the vulnerabilities with which he worked. Those included the family disposition to depression, which threatened to overcome him when he suffered physically in those last years. His letters to Bishop Will Scarlett and Justice Felix Frankfurter discuss his actions to heal the depression. Students sitting with him in his home in his closing seminars could not detect the depression which he rose to overcome. Through these vulnerabilities they became, in my estimation, the greatest thinkers of all of the contemporary scientists, philosophers, and writers I've studied. There is another book to write about their overcoming of their traumas, and perhaps the president of Union Theological Seminary, Serene Jones, can initiate it with her interdisciplinary study of trauma and Christian faith.[24] Niebuhr had rejected fine offers at Yale and Harvard Universities to remain at the seminary and close to its church context. Tillich coming from the university and less committed to the church than Niebuhr found its ethos strange at first, but it protected and nurtured him into his greatest achievements. There were conflicts within the community, but it remained the secure protector and basic community within which and from which they influenced the country.

The best known story of Niebuhr and Tillich resides in at least three versions. Robert McAfee Brown shared his version with me.

> You know the story about a student referring to Tillich in Niebuhr's class in relationship to nature, creation or something like that... Reinhold Niebuhr responded in an offhand way, "Aw, Tillich is nothing but a damned nature mystic." The word rapidly made its way to Tillich, and the next morning, after chapel, as Reinhold is bustling along Claremont Ave. there was Tillich admiring the spring crocuses. "Ah yes, Reinie, "he said, "Ze damn nature mystic is vorshipping ze flowers."[25]

Their fight most known to the public was whether or not Picasso's *Guernica* protesting and prophesying modern aerial warfare was "the most Protestant painting" as Tillich asserted. Probably the depths of the debate were rooted in Tillich's inclination to find the genius of Protestantism in protest and religious substance in Catholicism. Niebuhr more polemical in criticism of Catholicism in those early years, found both in Protestantism. As early as 1970, Niebuhr would list the ecological issue as one of the three major issues to be confronted by the nation as it began to prepare for its bicentennial celebration in 1976. But he never had Tillich's mystical association with nature as his world was that of the human historical. While he knew the human was rooted in nature, he emphasized more than his friend the transcendence from nature.

Someone shared an imaginary sequel to the well-known debate. Reinie conceded to Tillich saying: "Paulus in matters and taste of art I am a moron." Paulus still struggling learning English did not understand *moron*. For three weeks he fretted wondering what school of art was *moron*. Just before phoning the new director of the Musem of Modern art, his daughter Mutie put him straight on the meaning of the term and saved him the call.

John Dillenberger wrote to me that the two played out games with each other wondering if they really knew what the other was doing or thinking. Once in the hall, Reinie said to Tillich. "Paulus, that's nothing but Schleiermacher," to which Tillich, beaming, said, "Of course." So the chiding, one of the other, was received as if that was not all that was being done. Deception, no. Rather I think a deep respect, not letting or assuming that the other was saying anything negative.[26]

When, in 1990, I surveyed Union students from 1932–1960 about Niebuhr, I was surprised to learn how many of them said they did not understand Niebuhr or Tillich. Harjie Likins said that in the late 1940s Tillich and Niebuhr were neck and neck in popularity among the students and that

> A story went around about the poor student who went to Tillich's lecture and was totally confused, so he went to Niebuhr for an explanation, but he could not understand Niebuhr on Tillich. So he had to end with John Bennett who explained Niebuhr's explanation of Tillich and then explained Tillich.[27]

The great respect they had for each other is affirmed in their public as well as private words. Niebuhr wrote: "There is no one in our generation who so completely masters the stuff, philosophical and theological, with which he is dealing as Tillich."[28]

The respect was surrounded by real friendship. Tillich confessed this deep feeling of friendship in his *Travel Diary; 1936*. But their friendship was also founded in common commitments. They were partners in the philosophy of religion field. Tillich had a great debt, perhaps his life, to Reinhold Niebuhr's telegram asking him to accept the appointment at Union and Columbia. Beneath that lay H. Richard Niebuhr's translation of *The Religious Situation* which introduced Tillich to the American academic world. Not only real debts and affectionate feelings, but partnership in practical work at the Seminary and beyond bonded them together. Elizabeth Niebuhr Sifton put it in her book *The Serenity Prayer*: "They were friends."

Beverly Harrison reflected on her experiences of them as a student.

> Tillich and Niebuhr's relationship was, of course, a matter of constant speculation amongst students in the 1950s. Many of us perceived them as "World's apart theologically" and looked for every opportunity to surface the

> difference, but neither was easily baited on the point, and limited their criticisms to "asides" in the classroom. Tillich was more diffident in this regard than Niebuhr, as I recall. However, Niebuhr's own diffidence as a theologian seemed also to result in caution when discussing differences with Tillich. He usually stressed his preferences for dealing with the historical realities of religion and his doubts about ontology as the entry point into theological reflection.
>
> My favorite Niebuhr/Tillich story derives from my walking into room 214 just behind Niebuhr one morning, before Christian ethics. Tillich's class was just leaving the room and he (Tillich) met Niebuhr at the door. I was caught, literally, in the midst of the exchange. Reinie said, "Paulus, I have been reading your new book. It's wonderful, wonderful—I think it may be the best thing you have written." Tillich literally blushed with pleasure and said something to the effect—"Reinie, Reinie—do you really think so?" I was a bit embarrassed to stand there, but I could not move on, so I continued to stand there as Niebuhr went on about his enthusiasm. Tillich was like a little boy in a candy shop, he was so pleased. When I finally got into 214 and sat down, I found myself very confused. Niebuhr had been talking about *The Shaking of the Foundations*, and while I also love that book, I wondered if it hadn't been some kind of a put down to insist that that was possibly Tillich's best book! I realized, of course, that Tillich had not heard Niebuhr's comment that way—but I wondered.[29]

This collection of comments from the halls of Union would not be complete without Owen Thomas's remembrance. His sense that Niebuhr was a friend and colleague of Tillich, but not a close friend, corresponds to the memory of Wilhelm Pauck. Thomas said: "They spoke German together. Tillich and Niebuhr were walking down the hall speaking in German. Tillich was speaking and Niebuhr was saying 'Ja, Ja, Ja.' (Then) 'Oh hell, yes!' "[30]

Roger Shinn, too, puzzled about the relationship between Tillich and Niebuhr.

> Richard Fox dug out what he could, but his treatment is not adequate. When Tillich arrived in this country, knowing no English, Reinie was one person with whom he could converse. As late as my time, I heard them occasionally exchanging comments in German as they passed each other in the halls. Each had a genuine admiration for the other. See Gilkey's angry review of Fox for an example of Tillich's admiration for Reinie. Many people glibly associated the two as "neoorthodox," a bad categorization for both. I think I once wrote in *Christianity and Crisis*, back in the days when I was one of their regulars, that I long puzzled over this categorization of Tillich until the reason dawned on me: he spoke with a German accent. There's one other possible reason. As Niebuhr once said in a friendly, jovial way, "Whatever heresies Paul Tillich goes wandering among, he always comes home to 'justification by faith.' "

But to back up, the two became strongly associated in the public mind. A sound reason is that each of them defended the other against critics of the prevailing liberal-rational type. So the critics of both tended to merge them. The phrase: "Niebuhr and Tillich," became almost one word in some circles, even sometimes at Union. But it was foolish.

There was one more reason for the popular association. When Tillich arrived in this country, Niebuhr immediately welcomed him and many of his friends (including Eduard Heimann and others from the New School) into the Fellowship of Socialist Christians, and they there found something of an American base. Actually, as Tillich's book on "Religious Socialism" shows there was a considerable difference between the continental group and Niebuhr's American group. But they shared many criticisms of the dominant American culture, and from the mainstream of American politics they looked alike.

One night (somewhere during my 1945–1949 period at Union) I found myself helping Reinie and Urusla clean up their kitchen after a party. We combined intellectual conversation with dishwashing in a very Niebuhrian way. Something led Reinie to comment, "You Know, I've just begun to realize how really different Paul and I are." I replied brashly—it was easy to be brash around Reinie—"Your students have known it for a long time." He laughed in his friendly way. We students knew it because we were getting Tillich's "system" in his lectures, Niebuhr, reading Tillich's early publications and entering conversation with him was slower in getting the impact of "the system."[31]

In conclusion it is fitting to end with suggestions of their mutual genius and how their thought compliments each other. Niebuhr wrestled for years with the dialectic of love and justice. At last, he talked about it as Christian love inspiring the struggle for justice utilizing power. Tillich provided a philosophy of love, justice, and power for Niebuhr's more pragmatic synthesis. Niebuhr's dialectic gives the push for the never-ending struggle for justice, and Tillich provides a rationale for their necessary relationship with each other and with power.Tillich provided an alternative metaphysic for the modern mind to be persuaded by the Christian perspective.

Niebuhr recognized the need for a persuasive metaphysic, and he supplied the social theory of relevance of the Christian view for the American public which was the second need in his estimation. Niebuhr developed the understanding of social thought and the example of constant action that Tillich's *Systematic Theology* called for, and Tillich's understanding of Spirit in that volume filled that lacuna in Niebuhr's theology. Tillich failed to write about the crucial importance of the black struggle in the American nation, and Niebuhr supported it, provided some conceptual thought for it, and criticized the nation for not responding to the revolution.

If Niebuhr relied too much on male symbolism, Tillich opened the door to feminine symbolism for the divine. If Tillich's Bohemian lifestyle (found in the brokenness of a defeated self and a defeated nation) was not a good representation of sexual ethics, Niebuhr's celebration of the family provided an antidote. Given they both were Euro-American-centric, Tillich's opening to further exploration of world religions began to overcome that limitation and to show new ways toward peacemaking.

Being born in empires, they learned to criticize those empires while still advocating realistic measures for their reformation and contribution to the wider community of humanity whose peaceful union was postponed to the indefinite future. They learned as chaplain and director of chaplains in World War I that the world was a very dangerous place. They never lost that sense of danger, and they also learned that the idealistic internationalism of Woodrow Wilson was limited in its capacity to maintain the peace. They knew that secular and parareligious ideologies magnified the danger. Historical inheritances made radical improvement very difficult. However beyond their Lutheran inheritance toward social pessimism, their liberal educations and values drove them to strive for social reform. Christian love inevitably sought social justice in their thought and action. Underneath these progressive measures lay a Christian faith that realized that the peace of God was different from the earth's peace. Niebuhr promised Tillich they could create a school. In a sense they succeeded in the greatness of Union Theological Seminary while they inspired it and established the ongoing relevance of Christian realism. To paraphrase the previous statement of Walter Lippmann: When will we ever see their like again?

Notes

Notes to chapter 1: The Great War

1. Richard Fox, *Reinhold Niebuhr: a Biography* (New York: Pantheon Books, 1985).

2. William G. Chrystal: *Young Reinhold Niebuhr* (St. Louis: Eden Publishing House, 1977). Chrystal brought out the story of Niebuhr's early enthusiasm for the American cause and his devotion to Woodrow Wilson's Fourteen Principles when he published the previously unknown writings of the young pastor.

3. Reinhold Niebuhr, *Leaves from the Notebook of a Tamed Cynic* (New York: Richard R. Smith, 1930) 14.

4. Chrystal, 88.

5. Ibid.

6. Ibid., 91.

7. Ibid., 99.

8. Ibid.,100.

9. See Wilhelm and Marion Pauck, *Paul Tillich: His Life and Thought,* 1 (New York: Harper & Row Publishers, 1975) 53-55.

10. Paul Tillich, "*Predigt gehalten nach den Kampen bei Tahure am 30, und 31 Oktober, 1915,*" Tillich Papers, Harvard University Archives, Cambridge MA; hereafter cited as Tillich Papers. My translation.

11. Ibid.

12. Quoted from Ronald B. MacLennan, "World War I and Paul Tillich: the Deconstruction and Reconstruction of Theology," from Paul Tillich, *Erganzungs-und Nachlassbande zu den Gesammelten Werken von Paul Tillich,* ed. Renate Albrecht andMargot Hall (Stuttgart: Evangelisches Berlagswerk, 1971) 100.

13. Paul Tillich, *Gessammelten Werken,* 13:70.

14. Paul Tillich, *A History of Christian Thought,* ed. Carl E. Braaten (New York: Simon & Schuster, 1967) 501.

15. Matthew Lon Weaver, "The Birth of a Religious Socialist: Paul Tillich at the Close of World War," unpublished paper (2008), used with permission. The following translations of the sermons are from this paper, 1.

16. Ibid., 9.

17. Ibid.,10.

18. Weaver, "The Birth of a Religious Socialist," 11.

19. Presented in MacLennan, "World War I."

Notes to chapter 2: Background of Two German Thinkers

1. E. Hershey Sneath, ed., *Religion and the War* (New Haven CT: Yale University Press, 1917).

2. Paul Tillich, *A History of Christian Thought: From its Judaic and Hellenistic Origins to Existentalism,* ed., Carl E. Braaten (New York: Simon and Schuster, 1967) 438.

3. There is more on Schelling in my earlier book *Paul Tillich's Radical Social Thought* (Atlanta: John Knox Press, 1980) 24-31. Also in reprint: (Lanham MD: University Press of America, 1986). Jerome Stone has an extensive analysis in "Tillich and Schelling's Later Philosophy," in *Kairos and Logos*, ed. John Carey (Cambridge MA: North American Paul Tillich Society, 1978) 11-44.

4. See: Fox, *Niebuhr* for a more thorough discussion of the essay.

Notes: to chapter 3: Between Emperor and Dictator

1. Paul Tillich, "Aufruf." Tillich Papers. James V. Fisher has written the fullest account of the *Bund Neue Kirche* and Tillich's association with the group in "The Politicizing of Paul Tillich: The First Phase," in *Tillich Studies: 1975*, ed. John J. Carey (Tallahassee FL: North American Paul Tillich Society, 1975) 27-38.

2. Tillich, *Gesammelte Werke* 13:154-60. Tillich, "Answer to an Inquiry of the Protestant Consistory of Brandenburg," trans. James Luther Adams, *Metanoia* (September 1971): 10.

3. Eberhard Amelung, "Religious Socialism as an Ideology: A Study of the Kairos Circle in Germany between 1919 and 1933" (doctoral diss., Harvard, 1962, university microfilms). Cf. John R. Stumme, *Socialism in Theological Perspective: A Study of Paul Tillich* (Missoula MT: Scholars Press, 1978).

4. Tillich, "Kairos," in *Die Tat* XIV (1922): Heft 5. Repr.: *The Protestant Era* (Chicago: University of Chicago Press, 1948) 32-54.

5. Tillich, "Das Damonishe, ein Beitrag sur Sinndeutung der Geschichte," in *The Interpretation of History* (New York: Scribner's, 1936) 77-125; suffers from poor translation.

6. Ibid., 85.

7. Tillich, *Gesmmelte Werke* 2:175-92.

8. The brevity of the discussion of the Frankfurt school is due to a few pages of it appearing in a later chapter, and also due to the fact that it receives a longer discussion in *Paul Tillich's Radical Social Thought*, 63-72. Also recommended is Guyton B. Hammond, *Man in Estrangement: A Comparison of the Thought of Paul Tillich and Erich Fromm* (Nashville: Vanderbilt University Press, 1965).

9. See Richard Fox, *Reinhold Niebuhr* for the discussion of Mayor Smith's appointment of Niebuhr.

10. Reinhold Niebuhr, "Race Prejudice in the North," the *Christian Century* 44 (12 May 1927): 584.

11. "The Battle of Detroit," the *Christian Century* 68/42 (21 October 1926): 1287-89.

12. Hubert C. Herring, "Business Cracks the Whip," the *Christian Century* 48/42 (21 October 1926): 1292.

13. "The Battle of Detroit," 1289.

14. Reinhold Niebuhr, "Henry Ford and Industrial Autocracy," the *Christian Century* 48/44 (4 November 1926): 1355.

15. Reinhold Niebuhr, "How Philanthropic Is Henry Ford?" the *Christian Century* 48/49 (9 December 1926): 1517.

16. Reinhold Niebuhr, "Ford's Five-Day Week Shrinks," the *Christian Century* 54/23 (9 June 1927): 714.

Notes to chapter 4: The World Tomorrow

1. *The World Tommorrow* (January 1927).

2. Miles Horton, *The Long Haul: An Autobiography* (New York: Doubleday, 1990) 37.

3. Ibid., 61.

4.Marshall Surratt, "Myles Horton: Activism and Gospel," *Christianity and Crisis* 50 (17 December 1990): 399.

5. Ibid.

6. Reinhold Niebuhr, *Moral Man and Immoral Society* (New York: Scribner's, 1932).

7. *The World Tomorrow* (4 January 1933): 20.

8. Ibid., 170.

9. Sherwood Eddy, *A Pilgrimage of Ideas: or The Reducation of Sherwood Eddy* (New York; Farrar & Rinehart: 1934) 214-15.

10. Reinhold Niebuhr, introduction to Sherwood Eddy, *Eighty Adventurous Years: An Autobiography* (New York: Harper, 1955) 9-12.

Notes to chapter 5: Opposition and Migration

1. The description of the events of 1933 is dependent on Hannah Tillich, *From Time to Time* (New York: Stein and Day, 1973); Wilhelm and Marian Pauck, *Tillich: His Life and Thought*, vol. 1 (New York: Harper & Row, 1976); and discussions with Mutie Tillich Farris.

2. Paul Tillich, "Zehen Thesen" in *Die Kirche und das dritte Reich. Fragen und Forderungen deutscher Theologen*, vol. 1, ed. Leopold Klotz (Gotha: Leopold Klotz Verlag, 1932) 126-28.

3. Quoted in Arthur Cochrane, *The Church's Confession under Hitler* (Philadelphia: Westminster Press, 1962) 80.

4. Translated by Andrea Boecherer in Ronald Stone's seminar on the thought of Paul Tillich. (Used by oral permission.) Published also in *Paul Tillich: Theologian of the Boundaries*, ed. Mark Kline Taylor (London: Collins Publications, 1987).

5. Tillich's early confrontation with National Socialism has been minimized in theological discussions of his resistance. In some cases this seems to have happened because his resistance was theological as well as political, and the early political opposition overshadowed his theological critique. This oversight may be because of interpreters' ideological loyalty to the Barthian critique in 1933 which was confined to theological and church critique. This seems to explain Arthur C. Cochrane's interpretation of Tillich's dismissal from Frankfurt as due to his left-wing politics. Cochrane knew of this text which is surely theological in its speaking of the cross shattering the swastika, and in its detailed exposition of the uniqueness of Protestantism over against Nazism. In *The Varieties of Protestantism in Nazi Germany*, Franz G. M. Feige (Lewiston MD: Edwin Mellen Press, 1990) notes the text in his bibliography as he records the works of Wilhelm and Marion Pauck, John Stumme, and Stone, but he doesn't seem to utilize the text or the secondary sources in his inadequate discussion of Tillich as a theologian and minister of the church in defiance of Nazism. See "Zehn Thesen" in *Die Kirche und das dritte Reich. Fragen Forderuundngen deutschen Theologen*, vol. 1, ed. Leopold Klotz (Gotha: Leopold Klotz Verlag, 1932) 126-28.

6. Paul Tillich, *The Religious Situation*, trans. H. Richard Niebuhr (repr.: New York: Meridian Books, 1956; ©1932 Henry Holt & Co.).

7. Reinhold Niebuhr, *Does Civilization Need Relgion* (New York: Macmillan, 1929).

8. Ibid., 163-64.

9. Ibid., 259.

10. Reinhold Niebuhr, *Moral Man and Immoral Society* (New York: Scribner's, 1932) xi.

11. Ibid., 234.

12. Norman Thomas. "Moral Man and Immoral Society," *The World Tomorrow* (17 December 1932): 565-57.

13. *Remembering Reinhold Niebuhr*, ed. Ursula Niebuhr (San Francisco: Harper/San Francisco, 1991) 30.

14. Richard Fox, *Reinhold Niebuhr. A Biography* (New York: Pantheon Books, 1955) 142.

15. H. Richard Niebuhr, "Letter to Reinhold Niebuhr, 1932," Library of Congress, Niebuhr Papers.

16. Letter to John C. Bennett in the correspondence file of Letters from Reinhold Niebuhr to Bennett in the Burke Library of Columbia University, New York City.

17. Letter to Ursula Keppel-Compton, Library of Congress, Niebuhr Papers, Box 58 (26 July 1931). He wrote her almost every day while she was absent from him in England. Many of the letters, but not all, are collected in her *Remembering Reinhold*.

18. The three paragraphs on emigration are taken from my *Paul Tillich's Radical Social Thought* , 86. And see Wilhelm and Marion Pauck, *Paul Tillich*, 157-59.

19. Speech before the Conference on Christian German Refugees, Riverside Church, New York City, 6 June 1936. See also Tillich, *Gesammelte Werke* 13:187-89.

Notes to chapter 6: On the Boundary

1. Paul Tillich, *The Interpretation of Histroy* (New York: Scribner's, 1936) viii.

2. Hannah Tillich, *From Time to Time.*

3. *Interpretation of History*, 29.

4. Ibid.

5. Ibid., 41

6. Ibid., 50.

7. Ibid., 61.

8. Paul Tillich, "The Christian and the Marxist View of Man" (Harvard Archive: Universal Christian Council for Life and Work, 1935; 2nd ed., 1959).

9. James L. Adams, Wilhelm Pauck, Roger L. Shinn, *The Thought of Paul Tillich* (San Francisco: Harper and Row, 1985) 76.

10. John R. Stumme, *Socialism in Theological Perspective* (Missoula MT: Scholars Press, 1978) 55.

11."The Christian and the Marxist View of Man," 5.

12. Ibid.,

13. Ibid., 9.

14. Ibid., 70.

15. A. James Reimer, *The Emmanuel Hirsch and Paul Tillich Debate* (Lewiston NY: Edwin Mellon Press, 1989) 107.

16. The discussion of the Hirsch-Tillich debate is reprinted with editing from my *Paul Tillich's Radical Social Thought* while noting and taking account of A. James Reimer's critique. Ibid. James A. Zabel, *Nazism and the Pastors: A Study of the Ideas of Three Deutsche Christen Groups*, American Academy of Religion Dissertation Series 14 (Missoula MT: Scholars Press, 1976) 22.

17. Paul Tillich, "*Die Theologie des Kairos und die gegenwartige geistige Lage.*" *Theologische Blatter* 13/11 (1934): 305-28.

18. Paul Tillich, *"Um was es geht,"* Theoloigsiche Blatter 14/5 (1935): 1117-20.

19. See Walter F. Benze, "Tillich's Kairos and Hitler's seizure of Power: The Tillich-Hirsch Exchange of 1934-35," in *Tillich Studies: 1975*, ed. John J. Carey (Tallahasee FL: North American Paul Tillich Society, 1975) 39-50.

20. Zabel, *Nazism and the Pastors*, 230.

21 Paul Tillich, *My Travel Diary: 1936. Between Two Worlds*, ed. Jerald C. Brauer, trans. Maria Pelikan (New York: Harper & Row, 1970).

22. Ibid., 145.

23. Ibid., 42, 85, 105, 168.

24. Ibid., 16.

25. Ursula Niebuhr, *Remembering Reinhold*, 119.

26. *The Essential Reinhold Niebuhr*, ed. Robert McAfee Brown (New Haven CT: Yale University Press, 1986), 92. See also Reinhold Niebuhr, *Christianity and Power Politics* (New York: Scribner's, 1940; repr.: Archon Books, 1969) 203-26. Originally published in *The Student World* (World Student Christian Federation, n.d.).

27. Paul Tillich, "The Kingdom of God and History" Published in the United Kingdom in 1938. Reprinted in *Theology of Peace*, ed. Ronald H. Stone (Louisville: Westminster/John Knox Press, 1990) 25-56.

Notes to chapter 7: Radical Religion

1. Reinhold Niebuhr, *Reflections on the End of an Era* (New York: Scribner's, 1934).

2. *Radical Religion* 1/1 (Augumn 1935):1.

3. "The Church and Political Action," *Christian Century* 51/31 (1 August 1934): 992-94.

3. *Radical Religion*. 1/1:5.

4. Ibid., 20.

5. "Pacifism and Sanctions," *Radical Religion* 1/2 (Winter 1935): 25-30.

6. Ibid., 36.

7. Wilhelm Pauck, review of *An Interpretation of Christian Ethics* in *Radical Religion* 1/2 (Winter 1935).

8. Ursula Niebuhr, review of H. Richard Niebuhr, Wilhelm Pauck, and Francis Miller, *The Church against the World* in *Radical Religion* 1 /2 (New York: Willet Clark and Co.,1935): 37-38.

9. "The Idea of Progress and Socialism," *Radical Religion* 1/3 (Spring 1936): 29.

10. Paul Tillich, "Historical Diagnosis," *Radical Relgion* 2/2 (Spring 1937): 17.

11. Reinhold Niebuhr, "The National Preaching Mission," *Radical Religion* 2/2 (Spring 1937): 3.

12. Reinhold Niebuhr, "The Oxford Conference on Church and State," *Radical Religion* 2/4 (Autumn 1937): 2.

13. Reinhold Niebuhr, "The International Situation," *Radical Religion* 3/1 (Winter 1937): 2.

14. Reinhold Niebuhr, "Socialist Decision and Christian Conscience," *Radical Religion* 3/2 (Spring 1938): 2.

15. "The Fellowship of Socialist Christians," in *Radical Religion*3/3 (Summer 1938): 44. The close relationship of the Fellowship to the Fellowship of Southern Churchmen meeting in Raleigh, N.C. was marked by the publication of their minutes in the same issue. Carl Hermann Voss who had been tutoring Tillich in English was now the pastor of the United

Church where the meeting was held. A minor note in the minutes was that Charles Mason, a student at Union Theological Seminary, had joined the Fellowship of Socialist Christians. Twenty-two years later when he was serving as district superintendent of the Methodist church in the Sioux City District he would give me my first copy of *The Nature and Destiny of Man* as I prepared to leave Iowa to study at Union. Other issues addressed by Niebuhr included the anti-Semitism of the Nazis, particularly as they took over Austria, the deteriorating international scene, more on the Red Army purges, tax policies, the Delta Cooperative Farm which was experiencing economic difficulty, and criticism of the Roman Catholic Church for its support of Franco in Spain and Mussolini in Italy. The remainder of the journal was dedicated to the Japanese conquest of parts of China, *the reconciliation of religion and radicalism*—which was possibly the most discussed issue during the journal's life—intellectuals and united front organizations, and analysis of the labor movement.

16. Reinhold Niebuhr, "The International Situation," *Radical Religion* 3/4 (Autumn 1938): 2.

17. Paul Tillich in *Radical Religion* 4/1 (Winter 1938): 36.

Notes to chapter 8: Christian Realism

1. "Christian Faith and the World Crisis" in *Witness to a Generation,* ed. Wayne C. Cowan (Indianapolis: Bobbs-Merrill, 1966): 1-6.

2. Alan Paton, "Journey Continued: An Autobiography," repr. in *Kent Quarterly* 9 (Fall 1989): 30.

3. See Reinhold Niebuhr, *Human Destiny* (New York: Scribner's, 1943): 249, for a short discussion of the evil of Nazism and the persecution of the Jews. Reprinted with pagination retained as part 2 in *The Nature and Destiny of Man: A Christian Interpretation* (New York: Scribner's, 1949).

4. Niebuhr, *Human Nature* (New York: Scribner's, 1941) 1. Reprinted with pagination retained as part 1 in *The Nature and Destiny of Man: A Christian Interpretation* (New York: Scribner's, 1949).

5. Ibid., 36.

6. Ibid., 12-18.

7. Ibid., 120.

8. Letter in author's possession. There being no known earlier extant text, the works by Elizabeth Sifton and Richard Fox establish the origins of the prayer.

9. "A symposium on Reinhold Niebuhr's *Nature and Destiny of Man,*" *Christendom* 6 (Autumn 1941): 568-76.

10. Paul Tillich, review of *The Nature and Destiny of Man, Christianity and Society* 6 (Spring 1941): 37.

11. Larry Rasmussen, "Reinhold Niebuhr: Court Prophet," lecture at Union Theological Seminary, November 1986. Quotation from Roger Shinn, *The New Humanism* (Philadelphia: Westminster, 1978) 160.

12. Reinhold Niebuhr, *Man's Nature and His Communities* (New York: Scribner's, 1965): 23-24.

13. Reinhold Niebuhr, editorials, *Christianity and Society* 5 (Spring 1940): 10.

14. Ibid.

15. June Bingham, *Courage to Change. An Introduction to the Life and Thought of Reinhold Niebuhr* (New York: Scribner's, 1961) 280.

16. Niebuhr, *Human Destiny*, 3.

17. Niebuhr, *Human Destiny*, 96. The argument moves from Plato through James Madison with the usual Niebuhr emphasis upon Augustine, Calvin, and Luther. Edmund Burke does not appear as part of this interpretation of significant political theory.

18. Niebuhr, *Human Destiny*, 321.

19. John C. Bennett, "Human Destiny—Reinhold Niebuhr: A Symposium," *Union Review* 4 (March 1943): 24.

20. Ibid., 25.

21. It was the relative neglect of Niebuhr's writing on symbolism that informed my including them in a book of essays of Niebuhr's that I chose and edited with Niebuhr's approval of the inclusions—*Faith and Politics* (New York: George Braziller, 1968) 3-31.

Notes to chapter 9: World War II

1. When one remembers that he came to New York City as an editor and as a professor, anyone interpreting Niebuhr needs to recognize that for most of his career he was a professor as well as a journalist. He had been a preacher, and he remained a journeyman preacher, mostly to colleges and universities. He fulfilled many other roles, but as he developed as a scholar and as an interpreter of America, the journalism continued. It had to be undertaken almost every week.

2. Karl Barth "Extracts from a Letter by Dr. Karl Barth to a French Editor" in *Christianity and Society* 5/2 (Spring 1940): 38. Note: The journal continued the volume and issue numbers from *Radical Religion*.

3. Ibid., 40.

4. Ibid., Niebuhr, 24.

5. Ibid., 28.

6. Ibid., Roberts, 43.

7. Ibid., Niebuhr, 5.

8. Reinhold Niebuhr, "The Socialist Campaign," *Christianity and Society* 5/3 (Summer 1940): 4.

9. Ibid., Niebuhr, "An Open Letter," 30.

10. Reinhold Niebuhr, *Christianity and Power Politics* (New York: Scribner's, 1940) 1-32.

11. See Ronald H. Stone, *Reinhold Niebuhr: Prophet to Politicians*, 78-79.

12. See Ronald H. Stone, *Prophetic Realism: Beyond Militarism and Pacifism in an Age of Terror*, 125-29.

13. Colm Mckeogh, "Niebuhr's Critique of Pacifism" in *Reinhold Niebuhr Revisited*, ed. Daniel F. Rice, 220.

14. Reinhold Niebuhr, "Christianity and the World Crisis," *Christianity and Society* 5/4 (Fall 1940): 5.

15. Liston Pope, "Ivory Towers and Battle Turrets," *Christianity and Society* 5/5 (Winter 1940): 21.

16. Wilhelm Pauck, "A False Catholic Protestantism," *Christianity and Society* 6/2 (Spring 1941): 9-16.

17. Reinhold Niebuhr, "America in the Hour of Decision," *Christianity and Society* 6/3 (Summer 1941): 3.

18. Therese B. DeLision, "Did Reinhold Niebuhr Care about Racism in America?" *Union Seminary Quarterly Review* 61/3-4 (2008). "Except for the years immediately preceding and during World War II, the issue of race never dropped out of the wide range of Niebuhr's religious and political commentary." In fact, his other World War II writings dealing with discrimination against African-Americans include: "Negroes and the Railroads," in *Christianity and Society* 9/2 (Winter 1943): 11; "The Negro Issue in America," *Christianity and Society* 9/3 (Summer 1943): 5-7; "Editorial Note" on Gunnar Myrdahl, An American Dilemma, *Christianity and Crisis* 4/16 (18 September 1944): 2; and the essay connecting racial discrimination with original sin, "Christian Faith and the Race Problem," *Christianity and Society* 11/2 (Spring 1945): 21-24. Particular issues of race oppression appear also in shorter notes in journals he edited.

19. Reinhold Niebuhr, "The Supreme Court and Jim Crowism," *Christianity and Scoiety* 6/3 (Summer 1941): 9.

20. H. Richard Niebuhr, "The Christian Church in the World's Crisis," in ibid., 16.

21. See: Ronald Stone, *Reinhold Niebuhr: Prophet*, 236-37.

22. Reinhold Niebuhr, "History (God) Has Overtaken Us," *Christianity and Society* 7/1 (Winter 1941): 3.

23. Roger Shinn, "A Buck Private's Look at the World," *Christianity and Society* 7/1 (Winter 1941): 27.

24. Paul Tillich, "I am an American," *Protestant Digest* 2/4 (June-July 1941): 24-26.

25. Paul Tillich, "Protestant Principles," *The Protestant* 4/5 (April-May 1942): 17.

26. *The Protestant* 4/7 (August-September 1941): 8-14.

27. Ibid., 14.

28. Paul Tillich, *War Aims* (New York: Protestant Digest, 1941).

29. The preceding paragraphs on *The Protestant* are dependent on my *Paul Tillich's Radical Social Thought*, 99-101.

30. *Remembering Reinhold Niebuhr*, ed. Ursula Niebuhr (San Francisco: HarperSanFrancisco, 1991) 185. Her volume is the invaluable source for the days that she and Reinhold were separated by the Atlantic Ocean.

31. The lectures are in Tillich's handwriting in the Paul Tillich Archive, Andover-Harvard Theological Library, and were presented for the first time in their outline form in *Paul Tillich, Theology of Peace*, ed. Ronald H. Stone (Louisville: Westminster/John Knox Press, 1990) 73-87. An earlier version of the paragraphs introducing the lectures is in the volume, 13-16.

32. The story of Roosevelt and Tillich is a combination of gossip around Union Theological Seminary in the 1960s and the story of Marion and Wilhelm Pauck based on an interview with Tillich as recorded in their volume, *Paul Tillich*, 204-205.

33. Quoted in Brown, 110. See also Fox. 201.

34. See Stone, ed., *Tillich, Theology of Peace*, 105-10.

35. Reinhold Niebuhr's vocation as a professor is the major theme of an earlier book, *Professor Reinhold Niebuhr* (Louisville: Westminster/John Knox Press, 1992).

Notes to chapter 10: A Voice Against the Third Reich

1. Some of the text is rewritten from the introduction to Paul Tillich, *Against the Third Reich*, ed. Ronald H. Stone and Matthew Lon Weaver (Louisville: Westminster/John Knox Press, 1998). Several of the entries from the speeches are taken from that volume containing fifty of his speeches, others are taken from Lon Weaver's translation of the speeches from the German edition and his translation of the still unpublished speeches located in the Harvard Archives. The entries of the speeches taken from *Against the Third Reich* are noted as *Against*, if taken from Weaver's other translations they are noted "Weaver" (copy in author's possession).

2. Jakub S. Trojan, interview in Prague, 1995. The late Professor Emeritus Eberhard von Waldow of Pittsburgh Theological Seminary interview, 1997 in Pittsburgh. Holly Cowan Shulman, *The Voice of America: Propaganda and Democracy, 1941–1945* (Madison: University of Wisconsin Press, 1990) 26.

3. Anton Gill, *An Honourable Defeat: A History of German Resistance to Hitler: 1933-1945* (New York: Henry Holt, 1994) 23-24.

4. Ibid., 129-31. 151-55.

5. Dagmar Herzog, "Berlin Underground," *New York Times Book Review* (7 June 2009): 13.

6. Ibid., 24, 43, 66, 67, 160-61, 175-79, 183-87, 192-94, 197-98.

7. Brown, 110.

8. *Against*, 16.

9. Weaver, 19-20.

10. *Against*, 53.

11. Ibid., 58.

12. Weaver, U16. The "U" preceding the page number means unpublished in either German or English, but present in Weaver's papers translated from the Harvard archives.

13. *Against*, 88-89.

14. Ibid., 98-99.

15. Ibid., 113-14.

16. Ibid., 130.

17. Ibid., 154.

18. Ibid., 184.

19. Ibid., 191.

20. An earlier version of the introduction to the speeches of 1944 appeared in *Against the Third Reich*, 223-24.

21. Ibid., 239.

Notes to chapter 11: A Voice for Democracy

1. Reinhold Niebuhr, "Note on Common Convictions of Fellowship of Socialist Christians," in *Christianity and Society* 8/2 (Spring 1943): 2.

2. *Children of Light*, 117.

3. Ibid., 118.

4. Ibid., 17.

5. Ibid., xiii.

6. Ibid., 9.

7. Ibid., 178.

8. Ibid., 190. This theological reference was not emphasized in the earlier reflections by Niebuhr on the race question. This element appeared later in "Christian Faith and the Race Problem" in *Christianity and Society* 11/2 (Spring 1945): 21-22.

9. Adlai Stevenson's comment was to his son, Adlai Stevenson III, and told to me at the American Academy of Religion meeting by John Burkhart.

10. Henry Clark, *Serenity, Courage, and Wisdom* (Cleveland: The Pilgrim Press, 1994).

11. Robin Lovin, "Prophetic Faith and American Democracy," in *Reinhold Niebuhr Revisited*, 230, 233-34.

12. Reinhold Niebuhr, "The Perspective of Faith on History," *Christianity and Society* 9/2 (Spring 1944): 6-7.

13. Reinhold Niebuhr, "Realistic Internationalism," *Christianity and Society* 9/3 (Autumn 1944): 4, 5.

14. Reinhold Niebuhr, "Reason and Interests in Politics," *Christianity and Society* 10/1 (Winter 1944): 4, 5.

15. Paul Tillich et al., *The Christian Answer*, ed. Henry P. Van Dusen (New York: Charles Scribner's Sons, 1945).

16. Tillich, *Gesammelte Werke*, 9:139-92.

17. Reprinted as Paul Tillich, *The World Situation*, Social Ethics Series 2 (Philadelphia: Fortress Press, Facet Books, 1965).

18. Ibid., 24.

19. Ibid., 26.

20. Ibid., 27.

21. An earlier version of this discussion is in *Paul Tillich's Radical Social Thought*, 108-11. The essay by Tillich is also reprinted in Tillich, *Theology of Peace*, 111-57.

22. Niebuhr's appreciation of British politics was reciprocated by many British political leaders, and a new book in England notes his political influence suggesting it even extended to elements of the reform of the British educational system under Tory leadership in 1944. *Reinhold Niebuhr and Contemporary Politics*, ed. Richard Harries and Stephen Platten (Oxford: Oxford University Press, 2010).

Notes to chapter 12: The Bomb

1. *Christianity and Crisis* 5/15 (17 Sept. 1945): 7.

2. Ibid., 5/17 (15 Oct. 1945): 7.

3. *Atomic Warfare and the Christian Faith* (New York: Federal Council of Churches, 1946) 11.

4. James G. Hershberg, James B. Connant, *Harvard to Hiroshima and the Making of a Nuclear Age* (New York: Alfred A. Knopf, 1993) 284.

5. Robert C. Calhoun and Georgia Harkness of the original critics dissented from the Dunn Commission of 1950 which represented the theologian's acceptance of the weapons. See Robert C. Bartchelder, *The Irreversible Decision 1939–1950* (Boston: Houghton Mifflin Co., 1961) 237-69.

6. Quotes from letter of James B. Conant to Reinhold Niebuhr, 6 March 1946, Reinhold Niebuhr Papers, Library of Congress.

7. Ibid.

8. Ibid.

9. *Christianity and Crisis* 10/21 (11 Dec. 1950): 161.

10. Reinhold Niebuhr, "The Hydrogen Bomb," *Christianity and Society* (Spring 1950): 5-7. Also "Ten Fateful Years," *Christianity and Crisis* 11/1 (5 Feb. 1951): 4.

11. Paul Tillich, "Correspondence," *Partisan Review* 39/2 (1962): 311-12.

12. Ibid., 312.

13. Reprinted in Paul Tillich, "The Hydrogen Bomb," in *Theology of Peace* (Louisville: Westminster/John Knox Press, 1990) 158-59.

14. *Christianity and Crisis* 21/19 (13 Nov. 1961): 200-204.

Notes to chapter 13: The Jewish Question

1. Ben Halpern, "Zionism," *International Encyclopedia of the Social Sciences* (New York: Macmillan, 1968) 593.

2. *Man's Nature and His Communities* (New York: Scribner's, 1965) 18.

3. Ibid., 19.

4. "Jews After the War," *The Nation* (21 February 1942): 214-16, 253-55.

5. Hertzel Fishman, *American Protestantism and a Jewish State* (Detroit: Wayne State University Press, 1973) 75.

6. Ibid.

7. *Christianity and Crisis* 16, 9 (May 28, 1956): 65.

8. *Pious and Secular America* (New York: Scribner's, 1958) 109.

9. Ibid.

Notes to chapter 14: Foundations of Postwar Political Philosophy

1. *Reinhold Niebuhr*, ed. Kegley and Bretall, 149.

2. H. Richard Niebuhr, "Reinhold Niebuhr's Interpretation of History," Reinhold Niebuhr Papers (MSS in the library of Congress, Washington DC) container 17.

3. Niebuhr, *Man's Nature*, 15. See: Ronald Stone, *Reinhold Niebuhr*, chp. 5 for the earlier version of this chapter.

4. Ibid., 24.

5. Ibid.

6. *Reinhold Niebuhr*, ed. Kegley and Bretall, 435.

7. *Reinhold Niebuhr:A Prophetic Voice*, ed. Landon, 34-35.

8. Ibid., 120.

9. E.g., Niebuhr, *Man's Nature*, 106.

10. Ibid., 111.

11. Ibid., 125.

`12. Reinhold Niebuhr, *The Irony of American History* (New York: Scribner's, 1952) viii-1x.

13. Henry F. May, "A Meditation on an Unfashionable Book," *Christianity and Crisis* 27 (27 May 1968): 120.

14. "Christianity's view of history is tragic insofar as it recognizes evil as an inevitable concomitant of even the highest spiritual enterprises." Reinhold Niebuhr, *Beyond Tragedy* (New York: Scribner's, 1937) x-xi.

15. *Reinold Niebuhr*, ed. Kegley and Bretall, 303.

16. Niebuhr, *Irony of History*, viii.

17. Ibid., 155.

18. Ibid., 157.

19. See: Stone, *Reinhold Niebuhr*, 44.

20. Niebuhr, *Irony of History*, 167.

21. Ibid., 2.

22. Ibid., 63.

23. Niebuhr and Sigmund, *Democratic Experience*, vi.

24. Reinhold Niebuhr, "The Negro Minority and its Fate in a Self-Righteous Nation," *Social Action/Social Progress* 35/54 (October 1968): 53-64.

25. Quoted in Bingham, *Courage to Change*, 224.

26. *Reinhold Niebuhr on Politics*, ed. Harry R. Davis and Robert C. Good (New York: Scribner's, 1960) 200.

27. *Reinhold Niebuhr*, ed. Kegley and Bretall, eds., 36.

28. *Discerning the Signs of the Times* (New York, Scribner's, 1946); *Christian Realism and Political Problems* (New York: Scribner's, 1953): and *Pious and Secular America* (New York: Scribner's, 1958).

29. Niebuhr, *Pious and Secular America*, 7.

30. Niebuhr, *Christian Realism*, 176.

31. Niebuhr's trust in the coherence of the world and man's ability to create models adequate to portray these coherences is most applicable in the natural sciences, in the human sciences dependent upon biology and chemistry, and in the areas of the social sciences amenable to statistics and predictions of probability. The emphasis upon coherence is qualified, and the mystery of human existence is emphasized in the tradition of Pascal to provide a basis for dealing with unique events, necessary rational contradictions, the failure to provide one scheme of meaning for all the structures of human life, and human freedom. Cf. ibid., 176-79.

32. Ibid,.175.

33. Ibid., 171-76.

34. William James, *Pragmatism, a New Name for Some Old Ways of Thinking* (New York: Longmans, Green and Co., 1907) 218.

35. Statement by Reinhold Niebuhr, personal interview, 24 March 1967.

36. William James, *The Will to Believe* (New York: Longmans, Green and Co., 1896) 17.

37. Ibid., 188-89.

38. Stanley Hauerwas, *With the Grain of the Universe* (Grand Rapids MI: Brazos Press, 2001).

39. James, *Pragmatism*, 73.

40. Ibid., 20.

41. *The World Tomorrow* 16/9 (1 March 1933) 203-205.

42. Ibid., 204.

43. John Dewey, "Unity and Purpose," *The World Tomorrow* 16/10 (8 March 1933): 232-33.

44. Niebuhr, *Moral Man*, xiii, 35, 212; Niebuhr, *Interpretation of Christian Ethics*, 207-208; Niebuhr, *Nature and Destiny*, 1:110-14; Niebuhr, *Children of Light*, 129; Niebuhr, *Faith and History*, 67, 68, 83, 95, 116.

45. E.g., Sidney Hook, "Social Change and Original Sin: Answer to Niebuhr," *The New Leader* 24 (8 November 1941): 1-7; Sidney Hook, "The New Failure of Nerve," *Partisan Review* 10 (January-February 1943): 2-17; George A. Coe and Reinhold Niebuhr, "Coe vs.

Niebuhr," *The Christian Century* 50 (15 March 1933): 362-64; White, *Social Thought in America*, 247-67, 277-79.

46. See Roger L. Shinn, "Some Notes on Reinhold Niebuhr's Use of Philosophy," (unpublished paper for The Society of Theological Discussion, n.d.) 2.

47. See Daniel F. Rice, *Reinhold Niebuhr and John Dewey* (Albany: State University of New York Press, 1993). Stephen C. Rockefeller, *John Dewey* (New York: Columbia University Press, 1991).

48. See: Stone, *Reihnhold Niebuhr*, 102-104.

49. Niebuhr, *Nature and Destiny*, 1:110.

50. *Reinhold Niebuhr*, ed. Kegley and Bretall, 141.

51. Reinhold Niebuhr, "The Pathos of Liberalism," *The Nation* 121 (11 September 1935): 303-304.

52. White, *Social Thought in America*, 255.

53. John Dewey, *Human Nature and Conduct* (New York: Modern Library, 1930) 13.

54. Dewey guarded himself against the charges of over-optimism by admitting the difficulties of applying intelligence to social problems but advocating the attempt in the face of no acceptable alternatives. "There is no need to dwell upon the enormous obstacles that stand in the way of extending from its limited field to the larger field of human relations the control of organized intelligence operating through the release of individual powers and capabilities. There is the weight of past history on the side of those who are pessimistic about the possibility of achieving this humanly desirable and humanly necessary task. I do not predict that the extension will be effectively actualized." John Dewey, "Authority and Resistance to Social Change," *School and Society* 44 (10 Oct. 1936): 466.

55. Niebuhr, *Moral Man*, 212-15.

56. Daniel J. Boorstein, *The Genius of American Politics* (Chicago: University of Chicago Press, 1943) 119.

57. Reinhold Niebuhr, "Theology and Political Thought in the Western World," *The Ecumenical Review* 9 (April 1957): 253-62.

58. *A Handbook of Christian Theology*, ed. Marvin Halverson (New York: World Publishing Co., 1958) 141.

59. Niebuhr, "The Death of the President," *Christianity and Crisis* 5/7 (30 April 1945): 4-6.

60. Statement by Reinhold Niebuhr, personal interview, 6 January 1967.

61. Reinhold Neibuhr, "Draft of Americans for Democratic Action Statement on Foreign Policy," 30 November 1955. Reinhold Niebuhr Papers (MSS in the Library of Congress Washington DC) container 1.

62. Though several of the preceding paragraphs on liberalism are taken from my earlier work, there is a more complete discussion of liberal political theory in *Reinhold Niebuhr: Prophet to Politicians*, 160-64.

63. Niebuhr, *Christian Realism*, 146; italics added.

64. Niebuhr, *Man's Nature*, 46; italics added.

Notes to chapter 15: Cold War International Relations: The Beginning

1. Reinhold Niebuhr, editorial notes, *Christianity and Crisis* 5/11 (25 June 1945): 2.

2. Ibid., 6-7. See, also, for another version: "Dietrich Bonhoeffer" in *Union Seminary Quarterly Review* 1/3 (March 1946): 3. This issue also called for funds for the ten fatherless children left by the executions of Dietrich's brother and two brothers-in-law.

3. Reinhold Niebuhr, editorial notes, *Christianity and Crisis* 6/5 (1 April 1946): 2.

4. Reinhold Niebuhr in Ursula M. Niebuhr, *Remembering Reinhold Niebuhr* (San Francisco: HarperSanFancisco, 1991) 189.

5. *Discerning the Signs of the Times* (New York: Scribner's, 1946).

6. "The Russian and American Race," *Christianity and Society* 11/2 (Spring 1946): 6.

7. "A Report on Germany," *Christianity and Crisis* 6/16 (30 September 1946): 6-7.

8. Mark L. Kleinmann, *A World of Hope A World of Fear: Henry A. Wallace, Reinhold Niebuhr, and American Liberalism* (Columbus: Ohio State University Press, 2000) 210.

9. Niebuhr, "The Fight for Germany," *Life* (21 Oct. 1946): 65-68.

10. Kleinmann's history is sympathetic to Henry A. Wallace and he particularly faults Niebuhr and Loeb for their tactics opposing Wallace. *A World*, 252-84. While he does deal with Wallace's later recantation of his trust of the Soviet Union, he, I think, following Richard Fox, does not regard Niebuhr's books since the 1952 *Irony of American History* as having great significance for the interpretation of Niebuhr's Cold-War perspective on foreign relations. Further reading probably would have led him to diminish his critique of Niebuhr and maybe even to have understood Niebuhr to be seeking cooperation with the Soviet Union to manage the nuclear issue as far as it was possible given their political struggle.

11. *Discerning the Signs*, 38.

12. Ibid .,40.

13. Ibid., 50.

14. Ibid., 51.

15. Ibid.,72.

16. Ibid., 143-44.

Notes to chapter 16: The Cold War Freezes

1. Ursula Niebuhr, *Remembering Reinhold*, 212. Her volume contains the details of his visits abroad found in his letters and reported in this chapter.

2. Reinhold Niebuhr, "Scientific Man versus Power Politics," in *Christianity and Society* 12 (Spring 1947): 33-34.

3. Reinhold Niebuhr, editorial notes, *Christianity and Crisis* 7/9 (7 July 1947): 2.

4. Paul Tillich, "The Disintegration of Society in Christian Countries," in *Man's Disorder and God's Design* (New York: Harper & Brothers, 1948) 53-64.

5. Reinhold Niebuhr, Assembly address published in *Christian Realism and Political Problems* (New York: Scribner's, 1953); republished in *The Essential Reinhold Niebuhr*, ed. Robert McAfee Brown (New Haven CT: Yale University Press, 1986) 101.

6. Ursula Niebuhr, *Remembering Reinhold*, 258.

7. Ibid., 260. Reinhold could laughingly in conversations with Ursula refer to the Congregational Church merger into the United Church of Christ with his Evangelical and Reformed Synod as creating "the one true church." Both his low-church background and his commitment to the ecumenical enterprise for the sake of church renewal obscured to his critics his devotion to the church which he served all of his life.

8. Pauck and Pauck, *Paul Tillich*, 222.

9. Paul Tillich, *The Protestant Era* (Chicago: University of Chicago Press, 1948) 93.

10. Ibid., xxi.

11. Ibid., xviii.

12. Paul Tillich, "Visit to Germany," in *Christianity and Crisis* 8/19 (Nov. 1948): 147-49. The most complete discussion of his summer, 1948 trip is in Pauck and Pauck, *Paul Tillich.*

14. Paul Tillich, *The New Being* (New York: Scribner's, 1955) 34-35.

15. Paul Tillich, *The Shaking of the Foundations* (New York: Scribner's, 1948) 103.

16. Ibid., 153-63.

17. Paul Tillich, "Das geistige Vakuum," in *Das sozialistiche Jahrhundert* 2/20 (15 Sept. 1948): 303-305. Translation by Matthew Lon Weaver.

18. Ibid., 185.

19. Ibid., 186.

Notes to chapter 17: Limits and World Responsibility

1. Ursula Niebuhr, *Remembering Reinhold*, 265. All of the details of the meeting are from the letters edited by Ursula Niebuhr.

2. Reinhold Niebuhr, "Peace through Cultural Cooperation," *Christianity and Crisis* 9/17 (17 Oct. 1949): 131-33.

3. Karl Barth, "No Christian Marshall Plan," *The Christian Century* 65/49 (Dec. 1948): 1330-33.

4. Reinhold Niebuhr, "We Are Men Not God," *The Christian Century* 65/43 (27 Oct. 1948): 1138-40.

5. Karl Barth, "Continental vs. Anglo-Saxon Theology," *The Christian Century* 65/7 (16 Feb 1948): 201-204.

6. Reinhold Niebuhr, "An Answer to Karl Barth," *The Christian Century*66/8 (23 Feb. 1948): 234-36.

7. Reinhold Niebuhr, "Streaks of Dawn in the Night," *Christianity and Crisis* 9/21 (12 Dec. 1949): 163.

8. Ibid., 164.

9. Reinhold Niebuhr, editorial notes, in *Christianity and Crisis* 10/17 (16 Oct. 1950): 130; and "The World Council and the Peace Issue," *Christianity and Crisis* 10/14 (7 Aug. 1950): 107-108.

10. Reinhold Niebuhr, "The Illusion of World Government," *Foreign Affairs* 27/3 (April): 397-88; repr. in *The World Crisis and American Responsibility*, ed. Ernest W. Lefever (Westport: Greenwood Press, 1958).

11. Reinhold Niebuhr, "The Challenge of the World Crisis"; repr. in Lefever, 11-48.

12. Reinhold Niebuhr, *Faith and History* (New York: Scribner's, 1949) 11.

13. Ibid., 124.

14. Ibid., 141.

15. Ibid., 165.

16. Ibid., 213.

17. Ibid., 238.

18. Ibid., 242.

19. Brown, 156.

20. Paul Merkley, *Reinhold Niebuhr, A Political Account* (Montreal: McGill-Queens University Press, 1975) 203, 214-15, 220-21.

21. Richard Fox, *Reinhold Niebuhr*, 137-38.

22. Arthur Schlesinger, Jr., book review of *Faith and History*, in *Christianity and Society* 14 (Summer 1947): 26-27.

Notes to chapter 18: Under Investigation

1. File No. 121-33418 on Reinhold Niebuhr provided by the FBI under the Freedom of Information Act, and in the author's possession. The file provided has 623 pages, but much material is blacked out. There are more files in other government agencies.

2. Reinhold Niebuhr, "The King's Chapel and the King's Court," *Christianity and Crisis* (4 August 1969).

3. File No. 100-392815 on Paul Tillich provided by the FBI pursuant to the Freedom of Information Act, and in the author's possession. The file provided has eighty-two pages, but much material is blacked out. There are more files in other government agencies.

Notes to chapter 19: Tillich's Later Social Ethics

1. Paul Tillich, *A History of Christian Thought : From Its Judaic and Hellinistic Origins to Existentialism*, ed. Carl E. Bratten (New York: Simon and Schuster, 1967) 292.

2. Ibid., 293.

3. Paul Tillich, *Systematic Theology*, 3 vols. (Chicago: University of Chicago Press, 1951, 1957, 1963) 1:4.

4. Ibid., 1:31.

5. Ibid., 1:5.

6. Ibid., 1:68.

7. Alexander Solzhenitsyn, "The exhausted West," *Harvard Magazine* 80/6 (July-August 1978): 21-26.

8. Quoted in Tillich, *Systematic Theology*, 1:11.

9. Ibid., 1:99.

10. Ibid., 1:72.

11. Ibid., 1:86.

12. Ibid., 1:117.

13. Ibid ., 1:76, 92-93.

14. Ibid., 1:220.

15. Ibid., 1:279-94.

16. Ibid., 1;270.

17. Ibid., 2:66, 74.

18. Ibid., 2;59.

19. Ibid., 3:283.

20. Ibid., 3:293-94.

21. Ibid., 3;356-57.

22. See Paul Tillich, *Christianity and the Encounter of the World Religions* (New York: Columbia University Press, 1963) 63-74.

23. Tillich, *Systematic Theology*, 3:344.

24. Ibid., 3:346.

25. Ibid., 3:347.

26. Ibid., 3:389.

27. Ibid., 3:391. While Tillich quotes a Marxist philosopher and even uses key terms from his religious-socialist writing like demonic, Kairos, expectation, Kingdom of God, they no longer are used in advocacy of a socialist economic system. His protests against technical reason, domination, and technological society are protests against these phenomena in socialist and capitalist societies. His earlier model had been Marxist enough that he recognized that an America without a proletariat was not fertile ground for a socialist revolution or coup. He remained more socialist than Niebuhr, joining the SDP in Germany. But in America in his later years he enjoyed the benefits of capitalism and worked for its development of the welfare side of its mixed economy toward greater justice or fragmentary fulfillment of the Kingdom of God.

28. Paul Tillich, "The Political Meaning of Utopia," in *Political Expectations* (New York: Harper & Row, 1971) 180. This essay was originally delivered in 1951 as lectures at the Deutsche Hochschule für Politik in Berlin.

29. Tillich, "The person in a Technical Society," in *Christian Faith and Social Action*, ed. John A. Hutchinson (New York: Scribner's, 1953) 137-53. Repr. in *Social Ethics : Issues in Ethics and Society*, ed Gibson Winter (New York: Harper & Row, 1968) 120-38.

30. Tillich in Hutchinson, *Christian Faith*, 153.

31. Paul Tillich, "The Effects of Space Exploration on Man's Condition and Stature," in *The Future of Religions*, ed. Jerald C. Brauer (New York: Harper & Row, 1966) 51.

32. Paul Tillich, "Moralisms and Morality" in *The Meaning of Health*, ed., Perry LeFevre (Chicago: Exploration Press, 1984) 100-15.

33. John J. Carey, "Morality and Beyond: Tillich's Ethics in Life and Death" in *Tillich Studies, 1975* (Tallahassee FL: North American Paul Tillich Society, 1975) 108.

34. Glenn Graber, "The Metaethics of Paul Tillich," *Journal of Religious Ethics* 1 (Fall 1973): 113.

35. Mark Lewis Taylor, "Tillich's Ethics between Politics and Ontology" in *The Cambridge Companion to Paul Tillich*, ed. Russell Re Manning (Cambridge: Cambridge University Press, 2009) 189-207.

36. Paul Tillich, "Ethical Problems of Moral Action"; speech given at Florida State University, Tallahassee, 2 March 1962.

37. Paul Tillich, "Problems in Christian Ethics"; speech given in Dallas, Texas, 28 May 1962).

38. Paul Tillich, *Morality and Beyond* (New York: Harper & Row, 1963) 65-81.

39. Tillich, *Love, Power, and Justice: Ontological Analysis and Ethical Applications* (London: Oxford University Press, 1954) 25.

Notes to chapter 20: On Justice

1. *Does Civilization?* 43.

2. John Rawls, *Theory of Justice* (Cambridge: Harvard University Press, 1971); Nicholas Wolterstorff, *Justice* (Princeton NJ: Princeton University Press, 2008).

3. *Nature and Destiny* 1:285.

4. Ibid., 296.

5. Harlan Beckley, *Passion for Justice* (Louisville: Westminster/John Knox Press, 1992).

6. Ibid., 191.

7. Ibid., 341.

8. Ibid., 340.

9. Conversation with James Cone at Union Theological Seminary, 9 Oct. 2009. James Cone's friendship and dialogue with me about race relations and Reinhold Niebuhr have been invaluable. James first warned me about dangers to my tenure at Pittsburgh Theological Seminary due to my activism on race relations in the streets of Pittsburgh, and antiwar activism in Washington D.C. For his first academic year we shared a hall at Union Theological Seminary as we did again when I returned to Union on a part-time teaching assignment. Our continuing conversations are a mixture of mutual criticism and support.

10. *Love and Justice*, ed. D. B. Robertson (Louisville: Westminster/John Knox Press).

11. See Sam H. Franklin, Jr., "Early Years of the Delta Cooperative Farm and the Providence Cooperative Farm" (Pittsburgh Theological Seminary Copy, duplicated for circulation, 1980) 21. He wrote of Niebuhr: "Not in the matter of day-by-day decisions, but in a broad sense, his influence is certainly one of the key facts in the history of our organization." He mentions the farms as one of Niebuhr's projects, including the Fellowship of Socialist Christians, Highlander Folk School, Fellowship of Southern Churchmen, and Americans for Democratic Action.

12. *Justice and Mercy*, ed. Ursula M. Niebuhr (New York: Harper & Row, 1974). As a graduate student at Union I arranged, in 1968, for Doris Liles, later Doris Liles Rockefeller, to type the manuscripts of his sermons from tapes available in the president's closet at Union Theological Seminary. These, along with other manuscripts in Ursula Niebuhr's possession, were combined with copies of his prayers which she edited to form the manuscript. The differing uses of the term justice in the book are taken from her collection of his prayers and the references to the theme of justice which she provided at the end of the book.

13. Written in 1963 in "Development of a Social Ethic in the Ecumenical Movement" in *Faith and Politics*, ed. Ronald Stone (New York: Braziller, 1968) 166-67. The essay in its entirety represents Niebuhr's concern for and knowledge of the evolution of the Christian ecumenical movement of the twentieth century. He detected a turn towards pragmatism and the noncriticism of mixed economies while the World Council of Churches was critical of both Communism and laissez-faire capitalism.

14. *Man's Nature*, 24.

15. Karen Lebacqz, *Six Theories of Justice* (Minneapolis: Augsburg Publishing House, 1986), 99.

16. Robin W. Lovin, *Reinhold Niebuhr and Christian Realism* (Cambridge: Cambridge University Press, 1995) and *Christian Realism and the New Realities* (Cambridge: Cambridge University Press, 2008).

17. *Reinhold Niebuhr and Christian Realism*, 191.

18. Ibid., 214.

19. *Christian Realism and New Realities*, 36, 71.

20. Robertson, *Love and Justice*, 20.

21. *Love and Justice*, ed. D. B. Robertson (Louisville: Westminster/John Knox, 1957).

22. Merle Longwood, "Niebuhr and a Theory of Justice" (unpublished paper, New York City consultation on the Political Thought of Reinhold Niebuhr, 2 March 1973. A revised version was published in *Dialog*).

23. *Christianity and Society* 8/4 (1943): 17. A fuller discussion of Tillich on justice compared to liberation theology from Latin America is found in Mary Ann Stenger and

Ronald H. Stone, *Dialogues of Paul Tillich* (Macon: Mercer University Press, 2002) 193-98. Some paragraphs of that discussion are republished here with slight editing.

24. Ibid.,

25. *The Socialist Decision*, 6.

26. Ibid.

27. Ibid. 139.

28. See Alistair M. Macleod, *Paul Tillich; An Essay on the Role of Ontology in His Philosophical Theology* (London: George Allen & Unwin. 1973).

29. Paul Tillich, *Love, Power, and Justice* (New York: Oxford University Press, 1954) 56.

30. Ibid. 71.

31. Reinhold Niebuhr. "Memorandum on Bicentennial," Letter to American Revolution Bicentennial Commission (March 1970). Niebuhr Papers, Library of Congress Washington D.C.

32. Reinhold Niebuhr, letter to Bethel Evangelical Church (22 January 1930). Niebuhr Papers, Library of Congress Washington D.C.

33. Richard Fox, *Reinhold Niebuhr*, 118-20. Fox's interpretation based on early access to crucial letters possessed by Ursula Niebuhr is quite thorough. He implies more criticism than I would of Niebuhr as he bores into Niebuhr's supposed inner thoughts. My view is tempered by my own experience in church integration and prices paid for the attempts.

34. Dr. Söllee and I were partners in teaching resistance to militarism at Ghost Ranch where we organized a protest at the Los Alamos Labs. On the occasion referenced she was a house guest, and we were visiting a white church in Pittsburgh and not my own integrated congregation of East Liberty Presbyterian Church.

Notes to chapter 21: Political Philosophy in the Cold War

1. Chapter 21 includes a revision of chp. 6 of Stone, *Reinhold Niebuhr*.

2. Quoted in Bingham, *Courage to Change*, 368.

3. John C. Bennett, *Christian Realism* (New York: Scribner's, 1941) 48.

4. Thompson, *Political Realism*, 48.

5. Theodore R. Weber, "Dissentiment dans la Maison Niebuhr: la crise des nomes au sein du realisme politique chretien," *Christianisme Social* 71 (Septembre-Decembre, 1963) 747-67.

6. Ibid., 754.

7. Raymond Aron, *Peace and War* (Garden City NY, Doubleday, 1966) 599.

8. Thompson, *Political Realism*, 50.

9. See: Stone, *Reinhold Niebuhr*, 118-20.

10. Reinhold Niebuhr, "Plans for World Reorganization," *Christianity and Crisis* 2 (19 Oct. 1942.

11. John H. Herz, *International Politics in the Atomic Age* (New York: Columbia University Press, 1962) 11.

12. J. Robert Oppenheimer, "Atomic Weapons and American Policy," *Foreign Affairs* 31 (1952–1953): 129.

13. See: Stone, *Reinhold Niebuhr*, 156-58.

14. Niebuhr's recognition of the role of the United States as both an imperialist and a status quo nation contrasts with Hans J. Morgenthau's division of a nation's foreign policies into one category or the other. "A nation whose foreign policy tends toward

keeping power and not toward changing the distribution of power in its favor pursues a policy of the status quo. A nation whose foreign policy aims at acquiring more power than it actually has through a reversal of existing power relations pursues a policy of imperialism." Hans J. Morgenthau, *Politics among Nations,The Struggle for Power and Peace* (New York: Alfred A. Knopf, 1962) 39. The difference between the two lay in the definition of imperialism, and they both agreed that the United States was committed to preserving the existing system while favoring adjustments within the system.

15. Niebuhr, *Man's Nature*, 82.

16. Ibid., 81.

17. Ibid., 83.

18. Reinhold Niebuhr, "The Social Myths in the Cold War," *Journal of International Relations* 21 (1967): 53.

19. Reinhold Niebuhr, lecture at Barnard College, New York City, 15 April 1963.

20. Ibid.

21. Ibid.

22. Niebuhr, *Nature and Destiny* 2:257-58, 265.

23. Niebuhr, *Nature and Destiny* 1:192.

24. Niebuhr, *Nature and Destiny* 2:258; *Power Politics*, 156; *Moral Man*, 6, 16.

25. E.g., Niebuhr, *Power Politics*, 123.

26. Reinhold Niebuhr, "Leaves from the Notebook of a War-bound American," *The Christian Century* 56 (5 Nov. 1939): 1405.

27. "Political power deserves to be placed in a special category, because it rests upon the ability to use and manipulate other forms of social power for the particular purpose of organizing and dominating the community." Niebuhr, *Nature and Destiny* 2:263.

28. Harry Rex Davis, "The Political Philosophy of Reinhold Niebuhr," (Ph.D. diss., University of Chicago, 1951).

29. Niebuhr, *Moral Man*, 7-8, 257; Niebuhr, *Children of Light*, 62-63; Niebuhr, *Reflections*, 151.

30. Davis, "The Political Philosophy of Reinhold Niebuhr," 61.

31. Ibid.

32. Niebuhr, *Nature and Destiny* 2:260.

33. Reinhold Niebuhr, "Politics and Economics," *Chrisitanity and Society* 7 (Autumn 1942): 7-8.

34. Davis, "The Political Philosophy of Reinhold Niebuhr," 16.

35. Niebuhr, *Moral Man*, 19.

36. Niebuhr, *Discerning the Signs of the Times*, 187.

37. Niebuhr, *Nature and Destiny* 2:258.

38. Cf. Morgenthau, *Politics among Nations*, 161-218.

39. Niebuhr, "American Power and World Responsibility," *Christianity and Crisis* 3 (5 April 1943): 2.

40. "The real contribution of Christian faith to problems of world organization lies not in imitating the utopianism of secular rationalities, adding only pious phrases to their dreams, but in encouraging men and nations to assume the responsibilities which inhere in the possession of power with as little pride as possible." Reinhold Niebuhr, "Power and Justice" *Christianity and Society* 8 (Winter 1942): 10.

41. Ibid.

42. Reinhold Niebuhr, "The Limits of American Power." *Christianity and Society* 17 (Autumn 1952): 5.

43. *Structures of Nations*, published in 1958 but not available to the first interpreters of Niebuhr's political philosophy; consequently excellent dissertations like those of Robert C. Good at Yale in 1956 and Harry R. Davis at Chicago in 1951 are incomplete interpretations of his thought.

44. Niebuhr, *Structures of Nations*, 1.

45. Ibid., 2.

46. Ibid., 3.

47. Ibid., 206.

48. Niebuhr repeatedly attacked the idea that capitalism is the cause of imperialism. *Structure of Nations*, 23; *Christian Realism*, 57.

49. Niebuhr, *Structure of Nations*, 202-203.

50. Ibid.

51. Niebuhr, *Structure of Nations*, 215; see also 25, 216, 295, and 298.

52. Ibid., 10-32.

53. Ibid., 11.

54. Niebuhr, "Perils of American Power," 90-91.

55. Niebuhr, *Structure of Nations*, 15.

56. Niebuhr's judgment as to the gravity of the situation in May 1956 was prophetic, but his estimate in September 1956, was mistaken. He had then written, "It is quite apparent, however, that the Suez crisis will not lead to war and that Nasser will not seriously challenge the international stakes in the waterway." Reinhold Niebuhr, "The Crisis in the Suez Canal," *Christianity and Crisis* 16 (17 Sept. 1956): 113.

57. "For the state of Israel is, whatever its limitations, a heartening adventure in nationhood. Whatever our political or religious positions may be, it is not possible to withhold admiration, sympathy, and respect for such an achievement." Reinhold Niebuhr," New Hopes for Peace in the Middle East," *Christianity and Crisis* 16 (28 May 1956): 65.

58. Reinhold Niebuhr "Seven Great Errors of U.S. Foreign Policy," *The New Leader* 39 (24-31 Dec.): 3-5.

59. There is also a tendency toward dismissal of Arab culture, seen in references to "the moribund culture of the Islamic world." Ibid., 4.

60. *Faith and Politics*, 208-12.

61. Reinhold Niebuhr, "The Dilemma in China," *The Messenger* 14 (4 Jan. 1949): 7.

62. Niebuhr, "The Limits of American Power," 5.

63. Ibid., 6.

64. Reinhold Niebuhr, "The Limits of Military Power," *The New Leader* 48 (30 May 1965): 16-17.

65. Ibid.

66. Reinhold Niebuhr, "Can Democracy Work?" *The New Leader* 45 (28 May 1962): 9.

67. Reinhold Niebuhr, "Pretense and Power," *The New Leader* 48 (1 March 1965): 6-7.

68. Ibid.

69. Reinhold Niebuhr, "The Fateful Triangle," *The New Leader* 48 (4 Jan. 1965): 18-20.

70. This term became characteristic of Niebuhr's talk about Vietnam in a manner similar to that played by role, sin, irony, and paradox in his theological language.

71. Letters to Will Scarlett.

72. Reinhold Niebuhr and Hans J. Morgenthau, "The Ethics of War and Peace in the Nuclear Age," *War/Peace Report* 7 (Feb. 1967): 3-7.

73. Niebuhr, "The Social Myths in the Cold War," 55.

74. Niebuhr and Morgenthau, "Ethics of War and Peace," 4-5.

75. "This study of the perennial patterns, recurring problems, and varied but similar structures of the political order was undertaken with an eye on our present perplexities." Niebuhr, *Structure of Nations*, ix.

76. E.g., "Perhaps the most significant moral characteristic of a nation is its hypocrisy." Niebuhr, *Moral Man*, 95.

77. Ibid., 108.

78. Niebuhr, "The Social Myths of the Cold War," 11.

79. Davis and Good, eds., *Reinhold Niebuhr on Politics*, 330.

80. Ibid., 328.

81. Ibid., 327.

82. Landon, ed., *Reinhold Niebuhr: A Prophetic Voice*, 102.

83. Ibid., 121.

84. Hans J. Morgenthau, "Another Great Debate," *The American Political Science Review* 56 (Dec. 1952): 984,

85. Morgenthau, *Politics among Nations*, 11.

86. "Contrast, for example his frequent assertion that 'politics is interest defined in terms of power' and a less-quoted statement in which he says that the 'political action can be defined as an attempt to realize the moral values through the medium of politics, that is, power.' [Morgenthau, "Another Great Debate," *The American Political Science Review* 56 (Dec. 1952): 987]." Robert C. Good, "The National Interest and Political Realism: Niebuhr's 'Debate' with Morgenthau and Kennan," *The Journal of Politics* 22 (1960): 613.

87. Niebuhr, *Structure of Nations* , 144.

88. Niebuhr, *Man's Nature*, 75,

89. Hans J. Morgenthau, *Scientific Man vs. Power Politics* (Chicago: University of Chicago Press, 1946) 207.

90. Hans J. Morgenthau, *In Defense of the National Interest* (New York: Alfred A. Knopf, 1951) 242.

91. Davis and Good, eds., *Reinhold Niebuhr on Politics*, 333.

92. Isolating the differences between Reinhold Niebuhr and Hans J. Morgenthau should not obscure their basic agreement. Niebuhr said on an occasion: "I wouldn't say that the views of Morgenthau, and myself are 'somewhat different.' We basically have common ideas with certain peripheral differences." Niebuhr and Morgenthau, "The Ethics of War and Peace," 3. Late in Niebuhr's life he exchanged letters with Morgenthau in which both jokingly attributed their better ideas to the other. However, I came to Niebuhr's attention because of a paper on Morgenthau's political ethics in a seminar in 1964 in which I distinguished their ethics much as in this chapter. He wrote me a nice tribute which though probably over-generous points toward his own further distinguishing his position from Morgenthau in his last book, *Man's Nature.*

93. He retired from Union in 1960 at the required retirement age of 68. He offered one course at Union in 1961, moved on to teach at Princeton and Harvard, and returned to Morningside Heights to teach one course at Barnard College in 1963. From 1964 to 1968 he offered a seminar in social ethics to students at Union Theological seminary, with limited

enrollment, first at the Seminary and then in his apartment at Riverside Drive overlooking Riverside Park and the Hudson River.

94. Niebuhr and Sigmund, *Democratic Experience.*

95. Ibid., vi.

96. Ibid., 9.

97. Ibid., 92.

98. Ibid., 3.

99. Ibid., 73.

100. Ibid. 184.

101. Niebuhr and Sigmund, *Democratic Experience*, 151-52.

102. Ibid., 146.

103. Ibid., 148.

104. Ibid. 85.

105. Ronald H. Stone, "An Interview with Reinhold Niebuhr," *Christianity and Crisis* 29/4 (17 March 1969): 51.

106. Letter to Ronald H. Stone, in author's possession (27 May 1969).

107. Seymour Melman, "How to Cut Military Budget by $14 Billion," *Commonweal* 91 (28 Nov. 1969): 274. Cf. Seymour Melman, *Our Depleted Society* (New York: Dell Publishing Company, 1965).

108. Published previously in Charles W. Kegley, ed., *Reinhold Niebuhr: His Religious, Social and Political Thought* (New York: Pilgrim Press, 1984) 68-74.

109. Reinhold Niebuhr, "Caribbean Blunder," *Christianity and Crisis* 25/9 (31 May 1965): 113-14.

110. John H. Swomley, *American Empire: The Political Ethics of Twnetieth Century Conquest* (London: Macmillan, 1970) 34.

111. *Christianity and Crisis* 29/4 (4 August 1969): 211-12.

112. "After Sputnik and Explorer," *Christianity and Crisis* 18/4 (17 March 1958): 29-30.

113. "The Limits of Military Power," *The New Leader* 38/1 (30 May 1955): 16-17.

114. Niebuhr, *Faith and Politics*, 215.

115. Ibid., 211.

116. Ibid., 203.

117. Ibid., 236.

118. Ibid., 218.

119. *Reinhold Niebuhr: Prophet to Politicians*, 207-210.

120. Swomley, *American Empire*, 35.

121. "An Interview with Reinhold Niebuhr," *Christianity and Crisis* 29/4 (17 March 1969): 51.

122. Ibid.

123. Ibid.

124. "Peace through Cultural Co-operation," *Christianity and Crisis* 9/17 (17 Oct. 1949): 131-33.

125. Told to Stevenson's son and relayed to the Rev. Dr. John Burkhart of McCormick Theological Seminary, Chicago, Illinois.

126. Reinhold Niebuhr,"The Democratic Elite and American Foreign Policy" in Marquis Childs and James Reston, eds., *Walter Lippmann and His Times* (New York: Harcourt, Brace and Co., 1959) 168-88.

Notes to chapter 22: Myth and Meeting

1. "Faith as the Sense of Meaning in Human Existence," *Christianity and Crisis* 26/10 (13 June 1966): 127-31; repr. in *Faith and Politics*, ed. Ronald H. Stone, 3-13.

2. "The Truth in Myths," in *The Nature of Religious Experience* (New York: Harper & Row, 1937) 117-35; repr. in *Faith and Politics*, 15-31.

3. Langdon Gilkey, *On Niebuhr. A Theological Study* (Chicago: University of Chicago Press, 2001).

4. "Biblical Thought and Ontological Speculation in Tillich's Theology," in *The Thought of Paul Tillich*, ed. Charles Kegley and Robert Bretall (New York: Macmillan, 1952) 216-29.

5. Paul Tillich, *Biblical Religion and the Search for Ultimate Reality* (Chicago: University of Chicago Press, 1955) vii.

6. Paul Tillich, "Reinhold Niebuhr's Doctrine of Knowledge," in *Reinhold Niebuhr. His Religious, Social and Political Thought*, ed. Charles Kegley (New York: Pilgrim Press, 1984) 89.

7. Niebuhr, ibid., 508-509.

8. Ibid., 523.

9. The major works on Tillich's symbolism are commented on by Michael Riposa, "Remarks Concerning Donald Dreisbach's *Symbols and Salvation* and Richard Grigg's *Symbolism and Empowerment*, in *Papers from the Annual Meeting of the North American Paul Tillich Society* (November 1994) 49-51. See also John Herman Randall, "The Ontology of Paul Tillich" in C. W. Kegley and R. W. Bretall, *The Theology of Paul Tillich* (New York: Macmillan, 1961) and Paul Tillich's response in the same volume, 335. Paul Tillich, "Theology and Symbolism," in *Religious Symbolism*, ed. F. E. Johnson (New York: Harper & Brothers, 1955) 107-16, is very important.

10. *Dynamics of Faith* (New York: Harper-Collins Books, 1957) 47-50.

11. Gary Dorrien, *The Word as True Myth* (Louisville: Westminster/John Knox, 1997).

12. In the interests of disclosure, I enjoyed a course with Langdon Gilkey on religious language, immediately after his studying philosophy of linguistic analysis at Oxford in a Union Seminary summer school, and wrote a paper on Tillich's use of religious symbols. Our final meeting was with Elizabeth Niebuhr Sifton after their presentations at the Niebuhr Society. The discussion was more on politics than religion, and both Gilkey and I were past our examinations of liberation theology which in my case had taken me to study projects in Latin America, to invite Gustavo Gutierrez to Pittsburgh twice, and to edit *Liberation and Change* for him and Richard Shaull.

13. Dorrien, *The Word*, 236.

Notes to chapter 23: Criticism of Niebuhr on Faith and Politics

1. In *Reinhold Niebuhr Revisited*, ed. Daniel Rice (Grand Rapids MI: Eerdmans, 2009) 260-85.

2. The discussion of the panel is an edited version of Ronald Stone, "The Realists and their Critics," in *Worldview* 16/6 (June 1973): 19-20. The panel discussion was presented in *Christianity and Crisis* 28/14 (5 August 1968): 175-90.

3. Valerie Saving Goldstein, "The Human Situation," *Journal of Religion* (April 1960): 100-15.

4. (Washington DC: University Press of America, 1980). As a sometime reviewer for University Press for America, I critically reviewed the book before its publication by the

Press. At the time I was partially persuaded by its argument and very impressed by its vigor, and I realize its importance today.

5. Goldstein, 110.

6. Plaskow, 34-35.

7. Ibid., 50. On the specific point of distance from the culture and on not interfering with women's struggle for equality, an example would be Niebuhr's 1948 essay celebrating secular society for being more advanced in granting equality than the church. He noted that at the time European women seemed to be pushing harder than American women for the right to be ordained and that the Danish parliament had granted it. Women in the American churches seemed to have more influence through their own organizations than women in Europe, but there the emphasis was on gains in secular society. He also ruefully reported the overturning of the ordination of the woman in Hong Kong whose cause he and Ursula had supported. "Women in the Church" in *Messenger* 13 (9 Nov. 1948): 6.

8. Ibid., 94.

9. Henry B. Clark, *Serenity, Courage, Wisdom: The Enduring Legacy of Reinhold Niebuhr* (Cleveland: Pilgrim Press, 1994) 171.

10. Susan Nelson Dunfee, "The Sin of Hiding: A Feminist Critique of Reinhold Niebuhr's Account of the Sin of Pride" in *Soundings* 60 (Spring 1982): 316-26. See also Susan Nelson Dunfee, *Beyond Servanthood: Christianity and the Liberation of Women* (Lanham: University Press of America, 1989).

11. Marjorie Suchocki, *The Fall to Violence: Original Sin in Relational Theology* (New York: Continuum, 1994) 32, 44.

12. As quoted by Lesley Hazleton, "Doris Lessing on Feminism, Communism and 'Space Fiction.' " in the *New York Times* (25 July 1982). htttp://mural.uv.es/vemivein/feminismcommunism.htm.

13. Aurelia Takacs Fule, "Being Human before God," in *Reinhold Niebuhr (1892–1992: A Centenary Appraisal*, ed. Gary A. Gaudin and Douglas John Hall (Atlanta: Scholars Press, 1994) 64.

14. Charles W. Kegley and Robert W. Bretall, *Reinhold Niebuhr: His Religious Social and Political Thought* (New York: Macmillan, 1961).

15. Ibid., 450.

16. Harold R. Landon, *Reinhold Niebuhr: A Prophetic Voice in Our Time* (Greenwich: Seabury Press, 1962) 24.

17. Ibid., 41.

18. Ibid., 79.

19. Ibid., 109.

20. Ibid., 119.

21. Ibid., 123.

22. Cornel West, *Prophetic Fragments* (Grand Rapids MI: Eerdmans, 1988) 142-43.

23. Ronald H. Stone, *Realism and Hope* (Lanham: University Press of America, 1977).

24. Oscar Cole Arnal, "A Canadian Socialist Christian Looks at Reinhold Niebuhr," in *Reinhold Niebuhr*, ed. Gaudin and Hall.

25. Paul Merkley, *Reinhold Niebuhr: A Political Account* (Montreal: McGill-Queen's University Press, 1975), 180.

26. Beverly Harrison, *Making the Connections: Essays in Feminist Social Ethics*, ed., Carol S. Robb (Boston: Beacon Press, 1985) 27-28.

27. Ronald H. Stone, "Karl Marx and the End of Religion," in *Social Action* 35/3 (Nov. 1968): 26-39. Also "The Revolutionary Anti-Kingdom of Karl Marx" in *Realism and Hope* (Lanham: University Press of America, 1977) 48-91.

28. Harrison, *Making Connections*, 59, 65.

29. Reinhold Niebuhr, introduction to *Marx and Engels on Religion* (New York: Schocken Books, 1964) vii-xiv. Another of his students, John C. Raines, has since published a new introduction to the Temple University reprint which he is certain is much more complete. Also, Reinhold Niebuhr, "Marx and Engels on Religion" repr. from his introduction to *Faith and Politics*, 47-54.

30. The internal characteristics of the three essays on Karl Marx, Adam Smith, and the "Comments on the Religious Assumptions of Adam Smith and Karl Marx" in the Niebuhr papers in the Library of Congress are very inconsistent with Niebuhr's published views on progress. A comparison with his published views of Karl Marx establishes the essays were not written by Niebuhr. Furthermore, writing style, sources used, and footnote usage are inconsistent with Niebuhr's established patterns. I've inquired but my best guess as to authorship was invalid, and I have been unable to locate the author.

31. Karl Marx, *Grundrisse* (New York, Random House, 1973).

32. Gustavo Gutierrez, "Freedom and Salvation" in *Liberation and Change*, ed. Ronald H. Stone (Atlanta: John Knox Press, 1977) 3-96.

33. Larry L. Rasmussen, introduction to *Theologian of Public Life* (London: Collins Publishers, 1988) 35-37.

34. William Inboden, *Religion and American Foreign Policy, 1945–960: The Soul of Containment* (Cambridge: Cambridge University Press, 2008).

35. Campbell Craig, *The Glimmer of a New Leviathan* (New York: Columbia University Press, 2003).

36. Quoted by Kenneth Thompson, "Niebuhr and the Foreign Policy Realists," in Rice, *Reinhold Niebuhr*, 158.

37. Ronald H. Stone, *Realism and Hope* and *Prophetic Realism*, 50-55.

38. Roger D. Spegele, *Political Realism in Political Theory* (Cambridge: Cambridge University Press, 1996) 230-44.

39. Ronald H. Stone, *Prophetic Realism*.

Notes to chapter 24: Criticism of Tillich on Faith and Politics

1. José Miguez Bonino, "Reading Tillich in Latin America: From Religious Socialism to the Exile," in *Religion in the New Millenium*, ed. Raymond F. Bulman and Fredrick J. Parrella (Macon GA: Mercer University Press, 2001) 19.

2. John Thatamanil, "Tillich and the Postmodern," in *The Cambridge Companion of Paul Tillich*, ed. Russell Manning (Cambridge: Cambridge University Press, 2009) 300.

3. Marc Boss, "Tillich in Dialogue with Japanese Buddhism: A Paradigmatic Illustration of His Approach to Inter-religious Conversation," in Manning, *Cambridge Companion*, 254-70.

4. Rachel Sophia Baard, "Tillich and Feminism" in Manning, *Cambridge Companion*, 273-87.

5. Tillich, *Systematic Theology* 3:292-94.

6. Anne Belford Ulanov, "The Anxiety of Being," in *The Thought of Paul Tillich*, ed. James Luther Adams, Wilhelm Pauck and Roger L. Shinn (San Francsisco: Harper & Row, 1985) 129.

7. Baard, 285.

8. Ibid.

9. Julia A. Lamm, "A hermeneutics of Revulsion: Response to Owen C. Thomas," in *Papers from the Annual Meeting of the North American Paul Tillich Society* (November 1994) 43.

10. Rene Tillich, " My Father, Paul Tillich" in *Tillich-Studien* 5 (Munster: Lit verlag, 2001).

11. Ibid., 13.

12. Ibid.,14.

13. Ibid., 18.

14. Ibid., 19.

15. See Mary Ann Stenger, "Thought and Life: Issues of Truth and Morality Response to Owen Thomas," in *Papers from the Annual Meeting*, 43-44. Stenger, part 2 in Stenger and Stone, 82-149.

16. Francis Ching-Wah Yip, *Capitalism as Religion: A Study of Paul Tillich's Interpretation of Modernity* (Cambridge: Harvard University Press, 2010) 101-37.

17. Paul Tillich, *Political Expectations*, ed. James Luther Adams (New York: Harper & Row, 1971) 123-80.

18. Ibid., 180.

Notes to chapter 25: Legacies

1. Roger L. Shinn, "Tillich an Interpreter and Disturber of Contemporary Civilization," in Adams, Pauck, and Shinn, *The Thought of Paul Tillich*.

2. Reinhold Niebuhr, *Discerning the Signs of the Times*, 170.

3. Paul Tillich, *The Eternal Now* (New York: Scribner's, 1963) 183-85.

4. Gary Dorrien, *The Word as True Myth* (Louisville: Westminster/John Knox Press, 1997).

5. Paul Tillich, *Theology of Peace*, 174-81.

6. Reinhold Niebuhr, "Memorandum on the Bicentennial" (10 March 1970). Reinhold Niebuhr Papers. Manuscript Division, Library of Congress, Washington, D.C.

7. The three essays are most easily located in the last anthology Niebuhr oversaw, *Faith and Politics*, 119-81.

8. Robert L. Stivers, "Resistance and Economic Globalization" in *Resistance and Theological Ethics*, ed. Ronald H. Stone, and Robert L. Stivers (Lanham: Rowman & Littlefield Publishers, 2004) 28-32.

9. Gary Dorrien, *Social Ethics in the Making* (Malden, Wiley-Blackwell, 2009) 683-88.

10. Mark Lewis Taylor, in *The Cambridge Companion to Paul Tillich*, 189-207.

11. Henry Clark, *Serenity, Courage, and Wisdom*, 176.

12. *Social Responsibility in a Pluralistic Culture*, ed. Louis Finkelstein (New York: Jewish Theological Seminary, 1971) 171-211.

13. I have discussed these rather fully in "The Contribution of Reinhold Niebuhr to the Twentieth Century" in *Reinhold Niebuhr His Religious, Social, and Political Thought*, ed. Charles Kegley, 60-68. See also the dissertation of Emmett C. Burns whose committee I served on, "Love, Power, and Justice as Central Elements in a View of Social Change: A

Comparison and Evaluation of the Thought of Reinhold Niebuhr and Martin Luther King, Jr. (Ph.D. diss., University of Pittsburgh).

14. Reinhold Niebuhr, "The Mounting Racial Crisis," *Christianity and Crisis* 23/12 (8 July 1963): 1.

15. "The Meaning of the Tragedy in Birmingham" (22 September 1963). Unpublished manuscript. The Reinhold Niebuhr Papers, Library of Congress, Washington D.C.

16. The comments on the seminar are taken from 16 December 1964 class notes and memory and written in 2010. The balance between the efficacy of law andsocial pressures, moral foundations, and community resistance was also explored in his book *Pious and Secular America* (New York: Scribner's, 1958) and in the chapter "Justice to the American Negro from State, Community, and Church."

17. Reinhold Niebuhr, foreword to *Mississippi Black Paper* (New York: Random House, 1965) 2 unnumbered pages. Reinhold Niebuhr papers, Library of Congress, Washington, D.C.

18. Ibid.

19. "The Negro Minority and its Fate in a Self-Righteous Nation," *Social Action* 35/2 (Oct. 1968): 53-64. *Social Progress* 55/1 (Sept./Oct. 1968).

20. Ibid., 64.

21. Andrew Young, quoted in *Christianity and Crisis* 21 (3 May 1971): 80.

22. Reinhold Niebuhr, "Memorandum on Bicentennial."

23. *The Legacy of Reinhold Niebuhr*, ed. Nathan A. Scott, Jr. (Chicago: University of Chicago Press, 1974) xvii-iii. Terry D. Cooper, *Reinhold Niebuhr and Psychology: The Ambiguities of the Self* (Macon GA: Mercer University Press, 2009) provides the most recent exploration of this side of Niebuhr's thought. Previously he had explored Tillich's psychology in *Paul Tillich and Psychology: Historic and Contemporary Explorations in Theology, Psychotherapy, and Ethics* (Macon GA: Mercer University Press, 2006).

24. Serene Jones, *Trauma and Grace: Theology in a Ruptured World* (Louisville: Westminster/John Knox Press, 2009).

25. Robert McAfee Brown, response to Ronald Stone's survey, in Stone's possession.

26. John Dillenberger, response.

27. Harjie Liken, response.

28. Charles W. Kegley, 217.

29. Beverly Harrison, response.

30. Owen Thomas, response.

31. Roger Shinn, response.

Index